PARADISE REFORGED

A History of the New Zealanders

From the 1880s to the Year 2000

JAMES BELICH

ALLEN LANE
THE PENGUIN PRESS

For
Jim and Valerie

ALLEN LANE
THE PENGUIN PRESS

Penguin Books (NZ) Ltd, cnr Rosedale and Airborne Roads, Albany,
Auckland 1310, New Zealand
Penguin Books Ltd, 80 Strand, London, WC2R 0RL, England
Penguin Putnam Inc, 375 Hudson Street, New York, NY 10014, United States
Penguin Books Australia Ltd, 250 Camberwell Road, Victoria 3124, Australia
Penguin Books Canada Ltd, 10 Alcorn Avenue, Toronto, Ontario, Canada M4V 3B2
Penguin Books (South Africa) (Pty) Ltd, 24 Sturdee Avenue, Rosebank,
Johannesburg 2196, South Africa,
Penguin Books India (P) Ltd, 11, Community Centre, Panchsheel Park,
New Delhi 110 017, India

Penguin Books Ltd, Registered Offices: Harmondsworth, Middlesex, England

First published by Penguin Books (NZ) Ltd, 2001

1 3 5 7 9 10 8 6 4 2

Copyright © James Belich, 2001

The right of James Belich to be identified as the author of this work in terms of
section 96 of the Copyright Act 1994 is hereby asserted.

Editing and book design by Richard King
Typeset by Egan-Reid Ltd
Printed in Australia by McPherson's Printing Group
ISBN 0-7139-9172-0

www.penguin.co.nz

CONTENTS

Preface 11

Prologue: Eden Before the Fall 15

Part 1 Better Britain, 1880s–1920s

Introduction 27

1. God's Lone Country 32
The Long Stagnation 32
The Exemplary Paradise 38
The Seventh Child 46

2. The Recolonial System 53
From Progress to Protein 54
Shifting Gear 68
Better Britons 76

3. Trouble in Paradise 87
1913 87
New Zealand in World War One 95
Dominionism 108

Part 2 The Great Tightening

Introduction 121

4. Social Harmony: The Touch of Class 126
The Decline of a Gentry 127
The Making of the New Zealand Working Class 133
The Rise of Farmer Backbone 146

5. Moral Harmony: A New Crusade 157
'Make Them Move': Moral Evangelism and its Allies 159
Drink, Death and Other Demons 170
The Mothers' Mutiny and Other Rebellions 181

6. Racial Harmony (1): Merging Maori? 189
The Race That Would Not Die 191
Young Maori: The New Collaborators? 200
Whitening Maori 206

7. Racial Harmony (2): Unmaking the Difference 216
Merging Pakeha 217
White New Zealand? 223
Islands of Difference 232

Part 3 Better Britain at Bay, 1920s–1960s

Introduction 243

8. Depression and Labour 245
Rewiring the System 245
Sugarbag Years? 254
First Labour 259

9. New Zealand in World War Two 270
The Sharp End 272
World War Where? 280
World War Two in New Zealand 287

10. Golden Weather? 297
1951 299
Long Slow Booms 307
Letting in Lolita? 316

Part 4 A People Without Songs?

Introduction 325

11. The Expatriate Game 326
Neanderthal Relatives 327
Waiting for Godwits 331
Cultural Overproduction? 341

12. Life During History 346
Pakeha Folkways 347
The Wild Child and Its Taming 356

13. Games Peoples Play 368
Sporting Society 370
Representative Rugby 378

Part 5 Beyond Better Britain, 1960s–2000

Introduction   391

14. 1984 and All That   394
Recolonisation's Last Stand   394
Right Turn   405
Post-Restructuralism: An Audit   413

15. Rainbow's End   425
Exit Britain, Enter World   426
Are You My Mother?   433
Terms of Trade   443

Part 6 Coming In, Coming Out

Introduction   463

16. Resurgent Maori   466
Revenge of the Cradle   467
The Treaty Strikes Back   475
Opting Out?   481

17. Escape from Nappy Valley   488
Baby Boom, Baby Bust   489
New Waves: Work and Feminism   496
Letting Out Lolita?   504
Out on the Street   511

18. One, Two, Many?   520
Towns and Arounds   522
New Migrations   531
Te Pakeha?   539

References   550

Index   592

Three Kings Is

Cape
Reinga

Bay of Islands

NORTHLAND
Whangarei

Hokianga Har.

Whangarei Har.

*Great
Barrier Is*

*Hauraki
Gulf*

Kaipara Har.

AUCKLAND

Coromandel
Peninsula

Manukau Har.

Waikato R.

Tauranga

Hamilton

BAY OF PLENTY

East
Cape

Kawhia Har.

WAIKATO

*Lake
Rotorua*

Rotorua

RAUKUMARA RA.

NORTH
ISLAND

*Lake
Taupo*

Mokau R.

Taupo

Waikaremoana

EAST COAST

Gisborne

Rangitaiki R.

New Plymouth

TARANAKI

. Mt
Tongariro

*Poverty
Bay*

Mt Taranaki

Mt Ruapehu

Mohaka R

Cape
Egmont

*HAWKE
BAY*

RUAHINE RANGE

Patea R

Napier

Whanganui R

Wanganui

MANAWATU

Rangitikei R

**Palmerston
North**

Manawatu R

TARARUA RA.

C. Turnagain

Farewell Spit

WAIRARAPA

*Marlborough
Sounds*

Castlepoint

WELLINGTON

Wairarapa R

Nelson

*COOK
STRAIT*

Blenheim

Cape Palliser

Cape
Campbell

SOUTH
ISLAND

KAIKOURA MTS

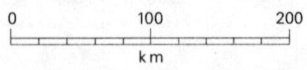

| 0 | | 100 | | 200 |

k m

Cape Egmont

Mt Taranaki

Farewell Spit

Kahurangi Pt

Marlborough Sounds

TASMAN BAY

MARLBOROUGH

NELSON

Nelson

COOK STRAIT

Westport

Cape Foulwind

Wairau R.

Blenheim

Buller R.

KAIKOURA MTS

Clarence R.

Grey R.

Greymouth

Taramakau R.

WESTLAND

Kaikoura Peninsula

Hokitika

Waiau R.

Hurunui R.

SOUTH ISLAND

SOUTHERN ALPS

CANTERBURY

Waimakariri R.

CHRISTCHURCH

Mt Cook

Banks Peninsula

Haast R.

L. Tekapo

Rakaia R.

Cascade Pt

L.Pukaki

Rangitata R.

Awarua Pt

Mt Aspiring

L. Ohau

Timaru

Milford Sound

L. Hawea

L. Wanaka

Queenstown

Waitaki R.

Oamaru

L. Wakatipu

Fiordland

Lake Te Anau

OTAGO

L. Manapouri

Otago Peninsula

Mataura R.

DUNEDIN

Waiau R.

SOUTHLAND

Taieri R.

Invercargill

Clutha R.

FOVEAUX STRAIT

Waipapa Pt

N

STEWART ISLAND

0   100   200

k m

PREFACE

This book is an interpretive general history of the New Zealanders from the 1880s to the present. It can be read as a stand-alone work, covering the making of modern New Zealand. It is also the sequel to *Making Peoples: A History of the New Zealanders from Polynesian Settlement to the End of the Nineteenth Century*. Historical writing is a context in which sheer mass is no necessary cause for pride, but together the two books do comprise the largest interpretive single-author history of New Zealand yet written.

Paradise Reforged traces the New Zealanders through the two great transitions of their modern history. The first transition, beginning in the 1880s, saw the demise of the remarkable system of 'progressive colonisation' that created the Pakeha people and marginalised the Maori people in less than half a century. There was nothing steady about its kind of progress, which was characterised by frenetic demographic and economic growth rates – among the highest in human history. This system of explosive settlement and extraction began its collapse in the 1880s, and completed it by the 1900s. Meanwhile, an equally remarkable replacement system struggled to its feet. My label for this is 'recolonisation'. This actually tightened New Zealand's links with its metropolis, Britain, to the point where 12,000 miles of distance were transcended and New Zealand became in many respects a virtual Scotland. Recolonisation made modern New Zealand an ideological and economic (though not necessarily a cultural and social) semi-colony of Britain, and a central thesis of this book is that it remained so to the 1960s. In some respects, New Zealand history and culture is still in a state of denial about this hard fact.

Yet, like Scotland's relationship with England, New Zealand's relationship with Britain had benefits as well as costs. This book tries to explore both, and to understand a system that transcends both conventional definitions of subordinate colonialism and the conventional national packaging of history. The concept 'recolonisation' – the tightening of relations between 'metropolis' and 'periphery' after an era of mass settlement – also has applications in Australian and Canadian history. Recolonisation consisted partly in the conviction that Australians, Canadians and New Zealanders were Britons too – indeed, in some respects better Britons than those of the homelands.

For a time, neo-Britons of the 'white dominions' also saw themselves as 'metropolitan': they were co-owners of the British Empire and of Old British culture and heritage. Living standards, egalitarianism and some other public goods were typically superior in the neo-Britains than in the Old, and it was often unclear who was exploiting whom. 'Recolonisation' is therefore also intended to imply a strand of inverse colonialism – the possibility of mutual exploitation, or symbiosis, between metropolis and periphery. This book conducts an internal debate about whether recolonisation was good, bad, both, or neither.

Recolonisation clung on somewhat longer in New Zealand than in Australia or Canada. Its demise here dates to the 1970s, and constitutes the second great transition of our modern history. Decolonisation, 1970s–90s, brought economic diversification, greater independence in foreign policy and collective identity, and a great socio-demographic 'coming out' of difference. It also brought slow economic growth, insecurity, trauma and challenge – all the more because it remains partly unrecognised. Recolonial transnationalism was partly replaced by the recent spasm of internationalisation known as 'globalism'. As New Zealand cultural and economic maturity gets belatedly to its own feet, there is a chance that it will be washed away or made redundant by globalising tides. This is one of many challenges brought by the era of decolonisation, whose midst is the present. Our chances of meeting them should improve if we take a clearer look at our past.

The rise and fall of recolonisation is the backbone of this book, but it is very far from the whole of it. The book is organised in three pairs of parts, each pair roughly associated with a period: 1880s–1920s, 1920s–60s, 1960s– 2000. The first part in each pair (Parts One, Three and Five) deal in what might be called 'over-history'; the second (Parts Two, Four and Six) in 'under-history'. 'Over-history' is closer to the conventional political focus of older general histories, but even here politics is mixed equally with economics, international relations, technology and ideology. 'Under-history' deals with social, demographic and cultural history, and with the story of the remarkable twentieth-century resurgence of the Maori people. Its themes range from class, gender and ethnicity to folklore, childhood, sport and sex. I range with varying degrees of comfort over these and other themes, seeking to understand stories as well as tell them, ungratefully second-guessing the specialists on whom I rely, and speculating into gaps where there are no specialists. As noted in the Preface to *Making Peoples*, this is a risky business. I accept the risks in the hope of conveying a whole history, of provoking experts into improving on my speculations, and of converting mere information into understanding.

The numerous debts I incurred in beginning this project are acknowledged in the Preface to *Making Peoples*. I incurred yet more in completing it. I am grateful to Raewyn Dalziel, Barry Reay, Judi Binney, Linda Bryder and Barbara Batt and all the other members of the University of Auckland History Department for their patience with a distracted colleague. The University's Research Committee supplied crucial financial help for the final phase of the research. The Marsden Fund and the Fulbright Foundation funded my work on a separate project – internationally applying hypotheses drawn from New Zealand history. There has been considerable cross-germination between this project and the present book, and I am very grateful for the opportunity for synergy. Several heroic individuals read all or part of the manuscript and provided comments: Jim Belich, Colin Feslier, Tim Hazledine, Richard Hill, John Hood, Melanie Nolan, John Pocock, Andrew Sharp and Rawiri Taonui. Others who helped in various ways include: Anna Ashwell, Angela Belich, Evana Belich, Tom Brooking, John Darwin, Derek Dow, Mike and Tricia Kyrke-Smith, Roger Louis, Joan Metge, Annette Mortensen, Erik Olssen, Jock Phillips, David Scott, Tainui Stephens, Huw Richards and Bronwyn Williams. I am especially grateful to Anna Gibbons for her help. Grace Tompkins, Dick Teare, John McNeill, Kevin Kane, Greta Van Zanten, George and Hilary Troup and my other friends at Georgetown University and the New Zealand Embassy in Washington helped re-energise me for the final sprint for the finishing line. My publisher, Geoff Walker, and his colleagues at Penguin Books have again been helpful and extremely patient. I am also grateful to Richard King, my editor; Anna King, who checked the references; and to Nik Andrew for the cover design. My wife, Margaret, and my daughters, Maria and Tessa, as always, provided the crucial support.

James Belich
March 2001

Eden Before the Fall

Until 10 June 1886, New Zealand's leading tourist attractions were the geyser-carved silicate Pink and White Terraces at Lake Rotomahana, near Rotorua. They were widely considered to be one of the natural wonders of the world:

> a fan-like staircase whose terraces covered more than 7 acres and glittered in the most delicate shades of pink, white, and turquoise . . . symmetrical terraces which required only the glint of sunshine or moonlight to bring out the unique tracery and colour of their beauty.[1]

On 10 June, the neighbouring Mount Tarawera, a volcano believed to be extinct, erupted in no uncertain terms. Rocks the size of houses were thrown 500 metres into the air. Smoke rose 11 kilometres high. Ash was distributed over 18,000 square kilometres. The noise was heard as far away as Christchurch. In the Manawatu, it was believed to be the sound of a Russian warship bombarding Wanganui. Lake Rotomahana was emptied of water, and 153 people were killed. At first, the Auckland newspapers reported with relief that the Pink and White Terraces had survived. 'Their loss would have been a world-wide calamity.'[2] Alas, they were not merely damaged but obliterated. By a freak of fate, an era of New Zealand history also disappeared in the same year. Like the Pink and White Terraces, it was extraordinary in its prime, and it ended with a bang.

The history of pre-modern New Zealand, the human lead-up to 10 June 1886, was the subject of *Making Peoples*, the 'prequel' to this book.[3] On present evidence, the lead-up lasted less than a thousand years.[4] At some point – my own guess is in or around the eleventh century AD – a group of Polynesian seafarers settled the islands of New Zealand, which some of them sometimes knew as Aotearoa – 'The Long Bright World'. The original group grew into a myriad of competing tribes known as the Maori people. Maori developed rapidly, forming a vibrant and varied culture in a blink of history's eyelid. From 1642, they encountered an equally dynamic and still more expansive culture, the European. By 1840, Britain, the leader of the European pack, had signed the Treaty of Waitangi with some Maori and begun organising settlement. Henceforward, the British Empire counted New Zealand among its prizes.

As noted in *Making Peoples*, the British colonised New Zealand in two senses. They sought to convert or conquer the indigenous Maori, with very mixed success, and they sought to reproduce their own culture in a new form, with very considerable success. Maori resistance to, and co-operation with, British colonisation is a great survival story. Remarkably, Maori were not destroyed by it. But booming settler numbers, helped at the crucial moment by a large imperial army, managed first to check, and then to swamp and marginalise them. Between 1881 and 1916, the last islands of full Maori independence fell under the sway of the Pakeha state. By 1900, Maori were 5 per cent of the population. The demise of independent Maoridom is documented in Part Two of *Making Peoples*. The amazing twentieth-century Maori resurgence is a theme of the present book.

The second type of colonisation produced a new people, half a million strong, in less than 50 years, 1840–1886. They came to be known as 'Pakeha', though not all like the term. The making of Maori, the making of Pakeha, and the traumatic encounter between them, are stories remarkable for their speed, not their length. They give the lie to the idea that histories have to be millennia-long to be interesting. Part Three of *Making Peoples* discussed the staggeringly rapid development of Pakeha between 1840 and the 1880s. This is the immediate backdrop of the present book, and it requires slightly more extended summary.

In 1885, English historian James Anthony Froude, biographer of that prophet of progress, Thomas Carlyle, visited New Zealand as part of a world tour. He was surprised to find an acquaintance, Professor William Aldis, living in a modest house on Mount Eden, Auckland, with only two servants. Far from seeing himself as rotting in colonial obscurity, Aldis, 'the most brilliant mathematician Cambridge had produced for half a century', looked back from Mount Eden on life in England 'as in comparison a sort of Tartarus, an abode of damned souls'. Froude himself was impressed by the 'Britain of the South', despite being asked about it by local journalists within two hours of landing – an enduring fate of Eminent Overseas Visitors. He made obligatory reference to the future New Zealander imagined by another historian, Thomas Macaulay, who had written of an heir of Empire sketching the ruins of Old St Paul's while standing on London Bridge. 'I have come to believe in that New Zealander since I have seen the country,' wrote Froude. But he did not find the South British paradise 'wholly satisfactory'. It was over-urban, under-rural, and much too deeply in debt.

It was disgusting to see, on one side, a beautiful country opening its arms to occupation, holding out in its lap every blessing which country life can offer; and on the other, cities like Auckland, crammed like an over-crowded beehive, the bees neglecting natural flowers and feeding on borrowed sugar.[5]

What Froude was observing was the phenomenon of 'progressive colonisation', a supercharged form of settlement, a frenzied crusade against nature and natives in honour of the nineteenth-century god 'Progress'. Progressive colonisation is my term for what may well rank as the most rapid form of cultural reproduction – the making of a new people from an old – in human history. 'Explosive colonisation' is an alternative name. Progressive colonisation dominated New Zealand history between the 1840s and the 1880s, but it was not restricted to this country. It also occurred in the other 'neo-Britains': Australia, Canada, South Africa and the United States. It was characterised by the large-scale opening-up of fresh lands for settlement, mass migration, steam technology, and abundant metropolitan credit from London or New York. It also featured an ideology so optimistic and seductive that people would gamble their children's lives on it, or readily see wild dream as sound scheme. Its leaders were engaged in a great colonising crusade, in which private and public benefits providentially converged. We can most easily distinguish *progressive* colonisation from other forms of colonisation by its speed. It could produce a mature socio-economic entity – a state, province or even proto-people – in a single lifetime. In the New Zealand case, the statistics were 2,000 to 500,000 people in 42 years, 1840–82. Progressive colonisation worked through an unholy alliance between myths and economics, an extraordinary system of dream-led growth through growth.

The solid core of progressive colonisation was the 'progress industry', and even it was not that solid. It included organised settlement – not only the instant townships of the 1840s, masterminded by Edward Gibbon Wakefield, but also a variety of subsequent schemes, ranging from the successful Irish settlement of Katikati in the Bay of Plenty to the unsuccessful Italian settlement of Jackson Bay in South Westland. From their emergence in 1853–56, elected governments, central and provincial, took over the colonising crusade from Wakefield's New Zealand Company, and operated on a much larger scale. Central government alone, under chief colonising crusader Julius Vogel, assisted out 100,000 European immigrants in the 1870s. Vogel was also prominent in another dimension of the progress industry – public works, notably railway building. But virtually every public authority in the country, from the Auckland Provincial Council to the Oamaru Harbour Board, engaged massively in public works: road, rail, harbour facilities, bridges, telegraph. Supplying immigrants and workers with housing, transport, timber, food, drink, news, shoes, clothes and draft animals locked the private sector, too, into the progress industry, and it also mounted development and settlement schemes of its own. Its equivalent of Vogel was Auckland entrepreneur Thomas Russell, who poured millions of other people's money into projects ranging from the Bank of New Zealand, through the New Zealand Insurance Company, to the draining of Waikato swamps. Public and private sectors alike sucked avidly at the teats of British credit. Progressive colonisation's leading import was money.

Allies of progress included the 'rush phases' of agriculture and sheep farming, when sheep and seed were grown to stock new farms, together with a range of extractive industries. These successively extracted and exported whales, seals, kauri timber and kauri gum, flax and gold. Progress itself warred against nature – mowing forests like grass, for example. Wars against 'natives', especially 1860–72, were in a sense another ally of the progress industry, bringing rapid economic growth to particular districts at particular times through military expenditure and military settlement. Settlement itself followed a spasmodic, rush-like pattern, with the prime benefits going to those first in.

James Froude believed that New Zealand's cities were growing at obscenely high rates, but that farming was languishing. He was a little unfair to the latter. Large- and medium-scale sheep farming for wool was important from the mid-1850s, especially in the South Island. Wool replaced gold as the leading export in 1872.[6] In the 1850s, provisions were supplied for a few years to Californian and Victorian goldfields. In the 1880s, in Canterbury, wheat boomed temporarily into a significant export. Apart from this, however, very little farm production was exported from colonial New Zealand and, outside town-supply districts, the 'normal' domestic market was also limited. The main market was domestic but *abnormal*: the progress industry and its allied rush phases, with their huge demand for food, leather, draft animals and oats. Archetypically, a new district would be deluged by a timber rush, gold rush or public works project such as rail-making, which brought with it large numbers of manual workers – the 'crews' of the progress industry. Roads, shops, pubs and farms would spring up to service their camps. The resulting settlement would either die after the rush phase ended, or skimp and scrape through to long-term viability. Given that most big towns began as organised settlements, it follows that colonisation in New Zealand was more often led by towns and camps than farms. Farms were given precedence only in retrospect, when a new era in which farming was more central rewrote the history of the old.

The motley 'crews' who staffed the rushes and the progress industry differed significantly from other sectors of society. They were wanderers or semi-nomadic workers: sailors, soldiers, whalers, sealers, navvies, lumbermen, goldminers and the like. These groups were mobile, male and prone to binge and to hit each other, and it is partly they who explain colonial Pakeha's high rates of drunkenness and assault. They did, however, share a loose culture, even a 'prefabricated community', which enabled strangers to fit in to teams of co-workers. This 'crew culture' had enduring effects on Pakeha, even after the crews themselves had gone. The term 'mate' is one possible legacy. 'Core' culture was the notional opposite of crew culture. Settled cores were people who stayed in one place, or who hoped or pretended to hope to do so. They struggled to generate local community against the de-socialising tides of immigration, emigration and geographic mobility within New Zealand. Their degree of success in the colonial era is a matter of debate, but historians agree that it was increasing from the 1880s.

The appropriate balance between local, regional and national history is an intriguing problem. A case can be made for telling New Zealand history from the inside out, rather than the outside in. Alternatively, one could argue that the nation as unit is too small, not too big – transnational and global streams join local and regional ones in the national whirlpool. For example, nineteenth-century New Zealand was in many respects part of a 'Tasman world' that it shared with eastern Australia. This book accepts 'national' as a pragmatic, though not entirely satisfactory compromise – a point of balance between internal and external forces. Certainly, by the 1880s, rail, telegraph and steamships were beginning to shrink New Zealand to a size in which countrywide communities of interest could be imagined. National organisations were beginning to sprout. Formal regionalism expired in 1876 with the abolition of the provinces after a life of only two dozen years. Informal regionalism remained significant.

Auckland, long an island of settlement and commerce in a Maori-dominated sea, was booming in the early 1880s. Thames gold was important; speculative investments were even more so; and Auckland's economy differed considerably from those of the southern provinces – less rail and wool, and more sailing ships and trade. Taranaki languished as it had done since the outbreak of the wars of the 1860s, but in the southern half of the North Island a beginning had been made in opening up the 'Great Bush' interior of Wellington and Hawke's Bay. Among the fringe provinces of the South Island, Nelson – once one of the Big Five – had failed to plug in to rail-led progress; Marlborough and Southland had their sheep; and Westland was beginning a shift from goldmining to coalmining, which was less lucrative. Canterbury and Otago rivalled Auckland as the richest provinces, but with much more wool, wheat and rail. Dunedin and Christchurch were the two largest cities in 1881, with Auckland close behind and Wellington well behind, though the capital was about to begin a climb as the hub of inter-regional steamshipping.

These cities had between 20,000 and 40,000 people each – not that small for a recently settled country of 500,000 people. Only two other towns (Napier at 5,700 and Nelson at 6,700) had more than 5,000 people in 1881.[7] There were 59 other boroughs, 63 rural counties and 314 road districts – enough local government for a country five times the size.

Life in the 128 cities, towns and counties of Pakeha New Zealand in the 1880s varied according to a host of factors, of which for the moment we will single out only race, church, class and sex. Lowland Scots Presbyterians were the leading ethnic-religious group in Otago and Southland; English Anglicans everywhere else, though almost matched by Catholic Irish in Westland. Germans, Scandinavians, Welsh and Chinese were the largest other groups – apart from Maori. Crews, who impact less on official statistics than do cores, seem to have been more pan-British than European. The American ship captain who brought James Froude to New Zealand preferred German and Scandinavian crewmen to English, Scots, Irish and Americans because the latter groups 'get drunk, get into prison, give me nothing but trouble'.[8] English, Scots, Irish and neo-British, including Americans, were the main ethnic components of crew culture.

Class was mostly 'loose' rather than 'tight', as yet a matter of shared lifeways rather than shared identity or countrywide community. Only a ramshackle colonial gentry approached tight class in 1880. New Zealand's gentry were sheep farmers, merchants, financiers, officials and professionals. They seldom descended from titled aristocracy; they worked quite hard themselves, and they often started as lower middle class, with more credit than cash. But they shared a common subculture, saw themselves as genteel, and were accepted as such, helped by a general broadening of definitions of gentility. There is little point in arguing about whether they were an upper class or an upper middle class in Old British terms. In New Zealand, there was no-one above them. From the 1870s, with the development of communications facilitating inter-action, especially for those with money, regional genteel élites networked into a New Zealand-wide élite that dominated big business, big farming and politics. This was the process by which loose regional classes become tight national ones. By the 1880s, the New Zealand gentry were a tight ruling class, but one that operated within strict limits, as we shall see.

As in Britain, women in colonial New Zealand suffered from massive political, legal, social and economic inequalities. They had no vote; husbands owned virtually all marital property; women had much less socially approved freedom than men; and, if they could get jobs, they were typically paid half as much. But there are some signs that women took advantage of changed circumstances, in this case the process of colonisation, to ease, though by no means remove, the constraints on them – a limited 'liberty of distance'. Genteel and middle-class women appear to have been able to travel more, send their daughters to school more, and engage more in valued work without loss of status. Men greatly outnumbered women among early Pakeha, and working women appear to have exploited their rarity value to select the husbands with the best prospect of achieving economic independence in the form of a small farm or business. Women's work helped make the prospect real – 'helping on the farm' was really a matter of being co-farmer or even principal farmer. The downside – and it was steep – was eternal drudgery and eternal pregnancy. Colonial Pakeha were certainly demographically progressive. The average family had six children around 1880.

Colonial Pakeha visions of themselves and their future were often surprisingly self-confident and optimistic, even grandiose. There was little hint of a colonial cringe when dealing with London governments or London financiers, partly because of a shared Britishness. Early Pakeha consistently saw themselves as the Britons of the South. They were less consistent about two variations on that theme: 'Greater Britain' and 'Better Britain'. *Greater* Britain prophesied that New Zealand would soon approach, or even equal and surpass, Old Britain in population and wealth, and become fully independent, though still attached to Britain by sentiment. *Better* Britain prophesied that New Zealand would grow much less and permanently remain Britain's junior partner, though a politically autonomous one whose citizens, man for man, were an improvement on the metropolis. To exaggerate for clarity, Greater Britain envisaged both qualitative and quantitative superiority – the American model. Better Britain envisaged qualitative superiority alone – the Scottish model. Pakeha collective identity was also 'Better British' in that it blended Scots and English more than did old Britain. Scots were greatly over-represented among Pakeha, of whom they comprised about a quarter, as against about 10 per cent in the British Isles.[9] Catholic Irish were much less welcome in theory, though they were sometimes assisted to immigrate when other sources of brides or labourers ran dry, or crossed the unpoliced Tasman on their own account. Catholic Irish made up about 14 per cent of the Pakeha population in the 1880s.

Britishness joined concepts of progress and paradise to comprise the three formal 'myths of settlement', a 'Pakeha prospectus' promulgated by colonising crusaders such as Wakefield and Vogel in numerous speeches and publications. Progress in New Zealand was to avoid the price that marred it in Old Britain: a loss of rural virtue; the vices of industrialism; and class tension and conflict. Progress was to be individual as well as collective – nobody came to New Zealand to be worse off. Opportunities for individual progress through prosperity and social promotion did not have to be equal, but they did have to be abundant and widespread. The formal theory was that working men and women would come to New Zealand, serve a long term as labourers or servants while they saved money, then marry each other and buy a small farm or business, so achieving promotion from the working class to the middle class. That there had to be a constant inflow of fresh labourers and servants was one way in which individual progress was locked in to collective progress. The Pakeha paradise complex offered a bewildering array of heavens on earth: a racial paradise where Anglo-Saxon virtue flowered; an investors' paradise, where Old Britons could safely entrust their money to New Britons; a workers' paradise full of well-paid jobs; a brides' paradise full of well-paid husbands; and a genteel paradise where a little money and status went a lot further than at home, and where gentility and the work ethic could be more readily reconciled.

These formal myths of settlement interacted with a set of informal myths, which reinforced the formal at some points and subverted them at others. These informal myths were an element of New Zealand *populism* – a tricky concept but an important one in this book. It is intended to indicate a set of firmly held convictions about the way life should be lived, which were widespread among the lower and lower middle classes of society. It vaguely imagined a community of the 'common people', ultimately gendered, colloquialised and stereotyped into the 'ordinary Kiwi bloke'. Populism can be romanticised. It was in fact capable of such things as extreme racism and sexism. New Zealand populism crossed class and was in some degree proto-nationalist, but it was also compatible with regionalism and pro-British imperialism. It was generally antagonistic to sectional interests, though not immune to capture by them. Typically, the enemies of populism were shadowy – absentee capital, absentee landlords, boardroom conspiracies, 'money power'. The informal myths of settlement quite quickly congealed into a 'populist compact' or 'Pakeha treaty', with which the ruling gentry had to compromise: it was this that placed the limits on their power.

Article One of the Pakeha treaty was egalitarianism: not the absence of class but the absence of extreme class distinctions, class oppression and direct gentry rule. The vote (for Pakeha men) had been more widespread in New Zealand than in Britain since the first elected assemblies of 1853–56. The ratio of electors to adult males was about 60 per cent in 1855 and 84 per cent in 1881.[10] Workers did not rule themselves, but they did choose which gentlemen would rule them, and the rule had to be hands-off, not hands-on. A few gentry dominated large estates like feudal lords, but most did not. Gentry power was exercised more as a class, through the institutions of government, than by genteel individuals. Cap-doffing, respectful address to social superiors, and tipping was much less common than in Britain, and the difference cut in early.

Article Two of the Pakeha treaty was class harmony, the absence of class conflict. In the 1880s, there were no tight countrywide classes apart from the gentry, though there were arguably moves in this direction among workers towards the end of the decade. But there were looser kinds of class, with shared subcultures though not shared collective identities. They included middle-class 'respectables' of various kinds, 'decent' working folk, and the 'disreputable' poor, who were not supposed to exist in New Zealand but did. Poverty was selective, seasonal and sporadic, not endemic, though this was small comfort to victims expecting a progressive paradise. Such divisions were widely recognised at the time; classlessness in colonial New Zealand was a retrospective myth, not a contemporary one. There are constant references to 'the various classes' and 'all classes'. But there is equally frequent reference to the need for these classes to work together in harmony. Indeed, in colonial politics such reference became almost obligatory.

The third and final article of the Pakeha treaty was that collective, and therefore individual, progress should be continuous, delivering a constant fresh supply of opportunity, but not just the kind of opportunity that Wakefield and company had in mind. Under the informal myths of settlement, working people did not necessarily want what the formal myths wanted them to want – social promotion, the desire to eventually move up a class. When they did want it, they wanted it more quickly than the prospectus had envisaged. Workers and servants alike were notoriously quick to quit in search of better prospects. When they did accept a long-term role as wage workers, and many did, they wanted opportunities not for *promotion*, but for the *adoption* of aspects of the lifestyles of the classes above them – while remaining workers. House ownership, horse ownership, easy access to high-status foods such as prime meat, and the availability of leisure are examples. These things were indeed much more accessible to Pakeha workers than to British workers. Adoption was as important as promotion to the informal myths of settlement, and progress in New Zealand was required to deliver both.

Readers of Australian, Canadian and American history will note resonances in all this. Progressive or explosive colonisation, progress industries, allied extractive industries, rush phases, myths of settlement formal and informal, the liberty of distance, 'crew culture' and 'populist compacts' were transnational phenomena. They were part of a pan-British (and American and Irish) system of supercharged settlement. It is this shared system that explains how different 'fragments' (particular sources of settlers) and different 'frontiers' (settler environments) could achieve similar results. There is a sense in which retrospective nationalisms artificially repackage the booming, rushing, ravaging development of nineteenth-century neo-Britains.

To the 1880s, the record of my particular package – colonial New Zealand

– was impressive, though by no means unmarred. 'Progress without the price, paradise without the serpent, and Britain without the Irish' had proven too hard an act for history to follow precisely. Colonial populism, sporadic but sharp poverty, 70,000 Irish and innumerable Australians had all slithered into the garden, but garden there still was. Migrants and money poured in, gold and babies poured out, grasslands and flocks grew at staggering rates, while resilient Maori were gradually forced back if not down. A flawed paradise, but still quite British and very progressive, sped down the rapids of history into the 1880s.

PART

I

Better Britain 1880s–1920s

INTRODUCTION

In 1884–85, Britain, with its Egyptian client-ally, found itself at war with the people of the Sudan, under Muhammad Ahmad, the Mahdi. The course of the struggle was followed avidly, via telegraph, throughout the British Empire. Interest centred on the Mahdist siege of the Egyptian garrison in Khartoum, commanded by General Charles Gordon, and on the relieving army creeping down the Nile towards it, reluctantly dispatched by Prime Minister Gladstone in response to public pressure. On 26 January 1885, two days before relief arrived, the Mahdists stormed Khartoum and killed Gordon, who was instantly deified.

> The empire, and indeed the entire western world, shared Britain's sense of loss and bereavement over Gordon's death ... he seemed to embody everything that was finest and noblest in the British Empire ... Nowhere were these feelings as strong as they were in the Australian colonies ... many felt that the colonies had lost a favourite son. Gordon had had many relatives and friends in the Antipodes – in Adelaide and Dunedin in particular.[1]

First prompted by a retired veteran of the New Zealand Wars, Commissary-General Edward Strickland, the Australian colonies tripped over themselves to contribute avenging troops. New South Wales, South Australia and Queensland offered contingents within three weeks of Gordon's death. The New South Wales offer was accepted, and by March 1885, 770 Australians had joined 400 Canadians in the Sudan. The Empire, for the first time, had marched.

Almost a hundred years later, Britain engaged in another distant war that was also big international news. In 1982, Argentine forces seized the Falkland, or Malvinas, Islands in the South Atlantic, and a British armada soon sailed to eject them – dispatched by Prime Minister Margaret Thatcher with a great deal more enthusiasm than displayed by Gladstone in 1885. Few of the millions who followed these events had much sympathy for the Argentine military regime, and the British tabloid press had a field day – 'Stuff That Up Your Junta!' But internationally there was a feeling that wars for Empire were things of the past, and there was talk in London political circles that a negotiated solution had been possible – giving Argentina nominal sovereignty but retaining British control – and that the Falkland settlers themselves had been willing to accept this.[2] Britain fought alone, with circumspect and semi-official help from the United States, and none from Australia and Canada. This time, the Empire did not march.

As we would expect, the New Zealand government attitude to these two British wars was markedly different. The relevant leaders were John Ballance, Minister of Defence in 1885, and Robert Muldoon, Prime Minister and de facto Minister of Everything in 1982. Both were able and independent-minded men, sons of Ulster, and staunch nationalists and Liberals in the New Zealand sense. They were exceptionally unenthusiastic in supporting Britain in one war, and exceptionally enthusiastic about supporting it in the other. The funny thing is that they somehow got these responses the wrong way round.

'Muldoon took a strong pro-British position. New Zealand broke diplomatic relations with Argentina almost immediately, without even awaiting a British request.' He provided a symbolic warship – to free up a British one for active service in the Falklands – and he published an article in *The Times* of London: 'Why We Stand With Our Mother Country.'[3] A century earlier, Ballance was not 'willing to commit New Zealand to any overseas military adventure and refused to send colonial troops to assist Britain in the Sudan'.[4] As in New South Wales, a New Zealand Wars veteran, Colonel Charles Rookes, was quick to prompt Ballance to send troops. 'In a letter I received from him,' wrote Rookes, '(written after the fall of Khartoum & death of Gordon) in reply to one I had sent him suggesting that a thousand of the best riders in the world could be formed in New Zealand & sent to the Soudan in a month . . . he negatived the idea & said his sympathies *were with the Mahdi*!'[5] What on earth was going on here?

Ballance and Muldoon were not necessarily typical of the public feeling of their day. Many New Zealanders favoured support for Britain in the Sudan; many opposed it in the Falklands. But Ballance and Muldoon were leaders, and they were (perhaps extreme) examples of quite widespread sentiments, not entirely out of step with the mood of their times. What, then, shifted New Zealand from apparently least loyal to most loyal of neo-Britains in the century after 1885?

Historians have not asked this question, let alone answered it. New Zealand's 'birthday' as an independent nation is variously dated to 1856 and the advent of elected government; to 1907 and the achievement of dominion status; to 1915, when adult nationhood was allegedly earned in blood on the slopes of Gallipoli; or to various other dates. The multiple births of the same entity should always have made us suspicious. A minority strand of opinion, dating from the 1930s and drawing from Marxist thought and later 'dependency theory', argues that New Zealand was very dependent in the 1880s and for the whole century thereafter. The master might have changed from British to 'international' capital, but not the dependency.[6] These views had little impact. The majority 'nationalist' view consistently argues that nationalism and independence grew naturally, steadily and gradually, but disputes the beginning and end points and the character of the growth.

One variant, loyalist nationalism, which held sway as the orthodoxy until the 1950s, stressed the earning of independence, freely given by an enlightened Britain, through loyalty, especially in war. This view permeated the school texts of the 1920s and was given more sophisticated expression by historians, such as W. P. Morrell in 1935.[7] It survives to the present in the notions that New Zealand's fervent imperialism of the first half of the twentieth century was fully compatible with nationalism, and that the nation was born on the slopes of Gallipoli. Another variant, popular nationalism, indelibly associated with historian Keith Sinclair, emerged with his classic *History of New Zealand* in 1959 and was given its fullest expression in his 1988 book, *A Destiny Apart*.[8] Sinclair argued that independent nationalism was unilaterally assumed by the people around 1900, not given by Britain. The people drove nationalism forward in progressive steps, with literary and political élites tagging along behind – sometimes a long way behind. Sinclair asserted that imperial fervour was partly mere official rhetoric, camouflaging popular nationalism. Both variants agree that war, especially that of 1914–18, consolidated national feeling though in different ways.

In short, the minority Marxian view graphs the story as a straight line along the bottom of a scale of independence. Both nationalist views draw incremental lines from low to high. Ballance and Muldoon involuntarily suggest the opposite: a line from high to low: that New Zealand became *less* independent after 1885. Did so strange a transformation, a shift from greater to lesser independence, against the expectations nurtured by the vast majority of our history books, indeed come about, and if so, how? This book's answer is a phenomenon we will call 'recolonisation'.

'Recolonisation', a major theme of this book, is my term for a renewal and reshaping of links between colony and metropolis after an earlier period of colonisation. In New Zealand's case, it reshuffled and tightened links with Britain between the 1880s and 1900s. It welded selected shards of the old regime together with fresh developments to form a new system in this period. The system had reached full fruition by the 1920s. It transformed New Zealand's economy, technology, politics, conceptual geography, history and ideology, and penetrated directly or indirectly into almost every other sphere. Similar transformations arguably occurred in Australia and Canada too, but the system was not multilateral. It was bilateral, with each recolonised neo-Britain establishing its own tight links with the homeland. In some respects, New Zealand and the relevant bits of Britain made up a single entity. Essentially, New Zealand became a town-supply district of London. London became the cultural capital of New Zealand.

Recolonisation's economic centrepiece was the 'protein industry': the mass export of frozen meat and dairy products to Britain, especially London. This transformed the New Zealand countryside; reduced regional differences; and created a powerful new class of medium farmers. The technological centrepiece, which drew on worldwide changes sometimes known as the 'Second Industrial Revolution', was the paradoxical emergence of a highly industrial and technological culture and a semi-industrial economy. New Zealand lived *as though* it were highly industrialised. In conceptual geography, New Zealand became smaller, its parts knit more tightly. It shifted away from Australia and towards Britain. In history, robust and ruthless town- and camp-led progress was written out, steady and virtuous farm-led progress was written in. In politics, relations with Britain became more deferential, but with a tacit price attached: the maintenance of privileged access to Britain's food, money and job markets. Recolonial collective identity was intense, but not nationalist. It was subnationalist, or 'dominionist' – a New Zealand identity fitting neatly within a British one. New Zealand's view of its future became more modest. It shifted away from the American model and towards the Scottish model; away from a destiny independent from, and even greater than, Britain's, towards acceptance of permanently smaller size and permanently junior partnership – smaller and junior, but very close, influential, and in some respects qualitatively superior. Quality replaced quantity as the centrepiece of New Zealand pride; Better Britain replaced Greater Britain.

It is easier to date the middle of an epoch than its beginning and end. Echoes of progressive colonisation persisted beyond the 1880s, to the 1900s. But, broadly speaking, the 1880s mark the beginning of modern New Zealand history. Not only were the 1880s the point where the majority of Maori began to live under some Pakeha control, but the decade also marked a huge shift in Pakeha history, from progressive colonisation to recolonisation. Before the 1880s, New Zealand imported people, goods and money at rates that were gargantuan in proportion to the numbers already here. After the 1880s, though growth eventually recommenced and even became quite respectable, it greatly diminished in rate and changed in kind. History slowed down.

Part One explores the period 1880s–1920s, when the new system emerged in the ruins of the old, replacing an extractive economy with a more sustainable one. Chapter One looks at the 'Black Eighties', at the advent of the reforming Liberal government in 1890 and its particular reforging of paradise during its long 1891–1912 reign, and at New Zealand's withdrawal from an

Australasian 'Tasman world' in 1901. Chapter Two outlines the new recolonial cultural and economic system that got up and running between the 1880s and 1900s. Chapter Three looks at the internal and external conflicts of 1912–22, including New Zealand's participation in World War One. By the 1920s, the recolonial system was firmly ensconced at the helm of New Zealand history.

CHAPTER ONE

God's Lone Country

Progressive colonisation in New Zealand was part of a still-greater process, as noted in the Prologue. Older neo-Europes, especially in the Americas, boomed through their own versions of steroid-boosted colonisation, progress by the dream-driven mass migration of people and money. New neo-Europes spawned from the same cause. The vast interiors of Canada and the United States, Brazil and Argentina sprouted fresh states, provinces and territories. The fruits of the new flocks and fields were shipped back to Old Europe, where Britain's growth was slowing. After earlier fluctuations, prices dropped in the late 1870s, and kept dropping to the 1890s.

The investors of England and Scotland, genteel widows to great companies, lost the sharp end of their confidence, symbolised by the collapse of the City of Glasgow Bank of 1878, followed by other banking crises to the 1890s. What one progressive colonial New Zealander, John Logan Campbell, had called 'ye Milch Cow John Bull'[1] began to go dry, her otherwise precocious calves far from weaned of the milk of human credit. On the pampas, prairies and grain seas of the Americas, progressive colonisation had sown the seeds of its own doom. The doom clouds wafted along the migration lines to New Zealand. Historians differ on their date of arrival and length of stay, but with some consensus on the years 1879–95, with the nadir in 1886–92. This was the 'Long Depression', the 'Black Eighties', when the promised land reneged on its promises, and tens of thousands got out.

The Long Stagnation

The Long Depression of the 1880s has a grim chapter of its own in most New Zealand history books, a cautionary tale of bubbles burst, but some scholars now dispute its very existence.[2] Defining 'depression' narrowly, they point out that prices dropped at least as fast as wages, holding up living standards for those in work, and that the 'frictional' unemployment of the 1880s was localised, seasonal and sporadic, not very different from that of earlier decades. They have a case. Unemployment statistics were a thing of the future, but the patchy figures available yield rates that do not seem that high: 'only 1 or 2 per cent of the labour force' in summer. 'The problem of unemployment seems to have been one of isolated pockets.'[3] The rate of landholding in proportion to the number of adult males also held up, and even increased slightly.[4] There was some investment in new industries; increased volumes of wool and wheat cushioned lower prices so that export values per capita did not drop much; and in most regions a degree of growth continued.

One could quibble at this new optimistic view. Men scraped together two or three pounds and crossed the Tasman rather than appear in the unemployment statistics, which were very incomplete anyway. Because those without property were readier to emigrate they reduced the ranks of adult males more than they did those of landholders. Unemployment might be low in summer, but it rose to 6 per cent or even 12 per cent in winter in large towns.[5] One estimate of the overall national rate in 1886 is 9 per cent.[6] Even the optimists concede underemployment – and the overemployment of long hours and low pay, especially for women and youths – was rife. Claims that most people 'toiled in poverty', and that beggars and vagrants 'lay in thousands under the hedge rows' may be exaggerated,[7] but many working people lived on the brink of poverty even in the 1860s and 1870s, and the 1880s were more likely to push them over.

In 1888, 5 per cent of the households in Freemans Bay, Auckland, received organised charitable relief.[8] The genteel and respectable did not apply for charity; the disreputable did not get it; and these classes made up half of the households in the locality. This implies that 10 per cent of decent working people in Freemans Bay received help, and more would have been too transient or too proud to apply, or looked too disreputable or able-bodied to get it if they did. Although no aggregates are available for rural areas, the evidence for a large increase in the number of wandering loners, or 'swaggers', searching for work or alms, does pile up.[9] While the optimists quite rightly point out that boom conditions ended in different regions at different times, they did end almost everywhere at some time. It remains true that the pessimists ignore the fact that falling prices cushioned falling wages, and that their estimates of joblessness are less convincing than lower ones. But something big did happen in and around the 1880s, even if it was not technically a 'depression'.

What the 1880s witnessed in fact was the end of progressive colonisation, and the end was permanent. Huge and long-term reversals at the broadest level of economic analysis, hinging on the years 1885–86, tell the tale. Until then, New Zealand's imports in most years far exceeded exports, with the balance made up by overseas borrowing. From then, exports exceeded imports with few exceptions for the next 90 years. There is a tendency to associate this change with the rise of exports; in fact the collapse of imports was initially more significant. Imports per head of New Zealand's population were running at £24 in 1874. By 1880 they had dropped to £11, and to £8 in 1890. Exports only fell from £16 per capita in 1874 to £12 in 1880; and they remained roughly at that level to the mid-1890s, when a steady rise began.[10] The change from net importer to net exporter reflects a change from an extractive to a sustainable economy, with the Long Depression – perhaps better described as the 'Long Stagnation' – as the period of transition. But the 'extraction' had been as much from the purses of Britain as the goldmines and native pastures of New Zealand, and the 1880s ended this too.

Between 1840 and 1886, public and private sectors, Vogelism and Russellism, worked in tandem to drag in from Britain a capital inflow of about £71 million. Reading billion for million gives a better idea of the impact. Money flooded in from Britain. Thereafter it flowed out to Britain. Public borrowing did not stop in the 1880s and 1890s, except for brief periods, but it could no longer keep pace with interest payments. Between 1880 and 1896, government interest payments exceeded new borrowing by £7.5 million.[11] This appears to have remained the case until the 1980s. The public debt ballooned out 'by virtue of the workings of compound interest',[12] not by new net capital imports. We are still paying for the progressive colonising crusade. The same reversal was even more marked in private capital migration, where, according to one estimate, outflows exceeded inflows by £15 million between 1887 and 1906.[13] British investors, who had been dominated by New Zealand entrepreneurs such as Russell to a surprising degree, mutinied and pulled their money out, or lost it. Only six of the 31 New Zealand–British public companies survived to 1910, and of those five had to be 'drastically reconstructed'.[14] Russellism disappeared, whereas Vogelism was only crippled, and hereafter overseas borrowing became largely a public affair – a platonic one as far as the net immigration of money was concerned.

British investment in New Zealand, government borrowing and economic growth did not stop, even in the depths of the Long Stagnation. But they did diminish so greatly in net impact and source that they changed in kind. The immigration of people as well as money dried up; indeed, there was net emigration in some years – the 'Exodus'. People who had not yet heard the news continued to flow in from Britain. But those who *had* heard the news flowed out to Australia in even greater numbers. In 1887–91, there was a net gain of about 16,000 on the migrant exchange with Britain. This in itself was a mere travesty of 1870s gains of over 100,000, but there was also a net loss of 25,000 on the exchange with Australia.[15] The overall net loss, 1885–90, was about 20,000.[16] This was the unkindest cut of all to the ultimate immigrants' paradise.

The population still grew considerably in the 1880s because birth rates, though beginning a long decline, were still high, and because it was not until 1886 that stagnation covered almost the whole country, pushing people across the Tasman rather than across Cook Strait. But it was now just growth rather than explosive growth. The population had doubled in the 1860s and again in the 1870s. In the 1880s, it rose by one-half; and in the 1890s by one-quarter. Even in the 1900s, when progress staged something of a last stand, it grew by only 30 per cent. This growth came mainly from local wombs and local purses, not British ones. 'Artificial' progress, boosted by the imported steroids of credit, became more 'natural'.

The optimists are right in suggesting that stagnation hit different regions at different times, but wrong where they imply that some escaped almost entirely. Progressive colonisation stopped first in Otago and Canterbury, which were especially sensitive to wool and wheat prices, about 1879. With minor exceptions, it stopped last in Auckland, about 1886, to which wool and wheat were not important. But stop it did. Auckland provincial district more than doubled in population between 1871 and 1886, while the cultivated area (mainly sown grasses for pasturing stock) increased sixfold. In the next fifteen years, the population increased by only one-third, and cultivations by only two-thirds. Otago and Canterbury doubled their population – and quintupled their cultivations – in the single decade of the frenetic 1870s. In the 1880s, cultivations increased only 70 per cent, despite the drive to increase export volumes of wool and wheat, while the population grew a pathetic 10 per cent.

Even the southern North Island (Wellington, Hawke's Bay and Taranaki), which one historian suggests was sheltered from stagnation by settlement of the bush-clad interior,[17] experienced a great drop in the speed of growth. Together, these three regions grew threefold in people in the 1870s, and sixfold in cultivations. In the 1880s, the increases were 60 and 50 per cent respectively – the 'opening of the Great Bush' proceeded at one-twelfth the rate in the 1880s that it had in the 1870s. The rate of growth in all these regions dropped to between a sixth and a tenth of what it had been before.[18] The great slow-down was also apparent in public works. The second-biggest spurt of rail construction was in the 1920s, when annual spending peaked at £5 10s per capita. In the 1870s, it had been £6, and rail-making costs per mile had increased fivefold in the intervening period. In other words, 1870s rail-making ran at over five times the rate of the silver medallist of the 1920s, with only a bronze medal in the 1900s, and no medal at all in the 1880s, 1890s and 1910s.[19]

'Getting on' changed down several gears for individuals and companies as well as regions, and here the gearbox seized completely for many. Some leading businessmen, such as J. C. Firth and Thomas Morrin of Auckland, and Waring Taylor of Wellington, went bust. Frederick Whitaker's eldest son committed suicide in the Auckland Club in 1887, 'depressed by his losses from land speculations'. His father, Russell's closest associate, 'could not assist him financially. He himself faced financial ruin.'[20] John Logan Campbell, later known as the 'Father of Auckland', was in such dire straits that he became 'tired of life and wished it were all ended'. His desperate struggles to meet his interest bill – giving up his carriage, ceasing entertaining, reducing his household staff to two maids and personally acting as the chief clerk of his brewery – were almost enough to make one feel sorry for him.[21] Other merchant princes suffered similarly, including Russell himself. Like Campbell, he recovered somewhat after 1895, and died in 1904 leaving £160,000, but this was a mere fraction of the millions that had passed through his hands.[22]

Many, perhaps most, of the leading colonising crusaders and substantial family firms also seem to have scraped through, though often as mere shadows of their former financial selves. The companies they were associated with fared less well, and small investors and businessmen still worse. Not only did the New Zealand–British companies that had helped lead progressive colonisation die like flies in London, but of the 122 companies formed in Auckland between 1881 and 1884, only five still existed in 1904.[23] Accountants and lawyers did quite well as undertakers to the insolvent, but they had to cut their rates by two-thirds, and Wyndham Street, Auckland, became known as 'Wind-'em-up Street'.[24] Colonywide, the rate of bankruptcies, most of them small 'getters-on' such as shopkeepers and master tradesmen, was quite staggering in proportion to population. The rate of bankruptcies in post-crash 1879 was almost eight times that of post-crash 1988.[25] There were 11,444 bankruptcies in the 1880s, on top of 4,000 in 1877–79.[26] In proportion to population, the total would be equivalent to about 100,000 today. One wonders how the 15,000 bankrupts would have reacted to the suggestion that there was no 'Long Depression'.

Once convinced that boosted progress had indeed stopped, people began searching for someone to blame. Decent and respectable people tended to blame a shadowy enemy of populism, which was taking firmer shape in the 1880s in a form that looked rather like the gentry. The gentry sometimes reciprocated. Russell described democracy as 'the curse of New Zealand' – in 1889, before it had fully arrived.[27] Campbell believed that 'the lower classes . . . had been living in a fool's paradise' – the very lowest level of the Pakeha heaven on earth.[28] All classes seemed prone to a sense of Original Sin; the colonising crusade had borrowed too many apples, and so let the serpent of stagnation into the garden. There was a strong tendency to attribute the end of progress to moral failings, nemesis following hubris, and to turn against the things associated with it. The antipathy to government borrowing, though very marked in the early 1890s, proved temporary. But a huge dent in collective self-confidence lasted longer, and an antipathy to banks, to big speculators and to town- and camp-led progress, or even the memory of it, lasted longer still.

The 'sin' of adventuring too far cannot wholly explain the crash of the 1880s, of course – or at least, not local sin. It was not, argues one economic historian, 'penance for past extravagance'.[29] As noted above, colonising crusades in other neo-Britains increased supply, while demand in Britain slowed, halving wheat prices in 1885 compared with 1877, and doing even more damage to wool. But stagnation struck Canada earlier, and Australia later, and, as we have seen, it took seven years to cover the whole of New Zealand. What explains these variations? Differing regional sensitivity to wool and wheat prices is part of the answer, as is the end of the rush phases in wool, gold and wheat around 1867, 1873 and 1878 respectively. Another factor may be that a need to freehold land absorbed genteel capital at the cost of investment in alternative export industries, though there was some development in this direction.

But there is something in the traditional metaphor of a bubble burst. While the crusaders kept faith, and kept pouring money into progress, it happened. At first, the fall in prices was seen as temporary, as it had been before. The confident or fanatical kept spending. The Bank of New Zealand built itself a headquarters in Dunedin for £30,000 at the very time progress in Otago was grinding to a halt, in 1879–83.[30] Big spending in the North Island clearly postponed stagnation there until about 1885. Progress seems to have held out longest in the Deep South. While neighbouring Invercargill stagnated, Bluff, where Joseph Ward, a creature of both old and new eras, was pouring borrowed capital into the Ocean Beach freezing works, kept booming until about 1888.[31] While some kept their nerve and kept spending, stagnation was ameliorated or postponed, and if enough lenders and borrowers had kept their nerve through the 1880s, who knows what might have happened? Banks and other lenders found that turning off the taps of credit was easier said than done. Like other high priests of progressive colonisation, such as Russell and Vogel, Ward was a great maker of converts. Golden tongues were reinforced by the hard fact that too many bankrupt clients could mean bankrupt banks – a fate that did indeed meet Ward's backers, the Colonial Bank of Otago, as well as Ward himself. Vast sectors of the economy were addicted to the great progressive steroid, credit – dealers almost as much as addicts. Its drying-up was cold turkey that some could not survive, and it dried up partly because people feared it would. Ideas about the potentiality of credit helped make progressive colonisation; ideas about the limits of credit helped kill it. There is a cultural history of economics.

The Exemplary Paradise

The Long Stagnation was presided over by various, mainly genteel, colonial governments, not hugely different from those of the 1860s and 1870s. The Stout–Vogel ministry of 1884–87 was an unholy alliance between Robert Stout, a usually liberal Dunedin jurist, and the chief crusader himself, Julius Vogel. Their successors, the so-called 'Scarecrow Ministry' of 1887–90, were uncomfortably led by Harry Atkinson, a Taranaki War hero and conservative capable of surprising spasms of radicalism in spheres other than economics. Stagnations or depressions do not make governments popular, and Atkinson was an exponent of what became New Zealand's panacea for them: retrench-ment, the art of living within contracting means, so guaranteeing their contraction. He lost the 1890 general election to a new alliance led by John Ballance. This alliance called itself *the* Liberals, and succeeded in entrenching the name in people's minds. It ruled until 1912, and its advent in 1890 ranks with the Treaty of Waitangi in 1840 as one of the dates twentieth-century schoolchildren were expected to know even if they knew nothing else. Its three leaders were a trinity around whom legends gathered: Seddon the Father, Ward the Son, and Ballance the Holy Spirit.

Ballance held office from January 1891, when the Liberals actually took office, to 1893, when he died despite a last-minute injection of champagne by his desperate doctors.[32] Stout was his heir apparent, but was out of Parliament and found Seddon firmly ensconced in the premiership before he could get back in. Stout was perhaps too intellectual for the times anyway. In 1887, he had 'threatened his constituents with complete retirement from politics should he be defeated'.[33] This is seldom a clever move for politicians, and he lost. Richard Seddon was a remarkable man: the first guardian of New Zealand populism who was actually a populist himself. Like a later Prime Minister, Robert Muldoon, he attached voters to him partly by deceiving intellectuals into thinking he was unintelligent. His ability to ride the crest of public sentiment like a bulky surfer was quite extraordinary. 'King Dick, as I am usually known' reigned from 1893 to 1906, when he died in office, and in retrospect he tends to dwarf his fellow premiers.[34] His predecessor, Ballance, is sometimes said to have been more use to his party dead than alive; and his successor, Ward, Premier 1906–12, has been described by an eminent Australian historian as 'a muddled man who could not even understand his own arguments'.[35] Muddled or not, Ward was a phoenix, rising from political death at least twice between 1895 and 1930, when physical death finally ran him down. Recent biographies have given a more rounded picture of two able and influential politicians.[36]

Beneath the big three was a second Liberal trinity, subordinate but not necessarily less significant. It included John McKenzie, huge small farmer's friend and union basher, the Liberals' chief evangelist of closer settlement on land to be obtained from anywhere at all. It also included William Pember Reeves, a brilliant young socialist, architect of both the Liberals' labour policy and their image in history. Finally, there was James Carroll, half-Maori and initiator of important new developments in Maori co-operation with the state. Chapter Six will argue that his historical reputation is not as good as it deserves to be.[37]

The key factor behind the Liberals' rise to power was a public sense that the populist compact was in danger, or had indeed been breached. Serpents – overt poverty, sweated labour, unemployment – had crept into paradise during the 1880s. Among the worst serpents was the fact that non-serpents were creeping out. Even Britishness was under some threat. The number of Chinese-born in New Zealand peaked at 5,000 in 1881 – a figure still not exceeded in 1976.[38] Liberals as diverse as Stout and Seddon were even more vehement in their condemnation of Chinese immigration than were non-Liberals. More subtly, great economic changes discussed below were focusing links with Britain more on London big business, and less on Britain as a whole. This shift was a matter of degree – London finance had always been important – and it was only beginning in 1890, but Ballance in particular made much of the malign influence of 'absentee capital' and 'overseas banks'.[39]

Land Monopoly and Absentee Capital, and their joint offspring, Absentee Landholding, were classically shadowy enemies of populism; tight class was another. Liberal rhetoric against genteel landowners was often fierce and struck fertile ground among voters. The guardians of the populist compact, the gentry, had failed in their trust and were increasingly looking like serpents themselves – a self-interested tight class or class community who were locking up the land in their great estates. Some gentry leaned left as far as they dared, and put forward a relatively ungenteel face in Atkinson, but the populist mantle slipped from their shoulders during the late 1880s. Their last strong-hold in national politics was the Legislative Council, the Upper House. In the early 1890s, this impeded some legislation and was blamed for the tardiness of more. The Liberals made much of this. 'The great obstructiveness of the Legislative Council . . . was of immense political value to the Liberal government. Indeed, it might not have survived but for this assistance.'[40] The Liberals both profited from and facilitated the recognition of the gentry as a tight class, an enemy of populism. We will see in Chapter Four, however, that their antagonism to the gentry was more bark than bite.

In 1890, the spectre of class seemed to grin from the bottom as well as the top of society. In the previous two years, there had been a sudden spurt of union forming, union joining and even union federating, culminating in the New Zealand Maritime Council, centred on seamen and waterside workers, and modelled on and allied to an Australian organisation of the same name. It was not very militant, but once the council found itself involved in the Australasian Maritime Strike in August 1890, it was no use telling this to the public. The strike was substantial and traumatic, but also limited, peaceful and orderly – 'by no means a violent or bitterly-fought conflict'.[41] It does not seem to have represented a widespread social conflict. It ended in victory for the employers.[42] The view that the Maritime Strike indicates the formation of a substantial tight working class, and that this class turned from the strike to the vote to play a crucial role in the Liberal victory, has been the subject of debate.[43] Those in favour may be overinfluenced by a desire to discover victory for workers in defeat, extending the long list of socialist Dunkirks; those against, by the myth of classlessness. Most labour activists at the time spoke in populist terms – advocating major improvements in conditions for 'the working classes' (the plural is significant) but also preaching class harmony. The three dozen Liberal candidates who received their endorsement in the 1890 election did exactly the same thing, and these men were overwhelmingly middle class.[44]

Populism and tight class were not wholly incompatible, but, to fit in with the former, the latter had to be well camouflaged and have strong alliances outside its natural constituency. There is some evidence for the emergence of regional senses of collective identity among workers in 1887–90, especially in Dunedin.[45] On one flank, this emphasised old, moderate, craft unionism, centred on skilled workers and a populist outlook; on the other, 'new' or 'industrial' unionism, with a more militant outlook and more 'unskilled' participation. There was considerable drift of ideas and people between the two wings. The *Otago Workman* sometimes preached class harmony with the best, but also saw the strike as 'the great battle of Armageddon long since predicted'.[46] When Armageddon fizzled out, some labour groups do appear to have made an organised entry into politics. But they succeeded in proportion to their moderation, to their acceptance of populism, not their militancy. In short, what we seem to have in 1890 is the embryo of a national working class rather than the thing itself.

This embryo gave some direct help to the Liberals, but its main effect was indirect. Tight class reared a second head to frighten the voters. Militant workers seemed to join land-monopolising gentry as an enemy of populism. Some on each side of Parliament advocated repressing worker discontent, but most saw stagnation and landlessness as its cause, and preferred a more moderate approach. Atkinson 'endeavoured to avoid being regarded as the instrument of the economically dominant classes by introducing a number of labour bills in 1890 and by adopting an attitude of strict impartiality during the Maritime Strike'.[47] Like successor governments in similar situations, the Liberals became more liberal through having to out-liberal Atkinson. Some Liberals were quite sympathetic to the strikers, and the party soon co-opted J. A. Millar, the strike leader. Organised labour, especially in Dunedin, responded with votes. But some Liberals, such as John McKenzie, chastised the strikers, and most expressed support for industrial harmony, not the strike.[48] In the end, the decisive factor was that the Liberal claim to be defenders of populism from class enemies above and below was more convincing than the government's claim. 'This is the greatest organised effort the Liberals have ever put forth,' wrote Ballance during the 1890 election campaign, 'and it will show what they can do against the classes.'[49]

It was, perhaps, not so much what the Liberals stood for that made them convincing defenders of populism, as who they were – even who they were *not*. They were an alternative to the early-settler genteel élite that had run New Zealand since the 1850s. Wellington members of the House of Representatives (MHRs) between 1856 and 1896 were two-thirds English, and 87.5 per cent 'high white collar' – genteel in our terms. Virtually all were overseas-born. Twenty-three out of 40 had settled in New Zealand before 1860. Nine of the 40 became Cabinet ministers.[50] By contrast, about a quarter of Liberal MHRs countrywide were New Zealand-born. This was hardly unexpected, a function of the passage of time, but what is more surprising is that over half of the migrant majority were Scots and Irish. Only a quarter of the migrants had arrived before 1860.[51] Ward's 1908 Cabinet of ten included five Scots, two Maori and an Irish Catholic prime minister.[52] This should not be mistaken for a rise in anti-English feeling – you could not get more Anglophile than Joseph Ward. But it was a changing of the guard. The four cities voted Liberal, but the majority of Liberal Cabinet ministers came not from the main settlements but from out-regions, like their three leaders. Liberal members themselves were predominantly middle class; few were either gentry or workers. All five Liberal premiers (including two very short-term incumbents) had been small businessmen.[53] In 1881, a leading newspaper complained about the rising young politician, Richard Seddon.

> His want of education; his incapacity to reflect; his aversion to anything like study or application; his entire ignorance of the subject he professes to be talking about; his Lancashire brogue; his intolerable use of his h's, render him a grotesque caricature of a legislator.[54]

You could say what you liked about Dick Seddon, but you could not say that he was genteel.

Ballance certainly saw himself as working in the interests of 'all classes'. 'The capitalist equally with the labourer must be identified, by residence and by fulfilling all the duties of a colonist, with the progress and destiny of New Zealand.'[55] Anyone who incited disharmony was, according to Seddon, 'an enemy' of New Zealand.[56] He who tried to 'set class against class', declared Ward, was a 'traitor to the best interests of New Zealand'. 'I do not want to do anything unfair to any class of the community.' He believed, above all, in a 'harmonious society'.[57] These comments show that the Liberal leaders, like most other people at the time, but unlike many historians, had no doubt that classes existed in New Zealand. This was taken for granted. It was not class itself, but tight and overt class and class disharmony that were the problems. The Liberals did not represent the workers against the genteel or vice versa; they did not even represent the decent and respectable against the genteel. They represented all classes against all class communities. Thus the Liberals slipped into the populist mantle that had slipped from the shoulders of the gentry in the 1880s.

Gaining power was one thing. Keeping it was another. One way in which the Liberal government marked a clear and permanent departure from its past was simple longevity. Before 1890, New Zealand ministries had an average life of sixteen months. The Liberal government stayed in power for almost 22 years, and its successors also had long runs – the Reform Party from 1912 to 1928, the Labour Party from 1935 to 1949, and the National Party from 1949 to 1984 (with two short breaks in 1957–60 and 1972–75). This was mega-shift indeed in terms of formal political stability. Liberal longevity is sometimes attributed to their introduction of a strong party organisation. But the best recent analysis suggests that Liberal Party organisation was not that strong, and anyway it did not get up and running until 1899.[58] Three other factors seem more important to Liberal longevity. As discussed above, the Liberals firmly grasped the mantle of guardians of populism in 1890, and they kept their grip on it, helped by the fact that they themselves seemed much more like members of the people than did their opponents.

Another factor behind the Liberal longevity was the weakness of the competition, which was bound up with the notorious absence of 'checks and balances' in New Zealand's parliamentary system. There was little in the way of a written constitution or a tradition of testing legislation in the courts that could constrain the will of Parliament. For the Liberals and their successors, 'Parliament' was effectively the House of Representatives. After serving its electoral purpose as enemy of the people in 1893, the Legislative Council, or Upper House, was effectively almost castrated and had little influence until its abolition in 1950. The provinces were long gone, and local governments were numerous but small and weak. The parliamentary Opposition was also weak – so weak in fact that between 1901 and 1903 it gave up the ghost completely and disbanded itself. New Zealand was briefly but literally a one-party state. 'Politics is dead,' wrote one Opposition leader, William Rolleston, at this time, 'Seddon is a great fact and must be *accepted* as such.'[59] The small size of the House of Representatives (74 seats 1890–99; 80 seats 1902–66), which enabled Cabinet to dominate Parliament, and the small size of Cabinet, which enabled the prime minister to dominate Cabinet, meant that astute leaders could remain in populism's driving seat for a long time.

A third key to Liberal longevity, as Rolleston's concession implied, was King Dick himself, under whose leadership they won five of their eight successful elections. Seddon's political mastery has yet to be fully unravelled, but a few points about it should be noted. He made at least as much use of direct and indirect patronage – jobs for individuals and public expenditure for districts – as his pre-1890 predecessors. But, in contrast to them, he consistently rewarded support rather than placated opposition. This provided an incentive for the former, but not the latter.

> He learned the lesson that concessions to 'disloyalty' only intensified the problem. He stabilized the party by making abundantly and blatantly plain . . . that only loyalty would be rewarded . . . Every dissident without exception languished in the wilderness.[60]

Another element of Seddon's success was his anti-intellectualism, or rather, his hiding of his own considerable intellectual lights under a bushel of bluff and, in some eyes, vulgar bombast. Sharing populist anti-intellectualism, and almost revelling in the scorn from intellectuals and other élites that this induced, was a key to the populist mandate. Seddon fooled some historians, and he fooled contemporary intellectuals, including his own colleague Reeves. 'Seddon,' wrote Reeves waspishly, 'was not encumbered with either theories or ideals. If you had spoken to him of Utopia, he would have asked you where it was.'[61] Reeves was wrong. 'We' did ask him, and he told us that it was here, in God's Own Country.

'God's Own Country' was Seddon's favourite phrase, an announcement that paradise had successfully been reforged. The announcement fell on ears made receptive by the insecurities of change, and gained conviction from repetition. Yet Seddon and his successor, Ward, could, and did, make a respectable case for its truth. One factor was the economic recovery that, for reasons discussed in the next chapter, cut in from the mid-1890s. Seddon, of course, took far more credit for this than he deserved. Both he and Ward repeatedly alluded to New Zealand having the world's highest living standards. This may not have been quite true, but it was not very far off. Gross national product per capita is estimated to have doubled during the Liberals' years in office.[62] The corrosive effects of inflation on this increase in prosperity were considerable, and hotly debated, but were nowhere near enough to erode the lot. But the distinctive Liberal contribution to the reforging of paradise was legislative. The Liberals reformed on four main fronts: land; labour; welfare and other state activity; and women's rights.

From 1891, the Liberals introduced a graduated land tax and a series of Lands for Settlement Acts, designed to buy great estates and subdivide them into viable farms available to the landless on easy terms. The graduated land tax was always a token measure. In practice, it was aimed more at raising revenue than at breaking up large farms; and it did not do even this very well – 1,500 wealthy taxpayers paid an average of about £40 each in 1892/3, which was hardly penal.[63] The Lands for Settlement measures had more teeth; a compulsory acquisition clause was introduced in 1894, and by 1912, 200 land purchases had been made, mostly from large estates.[64] The Liberals also bought large tracts of the remaining Maori land in the 1890s, for subdivision among Pakeha, although Carroll managed to slow sales greatly between 1899 and 1911. We shall see in Chapter Four that Liberal 'busting up' of great estates is more likely to have delayed than to have hastened the decline of the gentry. Furthermore, private subdivision exceeded state subdivision by at least a factor of five. But the Liberals also introduced a system of Advances to Settlers, supplying cheap credit to buy and develop farms. We shall see in the next chapter that John McKenzie was not the father of the coming golden age of New Zealand farming, but for many individual farmers he was the midwife. When the Liberals talked closer settlement, they meant it. It was their panacea for all ills, including unemployment and immorality in the cities. 'Our policy,' announced Seddon in 1893, 'is simplicity itself for it commences with the settlement of the people on the land and ends with it.'[65] The idea of solving social problems by increasing the number of sturdy yeomanry struck a strong chord with the myths of settlement.

Between 1891 and his exile to London in 1896, W. P. Reeves introduced a raft of labour legislation that was to have enduring consequences. He was helped by his energetic Secretary of Labour, Edward Tregear, who once proclaimed: 'I *am* my brother's keeper.'[66] Their masterpiece was the Industrial Conciliation and Arbitration Act of 1894 and the state-led compulsory arbitration system that developed from it – unsurprisingly, voluntary conciliation proved to be less effective.[67] The purpose of the arbitration system was to encourage unionisation but prevent strikes, and it succeeded in this between 1894 and 1906. 'How the Unions piled up on me!' wrote Tregear.[68]

By 1912, there were 322 unions with 60,000 members.[69] Craft unions favoured the arbitration system; employers came to do so too. Only the strongest industrial unions were unenthusiastic, seeing the system as a placebo for weak workers. Other measures included legislation regulating the employment of women and children, the institution of half-holidays (important in the rise of sport) and the formation of the Department of Labour itself.

The Liberals introduced a number of welfare measures, notably old age pensions in 1898. The measures were neither numerous nor generous, and to credit the Liberals with the creation of the New Zealand welfare state may be going too far. But they did begin the extension of state action into the welfare arena, and into many others. The Liberals did not create New Zealand's strong state, which had inherited the power of imperial governors, independent Maori and the provinces by 1876. But they did boost it substantially. Between 1890 and 1912, Post Office and Railways employees tripled, and total state employment quadrupled to about 40,000. These figures, however, need to be seen in the context of a doubling of the population and of the gross domestic product per capita in the same period. The proportion of GDP spent by the state in 1910 was much the same as it had been in the 1870s – about 10 per cent.[70]

In the long term, the Liberals' greatest legislative legacy was the one for which they could claim least credit: the introduction of votes for women in 1893. In November of that year, the women of New Zealand voted in parliamentary elections for the first time. This was proclaimed as one of several 'firsts', along with land and labour legislation and the old age pension, which gave New Zealand its status as the exemplary paradise among the nations. Some Liberal politicians, notably Seddon, publicised it after the event much more energetically than they had worked for it. International precedence really depends on definitions of 'nation'. Pitcairn Island gave women the vote in 1838, Wyoming in 1869, and Utah in 1870. But New Zealand was certainly in the forefront of women's suffrage – a quarter-century ahead of Britain, for example.

The achievement of suffrage in 1893 was not the only advance for New Zealand women in the late nineteenth century. Women ratepayers had voted in some local body elections since 1867, and several suffrage bills had come before the colonial Parliament in the late 1870s and 1880s, one of which, in 1878, failed by quite a small margin.[71] Elizabeth Yates of Onehunga was elected the first female mayor in the British Empire in 1893. The legal doctrine that made married women inferior beings before the law, already eased by the Matrimonial Property Act of 1884, was further modified by the Divorce Act of 1898. Aspects of male dominance in law remained in place until very recent times, but the late nineteenth century did see major gains for females. One historian has argued that these law reforms were as important as the vote.[72] Women remained well short of full political or legal equality, still less economic equality. They did not become eligible to stand for Parliament until 1919, and the first woman MP was not elected until 1933, well behind Britain. But what we are looking at does seem to be a real, substantial and inter-nationally early improvement in women's rights in and around the 1890s. Why this occurred is an important question in New Zealand history. It is discussed in Chapter Five.

The Liberal government of 1891–1912 was transitional between two eras: progressive colonisation and its successor system, recolonisation. The shift between the two was less obvious in the 1900s than it had been in 1890. The extraction of gold, flax, kauri timber and kauri gum experienced an Indian summer in the 1900s, as did public works, and at the time it must have seemed that 'God's Own Country' might be progressive colonisation revived. Ward was less cautious about borrowing than either Seddon or Ballance, and was sometimes said to be 'out-Vogelling Vogel'. But the Liberals' version of paradise was really much more modest than that of Vogel and the other colonising crusaders of the preceding era. It boasted not of being a Greater Britain in the making, but of being the 'world's social laboratory', more an exemplary paradise than a dynamic one. There was, perhaps, an underlying insecurity behind this strange (and enduring) pride in being the world's white rat. There is a sense in which the Liberals were presiding over changes they neither controlled nor fully understood. It is to these changes – in conceptual geography, economics, technology, and culture – that the rest of this chapter and the whole of the next are devoted.

The Seventh Child

One great change in which the Liberal government did play a significant supporting role was the departure of New Zealand from its old, Tasman, world in 1901. In that year a new entity, the 'Commonwealth of Australia', came into being, and New Zealand was not part of it. New Zealand's reasons for not federating have been the subject of an unusually substantial historical debate,[73] but what this debate has failed to bring out is that, before 1901, New Zealand *was* part of 'Australia', to the extent that any such thing existed. In a sense, non-federation was, by default, a declaration of independence, or at least a transfer of dependence. It also meant that, on 1 January 1901, New Zealand suddenly became small.

If Pakeha New Zealanders in 1900 used the concepts 'We' or 'Us' to include people they did not know personally, they might be referring to any one of a series of 'imagined communities', each a subsection of the next. At the bottom of the series were regional identities, whereby 'We' meant the people of Canterbury or Northland. At the top was a trio of vast, race-influenced identities: 'whites', including both Europeans and neo-Europeans; the 'English-speaking peoples', including Americans; and the (white) Empire – the Britons of Old Britain and the dominions. In the middle of the series were at least two further sites of 'Us'. One, of course, was New Zealand, *the* Britain of the South. The other was 'Australasia'. Coined by the French in the eighteenth century to include New Guinea, 'Australasia' soon gained its modern meaning: Australia plus New Zealand. It was only one of many names the two countries shared: the Great South Land; the Southern Continent; the Sealing Islands; the Antipodes; South Britain and its variants; the Seven Colonies, shortened locally to 'the Colonies'. 'Australia' itself, or 'the Australian colonies', was sometimes used as a contraction of 'Australasia', and could include New Zealand – even in the mouths of New Zealanders. When greater geographical precision was required, we sometimes find the formula 'Australia, New Zealand and Tasmania', indicating a great archipelago in which New Zealand was no more separate than Tasmania. The terms 'Australia and New Zealand' were often linked on the tongue by de facto hyphens, like Trinidad and Tobago or Hansel and Gretel.

'Australasia' was a very loose, vague and semi-tangible imagined community. But it was real; there were many links beyond the conceptual. All seven colonies were neo-Britains. Sydney and Old New Zealand were an important metropolis and hinterland for each other before 1840. In the 1860s, gold-rush Westland was economically and demographically part of Victoria rather than Canterbury. Also in the 1860s, thousands of Australians helped Pakeha fight Maori, and Australia was New Zealand's main trading partner. The embryonic Victorian colonial navy fought in the Taranaki War in 1860–61; several thousand Military Settlers and several hundred Armed Constabulary were recruited in Australia later in the 1860s. The New Zealand Wars were Australia's first overseas conflict. In proportion to its population of the day, it contributed roughly as much to fighting Maori as it did to fighting Boers. Careers in banking, insurance, or seafaring and shearing; commercial travellers, sports teams and evangelists – all had Australasian circuits.[74] The visiting circus, opera and theatre troupes, discussed in Chapter Eleven, were not Australian gifts to New Zealand – partly because Australia did not yet exist, and partly because they had substantial New Zealand participation. They were joint Australasian expressions of a still-wider pan-British culture. Above all, people and money shifted across the Tasman, a constant ebb and flow. It was relatively more important to New Zealand, but not always by much. New Zealanders are said to have made up 17 per cent of the very high 1880s emigration to Victoria.[75]

Most of the people crossing the Tasman probably did not see themselves as migrating, but as shifting and wandering within a single system, a linked constellation of colonies. This was certainly true of 'Tasmen' crew, whose seasonal round could cross the Tasman almost as easily as Cook or Bass Straits. One shearer made the trans-Tasman return voyage 40 times, and many sailors must have exceeded even this.[76] A distinction was routinely drawn between 'inter-colonial' and 'overseas' trade and shipping. The former was trade among the seven Australasian colonies, even though it too – for New Zealand – involved crossing seas. 'Inter-colonial' was a category between foreign and domestic, and closer to the latter. When you have half your contacts and experience in one place, and half in another, there is an incentive to imagine a community that links them. Interstate and inter-regional migration helped form Australian and New Zealand collective identities, especially in the twentieth century. In the nineteenth, something similar was happening with Australasia.

Australasia was loose, not tight; it had little solid form. New Zealand was not part of the short-lived nominal domain of Charles FitzRoy, early New Zealand Governor Robert FitzRoy's brother and 'Governor General of all Queen Victoria's Australian possessions' in the early 1850s.[77] But it did spend its first year as a political entity as part of New South Wales. That colony met New Zealand's first budget deficit, and Lieutenant-Governor Hobson signed the Treaty of Waitangi as a subordinate of Governor Gipps. As noted in *Making Peoples*, there may be scope for enterprising lawyers to make both New Zealand's national debt and Maori claims for recompense under the treaty the responsibility of the New South Wales exchequer. New South Wales, known in New Zealand in the 1820s as 'the Colony', has a certain primacy for us as well as for Tasmania, Queensland and Victoria, though convicts made it a disreputable parent in some eyes. Apart from this, New Zealand had little formal connection with Australia. But the mainland colonies and Tasmania had little formal connection with each other either. Until 1901, there was no such thing as a formal Australia; and to the extent that it existed informally, as 'Australasia' or its variants, New Zealand was as much a part of it as any. New Zealand not only failed to join something new in 1901; it abandoned something old – the Tasman world.

Historians and contemporaries have adduced many reasons for the New Zealand decision not to federate, which was made after spasmodic discussions dating from the early 1880s. One set centres on leadership. It is said that Seddon, in particular, preferred being a big fish in a small pond. 'Prince Dick' just did not have the same ring. But Seddon might have been a big fish in the federated pond – 'Seddon was as popular in Australia as in New Zealand'[78] – and self-confidence was the last thing he lacked. Other leaders appear to have been more divided than some historians assert. Some were always opposed to federation, but Atkinson initially backed it, as did Ward and Stout. Old George Grey, the great governor of the 1860s and not-so-great premier of the 1870s, 'at times sounded favourable'. A Liberal minister alleged that several of his colleagues, including Seddon, had favoured federation until he dissuaded them.[79] A survey of most members of Parliament in 1899 showed twenty in favour of federation, nineteen opposed, and twenty-five undecided or determined not to comment. It has been shown that an organised federation movement in New Zealand did exist, though it was not very impressive.[80] It seems that the New Zealand public were generally apathetic to the issue of federation, and this is often cited as a major factor in leaving Australasia. But public apathy could as easily have facilitated federation as hampered it. It was also a feature of the debate on the abolition of the New Zealand provinces in the early 1870s, and they did federate. Opinion against federation hardened after the fact. In 1901, submissions to a royal commission on whether to seek late entry were mostly against it.[81] This was partly because the new Australia declined to allow New Zealand the right of later entry under the original terms, but also because direct links with Britain were tightening as those with Australia loosened.

It has been noted, rightly, that economics was important in New Zealand's decision. In each year 1861–68, the Australian colonies took most of New Zealand's exports. They provided most imports in some years as well. Australia was New Zealand's 'major trading partner', but this formulation conceals the degree to which they were part of each other's internal markets, their trade more akin to interprovincial than international. There were some tariff barriers, but Australasia was to some extent a single market for goods as well as labour. Gold was sold to Australian banks and mints, and as its flow diminished in the 1870s and 1880s, so did exports to Australia: from 46 per cent in 1870 to 17 per cent in 1890. Imports declined from 35 to 17 per cent in these years, too. This economic separation was probably a factor in non-federation, but can be overstated. In 1900, the Australasian market was still significant at 14 per cent of exports and 17 per cent of imports.[82] There seems to have been somewhat more willingness to consider federation in the 1880s than the 1890s, at least among political leaders, and this shift moved in the contrary direction to that of the Australasian trade. The shift in opinion could be related to the different timing of stagnation on the two shores of the Tasman. In the 1880s, New Zealand was a sinking ship looking to join a rising one. In the 1890s, the situation was reversed. Terrible droughts may also have made joining Australia seem less attractive. But the shift in opinion was not huge, drought in Australia could boost demand for New Zealand products, and confidence in the return of Australasia-wide prosperity was considerable by 1900. The Australasian market was still important to New Zealand in that year, and though free-trade sentiment in New South Wales gave some hope of minimising the economic damage non-federation would cause, it was clearly probable that there would be some.

Other suggested reasons for not federating included geographical distance – 1,200 impediments to federation, in one politician's phrase. Yet, in an age where shipping remained the cheapest form of transport, the Tasman Sea was more bridge than barrier. It was certainly more easily crossed than the central Australian desert. A transcontinental railway did not reach Perth in Western Australia until 1917. Incipient nationalism is a more convincing explanation for New Zealand's cold feet. Myths of 'select' settler stock, the absence of convicts, and a climate allegedly conducive to racial improvement meant that 'many New Zealanders felt superior to Australians'.[83] This combined with a sense of 'a destiny apart', focusing more on the Pacific and less on Asia and its teeming hordes – for whom some feared Australia might serve as a gateway to New Zealand. Myths of racial harmony also figured here, as did the notion that New Zealand was more British – it did have fewer Irish and more Scots than Australia. It is true that New Zealanders had a sense of collective identity, almost before it had settlers. It was derived from the unholy alliance between formal and informal myths of settlement, from ideas of the progressive British paradise. What is less clear is whether a similar sense of identity was absent in Australia, and whether New Zealand's collective identity, and the hopes for the future it implied, were more threatened by staying in than by staying out.

A contemporary New Zealand commentator wrote of the debate on federation: 'What is this mild hankering after the flesh-pots and birth-stains of the Otherside?' This has been quoted to help explain the decision against federation, but it does not.[84] It concedes that there was a 'mild hankering'; Tasmania had no fleshpots either; Victoria and South Australia had no convict 'birth-stains'; and 'othersiders' was also a West Australian colloquialism for the people of east Australia. Western Australia had a destiny apart, too, which was beginning to look more promising in the 1890s through gold and diamond mining; and it also had a different outlook from its six sisters – across the Indian Ocean. Tasmania might conceivably claim similar evolutionary advantages to New Zealand in terms of climate and diverse environment. South Australia did not have convicts, and it did have 'better stock'. Indeed, it had corporate stock, a founding Wakefieldian company, just like New Zealand. It is easy to find factors that distinguish New Zealand from some Australian colonies, but not from all. Some even had almost as few Irish – and New Zealand had more of them than it cared to emphasise – and almost as many Scots. Public apathy was also a feature of the federation debate in most Australian colonies.[85] A recent study claims that Australian 'national sentiment was weak and played little part in Federation'. One of its chief architects, Alfred Deakin, claimed that federation was 'secured by a series of miracles'.[86]

A people can have more than one identity, as long as they are compatible. It is not obvious that a formal Australasia would have been any more damaging to New Zealand identity than an informal one. New Zealandness, Australasianism – and Britishness – were not mutually exclusive. There was very little that was anti-British about federationism in Australia. New Zealanders did fear a loss of autonomy to a federal government, though not necessarily more than other colonies. But in the high days of progressive colonisation, up to the 1880s, federation might have been seen as an opportunity of taking a short cut to 'Greater Britain'.

This is not to say that tighter relations with Australia, and especially its convict colonies, fitted comfortably with a Greater British future for New Zealand. Myths of New Zealand superiority were already too strong for that. But the same myths might have led to a belief that New Zealand was likely to take a lead in any federation. The most optimistic New Zealand prophets of progress, confident in their political and business talents, and in their country's natural advantages, envisaged a New Zealand takeover of Australia, not the other way round. Since the 1860s, some had been referring to this very prospect.

> With the exaggeration of phrase to which the English New Zealanders are prone, they prophesy a marvellous here-after for the whole Pacific, in which New Zealand . . . is to play the foremost part, the Australias following obediently in her train.[87]

A sense of sibling superiority was not necessarily one of antagonism or incompatible difference, as Australia has since shown in reverse. New Zealand–Australian separateness, difference and antagonism were largely a twentieth-century invention read back into the nineteenth century, as we shall see in a later chapter – more a product of non-federation than a cause of it. Above all, a Greater British New Zealand uncomfortably merged with Australia was arguably better than no Greater Britain at all.

Before 1901, New Zealand was not small in its local context. It ranked third of the seven colonies in population and production, and it was closer to the big two, Victoria and New South Wales, than to the small four. It was this, as well as myths of superiority, which gave rise to hopes of New Zealand leadership, which can seem ludicrous in modern Australasian eyes. On 1 January 1901, New Zealand suddenly shrank to about a quarter of its previous relative size. From an association of equals, or one dominated by a big three that included New Zealand, it became very much the junior partner in Australasia. The seven sisters had become two, and one was pretty big. Loose junior partnership fitted even less well with ideas of Greater Britain than tight equal partnership. A dwarfed sister made a poor prospective giant. This interacted with the bruises of other blows to Greater British optimism – the trauma of the end of progressive colonisation and the advent of the Long Stagnation. Greater Britain and the Tasman world were staggering by 1890; they fell in 1901, lurched back to their knees in the 1900s, fell again, gasped a few times, and expired in succeeding years.

Even loose membership of an Australian-dominated Australasia lost its lure, and it also lost its economic substance. Between 1900 and 1920, the Australian export market for New Zealand produce collapsed from 14 to 5 per cent, and remained at or below that level to the late 1960s.[88] If one shore of the Tasman world had disappeared in this period, the other might not have noticed it for a while in terms of trade. Before 1901, 'Australia' was a mere geographical expression; it was 'Australasia' that had some substance. Afterwards, they switched places. In 1922, one prominent New Zealander appealed for 'Australasia' to be stricken from the language on the grounds that 'it gave people the impression that New Zealand was part of Australia'.[89] By 1960, another could write that 'the term "Australasia" has been banned for many years – informally, as far as I know, but by common consent – in the New Zealand Press'.[90] Important residues of the Tasman world survived, until about 1920 at least, notably in popular culture and the labour movement, and various elements of the continuing Australian–New Zealand relationship are discussed in later chapters. But 'Greater Britain' and the merged Tasman world both substantially ended in 1901 and, for the New Zealanders who made the decision not to federate, their demise was predictable. What was worth this price, the sacrifice of both a past and a future?

CHAPTER TWO

The Recolonial System

'If "the Battle of Hastings 1066" is the best known date in England's history, the best known in New Zealand's should be "the Voyage of the *Dunedin* 1882".'[1] For those uninitiated in this great secret, the *Dunedin* in 1882 made the first-ever passage from New Zealand to Britain carrying a refrigerated cargo of 5,000 dead sheep and a little butter. The subsequent rise of refrigerated exports, and the associated creation of sheep-meat and dairying export industries, is indeed one of the most important of all New Zealand stories. Meat, cheese and butter have their differences, but each is a source of protein, and together they constituted the great New Zealand protein industry. In 1881, New Zealand shipped no frozen meat, cheese or butter to Britain or anywhere else. By 1901, it exported over 100,000 tons of meat and dairy products. By 1921, the figure was 340,000 tons; by 1941, 500,000 tonnes.[2] Wool remained important, at about a quarter of exports by value. But from the 1900s, it ran a distant second to protein, which comprised about two-thirds of exports. Exports became even more important to New Zealand than to other neo-European economies, and protein was its most important export.

While there were a few forays into other markets, Britain was over-whelmingly the destination. The protein industry was vital to New Zealand – and quite important to Britain. By 1950, New Zealand was Britain's fourth-biggest supplier, by value, of all products – behind Canada, Australia and the United States on an absolute basis, and dwarfing all three on a per capita basis. Incredibly enough, little New Zealand supplied a similar percentage of British imports to that provided by France and Germany combined.[3] Because distribution was disproportionately concentrated in London, that city lived on New Zealand protein to a significant degree. The town-supply district of London had shifted 12,000 miles to the south. What we are looking at here is not some dry-as-dust development in narrow agricultural or economic history, but a geographic miracle, a staggering conquest of distance. Further-more, it was this great New Zealand–British protein industry that under-pinned the whole recolonial system.

From Progress to Protein

From a purely technical perspective, refrigeration was the knight in icy armour that rode to the rescue of the New Zealand economy in the 1880s. The refrigeration of food was in itself old hat. Natural refrigeration, in the form of ice, was used to take Scottish salmon to London in the eighteenth century, and North American beef and even dairy products, to market in the mid-nineteenth. It was the advent of steam-powered mechanical freezers in the later nineteenth century that revolutionised the preservation and exporting of food. The first fully successful mechanised refrigerated shipment was from Argentina to France in 1877. To some extent, New Zealand was merely getting a share of a new British market opened up by refrigeration. But the simple technical explanation only takes us so far.

Britain had long been importing meat, chilled, tinned, cured and live, as well as dairy products – fresh butter from Denmark and cheese from Canada. Refrigeration does not by itself explain the fivefold increase in British meat imports between 1870 and 1900.[4] Obvious explanations might seem to be an increase in British affluence and a decline in British farming. Yet, while British historians do not agree on much, they do seem to agree that per capita economic growth in the 1880s–1920s period was modest, and population growth even more so.[5] Why did British demand for imported protein burgeon so much faster than incomes or population? While the details are disputed, there was a steady decline in British farming from the 1870s, largely because of the competition of cheaper imported produce. In 1870, most British food was home-grown; by 1900 most was imported.[6] But this was most true in wheat, not livestock products. British pastoral farming actually grew, 1870–1900 – domestic meat production went up 50 per cent.[7] What we seem to have here is an explosion in British protein consumption, rather than a decline in domestic production, and one driven by something other than simple rising affluence. The importance of this sudden rise of the British carnivore for New Zealand requires a brief foray into British cultural, social and culinary history.

In Northern Europe, even in ancient times, butter was the food 'that distinguishes the wealthy from the lower orders'. In Britain, by the eighteenth century, 'butter was everywhere' in genteel cuisine; Mrs Beeton's most common ingredient, featuring in pies, puddings and desserts, and as a spread and a sauce. 'Melted butter, with a dusting of flour in it, was perhaps the commonest sauce on the tables of the well-to-do throughout the eighteenth century; while white flour sauce, with little or no butter in it, was the equivalent among the poor and the thrifty.' Butter was edible gold, a folk symbol of status. Cheddar cheese, too, was extremely rich in cream, 'more expensive than other cheeses', and in the eighteenth century 'seldom seen but at noblemen's tables'. Continental visitors at this time were often struck by the English love of meat. 'Roast meat is the Englishman's delice and principal dish . . . I do not believe that any Englishman who is his own master has ever eaten a dinner without meat.' Though often portrayed as a defining characteristic of archetypal English, the regular consumption of prime cuts was restricted by class. Poorer country folk ate offal and scrag ends, selling the best parts of pigs if they had them; and poorer urban workers seldom ate meat at all. Prime cuts were a symbol of being one's 'own master'.[8]

In the eighteenth and early nineteenth centuries, certain genteel customs percolated into the upper ranks of the middle classes, some culinary preferences among them. By the later nineteenth century, such customs had also become an aspiration of those further down the social order, including the 'lower middle class' of white-collar workers that was emerging at this time. This new urban group, together with the middling respectables above it, and the upper rungs of the working class below it – skilled and semi-skilled urban workers – all appear to have enjoyed a slow but fairly steady rise in real incomes in the late nineteenth century, and to have increased in numbers. They put their disposable cash to new uses, so creating a discretionary mass market for the first time. They adopted some genteel activities, such as participatory sport and leisure travel, and they bought 'better' food when they could afford it. Cross-class adoption could work both ways; a taste for gin and oysters, for example, seems to have drifted up. But genteel gin consumers could not match the mass of those below in creating new markets, though some tried hard. The new mass consumers wanted much meat instead of little meat; prime cuts instead of scrag ends and offal; butter instead of dripping; and full-cream cheese instead of lesser varieties – and carpets instead of bare floors – if they could get them cheap. Enter the neo-Europes, newly opened by a progressive colonisation that could no longer survive of its own momentum, and newly linked to Britain by refrigeration and big steamships.

At first sight, New Zealand seemed reasonably well placed to join the rush for the new market, right from the outset. Dairy production for the domestic market already existed in 1882, and there was even some processing, the 'milling' of butter from various farms by storekeepers. Sheep production hardly had to be expanded at all. In the 1870s, farmers had had to drive surplus sheep over cliffs, or boil them down into tallow for soap and candles. Efforts to preserve and export sheep meat had begun. A Southland plant sent sixteen cases of preserved meats such as tongue to England in 1870. In 1871, a Dunedin canning works employed 50 people and killed 300 sheep a day, and there were similar efforts elsewhere.[9] There was protein; there was a market; all that was necessary was to bring them together. Hence the significance of the voyage of the *Dunedin* in 1882, and of the legendary heroes who commissioned and organised it – notably the Scots-New Zealand entrepreneurs Thomas Brydone and William Soltau Davidson. The status is not undeserved. Their travels and travails were epic. Brydone and Davidson ceremoniously lugged the first frozen sheep onto the *Dunedin* in late 1881, only to have the ship's refrigerating machinery fail. The First Four Sheep and their fellows were sold off for a song in Dunedin city, and the ship had to be restocked. During the voyage, the *Dunedin* nearly added frozen captain to its cargo when John Whitson was overcome by cold in the hold when checking on his precious passengers and had to be dragged out by his legs.[10] Brydone and Davidson did not invent mechanised refrigeration, still less refrigeration itself. They borrowed their technology from overseas pioneers, notably from Australia. But they did utilise its potential more quickly, comprehensively and effectively than its inventors.

In 1882, then, all three of the necessary components of the protein industry were apparently in place: New Zealand supply; British demand; and some sort of link between them. But there were hitches, and they were numerous and major. The *Dunedin*'s cargo was frozen on board ship, but, as the mechanical problem of 1881 showed, this was not satisfactory. Land-based freezing works and refrigerated rail wagons were needed. It also quickly became clear that factory production of butter and cheese was preferable to farm-made and milled products. A small dairy factory cost only £1,000–2,000, but had to be within three miles of the supplying farms in order to allow the farmer to cart in his milk daily, so there had to be a lot of them. A large freezing works could cost £50,000 or more. As a result of overinvestment in the 1870s and stagnation in the 1880s, capital and credit were hard to come by. This not only hampered the development of processing facilities, but also the adaptation of farms themselves to protein exporting, which required more fencing, more equipment, more fertiliser and better grasses than did wool farming or small-scale mixed farming for the domestic market. New Zealand had a great many rural landholdings in the 1880s, but most were too small, too undeveloped or too undercapitalised to be viable farms. With the collapse of progressive colonisation, both genteel large farmers and aspirant small farmers were crippled by lack of capital or credit. They might well have been doomed to watch the new protein-exporting opportunities pass by just beyond their grasp.

There was a set of even more serious problems with the British end of the fledgling protein industry, and with the link mechanism between Britain and New Zealand. The first voyages demonstrated a need for refrigerated storage in Britain and for an efficient distribution system. In the early 1880s, the arrival of two meat ships at the same time, with cargoes that became perishable as soon as they left the refrigerated hold, meant a glut. 'There were times,' wrote Davidson, 'when . . . the east End of London was traversed by hawkers selling the fore-quarters of mutton for "an old song" – sometimes accepting a sporting price for the whole barrowload!'[11] There may have been a silver lining in this cloud – the development of a taste for New Zealand mutton in East Enders through virtually free samples – but long-defrosted meat could as easily have the opposite effect. Another problem was shipping itself. The *Dunedin* was a sailing ship; steam powered the freezing chambers, not the ship, and its voyage took 98 days. This was too long for a regular mass protein trade, but refrigerated steamers were expensive to build and run. Added to this, freight and passengers bound for Britain from New Zealand often trans-shipped in Australia, lengthening the voyage still more. There was little 'direct' communication – no regular, cheap, fast and reliable rails on which the protein industry could run.

Yet another problem was the competition. Formally at least, Britain was a fairly free market until 1932. Much larger economies, with more developed protein export industries, competed with New Zealand in it. Canada, for example, had fifteen times as many cheese and butter factories as New Zealand in 1901, and dominated the British imported cheese market.[12] Denmark dominated the British butter market. South America shipped preserved and tinned meats and meat extracts to Britain from the 1860s; the United States began shipping chilled beef to London in 1875; and Australia and Argentina had successfully shipped frozen mutton to Europe by 1880. On top of all this, there was strong consumer prejudice against both foreign food and frozen food. Below the upper classes, the English diet was not noted for adventurousness. Wogs began at Calais, if not the Welsh border. Frozen meat was not only foreign but had also been dead for months, even years. Persuading people to actually eat it must have been quite a feat. At best, frozen meat carried the stigma of other forms of preserved meat, such as colonial tinned meat, the last resort of the British carnivore. Fresh and frozen meat was at first sold by different kinds of retailers, and the socially mobile did not like to be seen shopping at the latter. To the new consumer, frozen food must initially have seemed more closely related to tinned than to fresh. Worst of all, the new British consumer did not like New Zealand protein.

Like other customs, the food preferences being adopted in Britain by the expanding middle class were changed in the process. The gentry liked strong-flavoured meats, notably game; their lower-class imitators did not, either associating it with poaching and poverty or simply disliking the taste and texture. The first shipment of frozen meat from Auckland in 1883 included 56 brace of pheasants; and backers such as Logan Campbell hoped for a genteel market.[13] But the new lower-middle-class British carnivores not only selectively adopted culinary gentility, but adapted it as well. They disliked the gamy taste and texture of New Zealand's dominant merino. A gamy saddle of mutton was an acceptable genteel dish; the new consumers preferred 'spring' lamb for their Sunday roasts – younger, blander, more tender meat. They wanted it in their spring, not New Zealand's. They also hated New Zealand butter, complaining frequently about its strong and 'fishy flavour'; and they were particular about their cheese, too, preferring rich and consistent cheddar to any kind of variety. The 'Butter and Cheese' section of the *New Zealand Official Yearbook* of 1893 congratulated itself that complaints had been 'less numerous' that year than before.[14] It was not much to celebrate.

All these problems were solved through the transformation of New Zealand production, but also by a tightening and subtle reshaping of links with Britain, and of New Zealand's image in Britain. The process was not instantaneous, though in sheep meats it was quite fast. Frozen sheep-meat exports to Britain hit 50,000 tons in 1891, after less than ten years, and 93,000 tons in 1901, before growing to 216,000 tons in 1921. Dairying grew more slowly: a mere 4,000 tons in 1891; 15,000 in 1901; and a massive expansion to 123,000 tons by 1921.[15] In both meat and dairying, the wartime 'commandeer' of 1915–20, when the British government automatically purchased all New Zealand production, helped bring the industry to its full long-term size. There were three key contributors to the supply side of the New Zealand–British protein industry.

The first was a new class of small–medium farmers in New Zealand, who typically owned and operated their own land, though often with large mortgages. Raised too high in farm-led folklore and politics, they were also mocked too much by an intelligentsia generally uncomfortable with them. Their development as a social and political entity is discussed in Chapter Four. In some ways it is useful to see them as a peasantry who made extensive use of cheap but efficient family labour – 'farmers' wives' were often very active farmers themselves. But they were an unusual peasantry in several respects. In international terms, their holdings were large, mostly ranging from 100 to 1,000 acres, and averaging 300–400 between 1898 and 1911, as the protein industry established itself.[16] Many were technically mixed farmers, producing modest quantities of wool, beef, pork (as a sideline to dairying) and fodder crops such as swedes and turnips. But their main crop was grass, and their main products were butter, cheese and sheep meat. They were the base producers of the protein industry. Because dairying in particular was slow to get on its feet after the advent of refrigeration in 1882, they scarcely existed before the 1890s. As crew were to progressive colonisation, so the small–medium protein farmers were to recolonisation, and they rose (and fell) with the recolonial system.

The new protein small farmers were more important in New Zealand than in most agricultural exporting countries. In South American countries such as Argentina and Uruguay, large farmers and companies dominated exporting, while small farmers produced for themselves and the local market. Some commentators believe that agricultural exporting was consequently more efficient in these countries because they had fewer, bigger players.[17] It is true that New Zealand protein production and processing were more decentralised, with more farms, more dairy factories and more freezing works than the competition. Yet New Zealand's individualist small farmers had an intriguingly high capacity for collective action. Most dairy factories and some freezing works came to be owned by farmer co-operatives, and, with state help, exporting was often collectively organised from 1915. The balance between centralisation and decentralisation, combined with cultural factors discussed below, yielded benefits in the form of a quick uptake of new methods and new technology. An Australian historian has suggested that New Zealand historians have been too modest about the achievements of New Zealand small farming, which he rates as exceptionally effective. 'A population of enfranchised smallholders constituted a social environment in which science and technology could best be applied.'[18]

Although the natural fertility of New Zealand soils tends to be over-rated, there was one major natural advantage in the form of climate. Droughts were rarer and less severe than in Australia, and sheep and cattle could be pastured all year round, instead of having to be housed and fed in winter as in Europe. This obviously reduced costs, and stock grazed out over winter naturally distributed their fertilising manure more than those kept in yards and barns. New Zealand farmers literally had to shovel less shit than their European equivalents. Still more important was access to credit, and it was here that the second key agent in the development of the protein industry came into play. The state's contribution is usually seen in terms of its direct input into the reshuffling of landholdings into units compatible with protein production, through the Lands for Settlement schemes in particular. These did subdivide some large farms into protein-sized units, and the extensive purchase of Maori land in the 1890s supplied more. But the Liberals' intervention in the supply of credit, notably through the Advances to Settlers programme, was probably more important. This enabled aspirant small farmers to buy privately subdivided large estates and to turn raw proto-farms into viable protein units. State advances also pressured banks to lower the cost of credit and ease access to it. Two considerations confirm the importance of credit in the establishment of protein farms. In Taranaki, the first protein province, dairy farming took off in the 1890s, when government and bank credit was available, not in the 1880s, when it was not.[19] Second, Maori traditions of commercial dairying and effective farming dated back to the 1830s or before. But, with the exception of Ngati Porou, they were initially unable to participate in the new protein industry because government and banks would not lend to them.

State contributions extended well beyond credit, into the organisation, quality control, marketing, and research and development of the protein industry – especially dairying. Even before the advent of the Liberals, government had investigated dairying potential in 1883 and appointed dairy-farming instructors in 1889. The Liberals established the Department of Agriculture in 1892, and from that date involved government in the grading and quality control of protein exports, including the introduction of dairy-herd testing and meat inspection from 1898. Government encouraged the use of lime as fertiliser by transporting it free by rail from 1898. Subsequent state-aided developments included research into the improvement of grass types and stock breeds, and the use of superphosphate fertiliser – matters discussed further in Chapter Eight. One economic historian argues that improvements in sown pasture, dating from about 1900, were as important as refrigeration itself in establishing the New Zealand protein farmer.[20] The Liberal government saw dairy farmers as their yeomen dream come true: the solution of social problems through closer land settlement.

The third key player in setting up the supply side of the protein industry were genteel entrepreneurs and their New Zealand–British companies, whose dynamic boom–bust history is discussed in *Making Peoples*. These were in part the very same colonising crusaders who had led progressive colonisation and boomed and busted with it, sometimes at the very time they led the shift to protein. Big landowners supplied most sheep for the frozen-meat industry until the 1900s. The gentry and other private entrepreneurs invested in freezing works and, to a surprising though lesser extent, in dairy factories. The new system was initiated by, and partly constructed from, the old. Brydone and Davidson, the *Dunedin* pioneers, were senior employees of the New Zealand and Australian Land Company, a giant amalgam of Scottish and Dunedin capital and enterprise. One major component, the Canterbury and Otago Association Limited, was founded in 1859. The company boomed in the 1870s and ended up holding 877,000 New Zealand acres. Apart from commissioning the *Dunedin*, the company set up the Edendale Dairy Factory in 1882, able to produce both butter and cheese. Though not the first dairy factory in the country, it was the first to export significant quantities, gaining a government bounty of £500 for doing so. It was the model for many of the hundreds of dairy factories – 259 by 1901 – that soon sprouted up.[21]

Other Dunedin entrepreneurs set up the New Zealand Refrigeration Company and built the first freezing works at Burnside. A parallel Auckland concern, founded in 1883, was the New Zealand Frozen Meat and Storage Company, which was dominated by Russellite gentry, including the man himself. It sent the pheasants; its first shipment rotted, and it suffered many other woes. But the company spent hundreds of thousands on the protein industry, established large freezing works and acted as 'an Auckland pioneer of butter exports'. John Grigg of Canterbury, Russell's partner and brother-in-law, had a few hundred sheep aboard the *Dunedin*, and chartered a refrigerated vessel himself the next year. The freezers failed and the sheep rotted, but Grigg persevered and formed the Canterbury Frozen Meat and Dairy Produce Export Company with other pastoralists, building the country's second freezing works, at Christchurch. Grigg also built a cheese factory at Ashburton. By 1891, there were 21 freezing works, with an annual capacity of four million sheep. The 'colonising crusaders' had always been prone to almost manic optimism, to rushing boldly into new enterprises. Their involvement in the protein industry could almost be deduced from an 1883 remark in an Auckland newspaper: 'Meat-freezing is assuming the character of a mania . . . there seems growing a universal rage for rushing into the freezing and export of meat.'[22] The New Zealand and Australian Land Company sold Edendale in 1903 and ditched its other New Zealand interests about the same time, becoming Australian–British. The New Zealand Frozen Meat Company collapsed in bitter acrimony in 1889, along with most other New Zealand–British companies. But before these companies disappeared, they invested a lot in the protein industry, dairy as well as meat. In concert with the new small farmers and the state, they resolved many of the protein industry's teething problems, notably that of British consumer tastes.

Farm production of butter and cheese was displaced by milder and more consistent factory production. In legend, and sometimes history, the emergence of the dairy factories is associated with that of co-operative ownership, where the factory was owned by the small farmers who supplied it. Co-operatives did become very important. But the factory system was pioneered by private owners, who dominated it until World War One. Respectable small-town entrepreneurs, such as the remarkable Taranaki mandarin Chew Chong and dairy magnate T. L. Joll, also of Taranaki, developed the legacy that was inherited by co-operatives. Models such as Edendale encouraged dual-purpose cheese or butter factories – to a greater extent than in Canada, for example – which enabled New Zealand dairying to adjust more readily to the milk-fat vagaries of the British market. The state energetically evangelised for co-operatives and factory production, genteel large farmers invested heavily in both, and crusading banks financed them. By 1900, only 11 per cent of New Zealand butter was farm-produced or -milled, and complaints about 'fishy tastes' were submerged in a golden stream of mild and consistent factory-produced salted butter.[23]

A few bolder cheese varieties eventually emerged, such as 'Old Port' and 'Blue Vein', the New Zealand Stilton, but these were developed later, or for the home market, not the Home market. As far as Britain was concerned, cheddar – 'New Zealand Factory-Made Full-Cream Cheese' – was almost the beginning and end of the range, and the new British consumers liked it that way.[24] The colonising crusaders had long taken an interest in select stock, and since the end of the sheep rush they had been experimenting with imported and locally crossed breeds of sheep that might be run more profitably on converted pasture than merinos. New Zealand was therefore able to convert from tough and gamy merinos to more tender and milder-tasting breeds such as the Lincoln, Romney and Southdown. In 1882, merinos made up the majority of the national flock; ten years later they were one-third of it, and eventually they became almost an endangered species on the hillsides they once dominated.[25] Sheep were killed younger to meet the new consumers' taste for lamb. They were bred smaller to meet demands for smaller, single-meal roasts. There were also efforts, in both meat and dairying, to adjust production and export to northern seasonal variations in demand. New Zealand became a land of eight seasons. What the new consumers wanted, they got. The British customer was always right.

The rise and rapid adaptation of New Zealand protein farming was intertwined with the development of finance, processing, distribution and shipping to form a sophisticated mechanism connecting the farms to their markets. This was the keystone of a wider recolonial tightening and reshuffling of New Zealand–British links. The link mechanism was complicated, and requires further research, but as far as private finance is concerned, it appears to have taken the form of a shift from indirect British investment, mediated through the colonising entrepreneurs such as Thomas Russell, to direct British investment, under tighter London control. Borrowing did not stop, but money began to flow out of New Zealand even faster than it flowed in – repatriated profits of British investors and the interest on debt exceeded new borrowing. The implications of this should not be exaggerated. All repayments eventually exceed the loan in all borrowing, of course, and the profits of the protein industry were such that New Zealand could fund a respectable level of 'natural' progress, and even its participation in World War One, largely from its own resources.[26] But, after the 1880s, New Zealand entrepreneurs no longer waltzed into London, whistled up a few stray millions like the Pied Piper, and led them south forever.

Purely British companies, such as the misnamed National Bank of New Zealand, took up some of the investment slack left by collapsed or chastened New Zealand–British concerns, although the born-again Bank of New Zealand remained the largest bank. There was a trend to more direct, and therefore more controlled, investment from Britain, and to fewer and larger investors and borrowers. English financial institutions were aggregating in the nineteenth century anyway – 441 banks in 1844 became 40 in 1913.[27] Fewer lenders left borrowers fewer opportunities to divide and rule. The British–New Zealand economic relationship was increasingly funnelled through large London companies. The government was the only New Zealand borrower London investors still trusted, with important implications for the role of the state. From the 1880s, 'New Zealand companies fell under suspicion, and all but a few have remained more or less suspect ever since . . . Investment on the scale envisaged by Thomas Russell had become unthinkable except in companies backed by a solid government guarantee.'[28]

The development of the processing and distribution dimensions of the New Zealand–British link mechanism is also a complicated story, but one in which published sources permit a little more depth.[29] To some extent, New Zealand companies dominated meat processing, and British companies dominated distribution in Britain, but both ultimately invaded each other's spheres. Dunedin's New Zealand Refrigerating Company, which merged with a Christchurch meat processor in 1905, was the largest New Zealand concern, supplying 25 per cent of the country's kill in 1915. Initially allied to William Weddell and Company, a large British importer of New Zealand protein established in 1887, New Zealand Refrigerating bought its own British distributor, Towers and Company, in 1915. New Zealand-owned Towers had 36 branches in Britain, supplied 6,000 butchers and was extremely profitable between 1915 and 1922 – a case of the Empire striking back.[30] From the other direction, Thomas Borthwick, a Scottish livestock trader originally based in Liverpool but eventually in London, sold New Zealand frozen meat from 1883 and became increasingly involved in the processing end from the 1880s. By 1931, Borthwick's owned four large New Zealand freezing works and provided 20 per cent of the country's kill.[31] Vestey Brothers, another big British meat trader, which operated in New Zealand as W. and R. Fletcher, moved in to New Zealand processing a little later, and on the same large scale. New Zealand interests in the freezing industry were strongest in the early stages and in the South Island. As the industry expanded in the North Island from the 1890s, and as the first freezing works everywhere were modernised, New Zealand's overstretched entrepreneurs had to give way to British capital. Expansion was particularly great in the North Island during World War One.[32]

By 1922, there were 28 freezing works in the North Island and fifteen in the South. Overseas ownership featured large in the North Island, less so in the South.[33] This tendency to increasing British direct investment from the 1890s also took place in such industries as goldmining, and was an important feature of recolonisation.

A hybrid British–New Zealand enterprise was Nelson Brothers of Hawke's Bay and London. William and Frederick Nelson, sons of a London gelatine manufacturer, emigrated to New Zealand in 1863 and farmed sheep and milled flax without much success. William returned to Britain in 1872, leaving Frederick behind. William came out again in 1880, backed by his family's London company, and began processing sheep into casks of tallow and tins of gravy. He married into the rich and genteel Williams clan, who joined him in the business. He began freezing in 1884, and ten years later was the leading producer of frozen meat in the country, while the London end of the firm, encouraged by W. S. Davidson, who was on its board of directors, became central in the meat storage and distribution system there.[34] An even more remarkable hybrid was Glaxo, a New Zealand company founded by Joseph Nathan, which began to export milk-powder products, notably baby food, to London in 1903. The business was boosted by World War One shortages in Britain, and by 1921 turned over £1.5 million. Until the Depression of the 1930s, the company was dominated by its Wellington end. 'London was thereafter dominant, though not always supreme.' London completed its takeover after World War Two, and the company moved into pharmaceuticals and vitamins. Its last New Zealand plant closed in 1996, when its global turnover was about £4 billion.[35] Until the 1940s, it would have been impossible to describe Nelson Brothers or Glaxo as solely New Zealand or British companies. The fact is they were both. But one does get a sense of a shift in control in Britain's favour – not necessarily to the dominance of the British end, but from New Zealand dominance to parity.

British ascendancy was more marked in the distribution of dairy products than in meat. Butter and cheese very soon came to be sold by the London firms of Tooley Street, a name better known to the New Zealand dairy farmer than Oxford or Regent. Tooley Street, which is as much a part of New Zealand as of British history, stretches along the South Bank of the Thames from Tower Bridge to London Bridge. New Zealand dairy products landed at Hay's Wharf, consigned to one of the 27 importing firms of the street. Each Tooley Street company had an agent in New Zealand who, between them, bought up virtually the whole output of the country's dairy factories. 'Tooley Street soon dominated the marketing system, and gained an almost complete monopoly.'[36] Even the New Zealand Dairy Board, after it was set up in 1923, operated through Tooley Street. Dairy producers could still pick and choose which Tooley Street firm they would do business with, and New Zealand gained other benefits from the new system. But, again, the investment relationship shifted from New Zealand–British to British–New Zealand. The same applied to the final element of the protein industry's crucial link mechanism: shipping.

While New Zealand companies, especially Union Shipping, dominated the coastal and intercolonial trades, the British trade, direct and indirect, was in the hands of various British firms, such as Albion and Shaw Savill. During the 1870s and 1880s, there had been New Zealand attempts to challenge this dominance. Now-forgotten squadrons of small sailing ships owned by such men as C. W. Turner of Christchurch sailed the high seas. The most substantial long-range shipping enterprise was the New Zealand Shipping Company, founded by local merchants and pastoralists at Christchurch in 1873, who as usual pulled British capital in after them. This company engaged vigorously, though not profitably, in the protein trade from 1883, commissioning large refrigerated steamers for the purpose, including five from Glasgow shipyards. Like the Union Company, New Zealand Shipping was taken over by the giant British P&O Line during World War One. But unlike Union, its New Zealand founders lost control to their British shareholders long before that, in 1887. 'From this time onward the NZS Co. was a New Zealand company in name only . . . the real power lay in the hands of the British shipping barons and the meat traders who held 90% of its shares.'[37] As in those of the other New Zealand–British companies who survived the stagnation, the balance of control shifted in Britain's favour.

This was in part a world trend towards the concentration of control in ocean shipping, both through the amalgamation of companies and the formation of formal or informal pools or cartels. Until World War One, the Britain–New Zealand sea lanes were controlled and 'heavily regulated' by the Davis Pool of British companies, and by the equally British 'New Zealand Conference Lines' thereafter. The shipping lines in turn were allied to meat distributors: the Tyser Line to Nelson Brothers, the Blue Star Line to Vestey's. This enhanced Britain's grip on the protein industry, but it also led to massive investment in new, bigger and better ships, which now sailed from London to New Zealand direct, apart from a few brief stops for refuelling. The *Dunedin* in 1882 had taken 98 days to reach Britain. A New Zealand Shipping Company steamer made the voyage in 49 days in 1883, encouraged by a government bounty. By 1892, that company's protein and passenger steamers were making the voyage in 39 to 42 days. The competition matched this, and ships grew in size and number, and declined in cost.[38] By 1899, at least 30 ships were engaged in the New Zealand–British trade. By 1917, the number was 99; and by 1939, 127.[39] These ships were big, cheap, regular and reliable. With other elements of the link mechanism such as the distribution system, they formed what was in effect a 'protein bridge', linking London to its new town-supply district, 12,000 miles to the south.

All this explains New Zealand's successful entry into the protein industry. But it does not explain why New Zealand, in proportion to size, did even better than other participants in the industry. Australia and Argentina also had bold entrepeneurs and massive British investment in freezing works and shipping. It is true that New Zealand was at best only a minor player in the export of beef. Beef tasted better chilled than fully frozen, and this favoured closer South American sources, such as Argentina. Argentina was also a big producer of sheep meats, as was Australia, and each had advantages over New Zealand, such as size, earlier entry to refrigerated meat exports and, in the case of Argentina, relative proximity. Yet New Zealand dominated sheep-meat exports to Britain from the outset, and by 1933 supplied more than Australia and South America combined – 52 per cent of Britain's imported mutton and 54 per cent of its lamb.[40] In dairying, Canada was Britain's traditional supplier of cheese, and Denmark of butter, which proximity allowed it to supply fresh. In the early 1900s, New Zealand supplied just 5.3 per cent of Britain's imported butter, compared with Denmark's 42; and a trivial 2.7 per cent of Britain's cheese, compared to Canada's 65 per cent. By 1933, New Zealand had a narrow lead over Denmark in butter, at 28.4 to 28 per cent, and a huge lead over Canada in cheese, at 67.7 to 20 per cent. Australia was well behind New Zealand in all categories of sheep meats and dairy products, as were all other suppliers.[41] New Zealand provided roughly half of Britain's imports of lamb, mutton, cheese and butter combined. These are absolute figures. In proportion to population, New Zealand was leader by a country mile, a protein exporter's paradise in actuality as well as myth. How is New Zealand's pre-eminence to be explained?

There are many partial answers, some touched on above. The absence of alternatives may have supplied exceptional motivation. New Zealand had less in the way of alternative markets and alternative industries than did countries such as Canada and Australia. The excesses of progressive colonisation in New Zealand may have bequeathed a greater surplus of grassland, aspirant farmers and frustrated entrepreneurs than in other countries. The social organisation of farming gave an edge over ranching countries such as Argentina, as noted above. Another set of explanations would focus on 'imperial preference'– the formal and informal advantages of the dominions in the British market. These were consolidated in the Ottawa Agreement of 1932, and could be said to explain the pre-eminence of New Zealand in 1933.

Yet New Zealand outdid not only Denmark and Argentina, but also Canada and Australia, and it was almost as pre-eminent in the 1920s – before Ottawa, although that agreement did provide a supplementary boost. Another set of explanations centre on quality.

New Zealand appears to have made a more precise and more effective adaptation to the desires of the British market, and to have achieved a substantial edge in perceived quality. This is the conclusion of modern British economic scholarship, not merely of parochial New Zealand rural legend. According to one British economic historian,

> New Zealand was the major overseas producer [in sheep meat], followed by Australia . . . with New Zealand predominantly the country of first-grade mutton, and Australia generally supplying a rather more inferior product . . . Most New Zealand mutton received favourable reports about its quality in the British press.[42]

New Zealand grading and quality control, perhaps because of the state's input, were seen as more reliable than those of the competition. New Zealand government representatives in Britain launched 'frequent prosecutions' of butchers trying to pass off Australian and Argentine meat as New Zealand. Another British economic historian notes that New Zealand lamb was 'the product which took the freezing process best of all'. Its price variations were closer to those of fresh British lamb than those of Australian and Argentine frozen lamb.[43]

With all due respect to both British economic history and New Zealand rural ego, can the quality edge really have been sufficient to explain a market leadership that was massive in proportion to New Zealand's size? Can it explain New Zealand's success in butter and cheese, where claims of superior quality are far fewer? New Zealand dairy products were as good as average, but it is not clear that they were better. Can a quality edge alone explain the breaking of mental barriers to the consumption of frozen and foreign food that New Zealand helped lead? I myself doubt that New Zealand agricultural superiority alone can explain all this, and suspect that a curious set of cultural factors was also at work. These are discussed at the end of this chapter.

Deep in rural folklore long lurked the belief that New Zealand farmers were being exploited by British shippers, financiers and protein distributors. It is true that a group of British companies did do very well from the New Zealand protein industry. But the notion of colonialist British exploitation does not, in the end, hold up very well. An outflow of capital to Britain existed, but it was not huge and it included interest on the British capital that had created the New Zealand infrastructure in the first place. After all, the average living standard in 'exploited' New Zealand was usually higher than in 'exploiting' Britain, if only because British capital was exploiting its own workers even more than New Zealand workers. New Zealand gained a secure, massive and growing market – one that did not require vast amounts of packaging, product innovation, or marketing. All New Zealand had to do was maintain the quality of supply and keep increasing the quantity. In ease, reliability, low transactional costs and the quality of transport links, London was almost a *domestic* market for New Zealand, though it was 12,000 miles away. In 1882, the *New Zealand Herald* had claimed that 'Virtually, the exportation of frozen meat makes the colony of New Zealand as much a province of England, as easy a source of supply for the London market, as Yorkshire or Devon.'[44] It was not true in 1882, but by 1922 it was coming close.

Shifting Gear

From progress to protein was clearly one of the great transformations of New Zealand history. The New Zealand–British protein industry was fully-fledged by the 1890s; crucial by the 1900s; became dominant in World War One; and remained so to the 1970s. Wool exports were also important throughout; but just as wool had partly simulated the progress industry before the 1880s, so it did with protein. Britain was its major destination, too. The effects and implications of the formation of the protein industry rippled out into the other dimensions of New Zealand history between the 1880s and 1920s, and merged with independent changes. We will encounter many of these ripple effects in subsequent chapters, but the broader contexts of the economic, technological and cultural shifts associated with the rise of protein exports need noting here.

The shift from progress to protein took place in a world context of technological change, sometimes known as the 'Second Industrial Revolution' and dated to the 1880s–1920s. This ultimately saw a move from coal fuels and horsepower to oil fuels and electricity; and earlier moves from iron to steel, small ships to big ships. It saw improvements in communications, beginning with submarine telegraph, which linked the world by the 1890s, and continuing into telephone and radio. It also saw the gradual spread of new techniques of factory production, an increase in the range and sophistication of consumer goods, the expansion of service industries and the rise of what might be called a popular cult of science. It greatly increased the capacity of states to control societies and to express their power in total war. In New Zealand, this set of changes merged with that stemming from the Long Stagnation, the end of the Tasman world and the rise of the protein industry.

Together, they caused processes of *narrowing*, or specialising, in both economics and ideology; of *concentrating*, in larger and fewer units; and *tightening* – of links with Britain, but also of the potential for social control and tight community. These shifts are less easy to date than the aspects of recolonisation we have discussed hitherto. They sometimes developed fully after the 1920s, and they often overlapped with the full development of trends they were ultimately to displace.

One kind of tightening and concentrating was an ongoing shrinking of space through developments in transport and communications. This by no means eliminated localism and regionalism, but it did reinforce wider zones in which collective identity could be imagined. New Zealand itself was one. Since the 1860s, technology had been reducing travel time and message time between the various parts of New Zealand. Better coaches, regular steam services, better mail services, and telegraph provided some sort of national network by about 1870. In the 1870s, this was strengthened by Vogel's rail network. The Liberals, particularly Joseph Ward, were also enthusiasts for transport and communications, and they expanded the postal network, the rail network and the telegraph and telephone networks.[45] The completion of the Main Trunk railway line between Auckland and Wellington in 1908 symbolised the maturing of this phase of national networking, which provided potential for increasing national homogeneity.

Space shrank internationally, too. As we have seen, the length of the voyage from New Zealand to Britain fell by about two-thirds between the 1870s and the 1900s. A submarine telegraph cable to Sydney was laid in 1876, connecting New Zealand to a telegraph link to Britain. Wellington could get messages from London in 24 hours, compared to three months only a decade before. By 1901, communication time was only four hours. Technology provided the *potential* for tightening relations between places, but not necessarily the thing itself. Cultural and economic energy had to flow down the wires technology had laid. New Zealand's potential links to Australia increased even more than they did with Britain, but this was not enough to revive the Tasman world. The scale and intensity of the economic and cultural interactions flowing along it were as crucial to the New Zealand–British bridge as was technology.

Between the 1880s and the 1900s, an unholy triple alliance of last-ditch progressive colonisation, the fledgling protein industry and the cheap labour created by the Long Stagnation combined to give the New Zealand economy an impressive appearance of diversity. The extractive, export-oriented allies of the progress industry – gold, flax, and kauri gum and timber – still featured quite large, providing about 20 per cent of exports between them in 1900. Flax milling employed 3,024 workers in 177 mills in 1896. In 1893, over 9,000 people, some part-time, were digging kauri gum. Northland kauri lumbering reached its peak in the 1900s. Gold exports exceeded £2 million in each year 1905–09. Some end-of-era industries were more eccentric. The last huia, a rare and beautiful native bird, were shot for hat feathers in the 1900s, and there were several attempts at ostrich farming to replace them. The enterprising Chew Chong and others exported £375,000 worth of edible 'Jew's ear' fungus to Canton by 1904. Rabbit skins in millions, and even canned rabbit meat made their way overseas. The fruit and tobacco industries have their origins in this period, and the first refrigerated protein exporters tried their luck at many products apart from sheep, dairy products and pheasants. For a brief period in the late 1880s and early 1890s, there were also significant manufactured exports. Not one of these export industries was really significant by 1930. Apples, symbol of the Fall, were the biggest at less than 1.5 per cent of exports, beating gold in the race for the very minor placings behind protein and wool. Recolonisation narrowed the New Zealand economy massively. This was not necessarily a bad thing in itself, but it did mean there were more and more export eggs in the profitable protein basket.

Recolonisation and the protein industry transformed the New Zealand countryside, and considerably homogenised it. Northland and Southland differed more economically in the nineteenth century than in the twentieth, when both had protein. Export protein, meat or dairy, could not be produced on native grasses, and the excessive conversions into alien grass in the eastern parts of the country during the 1870s now came into their own. The estates and medium farms of these regions had traditions of mixed production, adjustable to the market, and they quickly developed a dual-farm system in alliance with hill-country sheep stations. Sheep were bred in the highlands and fattened for freezing in the lowlands and downlands on separate farms. The lowland 'fat lamb' farmers provided exceptionally luscious pastures, fields of rape, turnips and swedes, rather like Hansel and Gretel's witch. Before refrigeration, dairy production was concentrated in town-supply districts. Around 1880, Auckland, Wellington, Canterbury and Otago produced 82 per cent of New Zealand's butter and almost all its cheese. Taranaki produced only 6 per cent of butter and 1.4 per cent of cheese.[46] But it was Taranaki, the Cinderella of progressive colonisation, that benefited most from the protein industry, and that in turn helped it to adjust to the new consumers' cheese and butter requirements. It was the only region to display recolonial growth rates so great that they were almost progressive. By the early 1890s, it exported more butter than the rest of the country put together, and during that decade its population increased 72 per cent, its grassland area 153 per cent, and its dairy production 234 per cent. The number of farms tripled between 1874 and 1886, and doubled in the next twelve years. A typical dairying unit in

1899 was an owner-operated 100 acres – viable at last – with 30 cows, valued at £1,200 and producing a moderately healthy annual income of £153 after expenses.[47] As elsewhere in the country, the protein industry carried small farmers, whom the progress industry had kicked off, across the invisible goal-line to medium status and independency – sturdy yeomen at last.

The proteinising of Taranaki subsequently became true of other parts of the North Island. In addition to the town-supply districts of Auckland and Wellington, which switched to overseas export, fertile, high-rainfall areas took up dairying between the 1890s and the 1920s: Wanganui, Northland and Waikato in succession. The North Island grew not only through dairying but also through farming sheep for meat. During the 1900s, sheep numbers overtook those of the South Island, a remarkable reversal. Most of the new northern farms, both sheep and dairy, were medium units, not large or small. In the North Island, the number of holdings tripled between 1886 and 1911, while they increased a mere third in the South Island. But the new northern farms were not necessarily taken up by North Islanders. About 100,000 people are estimated to have migrated from the South to the North Island between 1886 and 1916, 55,000 of them from Otago, and money followed people and sheep. A typical adult male migrant was said to be the son of a South Island farmer coming north for a farm of his own, equipped with experience and a little family money. Another trickle of southern money came from deposits in Dunedin banks, funding development much further north.[48] 'Recolonisation' was partly of north by south. The new system wrought its changes in secondary industry as well as primary industry, town as well as country.

In 1884, the eminent civil engineer William Blair addressed the newly formed New Zealand Manufacturers Association:

> The greatest advantage we possess is that the Britain of the South is inhabited by identically the same race as the Britain of the North. The race that has made England supreme in all matters commercial and mechanical, and which is improving on itself across the Atlantic. The manufacturers of England deny us the right of developing our industrial instincts. We are to be the 'hewers of wood and drawers of water' 'roughing it' in the far distant Lebanon, while they, the skilled workmen, abide at home in Jerusalem earning higher wages in ease and comfort . . . Before this condition of things is conceded we must assume that the Colonist has left his brains at home, and only brought muscle with him to the wilds. It is in reality the other way about. Through natural selection in coming abroad the average colonist is all around a better man than his compeer who stays at home. This being the case, why should we stifle our natural instincts, and accept an inferior position?[49]

Between the 1880s and the 1900s, it may have seemed that Blair's hopes were being realised, though at a price. From the 1880s, New Zealand manufacturing expanded, with increasing emphasis on steam power and cheaper (female) labour. Between 1881 and 1891, males employed in factories increased 62 per cent, females 112 per cent, and horsepower 145 per cent.[50] Manufacturing came to include a certain amount of heavy industry; fuels and power sources were locally produced, not imported; and there were even exports of factory-made goods. Economic historian W. B. Sutch wrote that they went to the four corners of the earth, and claimed that, in the 1880s, 'New Zealand was becoming a miniature England'. For better or for worse, he implied, this embryonic industrialised future, which promised more independence of Britain, was then aborted by the new emphasis on agriculture and the British market.[51] Sutch was right about the increased economic dependency, though 'economic integration' may be a better term. He was also right about the increased importance of agriculture. But he was wrong about the decline in industrialisation. Recolonisation was a system that merged industry and agriculture, as well as the New Zealand and British economies.

Statistical factories employed an average of only ten people each in 1881, eleven in 1891, and still only fifteen in 1921. These factories accounted for 15 per cent of all production by value in 1900, compared with farming's 60 per cent. But these figures obscure the scale and importance of manufacturing. Most 'factories' were really small workshops, and some of the rest were quite large in local terms. By 1929, 3 per cent of factories and mills employed 50 per cent of manufacturing workers.[52] The processing of farm products was credited to farming in the main set of production statistics – hence the 15 per cent in 1900. In reality, half of all production that year passed through factories or mills. The processed proportion continued to increase. By 1921, it was three-quarters of all production. The value of factory and mill production, including raw materials, grew a massive 1,100 per cent between 1881 and 1921, and the value they added by about 700 per cent, while the proportion of the workforce employed only doubled.

The big factories were of two kinds: factories proper and 'mills'. The distinction is that factories proper create finished products from multiple inputs (as with a factory producing shoes from leather, hobnails and rubber) while mills process a single raw material, not necessarily into its final form (as with the milling of wheat into flour). There are, in turn, two subcategories of milling: renewable and extractive. The former processes renewable materials such as wool, wheat and protein products. Extractive mills process non-renewable materials, or materials they do not trouble to renew, such as flax and native timber. They are closely related to mining. Part of the huge growth in manufacturing, 1881–1921, was in factories proper. They fabricated or assembled a growing range and quantity of consumer products from milled materials and components. As international technology and manufacturing techniques grew more sophisticated and recolonisation created increasing pressures to 'buy British', the imported proportion of components and machines grew, and New Zealand heavy industry and 'self-sufficiency' both declined.

The bulk of manufacturing growth, however, was in the renewable milling of protein for export. Meat processing was already the biggest 'factory' sector by value in 1891, though not yet by number of employees. Meat was exported in whole carcasses, and its processing was actually finished overseas, by British butchers who cut it up into saleable joints and cuts. In short, recolonisation saw New Zealand industry grow greatly – much more in output than workforce – and concentrate into larger units. But it also became more dependent, more closely integrated with its overseas partner. It increasingly specialised in the factory finishing or assembling of materials milled (and partly fabricated) overseas, and the renewable milling of materials for finishing overseas. In both cases, 'overseas' was mainly Britain. New Zealand was increasingly locked into the two-nation system in both milling and factory production. It had part of an industrial economy, not the whole of one.

The recolonial reshaping of secondary industry also affected extractive milling, mining and transport. During recolonisation, renewable milling grew and extractive milling shrank relatively, as protein boomed and extractive resources were creamed off. Mining employed 7.5 per cent of the workforce in 1881, equal to manufacturing. It employed 1.5 per cent in 1921, one-eighth the number in manufacturing. Furthermore, the surviving mines and extractive mills tended to become larger and more stable. Before the 1880s, gold- and coalmining, like flax and timber milling, had been quite mobile, creaming off natural resources quickly then moving on. From the 1880s, coalmining exhausted shallow deposits, and concentrated on the deep seams of Huntly and the West Coast, settling down on them long term. Goldmining, too, moved into a new phase – to the crushing of quartz, with giant stamper batteries and complex separation techniques using cyanide. Quartz-mining operations such as those around Reefton and Waihi sat in the same place for half a century or more. The workforces of individual operations in both coal and gold became larger, more stable and sedentary – more like mills. Though in relative decline, mining remained important. As with factories and renewable milling, productivity per worker increased greatly, and there was even absolute growth. Gold output was high in the 1900s, before beginning a long decline. Coal output increased fourfold between 1881 and 1921. Its special recolonial role was to power the trains, coasters and transoceanic meat ships that supplied transport to the protein industry.

In shipping, as we have seen, control tended to concentrate and move to Britain, and there was also a concentration of the New Zealand workforce – partly to meet the demands of the protein industry, and partly in response to improvements in shipbuilding. The size of ships increased so greatly that though tonnage per man dropped, crews grew in size. They sailed fewer, larger, ships and were employed by fewer, larger, companies. Larger and fewer ships and increased freight volumes – imports, protein products, coal and the bulky fertilisers coming into use in the 1900s – led to larger and fewer ports, with a preference for those near the major protein-producing areas. Secondary ports lost out and wharf workforces grew, despite the increasing use of loading machinery. By 1913, the port of Wellington employed 1,600 water-siders.[53] Coalmines, goldmines and freezing works also had large staffs. Such workplaces not only became larger but also more strategic, because of their role in the protein industry. An unloaded sheep, or a sheep on an unmanned or unfuelled ship, was as little use for export as no sheep at all. All this increased the potential power and solidarity of the relevant trade unions.

What happened, then, between the 1880s and the 1920s was not industrialisation per se – this already existed in 1881 to a surprising extent – but a gradual transformation of secondary industry: from extractive to sustainable; from mobile to sedentary; from smaller to larger; from diverse to specialised. Secondary industry gradually disentangled itself from its key partner of the nineteenth century, the progress industry, and intertwined itself with a new one: the protein industry.

All this does not mean that New Zealand was becoming a less technologically sophisticated society. Another change that seems to have accompanied recolonisation was the rise of a popular cult of science and technology. This was an international phenomenon, but it seems to have been curiously acute in New Zealand. The patenting of inventions rose from a rate of less than one per 10,000 of population in 1881, to 17.5 in 1921.[54] Photography was a leading edge of popular technology at the time, and New Zealand was said to have six or seven times the number of photographers per capita as the United States in 1900. New Zealand was a world leader in the photographing of naked men. Aucklander Hermann Schmidt won 22 international awards for his studies of this subject in the 1920s.[55] New Zealand even contested the lead in some technical spheres. Its prominence in goldmining and, later, agricultural science and technology have economic explanations. An international reputation in police fingerprinting techniques, the invention of stamp-vending machines, and Richard Pearse, who gave the Wright brothers a powered flight for their money, are less easily explained. Fascination with science was not restricted to eccentric inventors. Recolonisation was the age of scientific management, scientific policing, scientific farming, scientific medicine, scientific homemaking and scientific motherhood. Recolonial New Zealand had the economy of a semi-industrialised country, but the attitudes to science and technology of a fully industrialised one.

One study of technology transfer in colonial contexts distinguishes two kinds: the transfer of technology itself; and of technology plus the infrastructure underpinning it, such as heavy industry to make and maintain the machines and the technical education and culture that produced the people to run them.[56] The former kind tended to be the fate of black colonies. In India, British sojourners were still running the railway system 90 years after its introduction. Like some other white colonies, New Zealand tended towards the second type of transfer. This was clearest in the transitional 1900s, when New Zealand had a surprisingly high degree of self-sufficiency and even heavy industry.[57] It was self-sufficient in its main power sources – horses, oats and coal – and its main building material – wood. It built its own railway wagons, stamper batteries and giant gold dredges, and some of its own steamships and locomotives. As machines became more complex and the economy concentrated on protein, however, New Zealand became less self-sufficient. Light industry grew with the rise of consumer goods. A new category was added from the 1920s with the emergence of assembly plants. But heavy industry declined and so, eventually, did self-sufficiency as petrol engines replaced horses and oil fuels replaced coal. Machinery and transport equipment increased from 4 to 14 per cent of all imports between the 1880s and the 1920s. Fuel, in the form of petrol, became a major import thereafter.

The protein industry privileged Britain as the source of imports, and attitudes and legislation did so, too. There was increasing official concern to show that Britain benefited from protein dependence on settler colonies, especially New Zealand. Official publications stressed it.[58] Policemen sitting promotion exams wrote essays on it.[59] Tariff policy reflected it, especially from the 1900s, with British goods taxed at lower rates than other imports. Technology itself now came from Britain. The physical infrastructure declined in New Zealand, but the cultural infrastructure – a technical orientation, technical education and a high output of technical talent – remained. The top end of the talent, however, now went to Britain – an 'expatriate game' discussed in Chapter Eleven in the context of arts and literature. In economics, technology and culture, New Zealand was part of a system not the whole of it, the two halves fitting together like those of a neatly broken glass.

Better Britons

Under progressive colonisation, New Zealand's rate of growth had been easily great enough to generate the kind of change trauma that scholars repeatedly rediscover and label 'demographic shock' or 'future shock'. Stagnation in the 1880s magnified the trauma – in this context the only thing worse than growing very fast is suddenly and unexpectedly stopping. The end of the Tasman world in 1901, tighter and more specialised links with Britain, the narrowing economy and the narrowing future discernible behind these things did not help either. Progressive colonial businessman and gentleman John Logan Campbell, the 'Father of Auckland', individualised the problem. He saw Auckland grow from no Pakeha to 100,000 in his own lifetime; his livelihood narrowed from merchant-entrepreneur to reluctant brewer, and became much more modest; his legacy shrank from a new, aristocratic Clan Campbell to Cornwall Park, and all this was quite hard on him psychologically. The genteel, Auckland-despising sojourner had to reinvent himself as its founding father.[60] Reshaped myths salved the wounds of a history that had not happened as it was supposed to, for New Zealand as a whole as well as for Campbell.

A sense of transition, of insecurity and uncertainty – indeed, something close to a collective identity crisis – can be detected in the New Zealand of the 1880s–1920s, partly masked by residues of the old ideology of progressive colonisation and, increasingly effectively, by the emergent new ideology of recolonisation. Identity crisis manifested itself in many ways, most discussed in Part Two. Poet Blanche Baughan hit the note in 1908:

> Ah, little Thor!
> Here in the night, face to face
> With the Burnt Bush within and without thee,
> Standing, small and alone:
> Bright Promise on Poverty's threshold!
> What art thou? Where hast thou come from?
> How far, how far! wilt thou go? [61]

Cultural crisis was resolved by a new ideology. Recolonisation was a cultural system as well as an economic one. The ideology had many faces, but its leading motif was New Zealand as 'Better Britain'. The progressive British paradise was comprehensively reconstructed. Progress was demoted. It came to mean modest, steady improvement or modernisation, which was sometimes regrettable – 'that's progress for you' – rather than meteoric growth which was always good. Its decline can be traced in diminishing projections of New Zealand's ideal population, from the Greater British 40 or 50 million in the 1900s, to ten or twenty million in the 1920s, to five million by the mid-twentieth century.[62] As the future contracted, so did the past. Ravening artificial amoral progress was replaced by the moral, natural growth of farm-first mythology; motley crews and entrepreneurial gentry on the make were replaced by enlightened and select pioneers and sturdy and virtuous yeomen-pioneers; dynamic sinners by steady saints. Past and future were rewritten for the new present. Britishness and paradise changed too, but belief in their new versions intensified as though to compensate for the decline of progress. New Zealand still offered paradise, but the promised land was now less varied, less bold. The shift was Greater Britain to Better Britain, from the Progressive British Paradise to the Exemplary British Paradise, from embryonic super-power to the world's social laboratory. The Liberal government's social legislation – and rhetoric – encouraged 'a New Zealand patriotism consisting of pride in New Zealand as a reforming country showing the way to the rest of the world and especially to the '"Old Country"'.[63]

Under progressive colonisation, Britishness had been asserted to attract fresh migrants and money, whether old British governments liked it or not. Britain helped Pakeha in their wars, not vice versa. In New Zealand as elsewhere, it was believed that settler colonies would become fully independent, on the American model, but through mutual agreement, not war. 'It had gradually become a common assumption that they would eventually obtain complete independence from the mother country.'[64] They were 'colonies which will probably rise into empires'. 'They are great communities at an early stage, and there is no reason why the names of New Zealand or Victoria should not one day sound as impressively in the ears of men as the names of England or France, Italy or Greece.'[65] Britain was being reproduced, not extended. Under recolonisation, Old British recognition of New Zealand's Britishness became essential – something that had to be proved again and again. New Zealand helped Britain in its wars, not vice versa. The new relationship was assumed to be permanently junior. New Zealand no longer aspired to Britain's greatness, but it did assert co-ownership of that greatness, as a junior partner – the Scots model. New Zealand was no longer to be both a qualitative and a quantitative reproduction of Britain. It was to be qualitative alone.

William Lane, a disillusioned Australian radical turned imperialist New Zealand journalist, encapsulated this new position in terms uncomfortable for modern New Zealanders:

> We have transplanted to these alien lands . . . the national ideals of the North, the racial vigour and aspirations of our sires . . . we have tried and are trying to keep the race clean and pure . . . to progress steadily and undeviatingly along the lines instinctively taken by the heroes and leaders of our ancestral

people. In a word, we seek to make of New Zealand a Better Britain . . . We do not want to found a new nation nor to fill the world with New Zealand's glory. We want, if it may be, to be chief among the children.[66]

These were not the aspirations of Wakefield, Vogel, Russell or George Grey.

The Better British recolonial ideology was woven from many strands, old as well as new. Pre-1880s myths of better stock and climatic determinism were dusted off. The New Zealand colonists were the best of British, carefully selected for superior genes by Wakefield and Vogel as though they were prize bulls and heifers. 'The stock from which New Zealanders are sprung,' claimed New Zealand historians in 1902, 'is not only British, but the best British.'[67] Britons flowered best in temperate climes, especially that of New Zealand. As late as 1925, it was claimed that New Zealand's 'weather conditions are conducive to the building of a fine race'.[68] New developments included proving Better Britishness in sport and war, discussed in later chapters, and the contribution of a benign and active state and its exemplary legislation, touched on above. There was also a reconstructed ruralism with its yeoman hero – postdated to the pre-protein era. Thomas Carlyle's archetypal Briton, John Bull, was a sturdy yeoman, whose racial virtues were guaranteed by rural life. In Old Britain, John had degenerated through industrialism, urbanisation and the associated vices. In Better Britain, he flowered anew, and better than ever, in both prospect and retrospect. Tributes to, and commemorations of, virtuous rural pioneers, and the publication of their memoirs (from which unruly crews were typically laundered out), flowered in the 1890s and 1900s.[69] In 1911, a newspaper reviewer celebrated one such memoir, *Looking Back*, with a synthesis of Better British myth.

We are the most English of England's possessions, and the secret of our likeness to the Old Land is revealed in the pages of 'Looking Back', for from the splendid specimens of the breed called British the best parts of the Dominion have sprung.[70]

Better British ideology melded an increasingly intense assertion of Britishness with a pre-existing popular self-image and an embryonic collective identity. It maintained that New Zealanders were even more loyal and closely linked to Old Britain than other neo-Britains, but also that they were in some respects superior to Old Britons. The self-image of New Zealanders asserted greater egalitarianism, ingenuity and self-reliance than Old Britons. The collective identity asserted New Zealandness and Britishness, with an assumption of compatibility so strong that it required no stating. These and other features of Better Britonism can be explored through a closer look at two of its manifestations: martial New Zealandness and collective self-promotion.

Between 1899 and 1902, Britain fought the Boer War, or Second South African War, against the Afrikaaners of the Transvaal and Orange Free State. Seddon seized upon the outbreak of war in 1899 to mount a competitive demonstration of loyalty to Britain. He was almost successful in getting New Zealand troops to South Africa ahead of those of other settlement colonies, but was bilked by a few New South Welshmen who had cheated by starting from Britain. The claim that New Zealand contributed more troops in proportion to population than other neo-Britains is now also said to be false.[71] But Seddon's enthusiasm was loud, consistent and practically expressed. New Zealand sent 6,500 troops to South Africa, which does appear to be a higher proportion than Australia (16,600) and Canada (8,400). The contrast with Ballance and the Sudan in 1885 is striking. The enthusiasm was not Seddon's alone. Huge crowds farewelled the departing contingents, and public subscriptions paid for a substantial part of the war effort.[72]

The New Zealanders lost 70 killed and 166 wounded in the Boer War, plus another 148 killed by disease and accidents. Their actual performance against the Boers is obscured by New Zealand martial mythology, which modern research has yet to fully penetrate. Testimonials to New Zealand military excellence were numerous and impressive, but not entirely convincing. It was even alleged that New Zealand horses were less likely than others to 'flap' under pressure.[73] Some New Zealanders distinguished themselves soon after their arrival, at Sligersfontein (15 January 1900), which became known as 'New Zealand Hill'. But groups of New Zealanders also surrendered to Boer parties on at least four occasions, and their bloodiest engagement, at Langverwacht Hill in February 1902, was more notable for gallantry than success.[74] This is one case, however, where the myth was more important than the actuality. Like later and greater conflicts, the Boer War held a mirror to the face of New Zealand collective identity and self-image. Key elements were that New Zealand's loyalty to Britain was second to none, but that New Zealand soldiers were superior to Old British ones.

Enthusiastic participation in the Boer War was not the only expression of this new militarism and imperial patriotism. It was also apparent in military policy and in public attitudes to it. New Zealand's system of volunteer units had been largely moribund since the end of major conflict with Maori in 1870. In the 1890s, however, New Zealand suddenly became more warlike. The number of volunteers increased from 5,000 to 18,000 between 1897 and 1902, and the climb began before the Boer War.[75] The whole orientation of New Zealand thinking on military issues shifted from local defence to contributing to an imperial war effort. The same was true of military training for boys. Military drill for schoolboys was first recorded in 1857, and encouraged by legislation in 1877. But it did not really take off until the

1890s – boosted in particular by the government provision of drill instructors from 1893.[76] In the 1900s, militarism intensified further with the development of the cadet system, which involved 30,000 boys by 1912; with the instant New Zealand adoption of Britain's Boy Scout movement in 1908 (discussed in Chapter Twelve); with Joseph Ward's donation of the expensive battle-cruiser *New Zealand* to the British navy in 1909; and with the introduction of compulsory military training between 1909 and 1912, at which Britain itself balked.

The rise of New Zealand militarism, 1890s–1912, could be attributed to the leadership of Seddon; to the visit of the imperial military icon Lord Kitchener in 1910; or to the excitement stemming from the Boer War. The above analysis implies that all three explanations are false. The rise actually pre-dated the Boer War, though it was clearly intensified by it. Under Seddon, wrote Reeves, 'Patriotism and Imperialism came into fashion'.[77] But Seddon, as usual, was riding and augmenting a wave, not creating it. Kitchener's real role was less significant still. His alleged role was an early example of a persistent recolonial habit: using the visit of an eminent British authority to legitimate an indigenous development. The new imperial patriotism was not universal, but it was popular rather than imposed. A voluntary organisation, the National Defence League, was 'well organised' and 'clamorous' in advocating compulsory military training, and 'exercised enormous influence'.[78] When New Zealand children played toy soldiers, they did so with due respect for imperial military icon Lord Roberts. 'The rule was that Bobs (Lord Roberts), on a white horse, was never allowed to be knocked down by the shells of an enemy, and whichever side drew him had to be victorious. A sense of guilt accompanied any accidental knocking of him over.'[79]

This conclusion contradicts that of Keith Sinclair, the historian to have discussed New Zealand nationalism in most depth. Sinclair maintained that the period witnessed the emergence of a popular nationalism, which despite official rhetoric was not imperialist. 'The mass of the people were unmoved by imperial questions, which failed to become electoral issues.'[80] How could imperialism become an electoral issue when almost all parliamentarians were agreed on it? Marriage was not an electoral issue either. Sinclair was right to detect an upsurge in New Zealand collective identity in and around the 1900s. But it was not popular independent nationalism. It was popular, and quite martial, Better Britonism. It is true that compulsory military service, which turned New Zealand into quite a highly militarised society by 1914, was not universally popular among those supposed to do the serving. In 1912–13, 10,000 young men were prosecuted for not attending training, nearly 7,000 were convicted, and 259 imprisoned.[81] This may reflect the strength of militant but anti-militarist working-class feeling, as well as 'pacifist' religious and liberal anti-militarism. Defaulters had some public support; five Christchurch youths became known as the 'Ripa Island Martyrs', and their release from that prison in 1913 was celebrated by a substantial crowd. Anti-militarists were not a majority, however – 2,500 people welcomed the martyrs; 130,000 welcomed the visiting battle-cruiser *New Zealand* the same year.[82] Most territorial soldiers accepted their call-up. Including senior cadets, New Zealand had almost 60,000 trained soldiers by 1914.[83] Their equipment was inadequate, and their training may have been, too. But, at around 6 per cent of the total population, this was a citizen army almost Prussian in scale.

What was true of martial New Zealandness appears also to have been true of Better Britonism in general. Sinclair dismissed William Lane, quoted above as an exemplar of the recolonial ideology. 'No-one could have been a less reliable guide to New Zealand opinion.'[84] Lane may have been extreme in his cringing tone, but you do not get to be editor of the *New Zealand Herald*, the country's largest daily, by being a voice crying alone in the wilderness. The pervasiveness of an ideology is not easy to test, yet there are signs that the recolonial idea of New Zealand as Better Britain was widely shared and persistent, and that it featured in informal as well as formal mythologies. 'The Best of British' and 'John Bull' were popular trademarks for New Zealand products. No-one was suprised that the 'Anglo-Special' bicycle was New Zealand-made, or that 'Britannia' featured proudly on boxes of New Zealand school chalk, as it did until the 1950s.[85] Brave New Zealand children were called 'little Britons' well into the century.[86] 'The central message' of New Zealand popular literature from the 1880s to the 1950s, was that 'the colonies provided a breeding ground for Britishness, perhaps even carried its destiny more effectively than Great Britain itself'.[87] Recolonial historians, both popular and scholarly, agreed with recolonial novelists. The pioneer settlers, wrote popular historian A. H. Reed, were 'a better class of people even than the average British town or village'.[88] The New Zealand volume of the *Cambridge History of the British Empire* concluded in 1933 that 'the Dominion thus is, and is likely to remain, more British even than Britain'. But it was a Britain without the mistakes, 'a revised edition of the Motherland'.[89]

New Zealand had a tradition of promoting itself internationally, especially in Britain, which dated back to the 1830s. Under progressive colonisation, promotions using a variety of media – books, displays, brochures and lectures – had centred on attracting money and migrants. Under recolonisation, on the face of things, they shifted in the direction of tourism. The physical focus of the tourism industry was the 'Thermal Wonderland' around Rotorua. Its attractions consisted of the ancient European spa tradition of 'taking the waters'; the local scenic wonders; and an informal reputation for 'dusky maidens'. This diversity of attractions enabled the Thermal Wonderland to survive the explosion of its top wonder, the Pink and White Terraces, in the Tarawera eruption of 1886. The efforts of Auckland entrepreneur Robert Graham were important in early tourism, but increasingly the industry was led by the state.[90] In 1901, the Liberal government established a Tourist and Publicity Department, said to be the first such institution in the world. State-led tourism expanded to 'natural wonders' outside the Rotorua region – to the other spas of Hanmer and Te Aroha, and to resorts at Mount Cook, Waitomo, Waikaremoana, Te Anau, Milford and Queenstown by 1926.

The state invested substantially in the promotion of New Zealand tourism overseas. Overseas tourism was clearly a big deal in the minds of New Zealand leaders and publicists. There was something strange about this. The domestic market, though restricted to the fairly affluent at this time, was probably more important for tourism than the overseas market. Overseas tourism was in fact tiny, almost to the point of economic insignificance. There were 5,000 overseas tourists in 1904; and still only about 12,000 a year in the 1920s. Compare this, even in proportion to increased host population, with the 1.5 million overseas tourists entering annually in the late 1990s. For all the hype, overseas tourism was worth no more than a large freezing works to the New Zealand economy. Furthermore, most of the tourists came from neighbouring Australia, as one would expect in the years before mass air travel. Yet publicity was directed primarily towards Britain. 'Overall, the highest concentration of New Zealand publicity was in London.'[91] 'Tourism' appears to have functioned as a proxy and focus for a much wider and more significant type of national self-promotion. The words 'tourist and publicity' in the department's title should have been inverted.

The promotion campaign operated at various levels, private as well as public. There was an exponential increase in the dispatch of picture postcards from New Zealand to Britain, from 1.4 million in 1903 to eight million in 1909.[92] The promotion campaign was one in which it was assumed private citizens would want to participate. 'New Zealanders travelling en route to Great Britain were supplied with literature "likely to assist them in dis-seminating useful information on their travels".'[93] Guidebooks to New Zealand proliferated from the 1890s. As in the 1840s and 1870s, they were joined by an ambiguous category of literature midway between information and advertising, including official publications. The promotional effort reached a new peak in the 1920s. Between 1920 and 1926, New Zealand's High Commission in London – which was the only full overseas diplomatic post –

sponsored at least 800 lectures and 47 displays and shopping days.[94] The High Commissioners, who were usually leading New Zealand politicians such as William Pember Reeves, doubled as managers of an ongoing promotions campaign.

The campaign was also expressed in exhibitions, to which New Zealand appears to have been particularly prone. 'New Zealand has had a weakness for Exhibitions from the first.'[95] Local exhibitionism was strong, especially in Dunedin and Christchurch, which hosted a dozen extravaganzas of increasing size between 1865 and 1926. Attendances at exhibitions in Christchurch in 1906–07 and in Dunedin in 1925–26 reached two and three million respectively.[96] New Zealand had been displaying itself overseas for even longer. It had a small display in London's seminal Crystal Palace exhibition of 1851, and much larger ones subsequently. Examples of extractive products such as gold, flax and kauri gum featured large in the early exhibitions, along with Maori artefacts and emigration advertising. Under recolonisation, some motifs persisted but there was also a change in emphasis. The wonders of New Zealand nature and natives continued to be emphasised. Indeed, Maori were probably more prominent in exhibitions after the 1880s than before. As explained in Chapter Six, elements of their culture were co-opted, along with thermal regions and fiords, to give New Zealand distinctiveness. On the other hand, exhibitions continued to emphasise New Zealand's Britishness, and its *tamed* natural purity as well as its wild nature. Clean, green rolling pastures, with contented cows munching lush grass, were in the foreground, great snow-capped mountains in the back. Added to this, examples of extractive products gave way to evocations of renewable products, notably protein. The 100,000 New Zealand lamb chops distributed at the International Health Exhibition in London in 1884 mark the beginning of this trend; the giant New Zealand butter sculptures at Old British exhibitions in the 1920s mark its full development.[97]

'Better Britain' does appear to have gained a long-term foothold in Old British minds. In 1948 Gallup polled Britons on emigration. Forty-two per cent of respondents were interested in emigrating, 4 per cent to the USA, 6 per cent to Canada, 9 per cent to Australia, and 8 per cent to New Zealand. That is, New Zealand's attractiveness per head of its population was four times greater than Australia's, over twelve times greater than Canada's, and 150 times greater than America's. New Zealand, writes a British historian, 'had acquired a reputation in the United Kingdom as the most loyal of settler societies, the most dutiful dominion. It was "the Britain of the South".'[98] Better Britain was better for Britons as an immigrant destination because it provided ruralism, freedom from urban and industrial pollution, and the virtues of an idealised England. So, possibly, did its food.

'Canterbury' did not sound as though it was very far from London at all. 'In the 1920s a leading member of the imported mutton trade observed that many of the housewives of London, who bought Canterbury lamb, imagined that they were buying lamb of Kentish origin.'[99] I myself doubt that the geographical education of Kentish housewives who could afford lamb was quite this bad. But what we may have here is a conceptual blurring that, while it did not quite extend to misplacing New Zealand by 12,000 miles, had an effect not wholly dissimilar, giving the consumer brand 'New Zealand' resonances of reliability, familiarity, home-like quality and an idealised rural Britishness. New Zealand protein brands and trademarks were certainly designed to exploit such resonances.

There was little variation in the imaging of New Zealand sheep meat. 'Prime Canterbury lamb' appears to have been the only major one. New Zealand was the key brand name, associated with frozen lamb as Biros are with pens. There is still a correlation between 'frozen lamb' and 'New Zealand lamb' in the minds of some older English. Association of the New Zealand product with the product as a whole was much less clear in dairying. In 1893, an expert wrote that New Zealand cheese and butter were 'not known by any special character like the dairy products of Denmark and Canada'.[100] It was not so much that brand names like 'New Zealand' and 'Canterbury' had a distinctive image in Britain, but that they blurred the difference between fresh and frozen, home and foreign. Londoners were probably aware, at least dimly, that their basic butter and cheese purchases came from New Zealand. Most labels said as much, showing cows on rich pastures, while emphasising that the contents were factory-made, and therefore reliable, not farm-made. They alluded not just to pastures but to the clean, green environment, as early as the 1890s. Food made in wide-open spaces, with unspoiled forests and mountains, was attractive to consumers in dirty, crowded, old London, and New Zealand protein was pitched accordingly.[101] A contented cow or lamb on lush green pasture with snowy mountains in the background became the symbol of the protein industry, even of New Zealand itself. The image was emphatically non-London, but vaguely British. The image might be vague, but all those involved in the protein industry, in New Zealand and Britain, and New Zealanders as a whole, had a vital interest in maintaining it. To risk a tongue-twister, Better British Butter helped make Better Britons, and Better Britonism helped make Better British Butter.

The 1948 Gallup poll was not broken down regionally, but it is a fair guess that New Zealand's attractiveness to Britons tended towards London and the south-east. It was the area where the rising middle class and the demand for new forms of protein was strongest. 'It was in London and the South East that new consumer and leisure patterns spread most rapidly.'[102] It was the area on which New Zealand marketers and distributors concentrated their efforts, and where a thin end of the wedge already existed. South-east England contained most of the English counties most prone to send immigrants to New Zealand during the great peopling period of the 1840s–80s. At least 100,000 people from London and the surrounding counties had migrated to New Zealand. Behind them, they left a much larger circle of friends, neighbours and relatives who had an idea of New Zealand as Better British, or at least British.

It was London and the south-east that engaged earliest and most enthusiastically with the new forms of protein, especially with the New Zealand ones. In 1891, 71 per cent of all frozen sheep-meat imports were shipped to London. In 1910, the figure was 66 per cent. In 1926–27, 90 per cent of New Zealand butter and cheese entered through London.[103] It was London, not the provinces, that most quickly overcame the prejudice against foreign and frozen meat. In 1907, 80 per cent of the meat sold in London was imported, mostly frozen, while 80 per cent of the meat sold in Dundee was home-produced. Some of the New Zealand protein landed in London was redistributed from there, of course, but the essential infrastructure of cool stores did not develop until much later outside the capital. Even when it did, the provinces tended to prefer leaner Argentine beef and lamb. There was a broadly similar division in preferences for Danish and New Zealand butter. The former was preferred in the north; the latter in the south. 'There appears to be no really satisfactory explanation for this regional variation in consumer tastes.'[104] The explanation may lie as much in New Zealand as in British history, or rather in that strange no-historian's-land between them. Whether it does or not, the Better British image ricocheted back to sender, from Old Britain to New Zealand, exaggerated as if in a fairground mirror. It was neither the first nor the last time that New Zealand came to believe its own advertising.

This chapter has tried to describe and understand the remarkable recolonial system that emerged in New Zealand between the 1880s and the 1920s. It was a cultural as well as an economic system, and it had important social dimensions too. It reinforced imperatives for social, moral and racial harmony – matters discussed in Part Two. Recolonisation and its harmonies were by no means uncontested, as we shall see. But the system survived challenges and outflanked exceptions sufficiently to dominate New Zealand history in the century after 1882. Recolonisation was not systemic in the sense of deliberate orchestration by back-room conspirators. It was systemic in that people with converging attitudes and material contexts made converging decisions, which melded into a matrix of relationships. This yielded economic profit and cultural satisfaction and so developed its own momentum, a cause–effect spiral. The recolonial system was symbolised by the giant meat ships. Carrying meat and talent out, machines and books back, and mailbags both ways, they were the corpuscles of a bilateral system – great ferries running like clockwork between the north and south islands of what was in some respects a single entity.

CHAPTER THREE

Trouble in Paradise

In 1912, the great Liberal government finally expired and was replaced by the Reform Party, which was relatively conservative despite its name. Over the next decade, early modern New Zealand and its youthful recolonial system faced various traumas and challenges, which can for convenience be packaged into three successive 'crises', 1912–22. The best known was an intense and terrible encounter with World War One, 1914–18. The aftershocks of war then combined with an influenza epidemic, economic recession and a degree of sectarian religious conflict to create another period of crisis, 1918–22. The first crisis of the decade, however, was the great industrial conflict of 1913.

1913

On Lambton Quay, a main thoroughfare of the city of Wellington, is the large bookshop Whitcoulls, once Whitcombe and Tombs. For many years, Wellingtonians have entered this shop to buy or browse a lot of overseas fiction and a little New Zealand history. Those who did so on 30 October 1913 would not have had to read their history. On that day a 'special' constable, said to have brandished his long baton once too often, ran into the shop, pursued by a group of angry unionists. 'Specials' were civilians recruited by the state as temporary police in emergencies. A regular policeman was severely injured trying to protect this special from his foes, but it was the booksellers who saved him 'by presenting firearms at the crowd'. As authors know, you do not mess with booksellers, and the unionists wisely vented their ire on other shopfronts outside. 'The ensuing destruction on Lambton Quay [had] never been witnessed in Wellington before.'[1] Perhaps a few New Zealand history books were knocked over in this fracas. If so, their fall constituted much of the historiographical impact of New Zealand's nearest approach to class war. The story begins at Waihi.

Waihi, at the bottom of the Coromandel Peninsula, is now a sleepy town that comes alive in summer as the base for a beach resort. In the 1900s, it had a population of about 4,000, over 1,000 of them employed in the local quartz goldmine, regularly described in the British press as one of the richest in the world. The British press was interested because the Waihi Gold Mining Company was directly British-owned, a reflection of the intensifying recolonial relationship.[2] The Waihi mine's gold production increased from around £100,000 a year in the late 1890s to over £400,000 in the late 1900s, but all was not well under this glittering façade. The problems were that the gold was crushed from increasing quantities of lower-grade quartz, boosting production costs, and that even the poorer ore was finite. The company responded with a fine example of scientific management: by applying new technology – electrification and the local use of rail; by expanding – into the neighbouring Waikino Mine; and by tightening work practices. This last included extending the use of competitive contracting, whereby miners were employed by labour-only subcontractors in gangs of fifteen or twenty to perform a specified amount of work for a specified price.[3]

As early as 1891, the Waihi goldminers had formed a union, but it apparently did little until 1900. From that date, it tried to resist the company's pressure through negotiation and the Arbitration Court. Like most workers, miners hated competitive contracting – as against co-operative contracting, where the workers had equal shares and elected their own foreman. Competitive contracting could increase dangers, lead to longer and harder work for less pay, and set workers against each other. The Waihi miners' resistance to low pay rates and tightening work practices had little success until 1911, when they opted out of the arbitration system, enlisted the aid of the Federation of Labour, and won substantial gains from the company. The FOL was a large and militant union organisation established in 1908, the first since the Maritime Council of 1890. It had 15,000 affiliates in 1912. It was radical, even revolutionary, in rhetoric, but effective at winning industrial disputes in practice. Some moderate affiliates tolerated the former to obtain the latter. The 'Red Fed' had been formed by West Coast miners. Several of its leaders were Australian, including Bob Semple, Paddy Webb and the late-comer Harry Holland, subsequently the first leader of the parliamentary Labour Party.[4]

From 1910, it was increasingly clear to the Waihi Gold Mining Company that scientific management was not going to be enough to solve their profit problem. The gap between ore crushed and gold produced continued to widen, increasing costs and rapidly exhausting the finite seams of quartz. The company decided on a more radical strategy: halving production. This improved profitability and ran down quartz stocks slowly – the mine did not close until 1952. But it entailed dumping much of the workforce, and tightening control of the remainder still more. To effect this, it appears that the company deliberately provoked the Waihi Strike of May–November 1912.

Union historians are sometimes too ready to detect employer conspiracies, and the evidence for this one is largely indirect. But it is strong.[5] Strikes hurt extractive mills less than renewable mills: finite raw materials not dug in one year could be dug in the next without reducing production long term. The company began cutting production before the strike and used it to complete the restructuring. It joined with Reefton companies in forming the Gold Mine Owners Association the month before the strike, and it refused to negotiate unless the union surrendered by re-registering under the arbitration system. The social and political impact of industrial unrest in New Zealand may have been of less concern to a British company than to a New Zealand one. The company-prompted formation of an arbitrationist union, which actually triggered the strike, was an unnecessary and provocative act. One union for one workplace was a basic Red Fed principle.

The 'country without strikes' had, in fact, seen over 30 strikes since 1906, with mixed results and little violence, and it was not immediately clear that Waihi was going to be different. For several months, the company did not try to reopen the mine with non-union labour – known to employers as 'free labour' and to unions as 'blacklegs' or 'scabs'. The atmosphere in Waihi was hardly pleasant, but the local police chief himself confirmed that there was no lawlessness from picketing and demonstrating strikers, and the struggle settled down to the usual contest between strikers' bellies and employers' wallets.[6] Three things escalated conflict: the involvement of the Red Feds; the involvement of the state from July; and the decision of the company to use state protection to reopen the mine thereafter.

The Red Fed leaders were initially reluctant to intervene. Either they felt the time was not ripe for confrontation, or their desire for ultimate confrontation was more rhetorical than real. Semple feared that they might be 'marching to their Sedan', where the French Emperor Napoleon III had met his Waterloo.[7] But Red Fed leadership of labour was still very insecure. On the right, its relations with political labour and the craft unions were poor; many unskilled unions remained unaffiliated; and on the left it was wobbling. The Industrial Workers of the World ('Wobblies') was formed in Chicago in 1908 and advocated worldwide industrial revolution through One Big Strike by One Big Union – a left-wing ideology known as 'syndicalism'. The Wobblies were used by the right as revolutionary 'bogeymen' until Bolsheviks inherited this mantle in 1917, but the loaded stereotype had a kernel of truth. Recent research has shown that they did have a brief but significant influence here, 1911–13. The same was true of the tiny but energetic Socialist Party, from about 1907.[8] To avoid being outflanked on the left, the Red Feds had to intensify their revolutionary rhetoric and, to some extent, their practice. They declined to call for support strikes and tried to keep the dispute local, but they took over management of the Waihi Strike and provided strike pay, which gave bellies some advantage over wallets. These factors combined to scare anti-union elements into unity.

The Liberal Government was at this moment staggering towards its fall. Thomas Mackenzie and a last-gasp ministry had taken over from Sir Joseph Ward in March 1912. While Mackenzie's ministry was not very sympathetic to militant labour, it did rely on three or four labour-sympathising MHRs for its majority. But in July, it lost a vote of no-confidence and the Reform government of William Massey took over. Massey, his party and the new protein-farming class from which he sprang are discussed in Chapter Four. It is enough to say here that he was able, vigorous and extremely antagonistic to strikers. A major difference between the Maritime Strike of 1890 and the strikes of 1912–13 was that, in the former, the state stayed fairly neutral; in the latter, it did not.

One of Massey's first decisions was to unleash the new Commissioner of Police on Waihi. Commissioner John Cullen, known to his own subordinates as 'Czar Cullen', was inclined towards harsh policing – 'I am naturally a strict man.'[9] He and Massey may have been acting on behalf of the employers in determining to suppress the Waihi Strike, but it is more likely that they actually believed revolutionary rhetoric and thought that the state faced a serious threat. They then proceeded to help create it. Overriding the claims of the local police chief that 'not one act of lawlessness . . . has been committed' by strikers, Cullen himself led 80 police into Waihi and began arresting strikers for such crimes as whistling the 'Red Flag'. Forty-five strikers were imprisoned by September. 'The evidence is hard to take seriously now.'[10]

Encouraged by the government's support, the mine company launched a wide search for strikebreakers, apparently selecting them more for pugilistic than mining skills, and reopened the mine. Striker picketing and demonstrations intensified in response, and Waihi erupted into a series of riots and street fights between strikers and strikebreakers. The police did limit the violence against the strikers, but they also managed it – preventing lynchings but encouraging beatings. The union store at Waihi and the union hall at neighbouring Waikino were stormed and ransacked, with police acquiescence, while company property does not appear to have been damaged. Cullen's confidential correspondence, revealed by recent research, shows that he deliberately orchestrated confrontations to ensure that the strikers were 'thoroughly cowed'. The strikebreakers, he wrote of one brawl that he had carefully brought about, 'dealt out many cut faces bleeding noses and black eyes . . . It was laughable to see the . . . strikers running at the end in all directions.'[11]

The climax came on Tuesday, 12 November 1912, when a large group of strikebreakers, leavened with police doing a strangely poor job of crowd control, stormed the union hall at Waihi. Unwisely lulled, it seems, by a promise of police protection, only half a dozen unionist men and women were guarding the hall. A few revolver shots were fired as the crowd entered, slightly wounding one strikebreaker in the leg. Another was fired later, hitting a policeman, Constable Wade, in the stomach. The enraged crowd caught one striker, Frederick George Evans, and beat and kicked him to within an inch of his life. Wade was taken to hospital, where he quickly recovered. The unconscious Evans spent over an hour on the floor of the police cells before being taken to hospital. He died the next day from a massive blow to the back of the head, among many other contusions.[12]

As we would expect, the events of 'Black Tuesday' wear their shroud of myth and controversy. There were claims that a strikebreaker shot Wade, then blamed it on Evans. It seems much more likely that the overwhelmingly outnumbered unionists drew their guns in a desperate attempt to save themselves from a terrible beating. With the veneer of state neutrality wearing precariously thin, between 1,000 and 1,800 strikers and their families were run out of town in the succeeding days, and the strike was broken. Waihi was the first, and perhaps the only, lethal civil strife in Pakeha society ever to occur. It intensified federationism greatly, right and left. Both sides now had myths and heroes, and a unifying threat. One side had a martyr. Harry Holland, soon recognised as the workers' leader, made the most of this in his instant bestseller *The Tragic Story of the Waihi Strike*, published early in 1913, which oozed outrage and revolution.

> Never a whirling sun that travels the uncharted roadways of space has glared [on] the scene of a more indescribable crime. Never a star that shines from the ether of God has hurled its far-flung rays upon a supremer tragedy . . . Waihi has furnished an indelible contribution to the history of world struggles for freedom; and out of its tragedy has sprung the magnificent promise of working class solidarity . . . even now the workers are preparing to unite industrially and politically for the overthrow of their class enemies. They are getting ready to write 'Victory' on every red banner of revolt.[13]

The prose could hardly have been more passionate, but this was still no call to arms. Holland advocated revolution, but through the strike and the vote, not the gun. Massey and Cullen were not so sure of this. More experienced right-wing heads, such as those at the Union Shipping Company, were apparently aware that revolution was preached more than practised, and that even the practice was not intended to be bloody.[14] But employers – and, increasingly, farmers and some urban middle-class groups – had no liking for revolution by whatever means. After Waihi all could see a militant working class expanding and hardening before their very eyes. In late 1912 and mid-1913, left organisations held remarkable unity conferences in Wellington, featuring moderate unskilled unions and even some craft unions, as well as radicals. Some 60,000 members were represented at one, the largest unionist assembly held in Australasia up to that time. This conference established the Social Democratic political party, forerunner of the Labour Party formed in 1916. It also established the United Federation of Labour, with Edward Tregear as nominal president but in fact under Red Fed leadership. The right's unity and attitudes hardened in response, a classic cause–effect spiral. The national secretary of the Employers Federation, the able and aggressive William Pryor, featured prominently. In October 1913, watersiders and miners, the old core of Red Fed support, struck or were locked out over specific disputes at Wellington and Huntly. 'The strike fever spread like a huge epidemic wave.'[15] The 'Great Strike' was on.

Massey and Cullen were determined to show the Red Feds 'that they were not going to be allowed to run this country'.[16] As strikes and demon-strations proliferated, especially in Auckland and Wellington, they mobilised the biggest expression of state power since the New Zealand Wars. With the agreement of their captains and the Governor-General, Lord Liverpool, Massey was briefly able to hijack two Royal Navy warships. The imperial government in London was not happy about this, and the navy was withdrawn from direct confrontation with strikers. But marines and machine-guns did land on the Wellington wharves, and heavy guns were trained on Auckland. Some New Zealand officials were imbued with the attitude that the state should act as referee in industrial disputes. The police chief at Auckland was removed from his post for softness towards strikers, and the commander of the army (then known as the Permanent Militia, Permanent Artillery or Permanent Force) had to be bullied into using troops. One measure was partly a concession to such sensibilities: the recruitment of temporary special constables, some mounted, and known as 'Massey's Cossacks'. The specials were most prominent in the numerous riots of October–November 1913; followed by the police, with regular troops in the background.

The notion that specials were temporary police was more form than content. At least half were members of the part-time Territorial Force set up in 1910; supply and support were provided by the Territorial administration and the Permanent Force. All troops, most police and some specials had firearms, but they appear to have actually used them on only one occasion. Horses were themselves weapons in crowded city streets, and the specials' batons were much more like heavy baseball bats than short truncheons.[17] The forces of the state seem to have amounted to about 10,000 all told. General

Godley, absent in England for consultations, wrote proudly of his army's performance while masquerading as police:

> At Wellington the Mounted Rifles, camouflaged in this way, had made short work of the strikers. Mounted and armed with stock whips, they rode through the town, and not only effectively dispersed riotous gatherings but pursued the rioters into the houses, and then dealt with them in such a manner that they had little stomach for a continuance of law-breaking.[18]

The usage 'at Wellington', rather than 'in Wellington', suggests a battle more than a city, which is fair enough.

Not all the Red Fed's 15,000 affiliates were active in the Great Strike, but support went well beyond the Red Feds; well beyond all activist organisations; and even beyond unionists and working people in general. Urban shopkeepers and publicans refused service to the strikebreakers and specials, and even a few small farmers supported the strikers. So did the disreputable denizens of such slum districts as Te Aro Flat in Wellington. Not only did the tight and militant New Zealand working class reach its peak size – perhaps a quarter or a third of all workers – but it established some sort of grip on the nether regions of populism. There were demonstrations, strikes, attempted general strikes, riots and street fights in many parts of the country, but in Dunedin and Christchurch they were relatively small scale and subdued. On the mine-dominated West Coast, the stronghold of organised labour, it was difficult to recruit specials, and the authorities here acted circumspectly, though there was some sabotage around Denniston. The situation was even more dangerous in Auckland, where between 5,000 and 10,000 people joined a general strike in November. 'You would imagine,' wrote one unionist to his mother, 'that Auckland was in a state of civil war, warship guns pointed at the town, armed men everywhere.'[19] But it was in Wellington, 30 October–5 November, that matters actually came to a head.

A huge riot on 5 November, when 800 specials rode through town to open the wharves, is sometimes presented as the climactic incident. A striker sympathiser drove a tram into the rear of the column; there were many cavalry charges and much batoning. Tregear witnessed the affair and described the specials as 'outcast scum'; the government responded by calling him a 'political skunk' – good examples of the contemporary standard of moderation.[20] Preceding incidents may in fact have been even more serious. The willingness to meet force with force appears to have increased greatly, something that can happen very rapidly in revolutionary situations. The leadership usually stopped short of advocating guns in preaching. In practice, many men on both sides carried them. Carrying revolvers was quite common in New Zealand at this time. It did not become illegal until 1921.[21] In October 1913, Wellington gun-shops sold out.

When the first specials entered Wellington, on 30 October, they were quartered at the army drill hall and police barracks in and around Buckle Street, under the protection of the Permanent Artillery. The strikers had 'almost taken control' of parts of the town, and Massey felt that 'there was absolutely no other place where they could be safe'. Tacks, ropes stretched across streets, barbed-wire barricades, and boulders rolled down onto the Hutt Road were employed against mounted specials. Arson was employed against a local baton factory. An angry crowd soon converged on Buckle Street, which was 'strongly held by Artillerymen, supported by two machine guns. This show of force apparently had the desired effect.' The crowd melted away but reassembled on 3 and 4 November in even greater numbers, 'joined by anti-authority elements from the neighbouring Te Aro slums'. During this semi-siege, there were various mêlées, and Cullen ordered mounted baton charges. In one incident, on the evening of 3 November 1913, concludes recent research, 'some specials almost certainly fired weapons . . . What is certain is that from windows and under verandahs in Taranaki and Buckle Streets, shots were fired at the specials.' 'Shots,' agrees another recent study, 'showered from the verandahs.'[22] A third source, journalist Pat Lawlor, witnessed the event: 'Stones, bottles and palings were hurtling in the direction of the barracks. The specials stood the onslaught for a while, and then they charged the mob. The sinister note of a revolver was heard and through the darkness firearms flashed and thundered.'[23]

Some of these shots might have been fired into the air, but two strikers and one special were wounded by bullets, in addition to several people severely injured by blunt weapons. Striker J. P. Hassett allegedly fired several shots at Cullen himself, but missed.[24] It was dark, revolvers have an effective range of only a few yards, and the low number of hits was probably not for want of trying. 'Revolvers Freely Used,' announced the *Sydney Morning Herald*. There was censorship of the New Zealand papers – Lawlor was not allowed to publish his account at the time. Colonel Heard, commanding the Permanent Force, felt that 'it was surprising that the casualties were so few'.[25] In short, the incident at Buckle Street was a bitter riot combined with a small gun battle. Until recently, it seems to have almost entirely disappeared from the collective memory.

Massey felt that 'we have got the upper hand', and that while the specials were 'out in force is the time to have something definite'. Colonel Heard noted that Cullen's tactics were often deliberately provocative, and eventually realised that this was part of the government plan. Many strike leaders, future Prime Minister Peter Fraser among them, were arrested for sedition. People realised that in the end tacks were no match for horses; fists for batons; revolvers for machine-guns. Active striker support never encompassed the majority of working people – the response to calls for a national general strike was disappointing. Specials and other strikebreaking labour reopened the wharves and crewed ships in place of seamen, who had belatedly joined the strike.[26] The Red Feds were crushed, New Zealand eased back from the brink, and victory clearly went to the state.

During the industrial conflict of 1912–13, one person was killed, five were shot and wounded, and scores injured by batons, hooves, fists and boots. This was not the Russian Revolution, but it does seem to have been something far closer to class war than most historians allow. Indeed, the degree of 'writing out' is reminiscent of that to which Maori–Pakeha conflict was once subject. In each case, powerful myths of racial and social harmony demanded a laundering of history. 'It should not happen here' easily becomes 'It cannot happen here', which easily becomes 'It has not happened here'. Pretending harmony from time immemorial is a way of making it happen.

New Zealand in World War One

Each week, a million New Zealanders indulge in the state-controlled lottery, a skill-free 'game' known as Lotto, probably descended from the ancient Chinese game of pakapoo. As in other countries, many watch televised lottery draws on Saturday night: the marbles roll, and often a new millionaire is made. Eighty-five years ago, the country's young men played a similar game, known sarcastically as the 'Art Union' after a predecessor of Lotto.[27] In a room in Wellington sat 233 drawers, containing 116,500 cards with numbers and names on them. The marbles rolled here, too, and thousands won first prize: a one-way trip to France.

The 'Great War' of August 1914–November 1918 was a struggle between two sets of European powers: the British, French and Russian Empires, known as the Triple Entente or the Allies; and the German and Austro-Hungarian Empires, known as the Central Powers, or Germany and the rest. From outside Europe, Japan and, eventually, the United States joined the Allies, and the Ottoman Empire joined Germany. Many other nations were involved, of whom the best known in New Zealand were 'poor little Belgium' and 'brave little Serbia'. They were so common a topic of conversation that Edward Tregear's five-year-old granddaughter found herself in disgrace for saying, 'Damn the little Belgians!'[28] New Zealanders in 1914 did not investigate the causes of conflict, and we can follow their example. World War One killed about ten million people; it killed them in a very strange way; and because the victims were proportionately as much New Zealanders as anyone, this issue is less easy to avoid.

While several hundred New Zealanders served in the British navy and air force, the country's direct contribution to these services was almost nil. What New Zealand did send was a vast army: 100,000 men, about 9 per cent of the whole population, over 40 per cent of all men of military age – equivalent at the time to ten million Americans. These men were sent to seats of conflict over 10,000 miles from their homes, by a country whose European foundations were still within living memory, and a staggering 58,000 of them were killed or wounded. World War One featured the highest casualty rates in military history – in New Zealand's case, about three times those of World War Two. About 1,600 of these casualties occurred in Egypt, Jordan and Palestine, where, between 1916 and 1918, the New Zealand Mounted Rifles Brigade took part in a series of British campaigns against the Turks, culminating biblically with the taking of Jericho by the Joshuas of Auckland. A further 50 casualties were inflicted by the Sanusi, or Senussi, a Libyan Muslim sect, during operations in late 1915 – a not-untypical Great War clash between two peoples who had never heard of each other.[29] Another 7,500 New Zealanders were killed and wounded during the disastrous Gallipoli campaign of 1915, fighting the Turks. The remaining 50,000 victims, all members of the New Zealand Division, met their fate at German hands in France, on the Western Front, in 1916–18.

If alien beings from another planet had looked down on the Western Front, they may well have concluded that the authorities on both sides had decided to eliminate their young single men by mutual agreement. For four years, the combatants notionally contested a long thin strip of French earth, the prize measured in metres of useless mud, the price in thousands of lives. Unprotected humans walked through shell craters, waist-deep mud and tangles of barbed wire, which would have been difficult enough without opposition, into storms of lead. Men came to know that their chances of surviving unmaimed were slim. Even the huge New Zealand casualty rate does not tell the whole tale here. The 'cutting edge', the front-line infantry, bore the brunt of these casualties. Service in support corps such as the artillery and front-line medical and supply services was very dangerous in comparison to most wars, but it was still nothing like the 'sharp end', especially during offensives. The New Zealand Division, usually of three brigades of four battalions each, had about 10,000 sharp-end slots. Each was completely refilled at least four times, fresh blades in the razor. If a wound did not maim you, you were fattened up afresh in a hospital in England or France then sent back to the slaughter. Men came to know that frontal attacks into machine-guns, normally the best tactic the Allied command could come up with, had very little chance of success. How did this strange system of slaughter emerge? Why did New Zealanders participate as individuals, often voluntarily? Why did New Zealand as a country so quickly promise 'any sacrifice', even to the 'last man and the last shilling'? What effects did this gargantuan war effort have, and what does it tell us about New Zealand society and ideology?

In recent decades, some British military historians have sought to resurrect the reputations of the Western Front generals, notably Douglas Haig, who ranks with Hongi Hika as the most lethal leader of New Zealanders.[30] They argue that 'attrition' – swapping lives until the less populous side ran out – was in fact the only way to beat the Germans, just as Haig and his ilk came to assert. Developments in military technology had indeed created an impasse. Firepower had drawn ahead of its ancient rivals, armour and mobility. It was this that reduced 'attack' to unprotected humans walking into storms of lead. There was no way through this problem; there were ways around it, but they were unattractive to the subculture that emerged in the British high command, and were never applied consistently or successfully. In the end, the Allies did win by swapping three lives for two. Parts of the problem were that technical change had outpaced tactical thought; and that the huge wartime expansion of armies had outpaced the pool of talented and experienced leaders. But among the generals a curious cult also emerged that emphasised quantitative over qualitative solutions, determination over imagination, and that persistently and almost wilfully deluded itself about the tactical realities of no-man's-land.

From the lowliest private to Major-General A. H. Russell, the Sandhurst-trained scion of the Hawke's Bay gentry who led the New Zealand Division in France, New Zealand soldiers came to recognise the slaughter system, and blamed it on the British.[31] The myth of New Zealand military superiority – to the British, let alone the enemy – flowered in World War One. As we will see, it had a modest kernel of truth, and to some extent became self-actualising. But it was not very true, especially earlier in the war. General Godley, the overall New Zealand commander, was a British regular officer – albeit the nephew of J. R. Godley, founder of Christchurch. He was an able administrator, with a sense of humour – when asked about Maori dietary requirements in 1915, he expressed the hope there would be enough Turks to go around. But he was unpopular with his men and was as much an inspiration-free zone as his British colleagues.[32] With the exception of Colonel W. G. Malone, I can detect little difference between British and New Zealand leadership at Gallipoli – and both appear to have been inferior to Turkish and German commanders, who were sacked more readily for incompetence.[33]

Even where the myth was true, it did not help. New Zealand civil and military leaders took great pride in their responsiveness to British military requirements, and made no effort to develop their own tactics and so insulate their men somewhat from the slaughter system. After taking some ground at the Battle of Messines in 1917, Russell wanted to thin his men out to prevent casualties from the counter-bombardment, but was not allowed. He even wanted to get the division transferred to Italy to get it away from British mismanagement, but he did not push this very hard, and the government would certainly have balked if he had.[34] Thousands more unnecessary casualties arose from the philosophy of aggressive stasis. French and Germans sometimes tacitly agreed to sit quiet in their trenches between battles. The British preferred to raid and bombard to gain the 'moral initiative', but for no tactical purpose at all. The New Zealanders were just as enthusiastic about this notion, and suffered heavy losses in these non-battles.[35] New Zealand officers noted, but did not do anything about, the miserly British issue of binoculars. German snipers and sergeants had these; to the British, they were appurtenances of the officer.[36] British and New Zealand anti-artillery bunkers may also have been inferior to the German – and the Maori ones of 50 years before – until quite late in the war. An Auckland unit lost 150 men to a bombardment lighter per square yard than that which killed ten at the Gate Pa in 1864. Most, though not all, New Zealand attacks were just as hopeless and useless as anyone else's. That this involved the comprehensive forgetting of the lessons of the New Zealand Wars, which the New Zealand Division and its Maori Pioneer Battalion were particularly well placed to learn, makes it all the more chastening.

Killing strangers for no personal benefit is an unnatural act, and deliberately risking your own life is more so.[37] The purpose of wartime military systems is therefore to turn normal people into deviants. In standing armies, this can be done by building up tribelike unit loyalties, with their own cultures, traditions and symbols such as flags, which grown men will actually die for. In new mass armies, the problem is a difficult one: two of several keys are the delusion of personal invulnerability – the irrational but strong conviction that whoever else gets killed, you will not – and the prospect of victory, with its personal reward, the heroic ending of danger. The Western Front was deficient in these incentives, and most New Zealand soldiers were fully aware of this. 'When things are going well,' wrote Private N. M. Ingram, 'one is keyed up with the hope of great results, and passes over the horrible part of it; but when one learns that thousands of valuable lives have been thrown away . . . somehow one sees and thinks of little but the awfulness of it all.'[38] Yet not only did most conscripts go fairly gracefully, but an even larger number of young men actually volunteered for a career as human fertiliser. Why did they don uniform, and why did they consent to be killed once in France?

Two facts prune down this problem. First, the 35,000 New Zealanders who volunteered before October 1915 had little idea of what they were letting themselves in for. The Boer War was the most recent precedent, and for New Zealanders it was not a lot more dangerous than the Huntly coalmine. The desire for adventure, to see the world, to 'do something', which some historians suggest motivated most volunteers, actually applied especially to this group. From mid-1915, long casualty lists began appearing in the newspapers, frank letters back slipped past the censors, and badly wounded men began returning. People began to realise that this war was an unusually lethal affair, though men may not have grasped the full truth until they reached the Front. Ironically, the early recruits received most social plaudits, but they were volunteering for a different, less dangerous, kind of war. Second, after this initial honeymoon of recruiting, resistance to both volunteering and conscription was greater than legend allows.

At the outbreak of war, New Zealand contained about 240,000 men aged between 20 and 45.[39] Around half these men eventually volunteered, and 92,000 passed the medical boards into uniform, in addition to 32,000 conscripts. Most volunteered for the real war – after mid-1915. Historians now tend to discount the direct role of official cultural pressures of imperial, racial and national patriotism in their decision. As indicated in the previous chapter, I think such beliefs did have a substantial grip on many New Zealanders at the time, and that this must have encouraged volunteering. Large numbers of young men had had an intense indoctrination in the military versions of these values in the years immediately before the war, in the territorials, the school cadets and the Boy Scouts. But external social pressures, often stemming from – or justified in terms of – official culture, were also important.

A large segment of society set out to push men to France by sheer moral force. Young single men who had not enlisted soon learned what it was like to be members of a persecuted minority. White Feather Leagues proliferated; 'shirkers' became objects of public opprobrium; sports organisations banned single men of military age. Young men were told to think of their future children. 'Think of the harm you are bringing on that innocent child when he, or she, in few years time is branded as the son or daughter of a shirker.'[40] No doubt it was considered better for such children not to exist at all, the sure fate of those with dead future fathers. Anti-shirker feeling was so vehement that eligible men who volunteered and had been rejected on medical grounds, or were exempted from conscription, found themselves obliged to wear badges to prove it.[41]

Women were central in the White Feather Leagues, and important in creating a warlike climate of opinion.[42] One motive may have been frustration at the passive role accorded women in the midst of collective crisis. Not content with sitting and knitting for Empire, some women flung themselves into paid and unpaid war work and the encouragement of volunteering. 'Equality of sacrifice' was another motive. If you had risked a son, the feeling was, then other mothers should do so too. There appears to have been a conception of family sacrifice, a tax in sons that should be evenly shared. The death of one son exempted the others when conscription was introduced. 'Equality of sacrifice' struck a deep chord among New Zealanders, and mothers were only one of the groups espousing it. Returned soldiers, for example, did so too. Some women remained unimpressed, preferring the sneers of the neighbours to the terminal telegram. Women of the Christchurch White Feather League, out for a day's shirker-hunting, were chased by other women off the streets.[43] But one has to note the prominence of safe groups – women, old men and married men – in pushing young single men to do the dying.

As this suggests, the militarist climate was strong but not all powerful, and different groups had different resistance to it. Young men acted in clumps, influenced by whether their friends and neighbours did or did not volunteer. Wanganui Rowing Club enlisted to a man early in the war, whereas only one out of 81 senior Canterbury cricketers joined up immediately.[44] Miners were heavily over-represented in early volunteering; heavily under-represented in late. The reverse pattern applied to professional men, and volunteering tended to increase over time among most middle-class groups, as well as among skilled workers. It decreased among the unskilled and rural workers.[45] This suggests that the social pressure to volunteer intensified over time, and that the higher classes were particularly susceptible to it.

Half of all eligible men volunteered; half did not; and it is hard to say which is the more surprising. The cultural and social pressures were immense; so was the known risk. The rate of volunteering was lower than in Australia or Britain, but it was only slightly lower than the former, which did not introduce conscription. After conscription was introduced in New Zealand, in August 1916, some men waited their turn instead of volunteering. Britain's ports and cities were actually bombarded by German aircraft and long-range guns, which made volunteering there a rather different matter. In late 1915, the New Zealand government surveyed 187,000 eligible men and found that 58.5 per cent professed willingness to volunteer for overseas service. The public had mixed feelings about whether to celebrate or mourn this figure. A further 23 per cent were prepared to volunteer for service in New Zealand, which was not much use to the war effort. Of the 34,000, or 18 per cent, who politely declined all forms of service, only eleven honest cowards gave being scared as their reason, though one man did volunteer to act as Minister of Defence.[46] Notwithstanding official denials, the introduction of conscription indicates at least a partial failure of volunteering. There were, it seems, three attitudes to the war among young men: enthusiastic or dutiful willingness to serve; overt reluctance; and covert reluctance. The last position, bowing to cultural and social pressure on the face of things but prevaricating as much as possible, is apparent when we look more closely at conscription.

Workers and pacifists were the backbone of overt resistance to wartime conscription. The most determined pacifist objectors tended to be religiously motivated, and they were subjected to a range of pressures as they resisted conscription. Their families were sent to Coventry by their neighbours; 273 were imprisoned; and fourteen were forced to the Front in a process objectively akin to sustained torture. Those jailed in New Zealand, were 'woken late at night and held upside down for an anal search for hidden objects' – and they were the lucky ones. The authorities were mystified by conscientious objectors' refusal to accept social norms. When the fourteen unfortunates persisted in taking off their uniforms, they were forcibly dressed in them, without underwear, and women were brought in the inaccurate belief that objections to nudity in mixed company would overcome their objections to uniform. These 'defaulters' passively resisted the machinery of state and society; other categories were more likely to evade it. They included socialists and militant workers, 'disreputables' automatically inclined to resist all authority, and Irishmen. The period was a high phase of nationalism in Ireland, culminating in the Easter Rising of 1916. The 1915 survey showed that the New Zealand Irish were least enthusiastic about volunteering; there was a major furore about the conscription of Catholic clergy – few went in the end. Some Irish defaulters and deserters are said to have joined the Irish Republican Army, to fight against the British rather than for them.[47] But most Irish New Zealanders co-operated with the war effort, keeping quiet about any doubts.

Militant labour's opposition to conscription was what the government feared most. Interestingly, its leaders denounced the ballot as an unacceptable extension of state control, the 'Prussianising' of New Zealand, the beginnings of 'the servile state'. The *Maoriland Worker* predicted civil war if conscription was introduced. There were strikes and rumours of miners collecting arms on the West Coast. But the feared major confrontation never came, for four reasons. First, the government used coercion, with an increasingly heavy hand. The definition of sedition was progressively broadened, and a future Parliament-full of labour leaders was imprisoned – 71 in all, including socialist and pacifist activists. Second, the government bribed the strategic unions – miners, seamen, wharfies and freezing workers. Their pay rises appear to have been above average, and their exemptions from conscription were, unofficially, virtually automatic, just like most farmers. Third, the most recalcitrant siphoned themselves off by evading call-up, or by deserting once called. As many as 5,000 never registered at all, entirely avoiding the state's statistical net, a basic weapon of social control. Only 200 were ever caught. Another 5,000 registered men were balloted but failed to respond. The state had these men's names, and a third were caught. Others went into uniform then deserted. Hundreds of these defaulters and deserters were smuggled out of the country, leading the government to introduce passports – your passport originates from a forgotten mass attempt to evade military service. Others hid out in the cities – in one case parents received six months' jail for concealing a deserter-son. Others again took to the hills, the bush, and the West Coast, where they were helped by sympathetic working people. Some were said to be still in hiding as late as 1920.[48]

Unskilled and semi-skilled workers provided most defaulters, but they also provided most volunteers, and the latter greatly exceeded the former. The key to this, and the fourth reason that limited worker resistance to the war, was of central importance in working-class history. The core of this class inherited and developed its own subculture, robustly populist as well as bigoted – oriented more to the tabloid *Truth* than to either radical journals or tracts on moral self-improvement. This subculture had its own definitions of decency, and links with disrepute and the old crews. It did not aspire to respectability and was normally resistant to evangelism from right or left. But in certain contexts, aggressive creeds did attract it, and both worker militancy and martial patriotism fitted this bill. In the period 1890–1918, the two creeds competed for the allegiance of the *Truth* group. Worker militancy had some success – hence the Great Strike of 1913 – and retained the support of a substantial minority. But, through the Boer War, the Age of Jingoism and the Great War, aggressive patriotism had more success. Pat Hickey noted 'the scars made by the specials' batons' on the Watersiders Band playing jingoistic tunes in Wellington early in the war.[49] Militarism weaned some workers from militancy.

Skilled workers and the middle class also resisted the pressure to fight, but they tended to try to do so covertly. Most Australians appeared to favour conscription, then voted against it in the referendum of 1916. New Zealanders had no referendum, and were possibly more amenable to conscription, but substantial minorities appear to have used loopholes in the system – to have preached willingness to fight more than they practised it. In 1917–18, there were 65 prosecutions for self-inflicted wounds in New Zealand camps. From late 1915, when it was known that conscription was in the air and that married men would be low on the list, there was a sudden rise in the marriage rate. Conscription did give married men a lower priority, but it was announced that men married after 1 May 1915 were to be treated as single, and the marriage rate declined greatly.

Only 16 per cent of men were lucky enough to miss each monthly ballot from the introduction of conscription to the end of the war. But some 37 per cent of registered eligibles were exempted on medical and other grounds. Your chances here varied regionally, according to the habits of local Military Service and Medical Boards. Some of the former were more willing than others to believe that 'a father could not manage a farm, or a town survive without two butchers'. For some reason, you had 24 times the chance of being rejected for goitre in Canterbury as in Auckland. The 1.4 per cent of balloted men rejected for defective intelligence included three lawyers, two teachers and a chemist.[50] Contemporaries and historians sometimes claimed or hinted that farmer militarism was more rhetorical than practical. I am not convinced this was generally true. Farming, like mining, was an 'essential industry' – a concept that gained currency during the war – and the rural sector was only slightly under-represented in the ranks. But married men, rural or urban, do seem to have loudly proclaimed their willingness to serve, and yet done everything possible to delay the day. They succeeded. By the time the barrel was scraped for married conscripts, the war had ended.[51]

Once in uniform, a discrepancy between legendary willingness to die and actual reluctance continued. About 3 per cent of recruits were returned as unsuitable – though this was a much lower rate than in Australia[52] – and self-inflicted wounds and malingering in hospital persisted, as they did in all armies. By 1917, the highest aspiration of soldiers on the Western Front was for 'a nice Blighty wound' – a wound serious enough to knock them permanently out of the war but not maim them too badly. The definition of 'too badly' became more flexible over time. Another form of danger evasion may have been the deliberate acquisition of venereal disease. A secret document reported that New Zealand troops contracted 12,000 cases of gonorrhoea and 4,000 of syphilis during the war, and some historians' estimates are even higher.[53] The New Zealand rate to 1917 seems to have been the same as the Australian – over 180 admissions annually for each 1,000 men. The Australians and other countries were quicker to officially introduce contraceptive sheaths, and their rates then dropped somewhat in comparison to New Zealand's. But sheaths were issued to New Zealanders in late 1917 – though only three for four days' leave in London. They were readily available privately well before this, partly through the efforts of the remarkable Ettie Rout. The authorities were concerned that men 'deliberately caught the disease to stay out of the front line . . . they would as soon be in VD hospitals as in the trenches'.[54] New Zealanders, like other soldiers, continued to have unprotected sex. Syphilis is a terrible disease, but there was one thing it was better than: being an infantryman on the Western Front.

Overt and covert resistance to 'volunteering' and to conscription was much more substantial than legend allows, but the fact remains that most men went when pushed, and that many did not have to be pushed very hard. A similar pattern applied once men were in uniform. New Zealanders entered their first experiences of battle, at Gallipoli, enthusiastically, and with the expectation of survival and victory. Thereafter, attitudes to going over the top were much more realistic and grim, and thousands preferred the clap to a bullet, but most still went. Why? The answers, I think, lie again in cultural and social pressures, and in the dehumanising effect of the slaughter system.

Concern about what the folk back home thought of you was no doubt a factor in inducing soldiers to fight bravely. The authorities certainly thought so and used the threat of public humiliation against defaulters, deserters and repeat VD cases. But this applied only if people at home knew what you did, and if you cared about it. Maintaining your repute at home gave no reason to be brave if no-one was watching, yet New Zealand soldiers sometimes were just that. Military resocialisation can loosen the grip of peacetime community. New Zealand soldiers believed that the folks back home would never learn about some aspects of their behaviour – an estimated 75 per cent visited prostitutes for example.[55] They also progressively cared less, as wartime norms displaced those of peacetime. Wartime community – the fear of letting down your mates – was also a factor in persuading men to go over the top, but it can be overstated. Mates were extremely transient beings in World War One; illness, death, wounds, transfers and leave made sure of that. Mates were 'here today and gone tomorrow'.[56] Military units, like the crews of progressive colonisation, were prefabricated communities, capable of enforcing some norms on virtual strangers. But these bonds also loosened in the face of mass death. Fear of military punishment was no doubt another factor. This could be brutal and humiliating, including crucifixion without the nails. But it was a doddle compared with lying crippled in no-man's-land, being eaten by rats bloated on human flesh, or drowning slowly in mud consisting partly of your own predecessors. If this was 'the fringe of hell', God save us from the real thing. No wonder that 'any possible penalty does not weigh very heavily with the average soldier'.[57]

Peacetime community and military community and institutions are parts of the explanation for individual participation in the slaughter system. Wider ideology was another. You did not preach to mates about how much you loved God, King and Country, and how willing you were to die for them. Yet I suspect myths related to patriotism were important. From the 1890s, the myth of inherent British military superiority – a function of race, not training – was an increasingly prominent part of the indoctrination of young New

Zealanders. The belief that New Zealanders were less prone to racial degeneration than Old Britons, and the legends and realities of their performance in the Boer War, combined with various other factors to give the myth special force for New Zealand British.[58] Because the myth of New Zealand military superiority flowered fully during and after World War One, it is difficult to distinguish cause and effect. But elements of the myth were in place by 1914; a cause–effect spiral may have been at work; and collective myths, even grandiose ones, do influence individuals. In the horrible and unfamiliar crisis of battle, New Zealanders sometimes behaved how they thought New Zealanders were supposed to behave: bravely.

As hopes of success and survival dulled on the Western Front, social, cultural and institutional factors continued to prevent mass mutiny – which occurred in the French army. But instead of the enthusiasm, or at least the grim determination of legend, a certain fatalism seems to have emerged. This emphasised the dehumanising effects of war, especially this war. Private Ingram kept exclaiming in his diary: 'What a Hell of a war this is! bundled about like so many cattle and not human beings . . . Hell! if this is war, give me a pig's life, humans were not born for this.' Even Cecil Malthus, an architect of the New Zealand version of the Anzac legend, wrote of one Gallipoli attack that 'we were all lined up for the slaughter'. Another private wrote: 'It was being gun-fodder material, mindless robots, that really got to me.' A dreary fatalism could subvert official norms such as enthusiastic patriotism, and unofficial ones such as mateship. While comradeship revived when leaving the line, it died going up. 'No-one cares if you are the next to be shot.' 'We were losing the feeling for one another, it was "every man for himself".' The Royal Army Medical Corps (RAMC) was known ungratefully as 'Rob All My Cobbers'. 'I now have no illusions about it. I know that it is just a butcher's shop, but as I have to go I'll go cheerily.'[59] This fatalism, I think, was one key to the strange social contract of World War One – people passively consenting to be killed, without much hope of survival or success. Resistance in the form of desertion and other offences punishable by courts martial peaked early in the New Zealand experience of the Western Front. Thereafter men became more passive.[60] Towards the end of the war, a New Zealand commander of British troops found much the same thing. 'I was very much struck by the nonchalance of the men . . . there was no life in them; their pulses were slower than usual.'[61] There is, I think, just a glimmer of similarity with the experience of the Jews during the Holocaust of World War Two. Both slaughter systems were so inconceivable, so removed from the realm of rational possibility, that they generated a kind of collective shock, masses of humans dulled into automatons. The best you could manage was a haggard and artificial appearance of hope or disbelief, which did not convince even yourself.

There are some signs that soldiers, including New Zealanders, questioned aspects of the ideologies that underlay acceptance of the slaughter system, though this fell well short of mass resistance. The soldiers were supposed to hate conscientious objectors. Yet the most famous of these, Archibald Baxter, records many acts of kindness from ordinary soldiers.[62] He subverted their reason for dying, but they almost admired him for it. There was some unofficial tolerance of shell-shocked and 'cowardly' comrades, especially late in the war.[63] Soldiers were also supposed to hate the enemy, and the official line at the time was that New Zealanders had nothing to do with the famous Christmas fraternisations in no-man's-land. In fact, while inconsistent and coupled with instances of the killing of wounded and prisoners in the heat of battle, there is some evidence that New Zealand soldiers developed an esteem for the Turks and Germans. This can be seen as chivalrous respect for gallant enemies – Orakau on the Dardanelles, with Mustapha Kemal as Rewi Maniapoto. Or it can be seen as what military systems fear most – the view that the opposition are fellow victims and that the leadership is the enemy. Legends of permanent deserters, military social bandits living in hiding or between the lines and including men from both sides, may have had some kernel of truth, and some New Zealand involvement. Even if they did not, the legends themselves are significant. A real but unofficial New Zealand hero, James Douglas Stark, was saved by his courage in battle from the consequences of his even more remarkable misdeeds. One of his nine courts martial charged him with 'abusing an NCO, firing ten rounds (not blank) at an NCO in a lavatory, half-strangling a Captain, and blaspheming the King, the Queen, and the Royal family'. 'Starkie' told proudly of how he and other Allied defaulters in a military prison at Le Havre helped seventeen Germans escape from their prisoner-of-war camp next door.[64] Was 'Starkie' admired by his fellow soldiers for his deeds or his misdeeds?

A sense of kinship with the enemy as fellow victims was coupled with a dislike of leaders and civilians. There are stories, a few probably true, of especially unpopular officers being killed by their own men. Despite the best efforts of commanders to orchestrate the reception of VIPs, visits by Massey, Ward and the Prince of Wales were greeted with a marked lack of enthusiasm, even hostility when they toured the front lines. Mutiny was not unknown, though New Zealand involvement in the Étaples riots of September 1917 has apparently been exaggerated.[65] Mutinous behaviour really flowered after the Armistice of 11 November 1918, which was received with quite staggering apathy among the troops. The survivors of the slaughter system were deadened if not dead. Military resocialisation had replaced peacetime norms; the slaughter system had reduced official military attitudes to fatalistic acceptance. Peace ended this, and New Zealand troops were left under very weak social control. All bets were off, and the survivors indulged in a bit of anarchy.

In late 1918 and early 1919, there were a number of riots, protests and mutinies among New Zealand troops in France, Britain and the Near East. In one, even the popular General Russell – known as 'Daddy' – was heckled and sworn at, and eyewitnesses felt bloodshed was close.[66] The Maori battalion was involved in several incidents. In one, a party of Maori stealing beer from a canteen shot two pursuing British soldiers. Another incident took place at Dunkirk on New Year's Eve, 1918. The following extract from the battalion commander's diary is quoted without comment in the semi-official history of the Maori battalion: 'They seem to have taken leave of their senses. It appears there was a bit of indiscriminate shooting going on, and when the piquet . . . attempted to arrest one of the offenders he resisted. Lieut. Wickham . . . tried to gain possession of the revolver, but was shot and died of the wound. Lieut. Angel was also slightly wounded.'[67] Such actions were not peculiar to the Maori battalion or directed solely against the military establishment.

Some soldiers came to feel antipathy to ordinary civilians, who, they felt, were not sharing their suffering, had no understanding of it and who might be profiting financially from the war. Civilians did not know what suffering was, thought the soldiers. This feeling extended to New Zealand civilians. One soldier wrote home that the 1918 influenza epidemic, which killed 8,600 people in New Zealand, was a storm in a teacup, and asked to be sent no more letters whining about it.[68] Malthus hated the Greeks of Lemnos, and there were derogatory remarks about British and French civilians.[69] But the antagonism was most prominent when the civilians were not white. On the voyage out of the first Australasian contingents in 1914, the Australian Anzac myth-master C. E. W. Bean observed in Colombo that 'the New Zealand men are not used to dealing with "real niggers" and place same on level with Maoris'. In Egypt, failing to notice the Pyramids, Godley cautioned against this attitude in a general order. 'The natives of Egypt have nothing in common with the Maoris. They belong to races lower in the human scale and cannot be treated in the same manner . . . Every member of the Force is charged with the enormous responsibility of maintaining the prestige of the British race.'[70]

Godley and Bean need not have concerned themselves. Pakeha were perfectly capable of distinguishing between Maori and Egyptians, and their respect for the former was a fragile flower anyway. They did not like or understand the Egyptians, and their inexperience led them to fear being duped even when there was no risk of it. During the New Zealanders' first sojourn, they tossed Egyptians in blankets, breaking the arm of one. 'How they did scream.'[71] They shot several for alleged theft and for not stopping when challenged, and at Easter 1915, in co-operation with the Australians, they sacked part of the Cairo red-light district. Racialism intensified post-Armistice anarchism among the Mounted Rifles Brigade immediately after the war. They rioted in Cairo in December 1918, and the same month paid a visit to the Palestinian village of Surafend, near Jaffa. A New Zealand soldier was found dead, and the perpetrator was assumed to come from Surafend. A well-organised but wholly unofficial party went out and sacked the village in retaliation. Historians now argue about this long-suppressed incident. But the debate is about whether there were over 40 innocent people killed, along with rapes and castrations; or whether there were only 20 or 30 killed, without rapes and castrations. The British General Allenby paraded the brigade, called them 'a lot of cowards and murderers', and had to beat a hasty retreat to save himself. There were no prosecutions.[72] Simple racism cannot in itself explain Surafend, which should be seen in the context of the dehumanising slaughter system. But it does show how far World War One could twist a group of New Zealanders.

Dominionism

Before 1899, as we have seen, New Zealand did not help Britain in its wars. But in the fifteen years after 1899, recolonisation, militarism and patriotism had helped reforge paradise. The Great War was seen from the outset as wider than previous conflicts, and there was no real possibility of New Zealand staying out. Its entry into a distant conflict with which it was not very directly concerned was shared by Japan, the United States and some South American countries, as well as by the other British dominions. This does not in itself indicate the absence of independent nationhood. The key here is not that New Zealand fought, but *how* it fought.

New Zealand's first move – indeed, one of the first aggressive Allied moves of the war – was to invade German Samoa. The dominion's leaders had long dreamed of Pacific empire, and this served New Zealand's perceived interests at least as much as Britain's. But there was very soon a hint that New Zealand's war aims were not its own direct interests. A 1,400-strong expeditionary force sailed on 15 August 1914. On 20 August, British naval authorities diverted it to New Caledonia, and it went on to seize Western Samoa from there. They did not inform the New Zealand government.[73] New Zealand had despatched its first solo army overseas, but within a week it did not know where it was. There were security reasons for this – a German squadron under Admiral Spee was at large in the Pacific, ready to intercept wireless messages. But this incident did symbolise the situation throughout the war. The decision to switch the Main Body, which embarked on 16 October 1914, from the assumed European destination to Egypt was made without consulting the New Zealand government.[74] We saw above how the New Zealand authorities failed utterly to insulate its troops from the deficiencies of the British military system. New Zealand controlled the reinforcement and aspects of the administration of its army; it did not control how it was used, or even where it went, and it did not try to. Indeed, where New Zealand authorities had the power they tried to be more British than the British, especially the other overseas British.

On the Western Front, 27 New Zealand soldiers were sentenced to death for desertion and mutiny. Five of these sentences were carried out. One historian attributes this to the tight imperial grip of the British military system. Another has convincingly disputed this, noting that it was the British who commuted 22 of the sentences. 'Indeed the reverse is true, and it was the New Zealand desire to be the best that sometimes led to a disciplinary zeal that was tempered by British experience.'[75] General Richardson, administering the New Zealand bases in Britain, considered the British treatment of conscientious objectors far too lenient, and was determined that New Zealand would do better.[76] By 1918, the New Zealand reinforcement rate was 150 per cent higher than the Australian, and New Zealand's leaders took great pride in this.[77] Massey and Ward, who jointly led a national coalition government between 1915 and 1919, were eager to offer a second division in 1917, and did manage an extra brigade.[78] This was eventually broken up for reinforcements, but in 1918 the New Zealand Division was among the best on the Western Front, if only because it was among the most numerous. It was therefore natural for generals to select it for difficult and costly missions. There cannot have been many single divisions that could boast 50,000 casualties, or about 400 per cent – and boast the New Zealand leaders did.

Sending 100,000 men through the mincer of the Western Front, with no control of how they were minced, was arguably not the only way of helping Britain win World War One. The archetypal New Zealand soldier had an alleged genius for mobile, open and irregular warfare. The Mounted Rifles Brigade was used for this, and the rest of the New Zealand army could have been, too. Instead, even the Mounted Rifles were blithely dismounted and flung ashore at Gallipoli. But the really curious missing dimension of the New Zealand war effort was the sea. Spee is not now a widely known name in New Zealand. It was, briefly, in 1914–15. The German admiral's ships cruised the Pacific for a while, 'bombarded and half-destroyed' Papeete,[79] and sank a pursuing British squadron off the coast of Chile before meeting their own doom at the hands of another squadron off the Falkland Islands. Spee's squadron also visited Apia on 14 September, and for a poignant if forgotten moment, New Zealand troops stared down the barrel of the heavy guns of the *Scharnhorst* and *Gneisenau*.[80] Perhaps because he did not wish to destroy the property of German planters, Spee held his fire. He did not visit New Zealand, but he could have. The Auckland naval defences constructed for the Russian war scare of the 1880s were reinforced. James Allen, Defence Minister and de facto Prime Minister of New Zealand for most of the war, anticipated a jolly 'evening's sport' if Spee dared attack the Queen City.[81] But this was mostly bombast, and it was lucky for Auckland that Spee did not arrive. One of his ships, the *Emden*, did very nearly get among the convoy carrying a large echelon of New Zealand troops in the Indian Ocean, before being sunk by an Australian cruiser. Lady Godley, accompanying the New Zealand convoy, claimed she heard the guns of the battle in her bath. The German raider *Wolf* laid mines and sank two merchantmen off the Northland coast in 1917. Worst of all, German U-boats sank 37 out of 99 ships engaged in British–New Zealand trade.[82] What measures did the New Zealand government take against these threats to its vital interests? The answer is, not a lot.

The 1909 gift of the *New Zealand* to Britain had ostensibly been made without strings attached. There were intended to be strings, but they proved breakable.[83] The dominion had been given to understand that its battle-cruiser would be deployed in the Pacific, and a New Zealand squadron of the Royal Navy, of no fewer than seven vessels, was part of the deal. The Admiralty progressively broke the 1909 deal, and although Allen complained loudly enough for the First Lord, Winston Churchill, to denounce his 'very foolish and retrogressive ideas',[84] his protests had little practical impact. Allen also took late and tentative steps to emulate the Australians by establishing New Zealand's own proto-navy. In 1914 he purchased the *Philomel*, an aged cruiser. Only a quarter of its crew were New Zealanders; it automatically reverted to Admiralty control in wartime; and spent 1915–17 cruising the Red Sea and the Mediterranean, losing a few New Zealanders in the process.[85] When it looked as though the Main Body might be inadequately escorted, Massey had no ships of his own, and was extremely reluctant to threaten to delay despatch of the troops. Instead, he threatened to resign if adequate escorts were not supplied. The New Zealand government had to hire two merchant-men and convert them to minesweepers to deal with the mines left by the *Wolf*. Damage to the protein bridge was repaired with new meat ships, which the British were very co-operative in providing, but New Zealand itself did very little to protect its recolonial lifeline.

Inherently, New Zealand has a very high rate of interaction with the sea. Nowhere is far from it; the country has an immense length of coast, and it also has a centuries-old tradition of building and using ships, inherited from two of the world's great maritime peoples, Polynesian and British. During

World War One, and throughout the twentieth century, no country in the world was more economically dependent on sea lanes. New Zealand could have afforded a modest navy. It spent £82 million on its army; gave the British one modern battle-cruiser and offered another.[86] Lack of sailors might have been a problem initially, but there were 500 New Zealanders serving in the Australian navy, and there was always conscription. A naval contribution would have helped guarantee escorts for the troopships, and helped provide protection against Spee, surface raiders in the Pacific, and U-boats along the protein bridge. It would have stimulated industry more than an army, ensured more New Zealand say in strategy, and left a more useful legacy after the war. It might have been just as useful to Britain as a military contribution, freeing resources for more binoculars, for example. But it did not happen, and was scarcely even considered. Why not? Why was New Zealand so determined to stand shoulder to ankle with Britain on the Western Front, to do exactly what it was told except more so, in disregard of its own direct interests?

During the Crimean War of the 1850s, the leader of the Italian state of Piedmont-Sardinia, Count Cavour, decided to help out Britain and France in their struggle against Russia. He sent several thousand troops, and a few bewildered Piedmontese and Russian peasants killed each other outside Sebastopol. Cavour had nothing against Russia. He wished to create a moral debt in the official minds of Britain and France, which would make them sympathetic to his desire to liberate and unify Italy. He succeeded, and French troops helped free Italy from the Austrians a few years later. Massey, Ward and Allen might not have known much about Count Cavour, but I think they were playing his game. The objective of the New Zealand war effort was to entrench and augment the special relationship with Britain that we have called recolonisation. The method was to create a moral debt in British minds to New Zealand in particular by exceeding the unquestioning loyalty and eager sacrifice even of the other dominions.

Aside from the reaction of militant labour, what the government feared most about the introduction of conscription was that it would 'tarnish the carefully cultivated image of New Zealand's war effort'.[87] This image involved the myth that all New Zealanders were eager to fight. When it came, conscription was justified on grounds, not of the need to press-gang the reluctant, but of 'equality of sacrifice' and 'national efficiency' – conscripted reinforcements flowed more smoothly and with less damage to the economy than voluntary ones. There is no doubt about where the 'carefully cultivated image' was aimed – London – and New Zealand's leaders spent much of their time there overseeing it. Massey and Ward, the country's two leading politicians, spent two of the three years between August 1916 and August 1919 outside New Zealand, in Britain or en route to it.[88] The prime minister of a country engaged in the culmination of a total war spent most of his time out of it, in the real capital of the New Zealand war effort – London.

It would be grossly unfair to suggest that this attitude was wholly cynical. New Zealand politicians sent their own sons as well as other people's. Basic affection for Britain, and the genuine and possibly accurate belief that defeat by Germany would ultimately be fatal to New Zealand, too, played a role. But the culture of recolonisation helped create New Zealand's war policy and was in turn tightened by it. There were other ways of helping prevent defeat than supplying meat for the mincer. And there was, perhaps, an element of cynicism in the constantly reiterated desire to be first, to outdo the other dominions. More government energy was devoted to this than to whether or not its army won particular battles. Greater attention to persuading other dominions to match New Zealand's contribution, to pace-setting rather than winning in the sacrificial race, might have delivered even more soldiers to the Western Front.

In an otherwise excellent study of conscription, one historian has hunted rather desperately for hints of independent nationalism. He asserts that 'many New Zealanders began to question the virtue of outstanding sacrifice, especially when performed mainly for the approval of Britain'. In the latter part of the war he discerns 'a new willingness to distinguish between British and New Zealand interests and to place New Zealand interests first'. He claims a mild nationalist reaction to the 'excessive enthusiasm of those who in 1915 had pushed New Zealand's commitment to a level unrivalled among the other Dominions'.[89] It must have been very mild indeed, and is not really borne out by his own evidence. By the end of the war, New Zealand had sent 19.4 per cent of all its males. Britain had sent 27.4 per cent, but the crucial point was that Australia and Canada had sent only 13.5 per cent each, while South Africa had sent 11.1 per cent of its whites.[90] 'Unquestionably, in proportion to her population, New Zealand contributed a larger percentage than any other overseas portion of the British Empire.'[91] The race to die for King and Mother Country was over, and New Zealand had won. Let James Allen have the last word: 'I do not want New Zealand to be in the position of Australia and Canada. We have a higher aim, a higher purpose, and I hope at the end of the war we shall reap a higher reward.'[92]

Class war and world war were not the only disasters to hit New Zealand in the decade after 1912. The British 'commandeer', or mass purchase, of exports continued until 1920, and with it the prosperity of an economy at full stretch. But this was followed by a sharp recession in 1921–22, and fluctuating export prices thereafter. There was also the terrible influenza epidemic of 1918, and a strange spasm of sectarian antagonism between Catholic and Protestant, which peaked with the trial of a Catholic bishop for sedition in 1922. Indeed, 1912–22 ranks with the 1820s, when the intertribal Musket Wars ravaged the Maori population, as New Zealand's worst decade for conflict, tragedy and death. Historians studying markedly different subjects speak of a semi-tangible sense of crisis and insecurity in the period, especially in the early 1920s: a 'general post-war unease', a 'nervousness' that society was 'in grave danger of decline and collapse'.[93] To some extent, these traumatic events challenged recolonial harmony, and its survival is testament to its strength. In other ways, trauma reinforced and consolidated Better Britain.

New Zealand's immediate reward for its efforts in World War One was anything but 'higher'. Prime Minister William Massey returned from one of his interminable London conferences aboard the ship *Niagara*, on 12 October 1918, bearing news of imminent victory and, possibly, the viral vectors of the world's worst pandemic since the Black Plague. At the height of the influenza in November 1918:

> Ordinary public life was suspended . . . Shops, offices and factories were closed, public services were curtailed or cancelled . . . schools, hotels, theatres and hairdressers' salons were closed by official decree . . . Between a third and a half of the entire population was infected with the 'flu . . . This 'flu was marked by the very sudden onset of symptoms, so that quite healthy individuals could be stricken and collapse within hours, some even dying the same day. There were no sure preventatives, except isolation, and no certain remedies . . . When they died, the bodies of the victims . . . turned dark purple or black, adding to the grief and horror of those nursing them.[94]

The 'Spanish' influenza pandemic of 1918 is said to have killed about 25 million people worldwide, and 8,600 in New Zealand. At 5.5 per 1,000, New Zealand's death rate was not huge on international comparisons. But there were three grim exceptions. One was young adult males, who were especially prone to die, a cruel double-jeopardy in wartime. Influenza contributed almost as many widows as the war. The second were Maori, whose death rate was six times that of Pakeha. Their trials are discussed in Chapter Six. The third, and worst, was Western Samoans, now under New Zealand military rule. Their loss was 7,500, a staggering fifth of the islands' population, and it was due at least partly to the failure of the New Zealand authorities to institute a quarantine. Including the Samoan toll, the number of deaths among people under New Zealand rule almost equalled those in the war. Like the class conflict of 1912–13, though for different reasons, the influenza epidemic of 1918 has until recently been swept under the carpet of history. Like the terrible but distant losses of the war, it must have contributed to the slow-burning sense of trauma in the New Zealand of the 1920s.

The final crisis of 1912–22 was an outbreak of sectarianism. The contending sects were Irish Catholicism and popular Protestantism. The correlation between Irish descent and Catholicism in recolonial New Zealand was around 95 per cent. Catholicism and Irishness reinforced each other. From the late nineteenth century, the Irish Catholic Church mounted a major resurgence among Irish abroad – its own brand of 'recolonisation'. Clergy streamed out from Ireland to the dominions, Catholic schooling was re-energised, and the Church became more assertive. New Zealand was no exception. In 1908, in the *Ne Temere* decree, the Pope pronounced that marriage to non-Catholics was not acceptable, which provoked an inchoate but angry Protestant reaction. A united Protestant movement emerged, which tended to exclude High Church Anglicans, whose ritualism it considered almost as suspect as Romanism. Otherwise, it was interdenominationally anti-Catholic. It converged with the long-standing Bible-in-Schools movement, which advocated the introduction of Protestant religious teaching into secular state schools. The controversy over the wartime conscription of Catholic clergy also fuelled flames. In 1916, the Easter Rising took place in Ireland, and was seen by British and neo-British Protestants as a terrible stab in the back for an empire at war. Simmering anti-Catholicism came to the boil in New Zealand, and Baptist preacher Howard Elliott formed the Protestant Political Association in 1917. Sectarian strife was restricted to public invective and public meetings, but it was surprisingly bitter for all that. At the highest estimate, support for Elliott reached 200,000, and many other Protestants agreed with his anti-Catholicism even if they found his expression of it too extreme. Allegations of child murder in convents were par for the course. New Zealand's sole twentieth-century spasm of religious sectarianism culminated with the trial of Catholic Bishop James Liston for sedition in 1922.[95]

At least one Catholic contemporary believed that 'sectarian frenzy came in more or less inexplicable cycles'.[96] The intensity of this particular frenzy, however, seems likely to have been influenced by the other traumas of the era: class conflict and war. Though their leaders were as anti-socialist as any, Catholics were over-represented in the working class and were thought to have a special relationship with the Labour Party. The conceptual slippages between Catholic, Irish, Socialists and 'traitors stabbing us in the back in a time of crisis' were easily made during and immediately after the war. Collective tensions often breed a need for scapegoats. Sectarianism, the after-effects of class conflict, the end of wartime prosperity, and the broader sense of trauma resulting from war and pandemic meant that, in 1922, the Massey government and recolonial harmony faced something of a crisis.

These rifts were closed, bridged or at least papered over by four converging sets of developments. Two, the achievement of social and moral harmonies, are discussed in the next two chapters. Of the remaining two, one was a cluster of contingent factors that helped defuse antagonism to Catholics from 1922. The second was the development of Better Britonism, through the crucible of war, into a secular religion. These factors led to a rapid and permanent decline in overt sectarianism in New Zealand from 1923.

The situation in Ireland itself, in the form of the Easter Rebellion of 1916, had helped cause the sectarian outburst of 1917–22,[97] and Irish current events also helped defuse it. In 1921, the British government and most Irish nationalists agreed on partition, splitting off most of Ireland from six counties of Ulster in the north, and conceding considerable independence to the former. This was followed in 1922 by the outbreak of civil war between nationalist factions, beginning with the assassination of Michael Collins and ending with the triumph of Eamon de Valera. The partition of 1921 defused sectarian tensions in New Zealand, and the killing of Collins and the civil war of 1922 led some New Zealand Catholics to turn away from the homeland. Neo-Irish attitudes to Old Ireland had always oscillated between nationalism and affection, and impatience bordering on contempt.[98] Fratricidal strife invoked the latter reaction, just as patriotic strife had invoked the former. As Chinese and Yugoslav New Zealanders could tell you, the Irish were not the last of our ethnic groups to be embarrassed by an exploding homeland.

Catholics made up about 14 per cent of New Zealand's population between the 1880s and the 1920s – a figure that remained roughly constant to the 1960s. This was a minority, but a substantial one, too large to be easy scapegoats. It was much higher than the proportion of Catholics in Britain. Furthermore, though Protestant anti-Catholicism was quite *popular*, it was not fully *populist*. Populism's enemies were typically shadowy conspiracies or tiny minorities, or indeed those who tried to divide the people by advocating tight class or sectarianism. Certainly *Truth*, the populist organ, was not impressed by Howard Elliott or by sectarianism. *Truth* described Elliott as the 'Arch-Nightman of Religion' – a reference to sewage collectors. It revelled in an incident in which 'Coward Yelliot' was beaten by the enraged brother of a nun he had accused of being pregnant, and celebrated his failure in the subsequent court case for 'Scathingly and Scorchingly Scotching a Slimy Sectarian Snake'.[99]

Elliott may have seized a lot of imaginations, but he did not seize *Truth*'s. He did not seize Prime Minister Massey's either, though allegations to the contrary have circulated for many years. Massey was an Ulster-born Presbyterian, of mainly Scots descent. He was a member of the Orange Lodge, an important Irish Protestant Friendly Society, and sometimes bowed to anti-Catholic pressures from his Reform Party, in which the Protestant Political

Association was influential. This led to the passing of some anti-Catholic legislation while Elliott was at the height of his power around 1920, such as the removal of state scholarships from Catholic schools and an Act directed against the Pope's *Ne Temere* decree on marriage. Massey may also have indulged in some anti-Catholicsm on his own account. It is said that he 'preferred not to accept Catholic candidates' standing for Parliament under the banner of his Reform Party.[100] But the fullest and most recent research on the subject concludes that 'Massey's attitude to the Catholic Church has been assumed rather than examined by most historians, who have denied him credit for escaping his Orange heritage.'[101] It was partly that he was too shrewd a politician to overindulge in anti-populist Catholic bashing. The obvious conservatism and loyalty to empire of some New Zealand Catholics, such as Bishop Henry Cleary, was another factor. Perhaps most important was the fact that Massey's own faith, while intense and Protestant, transcended sectarianism and arguably transcended religion itself.

This new cult was a development of Better Britonism. We might call it 'dominionism'. Better Britonism, as discussed in the preceding chapter, had three key components: a strong New Zealand collective identity as Better Britons; a patriotic and martial British 'imperialism'; and an assumption of full compatibility between the two. It was on the rise from the 1890s, and was already formidable, though by no means uncontested, before 1914. But it was World War One that transmuted an ideology into something close to a cult, a secular religion, complete with martyrs – no fewer than 18,000 of them, counting men died of wounds or killed by disease or accident. The cult also had state endorsement, shrines, a sacred day, and even a powerful order of 'monks' who would protect the cult against any threat.

Historians have not always appreciated the depth of the trauma of World War One in the New Zealand of the 1920s. The killed and wounded amounted to about a quarter of the male population of military age. Virtually every person in New Zealand had had a close relative or friend killed or maimed. The way in which most died on the Western Front led to the tiny, gnawing – and tragically accurate – suspicion that their sacrifice had not been for much. This suspicion had to be deeply suppressed, buried under as many mattresses as possible like the princess's pea. A cult of 18,000 Kiwi Christs emerged, whose sacrifice simply *had* to have been for a noble cause.

The cult's sacred day was April 25, Anzac Day, named after the acronym of the Australian and New Zealand Army Corps. The day technically commemorated the initial landing at Gallipoli in 1915, which had been dominated by Australians. The Gallipoli campaign itself had been very much a secondary theatre to the Western Front in terms of New Zealand casualties. But these mere facts had to bow to stronger forces. The Day was officially enshrined in legislation in 1921–22. Commercial use of the world 'Anzac' was banned. Government was following public opinion here, not leading it. Many communities were already celebrating Anzac Day by 1917. The Day quickly became 'the most solemn and most widely attended day of commemoration in New Zealand'.[102] Anzac Day activism was led by the 'monks' of the new cult, the Returned Servicemen's Association. Formed in 1915, it had 57,000 members by 1920. RSA clubs, RSA journals and the association itself became 'a potent force in politics and public opinion'.[103] Membership tapered off in the early 1920s, but then – intriguingly – began growing again from 1926.[104] The RSA expressed strong views on many issues of the day. They were not as consistently conservative in the 1920s as they later became. But one predictable and consistent attitude was the preservation of Anzac Day as a sacred – yet somewhat secular – ritual.

The most physical expression of the new cult was the erection of shrines to the fallen in almost every city and town, large and small, in the country.[105] A walk through any such community today shows the substantial thought, effort and money that went into these war memorials. It also shows that the World War One roll of honour for the dead is longer that that for World War Two, which was often simply added to the existing memorial. The memorials were usually of stone, and sometimes had more a pagan than a Christian flavour in design. Crosses were rarer than in Britain. The Protestant churches participated fully and enthusiastically in Anzac Day from the outset.[106] But they soon found that their new ally was stronger than they were.

> The deaths of sons, husbands and friends were closer for many people than the death of Christ had become. Churches were filled to overflowing only on Anzac Day. The clergy often expressed the hope that other holy days . . . might be granted similar respect . . . The people had however, found comfort and hope in this new day, benefits which apparently were lacking on other religious festivals. The ritual of Anzac filled a psychological need . . . and helped New Zealanders to cope with their losses, by making them feel part of a nation united in its determination to keep faith with the dead.[107]

The cult of Anzac was so powerful that even the Catholic Church sought to compromise with it. Some Catholics such as Bishop Cleary, a founder member of the RSA, had long been strongly dominionist, and by 1930 Auckland Catholics were participating in Anzac Day parades.

The cult of Anzac was also strong in Australia, but this did not indicate the deep Australasianism the name itself suggests. Australians more or less ignored the 'NZ' in Anzac; New Zealanders, to a lesser extent, did likewise with the 'A'.[108] This might seem to indicate that the cult reflected an emerging nationalism, and many historians have suggested as much. Like Better

Britonism, dominionism did assert a strong New Zealand – or Australian – collective identity, but in neither case was it independent nationalism. The 18,000 Christs had not died in a cause that could be easily or directly related to separate New Zealand national interests. The nobility of their sacrifice depended on the conceptual merging of British and New Zealand interests. In the iconography of war memorials, imperial and classical images were common; ferns, kiwi, and New Zealand flags were rare.[109] The essential Britishness of dominionism was expressed at both the top and bottom of New Zealand society.

At the top, Prime Minister Massey was a 'British Israelite', convinced that the British, broadly defined, were God's chosen people, destined to rule much of the world and to lead the rest of it. He had a 'mystical faith in the divine mission and permanency of the British Empire'. For him, 'loyalty to the British Empire and a deep faith in the positive characteristics of the British people' were key tenets. London, in Massey's own phrase, was 'the Mecca of every British citizen'.[110] At the bottom, every state-school child in the country learned versions of the same creed. During the war, the *School Journal*, founded in 1907, increasingly preached the dominionist gospel, including 'the need for sacrifice'. 'Expressions of mass loyalty and individual conformity were increasingly regarded as true patriotism.' A new history curriculum stressed race and Empire even more than the old. Flag-saluting ceremonies at schools were made compulsory in 1921, and teachers were forced to swear a loyalty oath from the following year. 'Schools became major vehicles for the indoctrination of sets of patriotic ideologies.'[111] A whole generation learned its history from a New Zealand text published in the 1920s, *Our Nation's Story*.[112] 'Our Nation' was Britain, not New Zealand. Whatever the case with the Christian Bible, the dominionist Bible *was* taught in schools.

PART

2

The Great Tightening

INTRODUCTION

Recolonisation and dominionism were allied to three massive social and cultural dimensions of change that took place at very roughly the same time, 1880s–1920s. They were three 'harmonies', processes of social, moral and racial integration. Part Two tells their story as a kind of social and cultural underside to the political, economic and ideological tale told in Part One. The three tried, as it were, to harmonise, homogenise and even pasteurise New Zealand society. They harmonised acknowledged differences, suppressed and camouflaged others, and purified and laundered both form and content. Clots of difference, including the cream of society, were homogenised out; the bacilli of tight class, sin, racial 'inferiors' and non-conformity were pasteurised out in practice, on paper, or both. The three harmonies can collectively be seen as a great tightening process. This Great Tightening was challenged, resisted, subverted and sidetracked to a considerable degree, but it had some success in both myth and actuality. The two went together, because writing resistance out of history through myth hampered its capacity to feed off its own traditions, and so dampened it in actuality.

One dimension of tightening was social, in a narrow sense of seeking to close or bridge the big social rift of class. In the colonial era, to the 1880s, few New Zealand settlers would have denied the existence of class differences; they were simply assumed. Lip service was sometimes paid to full equality and even social sameness, but the thrust of colonial egalitarianism was populist. Populism demanded that status differences be kept within bounds; that overt deference up and patronage down be minimised; that there be opportunities for promotion and adoption; and that the classes work in harmony, rather than exclusively for themselves. Classes, said populism, should be loose, not tight and selfish. The Long Stagnation had broken the populist compact, as we have seen. The supply of opportunity dried up and poverty stalked the land. As a result, the mantle of populism shredded off the ruling gentry, and they were left naked for all to see as a tight class, guardians of populism turned enemies. They were therefore sacked in 1890 and replaced by the Liberals.

The Liberals teamed up with the great economic and cultural changes of recolonisation to reforge a new paradise, emphasising quality against progressive colonisation's quantity. As we have seen in Chapter One, most Liberal leaders stressed populism above everything as the central tenet of their ideology, and they had some success in restoring a new version of it. They were helped by the facts that their urban middle-class core was not a class community, or tight class, whereas their potential opponents were. Two new tight classes were added to the gentry in and around the Liberal era. They were drawn from workers and farmers, though they did not include the whole of their 'natural constituencies'. The working-class challenge to recolonial harmony came to a head in 1913, the year in which New Zealand came closest to violent revolution. Populism survived the challenge and managed to restore the façade of social harmony and some of the substance. Farmers held political power for most of the period 1912–35, like workers in 1935–49, only because they adopted the mantle of populism, though they sometimes wore it as cape or kilt rather than full-body garment.

Another dimension of tightening was moral: a many-faced drive for purity and virtue, a partly religious but mainly secular crusade centred on 'moral evangelism'. This attacked the vestigial looseness, disorder and immorality of progressive colonising society. It sought to exorcise numerous demons, such as disorder, dirt, disease, drink and difference, to name only the Ds. It tried to tame games by organising sport. It sought to convert or conquer the remnant crews and lone atoms of progressive colonisation, independent Maori and wild colonial children. Moral evangelism preferred conversion – restoring, strengthening or creating the individual's willingness and capacity to conduct him- or herself according to its tenets. But it did not shrink from conquest. One newspaper advocated 'hygenic dictatorship' by the state: 'If people will be filthy they must be made clean by force.'[1]

Moral evangelism dared to invade the most inner of sanctums: individual and family life, the mind, the genitals, the cradle and the womb. It was helped by new explanations for misconduct, social and biological rather than individual. This new crusade did not seek to enforce static standards; it tightened them, moving the goalposts of acceptable behaviour. It was full of contradictions, yet prone to totalism. In its hands, sexual moderation became sexual puritanism; temperance became prohibition. Moral evangelism was not the crusade of a few do-gooders, but a mass movement. It used women as its shock troops; the feminists among them sought in turn to use it; and votes for women in 1893 were largely the result of this mutual exploitation. Who ultimately subverted whom is a major question in New Zealand women's history.

The third dimension of the Great Tightening was racial. Racial thought has rightly been discredited in the last half-century, but this has led to two more ambiguous tendencies among historians of the subject. One is to hunt out and denounce racism in the past without investigating its effects, tearing up shoots but leaving roots intact. The other is to reject such denunciations as unhistorical: almost everyone was racist, why castigate people for being creatures of their times? This view has merit but too often slips in to a tendency to downplay or ignore the role of racism in the past. We should not necessarily castigate people in the past for holding racialist views, but we should try to understand the effects of those views on history. In fact, racial ideology has played a major and underestimated role in New Zealand history, not only through its power to exclude, but also through its power to include. Internally, recolonial ideology emphasised racial purity or ethnic homo-geneity, which helped diminish, or at least contain, the sense of regional difference in the Scottish south, the Irish west and the Maori north-east. The staggering falsehood that New Zealand was '98.5 per cent British', which Britain itself could not boast, was its catch-cry. Apart from various statistical sleights, this required a broadening of 'Britain' to include the Irish, still a feature of some New Zealand usage. There was also a simultaneous narrowing of 'Britain', Anglicising Scots, Irish and Welsh to the point where even Celtic New Zealanders could see England as 'Home'.

It is an extraordinary fact that New Zealand was more tolerant of racial difference in the nineteenth century than in the first half of the twentieth. Those less-acceptable ethnic groups, Asians and Southern Europeans, that did manage to sneak in were not allowed reinforcements. Sinophobia, the reflexive hatred of the Chinese, became especially marked. Northern Europeans were much more acceptable, but even they were under heavy formal and informal pressure to assimilate. Racial harmony enlisted Social Darwinism and Aryanism, two clusters of racial concepts that were burgeon-ing internationally in the late nineteenth century. They are not easy to define briefly, but at least in the popular understanding Social Darwinism emphasised a struggle for existence, *within* as well as *between* races, in which the fit should succeed and the unfit fail. Aryanism argued that the most fit in the world was a Northern European master race, a collective 'new Adam'.[2] This race, or group of races, was of Caucasian origin, was responsible for almost everything good that the world had ever seen, and had remarkable powers of co-option, of inclusion as well as exclusion.

Racialism fused readily with the ideologies of Better Britonism and dominionism. It also fused with a global trend towards 'totalism', a broadening belief in the need for comprehensive social integration. The term is intended to suggest both a tendency to go the whole hog – for temperance to become prohibition – and to see society as a whole, a totality. Society needed more of its people more of the time. Until the mid-nineteenth century, states and ruling classes controlled people harshly but not intensively. Because shared ideologies and identities were limited, coercion was severe. Rulers rode shotgun on the fringes of the herd, policed crises harshly and clipped wool once a year. As the century unfolded, the means for more intensive control, such as improving statistics and communications, became much greater, and so did the perceived need. Racial and national ideas, which said that herd and herders were related, intensified. Mass warfare – the American Civil War of 1861–65, the Franco–Prussian War of 1870–71 – changed concepts of the value of the masses to society. These ideas merged in the variant of Social Darwinism that saw mass warfare as the inevitable, almost desirable, grand test of racial fitness, and racial deterioration as the main threat of failure. The clash of superpowers was Britain's problem, but recolonisation and dominionism encouraged New Zealand to see Britain's problems as its own.

A central issue for racial harmony, of course, was the Maori. From 1900, Pakeha gradually came to accept that Maori were not dying out after all, and a remarkable effort was made to racially incorporate, or 'whiten', them – initially in rhetoric and symbol more than in practice. Significantly, this process began when Maori were still believed to be safely dying out. Their culture and history was being collected, laundered and embalmed by Pakeha savants to prepare it for use in posthumously providing New Zealand with a rich past, runes and ruins. The Maori mummy woke up in the midst of the process. Maori disengagers – those who minimised their relations with the state – resisted assimilation and protested against it in various ways. Engagers – those who co-operated with the state – tried to bend it to their own purposes, like feminists with moral evangelism. In all, the drive for racial harmony succeeded well enough for New Zealand to claim that it was racially pure, and that the race was basically British, but Better British. Making the Irish, Northern Europeans and especially Maori racially 'British' was not easy to do, and it is not easy to explain, but the attempt is made in Chapters Six and Seven.

Racial harmony served its social and moral relatives, and it served recolonisation itself. It buttressed the ideology of the recolonised British–New Zealand system, asserting the strongest possible links of kinship between its two ends: kinship. Moral and racial improvement marched on together hand in groin. The assertions of social harmony, moral excellence and racial purity combined with the steady affluence flowing from the recolonised economy to make the case for Better Britain. Unlike Greater Britain, it would never be a superpower; its world empire would be by proxy. It would always be small and select, an exemplary paradise, 'God's Own Country'.

Increasing social integration and 'social efficiency' were features of recolonisation and harmony. In 1868, the New Zealand government scrabbled and borrowed desperately to muster a paltry two or three thousand troops for a war on its own doorstep, against the great Maori resistance leaders Titokowaru and Te Kooti. Fifty years later, in World War One, with only four times the Pakeha population, it mobilised 40 times the troops, paid for them itself and projected them across the world. What so revolutionised Pakeha society that its capacity to project military power increased tenfold, despite the large war being at the other end of the earth, and the small in its very midst? The short answer is recolonisation and the Great Tightening, in concert with the state. Recolonisation and harmony harnessed New Zealanders, increasing their capacity to pull together, and increasing the size and centrality of the state. War in turn beefed up the state, as wars usually do.

The direct effect of World War One on the New Zealand state was substantial. Tax revenue and public debt both more than doubled. The new borrowing was from New Zealanders – overseas (i.e. London) debt actually dropped during the war, from 83 to 50 per cent of all public debt.[3] Some 90,000 people were paying income tax by 1922, compared with only 3,500 thirty years earlier.[4] The state confirmed its position as the biggest lender to New Zealanders with massive loans to returned servicemen, for businesses as well as farms. It also became the biggest borrower *from* New Zealanders. Investment in the state may have increased people's sense of commitment to it; borrowing from it certainly did. Contrary to its ideology and its rhetoric, the Massey government oversaw a 40 per cent expansion in the state share of gross domestic product between 1912 and 1924. 'Claiming always to believe in private enterprise, his [Massey's] administration had become the most interventionist in New Zealand's history.'[5] The state became increasingly important in economic management, social engineering and 'national efficiency', a wartime phrase. It also became the chief instrument for meeting major challenges to social, moral and racial harmony, and to recolonisation itself. The growing state bureaucracy sometimes resisted becoming the agent of particular groups, with mixed success. It retained elements of neutrality and developed its own momentum. Under the Labour government of 1935, the warfare state became the welfare state, with great humanitarian deeds to its credit. But when the consensus or need was great enough, the state was a powerful agent of recolonisation and the Great Tightening.

CHAPTER FOUR

Social Harmony: The Touch of Class

The power of the myth of classlessness in New Zealand is such that historians talking class risk being dismissed as frothing radicals or – still worse – as unfashionable. Using broad horizontal categories such as class does risk papering over subtleties and differences. But the purpose of history is not, as too many historians imagine, to faithfully photograph chaos. We need to detect and understand processes that cause change and continuity in apparent chaos, or at least impose meaning on it. To do this we have to speak of rough patterns and categories, ideally at minimal damage to the facts. We need to remind ourselves that class cultures or subcultures are merely large groups of people, cutting across boundaries such as region, who live in broadly similar ways that distinguish them from the rest of the population, perhaps quite subtly. The distinctions are blurred at the margins, clearer at the cores.

Making Peoples posited four 'class cultures': genteel (upper class), respectable (middle class), decent (working class) and disreputable (un-employed, irregularly employed or illegally employed). Each has roots in a particular relationship of work and property, labour and capital, but they can drift away from these roots. Through 'class-cultural mobility' or adoption, one class could pick up selected characteristics of another. Each class could be subdivided – the middle class in particular. As the twentieth century wore on, an 'upper middle class' of professionals, managers and industrialists increasingly merged with, even absorbed, the gentry. One can also speak of 'middle' and 'lower' middle classes: a *petite bourgeoisie* of small–medium urban proprietors, a farming 'class' of small–medium rural proprietors, and a lower middle class of white-collar workers. Groups such as tribal Maori and the crews could exist outside the class cultures. Even class community, the tighter kind of class, is merely a wide group of people who, as well as sharing a class culture, come to imagine that they have a community of interest without actually knowing each other. A class community need not embrace the whole of the people in its class culture, though it needs at least a widespread and substantial minority. Using class analysis does not necessarily lock one in to a particular view of historical change. But the cohesion and breadth of class communities, and the reactions they generate in others, can make them important agents of change. Class communities are not necessarily dangerous to the status quo, but they can be.

This chapter inquires into the fate of what it argues were recolonial New Zealand's three class communities. One was the declining gentry. The others were two emerging tight classes: the class-conscious section of decent working people; and a rural and respectable middle class – the new protein farmers.

The Decline of a Gentry

In *Making Peoples* it was argued that the 1870s saw the emergence of the New Zealand gentry, which had both rural and urban wings, as a nationwide class community and as a ruling class. We have also seen that advent of the predominantly middle-class Liberals marked the end of gentry rule, although the disparate supporters of the Liberals never forged themselves into a single tight class. At some time between the 1890s and the 1940s, the gentry also lost social and economic leadership and ceased to be important as a class. Class communities are tough beasts; once formed, they do not give up the ghost easily. What explains the decline of this one?

Traditional explanations for the demise of the gentry deal only with their rural wing. They include the economic circumstances of the recolonisation era: stagnation; the rise of the protein industry; close-settling sentiment; and the actions of the Liberal government. These explanations have considerable merit. To some extent, the protein industry inherently favoured family farms over great estates. Intensive farming for meat and dairy production required much greater handling of stock than extensive farming for wool, and therefore more labour per acre and per stock unit. Family labour was the cheapest available. One historian has argued that the Long Stagnation of the 1880s did not greatly reduce the incomes of the landed gentry, and it is true that increased volumes did compensate to some extent for falling prices.[1] But some of the figures cited to show that the incomes of rural gentry held up exclude debt levels, and in the 1880s these were high. Urban gentry may have suffered even more from the Long Stagnation. Though most survived, their local and New Zealand–British companies did not, as we have seen, and many fortunes went with them. Neither urban nor rural wings of the gentry were destroyed by the Long Stagnation, but both were teetering.

High debt levels stemmed partly from an 1870s frenzy of genteel free-holding, a response to the pressure for closer settlement. The gentry were not consistently opposed to close settlement; on the contrary, a surprising number actively encouraged it. They, too, wanted sturdy yeomen; small farming and large farming could be complementary; and subdivision could be profitable. But you had to own land freehold to subdivide it. Partly to secure their improvements, partly to defend against closer settlement, and partly to take advantage of it, the gentry freeholded millions of acres in the 1870s with borrowed money. Stagnation in the 1880s therefore found them overburdened with debt; increasing volumes to match falling prices also required capital; and the situation was made doubly frustrating by new and rich opportunities for investment in the protein industry passing them by.

From 1892, the Liberals introduced their 'Lands for Settlement' Acts, designed to buy great estates and subdivide them into viable farms available to the landless on easy terms. A compulsory acquisition clause was introduced in 1894, and by 1912 no fewer than 200 purchases had been made, mostly from large estates.[2] This could easily be taken for a successful attack on the gentry, and Liberal leaders did indulge in anti-genteel rhetoric, as we have seen. It is also true that freehold estates and stations over 10,000 acres declined from 262 to 171 between 1892 and 1910, and that their total acreage halved. But as we shall see, this change was not as big as it looks, and government purchases were directly responsible for only a quarter of it.[3] Examined closely, much of the Liberals' anti-genteel rhetoric was qualified – absentee land-owners were the problem, thought Ballance, not local capitalists. Reeves' famous reference to 'social pests' was aimed more at large estates than at their owners.

When we look at practice, as against preaching, we find an even bigger discrepancy between form and content. Compulsory acquisition was used occasionally, and some gentry parted from their land with great regret, but most rushed to the slaughter, jostling each other in their eagerness. Four or five times the amount of land bought was voluntarily offered for sale under the Lands for Settlement Acts.[4] The gentry had overcapitalised in land, and there were few rich buyers. Private subdivision occurred on a considerable scale but was held back by lack of money for surveys, roading and, often, mortgage finance to encourage buyers. In the 1890s, the government helped solve the problem – not only through Lands for Settlement but also through 'Advances to Settlers' measures, beginning in 1894. These enabled more small and medium farmers to buy land with some hope of developing it – an impact reinforced by their side effect of forcing down interest rates on private rural credit. Some genteel sellers took their money and ran, but many, perhaps most, sold off only part of their landholdings.[5] They used the money to develop the rest and otherwise take advantage of the opportunities created by the recovery of wool prices and the new protein industry. Farm-service industries, such as stud farming and stock and station agencies, appear to have been another favoured form of investment. Money gained from private and public subdivision was also used to invest in urban industries – the newly mobilised capital of the rural wing of the gentry reinforced the battered urban wing. It may be more true to say that the Liberals' land purchases saved the gentry than that they destroyed them.

The Liberals' bark was enough to prompt a few nervous gentry into emigration; and it encouraged popular antagonism. But the bark was a lot worse than the bite; and the public bark was worse than the private one. 'John McKenzie [Minister of Lands and crusader for smallholdings] helped me very much,' wrote a large South Island runholder in difficulties with his leases, 'though he does not want it talked about.'[6] On the urban flank, gentry in business together with their surviving companies found that their worst fears about the Liberals were groundless. Some, like the reconstructed John Logan Campbell and the Union Shipping Company, were virtually considered public institutions, icons of populism rather than enemies of it. 'The [Union] company's interests are so closely interwoven with those of the colony that it is almost regarded as a national institution,' stated the 1893 *Official Yearbook*.[7] The company developed very close relations with Ward in particular. 'Big business and the Liberals had enjoyed a generally satisfactory relationship.'[8] Ward, despite his Irish Catholicism and middle-class roots, was an aspirant to genteel status.[9] Prices paid for genteel estates under the Lands for Settlement Acts often appear to have exceeded market rates.[10] This is not to suggest a secret pro-gentry Liberal conspiracy. There was some tension between populism and practical (as against rhetorical) enmity towards a whole class. The Liberals were not socialists, with or without doctrine. They were more interested in closer settlement than in hunting gentry. But if the Liberals and the other traditional factors did not push the gentry into decline, what did?

The decline of the gentry was relative as well as absolute. The New Zealand gentry had always been quite broadly defined, and willing to co-opt respectable newcomers who met at least some of the necessary criteria. From about 1900, new groups joined the gentry at the top of the socio-economic heap in numbers and with attitudes that could not easily be absorbed.[11] The expansion of services meant that many new occupations sought to professionalise; new subclasses of professionals, such as dentists and accountants, emerged, and professional status diminished as a route to gentility. Even the highest white-collar professions such as the upper levels of medicine and education came to place more emphasis on professionalism, scientific expertise and vocation, and less on gentility. These professionals increased in number in the decades around 1900, and were joined by another group with similar attitudes: a new type of 'scientific' and professional business manager, more cautious and less concerned with the leisure ethic and social leadership than the genteel owner-entrepreneurs who had preceded them. The top rung of respectable manufacturers, especially of consumer goods, also increased in wealth and numbers; as did medium farmers. Neither of these groups necessarily aspired to gentility. Overall, the balance shifted from gentry incorporating respectables towards respectables incorporating gentry. The survival of a class culture, or any culture for that matter, depends not so much on the exclusion of newcomers as on the capacity to absorb newcomers, or at least their children.

These changes were accompanied by a widening diffusion of some genteel characteristics to the point where they were devalued as class markers. This occurred in political leadership and in the playing of sport, but is most easily traced in secondary schooling. By the 1870s, the gentry had succeeded in establishing a small network of secondary schools for their own children.[12] Some were entirely private; most were endowed with land from the public estate, but charged substantial fees even for day pupils, and still higher ones for boarders. There were perhaps a dozen such schools in 1875. A scramble for endowments after provincial abolition, together with the 1877 Education Act doubled the number by 1885; and it remained roughly constant thereafter to 1900, when they still had fewer than 3,000 pupils.[13] They are sometimes said to have been modelled on English grammar schools, but this may stem from egalitarian myth, and the newer English public schools such as Rugby seem more likely prototypes. In New Zealand as in England, these 'public' schools pioneered organised sport. They featured fags, prefects, corporal punishment and Arnoldian principals trained at Charterhouse and Trinity and known as 'the Man'. In a word, they taught gentility.

Young gentlewomen were quite well represented; the non-genteel were not. In 1900, fewer than 10 per cent of primary school leavers went on to secondary school, and only 650 free places were provided.[14] From 1877, and especially from 1886, there was some compensatory development in primary schools and district high schools, discussed below. But broadly speaking, nineteenth-century secondary schools, like sheep stations, were gentry country. From the 1880s, however, the genteel schools came under increasing pressure to widen their intakes. They resisted fairly successfully until 1900, when Richard Seddon, that walking public opinion poll, took a hand, along with the reforming Secretary of Education, George Hogben. Rolls tripled in the 1900s, to about 9,000. An even bigger expansion followed under the Reform government of 1912–28, which boosted pupil numbers to about 30,000. By 1917, 37 per cent of primary school leavers went to secondary school, with the figure reaching 47 per cent in 1922, by which time secondary education had become a majority experience for the middle class, though not yet the working class.[15] This expansion damaged secondary schooling as a gatekeeper of gentility. It did not destroy it. Schools such as Christ's College in Christchurch and Wanganui Collegiate retained a special status. But other schools now provided a comparable, if somewhat less prestigious, education. Secondary schooling remained a minority experience until the 1930s, but the minority was increasingly large, including most middle-class children as well as the genteel.[16]

The widening of educational opportunity was largely the result of popular pressure, as we will see later in this chapter. Another long-standing popular sentiment also dealt a blow to the gentry from the 1900s: the ongoing servants' mutiny, lessened but not halted by the depths of the Long Stagnation. The mutiny intensified in the 1900s, when a long-term decline in the proportion of the workforce in domestic service began. Desperate efforts in the 1900s to establish training colleges for Maori servants, in which the genteel feminist Anna Stout was prominent, met the disapproval of Maori elders and came to little.[17] Servant numbers recovered somewhat in the 1920s and 1930s, before plummeting to insignificance after World War Two.[18] Improving domestic technology could not replace servants for the gentry, though it might for the respectable. Servants not only permitted leisure, even for working gentry, but were vital to genteel status and ritual. Gentility was allergic to removing night-soil and to serving itself in company. As noted in *Making Peoples*, you could not tell callers yourself that you were not at home.

The old gentry lived longer than the mass of the people, but those who had established themselves in between the 1840s and the 1870s were dying off during the period 1890–1920. It has been suggested that their sons and grandsons were less dynamic, and they may also have been shorter-lived. For various subcultural reasons, it is possible that the gentry were more prone to volunteering during World War One. They were certainly very prone to becoming officers, and the lower officers had higher casualties than other ranks. Indeed, becoming a junior infantry officer on the Western Front was something very close to a death sentence. The upper middle classes contributed about 60 per cent of commissioned officers, compared with unskilled labourers' 2 per cent, and the death rates of soldiers from élite schools and universities was above average.[19] The differing wartime fates of potential leaders in this and other groups, such as farmers, labour activists and alienated Maori, warrants further research. They might have survived better than gentry.

The decline of the gentry to 1914 was more relative than absolute, and it was also perhaps more apparent than real. The dreaded label 'Enemy of the People' was nearly pinned to their tail around 1890, and Liberal preaching did not help. As the twentieth century wore on, New Zealand's recolonial need to claim populist egalitarianism and homogeneity intensified. It became increasingly unwise to be caught being too genteel, or to consume too conspicuously. The gentry 'disappeared into seclusion. Their social life went on but away from the public gaze.'[20] There was an increasing incentive to camouflage gentility. Lands for Settlement cash was especially important here. It enabled gentry to reduce their estates below the level that caused public offence, spread their investments, lower their profile and so weather the egalitarian storm. Estates over 10,000 acres declined and were increasingly restricted to the high country, but the number of estates over 5,000 acres increased 50 per cent, as did their total acreage and average value per acre.[21] The dispersal of landholdings through partible inheritance was sometimes more apparent than real. Estates subdivided within families were often still run as one unit.[22] The false association of gentry with sheep stations alone, still a feature of some historiography, may have helped here, too. High-country stations were relatively inoffensive to close settlers, who could not use that type of land anyway, and one could believe that the vestiges of the gentry had withdrawn to isolated and marginal back country, where they could safely be left to provide a bit of local colour.

The Liberal government did not destroy the New Zealand gentry, and, until the 1940s, nothing else did either. There are signs that substantial overt gentility survived to World War Two. Genteel farmers on horseback and dressed in suits still supervised farm work in the 1920s and 1930s. An important study of social status in rural South Canterbury by an American anthropologist shows that the 'two table' tradition, family and employees eating separately, was quite strong to the 1940s.[23] Refined manners, servants and élite education were still considered hallmarks of gentility, as distinct from being merely wealthy. This study, and scraps of other evidence, hints at a continued propensity for in-marriage among old families. The hunt for servants was still strong in the 1920s.[24] Old money still dwelt in companies and law firms in the cities. The sons of Charles Clifford and John Grigg dominated the protein industry in Canterbury well into the twentieth century, and continued to provide social leadership in such things as sport and horse-racing.[25] Some clubs and some schools remained quite genteel. The gentry re-established an important if secondary position in the governments of 1912–35. Old manners could also survive for a while without old money. The Auckland Ladies Benevolent Society was, in 1917, delicately helping 'decayed gentlewomen who would rather die of starvation than go to the Charitable Aid Board'.[26]

But the gentry were relatively, apparently and really less important after World War One than they had been before; and they became less important still after World War Two. Even the Labour government of 1935–49 was not quite fatal to gentility, but it was not at all good for it. Both world wars reduced the availability and increased the cost of farm labour, a crucial factor in the break-up of some large holdings. In both wars, income tax rocketed, as did antagonism to conspicuous consumption, and this hurt both rural and urban gentry. Populist attitudes intensified further from the 1930s. In the late 1940s, a genteel Canterbury farming family tried to give a temporary worker his meal in the kitchen, rather than in the dining room with the family. 'I can see him now, walking past the window – he walked off. That was a very big lesson my parents learned.'[27] Domestic service, which revived temporarily during the 1930s depression, went into an even steeper decline in World War Two; secondary schooling and alternative élites burgeoned anew.

It may be that, even today, diligent search could rediscover the gentry as it sometimes rediscovers birds long thought extinct. There were still 400–500 farm holdings of over 10,000 acres in the 1960s, before the rise of corporate farming – 50 of them over 50,000 acres.[28] At least a few of these stations were still held by nineteenth-century genteel families. The odd scion of the old gentry could be found in Cabinets as late as 1984. Contemporary folk culture still whispers of old money and *the* old-boy network, and there are still native-born New Zealanders with 'plums in their mouths'. Something like a New Zealand genteel accent appears to have emerged by 1912, and exists to the present. It is more like received English pronunciation than general New Zealand speech, but is still distinctively New Zealand – a 'refined' New Zealand English.[29] But, in my experience at least, its speakers are over 50 years old. If gentility does still exist, it is vestigial and well camouflaged in the upper levels of respectability. Rather than vampires who come out only at night, this secret gentry is not very alarming. If found, there is a case for its preservation on offshore islands, such as Britain.

The Making of the New Zealand Working Class

Some historians have doubted that a 'tight' working class, organised, politically aware and conscious of its own unity, has ever existed in New Zealand. Previous chapters have indicated my view that there was indeed no nationwide tight working class until about 1906. Yet the absence of tight class is not the absence of a history of working people. Unionism is one institutional shape this history takes, and proto-unionist activity and sentiment in New Zealand can be traced back to the beginning of European settlement in the 1830s. Carpenter Samuel Duncan Parnell made his famous stand in favour of an eight-hour day in 1840 in Wellington. A prospective employer told him that 'in London the bell rang at six o'clock and if a man was not there ready to turn out he lost a quarter of a day'. 'We are not in London,' Parnell retorted.[30] There was a meeting in Barrett's Hotel, Wellington, the same year, which advocated the eight-hour day for all, 'anyone offending to be ducked into the harbour'.[31] Small unions, mainly of skilled craftsmen, date from the 1850s. Some united into regional Trades and Labour Councils from the 1870s, and there were various attempts at unionising unskilled workers from about 1880. At this time, the eight-hour day was an aspiration for many and a reality for some, and colonial New Zealand was a distinct improvement on Britain for most working people. These developments reflect, not the early emergence of a tight working class, but a deep integration of New Zealand populism and ideas of the dignity of labour. The eight-hour day meant that there was life outside work. Parnell and his prospective employer had called each other 'Mister'.

New Zealand unions were of two types, reflecting a broader distinction among working people. One comprised craft unions, guilds of skilled workers who had served an apprenticeship. They were designed to protect their artisan status and keep others out. The other comprised industrial unions of 'unskilled' workers, with more-or-less open entry. The distinction between the two was not hard and fast, but it is useful. Craft unions virtually monopolised the history of organised labour before 1880, were dominant for 25 years thereafter, and remained important to the 1920s at least. Industrial unions scarcely existed before 1880, and were not strong until about 1906, but became dominant by the 1920s. Craft unions tended to be small, moderate and regional, as well as skilled. They preferred political to industrial action. Industrial unions tended to be larger, more militant and national, as well as unskilled. Until 1913, they were more oriented to industrial than to political action. The distinction was not just a matter of types of union but also of diverging subcultures. 'Craft workers' and 'class workers' is another way of describing it.[32]

Craft workers were very far from the quislings of militant class-worker polemic. They were quite capable of political activism and radicalism, and were important and persistent contributors to improvements in the workers' lot. But they were inherently less oriented to tight class than were unionised unskilled workers. Craft actually cut across class, linking middle-class 'masters' – artisans who had acquired their own business – to the working-class journeymen and apprentices they employed. 'Master' and 'man' worked together and included each other in their imagined communities – there is a close analogy with working farmers and farm workers, as we shall see. Craft workers were more closely integrated into local communities than were unskilled workers. In the Dunedin suburb of Caversham, they were pillars of Protestant churches and Friendly Societies, which their unions resembled. From the 1880s, craft workers and their unions faced the problems of ongoing industrialisation and the advent of 'scientific management'. The former increased the scale and mechanisation of factories, as noted in Chapter Two, which threatened the small master craftsman and his workshop. The latter shifted control of the production process from worker to manager. Both combined to boost the number of 'semi-skilled' workers, notably machine operators. From 1900, the rise of technical education provided an alternative to apprenticeship.

The Caversham evidence suggests that craft workers resisted these pressures quite well – indeed, unusually well in international terms. Some masters became factory owners themselves, but retained a sense of unity with their skilled workers. Other craft workers entrenched themselves as privileged employees in factories, a distinct cut above semi-skilled workers, let alone unskilled. Semi-skilled categories survived best when they accepted subordination to the skilled. Craft culture was even capable of excluding the unskilled altogether. Disreputable 'itinerant labourers' were sometimes distinguished from decent 'working men'.[33] The power of craft – rooted in integration in the community, the relatively small scale of the economy and an orientation to populism rather than class conflict – was an important factor in New Zealand labour history.

Dividing labour sentiment between craft and class helps us understand the events and non-events of the period 1888–1906. In 1888–90 came a surge of unionisation, culminating in the Maritime Strike of late 1890.[34] Union membership exploded from around 3,000 to anything between 21,000 and 63,000.[35] The unions grouped in the Maritime Council comprised 8,000– 9,000 unskilled men, the strike lasted almost two months, and the rhetoric of radical socialism was heard. But, as suggested in Chapter One, the strike reflected the embryo and the shadow of a tight working class, rather than the mature thing itself. 'The 1890 strike was remarkably peaceful [it was] by no means a violent or bitterly-fought conflict.'[36] The strike was not very widespread; it was defeated relatively easily; and the number of unionists dropped almost as fast as it had risen. 'We were licked – and licked, and it must be said that we were also kicked and kicked very hard indeed . . . There was no bargaining about terms.'[37] Moreover, the strike was followed by fifteen years of industrial peace, when the exemplary paradise gained its reputation as 'the country without strikes'.

One factor in the weakness of the 1890 strikers and their relatively easy defeat was that they lacked the support of craft workers, who dominated the labour movement at the time. Another was the rapid and co-ordinated reaction of the employers. A major player was the Union Shipping Company, the 'Southern Octopus', whose tentacles were everywhere in New Zealand history in the 1890s and 1900s.[38] The Australian shipping companies had decided the time was ripe to force a showdown with their own militant unions, and it is said that Union Shipping reluctantly acceded to their wishes, so stretching the strike across the Tasman. But Union Shipping was not the sidekick of its Australian confrères; it was the biggest and most dominant member of the Australasian Ship-Owners Federation, and might well have been able to prevent or limit employer aggression in Australia, let alone New Zealand, if it had chosen to. Instead, it 'reluctantly' rejected various very conciliatory bargains offered by the New Zealand Maritime Council, which was in fact always quite moderate and which hoped to keep the strike out of New Zealand. The company then 'reluctantly' persecuted ex-strikers with great vigour in the years after 1890, forcing many out of the country.[39] Leading New Zealand protein companies felt even more strongly than Union Shipping. 'The unions are becoming so oppressive,' declared Nelson Brothers, 'we think the present an opportune time to knock down the whole system, for we shall never have a better chance.'[40] The Maritime Strike and the employer counter-strike were less Australian developments that overflowed to New Zealand than manifestations of a still-united Tasman world.

'Fifteen years of industrial peace' could easily be read as 'fifteen years of industrial quiescence', but this would not be fair. Craft workers were active allies of the Liberals and their new arbitration system, and would have been with or without the 1890 strike. The arbitration system created and protected craft unions, and constrained industrial ones. There were Liberal-Labour members of Parliament from 1891, mainly craftsmen. Seddon set up a national Liberal and Labour Federation in 1899 to encourage the labour vote.[41] He also declared Labour Day an official holiday the same year. It was celebrated on 28 October, commemorating Parnell and his eight-hour day, not 1 May, which celebrated international socialism.[42] Seddon's populist style appealed to craft workers. In Australia, where arbitration came later, where craft workers and the Liberal-Labour nexus were weaker, and where there was no Liberal Seddon, independent and strong Labour political parties emerged in the 1890s and 1900s. In New Zealand, they had to wait until 1916.

Broad labour sentiment – respect for manual work and for the rights of the working man – had deep roots in New Zealand. Yet a tight working class and a strong and independent Labour Party were relatively late developers, both emerging in the decade 1906–16. It is the dominance of craft ideas over class ideas to 1906 that reconciles these two facts. Yet a tight working class and a strong Labour Party did eventually emerge, and they did so against the odds. The strength of craft, populism, Liberalism and the arbitration system all militated against them. Why, then, did a tight working class capable of shaking the state in 1912–13 emerge from the infertile ground of recolonial New Zealand?

The New Zealand class conflict of 1912–13 can be seen simply as a local manifestation of an international rise in labour activism and socialist and syndicalist thought. Tracts such as those of Henry George and Edward Bellamy did find a mass market in New Zealand. Utopian socialism may have had quite deep roots in New Zealand; thinkers such as Robert Owen and William Morris had early influence. Karl Marx, not yet demonised by the Russian Revolution of 1917, also had his readers. Cheap printing and the wide availability of presses, a function of infrastructural technology transfer, enabled the left to produce a stream of pamphlets to compensate for the general antagonism of newspapers. The Red Fed's own *Maoriland Worker* sold 10,000 copies a week in 1911–13, and there were a few other left-leaning journals. But talk was probably the main medium for the yeast of unionist and militant ideas. As noted in Chapter Three, a Socialist Party formed in 1907, and socialist and syndicalist activists from America and Britain preached to New Zealand workers, who also preached to each other. Between 1907 and 1913, 'grim dungareed orators', evangelising workers at every 'smoko', were joined by a steady trickle of overseas activists who lectured around the country, sometimes to large crowds.[43] Chatting workmates, especially in large workplaces, were possibly even more important.

Class-conscious New Zealand workers were more Australasian in outlook, and perhaps more pan-British, than other sectors of the population. When conservative politicians raised the spectre of outside agitators in 1913, Red Fed leader Paddy Webb responded by denying that Australians, British and Irish were foreigners. In the 1900s, 'New Zealand working men, especially the unskilled, do not seem to have considered themselves distinct from Australians.'[44] There was, perhaps, an incentive for unionism to cross national boundaries within linked labour markets. Otherwise employers could too easily coerce militancy in one country by using non-union labour from the other – a long-term game in trans-Tasman shearing, for example. Socialist and syndicalist ideology also tended to be international – or pan-European, to be more precise. But internationalism in New Zealand in the 1900s cut across other developments – the growth of Better British nationalism and the split with Australia. The Tasman world in 1912–13 was weaker than in 1890. Many labour activists were Australian, toughened in bitter industrial struggles in the mid-1900s. But they were immigrants, not visitors. In contrast to the Maritime Strike the actual disputes of 1912–13 were not imported. The 1890 conflict was a trans-Tasman one; the 1912–13 conflict was a New Zealand one, with very limited Australian support.

The international labour movement may explain the leadership and the explicit motives of the tightening working class of 1912–13, but it does not explain the implicit motives or the fact that the leaders had followers. Four sets of factors can be identified: the implications of the broad systemic change of recolonisation; the rise to prominence of a new birth cohort, the New

Zealand-born; a decline in the supply of opportunity for working people; and a reaction to 'negative referents' – scapegoats who helped unite the working class – Chinese immigrants and working women.

The craft workers who dominated the New Zealand labour movement to 1906 were largely creatures of the domestic economy – metal, wood, food and clothing trades whose output went to the local market. This market boomed under progressive colonisation and experienced its Indian summer in the 1900s. Meanwhile, from the 1890s, the new recolonial economy rapidly overtook it in importance. The speed at which this took place varied regionally. Wellington and Auckland grew faster than Christchurch between 1881 and 1911, and very much faster than Dunedin.[45] Certain kinds of unskilled workers had a strategic position in the new economy. They included freezing workers, who processed protein; watersiders and seamen, who loaded and shipped it; and coalminers, who provided the fuel for the ships. As the economy shifted balance with recolonisation, class-prone industries were favoured over craft-prone industries. In the recolonial industries, workplaces grew in size, which facilitated the organisation of labour. The occupational subcultures of seamen, wharfies, freezing workers and coalminers were quite union-prone. These were in fact the groups who, between 1906 and 1913, struck most, unionised most and provided most support for the Red Federation of Labour in 1913. They did so much more in Auckland and Wellington than in Dunedin or Christchurch. To some extent, the new recolonial paradise forged its own working-class troubles.

The second factor behind the class crisis of 1912–13 may have been a matter of birth cohorts. Different generations can have different histories, and this is yet another largely unploughed field in New Zealand historical scholarship. The annual number of births in New Zealand first reached five figures in 1870, and continued to rise until 1884. A decline then began – even in absolute numbers, let alone birth *rates* – and the 1884 level, nearly 20,000 births, was not reached again until 1901. If you ever have to guess the birth year of a New Zealander born in the nineteenth century, 1884 is the best bet. The working-class cohort born during the height of progressive colonisation had better, though still basic, educations than their predecessors, and less restricted childhoods than their successors – as we will see in Chapter Twelve. They came from larger families than any subsequent generation, and they were more likely to have been brought up by other children – their colonial-born elder sisters. My guess is that they were less concerned about social mobility, or promotion, than their migrant parents, but more concerned about cultural mobility, or adoption. Nurtured in the unofficial myths of settlement, they may also have been more committed to egalitarianism – the absence of very overt status difference – and more willing to consider new collective identities. Though many leaders and activists in the worker mobilisation of 1912–13 came from overseas, this rather peculiar New Zealand-born generation provided many of the rank and file. 'According to many sources,' writes a leading labour historian, 'the New Zealand-born seemed more confident or careless of the future.'[46]

The third, more complicated, factor behind the rise of the working class was a pattern in the supply of opportunity for working people in the 1890s and 1900s. There were three main taps of opportunity, which turned off and on, up and down. One was promotion through the acquisition of small businesses. For the skilled, this could be one's own workshop or even factory, the shift from journeyman to master. For the unskilled, it meant 'open independencies', such as farms, pubs and stores, which required no formal qualifications. The second tap was promotion into safe, comfortable and allegedly middle-class white-collar jobs in offices, shops, and the state services. The third tap, opportunity for 'adoption' rather than promotion, was the co-opting of selected aspects of the lifestyles of higher classes.

Opportunity for promotion of the skilled to self-employment declined in the 1900s. Access to open independencies also shrank substantially but unevenly. There was one hotel to every 357 people in 1881; one to every 911 in 1915; one to every 1,542 in 1945, when your chance of owning a pub was at best one-fifth that of your grandparents.[47] The story in storekeeping was more complicated but broadly similar. Small general stores, as against large general stores and small specialist shops, appear to have declined greatly. In Hastings, their number fell from 27 in 1907 to four in 1934, despite a tripling of the population.[48] This development can still be traced in small-town archaeology – the country is littered with the sites of dead stores killed by shrinking travelling time. Getting on to farms, the archetypal open independency, had a still more complex pattern. We can trace it very roughly by looking at the number of landholdings above and below 100 acres as a proportion of all males twenty years or older. One hundred acres is a very rough boundary between marginal small farms on the one hand, and medium–large farms on the other. The proportion of small farms (below 100 acres) to men dropped between 1874 and 1881, rose slowly to 1886, boomed to 1896, then dropped substantially and steadily to 1921. The long-term change was from 12.9 per cent in 1881 to 10.6 per cent in 1921, but this conceals a high peak of 17 per cent in 1896. The percentage of medium and large farms (above 100 acres) to men rose very slightly between 1874 and 1881, then dropped to 1886, unlike small farms. The pattern then chased that of small farms by booming from 8.9 per cent in 1886 to 11.7 per cent in 1896, before dropping fairly steadily to 10.9 per cent in 1911.[49]

Between 1881 and 1911, medium–large farms eventually replaced small farms as the most numerous type of landholding. Medium farms tended to push out both smallholdings and large estates, though not high-country sheep stations. On our definitions, the protein industry did not make *small* farming more viable. Even dairying had a size threshold of around 100 acres that full economic viability found it hard to cross. What protein did do was create a window of opportunity, roughly 1886–96. I suspect it was actually helped in this by the Long Stagnation, which lowered land prices. The Liberals' closer settlement measures must also have helped, but perhaps not much. The window of opportunity opened well before they were implemented, and was most marked in regions where these measures had least effect, such as Taranaki and Wellington. A few people got directly inside the passing bus of opportunity by acquiring medium farms straight off; more grabbed hold of the outside by acquiring small farms. Some of these made their way inside by moving from small to medium; more were shaken off, moving from small to nothing. Most people, of course, missed the bus completely.

For an unskilled person, the very best chance of acquiring a landed independency was probably to obtain a small farm in the 1880s, when they were cheap, and convert it to a medium farm in the 1890s. The window of opportunity opened about 1886, both for acquiring small farms and for converting them into medium farms. A sample of land selectors in special settlements 1890–93 suggests that 44 per cent were unskilled workers, 30 per cent farmers and farmers' sons, 12 per cent skilled workers, and 10 per cent rural workers, presumably also unskilled.[50] The cloud of stagnation had a silver lining. People who saved in boom and bought in bust were exploiting the turn of an economic tide both ways. This could have led briefly to increased access to open independencies other than farming as well, before they began their long decline in the twentieth century. But it was probably mainly through farm formation that the self-employed proportion of the workforce rose greatly between 1886 and 1896, then declined, with minor fluctuations, to the late 1980s.[51] In the decade after 1896, while aspirations rose, the chances of unskilled workers obtaining their own farm or other business diminished.

The second tap of opportunity was white-collar work, notably in offices and shops. This expanded greatly from the 1880s. Most new jobs in the 'commercial' category, for example, which included shops, banks and most offices, were white-collar, and this category almost tripled between 1886 and 1911, from 5.2 to 14.4 per cent of the workforce.[52] The rise of white-collar work was an international phenomenon, caused by such things as technical change, increases in the availability of consumer goods, and the entry of public and private services such as health, education, insurance and banking into the mass market. It can be, and has been, argued that white-collar workers are really working class, and that their belief in their own respectability is a matter of 'false consciousness'. But working people were attracted to work that was cleaner, less dangerous and more secure than manual labour. They were attracted for their children, not themselves. It was difficult for unskilled adults to acquire the educational prerequisites for white-collar jobs. But workers had very large families up to the 1880s. They might dislike the banks and the civil service, but that they liked nice safe billets for their offspring in them is enshrined in folklore. It can also be traced through a remarkable working-class drive for education – education of a particular type. The architects of the 1877 Education Act, notably the genteel Charles Bowen, did not object to a few talented decent youths being helped to the highest levels. But, broadly speaking, they wanted to educate workers to be better workers. Children, stated Bowen, whose 'vocation is honest work waste in higher schools time which might be better devoted to the learning of a trade'.[53] The conflict between the middle-class desire for a 'technical' education for workers and the workers' own desire for an 'academic', or commercial, education was to be an enduring one, and workers had considerable success in subverting the system.

A major early example of this emerged with the introduction of the Junior Civil Service Examination in 1886. Other white-collar employers quickly began using this as a credential for recruitment. It was an academic exam pitched at pupils ending their first two years of secondary school, and, as we have seen, working-class children rarely made it into these. Instead, their parents pressured more and more primary schools into growing larger and larger 'secondary tops', in the form of either district high schools or 'standard seven'. District high schools were not numerous until after 1900. Standard seven was initially more important and subversive. It had no formal existence in the official curriculum; it was created largely by popular demand, and focused on providing academic training – partly for the Civil Service exam, partly as a credential for white-collar work in itself. Enrolments in standard seven increased sevenfold between 1882 and 1898, to 5,429. This may not seem a lot of children, but it was more in one year than the increase in all farm holdings, small, medium and large, over the five years 1896–1901. Working-class Westland had the highest standard seven enrolments in the country. Ten per cent of successful Civil Service examinees in 1893 came from Hokitika, Greymouth and Kumara, a hugely higher proportion than these towns' share of the population.[54]

Standard seven represented quite a successful working-class educational revolt. It suggests that quite a high proportion of the new white-collar workers of the 1880s and 1890s were from decent families. More speculatively, it can also be suggested that some but not all of these gains were reined in during the

1900s. This decade saw the growth of secondary schools proper; their entry into the credentialling market; and the devaluation of standard seven and the Civil Service exam as credentials. Standard seven enrolments dropped by 3,300, to 2,100 in 1912. Secondary school enrolments grew more than enough to compensate for this, but it is not clear that the two serviced the same people. Less than a third of the growth in secondary schools came from district high schools, which probably had easier access for the children of workers and small farmers; and even 'free' places in secondary schools had hidden costs, for such things as books and uniforms. Unlike standard seven, the new places in secondary schools may have gone more to the middle class than the working class. The rate of growth in white-collar jobs was diminishing anyway in this decade. This could mean that another window of opportunity for mobility closed as well as opened between the 1880s and the 1900s.

The third tap of opportunity did not involve promotion at all. It was the chance to adopt and adapt selected characteristics of other classes' lifestyles. For New Zealand workers, old favourites included the genteel practices of owning horses and houses, and of hunting and fishing. The genteel and middle-class customs of eating rich cheese and butter, and lots of prime meat, were also adopted – earlier in New Zealand than in Britain. 'Leisure' – time to yourself – was another adoption from gentility. The middle class adopted it around 1900, reconciling it with the work ethic by making leisure as work-like as possible, disciplining recreation into moral improvement. Craftsmen whose skills were in high demand under progressive colonisation had long been able to lever some leisure out of their employers. During the 1870s, some skilled workers achieved the 'four eights' – eight hours' sleep, eight hours' play, eight hours' work and eight shillings a day. The play was arguably as important as the pay. The unskilled aspired to leisure, too.

Returning prosperity and the arbitration system met this aspiration to some extent in the later 1890s and 1900s. But it is noticeable that many disputes were over non-wage issues, such as whether or not the journey between mine entrance and mine face should be considered part of the miner's working day. There was a great broadening of the adoptable menu, for which the workers of the 1900s required more money and more free time than their parents. Organised sport, union meetings, political meetings, and the social activities associated with these, required time. The increasing range of consumer goods required money. Real wages appear to have risen somewhat between 1896 and 1907, though there is some difference of opinion about this. There is more dispute about what happened to real wages in the next five years, but they probably either stayed static or dropped. Big increases in rents in Auckland and Wellington make the latter most likely in these cities. At the same time, except for a brief recession in 1908–09, protein prosperity kept flowing for non-wage-earning sectors of society. Even the lower ranks of the middle class could afford bicycles, coal ranges, better housing, modest holidays and photographs of themselves. Workers wanted these things, too, and they were not getting them in the late 1900s.

A prerequisite of tight working class is that workers expect to remain in their class for their whole lifetime. If promotion to the middle class is the common expectation, then it is much harder to organise and politicise, and for class community to develop. Where expectations of promotion (and adoption) have risen, then supply suddenly slows, resentment of this joins decreased social mobility to create the preconditions for tight class. In terms of getting on for decent people between 1880 and 1912, the broad picture seems to be one of a brief but traumatic halt to individual progress in the early 1880s, and a recovery in the late 1880s and 1890s. This recovery combined with other factors to boost expectations, but failed of its promise in the late 1900s. It is more or less a commonplace among those who try to explain popular revolutionary action that sheer want is not the key. Fluctuating and unevenly distributed prosperity can more easily generate the dangerous politics of disappointment.

The fourth possible key to the rise of a tight New Zealand working class was shared and intensifying racism and sexism. New Zealand workers shared a dislike of Asians, discussed mainly in Chapter Six. Anti-Chinese feeling was extraordinarily virulent and widespread in the 1900s. Nothing unites like the denigration of a shared antitype, and it has been suggested that 'hatred of the Chinese may have been a key catalyst of class'.[55] Gender attitudes may also have played a role. Between the 1880s and the 1900s, a number of significant changes took place in women's paid work, some against the grain of formal or official expectations.[56] The female proportion of the paid work-force jumped from 13 to 18 per cent during the 1880s, then grew more slowly to 22 per cent in the 1920s.[57] Domestic service was the middle classes' favourite occupation for working-class women, but they themselves saw it as a last resort. The proportion of paid women workers who were servants dropped from half in 1881 to a quarter in 1911.[58] Instead, they turned to new oppor-tunities: first, in the 1880s, to factories (especially clothing factories); and then, in the 1890s, to white-collar clerical jobs. The number of women in industry doubled between 1886 and 1906, with the great majority working in the clothing industry.[59] Women's share of the new and growing white-collar workforce increased from 2 per cent in 1891 to 40 per cent in 1921.[60] The total number of women in waged work rose from 20,000 in 1878 to 90,000 in 1911.[61] Some of this increase was due to dire necessity – the Long Stagnation of the 1880s. But the increase continued into more prosperous times. The proportion of women participating in the paid workforce increased from 25.8 per cent in 1896 to 28.1 per cent in 1911 – the highest rate until the 1960s. Liberal protective legislation sometimes reduced the marketability of women's labour, but it did improve conditions. Men retained a huge pay advantage, but it diminished significantly – women averaged about 50 per cent of male wages in 1880; 60 per cent in 1910.[62] The number of women in professions, principally teaching and nursing, increased almost fivefold between 1881 and 1911, and the organisation and remuneration of teaching and nursing improved somewhat.

Some male unionists supported the organising of women workers, and even equal pay. But most did so only to deprive women of their competitive edge over men in the job market. A strong antagonism to women in work was marked among working men. This is not unexpected in industries where women threatened male jobs, but it extended to industries that remained male preserves, and seems to reflect a deep hostility to the feminisation of wage labour. Red Fed rhetoric oozed masculinity; arbitration was alright for women; industrial action was the proper course for real men.[63] The brawny arm holding the hammer had thick hair on it as far as these blokes were concerned. Masculism, perhaps, joined racism as a unifying and activating force in the New Zealand working class.

It was these four sets of factors, it seems to me, that combined to create the tight New Zealand working class of 1913. They may also have combined with another development, even more amorphous and difficult to test. There are a few hints that support for the strikers of 1913 extended beyond the tight working class. In the 1890s, in Dunedin at least, it was relatively easy for skilled workers to move up to self-employment. Olssen's Caversham study suggests as many as 30 per cent of skilled workers managed it over twelve years. But this tap, too, turned down in the 1900s. 'The Caversham data suggest a decline in the opportunity to become self-employed' between 1890 and 1914.[64] The chances of making it from journeyman to master diminished, and this may have influenced the (very limited) support skilled workers gave the Great Strike in 1913.[65] There are indications that some urban petty proprietors also supported the Great Strike, an intriguing development.[66] The explanation may be that the concentrating and modernising tendencies of the economy in the 1900s not only reduced access to small independencies, but also threatened the more marginal of those that did exist. Furthermore, it was probably more likely in 1913 than in any later year that a small publican, shopkeeper or small farmer had once been an unskilled urban worker. The exceptional social mobility of the 1890s saw to this. These alliances, combined with the support of a few middle-class intellectuals such as Edward Tregear, and the sporadic support of the disreputable, may have given labour in 1913 some tinge of populism – an insecure and, as it proved, fleeting grip on the lower reaches of the populist mantle.

At the heart of the activist labour movement of 1912–13 were miners, seamen and wharfies – men-only occupations. The three also had other things in common. They were particularly subject to the concentrating and tightening processes described in Chapter Two, and they were strategic industries as far as the protein industry was concerned. They were also heirs of the crews who had staffed progressive colonisation. By 1912–13, they were less transient than the old crews, but more transient than, say, factory workers. Their transience had some pattern in it – it was more shifting than wandering. They shifted regions in the same job, and shifted jobs in the same region, sometimes into each other's occupations; older seamen often became watersiders, for example. Their trades were still extremely dangerous, and they had an ambiguous attitude to these dangers. Encouraged by unionism, they resented employers profiting from the risks to their life and limb, but such risks helped define their self-image. They drank heavily and considered fisticuffs among themselves socially acceptable.[67] It was rather as though wandering crews had been captured and forced to work under a new system, much more controlled and stationary than the old. They did not like it, and the same factor that permitted employers to organise them more tightly allowed unionists to do so too.

By 1913, New Zealand was among the most unionised country in the world. There were about 70,000 unionists, 15,000 of them affiliated to the Red Feds. Unionism was particularly strong in the strategic industries: 61 per cent of shearers were members of their union; as were 70 per cent of seamen and 123 per cent of wharfies (many men not currently working on the waterfront retained their membership).[68] The rhetoric of class conscious-ness and class conflict was quite pervasive among these workers, and rhetoric can beget reality. '"Class conscious labour" is in the stirrups,' noted an Auckland newspaper in 1911, 'and there is no telling how far it will ride.'[69] It rode to Waihi and to Wellington, and it rode as class.

The defeat of 1913 did not result in the demise, or even numerical decline, of New Zealand's new, tight, working class. War and its high demand for labour, combined with the full development of the recolonial system, allowed the strategic unions to recover from the defeat of 1913 far more quickly than from that of 1890. Union membership rose to about 100,000 and remained at that level throughout the 1920s.[70] A new union federation, the 'Alliance of Labour', emerged in 1919, led by the formidable 'Big Jim' Roberts. The strategic unions were involved in a number of major strikes between 1920 and 1924. Indeed, these industrial troubles could be ranked with the other traumas of the period: the aftershock of war, the influenza pandemic and the outburst of sectarianism discussed in Chapter Three. But trade union membership was low in comparison with Australia.[71] On the political front, after several false starts, the direct ancestor of the modern Labour Party formed in 1916.[72] Initially, it was quite radically socialist. Many of its leaders, such as Harry Holland, Paddy Webb and Bob Semple, had also been leaders of the Red Feds. The party quickly became a formidable force in New Zealand politics, with a quarter of the total vote as early as 1919, and its geographical distribution shows that there was a strong correlation between this vote and the tight working class. Yet 1913 did mark a shift from general strikes and potential revolutionary socialism to political action and evolutionary socialism. 'Guild socialism', which preached socialist ends through constitutional means, became influential.[73] There were no more general strikes, and the Labour Party vote remained capped at roughly its 1919 level throughout the 1920s. The period 1906–13 was an exceptionally radical moment in New Zealand labour history, a blip in the graph smoothed out by retrospect. What reined in the Labour movement after 1913?

Defeat itself, in 1913, demonstrated the limits of industrial action when employers were backed by the state. The lesson was hammered home by the failure of strikes in the early 1920s. From about 1925, Roberts and the Alliance of Labour shifted quietly to more moderate measures. 'Alliance militancy was dropped overboard so surreptitiously that nobody heard the splash.'[74] From that point at least, the partnership between unions and Labour Party was quite close,[75] though integration was not as full as it was to become after 1935. Yet both the union movement and the Labour vote remained limited in the 1920s. War must have been a factor here. As noted in the previous chapter, war weaned workers from militancy to militarism, and thereafter dominionism kept them weaned. Eventually the Labour Party, like the Catholic Church, had to compromise with dominionism. But another factor in limiting the labour movement between 1913 and the 1930s was the development of a seductive strategy by their opponents, the conservative Reform government. This government was dominated by a new and powerful New Zealand class: the farmers.

The Rise of Farmer Backbone

In England around 1850, 40-year-old engineer George Patterson made a double-page watercolour drawing of a washing mangle. From this evidence, his son's biographer was able to deduce that he was thinking of getting married.[76] Within a year he had indeed married and embarked with his wife Elizabeth and over £1,000 for New Zealand. In 1852, he landed at

New Plymouth and bought 150 acres of land. Elizabeth bore one dead baby and one live one, then died herself – of consumption, or tuberculosis. George immediately returned to England for a replacement, Susannah, and machinery for a sawmill. In Taranaki, Susannah built up a family of eight children, of whom only a quarter died, and she and George built up assets of about £2,000. 'We were very happy and contented. Then the Maori wars began.' The Pattersons' mill and farm were soon among the many victims of the First Taranaki War, though 'Father left a Maori testament on the table and our house was not destroyed'. George received government compensation, but on 24 February 1864 he was ambushed by Maori warriors and became one of the few victims of the 'Second Taranaki War'. Susannah died of typhus the same year, and the children were brought up by a nasty pair of foster parents. One child was sent to school with a sign around his neck: 'This is a boy who wets his bed'; a girl had gorse tied under her chin to stop her hanging her head; and the family fortune seems to have disappeared.

After a token education and a spell of cattle droving, one son, James Patterson, became an apprentice blacksmith, finally settling in 1885 in the Taranaki bush town of Manaia, where he set up shop on his own account. Apart from his blacksmithing business, he made, bought, sold and hired out buggies and carts, laboured clearing bush for others, and bought land himself. James got his start during the Long Stagnation, perhaps helped by low land prices, and he even managed to make money against the tide – he was worth £2,632 by 1890, and £5,258 by 1894. Good judgement and good fortune were among the keys to this. But one has to give pride of place to hard work. A friend told James's wife, Kate, that life was 'downright slavery for you and the children', and to say that James subscribed to the work ethic is to understate the case. He was addicted to work. Even as late as the 1900s, when he was prosperous, he often worked all night. In old age in the 1920s, when he was rich, he had to be forced to take a holiday at the Te Aroha spa by his wife's illness. While there, he got bored and hired himself out as a day labourer just for the fun of it.

James Patterson began dairy farming around 1890 – as a nine-cow supplementary activity, not for export. But this and his technical background (he had a hand-separator as early as 1892) positioned him well to move into the protein industry around 1900. Initially this was supplemented by contract roadmaking – his crew lived at 'Patterson's Camp'. But dairying rapidly became his mainstay, and no-one in twentieth-century Taranaki would have described J. J. Patterson as anything other than a dairy farmer. From an urban liberal perspective, he had all the less likeable characteristics of this class. He was ignorant, bigoted and politically conservative. He rode to riot if not battle against Titokowaru at Hastie's Farm in 1886. He rode to riot again in 1913 with Massey's Cossacks, and assailed what he called 'brutes' and 'riff-raff' with his huge club, the 'Olive Branch', on the streets of Wellington. He was a staunch supporter of Bill Massey and Reform. He was also a good parent and employer, who showed surprising flashes of enlightenment. He never used corporal punishment on his own family, he helped his wife with the washing, and he taught his daughters to swim in the sea and to handle horses, as well as ensuring they received the education he himself had never had. One daughter obtained a medical degree from Otago University in 1922, and went on to postgraduate work in London. James was modest, even diffident, embarrassed by his own lack of education. He had no aspirations to gentility for himself, though he may have harboured some for his daughters. He was hardworking to a fault, shrewd, innovative, and indomitable, not least because he survived the sheer mercilessness of dairying – cows needing milking do not care one whit if you are tired, sick or dead. He was the quintessence of the dairy farmer, salt of the New Zealand soil.

The 'cow-cocky' became a major icon of Pakeha popular culture. He was a neighbourly, unpretentious archetype, looked upon from the city with a degree of benign contempt as well as sneaking respect. But he was the single most important archetype of Better Britain: Trev Bull, John Bull's Antipodean nephew; J. J. Patterson exemplified him more than most – in kind, not degree. Patterson was quite possibly the biggest dairy farmer the world had ever seen. He weighed eighteen stone in his prime, and when he died in 1937 he owned 35 farms and 4,000 milk cows.

Before the 1880s, there had been two extremes in New Zealand farming. At one end were the owners of large sheep runs, producing wool for export. At the other were struggling 'semi-farmers', with holdings below the threshold of viability, who produced various kinds of food for the domestic market and often undertook wage work outside the farm as well. These extremes persisted after the 1880s but diminished in importance. Increasingly, they were shouldered aside by the two new protein-exporting categories: sheep-meat farmers and dairy farmers. The development of these industries, 1880s–1920s, was covered in Chapter Two. Sheep-meat farms, which might also produce wool on the side, tended to be medium sized, with 500–2,000 acres and a similar number of sheep. They could align themselves to big wool-farming runholders as easily as to dairy farmers. Dairy farms tended to be small, with 100–200 acres and half that number of cows. Especially while getting established, dairy farmers could readily align themselves with struggling semi-farmers. Most sheep-meat farmers and virtually all dairy farmers worked on the farm themselves, whether or not they employed paid labour as well. Especially on poorer farms, their wives and children worked, too. In 1939, 41 per cent of the people working on a sample of dairy farms were members of the farmer's family, half of them female. Paid labourers contributed 23 per cent, and male farmers themselves 33 per cent.[77]

Farmers, of course, were by no means the only inhabitants of rural New Zealand. Outside the high country, all farming districts had some kind of centre, supplying goods and services and transport or processing facilities. In the nineteenth century, these small country towns tended to be dominated by their own élites of small businessmen and professionals. From the 1890s, however, medium farmers were increasingly integrated into the leadership of country towns, and these towns increasingly voted for farmers' political parties.[78] A network of stock and station agencies, supplying farmers' inputs, sometimes buying their outputs, and often extending credit, grew with the protein industry and was a crucial component of it. There were also rural labourers of various kinds: permanent hands, a single man or 'married couple'; itinerant individuals; and seasonal gangs of workers, notably shearers. Sharemilkers were an intermediate category between working farmers and farm workers.

The unity of all these rural groups was not obvious or automatic. Wool, meat and dairy farming had different patterns of development and regional distribution. The difference between an affluent meat farmer, verging on runholder status, and a struggling dairy farmer, verging on bankruptcy, was considerable – arguably greater than the difference between the dairy farmer and an urban worker. Consequently, dairy farmers were quite prone to spasms of political radicalism, and produced their own political parties and movements in the 1920s and 1930s. Under an important but limited layer of egalitarian attitudes, and a genuine respect for skill, status differences also persisted. Runholders outranked farmers, sheepmen outranked dairymen, and old money outranked new. 'The stratificational pattern that I encountered in South Downs in 1981,' writes one researcher, 'was essentially a modified version of what I have described for 1921.' Any kind of farmer outranked any farm worker. In South Downs, the two groups drank in separate bars as late as the 1980s.[79] Farmers saw the businessmen and stock and station agents of their local town as equals, but sometimes resented their role as arbiters of credit.

Despite this potential for division and weakness, the story of the socio-politics of New Zealand farming from the 1900s is one of strength and potency. Divisions did persist, especially between struggling dairy farmers and the rest, but the degree of unity was more significant. 'Country' political parties, representing dissatisfied farmers, emerged in the 1920s and 1930s. But, in striking contrast to Australia, their supporters usually returned to the mainstream of farmer politics. Reform and its successor, the National Party, retained the loyalty not only of the farmers but also of a substantial set of allies. Somehow, the new protein farmers integrated themselves into a nationwide tight class, a potent force in economics and politics. More than this, they formed the heart of a wider alliance, including rural labourers, the businessmen of country towns, and often the middle classes and even some of the lower classes of the cities as well. From the later 1900s to the early 1980s, something like a third of members of Parliament were farmers, and farmer-dominated governments ruled between 1912 and 1935, and then again for most of the time between 1949 and 1972. Yet throughout the twentieth century, farmers and their families never amounted to more than 20 per cent of the population, and usually much less. How did farmers forge themselves so successfully into a tight class? How did they convince themselves and much of the rest of society that they were the 'backbone of the country', even its natural rulers?

Some answers are obvious enough. All nationwide tight classes, gentry and workers as well as farmers, require a nationwide network of transport and communications, forming a zone in which community can be imagined. This did not exist in New Zealand before about 1870, and was not substantial until the 1880s, when national associations began to sprout, including a farmers' league (1886) and a farmers' union (1889). The binding network thickened in the 1900s, with the completion of the national rail network and the rise of the telephone. A longer-lived farmers' union formed in 1902, a sheep owners' federation in 1910, and a farmer-dominated political party, Reform, in 1909. The network thickened again in the 1920s with the spread of rural telephone in the form of 'party lines' and the advent of the motorcar, which farmers acquired early. Associations of rural women formed in this decade. Agricultural and pastoral associations, their annual shows, and regular commercial stock sales were also sites of farmer class formation. Agricultural and pastoral associations date from 1843 but flowered from 1892, when the first nationwide conference was held. The network of associations and their annual conference 'reached its peak of energy, influence, and usefulness in 1911'.[80] The structure of the dairy and sheep-meat industries also facilitated community among farmers. Dairy farmers took their cream to local factories, which they often co-owned. Big high-country sheep farmers and medium low-country sheep farmers were integrally linked by the fat-lambing system. More speculatively, dairy farmers, like urban workers, may have found unity in a shared reaction to the partial 'unleashing' of working women.

The archetypal New Zealand dairy farmer of the twentieth century was very male, but his predecessors were, to a very considerable extent, female. Dairying, like orchards, market gardens, poultry and pig keeping, were part of the farm woman's domain in the nineteenth century. As these industries became more commercially viable and specialised, men took them over. The work of women and children remained important on dairy farms, but its profile was lowered. James Patterson, whose own wife and children had worked to establish his dairying operations, would not employ sharemilkers who said their wives would work with them. The woman's place, thought the established Patterson, was at home with the children. During a transition period around 1900, there may well have been a tension between such work as dairying and the masculine self-image. If so, it has of course been blotted right out of both history and legend. Machines and masculinity had come to be associated, and increasingly sophisticated technology may have eased such a tension. This could help to explain the readiness with which working farmers, traditionally a conservative breed, adopted new technology in New Zealand. The more sophisticated the gear in your milking shed, the easier it was to forget that what you were doing had been very definitely women's work in your parents' day. A collegial assertion of threatened masculinity might also have helped in the formation of farming class community, as it did with wage-working men. This may seem far-fetched, but there must have been some way in which the new protein-exporting dairy farmers of the 1900s accommodated the fact that they were doing what, in their childhood, had been women's work. There is no mistaking the assertive masculinity of both workers' and farmers' occupational subcultures. Women continued to work in dairying, but this was minimised, denied or written out. 'The business of farming is conceived as inherently masculine.'[81] As late as 1990, according to male farmers at least, 'farming was a male preserve'.[82]

The relationship between working farmers and farm workers had some similarities to that between skilled workers and master craftsmen, noted above. It depended on the belief that farm workers could, with luck, effort and a bit of state help, become farmers themselves. Sharemilking was an important mediating stage: a stepping stone that facilitated promotion from worker to owner. A sharemilker milked his own or someone else's herd on someone else's land for a share of the profits. Yet in practice farms were 'out of reach of all but the most successful sharemilkers'.[83] Windows of opportunity to acquire farms opened up in the 1890s and 1900s, as we have seen, but tended to close thereafter. The number of dairy farmers rocketed from 452 to 15,000 1891–1911,[84] but grew more slowly after that. The total number of farm holdings over 100 acres reached 40,000 around 1920 and remained at about that level.[85] After 1920, inheritance, often concealed by purchase within the family to avoid death duty, was the most common form of farm transfer. As late as 1990, 'farmers continue to be five times more likely than any other business people to have had parents in the same business'.[86]

An exception to the closure of opportunity was postwar soldier settlement. After World War One, the state assisted over 10,000 returned servicemen
onto farms. The failure rate of these soldier-farmers may have been exaggerated, but even so, over a third had left their farms by 1934.[87] Generally,
farm workers' aspiration to become farmers themselves was not very realistic.
But rural workers often acted and voted as though it was, which extended
the political power of farmers beyond their own class. Farm workers had
always been notoriously difficult to unionise.[88] In 1896, the Hawke's Bay
Workers' Union had 600 members, as against 2,000 in a rival populist
organisation, the Free Association of Employers and Workmen, whose
president was protein magnate William Nelson, and which advocated
'mutually beneficial relations between all classes'. Outside the cities and mining
districts, 'workers and employers had strong common interests . . . Little
sympathy existed for militant unionism. In so far as class feeling existed, it
was directed against the large estate owners.'[89]

The farming class first emerged immediately before World War One, at
roughly the same time as the tight working class and partly in response to it.
Reform, and its amorphous precursor, both led by Bill Massey, sat at around
a third of the vote in the three elections 1905–11. In 1914, its vote jumped to
almost half. Massey also rode the crest of militaristic dominionism more
effectively than either of his two rival parties, Labour and the Liberals. Behind
all this, of course, was the rise of the recolonial economic system. Farmers
portrayed themselves as the Chosen People of the new system and, therefore,
of the country as a whole. More surprisingly, other sectors of society accepted
the portrayal.

As early as 1902, William Pember Reeves spoke of an 'agrarian cult'. 'So
fashionable has the agrarian cult been, that, at times, to be a townsman has
almost been to wear a badge of inferiority'.[90] By the 1930s, such thinking had
become a truism.

> The rural bias has had a very marked influence on contemporary thought
> in New Zealand. The tradition of regarding the farmers as the 'backbone of
> the country' has become firmly established not only in the minds of rural
> dwellers but in the estimation of most of the townsfolk as well. The farmers
> contend that the urban industries are parasitical in that they depend for
> their very existence of the lifeblood of the farmer. Curiously enough there
> is no violent country versus town controversy – the country wins hands
> down. Anything in the nature of an adequate reply to the calumnies heaped
> on the urban dweller by the farmer at every conceivable opportunity would
> be shunned by any self-respecting [newspaper] editor as rank heresy. Even
> the Manufacturers Association is almost apologetic in the haste with which,
> in advancing its claims for assistance in various forms, it seeks to dispel any

suggestion of an attack on the rights and privileges peculiar to the farming community.[91]

Examples of the Farmer Backbone mantra, which portrayed New Zealand as one large farm, could be multiplied indefinitely, and were voiced as recently as 1990 by a National Party Cabinet minister.[92]

This cult of the farmer had some roots in reality. The protein industry was increasingly dominant in the New Zealand economy, and farmers were obviously its base producers. But, objectively, other links in the chain were just as vital. The New Zealand–British shipping and meat companies and the workers of the strategic industries are two of several possible examples. An unfrozen, unloaded, unshipped sheep carcass was almost as little use as no carcass at all. There was myth, as well as reality, in the exalted role of the recolonial farmer.

Primacy in the new system was read back into the past. The New Zealand version of the Sturdy Yeoman, a hardworking, independent and virtuous pioneer farmer, was a stock figure in nineteenth-century ideology. Pioneering, the opening-up of the land for settlement, was credited to his individual efforts. In reality, settlement was more often led by camps and towns than by individual farms.[93] In any case, the highly mechanised, highly collectivised, export-oriented protein farmer of the twentieth century differed drastically from his nineteenth-century forebear, who, mythically at least, was isolated, unmechanised, individualist and self-sufficient. Yet the new protein farmers were able to gather up the threads of pre-existing rural mythology and harness them in the interests of the new farming class. The backbone concept allowed sectional interest to portray itself as national interest, and so reconcile itself with the populist compact. This enabled farmers to form a wider alliance outside their class earlier and more consistently than workers, and to keep their profile as a tight class below the level that would attract populist hostility. They therefore achieved political power earlier, and held it for longer, than did their working-class rivals. One could speculate that the hybridity of New Zealand culture, which under recolonisation was British as well as New Zealand, helped here, too. New Zealand was supplying rural product and rural virtue, not only for itself but for highly urbanised Britain. Its ruralism therefore had to be all the stronger, to compensate for the great wen of London, not merely Auckland and Dunedin. Farmers were as much beneficiaries of the ideological dimension of recolonisation as of the economic one.

Keeping the balls of farmers' economic, political and ideological centrality simultaneously in the air was no easy juggling feat. The master juggler appears to have been 'Farmer Bill' Massey,[94] leader of the parliamentary Opposition from 1903, of his creation the Reform Party from 1909, and Prime Minister from 1912 to 1925. We noted in Chapter Three that Massey's reputation for anti-Catholic bigotry may have been exaggerated. His overall competence may also have been underestimated. He may have been a key founder of the farming class, as well as a product of it. He certainly contributed substantially to its firm grasp of the populist mantle, to its wide electoral alliance, and to a strategy that took the wind from the sails of its rival, the tight working class. The strategy consisted in turning up the taps of two kinds of opportunity: for secondary education, which gave access to white-collar jobs; and for home-ownership, which was widely believed to give even workers a 'stake in the country', to convert them into a virtual middle class.[95]

In 1912–13, it had been principally Massey who brought the stick of state down with a thump on the rebellious tight working class. Thereafter, however, his main instrument was not the stick but the carrot. He was a leading prophet of militarist Better Britonism in World War One, and led the charge in subsequently sanctifying it into dominionism. These powerful patriotisms transcended class and attracted many workers as well as middle-class people, as we have seen. Massey's other carrots were more pragmatic. One was expanding secondary school education, for which, as we have seen earlier in this chapter, workers were especially eager. The Liberals are often credited with the great expansion of secondary education, but, under Massey, expansion was even more spectacular. Government expenditure on education tripled between 1912 and 1926. As a proportion of all state spending, a measure that adjusts for inflation, increased taxation and increased national wealth, expenditure on schooling increased by half – from 10.9 to 16.2 per cent, between 1912 and 1926.[96] The actual number of secondary school students rose from 9,000 in 1910 to 31,000 in 1930.[97] The proportion of primary pupils going on to secondary school was about 37 per cent in 1917; 47 per cent in 1922; and 55 per cent in 1932.[98] Moreover, by 1922, 93 per cent of secondary school places were free.[99]

Under Massey, the expansion of home-ownership among wage earners was almost as dramatic as the expansion of secondary schooling. The proportion of working household heads owning their own homes rocketed from 36 to 49 per cent between 1916 and 1926. The increase can be directly attributed to state intervention. One form was rehabilitation loans to returned servicemen, which financed urban houses as well as rural farms. The other major form was state advances to workers, which, ironically enough, increased substantially under 'Farmer Bill' Massey. From 1923, the proportion of a house purchase or construction price that the state would lend increased from 75 to 95 per cent. By 1929, a total of £16 million had been advanced to help almost 21,000 workers into their homes. Two-thirds of the advances were made in the 1920s. Total state aid for housing has been estimated at £3 million–4 million a year between 1920 and 1931.[100] This presumably had the usual side effect of easing the barriers to, and lowering the cost of, mortgages from the private sector, which had to compete with that generous lender, the state. By the late 1920s, the New Zealand rate of home ownership was allegedly the highest in the world.[101]

Massey rightly calculated that workers who owned their own homes and sent their children to secondary school were unlikely revolutionaries. But there were several respects in which workers' gains from Massey's housing and education strategy were arguably more illusory than real. One was that the high symbolic significance of home-ownership was at odds with its low economic significance. Home-ownership did have real social and economic advantages, such as security from the whims of landlords and a role as a saving scheme for retirement. Even in cities, home production in the form of vegetables, fruit, eggs and poultry remained important until the 1960s. But this could be carried out in rented homes, too, and was seldom an urban family's main source of income. Increasingly in the 1920s, homes were mortgaged – two-thirds by 1926.[102] Owning one's home provided the illusion of a 'landed independency', of an economic 'stake in society' or viable landholding. For workers, it amounted to real adoption of middle-class lifeways, and was therefore some advance. But it did not amount to real promotion to the middle class through the ownership of a means of production. As noted in *Making Peoples*, lawn mowing was a ritual harvest, not a real one.

White-collar work arguably had some of the same characteristics. Such workers were very often as low paid, as subject to the boss and in as little control of the production process as blue-collar workers. They did not own their means of production either, and it could be said that their membership of the middle class was as illusory as that of home-owners. Moreover, while secondary education expanded greatly in the 1920s, the white-collar jobs to which it was supposed to lead did not. Male employment in what we can assume were white-collar jobs – the commerce, finance, service and public administration sectors – exploded between the 1880s and World War One, but reached a plateau, or even declined, after it. It totalled 25 per cent in 1921 and 21 per cent in 1926. Categorisation changes may account for the decline.[103] But we can be reasonably sure that there was no significant increase in white-collar jobs for men in the 1920s, though the situation may have been a little better for women. In other words, the increase in white-collar-credentialling opportunities at secondary schools was not being matched by an increase in actual white-collar jobs.

New Zealand working people actively sought their own homes and secondary education for their children in the 1910s and 1920s. Massey actively helped them to acquire both, and so reduced the potential for working-class political and industrial activism. One should not patronisingly dismiss the workers' desire for homes, schooling and white-collar jobs as 'false consciousness', an ideological trick that suborned elements of the working class into believing they were middle class. Owning one's home did have some advantages; secondary education had benefits other than access to white-collar jobs; and white-collar jobs were generally safer, cleaner and easier than blue-collar ones, even if they were not more independent or better paid. Yet Massey was manipulating a mythology at least as much as a reality in his successful attempt to restore social stability after the troubles in paradise of 1912–22. Between 1913 and 1935, the myth of substantial opportunity for workers outranked the reality of limited opportunity as an historical force. This helped clear the field for the long reign of Farmer Backbone.

CHAPTER FIVE

Moral Harmony: A New Crusade

In May 1918, the alert Constable Tricklebank was patrolling along Upland Road, in an affluent suburb of Wellington, looking in windows. In one house he noticed men and women, smoking, drinking and dancing. Professional antennae fully erect, he observed shades being drawn on the bedroom windows. The house, he established, was rented by women only. The occupants were promptly charged with keeping a bawdy-house. 'It was impossible to contemplate, the Magistrate concluded, that men would visit women living alone and take alcohol with them if the place was not a brothel.'[1] One harlot was reluctantly released after a medical examiner certified her virginity, two others were convicted, and another den of vice bit the dust at the onslaught of a great crusade.

From the 1880s to the 1930s, a crusade for moral harmony tightened up New Zealand society like a giant spanner, and its after-effects kept things tight until the 1960s. It had many causes, conflicting as well as converging, and many effects – good, bad and neutral. It had numerous enemies and allies, who sometimes switched roles according to time and context. Despite contradictions, it had a certain cumbrous unity. Its weapons included reconditioning the individual's capacity for self-restraint, but if this failed, it used social pressure: shame was to it what sin had been to evangelical Christianity. We should be cautious about sneering at the past. The crusade for moral harmony, or 'moral evangelism', can be credited with great achievements, such as votes for women and lives for children. The Great Tightening it achieved was incomplete – contested, resisted and subverted. But it did exist powerfully, and it is not, I think, too unhistorical to note and dislike some of its worst excesses.

Book censorship tightened in the 1890s, restricting 'offensive publications' such as the works of Balzac and Zola and the *Illustrated Marriage Guide*.[2] Cinemas, which mushroomed from 1910, were described in 1916 as 'a curse to the community', and linked to venereal disease and female smoking. Film censorship was introduced during the war, and as with many other restrictions it was left in place in peace. In 1932, 262 films were banned or cut. Two years before, New Zealand joined Mussolini's Italy as the only countries to ban *All Quiet on the Western Front*.[3] There were moral panics about vagrants in the 1880s, youthful larrikins in the 1890s, Chinese in the 1900s, socialists in the 1910s, and almost everything in the 1920s. There were intense social obsessions with sexual impropriety, prostitution, masturbation, venereal disease and uncontrolled motherhood and childhood. In Wellington, nude bathing at Thorndon was stopped in 1892, and Newtown Park was patrolled to prevent 'unseemly activities' from 1895.[4] Between 1918 and 1924, government-authorised health patrols of uniformed matrons roamed Christchurch streets and parks in search of courting couples. Women volunteers in Auckland in 1915 formed a vigilance committee to carry the search to the back seats of the new cinemas. All entertainment involving close contact between the sexes was frowned upon. 'Dancing,' announced a writer in the feminist *White Ribbon* in 1909, 'endangers the purity of our young people' because it sent 'blood powerfully to the pelvis'.[5] Around 1900, regulations were passed compelling farmers with fields fronting the public road to persuade their exhibitionist cattle to mate in the back paddocks, for reasons of public propriety. This law remained on the books until the 1950s.[6]

The Minister of Health in 1916 warned that venereal disease was transmitted 'in lavatories, privies and barber's shops, by the use of towels, the kissing of children, and the smoking of infected pipes'. Dr Daisy Platt Mills agreed that 'indiscriminate kissing' was a major problem. The minister advocated the quarantine of prostitutes, and was supported by the Wellington Superintendent of Police:

> Avaricious money-making harlots . . . are all at liberty to contaminate the nation from end to end . . . One cannot wonder at the number of young people wearing glasses, artificial teeth and other evidence of constitutional weakness when these female vultures are able to fatten and become wealthy.[7]

Prostitutes shouldered the blame for venereal disease, as did women in general for pregnancy. 'Pregnancy was always suspected when a young unmarried woman killed herself.' One domestic servant committed suicide in 1910 after incorrectly diagnosing herself as being with child. A fifteen-year-old virgin servant-girl killed herself because of rumours about her love life. A pregnant daughter of 'very respectable parents' did so because she was unable to bear the shame.[8] Her household seems to have been an exceptionally pure shrine to the Age of Shame; a sibling had also committed suicide. A dozen Auckland suicides were caused by the revelation of other forms of unacceptable sexual behaviour, including homosexuality, child molesting and masturbation.

The moral panic over self-abuse was quite extraordinary, perhaps because it was the symbolic opposite of self-restraint. 'Pile all other evils together – drunkenness swindling, robbery, murder; add to these, all sickness disease, pestilence, and war; and all these combined do not produce a tithe as much misery as this secret sin.'[9] In 1890, an 'inveterate masturbator' at Seacliff Asylum in Dunedin had her ovaries and clitoris removed by Dr Ferdinand Batchelor on the advice of Frederic Truby King, a leading crusader. 'Dr King's idea being as far as possible to obliterate the whole of the genital tract.' Such actions were uncommon, but one was enough.[10] Male masturbators in state care escaped with nothing more than electric-shock treatment, applied to the testicles.[11] Masturbation, blared medical science to hordes of petrified self-abusers, caused

> Lassitude, Weakness of the Back, Pain across the Loins, Confusion of Ideas, Defective Memory, Aversion to Society, Despondency, Offensive Breath, Palpitation of the Heart, Incapacity for Study or Business, Spots and Specks before the Eyes, Pimples, Blotches &c.[12]

That it also caused impotence was so well known it was not worth mentioning. Eliza Frikart, an unorthodox pioneering woman doctor, offered cures at a guinea a bottle in 1893 for those who 'through Folly or Ignorance have Sapped their Vital Energies', but, as with unmarried pregnancy and venereal disease, escaping the consequences of vice was frowned upon. Frikart left a rapidly tightening New Zealand after practising for a year, abandoning poor self-abusers to their fate.[13]

Anti-intellectualism was reinforced by the folk belief that 'study or sedentary work could contribute to a decline of sexual potency'.[14] Masturbation was not good for police work either. The police surgeon around 1900 wished to reject all recruits who showed signs of 'masturbation in boyhood', but the Commissioner overruled him – perhaps for fear of too great a damage to intakes.[15] Irregular excretion in babies, warned Truby King, led to 'intolerable itching' and soon 'the vice of masturbation is contracted'. Regular bowel movements – fundamental discipline – was the answer. 'If a baby refused to co-operate, the mother was advised to tickle the anus with a feather', a cure arguably worse than the disease. They were not to play with, cuddle or otherwise spoil their infants. 'Baby must NEVER sleep in bed with his mother.' 'Mothers often say, "My baby's bowels will not move at a certain time." MAKE them move.'[16]

'Make Them Move': Moral Evangelism and its Allies

The crusade for moral harmony was a knot of many strands. The strands' thickness varied and the knot was constantly rewoven – an historian's nightmare. Many strands had overseas origins, but some found particularly fertile ground in New Zealand. Moral evangelism itself, also known as the 'Social Purity' movement, dates back to the early nineteenth century. In Britain, the United States and Germany, it had taken the form of various campaigns by the genteel and middle class to civilise the workers – to convert or to tame the savage within. Organisations using the term 'Social Purity' in their names had appeared in New Zealand by 1885. Two campaigns that exemplify the movement were prohibition – the attempt to ban alcoholic drink – and the rise of a 'cult of domesticity' aimed at increasing, exalting, improving, disciplining and controlling motherhood and home life. In New Zealand, the former flowered from the 1880s, and the latter from the 1900s. There were many associated changes dating from the same period, such as a tightening of immigration, censorship and sexual laws; attempts to tame childhood, residual crew and errant male culture; and shifts in attitudes to death and leisure. Some of these campaigns, the consequences of the crusade, are discussed in the next section. Our focus here is on the crusade's five major allies: the state; the medical profession; race and patriotism; religion; and feminism.

The state had an important but ambiguous role in moral evangelism – part constraint, part tool, part agent, part victim. It balked at the full prohibition of alcohol, for example, and generally failed to move as far or as fast as extreme moral evangelists wanted. Yet hundreds of statutes served the crusade – 44 restricting alcohol consumption alone between 1881 and 1913.[17] From the 1890s, the state showed 'a lessening level of tolerance for many activities . . . expectations of public order were growing'. By the 1900s, 'the state, through the police, was requiring stricter codes of public and private morality'. The police force professionalised, stopped carrying rifles and bayonets (though the universal issue of Colt revolvers continued to 1905), and expanded its role. 'There were no limits to what we had to do.'[18] 'Matters once the responsibility of parents were being handed over to the police.'[19] The police themselves were cleaned up in a succession of commissions of inquiry. In 1898, Inspector Emerson provoked public outrage and questions in Parliament by urinating into a hand basin on a crowded steamer – something that would hardly have occasioned even a disapproving glance twenty years earlier. There were crackdowns on gambling, prostitution and boxing – whose dangerous bare-knuckle version had long been a favourite spectator blood sport of the working class.[20]

Professionalisation was another ally of moral evangelism, notably in medicine. Doctors exploited the rise of science and a close, if sometimes uncomfortable, partnership with the state to entrench their leadership in the medical industry. Doctors clashed with the state in the 1920s over control of the birth process and over the introduction of free health care in 1938. But 'the state took an active role in supporting medical incomes and providing an infrastructure on which the profession depended'.[21] Helped by the state, doctors asserted their dominance and improved their status and incomes from the 1890s. Doctors were also helped by improved gatekeeping – the establishment in 1874 of the Otago Medical School, tightening registration and, from 1886, an increasingly powerful professional organisation. This organisation recolonially changed its name from the New Zealand Medical Association to the New Zealand Branch of the British Medical Association in 1896. Doctors were able to offer competing medical groups the alternatives of subordination or marginalisation. Nurses and chemists accepted the former; homeopaths the latter; midwives a bit of both. The extent to which medical systems are socially constructed can be exaggerated, but an exhaustive recent study does seem to show that doctoral dominance was due at least as much to superior politics as to superior medicine. There were, of course, many morally liberal and rationalist doctors; yet the influence of the new morality on others is very marked. They preached it with a special authority, becoming medicine men (and women) of moral evangelism.

Race and patriotism permeated at least the rhetoric of moral evangelism, stimulated in the 1900s and 1920s by 'moral panics' about low birth rates, and racial deterioration. Inside the nation, it was thought, immorality and social welfare encouraged the unfit to procreate, while selfishness and contraception discouraged the fit. Outside the nation, lesser races were breeding like flies and threatening to swarm into a 'Yellow Peril'. As early as 1884, fears were expressed about the 'decline of the race' and the need to 'populate or perish'.

> Myriads of the wretched are encouraged even to go on breeding swarms of still more wretched beings, who are carefully protected, and live to be a curse to themselves and all around them. Nature's law of the survival of the fittest or strongest is set aside, and a false moral code has taken its place.[22]

Many similar comments between the 1890s and the 1930s could be quoted. During World War One, it was found that two-thirds of recruits did not make the top fitness grade, and this stimulated fears of racial deterioration. According to a 1925 committee of inquiry:

> It has rightly been decided that this should not only be a 'white man's country,' but as completely British as possible. We ought to make every effort to keep the stock sturdy and strong, as well as racially pure . . . The Great War revealed . . . [New Zealanders as] some of the finest men the world has ever seen . . . It also revealed that an inferior strain had crept in . . . Surely our aim should be to prevent, as far as possible, the multiplication of the latter type.[23]

As late as 1950, the country's most widely read general history warned that 'New Zealanders find themselves in danger of being trodden down by hungry hordes . . . Artificial means of checking population have been rife . . . A sort of race suicide was taking place in what should have been an earthly paradise.'[24]

One solution was a powerful campaign against contraception, which involved the state, the media and the Protestant churches as well as Catholics. Another was 'eugenics' – a form of racial engineering that encouraged the 'fit' to breed, and discouraged the 'unfit', with most emphasis on the latter. This 'science' originated in 1869 with Englishman Francis Galton, whose interest in hereditary genius may have been stimulated by the fact that he was related to Charles Darwin. The idea received Darwin's own imprimatur in *The Descent of Man* in 1871, and percolated into New Zealand thought thereafter. It enjoyed quite a vogue between the 1880s and the 1930s. A Eugenic Society was formed in 1910, and 'eugenic ideas were widely held by even the most progressive members of society', including liberals and feminists.[25] Strictly speaking, eugenics and moral evangelism were not wholly compatible. There was little point in moralising to intrinsically unfit, immoral or criminal types once the genetic die had been cast. Eugenically, what one had to do was eliminate the troublesome genes by preventing the procreation of the 'unfit'. For countries outside Nazi Germany, where the Final Solution was used, this meant either compulsory sterilisation of the unfit or their segregation in institutions where they could not breed. Some democratic countries did use compulsory sterilisation; the 1925 commission advocated its use at the discretion of a 'Eugenics Board'; and there may have been a few actual cases in New Zealand. But segregation was generally preferred to sterilisation, and even that does not seem to have been applied very comprehensively or intensively.

A blurring of concepts, very common in the social history of ideas, softened New Zealand's relationship with eugenics. There were some measures to influence breeding, to ensure that more New Zealanders were Born Fit, but there were many more measures aimed at ensuring that those already born were Made Fit. Biological theory somehow translated into environmental practice. The practical emphasis was on nurture, not nature – improving the race through social discipline, not racial discipline.

> We believe in improvement through the survival of the fittest and the general tendencies of the fit to pass on their qualities through heredity . . . Of course tendencies are inherited, but observant and thinking men are coming to recognise more and more the fact that hereditary tendencies can be overcome by environment in the great majority of cases, and can always be greatly modified by suitable conditions of life and training.[26]

The author of these lines, Dr Truby King, ranks as an arch-prophet of moral evangelism, and was also a key agent of its pragmatic marriage with patriotism and racialism – in forms other than the strictly eugenic. Described by Keith Sinclair as 'arguably the most influential man in Pakeha society',[27] King was born at New Plymouth in 1858. An expert on motherhood and infancy, as we have seen, he argued that order, regularity and discipline were the keys to both, and that the proper management of both was the key to success for children, races and empires. In 1907, the Plunket Society was formed to propagate his ideas. King and Plunket did reduce infant mortality – though not to the extent that they claimed – and in some respects they did improve the experiences of motherhood and infancy.[28] But, to quote Erik Olssen, 'rooting out self-indulgence and imposing self-control obsessed King. Better health for babies, valuable in itself, was also a means towards that end.'[29]

King also preached a kind of race motherhood. 'If we lack noble mothers we lack the first element of racial success and national greatness. THE DESTINY OF THE RACE IS IN THE HANDS OF ITS MOTHERS.'[30] In the 1920s, Plunket Society literature stressed that 'Perfect Motherhood is Perfect Patriotism'. 'King defined moral responsibility for women as the bearing of babies for the white British Empire, to ensure that race suicide would be averted.'[31] This collectivised and racialised 'cult of domesticity' was a more important racial ally of moral evangelism than was eugenics. Moralists evangelised not only for themselves and their neighbours but for King, Country and Empire. Their messages drew urgency from the overriding need for physically and morally healthy soldiers and mothers. The 'cult of domesticity' was reinforced by the concept of 'race motherhood'. Mothers were the basic cells of the coral reef of Race and Empire.

Religion was a close and obvious ally of moral evangelism, but the relationship developed ambiguities. Official adherence to the three main Protestant denominations remained roughly constant or fell only slightly between the 1880s and the 1920s. Anglicans (who were mostly English) were just over 40 per cent; Presbyterians (who were mostly Scots) were about 24 per cent; and Methodists were 9–10 per cent. But we need to distinguish between the denominations professed in censuses and actual church attendance. Between 1874 and 1886, there was a substantial upsurge in churchgoing, but the picture thereafter was one of long-term decline in the major Protestant churches. Between 1891 and 1926, the proportion of people aged fifteen years and over who regularly attended church fell from 24.5 to 15 per cent among Anglicans, 48 to 28 per cent among Presbyterians, and 93.5 to 40.7 per cent among Methodists. Catholic attendance figures remained high at 50 per cent or more, but for Protestants, 1886 began a decline in churchgoing that continues to the present.[32]

One could explain this discrepancy by dismissing 'adherence' as being merely nominal, focus on churchgoing, and suggest that Protestant Pakeha were becoming less and less religious. But there are strong indicators to the contrary. The outburst of religious sectarianism in the early 1920s demonstrated that religious issues still cut to the public quick. Urban unskilled men had never been great churchgoers, but there is no sign of moral-religious collapse in the first decades of the twentieth century among the women, skilled workers, the middle class and rural people. The small North Canterbury town of Oxford, population 1,800, had ten churches and ten Sunday schools in the 1930s – 'there are no heathen'. Some of these Oxonians believed that proto-human fossils had been 'put there by the devil to shake our faith', and that Darwin had recanted on his deathbed. 'You can believe you are descended from monkeys if you like,' ran one sermon, 'but I am not, I am not, I am not!'[33]

The general impression of mainstream New Zealand in this period is the very opposite of irreligious. There was a strong tradition of piety and family use of the Bible, despite low church attendance.[34] Prohibition, the favourite moral cause of the more active Protestant churches, repeatedly associated with godliness, enjoyed widespread support. Regular election votes on prohibition received over 40 per cent from the 1890s to the 1920s, and actual majorities in 1905–11. This was also an era in which revivalism, fundamentalism and Protestant sects with elements of both featured quite prominently. Baptists increased 50 per cent between 1891 and 1926, and Brethren tripled, while their larger rivals languished. The Salvation Army marched into New Zealand in 1883, and its adherents rocketed to 1.5 per cent of the population by 1891.[35] American revivalists preached to substantial crowds in 1902 and 1912–13, and revivalism flourished in Auckland in the 1920s.[36]

One historian has suggested a decline in Sabbatarianism – belief in the sanctity of Sunday – and used this to indicate a general decline of Protestantism.[37] Yet New Zealand, in this period and beyond, is surely known for exceptional Sabbatarianism. Visitors complained the country was 'closed on Sundays' until the very recent past. Sunday newspapers were not legalised until 1965, and first-class cricket was first played on Sunday in 1968.[38] Sunday shopping and Sunday liquor sales had to wait until the 1980s and 1990s respectively. In 1928, the mayor of Christchurch objected to the idea that the famous aviator Charles Kingsford-Smith should arrive on a Sunday, as though he could have circled until Monday.[39] In 1930, two Thames clergymen objected to children using swings on Sunday, and in 1932 a Chinese market gardener was fined £5 for picking peas on a Sunday.[40]

What we may have here is decline in Protestant churchgoing without a decline in a broader religiousness. Conventional denominations were being weakened, as well as supported, by alliance with other ideologies: a vague and vaguely interdenominational Protestantism that did not necessarily require regular church attendance. It was closely associated with, but perhaps also to some extent displaced by, rising moral evangelism. One of the most astute foreign observers of the exemplary paradise in the 1900s, André Siegfried, detected in New Zealand spiritual and moral sentiment 'a strange narrowness which seems anchored to the very depths of the New Zealand soul, which perhaps regards it as a social and national tradition even more than a religious one!'[41]

In 1913, the Methodist Church feared it was being displaced by 'a new social propaganda'.[42] Historians of religion have noted something similar. 'The Protestant churches joined eagerly in [moral evangelist] campaigns, but this was not necessarily evidence of their strength. Although it was a moral community it was also a secular one.'[43] Moral evangelism, like Better British dominionism, was partly an ally of religion, partly an alternative. The impression of a strong secular element in New Zealand's moral ideology is reinforced by the importance of scientific rationalism, which appeared in a wide variety of guises in the period 1880s–1920s. They included rational dress, rational recreation, rational nutrition, scientific management and scientific motherhood.

The Catholic Church's relationship with moral evangelism was still more ambiguous. Moral evangelism was sometimes seen as another attack on Catholic Irish difference. It was feared, for example, that prohibition would ban the use of wine for Holy Communion. Protestants were content with unfermented grape juice . 'One excellent Presbyterian minister, lately deceased, once informed us that, in his view, the mere eating of raisins by the communicants would satisfy the purpose of the institution.'[44] Yet the Catholic Church, too, forged a close alliance with some moralist campaigns. From the late 1870s to the 1930s, Redemptorist missions preached powerfully against moral as well as religious sin, terrorising children in Catholic communities with a 'fearful picture of the torments and tortures of the damned'.[45] The Catholic Church led the campaign against that terrible demon, contraception, which would depopulate New Zealand and leave the field clear for the Yellow Peril. Bishop Cleary of Auckland feared 'the menace of the prolific Oriental' at a time when 'the white nations' were defying divine law by using contraception. Unless New Zealanders mended their ways, he prophesied, 'slant-eyed Orientals will yet sit by the hearths that we, by our sins, shall in due course leave childless and desolate'. He was matched in fervour by Baptist minister J. J. North: 'Lust, using the implements of France . . . is destroying the fountain of life, and is openly threatening this country with early destruction at the hands either of yellow races or by the action of slow attrition.'[46] Racialist dominionism joined moralism and conventional religion in New Zealand's Holy Trinity.

Moral evangelism's fifth great ally was 'first-wave' feminism: the late nineteenth-century women's movement. The movement can be traced back to the writings of John Stuart Mill, culminating in *On the Subjection of Women* in 1869; to the Seneca Falls Convention of women in the United States in 1848; and to the French Enlightenment and beyond. It sought increased rights and freedoms for women, *and* the reinforcement and revaluation of the traditional roles of wife and mother. Radical versions placed more stress on the former, moderate versions on the latter. Like moral evangelism itself, the movement was international, but it struck fertile ground in New Zealand, and struck it quite early. Mary Ann Muller published a feminist pamphlet in Auckland in 1869. Women's suffrage in 1893 is generally seen as the movement's defining achievement, though we will see below that gains extended further than this. Male politicians at the time sometimes implied that the vote was freely given to women by the enlightened men of New Zealand, and it is true that there were important male leaders of the suffrage movement, such as Sir John Hall. But the historical consensus is that women themselves were the key activists. It emphasises a remarkably talented group of feminist leaders, including Kate Sheppard, Margaret Sievwright, Amey Daldy and Anna Stout.[47]

Current discussion may place too much weight on the suffragist élite, replacing an overemphasis on great men with an overemphasis on great women. There is a case for distinguishing between conventional, formal middle-class feminism on the one hand, and populist, informal lower-class feminism on the other. This issue is discussed further in the final section of this chapter. But the feminist leaders deserve full credit for their deeds, and these were substantial and internationally early. The 1890s saw not only legislative triumphs, such as the vote and the Divorce Act of 1898, but also a proliferation of women's organisations. No fewer than 44 were formed in this decade, compared with sixteen in the 1880s and five in the 1870s. They included the National Council of Women, established in 1896.[48] Why was first-wave feminism so strong in New Zealand in the 1890s?

Some answers may lie in the colonising process itself. New Zealand feminism was unusual but not completely exceptional. It shared the early achievement of suffrage with a few other English-speaking polities – three states in Australia and four in the Midwestern United States – at a similar stage of development. Each experienced the displacement of progressive colonisation by some form of recolonisation, and therefore a perceived need to tame a 'frontier wildness', which was actually diminishing anyway. These polities also shared a 'Britonnic network' that enabled them to transmit ideas to and from each other. New Zealand, British, American and Australian feminist speakers, news and literature flowed from end to end of the network and back.[49] It does not follow from this that New Zealand feminism was simply derivative; it gave to, as well as took from, the transnational network. Another factor was that, while lady philanthropists had always been seen as central to moral evangelism, in England and the older parts of the United States they had well-established mechanisms of intervention: large and mature voluntary organisations; philanthropic traditions; and the social leadership of tight communities. In New Zealand, where gentry rule was indirect when it existed at all, these mechanisms were weaker. There was an incentive to operate through the state instead, and therefore to enter the arena of public politics.[50]

New Zealand was also exceptionally Scottish in comparison to the other neo-Britains. About a quarter of Pakeha were ethnically Scots, and the next chapter will show that even this may understate Scottish influences. Scots are said to have been more egalitarian than the English, and this applied to gender as well as class. A disproportionate number of New Zealand feminist leaders – almost half of one sample of 21 – had Scottish backgrounds.[51] Partible inheritance, which divided estates among all offspring including daughters, was the Scottish practice, while primogeniture, where everything went to the eldest son, was more common in England. It was the Scottish practice that applied most often in New Zealand, and this was also true in education, which Scots thought suitable even for girls.

New Zealand women do seem to have been exceptionally highly educated. Of all 118,000 public primary pupils in 1891, 48.7 per cent were girls. Boys slightly outnumbered girls in the 5–14 age group, and there were 1,700 more girls in private schools than boys, so there was very nearly parity in primary schooling.[52] At first sight, this is what one would expect from compulsory education, but the 1877 system was compulsory only in name. Fully 22 per cent of eligible children still did not attend school in 1891. It is said that, before 1877, parents preferred to send sons to school, but this was clearly not true afterwards. Truancy remained high, but, according to a study of Otago in 1902–07, it did not select for gender.[53] Near-parity in education was also true at secondary and tertiary levels, which until the 1900s were upper- and upper-middle-class domains. In 1886, 40 per cent of secondary school students were girls; by 1900 the proportion had risen to 45 per cent. By 1893, women 'constituted over half the number of university students in New Zealand'.[54] My impression is that these proportions were high in international terms. We will see that the type of education that girls received was sometimes aimed at domesticating them rather than liberating them, but relatively high levels of female education may have been both a cause and a consequence of relatively high levels of feminism.

Whatever its roots, feminism was a powerful ally of moral evangelism, but not necessarily a faithful one. The alliance was often close, but sometimes conflictual. It is not always clear who was using whom, and exploitation was often mutual. The alliance was closest and least problematic on prohibition, but sometimes contentious on education and motherhood – matters discussed further below. In general, moral evangelism expanded the image of women as moral guardians of the home to more public spheres. It asserted that they were its natural shock troops. They were conceded rights that might strengthen them in the role, such as the vote, but not freedoms that might distract them from it, such as open access to jobs. The concept of domestic motherhood was revalued, and joined by one of social motherhood – and racial motherhood. Race, by nature, and morality, by nurture, was held to reside in the mother, as though fathers were a bunch of storks. Racial motherhood joined domestic and social motherhood. This exalted conception of motherhood could be a padded prison or a socially valued citadel from which feminists could foray.

Moral evangelism was strongly resisted by various sectors of society, as we will see in the next section. The resisters tended to be from the lower classes. But it would be wrong to see moral harmony as something wholly imposed from above. A convergent shift in popular attitudes is discernable in spheres ranging from death to picnics. Annual community picnics at Taieri were initially sponsored by the local landowner, from 1859, and subsequently became known as school picnics, although they catered for all ages. They featured sports such as athletics and wrestling, lolly scrambles, with a 'married ladies race' as 'the great event of the day'. The traditional keg of beer became larger as the years passed. In the 1880s, local moral evangelists achieved the withdrawal of children from the event in favour of a separate, more controlled and decorous version, and the adults' version faded out.[55] This taming of public play seems to have been general. 'In the nineties the publicans' booth disappeared from the picnics.'[56]

Research into terminal social history in New Zealand is very sparse, but it seems that attitudes to death also tightened. Public grieving over deaths, the shared enemy, helped preserve imported folk customs and unite virtual strangers in the nineteenth century and in frontier-like communities in the twentieth. Generally speaking, however, it became more private, restrained and professionalised, more the realm of the doctor and the undertaker; less that of the community. A study of suicide in Auckland shows that professional coroners increasingly clashed with amateur juries during post-mortems on self-inflicted death, and virtually displaced them from 1909. Juries normally tried to soften the social stigma for the suicide victim's family with findings of 'insanity', often clashing with coroners, who saw most suicides as 'felonies'. Up to the 1900s, juries succeeded, and 80 per cent of suicides in Auckland were attributed to insanity. Coroners had their way thereafter, and by 1930 the insanity figure had dropped to 5 per cent.[57] Robbing the state of a citizen was no longer a victimless offence.

Moral harmony was to some degree internalised. In 1930, the Inland Revenue Department received five voluntary and anonymous repayments in a single month from taxpayers with guilty consciences.[58] Non-governmental organisations imposed their own versions of moral evangelism – in the provision of welfare, for example. Friendly Societies, which expanded their membership from 21,000 in 1886 to 95,000 in 1926,[59] had strict moralist rules about the provision of benefits. 'Not even the most regular contributor could expect to draw a benefit . . . if the illness or accident was caused by "fighting . . . or any intemperate, improper, or immoral conduct" [including] running, leaping or act of bravado . . . Any member found drinking, fighting, or gambling while in receipt of the sickness benefit was fined and the benefit withdrawn.'[60] These rules were similar to those imposed by the state on recipients of the old age pension from 1898. 'The moral character stipulations in the 1898 Act, which were policed vigorously for a time, had few parallels in . . . British pension legislation. This was a decidedly New Zealand measure.'[61] As this suggests, moral evangelism, while international, appears to have been stronger in New Zealand than in most other countries. Some New Zealand strands of the knot were thicker and tangled more tightly.

Contributing factors here may have been perceived needs to sweep away the residue of crews and chaos left by progressive colonisation, and to expiate the sin of stagnation through social and racial purification. A curious and persistent New Zealand puritanism, extremism, or 'voluntary totalitarianism', was another factor. People considered it their right and duty to impose their own code on others. One could see this as part and parcel of moralism itself, but this may not be entirely fair. In the history of New Zealand, the totalitarian tendency exists outside moralism. Neither the social evangelisms of the left nor the market evangelisms of the right were ever prone to tolerate argument, qualification or compromise. A world fad easily became a New Zealand fetish. Above all, perhaps, was the great reshuffling and systemic change of recolonisation itself. The new system demanded homogeneity, harmony and purity to buttress Better British ideology, and added dominionism and moralism to religion in its holy trinity. There was an element of slow-burning but massive 'moral panic', or change trauma. Collective identities under threat need causes, even scapegoats, to assist in defending and adapting themselves. We will see that the Great Tightening partly invented the demons it attacked.

Drink, Death and Other Demons

Among moral evangelism's best-known campaigns was a long-term mass assault on the 'demon drink', 1880–1920. Moral evangelism did not begin the crusade against drink. New Zealand's first temperance society was formed in Northland in the 1830s, and a number of temperance organisations, many of British origin, made their appearance thereafter. Symbolically enough, the first book published in English in this country was *A Report of the New Zealand Temperance Society*, in 1836.[62] While some temperance organisations advocated 'total abstinence' as early as the 1840s, others were oriented more to the mutual encouragement of self-control rather than state control, and to the elimination of strong spirits rather than wine and beer. James Busby saw no contradiction in being both a winemaker and drinker and a member of the first temperance society. Early temperance organisations included the Independent Order of Rechabites, an abstemious Friendly Society that was founded in Britain in 1835 and appeared in New Zealand as early as 1843. Both the Rechabites and another organisation, the Band of Hope, were quite strong in Auckland from 1863, when soldiers assembling for the Waikato War brought drunken mayhem to the streets.[63] It was from the 1880s, however, that the crusade against drink really took off and shifted from temperance to prohibition, or total abstinence. Moral evangelism was central to both these changes.

Prohibitionists included agnostics, like Robert Stout, and others influenced more by moralism than religion. But key players were the Protestant churches, especially the more evangelical among them, and the women's movement. 'The evangelical community tended to regard prohibition as the reform crucial for the redemption of New Zealand.'[64] Over half the 400 leaders of the prohibition movement, 1894–1914, were Protestant ministers of religion – very few of them Anglican.[65] Some saw prohibition as a means of regenerating churchgoing, as well as the moral fibre of society at large. Prohibition and the women's movement were intertwined from the start. The Women's Christian Temperance Union was formed in 1885 as a result of a visit by an American feminist prohibitionist, Mary Leavitt. The WCTU and its leaders, notably Kate Sheppard, were major actors in both temperance and suffrage movements. Feminism, religion and prohibition usually meshed quite neatly. 'We demand for our homes and our children the total Prohibition of the liquor traffic; Prohibition by law; Prohibition by politics; and Prohibition by woman's ballot, which may the Lord hasten.'[66]

Between 1880 and 1920, the prohibition movement chalked up about 50 laws controlling liquor consumption, beginning with the Licensing Act of 1881. Prohibition organisations formed the New Zealand Alliance in 1886. In 1894, the 'licensing poll' was introduced, held along with general elections, and offering various local prohibition options. Prohibition started strongly in 1894, received majorities in the three referenda between 1905 and 1911 – when the liquor trade was only saved by a provision for a three-fifths majority – and ran at over 40 per cent until 1928. Twelve licensing districts voted for local prohibition in 1908, and if it had not been for the three-fifths rule, the number would have been 50 out of 80 electorates. Voting for national prohibition was introduced in 1911, when it received 55.8 per cent of the vote. World War One saw the abolition of the three-fifths rule, and in the 1919 referendum booze only squeaked home through the votes of the troops still overseas.[67]

In August 1916, women were banned from 'that fair-gilded deadly Temple of Sin', the pub, after 6 pm, and 'anti-treating regulations' were introduced. Groups of drinkers were forbidden by law from buying each other drinks in rounds, and from 'shouting' the group. This little gem of interventionist puritanism did not outlast the war. Other laws against barmaids – wicked sirens who lured men to drink – lasted from 1911 to 1961, and 6 pm closing – for men as well as women – prevailed from 1917 to 1967. 'Six o'clock closing' became a folk symbol of the Age of Moral Harmony. Restrictions on pub hours appeared in Britain and Australia at the same time, but there was an important difference between northern and southern versions. In Britain, pubs opened at lunchtime, closed in the afternoon, and reopened in the evenings. This prevented workers who took lunch at the pub from staying all afternoon: it supported the work ethic in the name of national efficiency. In New Zealand and Australia, workers could still spend all afternoon boozing, but not the evening. This disciplined social life in the name of moral evangelism more than work in the name of national efficiency.

Temperance was preached with genuine crusading fervour, and aroused the strongest of feelings. There were riots between pro- and anti-temperance factions in the 1880s.[68] The rhetoric of temperance 'wowsers' is easy for a latter age to mock: 'There's a cloven hoof in the tankard's foam.' But why was drink the most hated demon of all for moral evangelists and feminists? Alcohol had been very dear indeed to progressive colonial New Zealand up to the 1880s. Consumption was staggeringly high, as were arrests for drunkenness and drink-related violence. Drink lubricated the notorious binges of unmarried male crew culture. In 1881, the small town of Oamaru, then a notorious binge centre, had 20 pubs, 32 illegal grog shops, and 12 brothels. The town went dry in 1905.[69] Drunken drowning was a major form of accidental death. In another small Otago community, Balclutha, in the 1870s, six men met this fate within a few weeks. In the 1870s, it was claimed that drink-related deaths amounted to 500 a year.[70] With the exception of a few 'disreputables', prostitutes and the like, women were excluded from crew culture, a leading site of drinking culture. Among the married, money spent on drink was lost to families, and divorce records are ridden with domestic violence by men against women, often oiled by drink.[71] On the face of it, the prohibition movement was a perfectly rational cause to espouse – for women in particular. Yet there were at least three curious things about it.

First, while it has long been assumed that women were central to prohibition, some research suggests they were little or no more prone to vote for it than were married men.[72] Feminists were prominent leaders of the movement, but male church leaders were even more prominent. The picture of primarily female 'wowsers' may be overdrawn. Second, though this is hard to prove, one gets the distinct impression that there was substantial inter-section between those who voted for prohibition and those who drank. Third, alcohol consumption, public drunkenness and related violence were all declining rapidly *before* the prohibition movement reached its peak. Rates of beer consumption, spirits consumption and arrests for drunkenness fell very dramatically between the 1860s and 1900 – to half, one-fifth and one-sixth respectively. There was a slight rise in all three indicators in the 1900s, during progressive colonisation's Indian summer, but to nothing like earlier rates, and prohibition sentiment was already well established by the 1890s anyway. The decline in consumption recommenced after 1910 and continued to the late 1930s.[73] The prohibition movement crusaded with increasing intensity against a shrinking problem. Like antagonism to the Chinese, discussed in Chapter Seven, antagonism to drink had an element of 'moral panic' or change trauma.

Prohibition failed in its ultimate objective, the complete elimination of alcohol consumption. But, like religious or socialist movements, it should not be judged wholly on its failure to achieve its millennium. It neither banned drink nor caused its decline – this was more likely related to the decline of those big drinkers, the crews. But the prohibition movement did steepen the decline and comprehensively tame the drinking process. The proportion of pubs to people in 1945 was one-fifth of its 1881 level. Barmaids, let alone dancing girls, were banned, and women were effectively excluded from public bars. The age of entry was increased from 16 to 21. The alcohol content of beer was progressively reduced to the point where getting drunk on beer was physically difficult. The promising wine industry went into remission between the 1890s and the 1960s. Drinking in pubs remained an important part of male culture, as we shall see, but it now took place behind darkened windows, from small glasses and at heavily restricted times. The demon drink survived, but, officially at least, it did so only in shackles.

Premature death from disease was another great demon attacked by moral evangelism from the 1880s to the 1920s. From the first mass European settlement in the 1840s, New Zealand had nurtured a reputation as a healthy country. It was helped by the fact that its disproportionately young population made its vital statistics look deceptively good.[74] An 'invalids' paradise' joined the menu of utopias offered to migrants, but was pushed only half-heartedly because incoming invalids could be vectors of infectious disease. Affluent but tubercular young Englishmen do appear to have become one of New Zealand's more pathetic categories of immigrant in the period 1880–1914, whereas in fact tuberculosis, or consumption as it was also known, was the country's leading killer.[75] Colonial New Zealand was healthier than Mother England in some respects, owing to less crowding and better nutrition as well as a younger population. But, to the 1870s, its state of health was not great. As in comparable societies, the next century saw great improvements. Life expectancy increased by twenty years; infant mortality decreased from one in ten babies under one year to one in a hundred; some lethal diseases such as typhoid and tuberculosis almost disappeared; others such as influenza and dysentery ceased to be major killers, allowing people to survive long enough to fall victim to heart disease and cancer.

This broad improvement in health began in the later nineteenth century, and the reasons are a subject of international debate. Apart from moral evangelism, possible heroes include the rise of scientific medicine; the rise of living standards, especially in nutrition; the rise of medical professionalism; improvements in sanitation by local authorities; and the establishment of public health systems. Each hero has its advocates, who tend to exaggerate the role of their favourite. The defeat of infant mortality, for example, was often credited to moral evangelism in the shape of the Plunket Society. But the beginning of the steady decline of infant death predates the formation of the society in 1907 by at least five years.[76] The percentage of central government expenditure devoted to health remained around 2–3 per cent for the whole period 1882–1932.[77] Death was not tamed by throwing masses of public money at it. But it was tamed somehow. Pakeha infant mortality halved between 1902 and 1924, and the overall death rate dropped about 20 per cent.

New Zealand evidence suggests that improvements in sanitation were more important to the commencement of the twentieth-century health boom than were improvements in nutrition, relative to Britain, which was already fairly good. On the other hand, sanitation, especially urban sanitation, started from a base almost as low as Britain. Colonial New Zealand cities were notorious cesspools. Even small towns such as Cromwell in Otago had severe problems as late as 1874, when a visiting doctor noted that the cleanest of its water tanks contained 'the debris of what had evidently passed through the alimentary canal of a horse'.[78] Christchurch, 'a damp fever-ridden swamp', had the worst record, with a death rate of twice the national average in 1875 – including infant mortality of almost one in five. From 1872, however, a series of measures brought some improvement. How far this was due to public health legislation by central government, and how far to the increased sanitary activism of local authorities, is unclear, though it seems that the latter predominated in Christchurch. That city gained a sewage system by 1882 and pressurised water mains and flush toilets by 1909. Between 1875 and 1911, the city's death rate fell from 30 per 1,000 to 10 per 1,000, which was about the Pakeha average.[79]

Urban sanitation generally appears to have improved significantly by the 1900s. This played its part in reducing death rates, and so too did the public health system. In the nineteenth century, public hospitals basically catered for marginal groups in society, such as the impoverished and the aged who did not have kin to care for them. They were deeply feared in folklore as places to which one went to die. After the abolition of the provinces in 1876, hospitals were to be run by regional hospital boards, which also administered charitable aid. The marriage between health and welfare was consolidated in an important Act in 1885, and persisted to the 1930s. Charitable aid was the nineteenth-century New Zealand equivalent of social welfare, but was very different from the post-1938 system. It was a ragged safety net with very large holes through which the undeserving poor were intended to slip. Like the education system, health administration between the 1870s and the 1930s was an uneasy compromise between local, regional and central authority, but with a marked trend towards the centre. A bubonic plague scare in 1900 led to the establishment of one of the world's first government departments of health. A system of maternity hospitals was established by Seddon in 1904, and a school medical service in 1912. The Health Department was greatly strengthened by further legislation in 1920, this time stimulated by the 1918 influenza pandemic. There were 38 public hospitals and related institutions in 1890, with only 6,700 in-patients. By 1925, the number of institutions had tripled and the number of in-patients had increased tenfold.[80] This was partly due to global developments in medical science and technology, which shifted treatment from homes to institutions that had specialists and equipment. It saw the entry of the middle classes into public hospitals for the first time, which in turn reduced the stigma against them.

Moral evangelism may not have contributed much to the taming of death in Christchurch, but it was deeply intertwined with the rise of a public health system. It helped shift hospitalisation from the margins to the mainstream. For example, it encouraged the transfer of the birth process from midwife to doctor and home to hospital as part of 'scientific motherhood'. By 1920, 35 per cent of births took place in hospitals; by 1935, the figure was 78 per cent.[81] This was probably good for infants but not for mothers, who not only lost control of the birth process but also appear to have suffered from increased rates of puerperal sepsis, or 'childbed fever'.[82] Public health officials, such as Dr Duncan McGregor, Inspector-General of Hospitals 1886–1906, were also leading moral (and racial) evangelists. Physical and moral wellbeing were thought to be closely linked, as were individual and racial health, humanitarianism and social control, dirt and disease, immorality and poverty. 'Good morals and good health,' announced Kate Sheppard in 1898, 'went together.'[83] A leading health crusader, Dr Elizabeth Gunn, made a quick strike on Stratford District High School to suppress an outbreak of masturbation, the perennial enemy, in 1921. 'I do not wonder when I see some of the septic foetid mouths of these children ... that they are listless, inattentive, and perverted.' All this was better than attributing illness to fate or magic – there was at least some chance of mending your ways – but not much. Victims were blamed more often, yet it remains true that they were also saved more often.

Tuberculosis, which caused 10 per cent of all Pakeha deaths in the late nineteenth century, was seen as a threat to the race, to be combated by sound habits – the 'person living a healthy life has nothing to fear from consumption'.[84] If sound habits failed, the tubercular were, from 1902, segregated in state sanatoria. Open-air sleeping, even in winter, was thought to prevent or even cure tuberculosis, and thousands of New Zealand houses today still possess sleeping porches and balconies, often converted into sunrooms, as monuments to this practice. In sanatoria, if hard work and fresh air failed to work their miraculous cures, the consumptive was at least prevented from breeding. Death rates from tuberculosis appear to have roughly halved between the late nineteenth century and the 1920s. Yet the rate of tuberculosis remained quite high, and did not fall dramatically until the mid-1940s. There was, it seems, a strange reluctance to attack the city slums known to harbour the disease, and a preference for inculcating healthy habits. This may suggest that the social-control motive had an edge over humane considerations, but the two were seldom separate in the minds of moral evangelists.

The merging of good morals and good health was perhaps best exemplified in the children's health services and the management of 'insanity'. The School Medical Service, established in 1912, examined 79,000 children in 1921. Reinforced by the School Dental Service in 1919, by the proliferation of health camps for children from about the same time, and by the Child Welfare Act in 1925, it disseminated healthy and moral doctrines with equal enthusiasm. 'Be upright in body and mind.' It used public humiliation and oppressive inspection rituals to achieve benign ends. Some saw its agents as 'persecuting fiends', 'a white league of avenging angels to harass and annoy'.[85] Increasing numbers of children, orphans and juvenile offenders, as well as the ill, were committed to public institutions. There, they were protected and cared for, but also disciplined and controlled – and sometimes paraded through the streets as an example to the more fortunate of what not to be.[86] The children learning toothbrush drill, spitting in unison on the count of 25, symbolised not only moralist regimentation but also an improvement in dental health.

In 1919, the *Official Yearbook* listed alcohol, syphilis, epilepsy and puberty as major causes of insanity. Minor causes included pregnancy, solitude, sunstroke, 'overstudy', sexual excess and, of course, masturbation. Definitions of many, though not all, forms of insanity, like other abnormalities, were designed to sustain norms and had to be changed to match them. Women, for example, who loudly rejected their roles as wives, housekeepers and mothers were at risk of being judged insane – probably to a greater degree under moral evangelism than before. In 1890, 41 per cent of a sample of women patients in the Auckland Lunatic Asylum were committed for 'threats to social norms'; by 1910 the figure was 54 per cent. Some used mental asylums to escape from oppressive family life, but it was a case of frying pan into fire. Asylums were unpleasant places at least until World War Two, relying mainly on work, discipline and electric-shock treatment to effect cures, and the social stigma against 'loony bins' persisted even longer. The evidence on committal rates is sparse and contradictory. One official source shows a substantial colonywide increase between 1874 and 1891, 35 per cent for men and 53 per cent for women. Another shows a near-doubling between 1880 and 1895. A recent study of committals to the Auckland asylum shows a near-halving of rates for both sexes between 1871 and 1911. Tossing people into the looney bin was a crude form of social engineering, and it may have been used more often early in the crusade than late, operating thereafter as a vague background threat for the many, and an actual hell or refuge for the few.[87]

Drink and premature death were key targets of moral evangelism. Another was unruly single men, notably the remnant crews of the nineteenth century and their legacies in broader male culture. Crews declined in numbers from the 1880s, with a brief and partial revival in the 1900s, when extractive industries like gold and timber, together with public works such as the Main

Trunk railway line, staged progressive colonisation's last stand. Their demise brought down crime rates for assault and drunkenness, and combined with the decline of transience in general to make society more stable and orderly. This merged nicely with the Great Tightening, which in turn did its bit in helping mop up the vestiges of the crews. The classic exit route for crews was emigration, and many took this path in the 1880s and 1890s. Others died, married and settled down, or retired into poverty in rural shacks or in the boarding-house quarters of the cities. The arbitration system and scientific management made employers more reluctant to hire the old, and indigent ex-crew became a target of moral evangelism from the late 1890s. The last survivors hung on to the 1920s. The 1898 Pensions Act, aimed by Seddon at his old miner constituents, was some help, but you had to be deserving as well as poor and old. Your pension could be stopped if you were seen in a pub, which the police were expected to patrol for drinking pensioners. Crewmen could manage being poor and old, but they had problems with being deserving. The proportion of those eligible by age and residence receiving old age pensions was only 27 per cent in 1903–04.[88]

Some aged crewmen were swept up into institutions. Public hospitals, especially in crew districts, had long doubled as old men's homes. Private charities preferred genteel widows to elderly male 'reprobates', and the aged, ill, and sometimes mutinous crewmen were left to the public system. The unpleasantness of these institutions can be exaggerated; at least one retired loner, James Cox, found his the most secure, comfortable and sociable environment of his life.[89] But they were grim and strictly regimented, and many old men got out when they could, and rebelled when they could not. Drink, violence and 'obscene exposure to a nurse' by old male inmates were problems in the Otago Benevolent Institution until the 1920s. One man was 'charged with stating that he had beaten the authorities for years and would do no work for them'. In 1909, William Garrick successfully sued the asylum's manager for forcing him to take a weekly bath. The crisis elicited this telegram to the Inspector-General of Hospitals, an epigraph for centralised bureaucracy: 'William Garrick declines to take a bath. What shall we do?'[90]

Outside public institutions, other ageing crewmen eked out their lonely lives, and sometimes ended them, in shacks or boarding houses. Between 1895 and 1904, they were the main contributors to a peak in the Auckland suicide rate. They would have echoed the sentiments of an old crewman's suicide note in 1922: 'No work, No friends, No money, Nowhere to go.'[91] The old boarding-house districts, haunts of single old men, still survived in the cities. They are sad places. Instead of fatally impacting on Maori, the heirs of the rowdy, robust agents of vice became extinct themselves. By definition, they had no biological heirs, though they did leave cultural legacies. Like

men, crew women emigrated, died, married or hung on. 'In most cities there
. . . appears to have been a small body of elderly vagrant women, hard core
inebriates and suspected promulgators of syphilis and gonorrhea.'[92] But by
the 1920s the taming of the crew was largely complete.

Decent working men in general were also targets of moral evangelism –
targets that it hoped to convert and improve rather than eliminate or isolate.
Working men were encouraged to improve themselves and be improved, and
they benefited from health reforms and pensions. Socialist, syndicalist and
militant unionist organisations sometimes formed alliances with aspects of
moral evangelism, but these normally proved temporary. The socialist Ettie
Rout led possibly the most successful of all campaigns against venereal disease,
but this met with the disapproval of feminists, moralists and racialists alike.[93]
Her advocacy of contraception and sexual knowledge was thought to make
woman a 'mere sexual convenience', save men from the consequences of sin,
and discourage breeding. The condom was seen as a dangerously effective
instrument of race suicide, the racial equivalent of a razor blade and a warm
bath. With all due respect to the sobriety of the left, some alliances between
socialism and moralism foundered on the issue of drink. Outside the left,
the upper rungs of decency were especially vulnerable to moral evangelism.
Skilled craftsmen – masters and journeymen – formed a cusp between decent
and respectable, as we have seen. Dissenting religion was strong among them;
their moderate unions sometimes functioned as moralist organisations as
well as Friendly Societies; and official Friendly Societies often also had a
moralist role. On the other hand, many respectables retained strong elements
of working-class culture, sharing the populist response to moral evangelism.

This populist response was mixed: it involved accepting, adapting and
even exaggerating some aspects of moral harmony and rejecting and
subverting others. Gambling declined in some forms but grew in others,
attaining a degree of respectability on the race course. The male masses kept
drinking despite moral evangelism. They drank unrespectable amounts in a
respectable way – in private, at home, but in bulk, leading to the rise of the
flagon, the half-gallon jar. Alternatively, they drank respectable amounts in
an unrespectable way: seven-ounce glasses of beer were the delicate little
vehicles of the six o' clock swill, downed fast and frequently in public bars
with décors notoriously reminiscent of inverted urinals. Mechanics' institutes,
followed by working men's clubs, originated as agents of the mid-nineteenth-
century forebears of moral evangelism, intended to fill the spare hours of
self-improving workmen with useful leisure, or at least harmless pleasures,
such as listening to or reading moralising sermons, or playing draughts and
reading newspapers. Generally speaking, these institutions experienced one
of three fates: they collapsed; were taken over by the respectable and kept

their refined curriculum, but lost their decent pupils; or they became camouflaged beer houses and lost their curriculum, but kept their pupils. In small communities such as Oxford between the wars they contrived to do both. The town's two pubs, which did booming business before World War One, teetered towards disrepute and bankruptcy, and public opinion formally favoured prohibition. The Oxford Working Men's Club, founded in 1887, lent books and encouraged self-improvement, but drew two-thirds of its income from bar sales and was the watering hole of 70 per cent of the town's menfolk.[94] It was a place of compromise between middle and working class, and between moralism and populism. Its leaders might have frowned down on *Truth*, the tabloid organ of New Zealand populism, but the two institutions had characteristics in common.

Truth found its way to New Zealand in 1906. It had been founded in Australia by John Norton, who was said to have coined the term 'wowser' and to have described Queen Victoria as 'flabby, fat, and flatulent'.[95] *New Zealand Truth* soon established its own strident tone and was run by self-proclaimed 'crusaders for the ordinary New Zealander, the common man'. It was intensely populist, repeatedly advocating politics that 'transcended sectional interests in the interest of the whole nation, the people' – 'the best interests of the people as a whole ... mutual co-operation and equal opportunity for all'. This might have been Seddon speaking, and *Truth* backed the remnants of the Liberals until the 1930s, against 'extremists' of right and left such as Reform and Labour. Like Seddon, it was a good public opinion survey, at least of a central core of populist, decent males. The rest of the press sneered at it; libraries and reading rooms did not subscribe to it, but it adapted to its mainly decent readers' prejudices – sometimes slowly but often fast. It was the nearest thing New Zealand had to a national newspaper, and by 1928 it was selling almost 100,000 copies a week. It was no perfect mirror, but it is to *Truth*, rather than the official pronouncements, the dailies or the small left-wing journals, that we should look for evidence of working-class attitudes, subtracting for a lurid lens.

It can be argued that *Truth* was the down-market face of the moral evangelism and the other harmonies. 'Above all else *Truth* allowed no deviation from the established laws and mores. It was a force for conformity and those it identified as non-conformists were to be persecuted.'[96] This is at least partly correct. The paper attacked inner-city slums as breeding grounds of 'depravity, crime, and all manner of vices', and advocated health, housing and sanitary reform. It trumpeted moral panic about venereal disease and eugenic fears with the best, arguing that 'New Zealand Must Be Cleaned' and explaining 'How We Breed Degenerates'. It persecuted adulterers, rapists, child-abusers, prostitutes, transvestites and 'nymphomaniacs'. It was very hostile to drunken driving, advocating harsh penalties for it; and fomented a moral panic about drugs in the 1920s, which encouraged the banning of cocaine and other drugs in 1927. It also hated jazz, a 'corrupting influence', the music of 'noisome and noxious niggers', but was less antagonistic to dancing than was the feminist and moralist *White Ribbon*. Like the formal ideology of the genteel and respectable, it was also militarist and imperialist, but not always Anglophile; racialist, but not anti-Maori.

Yet it seems to me to be a mistake to see *Truth*, and the populist culture of which it was a distorted reflection, as accepting the whole of 'established laws and mores' and formal conformism. Its journalists haunted the criminal and divorce courts with a prurient as well as puritan agenda: 'While she believed he was at the cheese factory making cheese . . . he was extolling the scenery at Mount Egmont to another young lady'; 'Faithless Wife Confessed, and Made Startling Allegations Against Husband and Colored Woman'; 'Nude Revellers in Midnight Bacchanalian Orgy'. *Truth* exposed frauds as well as scandals, and both attacked and advertised quack cures. It attacked 'slumlords' as well as slums, monopolies as well as Marxists. It 'repeatedly told its predominantly working-class readership that wowsers were the enemy of the "people"'. Apart from drink, it defended other decent amusements such as the cinema – it sometimes opposed censorship – and gambling, along with the sports associated with it – boxing, billiards and especially horse-racing, for which it was the chief source of tips. It backed the 40-hour week, and opposed beauty shows, which it said 'reduced the nation's girlhood to the level of prize cattle'. It policed the police for corruption and excessive harshness, and sometimes showed sympathy for crimes of poverty.

Both *Truth* and the culture it symbolised 'believed in publicity and humiliation as deterrent and punishment'. Despite many libel actions, it persisted in naming names and personally exposing sinners and deviants. But its definitions of sin and deviation converged with those of moral evangelism only about half the time, as did its type of sanction. *Truth* and its ilk seem to me to be a modern form of charivari – the ancient folk practice of publicly humiliating those who transgress, through a ritual group display of cacophonous noise, such as 'tin-canning' and impromptu theatre. Its sensationalism and persecutions were more village-oriented than those of modern tabloids – more concerned with misdeeds among the neighbours than among the great. Its norms were not those of formal ideology, but of populism, which was both ally and enemy of the moralising crusade. Yet its methods, the national application of informal community sanctions, were further evidence of a tightening, but not fully tight, society.

The Mothers' Mutiny and Other Rebellions

The Great Tightening was never wholly successful. We will see in Chapter Twelve that it took a long time to tame wild colonial children, and there were many other low-key mini-mutinies. The tight liquor laws were regularly subverted by illegal distilling, notably the Deep South's 'Hokonui hooch', illicit bars and the late-night closing of regular pubs. The last was particularly prevalent in Westland, stronghold of the working class. Here, six o'clock closing was a standing joke – publicans allegedly had an informal arrangement with the police to take it in turns once a year to be arrested for late closing. Illegal gambling was widespread, notably in the form of bookmaking – off-course betting on race horses, which became illegal in 1911. Juries were reluctant to convict 'bookies' – a good example of a legal crime not being considered a social crime.[97] Some mothers took their Truby King doctrine with a dose of salts. Forbidden dummies were found hidden in cots. One mother, assuring the Plunket nurse that breast milk was all that baby consumed, was undone by an older child announcing, 'He does have potatoes and gravy sometimes.' One low-key rebellion occurred in the choice of reading matter. Hundreds of communities (at least 361 in 1887) ran public libraries, largely for the edification of the working class. Collections consisted mainly of uplifting works of non-fiction, but borrowers generally declined to uplift them. Some 86 per cent of issues (in marked contrast to holdings) were fiction at Auckland and Wellington public libraries in the 1890s.[98] But of all the mutinies against moral evangelism, that of mothers was the most extraordinary.

   The drive to control and discipline motherhood, and to discourage illicit motherhood, was also a drive to encourage legitimate maternity. Many feminists supported this drive, and historians believe that most women accepted it. 'Feminists never denied the centrality of motherhood to women.'[99] Many women believed the 'populate or perish' ideology.[100] 'I am certain that the rhetoric of nurturant motherhood was not used expediently by these women. The ideology had been internalized.'[101] From every side, for their own self-fulfilment and for the sake of society and the race, 'fit' married women were urged to breed. But they did not. Between 1881 and 1926, the rate of child-bearing among women aged fifteen to forty-five years more than halved, and it remained low to the late 1940s. The steepest decline came between 1881 and 1896, when the rate fell 40 per cent, compared with 7 per cent over the next fifteen years, 1896–1911, and a further 22 per cent over the fifteen years after that.[102] 'From 1876 to 1901 the Pakeha population went through a remarkable fertility decline, from an estimated total fertility rate of 7.0 live births to only 3.5.'[103]

This Great Mothers' Mutiny was again an international trend, but New Zealand led the pack. The 1893 *Yearbook* noted with concern that the birth rate had been the highest in Australasia in 1880, but was lowest by 1892, when it was also lower than that of England, Wales and Scotland.[104] It has been suggested that the Pakeha baby bust was the world's most rapid.[105] In Britain, the genteel and respectable slowed their breeding earlier than others – perhaps as early as mid-century. The lower classes experienced their big drop much later, between 1901 and 1931.[106] In New Zealand, the higher classes may have slowed later than Britain, but the lower clearly slowed much earlier. There were substantial class, regional and rural–urban differences, but birth rates in all classes and most regions dropped quickly and steeply.[107]

This demographic revolution had all sorts of implications. High birth rates, like high immigration rates, encouraged belief in a Greater British future; low rates helped the shift to Better Britain – preferring quality to quantity made a virtue of necessity. The spread of eugenic fears was a reaction to the baby bust, a womb-led ideology. Pre-bust children had twice the siblings and half the potential parental attention of post-bust children, with substantial effects on the nature of childhood. Post-bust mothers spent half the time attached to a foetus or dependent infant, a change arguably more important than the vote. Yet the Great Mothers' Mutiny has received remarkably little attention from historians of New Zealand women.

Working out just how and why this massive baby bust came about is not easy. The evidence seems incomplete and confusing, and one must resort to analogies with overseas research. New Zealand demographers attribute about two-thirds of the decline to 'shifts in patterns of nuptiality' – less and later marriage. I doubt that later marriage was crucial. The 1880s rise in marriage ages was not great – not nearly enough to explain a 40 per cent drop in birth rates. Average ages at marriage actually declined between 1890 and 1930, and the average ages of new mothers stayed static or declined slightly from 1913, and probably before.[108] Less marriage was an important factor. The number of adult males 'never married' at census time stayed fairly static between 1881 and 1911, at a high 40–43 per cent – the crewmen and unskilled workers that nobody wanted. But the proportion of women 'never married' rocketed from 15 per cent in 1881, to 22 per cent in 1891, to 28 per cent in 1901, and remained at about that level to 1911.[109]

An equally important factor, perhaps, was a tendency to stop breeding earlier in married life. A statistical analysis of birth rates by age cohort shows that, between 1912 and 1935, the fertility of older mothers declined very much more than that of younger mothers.[110] The same may hold true for the earlier period. British research discounts rising ages at marriage, and sees stopping breeding earlier as the main cause of the baby bust.[111] I think this, coupled with a trend towards less marriage, was also the case in New Zealand. But the bust came earlier and stronger to the mass of the population in South Britain than in North.

Contraception was probably not the main mechanism of birth control. The invention of vulcanised rubber was improving such contraceptives as the sheath in the later nineteenth century; they had previously been made from animal intestines and were known in England as 'French letters' and in France as 'English overcoats'. They were available in New Zealand by the 1900s at the latest. In 1907, the Chief Health Officer was able to buy a dozen different types, no doubt as part of his official duties. But they were not yet very widely or easily available, and they were not reliable or cheap. (As late as the 1930s, condoms cost a shilling each, with a 'washable' variety at seven shillings and sixpence.) Much the same could be said of the pessaries, intra-uterine devices and abortifacients also in use, even though 'Dr Hall's Capsules' for 'restoring menstrual flow' came in extra-strength versions for 'chronic and obstinate cases'.[112] The ancient rhythm method was no good either, because both folk medicine and the few professional medics who would advise on such things had got the rhythm wrong.

Coitus interruptus was probably important, in the tradition of Margot Asquith. 'Henry always withdrew in time, such a noble man.'[113] But noble or not, he failed to pull out fast enough and withdrawal was not reliable: Margot had five children, three of them still-born. Abstinence later in marriage seems a stronger possibility. It was the only socially approved method, and, perhaps more importantly, it was the easiest, cheapest, safest and most reliable. There was no great difference between the decline in Protestant and Catholic birth rates in New Zealand, despite the strong strictures against contraception among the latter.[114] An important effect of the rise of effective contraception later in the century may have been the restoration of sex to late marriage. Abstinence with occasional lapses might have been backed up by coitus interruptus, with this in turn backstopped by abortion. The New Zealand evidence suggests that married women, rather than unmarried ones, were the main users of abortion, and that it was quite common – one 1916 estimate suggested a fifth of all pregnancies were aborted.[115] Abortion by do-it-yourself methods, by dubious abortifacients or by quack practitioners could be dangerous, and New Zealand had an internationally high death rate from septic abortion in 1932, and perhaps before. Most of the victims were married. But there were also reliable practitioners, male and female. Popular attitudes to such people were far less condemnatory than the law or official norms. It was difficult to get juries to convict abortionists, just as with bookmakers.

Unmarried women had different strategies. The social stigma against unmarried motherhood was extremely strong, more so than ever under moral evangelism. Some women rejected it, kept their babies and so accepted disrepute unless they could convincingly invent an absent husband. Most bowed to it. Some gave their children up to grim orphanages or to familial or stranger adoption. The pressure to take the last option intensified as the twentieth century unfolded. Others used socially disapproved means to evade social disapproval. Desperate young pregnant women who could not or would not marry committed suicide, procured abortions or participated in a widespread form of covert semi-infanticide. Unmarried parents did not often kill their children, but they quite often allowed them to die. Illegitimate babies were two and a half times as prone to die in infancy as legitimate ones,[116] and the process was sometimes helped along in the childcare institutions known as 'baby farms'.

The most notorious baby farmer was Williamina 'Minnie' Dean of Southland. Between 1889 and 1895, 26 children 'passed through her hands', of whom at least six died. Three were found buried in the garden of her home, The Larches, in Winton, Southland. It was said that she had concealed another corpse in a hatbox. On 12 August 1895, Minnie Dean became the only woman to be hanged for murder in New Zealand history. Dean entered Pakeha folklore as a witchlike figure. Children chanted, 'Minnie Dean will get you'; parents told troublesome kids to behave, or they would be given to Minnie Dean. It was said that no flowers would grow on her grave. A type of hatbox became known as a 'Minnie Dean', and quickly went out of fashion. Decades after her death, Southlanders would pull out a type of wildflower associated with her if it appeared in their gardens.[117]

Dean was in fact a scapegoat for a quite widespread practice that even informal populist culture was reluctant to confess to. Her death rate – six out of 26 – was probably not untypical. A few other cases of baby farming are known, ranging from one in Mount Eden, Auckland, in 1881, to another in 1923, when four infant skeletons were dug up in a back garden in Newlands, Wellington.[118] The most telling evidence of prevalence is the illegitimate-infant death rate, so much higher than the legitimate. Mothers of illegitimate children faced social ostracism, and £10 or £20 to someone like Minnie Dean could solve the problem. It was quietly accepted that the child's chances of survival were not good. 'It is perfectly well understood that the sooner the child dies the better pleased all concerned will be.'[119] Unmarried mothers were clearly victims of this process, and fathers were irritatingly likely to escape scot-free, but the worst victims were obviously the infants. If we want to uncover the hidden successes of populism, of the mass of the people in resisting the evangelisms of right and left and exerting some control over their own lives, we have to take the bad with the good.

Why did New Zealand's birth rate drop so dramatically? One factor was probably the decline in infant mortality. Deaths of legitimate children under one year old fluctuated with epidemics and the like, but the long-term trend was downward from the 1880s.[120] The decline was slower than the decline in birth rates, but it may have had a significant psychological impact. Children ceased to be 'little angels only lent', and families no longer needed spares to guard against the Grim Reaper. Urbanisation, the displacement of family economies with male breadwinners, and the spread of education are also said to have played a role. More education and a decline in the importance of children's work were interlocked. Children continued to engage in paid and unpaid work despite 'compulsory' education – labouring before and after school, attending irregularly, or not attending at all in peak working seasons. But they did so progressively less as attendance regulations and legislation limiting the employment of children tightened.[121] Labour-saving technology may have reduced the need for children's work. It has been suggested that dairy-farming areas kept breeding against national trends until the advent of the milking machine in the 1890s, when they suddenly slowed. Like the state, large families helped set up the dairy farmers and were then unceremoniously dumped.[122] For the genteel and respectable, the high costs of educating their children in secondary schools may have discouraged large families, as in Britain. There were also hidden costs even in 'free' schooling – lunches, slates, donations, transport, clothing that did not bring disrepute on parents. More schooling and less work therefore made children more expensive and dependent, which was an incentive to have fewer of them.

Marriage, household and family formation had long been associated with economic prosperity and confidence. The Long Stagnation in and around the 1880s was obviously a factor in beginning or greatly accelerating the decline in birth rates, or at least in spreading it across classes. New Zealand's unusually prompt and massive demographic response to 'depression' could be explained by the trauma of futures lost. People's expectations had further to fall than in some other places, and a loss of faith in collective progress could have been coupled with less confidence in individual progress, with corresponding caution about large families. But the trauma was just as great in other neo-Britains such as Victoria, while the breeding reaction, apparently, was not. Moreover, we have seen that stagnation in the period 1886–96 saw an increase in access to farms – individual progress collapsed less completely than collective progress. Above all, the long-term correlation between economic boom and bust and baby boom and bust is not very strong. The decline in birth rates was even steeper in the early 1880s, when stagnation covered only part of the country, than in the late 1880s, when it covered the whole of it, and the decline steepened again in 1891–96, when there were some signs of recovery. Generally, economic recovery did not lead to reproductive recovery. Birth rates were briefly boosted a little in the early 1900s, but there was another steep decline from 1906, which hard economic times cannot explain.

Who made the decision to control family size? It is tempting to stress the male role, or shared decisions, in reaction to the dubious belief that birth control is the woman's business. It has been suggested that, among the higher classes in Britain, the decision to restrict breeding was male-led. Pater received the bill from Eton for Number One Son, looked at the prospective family budget over the next few years, and washed out the condom or moved into the spare bedroom. But an alternative form of controlling schooling costs was by not educating girls, and as we have seen, New Zealand families rejected this. No doubt some decisions were male-led, and more were shared. Yet women had the most powerful motives for controlling their own fertility. 'What is the life of the average middle class New Zealand woman worth . . . spent as it is in a daily round of drudgery . . . How . . . can she be expected to look forward with anything but dread to the prospect of another child?'[123] The evidence is particularly sparse in this area, but my guess is that the fall in birth rates was women-led, that it was intended by women to improve their own quality of life as well as that of the children they did have, and that this was an expression of *populist* feminism, the Great Mothers' Mutiny.

The Mothers' Mutiny, 1880s–1930s, is an unsung heroine of New Zealand women's history, and it was not the only one. Several developments suggest that lower-class women, as well as their higher-class sisters, took advantage of the changing circumstances to improve their lot. Working women seem to have engaged eagerly with suffrage, despite the complete absence of a tradition of public politics. An impressive 78 per cent of eligible women registered for the vote in 1893, despite having only six weeks to do so. Some 83 per cent of these actually voted, compared to 75 per cent of all registered voters, indicating that the women's turnout was far better than men's.[124] Moral evangelists and formal feminists would have approved of this, but they would not have approved of other developments, in work, education and sex, any more than they would have approved of the mothers' mutiny.

As we saw in the last chapter, the amount and quality of women's waged work improved substantially between 1881 and 1911 – shifting away from undesirable domestic service and towards desirable office work. Official norms, moral evangelism and sometimes even formal feminism did not approve of these developments, but they happened anyway. A powerful drive to train girls to be girls, to give them a different school curriculum that emphasised domestic skills such as cooking and sewing was also resisted. Truby King and other moral evangelists preached long and hard about the 'evils of cram', about the malign effect of intensive academic education for girls, which they believed ruined them as wives and mothers. They were horrified by a survey in 1915 that found that girls were the highest academic achievers in nineteen schools out of 22. They convinced the state, and domestic sciences permeated school and even university curricula from the 1900s. Domestic education was 'imposed on the schools by the [Education] Department'. But girls and their parents preferred academic and commercial courses that might equip the former for preferred jobs. Domestic courses 'consistently lacked popularity'[125] and had 'an unhappy and unpopular career'. By 1939, the proportion of girls studying 'Home Life' in Auckland secondary schools was only 1 per cent, while 18 per cent did commerce and 45 per cent academic subjects.[126] Market pressure for commercial courses was substantial from the 1900s. It led to the establishment of private commercial colleges, and so forced schools to offer such courses themselves.[127]

Girls embraced evil 'cram' as eagerly as they rejected noble mass motherhood. A more ambiguous development – or perhaps continuity – was the surprising prevalence of a form of premarital sex. Some statistics suggest that, in 1913, about one-third of legitimate first births of women under the age of 30 (the great majority of brides) took place within seven months of marriage.[128] Taking account of illegitimate births and abortions, contraception and the fact that even without contraception not all sexual intercourse results in conception, it may be that a narrow majority of New Zealand women in 1913 engaged in premarital sex. In most cases, they did so with husbands-to-be, and there must have been an unspoken tolerance of this by the community. This suggests a folk custom of trial marriage or 'proto-marital sex', rather than widespread promiscuity. But it still jars strikingly with our preconceptions about chaste grandmothers, and with the dictates of moral evangelism. The Mothers' Mutiny, the entry into uncovenanted work, the rejection of domestic education, and the practice of proto-marital sex all suggest a populist feminism that clashed much more with moral evangelism than did formal feminism. They also suggest that too great a focus on élites is a problem in New Zealand women's history as well as men's history. Populism is the dog that does not bark in the conventional versions of both histories.

The twenty years around 1900 was a period of improvement in the lot of many New Zealand women, of which the vote was only the tip of the iceberg. As in the colonial era, women took advantage of contextual change to ease or partially subvert some of the restrictions placed on them. As in the colonial era, however, this loosening of bonds was followed by some 're-leashing' – 'male backlash' may be too strong a term for an amorphous reflex. Formal feminism lost impetus from the mid-1900s, in the opinion of some of its own leaders. The National Council of Women 'went into recess in 1905 and active feminism disappeared for some years'.[129] Middle-class women did not share in the modest expansion of university education after 1918. Women were 35 per cent of graduates from Canterbury University from its foundation in 1873 to 1914; 25 per cent between 1959 and 1975.[130]

As for lower-class women, their participation in the workforce ceased to grow from World War One. Neither the self-aware working class nor the arbitration system were of much use to women workers. The former was deeply masculist – indeed, the entry of women into work in the 1880s–1900s may have been a factor in its emergence, as we saw in the last chapter. From the late 1900s, the arbitration system developed the concept of the family wage, which tended to marginalise female employment. It can be seen as an aspect of the 'cult of domesticity', which contributed to some successful 'domestication' of both men and women. The concept of the 'family man' increasingly contested that of the 'man's man' – Kiwi bloke and his mates.[131] The number of married women in waged work decreased substantially. I suspect a key agent of the re-leashing process was World War One. It was men who made the ultimate sacrifice and, in doing so, reasserted masculine dominance. In the crudest sense, the war eliminated the oversupply of men and produced the part-tragic, part-heroic Maiden Aunt – women who never married, in some cases because their husbands-to-be had died on the Western Front. Less crudely, the 18,000 Christs of dominionism were all male, and New Zealand society, including women, conceded that it owed a debt to them and their surviving brothers. If World War One did not exist, New Zealand masculism may have had to invent it. Populist feminism did not conquer moral evangelism, but it did force some compromise on it, notably families of half the size the cult wanted them to be. Some of its gains and those of formal feminism were reined in between the wars, but not all. This was an old story in women's history – three steps forward, two steps back.

CHAPTER SIX

Racial Harmony (1): Merging Maori?

Recolonial New Zealand claimed the strongest of all possible ties to its British partner: blood. The blood was not only that spilled by New Zealand soldiers in Britain's battles, but also that of kith and kin, the whole New Zealand people, the Britons of the South. British and New Zealanders were the same race. In New Zealand official statistics, 'foreigners' did not include fellow Britons from however far away, even if they had arrived yesterday, as long as they were white. When combined with the Great Tightening, which emphasised conformity above all, the racial imperative broadened to include homogeneity as well as Britishness. The slogan, repeated ad nauseam in official and unofficial texts, was that New Zealand was '98.5 per cent British' – the 0.5 per cent was there because Australia claimed to be '98 per cent British'. These racial imperatives were important to New Zealand. It met recolonial needs for collective identity and the security of sameness. It made the British Empire ours, too. It meant that, if asked why it should have privileged access to Old British produce, job and credit markets, New Zealand could answer: kinship, blood, race.

These recolonial racial imperatives faced problems, however, of which the most obvious was Maori. They were never less than 5 per cent of the population, even at their demographic nadir around 1900. One way of dealing with this, discussed below, was the remarkable process of 'whitening' Maori, of reinventing them into a European-descended race of honorary whites. When Maori ethnic difference was conceded, it was handled in one of several other ways. Early in the twentieth century, it could still be dismissed as a transitory difference, a blip in racial homogeneity, because many believed Maori to be dying out. When they declined to die physically, Pakeha believed that they were rapidly dying out culturally: becoming Brown Britons through intermarriage, individualisation, modernisation and assimilation. Dying or not, Maori were thought to have an exceptionally benign relationship with their neo-Europeans, so much better than that of Australia, South Africa and the United States. To the extent that Maori–Pakeha racial difference existed,

New Zealand was a paradise of racial harmony. A racial utopia joined the socially and morally harmonious 'tight society', the virtuous social laboratory and the classless exemplary paradise.

The enduring myth of exceptionally benign Maori–Pakeha relations, of New Zealand as a paradise of racial harmony, is an easy target for historians. New Zealand race relations in the twentieth century *were* better than those of South Africa or the United States, but better is not great. The fact that New Zealand is larger than Liechtenstein does not make it big. Maori entered the century at the nadir of their demographic fortunes, and massive problems persisted. On almost every demographic, social and economic criterion Maori were – and often still are – disadvantaged in comparison to Pakeha. Their political influence was limited and fragile, their protests often ignored. They were subjected to an official policy of assimilation, which proclaimed them to be 'better blacks', but was explicitly intended to reduce them to a 'golden tinge' on the faces of New Zealanders. In the words of William Herries, Minister of Native Affairs between 1912 and 1921: 'I look forward for the next hundred years or so, to a time when we shall have no Maoris at all, but a white race with a slight dash of the finest coloured race in the world.'[1] Unofficially, Maori were often subjected to low-profile but widespread forms of Pakeha discrimination and prejudice at least until the 1960s. 'Maori bugs' were evil-smelling insects; 'Maori time' was being unpunctual. Unflattering stereotypes of Maori featured quite large in Pakeha popular culture, as patronising jokes and as lessons in what not to be.[2] Yet despite all this prejudice and disadvantage, there is a stubborn kernel of truth in the myth of relatively good Maori–Pakeha relations.

In 1959, a man named Harry Bennett was refused service in an Auckland lounge bar on the grounds that he was Maori, and it was found that such petty discrimination was quite widespread. A survey of hotels in 1958 indicated that one-quarter refused to accept a booking by letter when a Maori name was supplied. It was a 'common practice' for advertisements for rental housing to say 'Europeans only'. In Pukekohe, the little South Auckland town that for some reason was the capital of New Zealand racism, Maori were discriminated against not only at pubs but also at the cinemas, at barbers' shops and at the public swimming baths. Their neighbourhood was known as 'the reservation', and a separate school for them had been established in 1952 after protests by Pakeha parents about Maori children mixing with their own. This symbolises the bad news about Maori–Pakeha relations in recolonial New Zealand.[3]

Yet Dr Bennett was senior medical officer at his local public hospital. His brother was New Zealand High Commissioner in Malaysia, and his father was an Anglican bishop. Seven of his brothers had been commissioned officers in World War Two.[4] His failure to get a drink caused a public storm. It was denounced by the Prime Minister and by the hotel chain concerned. Anti-discriminatory legislation was tightened in consequence. All this is quite hard to imagine in the South Africa, Australia or United States of 1959. Maori had been accorded political rights and theoretical equality before the law since 1840. They had had four seats in the New Zealand Parliament since 1867 – a hundred years before Australian Aboriginals became full citizens. All Cabinets had Maori ministers between 1892 and 1934, and a Maori was Acting Prime Minister in 1909 – try that on for size in the other settler societies at the time. Maori were members of national sports teams from the time such things first emerged in the 1880s, and graduated from universities from the 1890s. Between the 1930s and the 1960s, Maori disadvantages in health, income and housing diminished substantially, with significant state help. Maori motifs were central, even dominant, in the symbolic representation of New Zealand. In the view of a recent Canadian study: 'From 1840 to 1960 Maori had not been subject to the oppressive family and child welfare measures that were used as part of the policies of assimilation in Australia and Canada.' 'In both Australia and Canada, the approach to establishing aboriginal status was much more rigid and harsh than was the case in New Zealand.'[5] There was good news, as well as bad news, about Maori–Pakeha relations in the first half of the twentieth century. We need to explain both.

The Race That Would Not Die

As the twentieth century opened, most Pakeha and some Maori believed that the Maori people were destined for extinction. At best, they were thought to face complete assimilation, becoming nothing more than that exotic 'golden tinge' in the blood of their conquerors. Though the 'fatal impact' of Europe on Maori during the nineteenth century has been exaggerated, the stresses of contact did halve Maori numbers during the century – to 45,000 in 1901, including 'half-castes living as Europeans'. Moreover, Maori had been swamped and marginalised by a rising tide of Pakeha. They were a small minority of 5 per cent in their own country. They had lost most of their best land, together with their powers of effective resistance and, therefore, of valued co-operation. Islands of political independence remained as late as 1916 in remote regions, but they were shrinking, and by 1900 most Maori were to some extent subject to the Pakeha state.

Socially, economically and culturally, however, most Maori remained semi-autonomous. Predominantly rural, they were isolated from, and marginal to, the urbanising Pakeha socio-economy. As late as 1937, it was possible to claim that 'the average New Zealander rarely sees a Maori'.[6] A few

Maori groups had managed to plug into new industries. Te Arawa had a sporadically profitable, if ambiguous, role in Rotorua tourism. Ngati Porou engaged substantially in sheep and dairy farming. But isolation, poor land and the lack of credit for the necessary new technology meant this was not an option for most. Maori access to the pension schemes of the Liberal government existed but was restricted and contested, and the schemes were miserly anyway.[7] Maori communities survived through a mix of activities: subsistence agriculture supplemented by gathering, hunting and fishing; and casual or seasonal work of various kinds. In the 1900s, this was quite abundant, owing to the last spasm of progressive colonisation. Maori took temporary waged work on public and private development schemes. They were heavily involved in the kauri-gum industry and in the logging of the last forests of high-value kauri timber. Maori in areas such as the Kaipara and the Hokianga worked as lumbermen and in timber mills, and received royalties for logging rights to their land. But as gum prices dropped, prime native timber ran out and public works diminished after about 1910, Maori were increasingly reliant on spasms of casual wage work for cash. When all went well, this disparate package of activities was sufficient to live simply, but Maori domestic economies were particularly vulnerable to recession and illness.

Continued land loss added to the problems. Under heavy government and economic pressure, the 1890s and 1910s saw spasms of land selling that reduced Maori landholdings from 11 million acres in 1891 to 4.8 million acres in 1920, almost all of it in the North Island.[8] This was still one-sixth of the North Island, but much of the land was remote rough country, and some of the best was leased to Pakeha at token rentals. Of the good land that remained in Maori hands, much was underdeveloped, but could not be improved without credit, which Pakeha banks would not provide. The Pakeha state, moreover, had imposed a system of tenure that divided land into units that were difficult to farm economically. Pakeha stereotypes of 'lazy Maori' were boosted by the sight – and alleged sight – of Maori-owned land lying idle. Where this did exist, it lay idle because of fragmented tenure and lack of credit – a sorry set of vicious circles. From 1920, with barely 5 million acres of Maori land left, much of it marginal, the bureaucrats of the Native Department at last developed doubts about the purchase of Maori land. 'Seeing that the Europeans have acquired about 62,000,000 acres of Native land, it might not be thought unreasonable to allow the Native owners to retain the small area remaining to them.'[9] Land selling tailed away, but the damage had been done.

Maori participation in World War One was substantial and significant, for reasons we will come to, but was proportionally lower that that of Pakeha. The cost in casualties was consequently lower as well, and was restricted mainly to tribes that had fought for the British in the wars of the 1860s, such as Ngati Porou and Te Arawa. About 2,200 Maori fought; 336 were killed and 734 wounded, a similar casualty rate to that of Pakeha.[10] The 1918 influenza epidemic, on the other hand, was particularly severe on Maori. The official death toll was 1,130, but many deaths went unregistered and the full toll is estimated at 2,160 – seven times the Pakeha death rate. Impact varied regionally: Thames and South Taranaki had twice the average of Maori deaths; Hawke's Bay and Rangitikei had half; and the East Cape was almost unscathed.[11] Patterns of contact influenced the number who caught the disease. The Urewera was preserved by a local constable who forbade travel for several weeks – the first favour the police had done Tuhoe for a very long time.[12] Patterns of response influenced the number who died. At Arahura, in Westland, where Emma Tainui organised effective nursing, there were many sufferers but no deaths.

There was not a lot Maori could do about the underlying causes of their high infection and death rates, however.[13] The lower immunity of isolated rural communities to influenza-type infections was one factor, and poor housing is also frequently cited. I myself suspect that inadequate nutrition was important. Reserves of food and access to shops were limited, and sub-sistence economics meant that you obtained your daily food by doing daily tasks. When a whole community was down with the flu, daily tasks did not get done. Even funeral rites, so central in Maori culture, were scamped in the darkest days of the pandemic. 'I used to look out the window and they would be pulling the bodies up the hill,' remembered one Hokianga Maori. 'There were no coffins, no tangis, no funerals. They were just wrapped up, hauled up the hill and put in a hole. We didn't even mourn them then. We just said things like, "Oh, our Joey's gone."'[14]

The influenza pandemic of 1918 seared itself into Maori memories. It was described as 'the severest set back the race has received since the fighting days of Hongi Hika'.[15] This is understandable, but not true. Pandemics in the high phase of Maori population decline, 1850s–70s, were more severe, and even in 1918 Western Samoans suffered much more than Maori. Moreover, the 1918 toll, terrible as it was, represented a blip against a trend, and the trend was Maori population growth. Influenza notwithstanding, the 'dying race' was striking back. The population increased slowly but steadily after the 1896 census and doubled over the next 40 years – to about 82,000 in the 1936 census.

The Maori recovery has been attributed to various initiatives in public health and health education, stemming either from the 'Young Maori' reform movement, discussed below, or from the Pakeha state. This is unlikely to be true, simply because the recovery seems to date from the 1890s, while Young

Maori and state initiatives dated from the 1900s. An alternative explanation is the maturing of a century-long process dating from the beginnings of mass contact with Europeans: the gradual development of immunity to some, though not all, infectious diseases. This was coupled with a steady growth in birth rates, dating from the mid-nineteenth century. The 1890s were the point where the two lines intersected. Death rates remained quite high – much higher than those of the Pakeha – but birth rates were now higher still. The various health initiatives beginning in the 1900s consolidated gains, and may have contributed to a later, even greater, decline in Maori mortality that began after 1940. This is discussed in Chapter Sixteen.

Defying a century of 'fatal impact' doomsaying, then, the 'dying race' got up from its deathbed and walked away. It did not walk aimlessly, head bowed, shoulders stooped, into an uncontestedly Pakeha new world. Maori responded to new circumstances in new ways, but along two main lines broadly similar to those of the later nineteenth century – 'disengagement' and 'engagement'. As in the previous century, disengagement involved a degree of self-segregation from Pakeha practices, if no longer so much from Pakeha people. Except in the Urewera mountains in 1916, when the prophet Rua Kenana's followers fought a gun battle with the police, it no longer involved armed resistance. But it did specialise in protest, notably a long succession of appeals to the Treaty of Waitangi and to the British Crown, which had signed it in 1840. The classic 'disengager' organisation was the King Movement.

'Engagement' no longer consisted in armed co-operation against fellow Maori, because there was no armed resistance. Instead, it embraced elements of the Pakeha system, economic, political and cultural, and sought to bend them from within in directions that favoured Maori. The Young Maori movement, led successively by James Carroll and Apirana Ngata, dominated the engagement strategy between the 1890s and the 1920s. From the 1920s, the old strategies of engagement and disengagement began to merge and blur. But both were aimed at advancement for Maori and at retaining Maori identity and cultural autonomy. Against the odds, each had some success.

Major centres of disengagement included parts of Northland, Parihaka in South Taranaki, and the Urewera mountains. Their demise as 'states within states' took place between 1898 and 1916, and is described in *Making Peoples*.[16] But these places and their associated religious movements remained foci of disengagement and cultural assertion after that. Rua Kenana remained active to his death in 1937, and branches of the Ringatu religion other than his also persisted.[17] Another staunch disengager was the King Movement, the great pan-tribal movement founded in 1858. In the 1860s, the movement, though centred on the Waikato region and the Tainui tribes, had influence countrywide. It narrowly lost the Waikato War against the British Empire in 1864, and survived as a diminished but independent state until the 1890s. The few Europeans in the King Country were told to obey Kingite laws as late as 1893, and the three volleys fired to celebrate the coronation of a new king the following year shows that the Kingitanga was still armed. After this, resources and independence diminished, and European settlement increased. The organisation came to be seen by outsiders as solely a Waikato or Tainui thing. Even among the core Kingite tribes – Ngati Maniapoto, Ngati Haua, and Waikato proper – there was dissension, a complex politics centred around attitudes to land selling and other forms of engagement with the Pakeha state.[18]

King Mahuta, who succeeded the great Tawhiao in 1894; King Te Rata, who reigned 1912–33; and King Koroki (1933–66) were all intelligent but somewhat diffident men, prone to stay out of the limelight and leave high-profile leadership to others. A key Kingite leader in the 1890s and 1900s was Henare Kaihau, the King Movement's first representative in the Pakeha parliament, where he served from 1896 to 1911. Massive, able, and charming, he was also described by Apirana Ngata as 'a crook'.[19] He persuaded King Mahuta to attempt a reconciliation with the Pakeha state, which involved the King holding a seat in the Legislative and Executive Councils in the 1900s. This proved to be 'a short-lived experiment in co-operation with Pakeha authority',[20] and Kaihau lost his influence when he lost £50,000 of the King Movement's money in failed investments. A second candidate for de facto leadership of the King Movement was the fiery Tupu Taingakawa of Ngati Haua, a son of Wiremu Tamehana, who inherited the title of Tumuaki, or Kingmaker. A leader of the Kingite Kahaunganui parliament, established in 1891, he opposed compromise with the state. In the 1900s, he effected a recon-ciliation with a revived version of the rival Maori parliament, Kotahitanga, and by 1910 was said to be acknowledged as leader of both. Taingakawa built up Rukumoana, in his own Ngati Haua territory, as a Kingite centre rivalling the King's Waahi. From 1912, however, he lost influence to the third and greatest Kingite leader: Te Puea Herangi.

Te Puea, a granddaughter of King Tawhaio, was born in 1883. She was an extraordinary woman of great charisma, generosity and determination, together with correspondingly robust vices. After a turbulent youth, during which she smoked, drank and 'had men for breakfast', she was returned to her vocation in 1911 by King Mahuta himself, who had to threaten suicide to persuade her to leave a Pakeha lover.[21] The young woman was already a significant leader by 1912, but really came into her own during the dark days of World War One. As we will see, some Maori enthusiastically backed participation in the war, intending to use it to help lever the state into measures favouring Maori. But for those in the King Movement, the scars of their own war were still too fresh and they were extremely reluctant to volunteer. As Rua Kenana and Pakeha conscientious objectors discovered to their cost, the Pakeha state at total war was particularly intolerant of dissent. When various attempts to persuade or pressure the Kingites failed, conscription was imposed on the Waikato – alone of all Maori. Quietly encouraged by their leaders, the young men refused to submit to it. Police visited Te Puea's marae in 1918. According to one historian, violence came close, but Te Puea ensured that resistance remained passive. Some 111 Waikato conscripts were imprisoned and harshly treated when they refused to serve. But none was sent overseas and all were released at the war's end without further penalty. This was seen as a victory by the King Movement, and was rightly attributed to Te Puea.[22] It was also she who held the people together and organised feeding and nursing during the influenza epidemic. She gathered together over a hundred children orphaned by the flu, who became her helpmeets in the projects of the future. These included the 'Te Puea Concert Party', which toured the country performing traditional songs and dances to raise funds. The funds were mostly spent on establishing a new marae, Turangawaewae, as an economic, social and cultural base for rejuvenating the King Movement. It eventually opened in 1929.

Te Puea is an example of the blurring of engagement and disengagement. She led the anti-conscription protests of World War One, but later began to work with Maori engagers and the Pakeha state. She developed close personal relations with Reform leader Gordon Coates and, later, Labour leader Peter Fraser. In 1946, such alliances combined with the long tradition of protest to bring about token, but symbolically significant, state compensation for the 1860s invasion. Te Puea continued to be willing to protest as well as to co-operate. She boycotted the centenary celebrations of the Treaty of Waitangi in 1940, to protest at King Koroki being forced to register under the Social Security Act of 1938. Te Puea died in 1952. She has been described as 'the most influential woman in New Zealand's political history'.[23] Certainly, she was the first of a series of important Maori women leaders in the twentieth century, beginning a long list that includes Whina Cooper and Eva Rickard. In 1966, Te Atairangikaahu became Maori queen, despite traditions demanding male inheritance. The twentieth-century Maori shift towards accepting female leadership remains, to my knowledge, unexplained. But it does demonstrate that Maori attitudes to gender are capable of changing themselves.

The most important new 'disengager' initiative of the twentieth century was the Ratana movement, a religious and political organisation founded by

Tahupotiki Wiremu Ratana after a divine revelation in 1918. Ratana was of Ngati Apa, a tribe of the Wanganui-Rangitikei region. He had marriage and kinship links with South Taranaki, the Maori Palestine that had generated a series of Maori-Christian religious movements since 1845. An immediate precursor was the Church of the Holy Spirit, founded in the 1900s by Mere Rikiriki, Ratana's aunt, who had been with Te Whiti at Parihaka in the 1880s. Ratana's personality, his creed and his social philosophy strike me as being particularly similar to those of Te Ua Haumene, prophet of Pai Marire in the 1860s. Ratana, known to his followers as the Mangai, or Mouthpiece, initially came to prominence through his practice of faith-healing, but it quickly became clear that his movement was the latest and largest of the long series of indigenously developed Maori-Christian religions. In the 1926 census, over 11,000 Maori (and 193 Pakeha) declared themselves members of the Ratana Church, 18.2 per cent of all Maori. Early support was strong in Auckland, Northland, Wairapapa and Hawke's Bay, as well as Ratana's home territory of Taranaki and Wanganui. By 1936, support was spread nationwide and the official figure was 20 per cent. Census figures understate the movement's actual influence, and one estimate goes as high as 40,000, or half the Maori population in the mid-1930s.[24]

Both Pakeha and Maori élites saw the Ratana movement as subversive. Like many Maori protest leaders before and after him, Ratana took up the Treaty of Waitangi as his political credo. In 1924, he and his entourage travelled to Britain and tried and failed to present a protest petition based on the treaty to King George V. Ratana also made fund-raising and goodwill tours to the United States, Canada and Japan. The last visit caused still further Pakeha antagonism up to and during World War Two, when Ratana supporters were suspected of pro-Japanese sympathies. Historians may have dismissed this possibility a little too blithely. 'Only a few [Ratana members] spoke in favour of a Japanese invasion.'[25] It was not immediately obvious to some Maori that Japanese would be even worse masters than Pakeha. But it remains true that Ratana shifted towards politics and engagement from about 1924, and to alliance with a Pakeha movement he saw as compatible with his own: the Labour Party. The first Ratana MP, Eruera Tirakatene, was elected in 1932 as an independent, but one allied to the Labour Party. By 1943, Ratana-Labour MPs held all four Maori seats.[26]

Maori antagonism to Ratana may have stemmed partly from the non-traditional and supra-tribal elements in his movement, which appear to have been quite strong. He required his MPs to sign an undertaking 'to work for the Maori people as a whole, rather than for any tribe or district'.[27] His followers, according to a recent study by a Maori historian, 'distanced themselves from their tribal identity', and the 'denial of tribalism' was central to the movement.[28] In this sense, the Ratana movement was a precursor of subsequent urban non-tribal organisations. Traditional tribal leaders were not keen on this, of course, and there was also hostility to Ratana from some established churches. Ratana followed the old Maori practice of allowing his followers to double-dip denominations – you could be Ratana *and* Methodist. The established churches, especially the Anglicans, were less keen on alliance. They had doubts about the full Christianity of the Ratana movement, based partly on the status of the Mangai himself, which some thought too Christ-like, and partly on the fears that its emphasis on angels masked polytheism. The Methodist Church, however, which had long been strong among Taranaki Maori, continued to co-operate with Ratana, even after he declared his movement to be a separate, though Christian, church in 1925.

Established rivals of Ratana also included the Roman Catholic Church and its successful Mill Hill mission to Maori, which dated from 1886. Roman Catholicism had been a denomination of dissent for Maori since the 1830s, and the fact that the Mill Hill fathers were largely Dutch may have facilitated disassociation from the Pakeha establishment. Roman Catholicism among Maori continued to grow between 1926 and 1936, despite the competition from Ratana.[29] In Northland at least, intense Catholicism is thought to have armoured Maori communities against the blandishments of Ratana.[30] On the other hand, lapsed Anglicans were a major source of Ratana adherents, so alarming that church that it bowed to Ngata's pressure to appoint a Maori bishop in 1928. Another Ratana rival, and another Maori denomination of dissent, was the Mormon Church. The Latter-day Saints had evangelised strongly among Maori from the 1880s, and had converted thousands. As in the early nineteenth century, some Maori even made the trip to the relevant Mecca, in this case, Salt Lake City, Utah.[31] There was the usual subliminal contest between European orthodoxy and compromise with Maori practices. As in other denominations, Ratana gave the latter a boost in the Mormon Church. The Mormon's American leaders were forced to treat Ratana with kid gloves when they noted in 1928 that 'of our membership at least 2,000 have signed up with the Ratana movement'. They became less inclined to dismiss the words of one Maori adherent who explained to them 'an old Maori belief that it is good to have two homes and two churches so that if one fails the other is still left'.[32]

The antagonism of some Maori, many Pakeha, and the established churches, coupled with its own policy 'not to publicise its teachings' except orally, has left the Ratana movement with less historical attention than it deserves. The direct role of the movement in Maori health and education, for example, is hard to discover but may have been substantial. The Mangai encouraged schooling and attention to hygiene and sanitation, and emphasised that he never opposed Pakeha medicine. Equally intriguing and mysterious is the degree of Ratana's social radicalism. Ratana emphasised Maori unity, as did both the Kingitanga and the Young Maori. But the other two organisations were *pan*-tribal; their 'Maori people' was constructed from tribal building blocks. Ratana's movement was more *non*-tribal, like that of Te Ua before him, and there are signs of similar rejections of hereditary chieftainship and some other traditions.[33] Just how far this went, or how far it extended to issues such as gender, I cannot say. But this fundamental social difference may have been a factor in the antagonism of Young Maori and some Kingites towards Ratana. Te Puea had her only encounter with Ratana in 1925, when her concert party was performing close to the Ratana Pa. Te Puea was with her female performers in a changing room when she was told that the Mangai was coming to see her. She ordered everyone to take off their clothes, and the Mangai fled 'nonplussed' after being 'faced with a room full of naked women'.[34] Other members of the Kingitanga, including Tupu Taingakawa, were more favourably inclined towards Ratana.[35]

A third Maori disengager or protest organisation, the Kotahitanga or Maori Unity movement, actually came from an engager background: 'kupapa' tribes that had backed the Pakeha or remained neutral in the wars of the 1860s. Kotahitanga dimensions, origins and persistence are hard to pin down. The movement is usually dated to 1892–1902, when it impacted most on the Pakeha record. But 1870s–1900s is probably a more accurate dating of its heyday. A variety of leaders and movements before and after that period have also been linked to it. Northland leaders were prominent, including descendants of the 1840s resistance leaders Kawiti and Hone Heke. Like Ratana, Kotahitanga stressed the Treaty of Waitangi, and Pakeha breaches of it. Northland Maori had maintained a house known as Te Tiriti o Waitangi at Te Ti, near the site of the signing, since 1875.[36] Regular meetings were held there. After one, in 1881, Maihi Paraone Kawiti declared that '[We] desire a Parliament of the leading chiefs of the Maori tribes to be constituted to carry out the intentions of the Treaty of Waitangi . . . without this Parliament our affairs will never be arranged as provided by the Treaty.'[37] The Kotahitanga movement was represented in the Pakeha Parliament by the able and charismatic Hone Heke Ngapua between 1893 and 1909, when he died prematurely. Heke sometimes opposed the Young Maori Party, led by Carroll and Ngata, but was more often allied with them, another example of the blurring of engagement and disengagement. The Kotahitanga Parliament went into recess from 1902, but its legacy was subsequently claimed by new waves in the complex and connected politics of Maori protest and unity.

Young Maori: The New Collaborators?

The most important engagement movement developed from the 1890s and was led by a group of bicultural Maori known from 1907 as the Young Maori Party. The most prominent leaders were Apirana Ngata, Maui Pomare and Peter Buck, all three of whom became knights and Cabinet ministers. The three had attended Te Aute College in Hawke's Bay, 'the seminary of a Maori élite'.[38] Behind them was James Carroll, the older politician who was in effect the father of the Young Maori movement. Carroll's Irish-Australian father was something of a 'Pakeha Maori' – a European assimilated into a Maori community. His mother was Ngati Kahungunu, and he was brought up in both traditions. Carroll entered Parliament in 1887 as Member for Eastern Maori, and from 1892 was a member of the Liberal Cabinet. In 1893, in an exceptional feat for a Maori politician, Carroll won a European seat in Parliament. Carroll was Minister of Native Affairs between 1899 and 1912, and Acting Prime Minister in 1909 and 1911, the first Maori to hold either post. As Ngata readily recognised, it was Carroll who was the real founder of the Young Maori movement. Carroll's initiatives in what he saw as Maori interests ranged widely. They included legislative measures, such as the Maori Councils Act of 1900, intended to encourage Maori-controlled reform in such areas as health and land development. This legislation managed to create a degree of Maori self-government in some regions, but its success was limited in the long run. It is land sale that tends to be used as the litmus test of Carroll's achievement.

As a youth, in 1870, Carroll had fought alongside his fellow tribesmen against the great resistance leader Te Kooti. He had been a kupapa, a pro-government Maori, and some critics believe he remained so – a 'cultural kupapa' or 'collaborator'. Like other Young Maori leaders, he sometimes advocated modernisation, individualisation and assimilation for his people. As a member of the land-hungry Liberal government, he was constantly under pressure from his Cabinet colleagues to facilitate the purchase of Maori land, and sometimes bowed to it. Carroll's government mounted the 'penultimate land grab', buying up 3.1 million acres of Maori land between 1891 and 1911, in addition to half a million acres purchased privately. But Carroll's achievement in slowing Maori land alienation tends to be overlooked. It was not until 1899 that he had really substantial influence over government land buying. When this is taken into account, the numbers speak for themselves – and for Carroll. In the 1890s, the decade before Carroll's full power over Maori affairs, land was sold at an average of about 360,000 acres a year. In 1911–20, the decade after Carroll, during the 'last land grab', it was sold at a rate of about 230,000 acres a year. In the 1900s, with Carroll's foot firmly on the brakes, it sold at about 50,000 acres a year.[39]

These figures suggest that Carroll maintained the appearance of co-operation with Pakeha, rhetorically accepting the official policy of land sale and assimilation while doing his best to slow the process under the table. Carroll had to be in the Pakeha car to apply the brakes. His historian critics, perhaps, have been deceived by appearances. Carroll not only slowed land alienation but sought to take initiatives that might improve conditions for Maori and preserve their culture. The best-remembered saying of this alleged assimilationist was 'Hold fast to your Maoritanga', to Maori culture and identity. This was also the approach of Apirana Ngata, Carroll's greatest successor. Between Carroll and Ngata came Maui Pomare, a Taranaki Maori who became a medic and Seventh-Day Adventist after his time at Te Aute. Pomare was prominent in sporadic government attempts to address Maori health problems, first as a bureaucrat (1901–10) then as a member of Cabinet in the Reform government (1912–28). Pomare was probably more genuinely assimilationist than either Carroll or Ngata were, but it is worth noting that his main expression of this, the advocacy of new attitudes to health and hygiene, had recently been as novel to Pakeha as it was to Maori.[40]

Ngata, who in 1893 became the first Maori to obtain a university degree, entered Parliament in 1905 and remained there to 1943. The peak of his official power was in 1928–34, when he was Minister for Native Affairs, but his influence spanned the whole period 1890s–1940s. Like Carroll, Ngata came from a kupapa background – in his case, Ngati Porou – and was a member of the Liberal Party. Along with his friend Peter Buck, a scholar whose encounter with politics was brief, Ngata was one of New Zealand's leading intellectuals, and arguably the greatest Maori leader of the twentieth century. Ngata was quite explicit about his and Carroll's dual strategy – and its risks. 'One foot on the Pakeha brake and the other on the Maori accelerator, how will the car stand it?'[41]

The Young Maori leaders nudged brakes and accelerators in a number of different ways between the 1890s and the 1940s. Carroll's slowing of land sales was not continued by Pomare, and a last major land grab took place in the 1910s. In 1921, however, Massey's lieutenant Gordon Coates took over Native Affairs, and land selling again slowed. Coates spoke fluent Maori and was strongly rumoured to have fathered a child by a Maori mistress before his marriage. He became a firm friend of Ngata and of Maori, an honorary 'Young Maori'. Ngata, through Coates, who was Prime Minister between 1925 and 1928, had considerable influence, despite their belonging to opposed political parties and Ngata's being out of office before 1928 and after 1934. Ngata's influence was further augmented by allied civil servants in the Department of Native Affairs, such as Te Raumoa Balneavis. During his spell as Native Minister, 1928–34, Ngata 'laid the foundation for the modern department', increased staff from 89 to 141, despite severe economic depression and general retrenchment, and shifted the culture away from that of colonial officials administering natives – to some extent at least.[42]

Ngata was influential in pressuring the Anglican Church to establish a Maori bishopric in 1928, and was also, with Coates, behind a series of legislative attempts to meet, or at least compromise with, Maori historical grievances. Arawa and Ngati Tuwharetoa Trust Boards were established in 1922 and 1926, with modest government funding and an acknowledgement of their rights to their lakes, Rotorua and Taupo. Royal commissions in 1920 and 1926–27 decided in favour of compensation to Ngai Tahu of the South Island for crooked nineteenth-century land sales, and to Taranaki and Waikato for 1860s land confiscations. Actual monetary settlements were negotiated later. From the perspective of the present, claims of 'full and final settlement' seem ironic, and the sums involved – a few thousand pounds a year in each case – seem little better than token gestures. But, in the context of the time – economic stringency, conservative government, commonplace racism – these were significant successes for Ngata's strategy.

One of Ngata's greatest crusades was his land-development scheme, which he hoped would 'paint the map of New Zealand with Maori farms'.[43] The scheme involved grouping Maori landholdings into economic farms, developing them through collective effort, and then running them either co-operatively, through employed managers, or individually. A supply of credit, the key obstacle to Maori participation in the new protein industry, was an important part of the scheme, as was negotiation to free the land from crippling liability for local body rates. Ngata's own Ngati Porou had long had an exceptional level of involvement in export farming. By the 1920s, they owned a quarter of a million sheep and had their own store and finance company.[44] From 1921, Ngata built on this to make Ngati Porou a model for the land-development scheme. The allegation that he preferred to focus resources on his own people contributed to his political downfall in 1934. But he freely admitted Ngati Porou's exemplary role and the importance of tribal rivalry, the age-old Maori change agent, in spreading the schemes. From 1928, with great patience, skill and understanding of tribal politics, Ngata encouraged the spread of land development to other tribes. By 1935, the farms (mostly dairy) created by the schemes supported about 12,000 Maori. Ngata was the initiator, but in some districts Maori engaged with the schemes at grass-roots level, and with great enthusiasm. In the Hokianga, for example, almost 20,000 acres were developed between 1932 and 1938, carrying 6,000 dairy cattle and providing at least some support for 3,000 Maori.[45] Ultimately, some farms proved too small or otherwise uneconomic. As historians have observed, poverty remained endemic, and 12,000 was in any case only a minority of Maori. But, especially in the context of economic depression, it was a substantial one. By 1936, Ngata had prised £1.5 million for Maori land development from one of the stingiest governments in New Zealand history. 'Did you ever expect,' he wrote to Buck with understandable triumph, 'that we should get so much assistance from the State?'[46]

Ngata also attacked Maori problems on the cultural front. Again with the help of Coates, he provided funds for research in Maori traditions and established a School of Maori Arts and Crafts at Rotorua in 1926. The school was crucial in the inter-tribal preservation and revival of the great Maori visual art of woodcarving, especially for meeting houses, the traditional centres and cultural repositories of Maori communities. The Ngati Porou carvers, brothers Hone and Pine Taiapa, trained there, as did the Kingite master carver Piri Poutapu, who alone worked on 64 meeting houses between 1922 and 1940.[47] Ngata himself organised and supervised the construction of 29 meeting houses between 1925 and 1950.[48] Ngata was also a sponsor of Maori scholarship and education. He was behind the setting-up of the Board of Maori Ethnological Research in 1923 and the Maori Purposes Fund in 1924, and himself published an important collection of traditional songs and sayings. The Maori language had been an optional subject at Maori secondary schools since 1909, and became compulsory in 1931. Ngata was able to have the language accepted as a university subject in 1923. The numbers were not great – seven students sat the examination in 1928 – but again this was an internationally exceptional development in settler societies.[49]

In education, Ngata was dealing with a long-standing engager institution that, like the Young Maori themselves, had its own mix of assimilationism and Maoriness: the Native School system. The system was established in 1867 and disestablished 102 years later, in 1969. From 1900, it grew steadily from 89 primary schools and 3,100 students to a peak of 166 schools and 13,600 pupils in the 1950s.[50] The Pakeha head of the system in 1887, James Pope, saw the schools as 'centres for spreading European ideas and habits among the Maoris'.[51] In some cases, that is precisely what they were. After a shift towards the immersion teaching of the English language in the 1900s, some schools punished pupils for speaking Maori in class. Factors such as this have given the Native Schools a bad press, but some research suggests that the schools were a 'site of struggle', in which Maori sometimes won. At one extreme was draconian assimilation; at the other were close relations between school and marae, along with good education, and the encouragement of Maori identity and arts, if not language.

Even the language issue has ambiguities. Often, Maori themselves wanted their children taught English because they realised that this gave them independent access to global knowledge. It was literacy in Maori only that had given Pakeha missionaries and educators a stranglehold over what Maori learned about the world. While the Maori language was strong at home, English at school was not a threat to it. In 1930, the great majority of Maori children spoke only Maori at home – allegedly as many as 96 per cent. Urbanisation from 1945 did much more damage to the Maori language than did the Native Schools. From the 1900s, there was a growing push to make curricula less academic and more agricultural and technical, keeping Maori in the occupations thought to be appropriate for them. Precisely the same push occurred in working-class Pakeha schools, as we have seen. In both cases it met resistance, and in some Native Schools there was a marked difference between official policy and actual practice. Certainly, the Native Schools appear to have been academically better for Maori than the mainstream system. In 1928, the number of Native School Maori pupils in the academically oriented standard seven was small, but it was five times as great as the standard seven Maori in mainstream schools. In 1967, when the shrinking system educated only about one in seven Maori children, two out of three Maori university students were trained in it.[52] Assimilationist Pakeha repeatedly advocated the abolition of Native Schools, which they would not have done if they were successful agencies of assimilation. Ngata and Buck headed off one such move in 1912. On the whole I suspect that the Native School system did more good than harm to Maori education, identity and cultural persistence.[53] The demise of the system in 1969 was not good news for Maoridom.

Another pre-existing engager institution with which the Young Maori allied was Rotorua tourism. This industry, dating from about 1870, was the biggest contributor to the small tourist industry nationwide. It was a joint venture between the government and Te Arawa, the local Maori, most of whom had sided with the government in the New Zealand Wars of the 1860s. Rotorua, the 'Thermal Wonderland', a town founded in 1882, became a key icon of New Zealand, and so did its Maori. Despite predictions that 'Rotten Egg Town will only last a short time', Rotorua thrived under the patronage of the state.[54] In 1907, it was described as 'the only State-owned State-managed town in Australasia'.[55] It is not altogether clear that the state was fully aware of what it was involved in. One hot pool was said to give off a laughing gas that caused 'delightful delirium'. Te Arawa offered 'a brief ordinary dance', or one 'complete with indecencies, which they said the gentlemen usually preferred, for £3/10'. Maori 'degradation', felt one visitor, 'could hardly have been carried further'.[56] But Arawa had been, and would continue to be, important partners of the state – using, as well as being used by, their European collaborators and visitors.

As early as the 1880s, tourism had made one section of Te Arawa, the Tuhourangi, 'the richest Maori tribe in the whole of New Zealand' with an income of well over £6,000 from the industry. The gold sovereigns serving instead of paua shells as the eyes of Tuhourangi carvings did not necessarily diminish Maoriness.[57] The destruction of the Pink and White Terraces in the Tarawera eruption of 1886 was a blow, but tourist numbers, though never high compared with modern figures, recovered quite quickly. Te Arawa's relationship with tourism is illustrated by an anecdote from Adela Stewart's classic, *My Simple Life in New Zealand*. She and her soldier-brother, recovering from the Second Afghan War, along with their spouses, visited Rotorua in 1882. 'Covetous natives' charged a toll at each geyser, then toured the tourists as the latter sat at dinner. The Stewart party dined at McRae's Hotel (twelve shillings and sixpence a day for bed and board) like zoo animals, with Maori spectators looking on. This was 'much to the disgust of my brother, who wanted to disperse them as he would have in India, but was dissuaded imploringly by McRae'.[58]

Te Arawa arts and crafts were an integral part of the industry – for performance and display, the decoration of meeting houses and as souvenirs. There may have been some adjustment to Pakeha tools and styles, and some commercialisation. Tene Waitere, 'by far the most prolific' Arawa tourist carver, operated in two styles, one for Pakeha and one for Maori.[59] But, adjusted or not, commercial or not, it was Arawa carvers who provided the skill base for Ngata's School of Arts and Crafts and for the revival of Maori carving. Te Arawa teachers predominated at the school. Ngata helped in the development of tourist facilities at Rotorua, and Te Arawa in turn helped him in his attempt to preserve and re-energise Maori culture. The Maori boys and girls diving for tourist pennies, seen as a symbol of Maori degradation at the hands of Pakeha commerce, might well have been diving for fun, pennies or not.[60]

The Young Maori had an inter-tribal agenda as well as an inter-racial one. James Carroll asserted that Maori were a united whole, 'tatou, tatou', 'a slogan for inter-tribal interdependence'.[61] In 1897, the young Ngata advocated that Maori should be 'possessed of a strong national sentiment, conscious . . . of a distinct and separate existence' from the Pakeha, though still co-operating with them.[62] He agreed with Buck that 'the development of a race consciousness must be based on a tribal consciousness'. But both hoped that 'a Race spirit and consciousness' will 'spread like an epidemic'.[63] This was a pan-tribal or nationalist agenda, though more compatible with tribalism than the pan-Maori sentiments of the Ratana movement. As in the nineteenth century, there was a national Maori history as well as various tribal ones.

Those Maori in the present who still deny this seem to me to disregard the facts.

The Young Maori in general, and Ngata in particular, have long been the heroes of one strand of historical literature, which celebrates their achievements and their prominence on the national stage, but also their alleged assimilationism. More recently, doubts have been expressed about their contribution, with the concept 'cultural kupapa' usually simmering below the surface. My view is closer to the older strand, but for different reasons. The claim that Young Maori had little influence at the grass-roots level of Maori society may be true of the 1900s, but it was not true of the 1920s. In the end, the main legacy of Ngata and company was not assimilation but a kind of benign segregation. While Pakeha spouted the rhetoric of assimilation, Maori had separate military, religious, sporting, welfare, land-development, educational and cultural organisations. Some, such as the Native Schools system, had mixed effects; others, such as welfare, had inadequate resources. But each helped preserve Maoriness and helped make a certain limited amount of space for it in state and society. In 1961, a list was compiled showing '297 instances of legislative distinctions between Maori and Pakeha', most permitting different organisations or procedures that Maori themselves wanted.[64] Under the rhetoric of assimilation was a reality of benign segregation, a set of storm sails under which Maoriness could ride out the tempests of endemic poverty and epidemic depression.

Maori, in sum, were in part themselves responsible for the limited but significant 'good news' about their history in the first half of the twentieth century. Protest and co-operation, engagement and disengagement, and a mix of each, were among their strategies; and Carroll, Ratana, Te Puea and, above all, Ngata, were among their leaders. There is a sense in which these twentieth-century strategies and leaders were functionally equivalent to the modern pa and great Maori generals of the nineteenth century. Ngata's brilliantly subversive co-operation replaced Kawiti's brilliantly innovative resistance as the leading guardian of Maori interests. Yet this question remains. Brilliant though he was, how did Ngata manage to prise benignly separate institutions, recognition of land grievances, and substantial state finance for Maori out of one of the most conservative, miserly and racialist governments in New Zealand's history?

Whitening Maori

A relatively benign European view of Maori had long co-existed with more negative stereotypes. It dated back to the early explorers and missionaries, and was encouraged by real and perceived differences in the behaviour of indigenous peoples on the two shores of the Tasman world. Australian Aboriginals were thought to be more primitive; New Zealand Maori more 'advanced'. Aboriginals sometimes showed a genuine disinterest in Europe and its things and thoughts; Maori often showed a genuine interest. From these and other strands, Europeans wove an image of Maori as the most convertible of 'savages', the most prone to 'civilise' or Europeanise. Maori were 'better blacks', so good that they could become almost white – with the help of European teachers. This 'White Maori' stereotype quickly found itself in competition with others, notably the 'Black Maori' and the 'Grey Maori'. Black Maori could be pathetic or ferocious, but in either case they were basically unconvertible. Any trappings of civilisation they seemed to take on were a mere façade, from which they would soon revert at 'the call of the Pah'. Grey Maori were a dying race, tragically but inevitably making way for the Pakeha by a law of nature. White was the most prominent stereotype to 1860, but war and the continued decline of the Maori population then boosted its rivals, Black and Grey. It was the Grey Maori, the dying race, that held the lead to 1885 and remained important into the twentieth century. But it was increasingly displaced by a resurgence of the White Maori stereotype.

The turn of the tide in the contest of stereotypes came in 1885, when Edward Tregear, the surveyor, scholar and civil servant who was to become founding head of the Department of Labour in 1892, published a remarkable little book, *The Aryan Maori*. Its basic argument was that Maori shared an ancient origin with Northern Europeans, including the British. Both were members of the Aryan master race, who had gone in different directions after leaving their ancient homeland north of India. With 'the wonderful spirit of enterprise and colonization which has always distinguished the race', the Aryan Maori had wandered all the way from the Caucasus to the Bluff.[65] Tregear based his case on such things as the memory of animals known to the ancient Aryans, unknown in New Zealand, but embalmed in the language of their Maori descendants, which shared Aryan roots with Sanscrit, Latin and English. For Tregear, the Maori 'tarahono' – 'he lay in a heap' – was obviously cousin to the Latin *taurus*, or bull. Tahere, 'he hung himself', was clearly linked to 'noosed cat'. 'Kahupapa', or bridge, was 'flat cow'; Ngati Kahungunu were 'cow-biters'. The Sanscrit *mih* was evidently the Maori 'mimi' (to urinate), but, rather than continue in this vein, Tregear noted that 'some of my best examples I am compelled to keep back on account of their not being fit for use here'. Tregear's evidence was not restricted to language. 'That the Maori had also some memories of India it is impossible to doubt when looking at the rock paintings in the Weka Pass. The picture is a rude but vivid representation of the first Avatar of Vishnu.'

Tregear's evidence was ludicrously thin and was laughed at, even at the time. One reviewer, Arthur Atkinson, joked in 1886 that ancient Aryans had come to New Zealand and seen a kakapo, a large ground parrot, eating grass like a bull. They had returned home and told the story of a *kaka* (cock in Sanscrit) eating grass like a *po* (bull). The legend survived in English in the form of the phrase 'a cock-and-bull story'.[66] Some modern scholars have also seen the Aryan Maori as a joke, or at best as an intellectual curiosity. But the joke is on us, because the book arguably ranks with the Treaty of Waitangi as a key text of Maori–Pakeha relations.

The Aryan Maori thesis was accepted and disseminated by a group of Pakeha scholars centred around Stephenson Percy Smith and the Polynesian Society, which he and Tregear founded in 1892.[67] It became part of a homogenised and Europeanised 'Smithed' version of Maori history. The package included legends of the Cook-like explorer Kupe, and the 'Great Fleet' of original settlers arriving in 1350, their First Seven Canoes playing First Four Ships. It also included the belief that Maori had displaced an inferior race, the mythical mainland Moriori, and the laundered legend of the New Zealand Wars of the 1860s, in which the courage and Christian chivalry of Maori resistance featured much larger than its effectiveness. The Aryan Maori was the master myth of this Smithed version of Maori history. Its acceptance was never universal, and the somewhat broader racial concept of 'Caucasian' was sometimes preferred to 'Aryan'. But the idea of a European origin for Maori was increasingly pervasive from the 1890s, and it persisted until quite recent times.

Historians agree that 'there was widespread acceptance of the notion of Aryan origins for Maoridom' in the early twentieth century.[68] 'It was widely believed that the Maoris were a "branch of the Caucasian race".'[69] By the 1900s, there was 'a general consensus of opinion that the Maori ... are a Polynesian, that is originally an Aryan race'.[70] Aucklanders in 1927 were treated to lectures on 'the reunion of two branches of the Caucasian race'.[71] 'Of all the other races in the world,' announced leading anthropologists in a centenary publication in 1940, 'the Maori most closely resembles in physical type the Caucasian race to which the white man belongs.'[72] In 1949, Prime Minister Peter Fraser was reported to be favourably impressed by the view that Maori and Celt 'both sprang from the same Caucasian stock'.[73] This belief survived into the recent past. *The Story of the Maori People* informed readers in 1968 that 'all the evidence points towards the racial origins of the Maori as being basically Caucasian.'[74] The 1960 edition of one widely read general history stated that 'racially the Polynesians are akin to the Europeans, being of the Caucasoid group'.[75] A 'revised edition' of another, even more widely read general history claimed, as late as 1974, that Maori were descended from 'a people called Aryans', as was 'our own Anglo-Saxon race'.[76]

There was also an indirect acceptance of the Aryan Maori thesis. This did not use the word 'Aryan', or even 'Caucasian', but instead portrayed Maori as 'better blacks' or 'honorary whites'. In the 1920s, the populist *Truth* pulled no punches over 'noisome and noxious [American] niggers', and almost choked on its own Sinophobia, yet was sympathetic towards some Maori grievances and was seldom anti-Maori as such.[77] 'Better blacks' were associated with New Zealand by the world – rather more, ironically, than Better Britons. Young British readers were informed that 'no finer coloured race exists in the world'.[78] Australians discovered in school textbooks that Maori were 'a far superior race to the Australian blacks'.[79] Like Better Britons, 'better blacks' proved their status in war and sport. The achievements of Maori rugby players and Maori soldiers were celebrated by Pakeha as solid evidence that the country was indeed a paradise of racial harmony. In 1921, a South African journalist complained telegraphically about his visiting rugby team having to play Maori, with 'spectacle of thousands of Europeans frantically cheering on band of coloured men to defeat own race' adding insult to injury. This received an indignant response from New Zealand rugby officialdom – not a subculture noted for its enlightenment. The Maori 'should not be looked upon as nothing better than a kaffir'.[80] In 1945, New Zealand military authorities held an inquiry into a series of fights between American and Maori soldiers, and reached a similar conclusion. 'It is apparent that US personnel do not appreciate the standing that the Maori has in our community, and are inclined to treat him as they treat the American Negro.'[81]

The survival and spread of the Aryan Maori thesis did not result from intellectual merit or weight of evidence, but from its cultural utility. Previous chapters have noted a collective Pakeha 'identity crisis' in the period 1880s–1920s, when the recolonial system was getting up and running. Optimistic ideas of a Greater British future declined after the bubble of progressive colonisation burst in the 1880s. An Australasian identity was no longer an option after 1901. Better Britonism and dominionism, the exemplary paradise, social harmony and moral harmony addressed these crises, but they needed help, especially in providing some distinctiveness from Old Britain, to set alongside indissoluble links. A distinctive history and a distinctive set of cultural symbols borrowed from Maori provided this help, runes and ruins for a runeless and ruinless land. The beauty of it was that such distinctiveness, the distinguishing 'golden tinge' in New Zealand culture, did not threaten the recolonial imperative of racial homogeneity and Britishness, because Maori were Aryan – virtually Brown Britons. 'Owing to his exceptional characteristics,' announced a leading newspaper in 1901, 'the Maori interferes in no way with our national homogeneity. His position is . . . unique.'[82]

There are indeed signs of a Pakeha co-option of Maori culture from the

1890s, finding in it symbols to represent New Zealand, initially without much concern for the original owners. Pakeha hockey teams and children were given Maori names; 'Kia ora' was advocated as a Pakeha greeting; and 'Maorilanders' became a populist by-name for European New Zealanders. Pakeha musicians and artists in the decades around 1900 were fascinated by Maori subjects, as was the country's leading woman photographer, Margaret Matilda White. 'Her fascination with Maoridom led to her most disturbing image; a self-portrait with a moko painted on her chin.'[83] Maori motifs were very common in two competitions for a national coat of arms in the 1900s, whereas they had not featured in an 1880s competition for a national song.[84] Increasingly, Maori symbols were used to represent New Zealand as a whole: Maori welcomes and Maori carvings for visiting VIPs; Maori haka before international rugby games; Maori performance groups and displays at New Zealand's exhibitions overseas.

Paradoxically enough, the Aryanised White Maori stereotype initially merged with its chief rival, the Dying Maori. Tregear himself had accepted that Maori were dying out. That Maori Aryanism was to be posthumous reduced the conceptual risks for its prospective Pakeha heirs. One could take over symbols, names and history without the bother of live Maori owners. From 1900, when it began to seem likely that Maori were not dying out after all, Pakeha had to fit live Maori into the new ideology. Racial incorporation of Maori as Aryans and Brown Britons was one solution. To the extent that racial difference was conceded, the notion of New Zealand as a paradise of racial harmony was another. Equally paradoxical was the fact that neither racial incorporation nor racial harmony were based on the *absence* of racism, but on Maori exemption from it. Both paradoxes were exemplified by William Pember Reeves. In 1898, he wrote that the average New Zealander 'regards a Mongolian with repulsion, a Negro with contempt, and looks on an Australian black as very near to a wild beast; but he likes the Maori, and is sorry that they are dying out'. A quarter-century later, in a new edition of the relevant book, the last phrase was replaced with 'and treats him in many respects as his equal'.[85] The final paradoxical thing about the Aryan Maori ideology was the strong possibility of Maori participation in it.

Maori input into the European White Maori stereotype, and related legends, was long-standing, beginning with the great Maori sponsor of missionary activity, Ruatara, in the 1810s. In 1899, Carroll suggested that the teachings of the 1860s Maori scholar Te Matorohanga be edited and copied for preservation. They were eventually transmuted into the *Lore of the Whare-wananga*, by S. Percy Smith. But before this they passed through mediating

Maori minds, including a 1907 committee of Maori elders, also instigated by Carroll.[86] There was an element of 'Carrolling' in 'Smithing'. The most prominent scholar of the Young Maori movement, Peter Buck, was an enthusiastic Aryanist. In 1930, he attempted to convert two American politicians, Democrats from the Southern states. 'The job was to show that the Samoan was a Polynesian of Caucasian descent and quite distinct from the negroid division of mankind. The two democrats were duly converted.'[87] Buck was subsequently enraged when he was denied American citizenship on the grounds of his race. 'This in spite of the opinion of anthropologists that the Polynesians are largely of Caucasian origin.'[88] His best-known book, *Vikings of the Sunrise*, obviously played on this concept.[89] As for Ngata, he had scholarly doubts about aspects of the Smithed version, such as the Great Fleet, and his acceptance of Maori Aryanism seems half-hearted. But he kept this to himself, and his public stance, and that of the Young Maori movement generally, was to actively but selectively support the Pakeha myth of the White Maori in three key areas: war, sport and symbolism.

When World War One broke out in 1914, Ngata, Caroll, Pomare, Buck and other Young Maori leaders formed a recruiting committee and set about organising a Maori contribution, as far as possible on their own terms.[90] The terms were a separate and united Maori battalion, a high-profile combat role, and the fullest possible official and public recognition. The first difficulties they faced were British reluctance to involve 'coloured' troops in a 'white man's war', and General Godley's hesitations about the quality of the Maori unit. Godley thought one Maori company commander was 'quite useless' – possibly the same officer that weighed 125 kilograms. These difficulties were circumvented quite quickly. By August 1915, only a few months after the initiation of their Pakeha brethren, Maori, too, had the honour of dying on the slopes of Gallipoli. The Maori combat performance at Gallipoli, and the haka 'resounding up the slopes of Sari Bair', impressed Pakeha military and public alike. Young Maori led from the front. Peter Buck accompanied the Maori contingent as medical officer, and earned a decoration.

Godley's doubts were partly assuaged. But he still had little sympathy for the Young Maori objectives and tried to break up the Maori contingent and distribute it as reinforcements among Pakeha units. Ngata and company protested strongly, to the extent of threatening to suspend recruitment, and Godley was brought to heel. He reorganised the contingent into the main constituent of a 'Pioneer Battalion', and it was as such that Maori served on the Western Front in 1916–18. 'Pioneers' were not support troops but combat engineers, as the name implied and Maori casualties proved. Maori earned many plaudits and Pomare, as a member of the War Cabinet, was not slow to remind his colleagues of this. The Maori had 'forever joined his name and *mana* with that of his pakeha brother. Henceforth he was the racial peer of any man on earth.'[91]

The other major set of difficulties facing the Young Maori war strategy involved recruitment at home. As we have seen, Waikato were not enthusiastic about co-operating, and the same was true of Taranaki and other nineteenth-century centres of resistance. The old kupapa tribes, Arawa, Ngati Porou and Ngati Kahungunu, along with Nga Puhi, were the major suppliers of recruits. But these groups alone could not meet World War One's appetite for fresh lives. Pomare became increasingly desperate in his efforts to maintain the numbers, and therefore the prominence, of the Maori battalion. In the end, as minister in charge of the Island territories, he turned to Niue and the Cook Islands to make up the Maori deficit. Cook Islanders and Niueans were not Maori, but they were near enough for Pomare's purposes. Pomare appears to have been ruthless in pressuring the islanders to volunteer. In the end, about 500 Cook Islanders joined up – a higher proportion than Maori.[92] The high Cook Islands contribution to the Maori battalion, and the modest overall Maori rate of recruitment, which at 4.5 per cent of the population was half that of Pakeha, was successfully glossed over by the Young Maori leaders. They used the deeds of the Maori battalion to increase respect for Maori among the Pakeha public, and to increase the sense of moral debt in the minds of Pakeha politicians and officials. Precisely the same strategy was used in World War Two, with much broader Maori support and even greater success. The strategy of high-profile loyalty in war creating moral debt was strikingly similar to that employed by Pakeha towards the British. The Maori performance in the two world wars did enhance their status, even 'whiten' them, in Pakeha eyes. Some Maori leaders had wanted to send a detachment to the Boer War in 1899 for similar reasons. They were not allowed, on the grounds that it was a 'white man's war'. Maori then had to be content with fund-raising and the composition of a song called 'Kiki te Poa' – Kick the Boer.[93] By 1939, it was inconceivable that Maori should be excluded in this way.

The central role of sport in New Zealand culture has a future chapter of its own. It is enough to say here that organised rugby union football rose above a miscellany of semi-organised sports from the 1890s, becoming the 'national game' in the 1900s, and the dominant sport by the 1920s. The Young Maori sought a prominent role in the game for their people from the outset. Tom Ellison, a Ngai Tahu educated at Te Aute, was captain of the first official New Zealand team in 1893. He is said to have proposed the black uniform with silver fern; he published *The Art of Rugby Football* in 1902; and was an important and innovative influence on the New Zealand game. There were apparently no Maori in national teams between 1894 and 1920, but Maori rugby continued to develop at local, regional and pan-Maori levels.[94] In 1904, a pan-Maori team beat the touring British side at Rotorua.[95] Te Aute College won the Hawke's Bay club championship in the 1880s and 1890s, and provided half the province's representative team in 1900. Maori teams toured Australia from 1910.[96] In the 1920s, Maori rugby came into full flower. The Prince of Wales Cup was presented for competition between the 'four quarters' of Maoridom; Maori teams played the All Blacks and the Springboks at home, and toured Britain. Maori All Blacks multiplied.

The traditional explanation for Maori success in rugby is that they were naturals at the game, with the logic sometimes following these lines: rugby was warlike, they were warlike, therefore they were good at it. Yet athletics, rowing and even cricket were more akin to traditional Maori activities than rugby, and they initially participated in these sports. A missionary wrote in 1832 that Maori cricketers were 'very expert, good bowlers'.[97] Two Maori were Australasian champions in pole-vaulting in the 1890s. Peter Buck, the Viking of the Sunrise himself, was New Zealand long-jump champ in 1903.[98] From the 1900s, however, as rugby rose in status, Maori concentrated their efforts on it. The Young Maori leaders were prominent in organising these efforts.

Carroll, Ngata and Pomare helped institutionalise Maori teams and competitions within the Rugby Union, delicately negotiating their way past assimilationist Pakeha hesitations about separatism. They established the Prince of Wales Cup in 1928. Pomare linked Maori feats on the battlefields of Europe with those 'on the battlefields of "Rugger"', and was soon echoed by Pakeha politicians.[99] Ngata, described by the resentful as 'the Mussolini of Maori football',[100] took great satisfaction from large Pakeha attendances at Maori games. A game between the New Zealand Maori team and the national team, the All Blacks, showed Maori were 'a match for, if not a better man than, the pakeha' even though the Maori lost 18–37. In 1930, 25,000 people, mainly Pakeha, watched the Maori team play Britain in a midweek game in Wellington. Ngata was convinced that Maori performance in rugby, as in war, enhanced Pakeha esteem.[101] Maori rugby, and the Maori role in New Zealand rugby, was made, not born. It was made at least partly by the Young Maori as part of a broad engagement with Pakeha mythology.

The third component of this engagement was in symbolism. The Young Maori co-operated with, even encouraged, a Pakeha tendency to adopt Maori cultural motifs as their own, and to use them to represent the whole nation. Buck emphasised to Pakeha 'the fact that the traditions of the Maori were the traditions of our mutual country and were as much theirs as mine'.[102] During the 1900s, Te Arawa carvings and those produced by the prolific Te Ati Awa carver Jacob Heberly were increasingly used as state gifts. 'Maori carvings became accepted as a powerful symbol of the new nation.'[103] The Young Maori leaders helped organise the welcomes for overseas dignitaries and the performance troupes at overseas exhibitions. Ngata specialised in the mass commemoration of great events. In 1934, he orchestrated Maori participation in the opening of the Treaty House at Waitangi, gifted to the nation by the Governor-General, Charles Bledisloe. Some 1,400 Maori from numerous tribes performed. 'The gathering,' wrote Ngata, 'will give us the opportunity for taking stock of where we are in the minds of our pakeha friends.'[104] Ngata also arranged the building of a finely carved meeting house, representing all the tribes, beside the Treaty House and as a Maori twin to it. Ngata was also prominent in the centenary celebrations of the Treaty of Waitangi in 1940. His masterpiece, however, was the celebration of the '600th anniversary' of the arrival of the Great Fleet in 1950, just before his death. Ngata the scholar had no doubt that the arrival could not be fixed with this accuracy, and did have doubt about the very existence of the fleet. But Ngata the political strategist was not about to pass up such an opportunity.

Why did the Young Maori engage with the Pakeha myths of the White Maori and the paradise of racial harmony, using war, sport and commemoration as their propaganda instruments? Buck's Aryanism aside, they had few illusions about the veracity of these myths, or the persistence of Pakeha racialism and Maori socio-economic disadvantage. I have speculated elsewhere that Maori Aryanism echoes an ancient Maori practice of retrospective marriage alliance, finding shared ancestors in the past to match links in the present.[105] Another motive, more pragmatic and less speculative, was that the White Maori stereotype was clearly the least of three evils. Not even Ngata's genius could completely reconstruct Pakeha images of Maori. All he and others could do was steer them away from the Black and Grey stereotypes, and towards the White.

The key motive for engaging with the Pakeha myths of the Aryan Maori and the paradise of racial harmony was to augment Maori status in the Pakeha mind – not for its own sake, but as a point of leverage. The explicit aim was, in Ngata's words, 'influencing Pakeha opinion to a more kinly attitude and respect towards the Maori'.[106] The implicit message to Pakeha state and society was this: If Pakeha wished to claim that New Zealand's race relations and indigenous people were the best and whitest in the world, fine. Indeed, Maori will help by supplying the battalions, the sports teams and the cultural symbols. But Maori will insist on some sort of quid pro quo, such as finance for the land-development schemes and a set of state-funded but benignly separate institutions. Like recolonial Pakeha attachment to Britain, Maori co-operation had a price attached. Ngata once privately confessed to Buck, in Maori, that 'it is I who must go about warding off the wrong doings of the

Pakeha so that the spirit of the Maori people may emerge'.[107] He tried to ward off the wrongdoings through brilliantly subversive co-operation, just as nineteenth-century Maori leaders had tried to do so through brilliantly innovative resistance.

This chapter has presented a more positive picture of Maori history, 1900s–40s, than is now customary. I make no apology for this. Maori cultural persistence and demographic growth occurred in the period, and it did so against odds as great, though different in kind, from those that faced Maori political independence in the nineteenth century. In the 1890s, few indeed, Maori or Pakeha, would have predicted this. The good news is more surprising and less recognised than the bad, and is therefore more necessary to explain. But we should not forget the bad news: a fragile Maori economy, vulnerable to recession, which hit hard in the 1930s; persisting high death rates; and widespread if petty racial discrimination. Nor should we forget that Ngata's leverage with Pakeha state and society, the Aryan Maori myth, was a product of the strength of New Zealand racism, not its weakness. Still, in the history of race relations in settler societies, you take your good news wherever you can get it.

CHAPTER SEVEN

Racial Harmony (2):
Unmaking the Difference

Maori were not the only problem with the claim that New Zealand was 98.5 per cent racially pure and racially British. For one thing, in terms of racial theory, 'British' was not a race at all, but a hybrid of (English) Anglo-Saxons and (Scots and Welsh) Celts. Another problem was the Catholic Irish, who comprised about 14 per cent of Pakeha. Catholic Irish had never been considered racially British and, after the formation of the Irish Free State in 1922, even their political Britishness was tenuous. Describing Irish as 'British' risked a punch on the nose in some countries. In New Zealand, it was common. There was also the question of racial reinforcement in the form of immigrants. The racially 'undesirable' were hard to keep out, and the racially 'desirable' were hard to get. Between the 1880s and the 1920s, immigration policy was progressively adjusted to minimise these problems. A gatekeeping system emerged, known informally as 'the White New Zealand Policy'. Yet 'undesirables' did slip in. In the first half of the twentieth century, at least 5 per cent of New Zealanders were neither British, nor Irish nor Maori. How did the '98.5 per cent British' slogan cope with that, and how did it cope with ethnic difference in general?

The short answer is that ethnic difference in New Zealand was *minimised* through increasingly tight control of the immigration gates; *reduced*, through culturally enforced conformism; *concealed*, through the pretended or partial assimilation of ethnic minorities; and *denied*, through a mix of myth, misunderstanding, statistical tricks and bare-faced lies. Ethnic differences within Pakeha were blurred and distorted; groups that were neither Maori nor Pakeha were written out or banished to outlying islands, geographical and conceptual. This chapter seeks to understand the homogenising-out of ethnic difference among non-Maori New Zealanders, and to assess the extent to which substantive difference did survive being minimised, reduced, concealed and denied. Is there a history of non-Maori New Zealand ethnicity? If so, what might it look like, and how did the tight society handle it?

Merging Pakeha

Ethnicity is a slippery concept, almost as problematic as class. It can be defined in at least four ways: how you identify yourself ethnically; how others identify you; an ethnic difference between your ways of life and those of other groups; and your ethnicity by descent. Ethnic descent does not necessarily mean much of itself. It used to be called 'race', with connotations of biological determinism, stereotyping and a tendency to rank difference as well as merely assert it. Intermarriage multiplies descent opportunities beyond population. It is quite possible that English, Scottish and Irish descent each extend to half or more of today's New Zealanders, giving us an inconvenient three halves. Yet ethnic descent can function as a proxy for substantive things, such as persistent cultural difference and a differentiated sense of community. You are unlikely to see yourself as Irish, be seen by others as Irish and to maintain a degree of Irish culture or ways of life if you have no Irish descent.

Problematic as it is, ethnicity is worth pursuing, but in New Zealand it is not easy. Ethnic difference has been concealed and denied by a connected set of semantic slippages and statistical sleights. 'British' was never an ethnic group any more than it was a 'race'. Though there was blurring and mixing in Old Britain, and though compound British cultures have developed, ethnic difference persists to the present. The English and Scottish use of the English language, for example, still differs more than that of Australians and New Zealanders. In any case, most of New Zealand's British genes were taken on between the 1840s and the 1880s, when English, Scots and Welsh were even more different from each other. 'British' is in itself an ethnic plural. To make matters worse, official statistics often used 'European' as an ethnic group, and still do, whereas Europe contains at least 50 ethnicities. 'European', 'British' and 'English' often blurred into synonyms in New Zealand usage. Another slippage was from technical status to ethnicity. Maori and Indian New Zealanders were technically born British subjects, and this was the '98.5 per cent British' slogan's only claim to validity. Yet it was almost always used with an implication of ethnic homogeneity, and kinship with Britain. In another sleight of mind, British and Maori New Zealanders were allowed their descendants in official statistics, but other ethnic groups were not. Instead, they were estimated on the basis of birthplace, which could amount to gross deception. For example, in 1945 only 18,000 New Zealanders were Irish-born, including Protestants. Yet the number of Irish Catholics alone exceeded 200,000 at that time. Ethnic minorities are still sometimes measured by the number of overseas-born, which usually understates their size substantially. In all, the historian of New Zealand ethnicity faces a conspiracy of silence in the sources – a silence that illustrates the power, pervasiveness, and persistence of the recolonial demand for ethnic homogeneity.

A pioneering attack on the 'spurious unity' of Pakeha was made in 1990 by Canadian scholar Donald Akenson, a leading historian of the Irish diaspora. He made a guess about Pakeha ethnicity that was much more educated than that bequeathed by recolonial ideology. Between the 1860s and the 1950s, according to Akenson, Pakeha were 50–53 per cent English and Welsh, 21–24 per cent Scots, and 16–18 per cent Irish. About a quarter of the Irish were Protestants, the rest Catholic.[1] One should also deduct about 2 per cent from the English and Welsh figure for Welsh, and note that these figures excluded Maori. Because Maori were never less than 4.5 per cent of the population, even on definitions that excluded some half-castes, the English were never a majority of New Zealand's whole population, though sometimes they did come close. But do statistics about ethnic origin actually mean anything? Did ethnic difference persist within Pakeha?

The traditional answer would be no, not much. It was assumed that Scots, Welsh, Protestant Irish and even Catholic Irish rapidly 'assimilated' into a 'mainstream', and that other ethnic groups did so as well. The tight society did place immense pressure on ethnic minorities to conform and assimilate. As late as the 1950s, even allegedly highly assimilable Dutch immigrants found that they had to 'conform rigidly to the New Zealand culture pattern'. This was the case in other societies, too, but 'the undeviating consistency and all-pervasiveness of this attitude' in New Zealand 'was certainly distinctive'.[2] Ethnic minorities in New Zealand learned to deny and camouflage their difference, as well as diminish it in actuality. Chinese New Zealanders interviewed around 1970 claimed that they were perfectly assimilated: the only minor differences were that they had different birth, death and marriage rituals; that they ate different food every day in a different way; that they brought up their children differently; and that they married other Chinese.[3] In 1968, a leading New Zealand anthropologist adamantly denied the existence of substantial Maori difference and dismissively listed its few vestiges: different living and authority patterns; different language for some; different cultural foci in the form of marae and meeting houses; different decorative art forms; some preference for different foods; different childrearing practices; and 'a personality pattern and outlook on life which is, by and large, different from that of the Pakeha'.[4] That was all.

We should not exaggerate the persistence of ethnic difference, but we should not insist on extreme and comprehensive difference, either. We should not expect it to take the form of people with two heads. We are looking for modern Maoriness, not the stereotyped, frozen, pre-contact kind; we are looking for *New Zealand* Irishness, not some reinvented, stereotyped metropolitan Irish kind – singing, boozing leprechauns, always dressed in green.

The 'mainstream' into which minorities allegedly assimilated was assumed to be English, or 'Anglo-Pakeha': to assimilate was to Anglicise. In fact, all ethnic groups at least partially adopted various developing 'compound cultures', lifeways prevalent throughout and beyond New Zealand. Of the New Zealand ethnic groups, the English were the largest contributors to these compound cultures. The notion of New Zealand's Englishness needs pruning, not uprooting. But it is not true to say that 'mainstream culture' equals English or Anglo-Pakeha culture. We can distinguish at least three types of compound culture, of which the first is global. Adopting Christianity, an Asian religion; writing in a phonetic, Asian alphabet; eating native American potatoes; smoking native American tobacco; watching modern American television and driving modern Japanese cars are not in themselves acts of Englishness. The second compound culture was 'pan-British', including American. It originated in the British Isles, but was essentially transnational, a creation of the British diaspora, owned by neo-Britains, including New Zealand, as much as by Old Britain. Its classic social expression was 'crew culture'. The Tasman world was a local manifestation of this pan-British culture. Even in the twentieth century, mainstream New Zealand culture continued to draw on it as well as contribute to it, a matter discussed further in Chapter Eleven.

New Zealandness itself was the third compound. English were major contributors, but so were local factors, including Maori, other compound cultures and other ethnic groups. Shared assimilation into New Zealand's mainstream culture did reduce ethnic difference, but not necessarily through Anglicisation. New Zealand's Scottishness illustrates this point. The proportion of Scots in New Zealand was roughly twice that in the British Isles. The great majority – over 80 per cent – were Lowlanders, many from around, but not in, the cities of Glasgow and Edinburgh. Scottish legacies may include an emphasis on education, even for girls; a willingness to get married in places other than church; a liking for milk; the celebration of New Year; the Boys' Brigade; and the habit of going barefoot without necessarily implying low social status. The New Zealand preference for partible inheritance over primogeniture may also be of partly Scottish origin. Other Scottish contributions include a liking for porridge, golf and shortbread, and the words 'slater', 'skite', 'shanghai', 'whinge' and 'wee', as in small. The practice of adding 'ie' is also Scottish: wharfie, crankie, footie, shrewdie. Other Scottish expressions in New Zealand English include: 'He wanted in'; 'They stopped with us for a week'; 'Wait on'; 'He slept in'; 'I didn't let on that I knew'; and 'He has no money on him' – a term of strong disapprobation.[5]

Scots met some basic criteria for ethno-cultural persistence. They had their own church, Presbyterianism, and some were 'ghettoised' – tending to settle in the same place. Both factors encouraged a degree of in-marriage. The ghetto was rather large: Otago and Southland. It is sometimes implied that the Scottish 'Old Identity' was swamped by the gold-digging 'New Iniquity' in the 1860s, but this does not appear to be so. Using Presbyterianism as a proxy for Scottishness, Otago and Southland were still about half Scottish in 1871, in 1956, and possibly the present, except for a more mixed student population.[6] In the south, Scots filled the role that English filled elsewhere. The local Maori, Ngai Tahu, whose pre-1848 Pakeha partners were more English and less American than in the north, may be more English than their local Pakeha.[7]

There were at least two intriguing groups of Highland Scots immigrants. One re-emigrated from Cape Breton Island in Canada to Waipu in Northland between 1854 and 1860, and established a community in which difference persisted well into the twentieth century. Church services were in Gaelic until World War One, and the practice of fostering children, sharing them out among families within the community without very much regard for direct kinship, lasted even longer. Most of the Waipu Scots came from only three Highland parishes.[8] The other Highland group were Shetland Islanders, who displayed a marked preference for New Zealand as an immigrant destination from the 1870s to the 1950s. It has been estimated that between 30,000 and 50,000 New Zealanders today have some Shetland descent. The population of the islands themselves in 1983 was only 23,000, making New Zealand more Shetland than the Shetlands. Shetlanders in New Zealand sometimes distinguished themselves from other Highland Scots, let alone Lowlanders, by emphasising their Norse heritage – the islands were ruled by Norway until 1472. Their festivals, and their knitting and fiddling traditions, survived at least to the 1950s.[9] The cases of the Waipu Scots and the Shetlanders suggest that the Highland minority of Scots tended to replicate what we will see was the experience of non-British migrant groups. The Lowland majority, on the other hand, appears to have replicated the experience of English migrants, and to have made almost as great a contribution to 'mainstream culture'.

Scots were both concentrated *and* widespread. In 1871, Presbyterians were not only dominant in Otago and Southland, but were also between 17 and 20 per cent of the Pakeha population of all other provinces except unusually English Taranaki and Nelson.[10] From the 1880s there was a second great Scottish migration, this time internal. Southern Scots came north in thousands, moving into the North Island dairying and fat-lambing districts opened for business by refrigeration.[11] For reasons including the emphasis on education and the fact that Otago had been the wealthiest province from the 1860s to the 1880s, Scots appear to have been disproportionately successful in many walks of life. They began a little better educated and a little better capitalised, and became over-represented in various élites. They were also disproportionately rural, raising the possibility of Anglo-Pakeha cities and a Scots-Pakeha countryside. 'It is most noticeable that everywhere the proportion of Scots in the country districts is far higher than in the towns.'[12] Because recolonial New Zealand took rural people as its archetypes, this further magnified Scots' impact on the national compound culture. A 1970s comic icon of this culture, Fred Dagg, might have been better named Fred McDagg. The Scottish values of Otago – being egalitarian and down-to-earth, but competent and successful – were highly regarded by rural people in neighbouring South Canterbury, which was predominantly English.[13] Scottishness was also an obvious cultural 'denomination of dissent' when New Zealanders wished to emphasise distinctiveness from the English. Remember, we are not looking for reinvented and romantic Highland Scottishness, kilt, dirk and sporran; but for mild New Zealand Lowland Scottishness: archetypally egalitarian, competent, undemonstrative and somewhat dour. Except in the south, Scots did 'assimilate' readily, but into something in which they had a very large shareholding – New Zealandness. In the south, others assimilated to them. Outside Scotland itself, there probably is no other country in the world in which Scots had more influence. For what it is worth – and it may be worth quite a lot – New Zealand is *the* neo-Scotland.

If one had to describe the leading influences on Pakeha in old ethnic terms, 'Anglo-Scots' is a lot more accurate than 'Anglo' alone – or than 'Anglo-Celtic'. The latter term implies an equal share for, and equal assimilation of, Catholic Irish, and this does not appear to have been the case. The prophets of progressive colonisation preferred to avoid assisting Catholic Irish immigrants, but were quite willing to resort to them when other cupboards were bare. Irish also entered of their own volition through Australia in substantial numbers. Consequently, the Irish proportion of Pakeha rose from around 10 per cent in the 1850s, to 18 per cent in the 1880s (including Protestants). But, in marked contrast to the Scots and English, the Catholic Irish were not allowed reinforcements thereafter. The absolute number of Irish-born peaked in 1881, then fell steadily thereafter. Reinforcements of fresh immigrants kept the number of Scots-born fairly steady, and the number of English-born actually rose.[14] This trend preceded the partition of Ireland in 1922, and was at least partly the result of a preference for English and Scots in twentieth-century government campaigns to encourage immigration. The myth of '98.5 per cent British' was trying to make itself true.

Yet, if we hold to the rule of looking for moderate difference coupled with a sharing of compound cultures, we find that New Zealand Irish ethnicity did manage to persist. Unlike the Scots, the Catholic Irish were not dominant in any large region, though they came close in Westland, where they were about a third of the population. What they did do was cluster or network in smaller localities – urban neighbourhoods such as South Dunedin or Grey Lynn in Auckland, and rural districts such as Temuka in South Canterbury.[15] Irish also clustered occupationally, in two jobs on the fringes of respectability: hotel-keeping and policing. About 42 per cent of the police were Catholic Irish in the 1890s and 1900s, and probably beyond.[16] New Zealand Irish had two key institutions that made for the persistence of difference: the Catholic Church and Catholic schools. Schools help generate community among parents as well as children, and Catholics, church and laity, put immense effort into expanding their own schools system. In 1950, 75 per cent of Catholic children attended 240 Catholic schools, which were arguably also New Zealand Irish schools.[17] The clergy running both church and school were disproportionately metropolitan Irish: missionaries of Irishness as well as Catholicism. Catholicism encouraged in-marriage. Historians have noted the willingness of Irish to marry other denominations, but over half still married other Irish Catholics, who were only about 14 per cent of potential partners. Irish women were more prone than men to insist that the children of mixed marriages be brought up as Catholics, and therefore to some extent as Irish. Irish female migration was disproportionately high in the 1870s, as the Vogellians sought brides to sop up and civilise their surplus males. The mixed marriages these women made may have spread Irishness rather than reduced it. Despite government adjustments to the immigration gates, despite the pressures of assimilation, the proportion of Catholic Irish remained stable at around 13–14 per cent.[18]

It would be an exaggeration to describe the New Zealand Irish as an oppressed minority, and there is a danger of overstating and stereotyping their persisting difference. Wary of this, Donald Akenson emphasises Irish economic and social success, and pours scorn on the notion that they were persistently crime-prone.[19] Yet in 1892, well after the 1840s–70s heyday of crime in New Zealand, Catholic Irish were 32 per cent of the prison population as against 14 per cent of the general population.[20] That Irish were disproportionately working class was one explanation of this. But a shared sense of being disadvantaged outsiders, and a subculture with different definitions of social crime, may also have contributed, as it did among urban Maori after World War Two. Overt sectarianism only flared in spasms. There were bitter sectarian riots at Hokitika in 1868, when the state genuinely feared armed rebellion, and at Timaru and Christchurch in 1879 over Orange Lodge marches by Irish Protestants.[21] As we have seen, there was another spasm between 1912 and 1922. Low-key antagonism among schoolchildren persisted at least until the 1960s. 'Catholic, Catholic ring the bell/Catholic, Catholic, go to Hell.'

Where ethnic antagonism could persist, so could ethnic difference and ethnic community. There is good evidence of tight Irish community in Christchurch between 1876 and 1915. Over 90 per cent of the married Irishmen who left wills named only fellow Irish Catholics as their executors; just one out of 76 named only non-Catholic executors.[22] Novelist Dan Davin and historian Peter O'Connor, New Zealand Irish themselves, bore witness to a strong sense of community among the Irish of Southland. Davin noted that 'religion tended to be identified with "culture"', and may have identified himself with an Irish bardic tradition.[23] O'Connor wrote of 'massive tribal gatherings, half picnic, half council of war, where between the Celtic songs and the wheelbarrow races their priests crooned to them of the sweets of victory to come'.[24] The wheelbarrow races may have been drawn from mainstream Pakeha culture, but the songs, the priests and the sense of tribal gathering were not.

White New Zealand?

New Zealand immigration policy to the 1880s had its racial and cultural preferences, but they were less strong than they later became. Wakefieldian and Vogellian colonisers were prepared to resort to Irish and Scandinavians, even to Italians and Australians, when English and Scots could not be had. Wakefield's willingness to have Catholic or even Muslim organised settlements if the price was right was a standing joke. A commission of inquiry into Chinese immigration in 1871 decided that it was not a problem. But, from the 1880s, New Zealand's immigration gates began to close, to all but the racially elect. Ironically, immigration was decreasing in importance from this time anyway. During the whole twentieth century, immigration in proportion to host population never reached anything like the rates of the great peopling period, 1840s–1880s. But there were still bouts of immigration, some of it state-assisted as it had been in the nineteenth century. One spasm occurred between 1903 and 1914; another between 1920 and 1927. The first spasm boosted the population by over 100,000, the second by about 80,000. Both spasms, and especially the second, were partly the result of government-assisted passages and publicity.[25] In the peak years 1920–26, about 60,000 British immigrants were assisted in, compared with about 30,000 in 1905–14.[26] The great majority were English and Scots.

Immigration policy discriminated positively in favour of Britons; it discriminated negatively against most other groups. Restrictive legislation began in 1881 and progressively tightened to the late 1920s. From 1897, prospective immigrants other than British and Irish were made to pass a language test, which from 1908 could be manipulated by officials to exclude almost anyone. The system remained largely intact at least until the 1950s, and arguably until 1974. Racism was not always overt, for diplomatic reasons such as the fact that India, too, was part of the British Empire. But informal racial restrictions lurked close to the surface and sometimes above it. Modern historians consistently describe this as the 'White New Zealand' policy, similar to that in operation in Australia and Canada and, from 1924, the United States. Indeed, one scholar has suggested that New Zealand's attitude was even tougher than that of the other neo-Britains.[27] That immigration policy, 1880s–1950s, was intensely racialist is beyond dispute. That it was 'white' is not so clear.

From the 1880s, there was an increasing tendency to racially rank past and prospective migrant groups. It was not a matter of simply preferring British to others, but of consistently ranking the others. At the top of this racial ranking were Northern Europeans, notably Germans and Scandinavians; in the middle were Southern Europeans, notably Dalmatians and Italians; at the bottom were Asians, notably Chinese and Indians.

Northern Europeans were not quite as welcome as English or Scots, but were considered a good second best, with an edge even over Catholic Irish. When New Zealand recognised that it could not get enough Britons, it was to Northern Europeans that it turned. Scandinavian-born and German-born New Zealanders numbered about 4,000 each in 1911, about 1 per cent of the population between them. But, as noted above, birthplace statistics were merely the tip of the ethnic iceberg. Because they entered from the 1840s in both genders, intermarried quite freely with neo-British, and bred enthusiastically, Germans and Scandinavians spread their genes throughout the Pakeha population. A recent study of New Zealand Germans cites three cases of early immigrant couples having between 1,137 and 3,500 descendants each (!), and calculates that 'there must be, therefore, at a conservative estimate, several hundred thousand present-day New Zealanders who are of German descent'.[28] This seems an exaggeration, but 100,000 or even 200,000 is conceivable. There were clusters of ethnic Germans in Nelson, Westland, Northland, Rangitikei, urban Wellington and Palmerston North, which was 8.5 per cent German in 1878.[29] The Lutheran Church, to which many Germans belonged, may also have provided a site for some persistence of ethnic difference. It still had about 4,000 adherents in the 1950s.[30] Each of the two world wars saw bouts of anti-Germanism. In the first, a university professor was arrested for burning rubbish in his incinerator on suspicion of sending smoke signals to U-boats.[31] But these spasms passed, and they had surprisingly little effect on immigration policy. German immigration renewed in 1928. Even in 1950, in the aftermath of World War Two, German women were allowed in, although men were considered too dangerous for the moment.[32] Both wars did cause German New Zealanders to lower their profiles and sometimes Anglicise their names. But not even world wars could permanently eliminate their status as favoured immigrants.

Scandinavians were the most favoured continentals of all, until the advent of the Dutch in the 1950s. Danes were the most numerous, followed closely by Norwegians and Swedes. As town names like Dannevirke and Norsewood attest, they clustered in Hawke's Bay in particular, where they were 7 per cent of the population in 1878. Unlike the Germans, they faced no wartime stigma and maintained, or revived, ethnic newspapers, such as *Scandia*, and ethnic clubs. In the early 1980s, it was claimed that 'Scandinavian clubs are the fastest growing ethnic clubs in New Zealand', and 300 people attended a 'Scandinavian convention' in Norsewood in 1983.[33] Intriguingly, the name implies some internalisation of the New Zealand tendency to lump Danes, Swedes and Norwegians together as 'Scandinavians'.

Like the Germans, Scandinavians had a high reputation for assimilation, and they do seem to have merged quite readily with the Pakeha mainstream, though specific research is lacking. They were thought to be 'settlers ready to adopt the culture and outlook of their British cousins'.[34] To Dr R. A. Lochore, a leading immigration expert and government official in the 1940s and 1950s, 'they scarcely seemed to be foreigners at all, they are so like us New Zealanders . . . Big capable men who can be relied upon to do a job and to stand by their mates.' 'English comes easily to them', because of a shared Viking syntax. Scandinavians 'were the least alien of aliens, melting away into the British population like snow on the Wellington hills'. Unfortunately, continued Lochore, 'all the Anglo-Saxon nations want Scandinavians for preference', which meant that New Zealand could not get enough. It had therefore to resort to less desirable types of Europeans, but in tiny doses, because its previous experience of them had not been good. The oldest Southern European group was Italian. Some 300 Italians were assisted out in the 1870s, and more trickled in slowly thereafter. The number of Italian-born approached 1,000 in 1936. Italians tended to cluster in Wellington, as did Greeks, who were even less numerous than the Italians until a surge in immigration after World War Two.

By far the largest Southern European group was that variously known as Dalmatian ('Dallies'), Croatian, Austrians, Yugoslav and 'Ngati Tarara'. The last name was given by Maori – whether as a transliteration of 'Dalmatian' or a jibe about speed of speech is not known. They came from the province of Dalmatia, on the east coast of the Adriatic Sea. Dalmatia was ethnically part of Croatia, but had been politically and economically separated for a long time. It was under Venetian rule from 1420 to 1797, and mostly under Austrian rule thereafter until 1919, when the kingdom of Yugoslavia was formed. Dalmatian sailors and wanderers first visited New Zealand in the 1850s. A steady trickle entered from about 1880, and focused mainly on the kauri-gum fields of Northland, where Dalmatians with little English language or capital could work as a group. One party of nine men won £1,000 each in a lottery in 1892. They are said to have returned home with gold-headed canes, omitting only to tell their admiring relatives the provenance of their new-found wealth. Assuming the streets of Auckland were paved with gold, the Dalmatian trickle grew into a small stream. The total inflow exceeded 8,000, 1890s–1920s.[35] New Zealanders of Dalmatian or Croatian origin are now estimated to total between 60,000 and 70,000.

Lochore conceded that Dalmatia was only on the edge of the 'crude Slav vortex', and that Dalmatians did become 'bigger and better peasants' in Northland but, he felt, they had little else going for them. 'Scarcely a week goes by but some Yugoslav comes before northern courts on a charge of sly-grogging, illicit gambling, disorderly behaviour, or tax evasion.' Your Dalmatian had his virtues, but was 'turbulent, headstrong, ungovernable, and unintimidable by any outwardly-imposed authority'. His comments about Italians, who initially came out as musicians 'in the traditional style, with barrel-organ and monkey', and whose sons 'played no games except cards', and about Greeks in their fish-and-chip shops 'reeking of boiling oil', were similar. In general, Southern Europeans were to be avoided. 'We naturally prefer northerners . . . from the cousin stocks of Europe.'[36] Lochore was no complete maverick. He was the government's chief advisor on immigration in the 1940s and 1950s. Similar views can be traced back to legislation restricting Dalmatian immigration from 1898. In 1907, the historian Dr Guy Scholefield described Dalmatians as dangerous 'non-Teutonic elements'; Slavs were 'rude and scarcely cultured above the plane of the Huns and Goths'; the 'untamed advance guard of barbarism'.[37] During World War One, there was a moral panic about Dalmatian loyalty, despite their general antagonism to their Austrian rulers. The issue was investigated by none other than John Cullen, of 1913 fame, recently retired as Commissioner of Police. Cullen concluded that 'after close intercourse with Jugoslavs I am now in a position to say . . . that they are not desirable persons to be allowed to remain in this Country'. They were seldom allowed to join the New Zealand army, but were required to labour on public works and interned if they refused.[38] Lochore's own book, published in 1951, carried a cautious endorsement from the Secretary of Internal Affairs. Its views were entirely consistent with 1950 Cabinet papers on immigration, except that the book was more moderate.

The papers recommended unambiguously 'that policy towards Yugoslav immigration be directed towards ending it'. 'Present policy is to look with favour only upon those applications from the "Northern" half of Europe . . . Entry permits from other European countries are, in the main, discouraged.'[39] In 1953, officials referred openly to 'the Government's policy to bring Yugoslav immigration to an end'. A careful study in the 1970s found 'clear evidence' of discrimination against Southern European immigration 'on the basis of nationality'. 'Preference is clearly expressed for "British", western or northern Europeans.'[40] 'The influx of Italians, Greeks, and Yugoslavs in Australia,' remarked another academic commentator in 1974, 'is looked upon with horror in New Zealand.'[41]

The third category of non-Maori and non-British New Zealanders was Asian. Two Asian groups of similar size were Lebanese and Syrian Christians, who totalled 1,400 overseas-born in 1945, and Indians, of whom there were 1,500. Though the first Indian settler in New Zealand arrived before 1810, few others did so in the nineteenth century – there were only 46 in 1896.[42] Indian inflow really began in the 1900s, and included a small group of Punjabis, mostly of the Jat caste, who can be 'loosely regarded as Sikhs'. The great majority, however, were Gujaratis from Surat, some of whom came to New Zealand through Fiji, where the importation of indentured Indian labour began in 1879. Like other immigrant groups, the Gujaratis seized a window of opportunity, immediately before and after World War One – a gap in the thickening gate of immigration law. As with the others, further immigration after 1920 tended to be restricted to the family members of those already here. 'Chain migration' was the name of the game, and your chain had to have started before 1920.

By far the largest group of Asian New Zealanders were the Chinese. New Zealand's links with China date back to the 1790s, when its seal furs sold in thousands in the markets of Canton. The link then lapsed, but revived in the 1860s, when Chinese came in to the South Island gold diggings. The Chinese-born population of New Zealand peaked in 1881 at 5,004, a figure not exceeded until after World War Two. New Zealand's share of a great Chinese diaspora was not huge compared with Australia or the United States, but the Chinese in 1881 came in ahead of the Germans as the largest ethnic group other than English, Scots, Irish and Maori. The total number of Chinese to enter New Zealand between 1871 and 1920 was 15,500, of whom many went home again.[43] Between the 1860s and the 1900s, when they began spreading more widely around the country, they were a very significant minority in parts of Otago, Westland and Southland. They tended towards marginal mining areas, which earlier diggers had failed to mine out or had found too difficult. They lived in their own communities, rarely dominating a whole settlement, but often forming Chinese quarters in Pakeha towns – Haining

Street in Wellington, Greys Avenue in Auckland. They had their own stores, teahouses and boarding houses, and obtained supplies of goods such as bottled condiments from China – enough to surprise archaeologists at some Otago sites.[44]

The early Chinese settlement of New Zealand was male. Only nine of the 5,004 of 1881 were women.[45] Like many European immigrants, the Chinese hoped to make their fortunes in 'New Gold Hill' (one of the many names New Zealand shares with Australia) and return home to their wives, who remained behind taking care of their children and parents, as was customary. Chinese migrants were so committed to this idea that they formed societies to send their corpses home dead if they could not make it alive. In 1902, one corpse ship, the *Ventnor*, went down en route to China, with the loss of almost 500 New Zealand Chinese bodies. The customary restriction of migration to men and the preference for sojourning over settling are factors in the failure of the old Chinese community to reproduce itself as it might have done. If they had reproduced as much as the Germans, whom they outnumbered in 1881, then a hundred thousand more New Zealanders today might have some Chinese descent. But sojourning was not the only factor in hobbling the old New Zealand Chinese ethnic group, in aborting its potential growth. The other was the growing determination of their fellow New Zealanders to keep them out if possible, and keep them few in number if not.

Asians ranked even lower than Southern Europeans on the immigration scale of desirability. Indians were discriminated against consistently, but not quite as much as the Chinese. The bond for good behaviour that Chinese immigrants had to pay eventually rose to £200 – twice as much as that for any other race.[46] 'Chinese,' stated government memoranda in 1950, 'are the only aliens who cannot freely obtain permits for the entry of their wives and children under our present immigration policy.'[47] Intellectuals and politicians such as Reeves, Stout, Tregear, Ward, Massey, Ngata and many others were explicitly antagonistic to Chinese immigration. Seddon, that walking opinion poll, led the pack. 'There is about as much distinction between a European and a Chinaman as that between a Chinaman and a monkey.'[48] 'I would rather a case of the plague here than see a hundred Chinese land.'[49] 'The chow element in New Zealand is like a cancer eating into the vitals of our moral being and slowly and insidiously encompassing the doom of its victim.'[50] Cartoons of evil Chinese appeared in trademarks for consumer products; children as well as their elders harrassed 'chows' and 'chinks';[51] and in 1905 Lionel Terry shot an old Chinese cripple in Haining Street, Wellington, claiming in his defence that the killing was no crime and that he was striking a blow against the Yellow Peril.

Terry was clearly what used to be called mad. He believed himself to be the Messiah, one up on his father, who was content with being the successor to Napoleon. Lionel Terry lived out his life in a mental hospital in the South Island. Just before his death in 1952, he was to be found 'seated on an elevated throne ... with long white hair and a beard which extended to his waist', advocating 'the trans-shipment of all Maoris to offshore islands'.[52] His crime itself did not necessarily indicate anything at all about public opinion. But his confinement was comfortable and loose; he escaped four times and was sheltered by rural people. 'Letters poured into newspapers, acclaiming him as a patriot.' 'Almost every person is in sympathy with Terry.'[53] It is not Terry's crime that tells us much about New Zealand attitudes, but the fact that he became something of a folk hero for it.

New Zealand Sinophobia was no pogrom, and it was not constant. It rose in the 1880s, killed only one or two Chinese, though it marred the lives of thousands, and began to decline from the 1930s. But it was quite strong, and existing explanations for it do not seem to me to be adequate. It intensified *after* the gold rushes, with which it is internationally associated. It does not correlate with economic depression, but increased in boom times as well. It correlates inversely with the actual Chinese percentage of the population, increasing as they became fewer. It did not stem from a class-specific fear of competition: workers were Sinophobic, but so were bourgeois and intellectuals. Chinese were castigated for not assimilating, yet were not allowed to assimilate. Pakeha would not marry them; Chinese women were not allowed in in any numbers until the 1930s. This strategy, of allowing in men for their labour but excluding women to strangle undesired ethnic minorities was later applied to other groups. Even the wives of long-term Chinese male residents were only allowed very restricted entry. As late as 1950, government officials were congratulating themselves on their clemency in letting a Chinese resident of 50 years bring in a wife he had married in 1898.[54] The intensity of Sinophobia in a country that took some pride in its alleged racial tolerance is something of a mystery. I myself suspect that it reflects the Pakeha identity crisis of the decades around 1900, arising from the Long Stagnation, and the collapse of progressive colonisation and the Tasman world. Racial scape-goating is a classic panacea for insecure collective identities.

Some whites were more favoured than others, and some blacks were more favoured than others – or at least slightly less disfavoured. Indians and Pacific Island Polynesians appear to have been somewhat less discriminated against in immigration policy than other coloured peoples. What template fits this dog's breakfast of racial ranking? It was not a 'White New Zealand' policy. A white Swedish woodcutter was considered more desirable than an equally white Russian woodcutter. The ostensible criterion for ranking was the perceived capacity to 'assimilate' into the mainstream. But the racial assumptions were very clearly the subtext. Even if the Russian woodcutter could read and write in English, while the Swede could not, the latter was still preferred. A superbly qualified Anglo-Burmese lawyer would always rank below an English labourer.

In my view, the racial template was Aryanism, which was already central in New Zealand racial ideology because of its capacity to incorporate Maori. References to 'the cousin stocks of northern Europe', by Lochore and others, made some such racial concept explicit. 'Teutonic', 'Nordic' and 'Germanic', though sometimes used as synonyms for 'Aryan', were not so inclusive of select non-Europeans. 'Caucasian' – increasingly the preferred racial label after World War Two – was not so exclusive. Aryanism had a flexible embrace, but median definitions included most Northern and Western Europeans, and excluded most Southern and Eastern Europeans. This definition very accurately describes New Zealand's preferred immigrants to the 1970s.[55] Aryanism also facilitated New Zealand's need to accommodate its numerous Scots, Welsh and Irish. Celts were not Anglo-Saxons or Teutons, but they were Aryans. Tregear's narrowest definition of Aryan consisted of the Maori and 'his Norse and Celtic brothers'.[56] New Zealand officialdom probed surprisingly deep into arcane corners of European racial theory. Cabinet was advised in 1950 that the only worthwhile Eastern European immigrants were Balts – who happened to be of Germanic descent. Northern Italians were less undesirable then Southern, presumably owing to Germanic legacies from the Lombards and Ostrogoths. Anti-Indian sentiment was reconciled with the alleged Aryan origins of some Northern Indians as follows: 'Unfortunately we in New Zealand know but little of the Aryans of India . . . Our knowledge is practically confined to inhabitants of central India, a degraded race.'[57] Aryanism was an exceptionally flexible racial myth, capable of linking as well as distinguishing. It could incorporate Scandinavians, Germans and Celts. It could also incorporate selected non-Europeans, such as Northern Indians, Maori and other Polynesians, by giving them proto-European origins. New Zealand's immigration policy was not white, but Aryan.

It would be just possible to present New Zealand racialism in general and Aryanism in particular as a hidden proto-Nazism, and highlight it on the dust jacket of this book as a sensational revelation. Lochore, who was probably responsible for the 1950 reports to Cabinet on immigration, was of the 'Hitler did have a few good ideas' school of thought. An 'unexpurgated' draft version of his 1951 magnum opus, *From Europe to New Zealand*, stated that 'the Nazi only wanted to become Herrenvolk [a master race] like the English . . . After the Scandinavians, the German is our nearest kinsman.' Lochore had a German doctorate, lectured to Nazi storm troopers in 1936, and became New Zealand's first ambassador to West Germany.[58] Some lines from Tregear's *The Aryan Maori* are literally interchangeable with lines from Hitler's *Mein Kampf*. 'That fire of mind and body which has caused the Aryan race to be the world's history-makers for the last four thousand years.'[59] Aryanism even seeped into the imagery of popular culture. Trademarks of New Zealand consumer goods used swastika motifs from the 1910s to the 1930s, including a Wellington sweet manufacturer's 'Swastika Confectioneries', and a line of agricultural tools that superimposed the swastika over 'Kia Ora', until it was replaced in 1939 with the profile of a goat.[60]

Such sensationalism, however, would be deceptive. Aryanism was more a matter of utility than conviction, and racialism was often qualified in practice. It was normally subject to what might be called 'personal exemption', the human capacity to stigmatise a group in theory but exempt particular individuals of that group in practice. Individuals of every ethnic group, including Chinese and Indians such as the Taranaki businessman Chew Chong and the Punjabi wrestler and 'star rugby player' Harbans Singh Pahilwan, were respected by the mainstream.[61] Anti-Semitism often cohabits with Aryanism, and it did exist in New Zealand. But it tended to be abstract, arising more from readings of the spurious *Protocols of Zion* than from hostility to the Jewish family next door. During World War One, Jews in New Zealand appear to have suffered more from having German names than from anti-Semitism.[62] New Zealand's Jewish community, which tended to cluster in Wellington and Auckland cities, was small but prosperous and prominent. Premier Vogel himself had been Jewish, and Jewish families such as Nathan, Levin, Myers and Hallenstein continued to be highly successful in businesses of various kinds. Maori, as we have seen, and Indians occasionally appealed to Aryanism themselves. During a flurry of anti-Indian sentiment at Pukekohe in 1926, Indians defended themselves by claiming that they were 'brothers and first cousins of the English people' and accepted the notion that some Indians were Aryan while other were not. 'We Sikhs and Punjabis are Aryans but the low bad-mashes [ruffians] of Pukekohe are Bengalese or Madresses.'[63] Ngata himself was not above putting the boot into the Chinese. 'Any integration between Maori and Chinese would bring racial contamination and moral degradation of the Maori people.'[64] Sinophobia in general thrived when a collective scapegoat was needed, 1880s–1920s, but declined from the 1930s. 'White Race Leagues' and 'Anti-Asiatic Leagues' rose and fell in much the same pattern.[65] Scandinavians, Germans and Irish made the Aryanist cut, as did Maori. The partial exemption of Maori from New Zealand racialism is an exceptional phenomenon in settler societies, and was arguably a benign one despite its dubious roots.

Yet the fact remains that racialism was central in recolonial ideology, 1880s–1960s. We should not necessarily castigate its exponents, who were creatures of their times, but we cannot understand New Zealand history without understanding it. The Aryan label on the package was ripped off during World War Two, of course, but some of the contents survived. Before this, recolonial racial ideology had constructed the immigration gates – an 'Aryan New Zealand' policy. The gates tell us not only what the gatekeepers wanted to keep outside, but also what they thought, or wanted to think, that they had inside: '98.5 per cent British'.

Islands of Difference

In the 1870s and 1880s, the people of the Panyu district of Canton lived in numerous small villages, including Stone Horse, South Village, View Hill and Round Hill. The favoured foods of all four villages were rice and pork; delicacies for special occasions included sugar dumplings, moon cakes, bean-curd cakes and bean-jam pies. The villagers worked extremely hard, but celebrated a number of festivals, including Chinese New Year, when they decorated their houses with red paper, wished each other joy and wealth, and feasted to the extent their means allowed. In all four villages, the men wore their hair in pigtails; they seldom drank alcohol but enjoyed tobacco and, in some cases, opium. There was at least one difference between Round Hill and the other Panyu villages. The others were in Canton, while Round Hill was in Southland, on the south coast of New Zealand. It was 'the southernmost Chinese settlement in the world'.[66]

New Zealand Chinese difference and community seldom existed as nakedly as it did at Round Hill in the 1880s, but it did persist. From about 1900, the Chinese moved from the goldfields of the South Island into towns large and small, all over New Zealand. The single men went home to China or lived out lonely lives in New Zealand, quietly but tragically, dreams unfulfilled. The few families (estimated to number a hundred in 1935) throve in businesses such as fruit and vegetable shops and market gardens, but faced increasing pressure to assimilate. A Presbyterian missionary, Alexander Don, who made a career out of trying to convert Chinese, pursued them from the goldfields to Dunedin and then to Palmerston North, but had 'strictly limited success'.[67] Some Chinese themselves tried to camouflage and to minimise their difference, as noted in the previous section. One can hardly blame them for appearing to bow to the prevailing winds of conformism. After the Japanese invasion of China in 1937, the government at last allowed in about 1,500 of their wives and children on temporary permits, which World War Two made permanent.[68] It was this accidental breach in the immigration gates that ensured the survival of the New Zealand Chinese as a substantial ethnic group. 'The emergence of racial islands in such a small country as

New Zealand,' warned the 1950 government report, 'must inevitably lead to serious maladjustments.'[69] But islands of difference did emerge and persist, and the Chinese 'island' was not the only one.

This chapter focuses on ethnic difference, but we should concede that assimilation in New Zealand did have major successes. The two largest ethnic groups, English and Scots, do appear to have merged substantially, though not completely – some Highland Scots may have been exceptions, as we have seen. Scots had much more importance in this mix than they did in old Britain. In this respect at least, New Zealand was indeed Better Britain. Protestant Irish – distinct from Northern Irish, many of whom were Catholic – should also be included in this 'mainstream', and so presumably should Welsh. Scandinavian and German levels of assimilation are less clear but may have been quite high. The 'mainstream', then, comprised 75–80 per cent of the total population in the first half of the twentieth century. Apart from Catholic Irish and Maori, the leading ethnic minorities were Chinese and Dalmatian. Italians, Greeks, Indians, Lebanese and Jews were also significant. How did these groups survive the powerful assimilating pressures of the tight society?

One key was clustering, both geographic and occupational. Geographic clustering was itself of two kinds. New Zealand's minorities were not drawn from across the whole of their home countries, but from tiny clusters of communities within them. We have seen that this was the case with the Shetlanders, the Waipu Scots and the Chinese. The Gujaratis were mainly from half a dozen or so villages in two small districts, Jalalpore and Bardoli, and Patel was the surname of many.[70] Most New Zealand Dalmatians originated from only nine villages in central Dalmatia. About 16 per cent came from the small island of Korcula; another 11.5 per cent from the single mainland village of Podgora.[71] Most Greeks came from three or four islands, and the original Italian settlers were mainly from Livorno.[72] In these tiny regions, pinpoints on a map, New Zealand was a name to conjure with, the local manifestation of an idealised 'New World'. In one Dalmatian village in the 1950s, if you wore your Sunday best on a weekday, you might be asked: 'Where do you think you are, Queen Street?' – a reference to the main street of Auckland. In another in 1980, you could see an exchange rate for the New Zealand dollar in the bank window, for the first time on a European tour since leaving London. The Shetland Islands have a similar conceptual relationship with New Zealand, but the assumption that this is 'unique among European communities' is mistaken.[73]

In New Zealand, many of the minorities clustered afresh. In the 1960s, there were 40 Greeks from Ithaca in Hastings.[74] Greeks in general clustered in Wellington, where over half lived in the suburbs of Mount Victoria and

Newtown. Dalmatians clustered in Northland, especially around Dargaville, to the 1920s and the decline of the gumfields. They then clustered in Henderson, still their capital, as well as in central Auckland and, to a lesser extent, central Wellington. Punjabis favoured a particular part of the Waikato, north-east of Hamilton. Clusters were not necessarily solid clumps. As with community in general, a network or 'patchwork' would do – a cousin next door, another around the corner, and two more in a neighbouring suburb. But the clusters could get pretty solid. A third of the houses in Panorama Road and Titoki Street in the Auckland borough of Mount Wellington are said to have been occupied by Dalmatians at one point. Most were from a single village – Zrnovo on Korcula, the Panorama Road of the north.[75]

Clustering at source and clustering at destination anchored 'chain migration'. Typically, a small 'clump' of Dalmatian, Indian or Chinese males would arrive together at Auckland or Dunedin, on the way to an entry occupation in which they could work together; the gumfields, the goldfields or contract labouring. They would bond further with each other and with co-nationals who had preceded them at some sort of 'staging post', at which information, advice and familiar company was available to the new immigrant. For Dalmatians, the staging post was the boarding-house district of central Auckland. For Punjabis, it was an establishment known as the 'Hindu Farm' in the Waikato, effectively a 'hospice for travellers'.[76]

Geographical clustering was coupled with occupational clustering. Minorities typically got into their own small businesses as quickly as possible, and helped friends and relatives into the same industry. 'Friends' and 'relatives' were categories that blurred among immigrant groups, as with the 'virtual kinship' practices of the Waipu Scots.[77] Greeks from Ithaca worked in restaurants and fish-and-chip shops; those from Mitilini in bootmaking, and those from Lesbos in hairdressing.[78] Chinese worked first on the goldfields, and then in market gardens and greengroceries, and to a lesser extent laundries and restaurants. Dalmatians began on the gumfields, and then moved into farming and the wine and fishing industries, and into quarrying, building and restaurants. In 1931, there were ten Dalmatian-owned restaurants in central Wellington. In 1944, there were 42 Dalmatian-owned businesses in central Auckland, including seventeen boarding houses. Of the 33 Dalmatians who settled in Taranaki before 1940, 26 went into restaurants and fish-and-chip shops – including fourteen men from Podgora.[79] The Punjabi entry occupation was scrub-cutting, in which they worked in gangs, followed by Waikato dairy farms.[80] Gujaratis also began with wage work such as scrub-cutting, then proceeded through hawking to fruit stalls, then to fruit shops, and later to dairies. As early as 1921, they had twice the general rate of self-employment.[81] Occupational clustering could operate against geographical clustering, because you could not have too many similar businesses in the same district or neighbourhood. But, especially in urban contexts, the two often went together.

Communal institutions of various kinds were another key to the persistence of difference. Apart from Irish and Maori, ethnic minorities seldom had their own schools. Some had churches. Jewish synagogues and Greek Orthodox churches were obvious foci of community. The Auckland and Wellington Jewish communities, each of about 500 families by the 1980s, centred on two religious congregations (liberal and orthodox), with associated religious schools, youth groups and clubs.[82] Some groups, however, shared a mainstream religion or did not have the critical mass in any particular locality to build their own church. Ethnic clubs were more common, and often had folk culture and sports groups attached to them. 'The Club' was the centre of community and social life for many Dalmatians in Auckland, from 1930. Indian societies were founded from 1918. The 'Country Section' of the Central Indian Association was Punjabi, the rest Gujarati.[83] Clusters, clubs and churches combined to encourage a degree of in-marriage, and this was further encouraged by ethnic attititudes – within and without the minorities themselves. Typically, male migrants would come first, establish themselves, and then bring over wives from their homelands, but in-marriage also persisted into the New Zealand-born generations to a surprising degree. Most New Zealand Chinese preferred in-marriage, at least in principle, and it was also preferred among New Zealand Dalmatians and Jews.[84]

In-marriage obviously required women from the relevant ethnicity, however, and until World War Two New Zealand's immigration gates were quite good at keeping out Chinese women in particular. This was an especially unattractive form of ethnic control: taking men, for their labour; relying on ethnic attitudes to prevent their marrying wives from the ethnic mainstream; and denying entry to women from their own group. Old single or separated men would either die or return home, and a potential blot on the ethnic landscape would be strangled before birth. But the same ethnic attitudes also encouraged in-marriage when women were available. After 1920, the laws that restricted entry to the family of migrants already in operated to the same effect. Thus laws and attitudes intended to encourage assimilation actually helped prevent it.

To add to the irony, immigration laws limiting entry to family members and to particular times and places encouraged New Zealand ethnic fragments to diverge from their country of origin. New Zealand Indian culture developed a strange mix of the denial of imported caste difference, in keeping with the local egalitarian ethos, and its unacknowledged persistence.[85] Even in New Zealand, higher castes were reluctant to marry Untouchables for example.

Even material Indian culture was not immune to adaptation. Faced with the absence of chapati flour, Sikhs persuaded storekeepers to stock wholemeal flour, a sufficient approximation of the real thing to make 'a passable chapati'.[86] They then got blacksmiths to make chapati pans from plowing discs – a Punjabi version of the iron patu produced by early Maori. Among Dalmatians, a 'New Zealand Croatian' language or sub-language has developed. It combines 'the language spoken in Dalmatia some 70 to 100 years ago' – itself a strange dialect in modern Zagreb – with English and Maori loan words and turns of phrase.[87] Its word for mainstream Pakeha is 'maslari', or 'butter people', an affluent folk but too benighted and ignorant to use olive oil. Maori and mainstream Pakeha are not the only cultures unique to New Zealand.

It is easy to get the impression that twentieth-century New Zealand consisted solely of the islands of Aotearoa. In fact, Wellington also administered a substantial chunk of the Pacific: the Cook Islands from 1890 (a New Zealand Resident preceded formal annexation by eleven years); Niue from 1901; Western Samoa from 1914; and the Tokelau Islands from 1925. New Zealand also shared the administration of Nauru – and the ruthless exploitation of its guano resources – with Australia and Britain between 1919 and 1967. All these islands were peopled at least partly by Polynesians like the Maori, but cultures varied between and even within island groups. Neither the political connection or the alleged Aryan origins of Polynesians helped Pacific Islanders gain entry to New Zealand itself before the 1950s. There were only 1,000 Island-born in New Zealand in 1921, and still only 3,000 in 1945.[88] Really large-scale Pacific Island immigration dates to the late 1950s, and even then they were initially allowed in as what the authorities hoped would be temporary guest workers. The important Pacific presence in New Zealand itself is treated in Chapter Eighteen.

New Zealand's aspirations for empire in the Pacific dated back to the early days of Pakeha settlement. George Grey and Julius Vogel were as ardent sub-imperialists as King Dick Seddon. Historians have tended to dismiss New Zealand's Pacific imperialism as 'baby playing emperor in the nursery', with some good reason.[89] New Zealand's overseas empire initially consisted of the Kermadec Islands, annexed in 1886, and its subjects comprised the islands' one settler family, the Bells. Parliament sang the national anthem on the formal annexation of the Cook Islands, in 1901, but the House was half empty. Even at full growth, in 1925, New Zealand's Pacific empire had a population of fewer than 100,000. After the occupation of German Samoa in 1914, New Zealand lost enthusiasm for the Pacific. It was, writes a leading specialist, 'marginal to New Zealand's interests'.[90] Yet 100,000 was not that small in comparison with New Zealand's own population. The Pacific Islands were among its nearest neighbours, and were ultimately to contribute large and important minorities to the country's own population. The real reason for historical and historiographical neglect in the first half of the twentieth century was recolonisation, which demoted the Pacific to a mere space between New Zealand and Britain. To a large extent, to say that New Zealand was in the Pacific was merely a geographical expression.

New Zealand's record in the smaller Island territories, the Cooks, Niue and the Tokelaus, seems that of a fairly benign bumbler, with spasms of less benignity and more efficiency. The enlightened and scholarly Frederick Moss, the first New Zealand administrator of the Cook Islands in the 1890s, when the population was about 8,000, was possibly also the best. His successor, Walter Gudgeon (1898–1909), who like Moss was something of an historian, encouraged the acquisition of Cook Island land by European settlers and the acquisition of Cook Island money by his own relatives. The longest-serving Cook Islands Resident Commissioner, Hugh Ayson (1922–43), does not appear to have done much, good or bad, except get drunk and beget illegitimate children. On the other hand, Maori medic Edward Ellison made a substantial contribution to the health of the Cook Islanders as Chief Medical Officer between 1931 and 1945. The forced recruitment of Cook Islanders for World War One, noted in the previous chapter, was not repeated in World War Two. Copra, bananas and oranges (and their juice) emerged as the leading export industries. But low prices for growers and low wages for workers limited the benefits for Cook Islanders themselves, as against New Zealand companies and middlemen. Orange and banana exports were greater in 1903 than in 1965.[91]

One gets a sense that Niue and the Tokelaus, in contrast to the Cooks and Samoa, used New Zealand rule almost as much as it used them. Niue did not wish to be grouped with, still less absorbed by, the neighbouring Cook Islands. Tokelauans felt the same about Samoa. Wellington was further away than Avarua or Apia. London was still further away, and Niueans in 1901 were irritated when they heard they were to be administered by New Zealand rather than Britain. They were even more irritated when New Zealand at first grouped them with the Cooks, but their protests led to separation in 1904. New Zealand officials displayed a similar difficulty in grasping Niuean and Tokelauan sentiments when decolonisation became an issue in the 1960s. Both island groups were tiny, with growing populations, mostly now living in New Zealand. They accepted autonomy, in varying and gradual degrees, but rejected independence. Their social and economic capital, though perhaps not their cultural one, was now Auckland. Their relationship with New Zealand had become intriguingly similar to that of New Zealand and Britain.[92]

The largest and most populous of New Zealand's Pacific responsibilities was Western Samoa. Samoans encountered Europeans in similar sequence to the Maori before them. European missionaries came from 1830, a mixed bag of settlers and traders – British, Germans and Americans – from about 1850, and the envoys and warships of these three states from the 1870s. Apia and Pago Pago did fine imitations of pre-1840s Kororareka during this period, and there were spasms of musket warfare between the two major tribal alliances from the 1840s to the 1890s. Formal European intervention was delayed by the sinking of German and American warships in Apia Harbour in 1888 by a providential hurricane, and by Samoan military successes against German punitive expeditions in the following decade. But, in an agreement of 1899, Samoa was split between the United States and Germany. After the New Zealand occupation of Western Samoa in 1914, it was run by a military administration until 1920, when it became a New Zealand 'mandate', a territory held in trust with responsibility to the League of Nations. Samoa became independent in 1962.

Samoan history in its colonial period, 1899–1962, is yet another subject to daunt the inexpert. New Zealand and Germany have reputations for the best and worst race relations in the twentieth century, and it is chastening to encounter the possibility that Germany's record in Samoa, under Wilhelm Solf, was better than New Zealand's. Being beaten into second place as humane colonisers by imperial Germany is not a good look. New Zealand politicians long claimed that New Zealand's experience governing Maori gave it special qualifications for Pacific administration – yet another incentive to maintain the myth of racial harmony. One revisionist history, which chastises New Zealand's record, may be somewhat prone to overstate a good case.[93] Other recent historians have revived the traditional defence of the New Zealand administration.[94] Their efforts, on the whole, are not convincing. New Zealand did have expertise that might have been useful in Samoa, such as that of Peter Buck. But it did not use it, and the case for the racialism and incompetence of New Zealand administrators in Western Samoa, at least between 1914 and 1935, seems strong.[95]

Samoans were Polynesian too, and therefore theoretically Aryan, according to the 'White Maori' racial ideology. One New Zealand official did use the notion of shared Aryanism to justify European–Samoan intermarriage, in marked contrast to Chinese–Samoan intermarriage, which was made illegal.[96] German settlers included their Samoan wives in a small local Nazi Party branch in the 1930s, again on the basis of shared Aryanism. This may be the world's only case of black Nazis.[97] But, among successive New Zealand administrators, the Aryan myth appears to have ameliorated racialism towards Samoans considerably less than it did that towards Maori. General G. S.

Richardson and Colonel Stephen Allen, administrators in 1923–28 and 1928–31 respectively, thought the Samoans 'destitute of reasoning power' with 'very undeveloped minds'. When they did learn quickly, it was 'the quickness of that great imitator the ape . . . and not that of the human species'.[98] New Zealand officialdom went to ludicrous lengths to maintain an image of European racial superiority. In 1929, the New Zealand film censor felt that, for Samoans, 'a picture with the famous dog Rin Tin Tin would be questionable as the dog frequently fights and overcomes the villain – a white man'.[99]

Such attitudes combined with disinterest in Wellington to create a New Zealand record in Samoa that was little short of disastrous, and that certainly included two specific disasters. The first was the influenza pandemic of 1918, which hit Western Samoa harder than virtually anywhere else in the world. A staggering 19.62 per cent of the population died, making it an absolutely exceptional demographic, and presumably social and cultural, catastrophe. The death rate was vastly higher than in New Zealand, even among Maori, which is not necessarily surprising given the epidemiological difference between a small island and a large landmass. But it was also higher than in American Samoa, which *is* surprising. Samoans attributed the disparity to ineffective New Zealand quarantine and relief measures. They appear to have been right, though the problem seems to have been due to incompetence and disinterest rather than malice.[100]

The New Zealand empire's second great disaster was the attempt to repress a Samoan nationalist movement, the Mau. The movement took shape from 1926, with peaceful protests and demonstrations increasing from 1927. It was led by Olaf Nelson, a Samoan-Swedish businessman, and Tupu Tamasese Lealofi, a high-ranking chief. The movement advocated greater local influence in government, and soon acquired the support of most Samoans. Both Richardson and Allen felt that 'rebellious Samoan children' needed a 'firm lesson'. The former deported 59 Samoans, including Nelson, in 1928. The latter created the environment for 'Black Saturday', 28 December 1929. On that day, during a peaceful protest in Apia, Allen ordered his special police force, recruited from New Zealand ex-soldiers, to arrest a wanted protester as a show of strength. The crowd resisted and threw stones. The police panicked and fired. Many Samoans were hit, and at least eight killed. They included Tamasese, who had been trying to restrain the protest.[101]

A policeman was beaten to death by angry protesters, and the allegation that a machine-gun was fired into the crowd appears to be untrue. But there is no doubt that trained New Zealand servicemen fired at least two volleys into an unarmed crowd. It was all rather embarrassing for the race relations paradise. 'New Zealand, which holds a world reputation for the results of the

Maori question, has come a cropper over this damned Samoa.'[102] Some Mau supporters took to the bush, where they were hunted by police and New Zealand naval columns until they submitted in 1930. Repression of the Mau, coupled with a halving of government expenditure on Samoa, continued until the election of the New Zealand Labour government in 1935.

For Samoans, there may be a silver lining to the clouds of New Zealand rule. The evidence appears to be that the New Zealanders were less benign than either the pre-1914 German administration of Western Samoa or the American administration of Eastern Samoa. But it was also less efficient and, perhaps, less wholeheartedly determined to convert or 'modernise'. The retention of culture and identity in Western Samoa, and possibly also of land, appears to have been higher than in Eastern Samoa or than it would have been in a German Western Samoa, had Solf's crusade to Europeanise continued. On the other hand, Solf and the New Zealanders alike favoured one basic Samoan institution – the matai, or hereditary chiefs – over another, the fono, or village council. Their support helped entrench and expand the matai. As elsewhere, the engagement of chiefly authority with colonialism reinforced both, and left Samoans with a more élitist legacy than they might otherwise have had. But, as with the Cooks, the Tokelaus and Niue, Samoa remained Samoan, an island of difference in the homogenising lands ruled by recolonial New Zealand.[103]

Better Britain at Bay
1920s–1960s

INTRODUCTION

At 10.46 on the morning of Tuesday, 3 February 1931, an earthquake shook the Hawke's Bay city of Napier. It lasted two and a half minutes, with a thirty-second break in the middle – just enough to fool you into believing that it was all over. Helped by the fires it started, the earthquake destroyed the town, causing £5 million worth of damage and killing 162 people in Napier, as well as 93 in neighbouring Hastings.[1] Bald statistics do not tell the story. In terms of 'impact on the community' – of friends, neighbours and relatives dead – the Napier toll alone was equivalent to over 10,000 killed in today's Auckland.

People coped, despite 525 aftershocks in the next two weeks. The homeless received help, food and shelter from their neighbours and from a British warship in the harbour; central and local government provided (somewhat miserly) financial relief; and memory focused on droller moments. A woman was said to have been thrown from an upper storey, landing in the street still naked in her bath, and was promptly given an overcoat by a policeman. Propriety was not forgotten even in the very moment of New Zealand history's worst civil disaster. Napier rose nicely from the ashes. It celebrated its rebuilding with a carnival in January 1933, and the rebuilding was carried out with some panache. The town eventually became the Art Deco jewel in sunny Hawke's Bay's crown. But this lay in the future. On 3 February 1931, there was only one comfort: the 1930s could hardly get any worse, could they?

They could. As Napier shook, the Great Depression of the 1930s settled on New Zealand 'like a new and unwanted stranger, a grey and ghostly visitor to the house'.[2] By 1933, New Zealand's export receipts were down 44 per cent on 1929 and the country was in its worst economic slump between the 1880s and the 1980s. Just as economic recovery was getting under way, in the later 1930s, the geopolitical situation deteriorated dramatically as Germany, Italy and Japan sought places in the sun. In September 1939, Britain and France reluctantly declared war on Germany, and New Zealand followed. In December 1941, Japan dropped its declaration of war on the American battle fleet at Pearl Harbour, and swept down East Asia and the Pacific towards New Zealand. World war raged until 1945, with New Zealand forces in the thick of it.

Depression and war were not only disasters in themselves, but also threats to the recolonial system. There were other threats, too, much more benign in human terms but equally dangerous to the status quo. In 1935, the first Labour government was elected. It was widely seen by contemporaries as the most radical outside the Soviet Union, and is widely seen by historians as the first genuinely independent government in New Zealand's history. Added to this, between 1918 and 1932 there was a significant shift in relations between Britain and the dominions, including New Zealand. The Balfour Declaration of 1926 announced that they were fully independent, and a 'British Commonwealth of Nations', nominally incorporating the dominions as equals, was superimposed on the 'British Empire' by the Statute of Westminster in 1931. It could be argued from this that recolonisation was maturing into independence. From the 1930s, increasing speed after World War Two, a decline in economic and geopolitical British power set in, yet another threat to the recolonial system. The period between the wars also saw a mass invasion of New Zealand by American popular culture: films, gramophone records, radio serials, novels and cars. These might be fun but they were not British, and 'Americanisation' was another big threat to recolonisation. It intensified during and after World War Two, when the possibility that Mother England would be replaced by Uncle Sam became very strong indeed. Part Three of this book explores New Zealand's response to these threats of massive change, 1920s–60s. Had the recolonial system reached maturity in the 1920s only to crumple under a succession of blows?

CHAPTER EIGHT

Depression and Labour

Part One of this book traced the development of the economic and ideological system of recolonisation from its origins in the 1880s to its maturity in the early 1920s. Part Two explored the matching growth of the tight society, with its three concordant harmonies: social, moral, and racial. In the 1920s and 1930s, the system faced challenges of three kinds. The first was a mixed set of developments in technology, in economic and political relations with Britain, and in cultural relations with America. The second was the Great Depression of 1929–35. The third was the advent of the first Labour government, elected in 1935 and then re-elected in 1938 with an even greater majority. The second and third developments are well-known watersheds in New Zealand history. They are the subjects of the later sections in this chapter. The first, mixed, set of changes has had a much lower profile, but gets what I hope are its just deserts in the next section.

Rewiring the System

During and after World War One, the importance of the dominions to Britain increased and became more obvious, both politically and economically. The extra political weight stemmed from their remarkable contribution during the war, which was much greater than anyone had expected. New Britons fought with the same commitment as the Old, and could no longer be easily dismissed as mere colonials. The dominions supplied more combat troops than India, which had many times their population.[1] They increased metropolitan British military power by between 20 and 30 per cent – more than Scotland, Wales and Ireland combined. The extra economic influence stemmed from a decline in Britain's global economic position, dating from World War One or before. Some historians attribute this decline to the weakness of technological and meritocratic cultures in Britain compared with Germany and the United States. Another explanation is that British capital had financed new infrastructures in the dominions (and America) rather than in Britain itself, leaving the metropolis with antiquated industrial plant and so unconsciously donating its economic future to its ungrateful offspring. Whatever the explanation, Britain between the wars 'retreated into the Empire', especially the dominions. For British industrialists, the dominions 'provided an escape hatch down which they hoped to disappear to avoid the agonies of modernisation and restructuring as competition increased'.[2] In 1913, the dominions provided 13.2 per cent of Britain's imports, took 17.5 per cent of its exports, and contained 26.4 per cent of its overseas investments. In 1934, the figures were 21.6, 23.3 and 41.4 per cent.[3]

The new political realities were formalised in New Zealand in various ways. The Governor was promoted to Governor-General in 1917 'in recognition of the growing importance of New Zealand, and in particular of the services which that Dominion has rendered during the War'.[4] In 1919–20, New Zealand itself, as well as Britain, signed the Treaty of Versailles ending World War One, and joined the new League of Nations. New Zealand participated in discussions with Britain and the other dominions that produced the Balfour Declaration in 1926 and the Statute of Westminster in 1931. Both declaration and statute asserted the full independence of the dominions and their equality with Old Britain, and institutionalised the British Commonwealth of Nations. Yet New Zealand declined to sign the Statute of Westminster until 1947, and the Governors-General remained Old Britons to 1967. New Zealand's leaders and constitutional experts, led by Massey, emphatically rejected any implication of independence or separation in the other measures. The leading subject expert is quite right to state that World War One and the consequent constitutional changes gave New Zealand 'an enhanced identity and a new status'.[5] But it is equally clear that neither the identity nor the status, still less the underlying economic and cultural realities, amounted to independence.

Canada, South Africa and the Irish Free State were interested in greater formal independence, Australia less so, and New Zealand least of all. On the Versailles Treaty and the League of Nations, New Zealand was carried along by its more independence-minded sisters. On the Balfour Declaration, it balked and insisted on a compromise in terminology to include 'the Empire' as well as 'the Commonwealth'.[6] On the Statute of Westminster, New Zealand (and Australia) spat the dummy completely and declined the opportunity for even nominal independence. Recolonial New Zealand was quite prepared to assert a share in the ownership of the black Empire, and even to help defend it in war, though not to help pay for it in peace. But, in its conceptual language, both 'Empire' and 'Commonwealth' were often code for white Empire and white Commonwealth, the cosy club of Britain and the white dominions. Recent historians generally acknowledge this, but what they fail to grasp is that this in turn was code for the bilateral recolonial relationship, similar but separate, between Old Britain and each dominion. 'Empire' and even 'Commonwealth' are concepts that have operated to obscure the more fundamental binary relationships.

The new economic realities were formalised at another conference between Britain and the dominions, in 1932 at Ottawa. The global Depression of 1929–35 created a sense of crisis. Britain seems to have suffered less, and recovered more quickly, from the Depression than New Zealand – its exports, on which it was less dependent anyway, fell 28 per cent by value compared with New Zealand's 44 per cent.[7] In marked contrast to New Zealand, meat consumption in Britain actually rose because of cheap and abundant imports.[8] But 28 per cent still hurt, and unemployment was very high. Canada, Australia and the rest of the Empire also suffered, and the British and neo-British leaders hoped that increased mutual aid could help them weather the storm. A complicated deal, or rather, set of deals, was struck that formalised and augmented the system of preferences already in place, so boosting the Empire and British shares of each other's trade. After Ottawa, food imports into Britain from the Empire went up 42 per cent, while those from other sources went down 32 per cent.[9]

New Zealand's market share benefited from this, at the expense of non-British protein exporters in Europe and South America, but not much.[10] New Zealand's recolonial relationship was 'natural', rather than artificially induced by legislation, and it was more highly developed than that of Canada and Australia, whose market shares now increased much more. For example, Australia's share of the British mutton market went from 3.5 to 25 per cent between 1924 and 1933, while New Zealand's share went from 41 to 54 per cent.[11] The Ottawa Agreement both masked and marked a long-term problem for recolonisation: the decline of British economic power. In the future, Britain would demand from New Zealand a more even balance of imports and exports. One benefit of the recolonial system to the 1920s was Britain's willingness to take between 74 and 87 per cent of New Zealand's exports while supplying only 46–47 per cent of its imports.[12] From the 1930s, apart from war years, this generosity began to diminish. For New Zealand at least, the Ottawa Agreement formalised, but only marginally enhanced, the existing economic relationship.

Constitutional and economic change was more apparent than real, but this was not true of technological change in the years between the wars. These years witnessed the mass advent of cinema and talking pictures, of radio broadcasting and gramophones, and of motor vehicles of all types. These were the potential vectors of an 'invasion' by American popular culture, discussed at the end of this section. Behind some of them were two new forms of power: electricity and oil fuels. From World War One, these increasingly joined coal in powering the country. As we have seen in Chapter Two, New Zealanders took to new technologies like ducks to water. The output of electric power increased almost ninefold between 1916 and 1931, then almost doubled again by 1936.[13] The electric lighting of city streets and homes, though not yet use of electric appliances such as stoves, became quite widespread. By the early 1930s, the use of electric power in industry exceeded that of steam.[14] Like electricity, motorcars first really boomed in the 1920s. There were only a very few thousand private cars in 1917 – 841 in the largest city, Auckland. There were over 100,000 motor vehicles by 1925; over 200,000 by 1930; and almost 300,000 in 1939, despite a slump in the rate of growth because of the Depression.[15] Motor vessels began replacing steamers from 1925, increasing speed and size still further. The meat ships grew from 10,000–15,000 tons to 15,000–20,000 tons, or even more. The *Dominion Monarch*, commissioned in 1939 for the British–New Zealand run, displaced 27,000 tons.[16] Coupled with increasing use of the Panama Canal, opened in 1914, this enhanced and strengthened the protein bridge on which the recolonial system depended. But it also reduced New Zealand's self-sufficiency in fuel. Coal came from New Zealand; oil did not even come from the British Empire, but from America and the Dutch East Indies.[17] This became a problem in 1942, when the Japanese rolled through South-east Asia. But a shift to more American and to British-controlled oil sources, in West Africa and the Middle East, handled this particular threat to recolonisation.

The new technologies featured prominently on the farm, which mechanised substantially in this period – quite early in international terms. Between 1919 and 1939, electrified milking sheds jumped from 7,000 to 29,000; other electric motors on farms from virtually nil to 50,000; tractors from 100 to 10,000.[18] Home separators, which separated out high-value cream, became almost universal at over 40,000 in 1923, and motor vehicles replaced horse-drawn in taking cream to factory.[19] This contributed to a 'grasslands revolution', a massive increase in farm productivity driven by science and technology. It continued to about 1972 and is usually said to have begun about 1920. Solely technological and scientific notions of the 'grasslands revolution' can easily underplay the importance of the social construction of the farming class and of the transnational recolonial system. With this caution, it is a useful concept, but it is probably more accurate to extend it back to 1882 and see it as having three stages. In the first, 1882–1918, the protein industry got up and running, with the help of steam technology. In the third, 1945–72, innovations such as aerial topdressing, milk tankers and improved pest control led to another productivity boom. It is with the middle stage, 1918–39, that we are concerned here.

Apart from electricity and petrol engines, the grasslands revolution, stage two, had three key elements. One was bird droppings: guano processed into superphosphate, and distributed over the land manually, from carts, trucks or tractors. There had been experiments with phosphate fertilisation from 1880, but it was in the 1920s that its use became really widespread. The second key was the development of a cure for 'bush sickness' – a mineral deficiency in soil that was prevalent in the central North Island. The problem was initially thought to be a lack of iron; addressing this happened also to provide cobalt, which was the real deficiency. The third key was the development of improved pasture, notably through the introduction of ryegrass and white clover, and improved stock, notably through herd testing.[20] The result was that, though the number of farms and the total farm acreage peaked about 1920, productivity increased and workforces fell. The big boom in productivity came in the final stage of the grasslands revolution, after 1939. But even in the troubled 1930s, volume increased by about a quarter. Sheep numbers increased only moderately, but the number of dairy cows climbed from about 700,000 in 1919 to 1,700,000 in 1939. The yield of butterfat per cow increased about a third. Together, the two factors massively expanded the dairy industry between the wars. Waikato and other hinterlands of Auckland joined Taranaki as leading dairying regions.[21] New Zealand's ratio of animals to people became even higher than that of Australia, and ten times that of Europe.[22] By 1940, its annual grass production was estimated at 80 million tons, enough to feed North America, if it had been wheat.[23] A grasslands utopia joined the ever-lengthening list of New Zealand paradises on earth.

Government scientists were heavily involved in all these innovations, and the development of a mature scientific establishment from the 1920s was important in rewiring the whole recolonial system. The diverse strands of New Zealand science had been gathered together by the state in the later nineteenth century. Government science chief James Hector, an able empire-builder, dominated the field between 1865 and 1903. Seddon was not a great friend to science – a fact symbolised by the tearing-down of the Colonial Observatory in 1906 to make way for his mausoleum.[24] But subsequent Premiers, Joseph Ward and Gordon Coates, were science enthusiasts. So too was Bill Massey, especially if the science was farm-oriented. By the later 1920s, a mature and quite impressive system of applied science had emerged, and it was crucial to the second and third stages of the grasslands revolution. Components included the privately endowed Cawthron Institute of Nelson (established 1921), the Department of Agriculture (1892), and Lincoln and Massey Agricultural Colleges (1880 and 1926 respectively). Some agricultural producer boards created their own research units after World War Two, such as the Meat Industry Research Institute (1955). But the centrepiece of applied science was the Department of Scientific and Industrial Research, established in 1926. At peak, in 1976, after continuous growth since 1935, the DSIR had twenty research divisions and over 2,000 staff.[25]

There are three possible explanations for the founding of the DSIR, which can be described as colonialist, nationalist, and recolonial. After World War One, with the rise of dominionism, Britain was eager to share the burden of scientific research with its white dominions. All were urged to reorganise and rejuvenate their scientific establishments along modern British lines. The head of British science, Sir Frank Heath, visited New Zealand at the government's invitation in 1926 and recommended the formation of the DSIR. On this colonialist view, New Zealand developed a substantial scientific system simply because Britain told it to. The second, nationalist, explanation attributes the foundation to New Zealand reformers, notably G. M. Thompson, who had been lobbying actively since 1913. Australia also set up its DSIR equivalent in 1926. That year, according to the nationalist view, 'marked the end of Australasian "colonial" dependence in science'.[26] On this view, Heath received credit he did not deserve, the real heroes were indigenous, and the founding of the DSIR in 1926 was a declaration of scientific independence.

It is true that attributing some major New Zealand development to the inspiration of a visiting British expert was common. Kitchener was credited with the establishment of compulsory military training, Otto Niemeyer with the founding of the Reserve Bank, and there were many similar cases. In each, the VIP visit was to some extent a rubber stamp on a done deal, a recolonial ritual. But, contrary to the nationalist view, the British connection in science was of real importance. It did not consist in the VIP visits, but in the transnationalism that the recolonial system provided. This leads to a recolonial explanation for the development of a substantial and effective New Zealand science system. Recent research shows that the British connection was important to New Zealand science in the critical 1920s in the most direct way possible. The Empire Marketing Board, established in 1923, provided 30 per cent of DSIR research funding in some years, and insisted on matching funds from the New Zealand government. Imperial Agricultural Bureaux in Britain contributed substantially to New Zealand pasture research. New Zealand gave as well as took in this relationship. 'New Zealand Wild White', a local adaptation of English white-clover strains, for example, 'was bound to have a wide utility', not only in New Zealand but 'for all first-class grasslands overseas'.[27] It was literally a Better British grass. The science system was more recolonial – oriented to Britain – than imperial – oriented to the Empire as a whole. New Zealand was much less enthusiastic about co-operating with Australian science than with British. In this sense, recolonisation, New Zealand applied science, and the grasslands revolution helped each other along.

Technological change also had its impact on the cultural front, and there was a recolonial subtext here too. Moving pictures were first screened in New Zealand in 1896, and purpose-built cinemas date from about 1910. In the 1920s, huge 'picture palaces' were built, such as the Civic in Auckland in 1929, the year talking pictures arrived. The Civic, renowned for its ceiling presented as a star-studded night sky, could seat 3,500 people and cost over £200,000.[28] By 1939, there were 576 theatres in New Zealand, and 30 million admissions a year, compared with only 550,000 admissions in 1917.[29] From 1922, radio joined cinema in revolutionising entertainment. In 1924, there were 2,800 licensed radio receivers in New Zealand. By 1930, there were 50,000; and by 1939, over 300,000. The first instant mass medium had arrived.[30] Broadcasting technology improved significantly in 1928, by which time a full national network of stations had emerged. The private but state-warranted Radio Broadcasting Company dominated until 1932, when it was bought by the government.

Radio and cinema were a threat to both moral harmony and cultural recolonisation, and were quickly seen as such. They were potential vectors of an American cultural invasion that was considered to be neither sufficiently moral nor sufficiently British. The tight society handled the moral problem with almost contemptuous ease. As noted in Chapter Five, it was very willing to chop and ban films by the hundred. Radio was also controlled by a mix of voluntary and formal censorship. As early as 1923, regulations banned material 'of a controversial nature'. Legislation was tightened in 1925, when anything 'of a seditious, profane, obscene, libellous or offensive nature' was also banned. Informal censorship extended the list to mildly risqué popular songs. 'In a corner of . . . the Broadcasting Board's head office lies a heap of gramophone records that New Zealand listeners will never hear.'[31] Between 1925 and 1932, music was restricted to no more than a quarter of broadcasting time, in any case.[32] If you turned on your wireless set at a certain time on Sunday, you would hear nothing – it was the time for silent prayer. Despite the new media, the tight society could sleep peacefully with moral harmony guarding the gate.

The new media represented more of a challenge to recolonisation. Since the first European settlement of New Zealand, there had been two great sources of Anglophone influence, Britain and the United States. American influences in the nineteenth century had been substantial in the form of New England whalers in the 1820s and 1830s, American goldminers in the 1860s, and less intense but longer trans-Pacific transmission of ideas, practices, technology and biota, such as the Californian pine. Americans and American ways of doing things were openly admired until the 1900s, culminating in the enthusiastic reception of the American fleet in 1908. New Zealand's Liberal legislation, in turn, was admired in the United States, and surprisingly widely publicised.[33] As cultural recolonisation (which developed more slowly than the economic arm of the system) intensified, however, American influence came to be viewed with increasing suspicion by New Zealand formal culture. Popular culture was less suspicious and Americans were still seen as relatives, but increasingly as relatives on the distaff side.

In 1914, 43 per cent (by value) of films screened in New Zealand were British; 32 per cent were American. From that time, world cinema was American-dominated, and the British industry struggled to compete. American movies became the norm on New Zealand screens – 350 out of 400 features in 1927. Hollywood was the leading edge of a wave of American 'global culture'; such things as American cars and American housing styles and fixtures also became popular in New Zealand in the 1920s. This aroused more concern in the recolonial New Zealand of the 1920s than the earlier waves of American influence. The Ottawa Agreement of 1932 consolidated Empire preferences for British goods, including films. Even before this, from 1928, New Zealand legislation had sought to load the dice in favour of British films through preferential duties. 'I say nothing against the American nation,' declaimed one New Zealand parliamentarian that year, 'but we ought to remember that we are British and as such we have a duty to encourage the production of films which depict the life of Britishers rather than Americans.'[34] Even without legislation, New Zealand cinema operators voluntarily discriminated against American films. Henry Hayward screened 'a big percentage of British films, even at a loss (on account of their inferiority) simply with the idea of encouraging the British Industry'. 'New Zealand,' the operators noted, 'has for some years past been screening a higher percentage of British films than has been screened in England itself' – a cinematic Better Britishness. The greater popularity and productivity of the American industry compared with the British meant this was ultimately a losing battle as far as feature films were concerned. But the proportion of British short films shown did increase towards 50 per cent in the 1930s. And recolonial attitudes did force compromise on American film distributors, who noted in 1929 that no films denigrating Britain should be shown in New Zealand, 'for the people are extremely sensitive on this point'.[35]

An attempted American invasion of the sound waves came somewhat later, in 1931, when American radio serials were first broadcast in New Zealand. They encountered establishment criticism from the outset. Some, wrote the head of the New Zealand Radio Broadcasting Company, 'would obviously never suit a 100 per cent British country like New Zealand'.[36] Protests were soon heard in Parliament about 'cheap American rubbish that we get over the air', with its dire effect on New Zealand speech, such as the introduction of the phrase 'Okay, baby'. After it took over broadcasting in 1932, the state progressively replaced American serials with British and Australian ones. There was a brief revival during the Second World War, owing to the presence of American servicemen, but 'in 1946 the importation of American serials was stopped'. They did not return to New Zealand broadcasting until the advent of television in the 1960s.[37]

The American invasion was seen off in terms of radio serials, but other forms of culture were less easy to control. Dime Western novels like those by Zane Grey,[38] American music and American cars were popular. American cars were arguably better vehicles than British, and were certainly better suited to New Zealand conditions. In 1918, 57 per cent of the cars imported into New Zealand (by value) were American. The figure then dropped to 34 per cent in 1921 and 24 per cent in 1930 – before the Ottawa Agreement. The proportion of British cars imported climbed from 28 per cent in 1921 to 75 per cent in 1931 – and reached 82 per cent in 1955.[39]

Intensifying recolonisation had its impact on local production as well as American imports. From 1921, some cars were imported as kitsets, and assembled in New Zealand. There was also some local production of films and radio material. The local film industry made a promising start. No fewer than fifteen feature films were made in the country between 1914 and 1927, with another seven made by 1936: a total of 22 films in 22 years. In the 44 years between 1937 and 1971, however, only six films were made.[40] A renaissance of New Zealand cinema production then began, and continues to the present. Other industries were to experience a similar 'recolonial gap'. In radio, both local and imported production was divided between two types of stations and programmes. The 'highbrow' strand, designated 'YA', was non-commercial, instructive, morally uplifting, and British. The 'lowbrow' strand, designated 'ZB' was commercial, entertaining, less moral, and less British. It tended to include first, more American and then more Australian programmes. From 1936, this division was personified by the intellectual and British Professor James Shelley, head of the YA service, and the populist and New Zealand Colin Scrimgeour, 'Uncle Scrim', head of the ZB service. With the sacking of Scrimgeour in 1943, it was Shelley and his trajectory that won out – a victory for good taste, perhaps, but also for recolonisation. This contest, and its result, was replicated in Labour Party politics at the same time, as we will see.[41] Indigenous radio icons did emerge, such as 'Aunt Daisy' (Maud Basham), a fast talker clocked at 200 words per minute, whose show was broadcast for 33 years after 1930. New Zealand radio plays (as against the costlier serials) were produced in quantity from the late 1930s. But they tended towards the British highbrow model. As with cars, local production did occur, but within a bi-national, recolonial system.

American media and material culture was far too powerful, popular and pervasive to exclude entirely. In both cars and radio, other dominions were sometimes used to mediate Americanism. Canada was an important source of cars in the 1930s, and Australia was an important source of radio serials. Both the Canadian cars and the Australian series were actually based on American models. The 1918–39 period was only the first round in a long contest between recolonial and American 'global' culture. But recolonisation did win the round on points. New Zealand's cinemas were American-dominated, but with qualifications, as we have seen. The roads and the radios were not American dominated. Throughout the whole period 1920s–60s, most cars were British, and the radio announcers' accents were English. American radio series were considered 'not acceptable' in New Zealand. Radio news services consisted largely of rebroadcasting the British Broadcasting Corporation's reports. 'They had the chimes of Big Ben. You always had to listen to the whole of the chimes by the way and they announced it two minutes before.'[42]

Sugarbag Years?

In mid-1929, for reasons still debated among economic historians, the booming American economy stopped growing and started shrinking. In October of that year, the famous 'Wall Street Crash' halved the value of the New York stock market, with ruined speculators 'falling like autumn leaves from upstairs windows', according to urban myth at least.[43] The Great Depression had begun. In striking contrast to more recent experience, recolonisation initially insulated New Zealand. 'In the short term, New Zealand brokers were blithely indifferent to this catastrophe' on Wall Street.[44] But indirect effects were soon felt. Many countries sought to shield their internal economies by imposing tariffs on imports of raw materials. Countries dependent on the export of primary produce rushed to the one remaining free market, Britain, and prices plummeted. By 1933, New Zealand's export receipts were down 44 per cent on 1929.

In New Zealand folk memory, and in some history books, the Depression of 1929–35 is both the great watershed and the great nadir of the twentieth century. As in the 1880s, the serpent of poverty slithered unchecked through paradise. Governments (the United ministry of 1928–31, led first by old Joseph Ward and then by George Forbes, and the United-Reform Coalition of 1931–35, led nominally by Forbes but actually by Gordon Coates) fiddled while New Zealand burned. These 'sugarbag years', when the unemployed made clothes out of hessian sacks from the Chelsea Sugar Refinery at Birkenhead, were indelibly etched into New Zealand memory. As it does with the 1880s depression, some modern scholarship has questioned this view. It notes that consumer prices fell even more than wage rates, so that real wages stayed stable or even improved, and that unemployment was not high in international terms, at less than half of the rates prevalent in Australia, America, and even Britain, where the Depression was relatively mild.

Refereeing between these divergent views of New Zealand's depression experience is no easy matter. Scholarly estimates of unemployment, for example, range from 10 to 32 per cent of the workforce.[45] The lower figure, slightly increased to 12 per cent, is most common, but appears to depend on counting only registered Pakeha male unemployed. If one counts women workers, Maori, underemployed and, above all, unregistered male unemployed, the higher figure looks more likely, though perhaps somewhat exaggerated. Depression income levels are also problematic. Real wage rates did hold up, even in the period 1932–35 when the arbitration system was suspended. But employers tended to dump their more highly paid workers, keeping their low-paid. The female minority of the workforce therefore suffered less unemployment than the male majority. Overtime was cut, many workers were paid for less than a full week, and the sector supplying most statistics (manufacturing) suffered less than those supplying least (construction and farm work).[46] Median incomes obviously fell far more than average wage rates, because unemployed and underemployed were getting next to nothing. Yet those who kept their jobs, or had other forms of income such as pensions or profits, do not seem to have suffered that much. The compromise conclusion, that there was depression for some and not for others, is tempting – perhaps too tempting.

Another way of assessing the mass impact of the Depression is to look at consumption. Even the consumption of food staples, theoretically the least elastic of markets, dropped significantly. Between 1929–30 and 1938, despite the fact that there must have been some recovery in the second half of this period, per capita consumption of beef and pork fell 30 per cent. Mutton, which was cheaper, dropped less. The purchase of potatoes, the cheapest food of all, fell by a third, perhaps because more people began growing their own. Spending on the modest luxuries of lower-income groups also fell sharply. Between 1929–30 and 1938, ice-cream consumption per capita dropped from eight to three pints a year. Between 1929 and 1933, beer consumption dropped 30 per cent, while betting on horses, consumption of wine and spirits, and the manufacture of cigarettes all roughly halved. Perhaps surprisingly, spending on the luxuries of high-income groups also fell, in several cases even more. Electric stoves continued to sell to a fortunate minority, but imports of coffee and brandy almost halved between 1929 and 1933; imports of motor vehicles and cigars dropped by over 80 per cent. The Depression may not have been harsh for high-income groups, but they cut their spending as though it was.[47]

The economic and psychological definitions of 'depression' have more in common than it might seem. What we appear to have here is a kind of collective clinical depression, where even the well-off drastically pulled in their horns. The tight society did not compel the rich to help their neighbours – charitable expenditure on such things as Health stamps dropped.[48] But it did demand that they share the suffering to some extent, and the sense of insecurity to a great extent. Like the consumption of imported luxuries, house-building and other forms of investment plummeted, while deposits in banks increased.[49] As in the 1880s, there was a strong sense of bubble burst, even of the permanent puncturing of prosperity. Historian William Morrell, writing in 1935, thought high unemployment would be permanent.[50] About the same time, leading politician Gordon Coates spoke forebodingly of the British market for New Zealand's products having finally reached its limit.[51]

On balance, the folk memory of a harsh depression appears to be more accurate than the minimalist portrayal of a mild one – these *were* the 'sugarbag years'. It was felt right across society – few failed to notice it – but it was not felt equally. Some of the worst horrors of Depression legend may have been rare, but they probably did occur. Poet and polemicist Rex Fairburn did time in a relief-work gang, and spoke of a widow and her son dying of starvation, unreported, and of a man driven mad by his inability to feed his family.[52] As late as 1938, a relief gang worked in such isolated and dangerous conditions that it lost 21 men in a flash flood.[53] Not all horrors were rare. A survey of primary schools in poorer areas of Christchurch in 1934 found what must have been a substantial minority of children (225) suffering from malnutrition, and what may well have been a majority (618) with inadequate clothing.[54] Abortions increased, as parents could not face another mouth to feed. One estimate implies an induced abortion rate of about one in five pregnancies.[55]

Government reactions, on the whole, reinforced the sense of despair. The United-Reform Coalition Cabinet of 1931–35 consisted of nine farmers and a lawyer, Downie Stewart, who resigned in 1933. The Prime Minister was George Forbes. Keith Sinclair predicted 25 years ago that some day a research student, desperate for a thesis topic, would find some good even in Forbes. That student has yet to emerge. Especially in 1933–35, the much more able Coates was the real leader of the country. Coates, as the only prominent personality in the government, became perhaps the most hated man in the country. He was the victim of rumours about heavy drinking and adultery, which were completely irrelevant if not necessarily completely untrue. But he has received a much better press from posterity, including the least likely of hagiographers, left-wing historians J. C. Beaglehole and W. B. Sutch.[56] Leader of a conservative party, Reform, Coates was prepared to attempt increasingly radical measures as the depth and length of the slump became apparent to him. His antidepressants, 1931–34, included various relief-work schemes for the unemployed; attempts to prevent foreclosures on farm mortgages; the devaluation of the New Zealand pound, which improved farm receipts; and the establishment of the Reserve Bank, which took control of currency and money supply from the six trading banks.

Coates was certainly a more able, humane and likeable man than contemporary folklore allowed. But historians may have swung the pendulum too far back in his favour. Of the measures listed above, only the last, the establishment of the Reserve Bank, can be described as a success, and it did nothing immediate for the jobless, the impoverished and the marginal. Mortgage relief and devaluation helped farmers, not workers, and the beneficial effects of devaluation even for farmers were apparently not great.[57] An unintended side effect was to force New Zealand to mint its own coinage for the first time, because British coins, which had been standard New Zealand circulation, could be smuggled back to Britain for a profit of 25 per cent.[58] The relief-work schemes were notoriously niggardly. Coates kept them so, not only for fiscal reasons but because he believed that better pay and conditions would prevent men from finding jobs for themselves. Yet there *were* no jobs. An unemployment benefit, or dole, did not join the relief-work schemes until 1934, after five years of greater hardship than was necessary. Coates was almost as keen on retrenching his way out of depression as Downie Stewart, his predecessor as finance minister. Cuts in wages were justified by the drop in prices, reasonably enough. But the system also cut for the sake of cutting. 'Even the meat allowance for cats in government offices was cut by a tenth.'[59] One unemployed man was told by an official to get rid of his canary.[60] Coates's budget of 1934–35, which returned a surplus of £1.6 million, must have rubbed salt into the wounds of the canary-free unemployed. To his credit, Coates later admitted that he could and should have done more to alleviate hardship. This historian, at least, agrees with him.[61]

It will come as no surprise that in these circumstances public frustration mounted. Radical organisations of the right, left and middle all gained support. The New Zealand Legion, the Communist Party and Social Credit are examples in each category. More dramatically, there was an intense spasm of mass rioting in all four main cities in April and May of 1932. They were, it seems, provoked by the government's rationing of relief work, niggardly though its pay and conditions already were. A 'food riot' had already taken place in Dunedin in January, but batons supplied to the police – in a sugarbag, appropriately enough – were not used. The same restraint was not shown in Auckland on the evening of 14 April, when an angry crowd of several thousand unemployed men demonstrated in Queen Street. Provoked by the police batoning of a spokesman, the crowd engaged the police in New Zealand's worst civil violence since 1913. Over a hundred people were hospitalised, most of the shop windows in Queen Street were broken, and there was a great deal of open looting while the crowd reigned in the city centre. Reinforced by sailors from a warship in the harbour, and by volunteers, the police regained control late that night.

There was comparable but smaller-scale violence in Dunedin and Wellington in the same period. Even in Christchurch, once thought to have been relatively immune to the Depression riots, civil violence was such that it resulted indirectly in two deaths.[62] The government showed that it could react decisively in some circumstances at least. Thousands of 'special constables' were recruited, secretly led by territorial troops, as in 1913. Again, 'great care was taken to hide the military character of this emergency police force'.[63] Parliament passed draconian legislation, facilitating arrests for 'sedition'. Some 185 prosecutions resulted from the riots; 72 men were imprisoned.[64]

Some historians claim that the riots of 1932 were the worst civil disturbances in New Zealand history. This is clearly untrue, and is further evidence of the downplaying of 1913. The numbers were smaller in 1932 than in 1913 – absolutely, let alone relative to population. Guns were not used and the demonstrators lacked the sense of solidarity and purpose apparent in 1913. Fairburn was amazed and delighted by the riots. 'The thought of a plate-glassless Queen Street almost gives me fresh hope for humanity . . . I didn't think they had the guts.'[65] Yet the surprising thing is not that the riots occurred, given the dire Depression circumstances, but that they were not even more intensive and extensive, and that they were not repeated. Some pundits thought that the riots presaged violent revolution, and the strength of the government's reaction suggests that it half agreed. But no such thing happened. Instead, the unemployed, underemployed and impoverished, perhaps a third of the total population by 1933, settled down into resignation – bewildered, sullen and bitter, but resigned nonetheless.

Historians agree on the resignation of the groups most disadvantaged by depression after 1932, but are less helpful in explaining it. One key may be that it was hard to find something or someone to blame. Popular feeling groomed Coates for the role, but he did not fit easily. He was too populist himself to be readily demonised, and it was pretty obvious that he was not to blame for the Depression. The disaster was global and inexplicable, mysteriously imported from the world. New Zealand populism was in some ways a conservative beast. To react dramatically, in either civil disobedience or radical electoral behaviour, it had to put some sort of face on its shadowy enemy.

First Labour

In late 1935, New Zealanders did react dramatically to the Depression, taking the electoral option. They elected the first Labour government, of 1935–49, led to 1940 by Michael Joseph Savage. Today, it is hard to visualise just how bold a move this seemed. Several of Labour's leaders were one-time 'Red Feds' who had been jailed for sedition in 1913, or for opposing conscription in World War One. The party, in being since 1916, unashamedly preached radical socialism. It had fully parted company with the Communist Party only in 1925, and only abandoned its policy of land nationalisation, which went down like a lead balloon with property owners both actual and aspirant, in 1927. Once in power, the government was soon seen, within and without New Zealand, as the most left-wing in the world outside the Soviet Union. The celebrations after Labour's winning its large majority included a greeting new to New Zealand streets: 'Hullo, comrade.'[66]

Contrary to some party legend, it was not that Labour achieved victory through a patient and steady build-up. The Labour Party in New Zealand was something of a slow developer in comparison to its sister parties in Australia and Britain. In the decade before 1931, as we saw in Chapter Four, Labour had been stuck on a vote plateau of less than half of its 'natural constituency' – manual workers – and a quarter of the total vote. One explanation for its eventual triumph in 1935 is simply the Depression, which tossed out incumbent governments all over the world. Yet in the 1931 election, the Depression, already two years old, was not enough to eject the Coalition, to overcome the entrenched dislike of voting Labour in sections of the working class, let alone the middle classes. As with that of the Liberals in 1890, Labour's victory in 1935 needs to be understood in terms of the Depression's corrosion of New Zealand's 'populist compact'.

As a working-class party, Labour itself could seem an enemy of populism, supporting one section of the people over others. Its moderation of policy, such as the rejection of land nationalism, from 1927 reduced this perception. So, too, did a change of leadership in 1933, when the dour and doctrinaire Harry Holland died and was replaced by the flexible and likeable Michael Joseph Savage. Savage was to become the most loved prime minister in New

Zealand history, the very face of a mild and benign populism. The full development of this reputation postdated the 1935 election and cannot therefore be cited as a cause of it. It stemmed partly from Savage's own 'almost indescribable charisma'; partly from his mastery of the mass medium of radio after 1935; and partly from his premature death in 1940, which occasioned mass mourning. The best way for politicians to secure their reputations with posterity is to die prematurely in office. In the 1935 election, however, it was not so much that Savage was popular hero, but that he was already a non-villain. His friendly face and manner could not be mistaken for an enemy of populism.

Yet it seemed clear to people that some such enemy was at work. Opportunities for social promotion, through the acquisition of farms or through secondary education, stopped expanding, then contracted. The plateau in farm numbers would have happened with or without depression, and various legislation from 1931 restricted the foreclosure of farm mortgages. But there were some foreclosures, and about 15 per cent of all farmers had already had to apply for mortgage relief by 1933.[67] The constriction of education could still more easily be blamed on a government that expelled five-year-olds from school, closed two teachers' colleges, and put 1,200 teachers onto the dole queue. Still worse, access to white-collar status was threatened by a drop of over 10 per cent in the number of secondary school students in 1932.[68] To top it all off, widespread home-ownership, that other bastion of the populist compact, also seemed to be under threat. Unlike farms, house mortgages were not significantly protected by the Coalition government. According to one estimate, there were a staggering 54,000 foreclosures during the Depression – close to one-third of all home mortgages.[69] According to another, the proportion of wage and salary earners owning their own homes dropped from 49.1 per cent in 1926 to 37.9 per cent in 1936.[70] This was breaking the Massey deal with a vengeance. All populism required for electoral retaliation was a face to put on the enemy. It found it at the bank, in the form of 'money power'.

Banks, like funeral parlours, are inherently unattractive institutions. They had never been popular with New Zealand populism. In 1890, they had been outranked by the gentry as perceived enemies of the people. In 1935, with the 1920s expansion of farm- and home-ownership based even more on bank credit than on state credit, it was their turn. The threat to ownership, actual for many home-owners and prospective for many farmers, obviously fed this feeling. It was given further focus by the idea of Social Credit: the belief that expensive bank credit could be replaced by an indefinite supply of cheap or free public credit. Social Credit has provided laughing stock for generations of historians and economists. But in the 1930s, with the financial causes of the Depression horribly inexplicable to most, it was attractive. Governments seemed to be able to find plenty of money to fight great wars. Why couldn't they do so to fight great depressions? The British father of the theory, Major Clifford Douglas, had many direct New Zealand disciples, and visited in person in 1934. Social Credit did not become a political party until 1953. In 1935, most of its supporters aligned themselves with Labour. The Labour leaders themselves did not need this encouragement to make attacks on the banking system and money power a major feature of their election rhetoric. With Democratic and Country Party candidates splitting the right-wing vote in rural electorates, this was enough to give Labour victory.

Labour's victory of 1935 was a landslide in terms of seats (55 out of 80) but not votes (46 per cent). Its victory was at least as much a vote against the Coalition, the Depression, the breaching of the populist compact, and money power as it was a vote for Labour. In 1938, however, Labour was re-elected with 55.8 per cent of the vote.[71] The increase in its vote between 1935 and 1938 was almost as great as that between 1931 and 1935. This post-election jump in Labour support, which surprised Labour supporters as well as opponents, was a consequence of the government's actions and prospective actions.

Labour's immediate measures, in 1935–36, were quick and generous. Five-year-olds went back to school; teachers' colleges reopened. Whether the cats in government buildings got their full meat ration back is unknown, but cuts to wages were restored in public and private sectors alike. A big public works programme absorbed some unemployment, and remaining unemployed and relief workers were given a Christmas bonus and a week's paid holiday. Normal working hours were reduced from 44 to 40 per week, and a minimum wage was introduced. Mortgage relief and protection against foreclosure was extended from farmers to workers. These actions go far towards explaining First Labour's high status in folk memory. People still remember the amazed and delighted reaction to the advent of paid holidays, hitherto a pipe dream for many. But Labour's two most important measures emerged fully only after the 1938 election. They were the renegotiation, but also reinforcement, of both the populist compact and the recolonial system. The former centred on the Social Security Act of 1938; the latter on the imposition of exchange and import controls the same year. These two sets of reforms were expanded and developed over time. But their fundamentals were to remain in place for the next 40 years.

The Social Security Act of 1938 delivered a pension at age 60, and unemployment and disability benefits to all who needed them – with the initial partial exception of Maori.[72] This was expansion along existing trajectories. A more novel departure was the introduction of elements of universalism into the welfare system. Despite the determined resistance of the medical profession, which eventually succeeded in undermining the intended free visits to general practitioners, a wide range of free health care was made available to all, needy or not. Similarly, a universal superannuation payment was made at age 65. Initially little more than a token, the intention was to increase it as government means allowed. Subsequently, other universal payments, such as family benefits in 1946, were added to the package. By 1942, government handbooks were already boasting that 'most people benefit somehow from our "social security" policy'.[73]

The debate between advocates of targeted and universal welfare benefits has become polemical in recent times. At one level, universal benefits are somewhat counterintuitive, and must have seemed so to many in 1938. Why should the public pay the health and education costs of the affluent, and give them substantial superannuation payments and family benefits as well? Labour had two answers. The first, which the government itself tended to emphasise, was that universalism eliminated the humiliation of receiving charity: one received benefits as of right. Social integration was increased by not singling out the needy. The second, which was not emphasised, was that universalism extended the benefits of a comprehensive welfare system to the middle classes, so increasing their willingness to pay for it. Universalism integrated both the needy and the middle classes into the new welfare society, but in New Zealand it was much less marked in 1938 than it later became, and even then universalism did not reach the heights of Scandinavian postwar welfare systems.[74] However, by then it did not need to, because full employment minimised the number of needy. It was full employment that made universalist social welfare affordable.

Other important reforms had also had an integrating effect. Compulsory unionism, introduced in 1936, greatly strengthened and expanded organised labour. But, coupled with the restored arbitration system, it also integrated labour more closely into the refurbished political economy. The unions became even more closely allied to the Labour Party after 1935, to the point where the two became closely intertwined. But this can mask the fact that the new integration of unions was systemic, rather than partisan. Unions remained closely integrated with the state for many years after the Labour Party fell from power. The introduction of guaranteed prices for dairy farmers, and increased state involvement in the marketing of their products, was another seminal measure. State aid to farmers was in itself nothing new, but the comprehensiveness of the Labour government's involvement (at first more in dairying than in meat or wool) was novel. Farmers were by no means uniformly enthusiastic about the semi-socialisation of their industry, but they accepted it. They, too, became deeply integrated into the renegotiated political economy.

Recolonial New Zealand to the 1920s had been characterised by the three harmonies: social, moral and racial. The first Labour government did not substantively contest any of these, even social harmony. Like all other successful New Zealand politicians since the 1850s, Labour leaders stressed that they served the interests of most sections of the community, not just their working-class base. What Labour did do was introduce a fourth, 'sectoral', harmony, an unholy alliance of rival sectors. After 1938, despite periods of friction, state, business, farming and labour sectors increasingly worked in concert, the situation sometimes described as 'corporatist'. Workers felt more comfortable under Labour, and business and farmers under the new National Party, which replaced the beaten Coalition in 1936. But any sector could work with any government. From 1949 to 1984, this system of sectoral integration and socio-economic security survived political change. This is the heart of the achievement that leads one international expert to describe New Zealand's first Labour government as 'the strongest that has ever existed in the English-speaking world'.[75]

The capacity of this political economy, now incorporating sectoral harmony, to restore and maintain the populist compact was considerable, but contingent on a renegotiation of the compact along existing trajectories. Security from poverty and unemployment, an issue from the 1880s, made another large step upwards in importance, owing to the 1930s Depression. Opportunity continued its more recent shift from farms, where the slots were already filled, to small businesses and white-collar jobs. First Labour restarted the expansion of secondary school places suspended during the Depression. Populism's other imperatives were the minimising of class distinction and the maximising of class harmony. First Labour had no problem at all with the former, and its hesitations about the latter soon proved to be more rhetorical than real. All this was successfully renegotiated, but the restoration and maintenance of the populist compact was contingent on another factor as well. Sectoral harmony needed the lubrication of prosperity to prevent friction between its parts. Social security needed prosperity, and the full employment it provided, to be affordable. Prosperity required some renegotiation not only of the internal political economy, but also of the recolonial system, and here first Labour's management of three key crises was much less sure.

In terms of economic indicators, although not necessarily of individual despair, the Depression reached its nadir in 1933. Export prices began to recover from that point, and farmers continued the grasslands revolution increase in output, which they had managed to maintain throughout the slump. Government spending, of course, increased sharply from 1936, and both this and the growth in export receipts contributed to a significant economic upturn. In 1938, however, this fragile new prosperity threatened to turn turtle with the advent of a crisis in economic relations with Britain.

Ironically enough, New Zealand had ended the Depression with a healthy 'overseas funds' balance, or accumulated export surplus, of £38 million. This began diminishing from 1936, partly because the recovering economy required high imports, and partly because British and New Zealand investors, fearful of the new socialist government, transferred their money elsewhere. New Zealand was prevented by the Ottawa Agreement from increasing tariffs on British imports to slow the flow. This left import licensing, whereby all purchases from overseas required government permission, as the main option.[76] The left of the Labour caucus, led by John A. Lee, strongly advocated import controls, but the more influential right, led by Deputy Prime Minister Peter Fraser and Finance Minister Walter Nash, were reluctant. The British were opposed, fearing that such controls would harm their importers, and many New Zealanders also opposed such regulationism and unorthodoxy. The government therefore postponed import controls until December 1938, after the election, despite the fact that the outflow of capital had become a flood earlier that year. Between April and November 1938, overseas funds declined dramatically, from £28.6 million to £8 million.[77]

In this context, the amiable, able but somewhat indecisive Walter Nash travelled to London in 1939 to arrange the normal roll-over of a British loan falling due and to obtain a new one. He walked into a series of meetings that were 'among the most distasteful in his life'. Nash's requests were initially refused point-blank; he was hauled over the coals by a range of British ministers and officials like 'an erring schoolboy'; and New Zealand was threatened with receivership, if not quite bankruptcy. Some commentators attributed Britain's attitude to its being short of money to lend, owing to the slump. But Coates had received the roll-over of a £10 million loan in 1935 without difficulty and on easy terms.[78] The key factor was clearly that the British government and economic establishment did not like New Zealand's new Labour government, its expensive policies and what they described as its 'economic totalitarianism'. We shall soon see that they were not enthralled by First Labour's pronouncements on international affairs either. Time for Britain to crack its whip.

Nash was not wholly without cards. Too great a punishment of an errant dominion was not good public relations for Britain, especially when the highly volatile situation in Europe in early 1939 placed a premium on the appearance of Empire unity. The Newfoundland option – suspending the constitution and taking direct control – was rejected by the British Cabinet, though it was voiced. British investment in, and export to, New Zealand was substantial, and Britain could not easily afford a New Zealand inability to buy imports, pay interest and remit profits. The British knew that the heresy of debt repudiation had been voiced in New South Wales. But Nash did not play his cards very vigorously. New Zealand's import controls were grudgingly accepted, but with a raft of conditions that minimised their impact on British exporters. Indeed, apart from a wartime blip, the import control system saw the percentage of New Zealand imports derived from Britain climb from 47 per cent in 1930 to 61 per cent in 1950.[79] The old loan was rolled over, and a minimal new loan granted, but on conditions Nash's biographer, Keith Sinclair, rightly described as 'humiliating'. Even some British newspapers thought the terms 'impossibly onerous; indeed blackmailing'.[80] Had peace persisted beyond 1939, these terms would have required substantial retrenchment in New Zealand, slowed or stopped the recovery from depression, reduced the standard of living, and possibly threatened the new social security system. As it happened, New Zealand's reshuffled socio-economy was saved by war.

This portrayal of the 1939 crisis in British–New Zealand economic relations is little more hard-hitting than that by Sinclair, which concluded that New Zealand remained a 'quasi-colony'.[81] But this book parts company with Sinclair and other historians in its assessment of a matching British–New Zealand disagreement in foreign policy, the second crisis of recolonisation in the late 1930s. On taking office in 1935, Savage had appointed his friend Bill Jordan as High Commissioner in London. In 1936 and 1937 in particular, Jordan – with Savage's full support – made a series of telling and widely publicised criticisms of British foreign policy. Under Massey, New Zealand had reluctantly accepted separate membership of the new League of Nations. Now Jordan used the league as a pulpit from which to denounce British appeasement of fascism, notably the lack of effective reaction to an Italian invasion of Ethiopia in 1935 and to a right-wing rebellion in Spain in 1936.

Labour's verbal attack on Britain has been explained in terms of the tradition of 'loyal dissent'.[82] New Zealand might openly disagree with Britain, but only in an effort to persuade the Mother Country to change its course of action, without in any way implying that New Zealand would not back it to the hilt whatever it did. It seems to me, however, that the initial Jordan–Savage position went further than this. Savage, for all his mild style, was less impressed by the British establishment than were his lieutenants, Fraser and Nash, who were themselves British, and was far less eager than they were to visit Britain. He had described New Zealand's Governor-General, Viscount Galway, as 'this bloody Pom'. When Savage did reluctantly visit Britain in

1937, he declared at an imperial conference, to the anger of other Common-wealth leaders, that 'New Zealand could not maintain her assurance of aid in time of war if Britain on her part refused to pursue a policy based strictly on the principles of the League and of collective security'.[83] This was ironic in relation to what Savage actually did do when war broke out in 1939, which was to wholeheartedly support Britain. But, without this advantage of retrospect, his statement was surely incompatible with the notion of 'loyal dissent'. Such a stand was more than a mere annoyance to Britain: it implied a threat to Empire solidarity and to the automatic support of the dominions, which supercharged British power in time of war.

Matters came to a head at the League of Nations on 28 May 1937, when Jordan was about to make a speech that the British feared would invoke a clause of the league's constitution demanding action on the civil war in Spain. According to a British journalist – and a New Zealand official sitting behind Jordan – the British Foreign Secretary, Anthony Eden, walked up and crossed out sections of the speech Jordan was about to make. Sinclair and other historians accepted Jordan's indignant denial, partly on the grounds that the New Zealand official was the young William Sutch, considered an unreliable witness. But a subsequent analysis of the incident suggests that it was true in substance, although Jordan may have changed his speech himself in response to British pressure. The draft of Jordan's speech included the offending passages, while the speech itself did not; the speech's conclusion sounded vague, as though its sting had been removed but not replaced; and Jordan's explanation of Eden's visit was contradictory – he said that Eden was correcting his own speech, but this had already been delivered.[84] New Zealand criticism of Britain became more restrained from 1938.[85] It seems likely that the British prompted the backdown by at least hinting at cracking their economic whip.

The Savage government of 1935–40 relieved human suffering and regenerated hope by refurbishing the populist compact, which was damaged and threatened by the Depression. It did so by introducing sectoral harmony and social security, which formed the basis of the New Zealand political economy for the next 40 years. This was a great achievement. As much by luck as good management, First Labour managed to reconcile this refurbished internal system with the external system – recolonisation – despite looming problems with the latter. Again, the technique of growing the state, through such measures as import controls, over cracks in the internal–external reconciliation was to prove a long-lasting one. This was the economic 'insulation' with which First Labour is traditionally credited. But it was insulation of the New Zealand–British recolonial economy, not an independ-ent New Zealand one. What First Labour did *not* do, contrary to some legends, was take major or lasting steps in the direction of economic and geopolitical independence. Keith Sinclair's belief that 'the Labour government increasingly stood for and strove for economic and political independence' cannot be accepted.[86] Like the right-wing ministries before and after it, First Labour was a recolonial government.

It could be said that Labour had no choice in this. New Zealand had thrown itself into the recolonial system voluntarily, even enthusiastically, between the 1880s and the 1920s. By the 1930s, the country was locked in and the key had been lost. It is true that the most radical nationalist measures, such as repudiating debt and withdrawing automatic support for Britain in war, were not very realistic options. Yet they were considered by some Labour leaders, and moderate moves towards independence may have been possible. Nash could have played his cards better in 1939, and Jordan could have told Eden where to go in 1937. Labour had no realistic choice about joining Britain in World War Two, but we shall see in the next chapter that it could have fought its war much more independent-mindedly. That these things did not happen was perhaps less a result of historical inevitability than of political contingency, symbolised by the third crisis of 1937–40, more widely known as 'the Lee Affair'.

The triumphant Labour caucus of 1935 was roughly evenly divided between a 'left', which advocated rapid economic and social reform, and a 'right', which advocated medium-paced social reform and gradual economic change. Both groups had abandoned the rapid imposition of full socialism. The right was led by Fraser and Nash; the left by John A. Lee.[87] Lee lived to become a caricature of himself, and his subsequent intemperate self-justifications have tended to obscure his importance in 1935–40. It is true that, even at the time, tact was not his strong point. He called the powerful union leader Fintan Patrick Walsh a 'shithouse' to his face – true but impolitic – and told his leader Savage, that he was 'mentally ill'.[88] But Lee also had a breadth of intellect, humour, and ability that the other Labour leaders lacked. A decorated veteran of World War One, a competent novelist, a man of immense energy and a fine colloquial orator, he was, like Savage, a person-ification of left-leaning populism, but with a harder edge.

One can make too much of the fact that Lee was New Zealand-born, while Fraser was a Scot, Nash an Englishman, and Savage an Australian. But it is true that Lee was more of a nationalist than either Nash or Fraser. Savage, also Antipodean, and less conservative and Anglophile than his two chief lieutenants, was in a sense Lee's natural ally. Lee did not make Savage's first ministry in 1935, and believed this was a result of antagonism dating from 1933. But Lee was in Savage's draft list of ministers, and Lee's actual appoint-ment – as sole undersecretary – could be seen as understudy to the Prime

Minister. However, Lee's resentment meant that the two fell out and behaved increasingly vindictively towards each other. Savage fell seriously ill in 1938, with what proved to be terminal cancer, though this was not known at the time. Lee and Fraser began shaping up to contest the succession.

Unlike Lee, Savage and Nash, Fraser lacks a scholarly biography at the time of this writing, and is not easy to assess.[89] He was a very able man indeed, at least as clever as Lee, and was capable of considerable enlightenment on some issues, such as cultural, educational and Maori policy. But he appears to have lacked some other virtues. Some close colleagues described him as a 'vindictive, bad-tempered and sadistic bully'; most agreed on his deviousness. 'Machiavelli had nothing on him.'[90] Fraser told Lee that he was trying to persuade Savage to appoint Lee to Cabinet. There is some evidence and a lot of probability that he was working in the opposite direction.[91] Some historians feel that Lee had no realistic chance of succeeding Savage as prime minister. At the time, it seems to me, Peter Fraser did not agree.

After the election of late 1938, Lee moved a successful motion that caucus should elect the Cabinet, which had been selected by the Prime Minister after the previous election. Savage refused to accept the decision of caucus but, instead of resigning, appealed to the Labour Party conference of 1939, which backed him. When war broke out in September, Lee's frustration rose to fever pitch. He believed he should be Minister of Defence, and this was not necessarily a function of egomania. Lee had the talent and experience; he had proven his administrative ability and pragmatism leading a massive state-housing scheme; and he had chaired a recent committee on defence that prompted a tripling of military expenditure and began long-delayed measures to give New Zealand some air power. But Savage (and Fraser) refused, and Lee retaliated unwisely. He published a lightly veiled attack on Savage, implying that he was too ill, physically and mentally, to lead the country. Savage, Fraser and Nash sacked him from his undersecretary's job and moved to have him expelled from the party. Lee had lost allies through his cruel attack on Savage, but Fraser and his allies must have believed that he might still carry the party conference of 1940. They loaded the dice by increasing the card vote of their union allies, and, at the crucial moment in the conference debate, Fraser produced a message from the very sick Savage saying Lee had made his life 'living hell'. Fraser claimed that Lee had, in effect, killed Savage, who did indeed die two days later. Lee was expelled and had to watch while Fraser – competently but recolonially – led New Zealand through World War Two.

For all his faults, John A. Lee may represent the lost chance of a more independent history that might have been. Counterfactual history is a risky business, but it does seem likely that a Lee government – or a Savage–Lee government – would have made the story of New Zealand in the war a very different one. Its failure to emerge resolved a serious crisis in recolonisation, reducing the possibility of a genuinely nationalist New Zealand government. First Labour was the lost chance of such a government, not the thing itself. As it happened, Savage's contribution to World War Two was restricted to opening the ball. On 3 September 1939, a few months before his death, he made his most famous radio speech, the declaration of war on Germany, in the very terms he himself had appeared to doubt in 1937. 'With gratitude for the past and confidence in the future we range ourselves without fear beside Britain. Where she goes, we go; where she stands, we stand.'

CHAPTER NINE

New Zealand in World War Two

The world war of 1939–45 was a global cataclysm that affected most people on earth and killed 50 million of them. It ended the histories of four nations as military superpowers – Germany, Japan, France and, ultimately, Britain. It dominated geopolitics for half a century, until the collapse of the Soviet Union in 1989. To some extent, we still live in its shadow. New Zealand's role in World War Two was less lethal than in World War One, but just as traumatic. New Zealand mobilised about 200,000 men from a population of 1.6 million, and lost almost 40,000 of them, killed, wounded or taken prisoner. During the war, New Zealand consolidated some old trajectories of its history, established some new trajectories, and rejected others. 'Postwar' New Zealand lasted until 1973, and arguably until 1984.

The received version of New Zealand in World War Two, and of the war in New Zealand, is a tangled knot of history, myth and memory. A desire to keep criticism within the club of old soldiers, and publicly emphasise the positives, persists. This merges with the idea of the Martial Kiwi: that the British were inherently good soldiers; that the Anzacs were the best of British; and that New Zealanders were the best of Anzacs. The battlefield joined the rugby field as the acid test of Better Britishness. The historical scholarship demonstrates that there are two ways to bury history – writing too little, and writing too much. The *Official Histories of World War Two* amount to 50 volumes, most large. Their standard is quite high, and gross censorship was carefully avoided, but they played perceived positives up and perceived negatives down. Apart from a small revisionist strand, dating from 1986,[1] subsequent histories, both scholarly and popular, tend to hold to the traditional line. Some very recent scholarship still claims that almost everything the New Zealand leadership did during the war was both wise and independent.

Such claims are not accepted in the following analysis. But the purpose is to open up, not close, the issues, and it is not to denigrate the New Zealand war effort, which was indeed massive and courageous for so small a country.

New Zealand's soldiers deserve understanding and admiration, as well as colder historical appraisals. To a degree, the myth of the Martial Kiwi managed to make itself true, as in World War One. Like the treatment of World War One in Chapter Three, this analysis centres on three questions. Did New Zealand fight as an independent nation; how well did it fight; and what insights might the first two questions provide into the broader patterns of the history of the New Zealanders?

When Micky Savage declared, 'Where Britain goes, we go', and launched New Zealand into global war, the great majority of his fellow New Zealanders entirely agreed with him. Their position could be seen as reflexively colonial, but historians have uniformly dismissed such a notion. They rightly point out that the New Zealand decision was less reflexive than Australia's; that New Zealand had long opposed appeasement of the fascist powers; and that genuine New Zealand interests were at stake. These interests extended beyond the defence of New Zealand to the survival of its British market and the British naval power that protected the protein bridge. The reasoning here is a little deceptive. New Zealand's decision was indeed less reflexive than Australia's, but this was because Australia was judged to be automatically at war (because Britain was) by its Prime Minister, Robert Menzies, an extremely Anglophile lawyer. The other dominions made much more considered decisions than either Australia or New Zealand – indeed one, Eire, remained neutral.[2] The New Zealand Labour government's dislike of appeasement was perfectly genuine but would obviously never have been enough to induce it to declare war if Britain did not. Rational consideration of strategic interest was secondary to shared British collective identity. If Germany, which liked protein too, had offered to take all New Zealand's exports, there would hardly have been some blithe shift from lamb roast to lamb wurst. New Zealand made its own decision for war, but the decision was determined by New Zealand's belief that it was British. This was not an act of cringing colonialism, but it was not an act of independent nationhood either.

It remains true that, in the context of the times, New Zealand's entry into the war was both reasonable and inevitable. But the decision to participate actively did not exhaust its options. One historian has recently made the astounding suggestion that the security of Britain could reasonably take priority over the security of New Zealand, even from the New Zealand point of view. 'A victorious Britain would be able to make good any reverses on the periphery, even the occupation of New Zealand.'[3] But New Zealand's interests did not converge wholly with Britain's. A British government might see the conquest of New Zealand as a tragic but acceptable price of ultimate victory; a New Zealand government could not. New Zealand should therefore have been more concerned about the possibility of war with Japan. The security of the protein bridge was even more important to New Zealand than to Britain, so New Zealand should also have been more concerned about that. Finally, the New Zealand government should have given an even higher priority to the survival and effectiveness of its own armed forces than a British high command, with numerous other responsibilities, could be expected to give. New Zealand could not have stayed out of World War Two, but it could have fought as a committed but independent-minded junior partner of Britain. Even from the dominionist perspective of the day, it could have sought to ensure that its resources were directed towards the common goal to best effect, and that that common goal did not entirely forget New Zealand. Alternatively, it could repeat the 'favourite child' strategy of World War One, giving top priority to what it thought would impress Britain most.

The Sharp End

New Zealand's Second World War took place in three vast theatres. One was its own Pacific. Low-level maritime warfare against German commerce raiders occurred in 1940. After Japan entered the war on 7 December 1941, New Zealand soldiers, sailors and aircrew served in the Pacific in thousands. These forces were intended first as forward defences of New Zealand itself against the Japanese advance, and then as attempts to maintain a New Zealand and British presence in what was increasingly becoming an American lake. New Zealand's Pacific war was very much the poor relation of the other theatres, in terms of both death and glory. It was a forgotten front – too close to home, not close enough to Home – and is discussed below with other home fronts.

New Zealand's second great theatre of operations was the air above Europe, to which its aircrews made a staggering contribution. Until the war against Japan got under way in 1942, the New Zealand air force was largely a training command for the Royal Air Force. Thereafter a New Zealand Pacific air effort was added to, but did not displace, this role. New Zealand airmen sometimes served in the RAF in titular New Zealand squadrons, but with no New Zealand government control. Some strove successfully to maintain a New Zealand identity; others were scattered among British units. 'It was almost impossible to find an RAF unit without at least one or two NZ airmen in it.'[4] Some seem to have become more British than the British. The first RAF officer to be captured was a New Zealander, shot down in the North Sea on 5 September 1939. He found his German captors 'good scouts', though he was 'pretty dashed lonely'.[5] The airmen's achievements merged into those of the RAF, and history has found it hard to separate them out and attach them to New Zealand martial mythology. Yet the facts, or at least the claims, are that a New Zealander, 'Cobber' Kain, was the first Allied air ace of the war;

that 18 per cent of German night-raiders shot down over Britain in May 1941 were credited to New Zealand pilots; and that over 300 other German planes and an almost incredible 138 Axis ships were destroyed or damaged by New Zealand-dominated squadrons, which also found time to drop a minimum of 20,000 tons of bombs on the Fatherland.[6]

As this suggests, the flow of New Zealanders to the Spitfires, mainly through the Empire Air Training Scheme, was substantial. A number of New Zealanders joined the RAF during or after World War One, and stayed on. The RNZAF, set up as a separate service in 1937, supplied 100 trained pilots to the RAF before the war, bringing the number of New Zealanders flying for Britain to 550 in 1939. No fewer than 11,529 New Zealanders served in the RAF by the end of the war.[7] Australia and Canada also participated in the Empire Training Scheme, but in at least the former case their contribution was proportionately about half that of New Zealand.[8] New Zealanders had better access than the British themselves to the privileged but dangerous status of aircrew as against ground staff, and they suffered the consequences: 3,285 were killed – 29 per cent of New Zealanders who served in the RAF, and 28 per cent of all New Zealand war deaths. A further 700 or so were captured or badly wounded. Because New Zealanders in the RAF were 90 per cent aircrew, they made up about 5 per cent of the British aircrew total. In addition, they are said to have made up 10 per cent of the aircrew of the British Fleet Air Arm in 1945.[9] Historians have missed the remarkable implications of these statistics. New Zealanders were proportionately more prone to serve as *British* aircrew, and therefore to die as such, than were Old Britons themselves.[10]

New Zealand airmen were disproportionately prone to promotion as well as death. Many New Zealanders held high commands, including the key fighter group and four fighter squadrons in the Battle of Britain. Who better to guard British skies than Better Britons? During the war, sixteen New Zealanders commanded RAF wings; 72 commanded RAF squadrons.[11] At least a dozen New Zealanders became air marshals in the RAF, during and after the war.[12] New Zealanders' leading role persisted into the much-reduced peacetime RAF. In 1948, about 300 New Zealanders held commissions, including a high proportion of the most senior commands.[13] As late as the 1960s, the RAF was still New Zealand-led: the RAF commanders in the Near East, the Far East and the Persian Gulf, as well as the Director of Organisation, the Chairman of Defence Research Policy, and the Chief of Air Staff himself.[14] This South British penetration of a North British armed service is perhaps comparable to the role of Scots generals in the British army in the nineteenth century. It is a remarkable example of what a later chapter will call 'the expatriate game' and 'cultural overproduction'. For the present, the point is that New Zealanders fought even more prominently and successfully in the air during World War Two than they did on the ground. It is just that they did not do so as New Zealanders.

By far the best known of New Zealand's three theatres of war is the Mediterranean, where New Zealand and its allies took on the Germans in Greece and Crete (1941), the Italians and Germans in North Africa (1941–43) and the Germans in Italy (1943–45). In 1945, at Trieste, some New Zealand leaders were also quite keen to have Tito's Yugoslav partisan army for dessert. New Zealand's role in these campaigns was remarkably substantial and prominent for so small a country, partly because the armies involved were also small. The Second New Zealand Expeditionary Force, based in Egypt from 1940, supplied, supported and constantly replenished the Second New Zealand Division. Its commander was General Bernard 'Tiny' Freyberg, a New Zealander who had become a British career officer after heroic deeds in World War One. Freyberg was equipped by the New Zealand government with a charter, intended to give him some independence from the British high command. The New Zealand Division constituted a third of the British combat troops in Greece and Crete, and one of the half-dozen key units of the Eighth Army, which fought Rommel's Afrika Korps in the Western Desert of North Africa. On the Western Front in World War One, the New Zealand Division was one of a hundred. In the Mediterranean war, especially the early phases, it was a significant player. It was also the site of some intriguing developments in New Zealand collective identity.

New Zealand's first four campaigns were an expedition to Greece (March–April 1941); the defence of Crete against German paratroop attack (May 1941); an offensive against General Rommel in the Libyan desert, code-named 'Crusader', (November–December 1941); and the defence of Egypt against Rommel's counter-offensive (June–July 1942). For New Zealand, though not in all cases for the Allied cause as a whole, each of these campaigns was a disaster similar in scale to Gallipoli. In the first, hopelessly inadequate Allied forces were predictably hustled out of Greece in a mere three weeks. In Crete, the Allies were again rapidly defeated, more narrowly but also more expensively. Almost half of the New Zealand Division, 7,300 men, and almost all of its equipment, were lost in these two campaigns. In the Crusader campaign, four out of ten New Zealand battalions, an artillery regiment and two out of three brigade headquarters were destroyed, with the loss of 4,600 men. During the defence of Egypt, the division narrowly escaped complete destruction at Minqar Qaim, and was heavily defeated in two subsequent attempts to counter-attack, with a total loss of over 5,000 men. In sum, the main New Zealand field army was crippled four times in these campaigns, and had to be painfully reconstructed four times.

Fortunately, New Zealand's Mediterranean war was a game of two halves, and the second was much better. From November 1942, the Eighth Army at last won a series of victories, notably the Battle of El Alamein, which by May 1943 had swept the Axis armies from North Africa. From late 1943 to early 1945, the New Zealanders then engaged in the arduous but ultimately successful Italian campaign. The New Zealand Division's performance in these later campaigns was not beyond criticism. The British command, itself now much improved, felt that Freyberg was too cautious during and after Alamein. From a New Zealand perspective, in the context of earlier high casualties, this was a forgivable sin. At Monte Cassino in Italy, however, Freyberg broke his own rule of refusing to participate in attacks he thought hopeless, and was defeated with heavy casualties. But, on balance, success was as marked in these operations as failure had been earlier, and a striking improvement in the effectiveness of the New Zealand Division was a contributor to it.

Did the New Zealanders in fact have an edge? Did the myth of the Martial Kiwi have a kernel of truth? Praise from outsiders claiming that this was so has often been quoted. Much was manipulated by the New Zealanders quoting it – a practice dating from the Boer War. German soldiers knew the New Zealanders not only as formidable enemies but also as 'the chaps with false teeth and wrist-watches'.[15] But some praise was not manipulated. Two days after Minqar Qaim, for example, Rommel described the New Zealand Division as 'among the élite of the British army' in a private letter to his wife.[16] As we shall see, the British were usually keen to keep the New Zealanders in the Mediterranean, even when it would have been less trouble to let them go home. They were regularly selected for important (and dangerous) assignments – though one factor here may have been their generous reinforcement policy, which meant the division was usually more numerous than most. The New Zealanders' rate of desertion and other forms of 'combat default' was less than half that of the British.[17] A Polish colonel in the British service, who as a commander of Long Range Desert Groups made up of various nationalities was in a good position to compare, rated 'the New Zealanders high on top'. Colonel Vladimir Peniakoff, known as 'Popski', provided the Martial Kiwi's dream testimonial. 'Gentle, playful and earnest, like serious children who do not break their toys . . . I consider the New Zealanders to be a superior form of humanity.'[18] Rejoining his countrymen after a long absence, the brilliant writer and soldier John Mulgan disagreed on their maturity but agreed on their other qualities. 'They are mature men, these New Zealanders of the desert, quiet and shrewd and skeptical.'[19] Perhaps there *was* something special about 'the Div'. Just as they deserved some blame for the early failures in the Mediterranean war, so the New Zealanders deserved some credit for the later successes. Both need to be explained.

The early disasters certainly require a better explanation than we have had from the received version. Extreme martial mythology, closely related to contemporary Allied propaganda, claimed that they were not disasters at all, and 'Dunkirked' them into moral victories. General Freyberg's official report on Crete almost doubled German numbers and almost tripled German casualties.[20] Despite continuous retreat, made obvious by the rapidly receding positions of the Allied forces, New Zealand newspapers reported the first clashes in Greece with great optimism. The Germans were said to be especially afraid of dominion troops. A 'trained neutral observer' was 'convinced that the new Anzacs, man for man without machines, are three times as good as the Germans'. German prisoners allegedly agreed – ' "Too good, too good" they say dejectedly.' There might be little armour or air support, but there was Kiwi ingenuity: 'A [German] tank with its hatches open came right up under a bluff where we were cooking soup. The crew fire, and one of us empties the scalding contents of the cauldron into the open tank.'[21] This genre of interpretation persisted to 1979, when one writer claimed that New Zealand's record of brigadiers captured by the enemy was 'second to none', surely one of the strangest boasts in all military history.[22]

The real cause of the disasters was a varying mix of adverse circumstance, British military problems and New Zealand military problems. Adverse circumstance was real enough, especially in Greece, where the Allied expedition was clearly doomed from the outset by German numerical and air superiority. This raises the question of what the Allies in general, and the New Zealanders in particular, were doing invading Europe and taking on the triumphant Wehrmacht with only two or three divisions. This question, with others of its ilk, is reserved for the next section. Adverse circumstance was the favoured official explanation of defeat, when defeat was recognised. For New Zealanders, British military weaknesses were the favoured unofficial explanation. By the end of July 1942, the New Zealanders, including Freyberg, 'were totally sceptical about the ability of the Eighth Army's higher command'. 'New Zealanders wondered whether their greatest enemy might be, not the Germans but British incompetence and insolence.' In particular, 'the New Zealanders bitterly disparaged the British armour'.[23] Better Britishness permitted the concept of Worse Britishness and, in a crisis, 'worse' could get pretty bad.

This unofficial New Zealand view was to some extent shared by the British Chief of General Staff, General Alan Brooke, who concluded in July 1942 that 'something was radically wrong' with his armies in the Middle East.[24] British military leadership was more imaginative and competent in World War Two than it had been in World War One, but that is not saying much, and old problems persisted. One was that rehydrating a small peacetime army to wartime size, combined with the continued influence of class, reduced the pool of leaders and led to the promotion of officers beyond their level of competence. There was a reluctance to dismiss old comrades who, while not necessarily incompetent, were not up to the demands of modern war. British military doctrine, unlike the German, continued to change more slowly than military realities, and in the early years of the war the Germans also had an edge in several categories of equipment. The problem with the British tank forces was not courage, as New Zealanders sometimes falsely alleged, but the takeover of tanks by the traditional cavalry regiments, with their aristocratic and somewhat amateurish ethos. The British artillery, with a more professional and technocratic ethos, was widely praised; the armour widely damned.[25] In the mobile context of World War Two, especially the Western Desert, all arms had to act in concert, hence the inclusion of infantry and artillery units in Panzer divisions. The British failed to grasp this, but either charged in brave tank-only masses, the Light Brigade on tracks, or were overcautious to the point of inertia.

The British forces gradually overcame some of these problems, but in the early stages of the Mediterranean war the New Zealand view had some substance. What it did not acknowledge was that, as in World War One, their division could have done more to insulate itself from British problems, and that it shared some of them. In the early campaigns, the New Zealand Division had problems at all levels – soldiers, officers, generals and government. All four disasters provide clear evidence of New Zealand command failure, as well as British. On Crete, for example, there was a real chance of success despite the shortage of air support and heavy equipment. The Allies outnumbered the Germans and had full knowledge of their plans through a broken code. The German paratroops themselves saw their eventual victory as 'almost a miracle', which came after 'we had ceased to believe in the possibility of success'.[26] But, while British and Australian units repelled all attacks, the New Zealanders failed to hold or retake a crucial position, Maleme Airfield, and so Crete was lost. The loss was clearly due to the inability of at least three New Zealand commanders to cope with the pace of modern war. The persistent effort to exclude a fourth – Freyberg himself – from blame is unconvincing.[27]

The sense that old comrades should close ranks against armchair critics persisted to 1986, when a book that had the temerity to suggest that New Zealand soldiers were no better and no worse than others aroused outcry. But closed ranks overlaid a contemporary insider's view, more accurate, but voluntarily suppressed. Two of Freyberg's most able lieutenants, Generals Kippenberger and Stewart, were scathing about New Zealand leadership on Crete. Kippenberger privately denounced 'the whole spiritless conduct of the defence of Crete'.[28] 'I considered then and still do,' stated Stewart, Freyberg's chief of staff, 'that General Freyberg made a balls of Crete.'[29] Yet Stewart praised Freyberg publicly. As general editor of the *Official Histories*, Kippenberger toned down criticisms, papered over failures and allowed Freyberg himself to 'correct errors'. Kippenberger described the Battle of Ruweisat as 'a tragedy of misdirection and mismanagement', but noted, 'we can't say this in a New Zealand Official History'.[30] That New Zealand command failure was all too prevalent in the early stages of the war is not solely the view of armchair critics.

The New Zealand Division also shared the British tension between experience and talent, and was not immune to the class problem either. The division's initial officer corps was drawn very largely from men with previous military experience and higher-class backgrounds. Thereafter, leadership democratised progressively as able junior officers were promoted and as more and more men were commissioned from the ranks. The proportion of officers commissioned from the higher classes halved between 1940 and 1945, with the steepest drops in 1941 and 1942.[31] My guess is that this was a factor in the simultaneous improvement in performance, and that the process occurred faster among the New Zealanders, whose ideology made them more comfortable with egalitarianism, than the British. Here is one possible explanation for the qualitative edge that the New Zealand Division did eventually establish over most British divisions. It was not that workers were more able than gentlemen, but if you choose your leaders from a pool of a thousand instead of a hundred, you tend to get better ones.

The New Zealanders may also have solved the problem of integrating armour a little faster than the British. In 1943, one of the New Zealand brigades was converted to armour. By that time, the desert war was over, and with it the most pressing need for infantry–armour co-operation. But well before, in September 1942, the New Zealand Division had integrated a British tank brigade, training with it and partly co-opting it into the division's institutional culture. The New Zealanders again had problems with other British armoured formations in the Battle of Alamein soon after, but not with its own adopted brigade.[32] New Zealanders may also have been less prone than the British to stick with conventional military doctrine, and this may have been most true of Maori New Zealanders. During the Crusader campaign, detachments of the Maori Battalion chalked up an 'impressive list of successes' while the rest of the division had 'taken a mauling'. Maori looted more than Pakeha, especially for symbols of victory, and this may have been one factor in these successes. The Maori were largely German-armed at this stage – some were arrested by a Polish unit in mistake for German native troops – and German weapons, especially anti-tank weapons, were superior. But other factors may have been the lesser attachment of the Maori to British military doctrine, and the fact that their Pakeha commander, a martinet, was temporarily absent, his place taken by young Maori officers who led from the front and used unorthodox tactics. These officers were too bold – they suffered heavy casualties, especially among themselves – but they did win engagements.[33]

This speedier solving of shared problems may have been one key to a New Zealand edge over most British divisions. But another set of factors was at least equally significant. As a national army as well as a division, the New Zealanders developed more sense of collective identity and solidarity, and a more intense institutional culture, than British divisions. Obviously enough, this increased military effectiveness, as did an inherited and shared martial mythology. As in World War One, it was not so much that the myth grew from its kernel of truth, but the reverse. The process went further in World War Two. Armies, especially civilian armies that have been through shared disasters, are capable of rapidly resocialising their members. The Second New Zealand Division was together for five years. It developed a very full support organisation – its own health, welfare, recreation and entertainment facilities, as well as the obvious military supply and support, its own ways of doing things. Some were similar to those in tight New Zealand. The division's newspaper did not allow correspondence, unlike other military newspapers, for fear of indiscipline and dissent. The Kiwi Concert Party, unlike British equivalents, is said to have avoided 'smut'.[34] But some elements of this temporary subculture differed from its New Zealand parent. 'The Div' became something of a society in itself, a martial variant of the genus 'New Zealander'. We can tell that writers like John Mulgan and Dan Davin missed it when they were away from it, and we can presume that others did so too. During one absence, Kippenberger wanted to be 'back home . . . back home with the division! Not back in New Zealand!'[35]

'The Div' came to exist in a space between the British high command and the New Zealand government. It sometimes used each to increase its autonomy from the other. It was a 'closed shop', hard for outsiders to break into, making its own promotions and demotions without much regard for HQ in Wellington. 'The policy adopted . . . was to try to settle our problems overseas and not refer them to Army HQ.'[36] The extreme example of this sense of autonomy was the collusion of the division's leadership with the British high command in dissuading the New Zealand government from withdrawing the division to fight the Japanese in the Pacific.

In 1944, Prime Minister Fraser visited his army in Italy. He wished to talk freely to private soldiers, partly to ascertain their views about the division staying in Europe, a controversial matter discussed in the next section. Brigadier J. W. Burrow decided that this was 'just begging for trouble', and secretly arranged that the meeting 'appeared casual but was in fact under careful control . . . I also told the regimental sergeant major to take what action he thought fit to discourage anyone from asking questions . . . As we moved away the PM said, "What a nice lot of men." "Yes sir, very nice," I said.'[37] Burrows not only deliberately deceived his own prime minister in time of war, but also published the fact with pride in his memoirs. For him, 'the Div' was self-evidently wiser than the government.

World War Where?

For most New Zealand memory, legend and history, 'World War Two' evokes the Mediterranean war. The foregoing section has added the air war in Europe to round out the picture. As far as actual death and glory is concerned, these theatres were indeed dominant. But another war happened in New Zealand and its Pacific front yard. For society, war reinforced both the Great Tightening and 'sectoral harmony', or socio-economic integration. For the government, the key issue was whether it should fight its own war or Britain's. In the Pacific Ocean, New Zealand faced, but did not necessarily face up to, two sets of threats. The later, and greater, was that of Japanese invasion. The earlier was a series of naval threats against economic targets of vital interest to New Zealand.

In 1939, the New Zealand navy, still a division of the Royal Navy, consisted of two cruisers and one minesweeper. Although half a dozen German surface raiders and tenders are known to have entered New Zealand waters between 1939 and 1941, at least one New Zealand cruiser, and sometimes both, served with the British in the Atlantic, the Red Sea and the Mediterranean. Nor, at first, was there much expansion of the navy. 'For some months after the outbreak of hostilities no special recruiting effort was made', and the New Zealand naval authorities hoped 'that the public will be good enough to refrain from writing to offer their services'.[38] Successful efforts were made to recruit for the Royal Navy, in which 7,000 New Zealanders eventually served. Meanwhile, the German surface raiders sank ships and laid mines, which sank more ships. The *Orion* and *Komet* sank four New Zealand merchantmen in the second half of 1940, including the 16,700-ton protein and passenger ship *Rangitane*. Subsequently the danger went under the sea, with German and Japanese submarines cruising the New Zealand coasts looking for targets on several occasions. In March and May 1942, aircraft from two Japanese submarines made reconnaissance flights over Wellington and Auckland, which did not notice them. As late as January 1945, a German U-boat, U-862, spent twelve days on the east coast after sinking a 7,000-ton American ship in the Tasman Sea.

Fortunately for New Zealand, submarines preferred to target the larger concentrations of shipping off the Australian coast, where they sank eleven vessels in the first half of 1943 alone.[39] Both Germans and Japanese did, however, attack what was technically New Zealand-controlled territory – Nauru and Ocean Islands, held as a joint mandate with Britain and Australia. In 1940, the *Orion* and *Komet* heavily shelled Nauru itself, and also sank five of the seventeen ships carrying phosphate from it to Australian and New Zealand farms. In August 1942, the Japanese invaded and seized Nauru, and held it throughout the war, causing problems on New Zealand farms and death and forced labour on the island itself.[40] A still more serious naval threat to New Zealand interests occurred mostly in the distant Atlantic, where 64 New Zealand–British protein ships, totalling 631,000 tons and about half the total fleet, were sunk by U-boats.[41] Forgotten episodes of New Zealand's war were fought out between U-boats and protein ships with Maori names. Five days short of its British destination, on 13 December 1942, the *Hororata*, carrying 10,000 tons of protein, was torpedoed in the wintry North Atlantic. 'Hundreds of boxes of butter were being washed out of the huge hole in her side, and floating away astern.'[42] The protein bridge, New Zealand's economic umbilical cord, was leaking even more badly than in World War One. What did New Zealand do about it this time?

New Zealand did belatedly build up a force of 24 small anti-submarine vessels and minesweepers, some New Zealand-built. The government also censored accounts of losses to U-boats from the newspapers.[43] But there was no naval equivalent of the New Zealand Division in the desperate Atlantic war against the U-boats, in which the country's vital protein bridge was clearly at stake. The situation was not much better at home. The naval official history itself berates the 'lamentable unpreparedness' of the navy in home waters as late as 1942. As they watched couples dancing to band music in bright lights on the promenade at Napier in January 1945, the crew of U-862 concluded that New Zealand did not know there was a war on. 'In New Zealand everyone seems to feel very safe.'[44] New Zealanders did in fact know that there was a war on. It is just that they thought it was somewhere else.

The sense of insulation from danger cracked only in 1942–43, as Japanese forces swept through South-east Asia and the Pacific, seizing a dozen countries in a few months, including Indonesia, New Zealand's main source of petroleum. The great British naval base of Singapore fell in February 1942, and the British eastern fleet was sunk or withdrawn, first to Ceylon and then to Africa. The only alternative Allied battle fleet, the American, lay at the bottom of Pearl Harbor. Some contemporaries drew comfort from the notion that the country 'could offer nothing to the Japanese which would make [invasion] worth their while', and historians tend to the same view. 'No attack on New Zealand was ever planned.'[45] But Fiji, for whose defence New Zealand had accepted prime responsibility and which was garrisoned by a New Zealand brigade group, clearly was a target. Moreover, there is unpublished evidence that casts doubt on the conviction that the Japanese would never have bothered with New Zealand itself.

During 1931–34, a young Japanese agriculturalist, Isamu Kawase, had trained at Lincoln and Massey Agricultural Colleges in New Zealand, and subsequently published two books on New Zealand agriculture and one on the country in general (1939) – the first of its kind in Japanese. Kawase was therefore the nearest thing that Japan had to an expert on New Zealand. In mid-1942, he was 'asked' by the Japanese navy to prepare five reports on New Zealand, with the alternative of going straight to the front. He agreed and was thereafter involved in several briefings on the possibility of invading New Zealand to both army and navy planning staff. Kawase's account, written after the war, was designed to counter allegations that he had been spying in New Zealand, and sometimes implied that, on the contrary, he had single-handedly saved the country from invasion by discouraging the naval planners. But most of his account – he warned one planner of the 'funnel of wind that is the Cook Strait' – has the feel of truth.

Kawase certainly did discourage some of the Japanese military's more Churchillian ideas, particularly those involving himself. He poured cold water on the prospects for rice production, and declined to be parachuted into New Zealand to agitate revolt among Maori, or to broadcast propaganda to them. The planners believed that there might be some support for the Japanese among Maori, and Kawase poured cold water on this, too. The belief in Maori sympathy for the Japanese was largely, but perhaps not wholly, unfounded. New Zealand authorities took it seriously enough to investigate it, and to arrange meetings with loyal Maori leaders to reassure the Americans.[46] Whatever the case with this, the Japanese planners persisted. On one occasion in 1943, Kawase 'spoke on New Zealand in front of nearly twenty members of military staffs', including Prince Takeda. On another, he was shown a booklet entitled something like 'The Landing Plan on New Zealand', copy No. 33. Kawase's fragmentary memories of the booklet indicate that the intent was to land forces at lightly defended harbours near, but not at, the major ports.[47] Military staffs normally plan for even remote eventualities, but not in Japan during World War Two, where planners were too few and under too much pressure from events.

The New Zealand government at the time, of course, had no knowledge of all this. But the plans do indicate that Japanese invasion was possible. This, to their credit, was precisely the assumption that the government made. They decided that invasion was a serious threat, with a preliminary battle to be fought in Fiji. British assurances that New Zealand was in no danger were rejected, and full mobilisation in New Zealand occurred in January 1942. Fiji was heavily reinforced – with all eight of New Zealand's anti-aircraft guns, among other units. The Battle of Midway in June 1942, in which the Japanese main carrier force was defeated by the Americans, was a turning point in the Pacific war, but only in hindsight. In August 1942, after heavy losses at Guadalcanal, the American Admiral Ghormley warned New Zealand to look to home defence.[48] Without hindsight, it was not until well into 1943 that the New Zealand government could discount all possibility of invasion. Even after that date, the case for shifting New Zealand's main war effort to the Pacific was considered very strong. The consequent debate about shifting the New Zealand Division from the Mediterranean to the Pacific was a turning point – or rather, an important *non*-turning point – in New Zealand history. To place it in context, we need to revert briefly to the former theatre.

From their forces' first arrival in the Middle East, Prime Minister Fraser and General Freyberg had had to wrestle with their British opposites for control. Freyberg stood up to his British commanders on some occasions, but he was a British officer himself and usually gave way on matters small and large. Officer training, which New Zealanders undertook at British facilities, was one issue. Some New Zealanders felt that these offered advanced courses in bootlicking and polishing, while the realities of modern war were taught poorly or not taught at all. There was a push to set up a New Zealand divisional officer training facility, but this was vetoed by Freyberg under British pressure, until October 1944. Nor did Freyberg use his government's permission to increase the inadequate British ration for his men. Freyberg did invoke his right of direct communication with the New Zealand government, but he usually allowed Middle Eastern Command to vet his messages.[49] Most notably, he did not make it plain to the New Zealand government that he considered the Greek expedition to be hopeless from the outset. The New Zealand government's consent to engaging in this campaign was therefore not fully informed. Even so, it set conditions – such as the availability of adequate air support – that were, in Freyberg's own words, 'lamentably and totally unfulfilled'.[50]

In subsequent campaigns, both Freyberg and Fraser struggled to make the British high command understand that their division was not just another division – one of Britain's 40 – but a national army, 1,000 of whose casualties were proportionately equivalent to about 30,000 Old British. Sometimes they succeeded – as when Fraser persuaded the Royal Navy to commit one last ship to the evacuation of Crete. More often they failed. When Freyberg hesitantly queried one of Britain's bold gambles with the New Zealand army and suggested that the New Zealand government might object, Anthony Eden replied: 'What, those dear old men, they would agree to anything.'[51] In the end, both Freyberg and Fraser were seldom prepared to overrule the British high command, if it really insisted, over the use of New Zealand troops.

There was a sorry epilogue to these events. In November 1943, British forces and a small New Zealand unit landed on the Greek Dodecanese Islands, but were counter-attacked and forced to surrender by the Germans. For the second time, New Zealand troops had landed in Greece to take on the Wehrmacht without the informed consent of their government – this time without even its knowledge. This was too much for Fraser. The New Zealand government, he wrote to London, 'were never consulted as to the use of their troops in this connection', nor was it or Freyberg even informed until after the troops had landed. The British tried to excuse themselves, for once to no avail. Fraser wrote that the New Zealand government dismissed the 'outdated, unhappy, and totally irrelevant' excuses 'unanimously and even contemptuously'. New Zealanders, he wrote 'were stupidly sacrificed without even consent for their inclusion . . . being asked from our Government'. This would arouse 'disappointment and bitterness' in New Zealand. The events have 'largely destroyed my own faith in the present Middle East Command'.[52] These were strong words from 'those dear old men'. But they came several thousand New Zealanders too late.

As the Japanese swept south in 1942, the question of whether New Zealand controlled its own armed forces took on an even more urgent edge. New Zealand in fact possessed the trained and experienced soldiers and airmen to give any Japanese invasion a hard time, but they were in Europe and the Middle East. Bringing home the soldiers was an option that had to be considered, and it was, on several occasions. After the fall of Singapore and the bombing of Darwin (which killed 240 people) in February 1942, the Australian government began the arduous process of extracting all but one of its divisions from British clutches in the Middle East and bringing them home to face the Japanese. New Zealand thought about doing the same, but decided against it. In November 1942, with Egypt finally secured by the victory at Alamein, the Australians ordered home their sole remaining division. Again New Zealand declined to follow suit – to the understandable rage of Australian Prime Minister John Curtin. When Axis forces were expelled from North Africa in May 1943, New Zealand declined a third opportunity to withdraw. Instead, it allowed its division to participate in the whole Italian campaign, 1943–45. Even when the *British* Chiefs of Staff suggested that the New Zealanders could be withdrawn after the fall of Rome, in 1944, the idea was not taken up.[53]

While the leadership of the New Zealand Division preferred to remain in the Mediterranean, this is not so clear of the rank and file. In early 1943,

Fraser told Parliament that the soldiers themselves were not upset by the return of the last Australian division, and that 'the men collectively did not wish to return home'. Frederick Jones, the Minister of Defence, who was visiting the troops, claimed that on the contrary, 'there is a general desire on the part of the men to return home', though they were understandably less enthusiastic about fighting the Japanese in the jungles of the Solomon Islands. Under pressure from Freyberg and others, Jones later changed his tune. The real attitude of the men can be measured by their reactions to a 'furlough scheme' that was being implemented at the same time. Over 6,000 of the longest-serving men were allowed to return home on leave, as compensation for the retention of the division in the Mediterranean. They arrived in New Zealand in July 1943 and, when the crunch came late that year, proved reluctant to return. In early 1944, what amounted to mutinies took place in various camps. About 1,000 men refused point-blank to return, and there was 'some loose, casual talk . . . about the possibility of armed revolt'. 'There is no foretelling what men who have faced but never feared the very cream of the German army might contemplate.' Military police fired shots in the air while arresting the ringleaders, and 200 were court-martialled.[54]

Fewer than one in six returned to the Mediterranean in the end, and at least one of those who did was told he was a bloody fool for doing so by those who had never left. 'What the hell did you come back for? I didn't think you would be such a b—— fool.'[55] Resentment at some fit men in New Zealand not having to serve, and an understandable desire to fight no more at all, were probably more important to the furlough men's attitude than some burning desire to fight the Japanese, who no longer threatened New Zealand directly. But the furlough affair does strongly suggest that the rank and file's desire to remain in the Mediterranean was an invention.

From 1942, New Zealand tried to mobilise a second division – known as 3 NZ Division. But, partly because a generous flow of reinforcements to the Mediterranean continued, it was never able to get this up to more than two-thirds strength. The American command in the Pacific was therefore reluctant to give the Third New Zealand Division major roles. It participated in three minor operations in late 1943 and early 1944, in co-operation with the Americans in the Solomon Islands. But in March 1944, the decision was made to disband it, to the despair of its able commander, H. E. Barrowclough. New Zealand naval and air force units continued to operate in the Pacific, but the New Zealand army did not.[56] It suffered a total of 300 casualties in the Pacific War, compared with 30,000 in the European war.

As recently as 2000, historians still claimed that the New Zealand government's decision to fight in the Mediterranean rather than the Pacific shows a 'strong grasp of strategic principles'. 'The decision to leave the division in the Mediterranean theatre was in fact based on a New Zealand assessment of New Zealand interests.'[57] Regrettably, the facts suggest otherwise. In May 1943, there was a large War Cabinet majority in favour of bringing the division home. Fraser talked his Cabinet around, 'though his own mind was not made up until the very last moment', and he 'almost wept over the distress which this policy was likely to inflict upon Curtin'.[58] The previous November, Fraser had formally requested the return of his division: 'It is felt that the place of the 2nd New Zealand division is . . . here in the Pacific.'[59] Fraser was himself talked around by a combination of his own dominionism and Winston Churchill.

Churchill, Britain's great wartime prime minister, was one of those inclined to snigger at New Zealand fears of Japanese invasion. 'There are many other far more tempting objectives for them.'[60] It is true that the direct Japanese threat to New Zealand disappeared in 1943, with American victories. But the threat to the Middle East had disappeared even earlier, with victory at Alamein in 1942, and the New Zealand government was convinced that New Zealand (and Britain) should play a major role in the Pacific to have any say in the postwar settlement there. It has been suggested that such an effort 'would have made practically no difference' in earning credit with the Americans,[61] but this was not clear at the time, and is highly debatable even in retrospect. One could say the same, with greater validity, about the Italian campaign. The benefits to New Zealand of inching bloodily up Italy were, surely, less than those of significant participation in the Allied reconquest of its own Pacific.

Churchill played his cards cleverly in his contest of wills with Peter Fraser. A frequent subtext in their correspondence was the favourable comparison of loyal, calm and enlightened New Zealand with Australia. Fraser did not exactly lap this up; unlike some of his officials, he valued good relations with Australia. But he valued 'New Zealand's favoured position as the good boy of the family' even more.[62] The British High Commissioner in New Zealand reported confidentially that Fraser 'is most anxious to find a solution acceptable to Mr Churchill and not to play Australia's game'.[63] One Australian revisionist history considers that the independence of Australia's own war effort has been greatly exaggerated. It notes that New Zealand – 'this diminutive dominion' – 'imitated Australia in subsuming her perceived national interest to that of Britain'.[64] In fact, New Zealand, as in World War One, competed with Australia in the dominionist game and, for what it is worth, it won again – its casualties were proportionately 50 per cent higher than Australia's.[65] Rubbing salt in the self-inflicted wound, during 1942 Churchill repeatedly fobbed off Fraser's increasingly desperate appeals for war materials, especially modern aircraft, of which New Zealand had none at all. This contrasted markedly with New Zealand's gifts of its sparse equipment, including two squadrons of bombers, to Britain in its hour of crisis in 1940.[66] One reads through the documents waiting for Fraser to at least hint at the obvious quid pro quo – some aircraft to face the Zeros in return for leaving the New Zealand Division in the Mediterranean. One waits in vain.[67]

Churchill's second card was the assertion that shipping was not available to bring home the New Zealand Division. Shipping was indeed very short, but there was always enough to ship protein to Britain and New Zealand reinforcements *to* the Middle East. Churchill's third card was the Americans. President Roosevelt appears to have sometimes inclined towards the switching of New Zealand's main war effort to the Pacific,[68] but usually supported Churchill in pressuring Fraser to leave his troops in the Mediterranean. From November 1942, Roosevelt also supplied American troops to garrison New Zealand (an earlier contingent of US Marines who arrived in June 1942 left again in July). Fraser initially dismissed an inexperienced American garrison as no substitute for New Zealand's own veteran army,[69] then came to accept it as such. As we have seen, Churchill also had an ally in the leadership of the New Zealand Division. In all, the evidence suggests to me that it was Winston Churchill, helped by our own recolonial mentality, who exercised the decisive influence on New Zealand's biggest strategic decision of the war.

World War Two in New Zealand

New Zealanders lost only half as many sons and brothers in World War Two as they had in World War One. The sons and brothers again did most of their fighting over 15,000 kilometres away from home. Whatever it should have been, the Pacific was a backwater in terms of combat, and the home front could be seen as the backwater of a backwater. Yet the war produced a galvanic effort from state and society. At peak in 1943, well over half the adult male population was in the armed forces (154,000) or the Home Guard (119,000). Women entered the armed services, voluntary organisations and the waged workforce in unprecedented numbers, and the Maori war effort dwarfed that in World War One. In 1942–44, over half the national income was devoted to the war. Furthermore, whereas World War One had taken New Zealanders to the world, World War Two also brought the world to New Zealand. New Zealand expected 100,000 Japanese. Instead, it got 100,000 Americans – the country's first mass encounter with foreigners since the gold rushes of the 1860s and the great migration of the 1870s. New Zealand's economic insulation had been challenged by the Depression of the 1930s, then re-established by a mix of luck and the Labour government. Now cultural and geopolitical insulation was under threat. What can war tell us about peace, about the underlying shapes of the tight society?

Backwater or not, New Zealand's home front is said to have hit the Axis propaganda machine's headlines on at least three occasions. On 5 May 1944, Nazi radio in Paris parlayed the furlough mutiny into the Siege of Hamilton. 'There has been a Mutiny among the troops due to embark for the European front in Hamilton. A state of siege has been proclaimed in the town.'[70] Earlier in the war, in Lyttelton Harbour, the fishing boat *Dolphin* breached some unclear wartime regulation and was sunk by a coast defence battery. A crewman was killed. The incident was censored from the local media, but German propagandist Lord Haw-Haw is said to have announced that the New Zealand navy had sunk its own battleship.[71] In 1941, a mentally disturbed Westland farmer and expert marksman, Stan Graham, killed seven police and Home Guardsmen during a famous manhunt. Again Lord Haw-Haw allegedly had a field day, claiming that Hitler had telegraphed Graham: 'Hold the South Island. Sending another man to take the North Island.'[72]

At least from December 1941, however, the war in New Zealand was no Goebbelsian joke. 'The man on the street . . . for the first time began to feel the war in the pit of his stomach.'[73] Recruitment, especially for the Home Guard, 'manpowering' (compulsory employment in essential industries) and preparations for local defence intensified. Those who doubt the seriousness with which the Japanese threat was taken might glance at the gun emplacements and tunnel complexes still to be seen in Auckland and Wellington. Blackout regulations were broadened and tightened. Breaches of them accounted for the majority of traffic prosecutions. In April 1942, pictures and documents were taken from the National Gallery, the National Archives and the Turnbull Library in Wellington and secreted in the countryside. They included portraits of deceased judges, which might profitably have been left to the Japanese. A statue of John Logan Campbell, Auckland's Dad, was taken from its pedestal in Manukau Road and buried in a nearby reserve. Such actions were not all state-led. At Farmers department store in Auckland, 'when the siren shrieked, each girl ran to a shelter, placed a cork between her teeth and cotton wool in her ears, then stretched herself on the floor and buried her face in a pillow'.[74] Bomb shelters appeared in thousands of private backyards,[75] and banks photographed their ledgers and sent the copies to safety – not even a Japanese invasion would free you from your mortgage.[76] If U-862 had visited in 1942 or 1943 instead of 1945, it would have found that New Zealanders did know that there was a war on, and that it was getting close to home.

Widespread fear may help explain New Zealand's worst bloodshed during World War Two – indeed, the worst since the siege of Ngatapa in 1869. About a thousand Japanese did make it to New Zealand, but only as prisoners. They were held in a camp in the sleepy Wairarapa township of Featherston, established in September 1942. Most were non-combat troops, who accepted imprisonment readily enough. But a couple of hundred were combat soldiers, who resented being forced to work for their captors. On 25 February 1943, a New Zealand guard shot a Japanese officer in the shoulder for refusing an order to move. About 240 prisoners began throwing stones and moving towards the 34 guards, who opened fire, killing 48 and wounding another 74. One guard was killed and six were wounded. A similar incident occurred in Australia the following year, and in both cases part of the problem seems to have been that Japanese combat troops, whose motto was never surrender, found it hard to accept imprisonment. But the numbers hit suggest rather a lot of shooting for the suppression of a riot by men without firearms. The incident was also suppressed in memory, even by those who heard about it at the time, and until recently the best New Zealand account of it was a stage play.[77]

Apart from Featherston, close engagment on the home front came not with enemies, but with allies. In mid-1942, a young girl saw men in strange uniforms walking down a New Zealand street. 'I took off back home at high speed shouting to my mother to "Get inside quick. The Germans are coming."'[78] Fortunately it was not the Germans, but the Americans. Substantial numbers of American troops, the First Marine Division, first arrived in June 1942, but they left again in July for the bloody beaches of Guadalcanal. Significant numbers from other units did not arrive until November, and it was not until 1943 that the Americans delivered much in the way of actual security from attack. But, that year and the next, they not only provided a comforting bulwark against the Japanese but also constituted New Zealand's first mass encounter with foreigners since the nineteenth century. Their numbers peaked at about 50,000 in July 1943, and totalled about 100,000 troops in camp, 1942–44. They were concentrated in and around Auckland and Wellington, and about half were Marines. These figures do not include ships' crews and troops on transports. The best estimate of total American visits is 150,000, and the figure might have been as high as 200,000.[79]

American reactions to New Zealand were predictable enough. 'No Scotch, two per cent beer, but nice folks.' 'Frankly, organised entertainment is pretty scarce in New Zealand.' There were no shoeshine boys, hotdogs or chewing gum, and 'one of the characteristics which the New Zealanders share with the British is a complete inability to make coffee'.[80] The Americans stimulated demand for commercial laundries, florists, gift shops, ice-cream, entertainment and liquor. They found six o'clock closing archaic, and circumvented it when they could. The relative sophistication of the Americans can be exaggerated. Many were farm boys, for whom Auckland and Wellington were big cities. They had not been able to get a legal drink at all, let alone after 6 pm, in the United States between 1919 and 1933, when prohibition ruled. But the American invasion was a prologue to a 'great opening' to the world that New Zealand was to experience from the 1960s, an early mass encounter with *difference*.

As the mass encounter began, in 1942, New Zealanders harboured various stereoypes of Americans, some positive, some negative. There was some sense of Anglo-Saxon kinship, gratitude for American help and generosity, and a Hollywood-induced aura of glamour. But there was also a sense of resentment at America's affluence and growing power, and a tendency to sneer at perceived American brashness, crassness and even naivety. This attitude would be hard to explain if New Zealanders thought of themselves as New Zealanders and nothing else. So small and isolated a country could not reasonably envy greater American power, or claim greater sophistication. The attitude only becomes comprehensible when we realise that New Zealanders thought of themselves as British too, citizens of a superpower whose geopolitical and cultural lead America was rapidly overhauling. Anti-Americanism was often a symptom of Better Britonism.

There was also resentment about American attitudes to Maori – not only among Maori themselves, but also among Pakeha. Americans, particularly from the Southern states, sometimes loudly objected to mixing with Maori in pubs and places of entertainment. Pakeha also discriminated against Maori, and sometimes denigrated them, but they did so less intensely and less overtly. As we have seen in Chapter Six, it was not that Pakeha rejected racialism, but that they partially excluded Maori from it. Such things as American use of the word 'nigger', and reluctance to take their rest and recreation on the same premises as Maori is said to have been one cause of violence between American and New Zealander servicemen.

Just how substantial inter-Allied conflict was is debatable. The 'Battle of Manners Street' in Wellington in April 1943, in which thousands of servicemen are said to have participated and at least two Americans were said to have been killed, was dismissed as largely legend in 1983.[81] Since then, however, historians have uncovered six incidents in which Americans and New Zealanders killed or wounded each other, and more in which they fought with fists, bottles and blackjacks, sometimes in large numbers.[82] Such incidents were officially suppressed, and these may represent the tip of an iceberg. 'Police statistics (and also, it seems, the censored newspapers) captured little of the disruption to order created by New Zealand and American service-men.'[83] American–Maori tensions in the Waikato are said to have resulted in the hospitalisation of 27 of the former at one time.[84] Where such frictions were not caused by race, they tended to be caused by sex.

New Zealand soldiers on home duty, in training for overseas fronts, or home on furlough numbered around 70,000 in 1942–44, and therefore outnumbered the Americans at any given time. Even Pakeha troops, let alone Maori, seem to have resented the American presence more than they saw them as saviours. That the Americans were better paid, better clothed and better equipped contributed to this, as did the growing feeling that New Zealand should be defended by New Zealanders. Another pea under the mattress, however, was the belief that Americans were having their evil way en masse with New Zealand women. In the New Zealand parody of a popular American song:

> If the army and the navy
> Ever gaze on heaven's scenes,
> They would see the angels sleeping with
> United States Marines.[85]

The pressure-cooker atmosphere of World War Two, fraught with individual as well as collective fears and tensions, was fertile ground for urban myth. Yet some male anecdote has the feel of truth. 'Let's face it, the bedroom commandos had it all their own way with Auckland women.'[86] One female attempt at comfort could only have made matters worse. 'Much of the love we gave to the Yanks we were giving by proxy to our own men too far away to touch.'[87] About 1,400 New Zealand women married Americans in New Zealand, with marriages in the United States bringing the total to perhaps 2,000.[88] Given that most American servicemen were in New Zealand for a matter of months rather than years, this rate does seem quite high. The illegitimacy rate increased over 80 per cent between 1939 and 1944, then dropped. Venereal disease followed much the same pattern, with a 70 per cent increase in registered cases of gonorrhea among women between 1941 and 1943, and a sharp drop in 1945.[89] These statistics are not conclusive. But, given that lavish American equipment included contraceptive sheaths, and that about 100,000 young New Zealand men were removed from the domestic scene, we do appear to be talking about some thousands of sexual relationships between New Zealand women and American servicemen.

A benign impression of the American invasion is much more common in female folk memory than in male. The Americans were the first foreigners most New Zealand women had ever encountered. They were different, but friendly, and their Hollywood accents made them seem exotic, yet familiar. They seemed sophisticated, romantic and generous – and more forthcoming and courteous than New Zealand men. *They* did not cluster in the corners at dances, drinking with their male mates. They 'made our men look boorish by comparison'.[90] We might speculate, tentatively, about a mini-mutiny by young New Zealand women, a brief affair with passing strangers that challenged traditional codes. If it existed, it was certainly not a product of formal feminism, which still frowned on such activity, but of populist feminism. It was populist feminism that gave us the Great Mothers' Mutiny, 1890s–1930s. As we shall see in the next chapter, its 1940s versions may have contributed to an opposite effect.

The picture of a proportionately gargantuan New Zealand war effort, up there with Germany and the Soviet Union as well as Britain, is not solely a product of local ego. Proportionately, mobilisation of both men and money was greater than in Australia, Canada and the United States. A comparative study of national war efforts concludes that New Zealand 'productivity per head of labour reach[ed] the highest level of any of the combatant states'.[91] Another study comments admiringly on Britain's overall war effort, then notes that 'the only allied nation to come near to equalling this was, rather oddly, New Zealand'.[92] This picture may need some pruning. Recent research suggests that the entry of women into the wartime workforce was not huge in comparative terms, and that the industrial effort generally has also been exaggerated. 'New Zealand's war effort encompassed neither a substantial general extension of hours nor a radical attempt to re-organise industry.'[93] Yet the economic war effort still seems quite impressive.

Rumours that some workers and businesses preferred profiteering to self-sacrifice were rife, but apparently inaccurate. Inflation (and therefore, presumably, profiteering and high wages) was less great than in comparable countries. The ratio of working days lost to strikes was much lower in New Zealand than in Canada, Australia and the United States.[94] Farming mechanised substantially during the war. Its paid workforce dropped by 22 per cent between 1936 and 1945; tractors doubled and electric motors increased 50 per cent. Dairy production held up despite losing the most labour, with harder work by unpaid families probably contributing as much as new machines. Meat production increased 14 per cent. New packaging techniques, developed to conserve sparse wartime shipping space, reduced freight costs.[95] Wool production increased rapidly, though encouraged by guaranteed prices rather than real demand. Local processing of wool doubled with the decline of shipping to Bradford (though it remained small), and the war proved 'a fillip to the wool industry'. The overall increase in farming output was not huge, at 13 per cent, but given the sharp decline in labour and other difficulties, wartime agricultural restructuring was quite impressive. It may have helped trigger the final phase of the 'grasslands revolution', which kept increasing farming productivity to about 1972.

There were also wartime developments in non-traditional primary industry and manufacturing. Dehydrated and canned meat and vegetable industries emerged, to supply US troops in the Pacific – vegetables were exported in quantity for the first time since the Australian gold rushes.[96] Wattie's Canneries, founded at Hastings in 1934, received a war boost, as did wine production.[97] American and New Zealand servicemen, desperate for alcohol in the tight society, were introduced to the sugary delights of 'Dally plonk', which Dalmatians themselves were seldom silly enough to drink. They could always make decent wine, and did so for their own consumption, but they could not sell it in a market that preferred beer, spirits and sugared ports and sherries.

Apart from weapons, including over 20,000 mortars, sub-machine guns, and automatic rifles, New Zealand produced 15,000 radios and 500 large boats and small ships – some of the last more efficiently than America, according to Americans themselves. Crown Lynn Potteries of Auckland substituted successfully for shortages of British and European tableware. New Zealand began producing its own tennis balls and, thanks to Mussolini, 'macaroni was made at Timaru'.[98] Manufacturing output increased 30 per cent by volume, and much more by value, and the New Zealand-made proportion of goods consumed rose from 60 per cent to over 70 per cent.[99] 'Many new manufacturing industries sprang up over the war years.'[100] Local cigarette production doubled; and a national totem, the gumboot, at last became home-made. 'An interesting wartime development was an upsurge of exports of manufactured articles',[101] including clothing, footwear, and electrical equipment, as well as munitions and ships. Manufactured exports rose thirteenfold from less than £1 million pre-war to £13 million.

Manufacturing for both export and domestic markets increased, imports decreased by volume, and the proportion of imports from Britain decreased too, with shifts to Australian and American sources. In 1943, helped by Lend-Lease, the United States temporarily supplanted Britain as the leading source of imports – the only time the latter lost first place between the 1860s and the 1980s.[102] Private savings doubled because of a dearth of things to buy. While public debt tripled, the proportion owed overseas – principally to London – dropped from 53 to 20 per cent.[103] Overseas debt also dropped absolutely, retired with booming export receipts; and overseas funds multiplied because of low imports, owing to belt-tightening in New Zealand and increased local supply of the local market.[104]

New Zealand economists at the end of the twentieth century would have been delighted by these figures; their nineteenth-century forebears would have been incredulous. Like that in World War One, the New Zealand war effort in World War Two, despite limits to overtime and the mobilisation of women, suggests a high degree of socio-economic efficiency, a surprising capacity to express power. Again the cause was a mix of growing state power, recolonial ideology and the ability of the tight society to produce concerted action, now assisted by the new fourth, sectoral, harmony.

On the face of it, the explanation for the intensity of New Zealand's war effort is an increasingly totalitarian warfare state. Government control of the economy, already substantial, tightened several notches. A wide array of regulations, banning such wasteful things as trouser cuffs and the use of heaters in business premises between 4 and 6 pm, provided rich ammunition for later anti-state diatribes. An elaborate Economic Stabilisation system was introduced in late 1942 to control wages and prices. It held the increase in wholesale prices to 6 per cent in the second half of the war, as against 17 per cent in the first half.[105] Rationing was introduced from 1939, beginning with petrol. Sugar and tea were rationed from early 1942, and a new raft of commodities from late 1943 – after the election. These included cheese, butter and meat, like rationing coal in Newcastle. 'Manpowering' regulations directed men to essential industries from early 1942, and were soon extended to women. A total of 176,000 workers were so directed. Employers were required to report absences of more than four hours, and manpower officials and police were entitled to pursue adult truants into pubs, cinemas, golf courses, tearooms and private homes. There were 163 such raids in early April 1944 alone, yielding 110 illicit absentees – fewer than one per raid, which seems rather counter-productive. But a total of 8,000 adult truants were fined for their misdeeds. Government encouraged many new industries, and itself ran several. Direct taxes went up 246 per cent to pay for all this. It was the war, as much as the first Labour government, that doubled state expenditure as a proportion of gross domestic product from 14 to 28 per cent between the 1920s and 1949.[106]

The state also augmented its power on many other fronts, notably through the Emergency Regulations Act of 1940. Censorship became comprehensive, presided over by a new 'Director of Publicity', J. T. Paul, and Prime Minister Fraser himself. It was stricter than in Australia or Britain. 'Catching the distributors of subversive literature,' announced the police on Fraser's instructions, 'had to take precedence over everything, short of murder.'[107] Two communist and socialist journals were banned, and so was the Social Credit News, though the only organisation to be made illegal was the Jehovah's Witnesses.[108] Other countries also banned this religious group for its strong anti-war views, but 'New Zealand was the last country in the Empire to lift the ban'. There were 45 convictions for subversive statements in 1940. Railway worker W. E. Aitken was sentenced to six months' hard labour for saying to his workmates, during an argument, 'I don't care if the British get beaten.' Men who stuck posters on lamp-posts saying 'No more troops overseas, New Zealand comes first' received the same prison sentence.[109] A Security Intelligence Service was established for the first time in 1941, and survived despite falling victim to an elaborate hoax by a conman in 1942.[110]

New Zealand's tiny group of 'enemy aliens', Germans and Italians, received quite harsh treatment. At peak in December 1942, 185 were interned.[111] The treatment of conscientious objectors was harsher still.[112] New Zealand allowed only 19 per cent of appeals against military service on grounds of conscience, compared with over 50 per cent in beleaguered Britain. Some 800 were interned, in camps deliberately designed to be uncomfortable, and 60 of the most obdurate were sent to civil prison for long terms. These men were banned from the civil service, and from voting, until 1951, and one was still being prevented from returning to his job as a schoolteacher in 1962. Two careful historians conclude that conscientious objectors in New Zealand 'received much harsher treatment than did those in Britain and other Commonwealth countries'.[113]

Kiwi totalitarianism, then, can go some way towards explaining the intensity of the New Zealand war effort. One could point to Peter Fraser, who was usually authoritarian and sometimes petty and vindictive. According to several historians, Fraser was characterised by 'intolerance of criticism and hatred of dissent', and led 'undoubtedly one of the least liberal ministries in the history of the country'.[114] But the notion of Fraser as wartime dictator can be overdrawn. Sidney Holland, who replaced Adam Hamilton as leader of the National Party Opposition during the war, might well have been even worse. The intensive war effort was not simply imposed on other sectors by the state, and it did not extend far beyond what the public were prepared to accept, or even demand. There was some dissent and complaint but Kiwi totalitarianism remained largely voluntary.

The war strengthened sectoral harmony, the unholy alliance between state, business, unions and, to a lesser extent, farmers. Union and business leaders, such as Fintan Patrick Walsh and James Fletcher, joined up with the state for the duration. Fletcher, head of the country's largest building company, who had previously helped the government with its state-housing programme, became Commissioner for Defence Construction with extremely wide powers. The unionist Walsh performed a not-dissimilar role in the Economic Stabilisation Commission. Both Fletcher and Walsh were close friends of Peter Fraser. Close personal cross-sector relationships were to prove a key to long-term sectoral harmony.

There was also widespread public demand for an intensive war effort – and for such things as harsh treatment of conscientious objectors and aliens.

The Returned Servicemen's Association generously suggested that the former should be branded and exiled to a desert island. 'Watersiders refused to work with men of Italian extraction.'[115] Volunteering for the services was slower and slighter than in World War One – New Zealanders now had no illusions about bloodless wars. But the acceptance of conscription, introduced in July 1940, was if anything more fatalistic. Other forms of volunteering were substantial. There was an unofficial mass mobilisation as well as an official one. A 'Women's War Service Auxiliary' was formed in 1940 by 69 women's organisations, and had a membership of 75,000 by 1942. Despite initial disinterest from the army, the Home Guard grew to 100,000 men within eight months of its establishment in August 1940.[116]

The Japanese threat of 1942–43 helped intensify the people's war effort, as it did that of the state. But both efforts were quite high before and after. The Home Guard and the women's volunteer movement were only two of many attempts explicitly to match activities in Britain. All were expressions of recolonial ideology, of a genuine shared identity with Britain, a desire to help it through danger. There was a substantial minority of sceptics, notably among resocialised servicemen, but they were well aware that they had to keep quiet. The Canterbury Education Board began its war by ordering instruction in 'what Britain and Britons stand for', and that 'every school day should begin with the song "There'll always be an England"'. After the war, with Britain perceived to be on the brink of starvation despite its victory, New Zealand continued to do more than its share, and this continued to be popular. The continuance of rationing, to make more food available for Britain, began to pall by 1949, but was accepted before that. Indeed, it was voluntarily enhanced by the public. New Zealand individuals sent 200,000 food parcels to Britain in the first quarter of 1947, and the total ran at about 800,000 a year – about two per New Zealand family. 'Helping Britain became almost an obsession for New Zealanders.'[117] 'The huge quantities of food parcels sent abroad were a remarkable expression of the desire of our people to assist and encourage their hard-pressed kin in the Mother Country.'[118] This was not simple charity. The London-bound parcels dwarfed the flow to European refugees, who were in more need. Like the young voices singing 'There'll always be an England' in Canterbury schools, the 800,000 parcels were stamped 'recolonisation triumphant'.

CHAPTER TEN

Golden Weather?

On 7 May 1945, Germany surrendered to the Allies, followed on 15 August by Japan. New Zealand celebrated VE (Victory Europe) and VJ (Victory Japan) Days with official thanksgiving services, parades, public holidays and a limited amount of impromptu rejoicing. Strangers kissed, and people danced in the streets – things New Zealanders normally do only after winning a yacht race. The victory days were constrained by heavy-handed government orchestration – people heard that Germany had surrendered on the afternoon of 7 May, but were ordered not to celebrate until the next day, after Britain had made its official announcement.[1] But victory still etched itself in people's minds like some benign earthquake. The clouds of doom lifted; the clouds of uncertainty did not. Postwar New Zealand was torn between two strong trends: a sense of irrevocable change, a world shattered and rebuilding in different shapes; and a desire to *restore* – to restore a past that, ideally at least, was more familiar and secure. The trajectories of change, to be accepted or rejected, came on three fronts.

On the social front, for Maori and women, World War Two seemed at first to offer prospects of what a later chapter will call 'coming out' – moving from socio-economic segregation and low status to participation and more equal status. The Maori war effort, expressed in high voluntary recruitment, voluntary war work and a movement into the waged workforce, even the urban one, had been very substantial. Through the Maori War Effort Organisation, established in 1942, it had also been Maori-led to a significant degree. Would these trends, to economic integration and urbanisation and to some Maori autonomy, continue after the war? These issues are discussed in Chapter Sixteen. Here, a short answer will do – yes and no. The economically integrative and urbanising trend did continue; the trend to autonomy did not.

Women also entered the waged workforce in unprecedented numbers during the war. Their contribution to the labour force went up one-third – more if women in the armed services are included – and they found their way into traditionally male occupations – as taxi drivers, tram conductors, farm labourers and many other forms of 'men's work'. Would this lead to permanent change in women's work and women's status? Again, this question is reserved for a later chapter, and here an even shorter answer will do: no. Rosie the Riveter doffed her overalls for a wedding ring and a maternity dress. Marriage became more romantic, the Great Mothers' Mutiny ended, and a baby boom, 1945–70, was on.

The second front of postwar change was in international politics and trade. Hot war was all too quickly replaced by cold war, in which the Soviet Union and its new satellites shaped up against its former allies. In 1949, final communist victory in a long civil war made China a prospective new ally for the Soviets. Matters came to a head with the Korean War of 1950–53, fought between the Communist Bloc and the West, largely but not wholly through unfortunate Korean proxies. There was never any question as to which side New Zealand would be on, but there was a question as to whether it would look to Britain or America for leadership and security, or opt for greater national independence within the Western alliance. There was a parallel question in terms of trade. During World War Two, dire necessity had greatly increased economic relations with America – and to a lesser extent Australia. Would this trajectory continue? The great global economic reconstruction and reshuffling after World War Two also offered opportunities for other markets, in Asia and continental Europe. Would these chances for external decolonisation, a managed end to the recolonial system, be taken?

A connected question applied to the third front of change, the internal system. First Labour and war had refurbished this to emphasise socio-economic security, sectoral integration and insulation through the agency of a growing state. The tight wartime system persisted after 1945. Rationing remained in place and, in 1949, a referendum was passed reintroducing compulsory military service, in case the Cold War heated up. The measure was sponsored by Prime Minister Fraser, an enthusiastic Cold Warrior, and it is sometimes implied that government manipulation determined the referendum. 'Only publicity in favour of conscription could be broadcast' on the radio networks, which were of course state-controlled. The majority for conscription – 533,000 in favour compared with 152,000 against – suggests otherwise.[2] New Zealand's tight society was consensual, not imposed. But the persistence of rationing, shortages of consumer goods, and other wartime constraints, as well as the tired old Labour government itself, was beginning to pall. Fraser's referendum triumph was reversed at the 1949 election, and First Labour gave way to First National, led by Sidney Holland.

The new National government was at least as conservative as Labour on the external front, in foreign relations and trade. But its initial position on the internal front promised major change. There was to be an end to the command economy, to sectoral harmony and to the mega-state. The economy was to be freed up, the warfare state was to be wound back, and those pesky unions, who had allegedly profited while their brothers bled, were to be taken down several pegs. Indeed, in the National government's rhetoric, some unions were ceasing to be merely pesky. Backed by the Soviet Union and global communism, they were making a 'very determined effort ... to overthrow orderly government by force'.[3]

1951

Among the young Irish New Zealanders who fled the country to evade military service in World War One was Patrick Tuohy, a seaman. After radicalising experiences in America, he returned to New Zealand, changed his name to Fintan Patrick Walsh, joined the fledgling Communist Party and became active in the union movement. An able and unscrupulous man – he was rumoured to have been involved in the murder of a strikebreaker in 1923 – he has been described as the nearest thing to an American-style gangster union boss that New Zealand ever had, complete with a personal fortune, allegedly dubiously obtained. But he left the Communist Party in 1924 and progressively moderated his policies and at least his official image, until a late spasm of militancy from 1958 to his death in 1963. Walsh took over the de facto leadership of the main body of the union movement during World War Two. With Angus McLagan, another ex-communist, who became Minister of Labour, he led the incorporation of the union movement into the state system, and continued to dominate the Federation of Labour (FOL) as long as he lived. He was very close to Peter Fraser, weeping openly at his funeral in 1950. Drying his tears, he was then able to establish a good working relationship with the first National government.[4]

F. P. Walsh's enemies could expect no mercy, and they tended to be clubs of which he had once been a member: the communist left of the union movement, the Catholic right, and the watersiders, or 'wharfies', traditional allies of his own Seamen's Union. The watersiders were led by the non-communist but very militant Harold 'Jock' Barnes, a man as tough and aggressive as Walsh, though less subtle. A strategically placed, traditionally militant union, prominent in 1913, the watersiders pushed hard for a share of wartime profits, taking their cut in leisure as well as cash through the system known as 'spelling', whereby each watersider worked only half or two-thirds of his paid hours. They were also widely believed to impose an informal tariff on imports, in the form of systematic pilfering.

The Labour government at first sought to restrain the watersiders through various port tribunals on which workers, as well as employers, were represented. As the watersiders continued their push for improved conditions to match rising prices and profits after the war, such measures became less and less effective. In 1949, Fraser, who had just deregistered the communist-led Auckland Carpenters' Union, verged on doing the same to the watersiders, who struck 28 times during that year. He had also considered 'drastic action' against them in 1947.[5] This danger passed, but watersider militancy continued. In 1950, they were expelled from the FOL for calling its leaders 'agents of the employing class',[6] and set up the rival Trade Union Congress. Outside the seamen, coalminers and freezing workers, they had few allies, but these unions were militant, strong and strategically placed in the recolonial economy.

In late 1950, Barnes and the watersiders again clashed with both the FOL and the government, the latter now National, and led by the aggressively populist Sidney Holland, who may never have read a book in his life but was a skilled if overexcitable professional politician and amateur magician. The trouble was patched up, but flared anew in February 1951. The trigger issue was whether or not a 15 per cent general wage order included or excluded a 6 per cent rise for the watersiders in the previous year. Inflation was high; the difference between the employers' top offer and the minimum acceptable to the watersiders was only threepence an hour; and the dispute in itself was soluble.[7] But there appears to have been a sense among leaders on both sides that the time was ripe for confrontation, which is what happened. The watersiders banned overtime, were locked out by the employers, and the great Waterfront Dispute of 1951 was on. The FOL, the media, the farmers, the employers and many other groups supported the government. The Labour Party seemed to sit on the fence, and the watersiders found themselves isolated except for the miners, freezing workers and seamen. After five months of bitter and costly industrial struggle involving about 20,000 workers, the state and its many allies crushed the watersiders and their few allies, dealing a blow to militant unionism from which it did not recover until the 1970s, if at all.

Curiously, historians have tended to see 1951 as the greatest industrial conflict in New Zealand history.[8] This is clearly not so: 1913 involved a much higher proportion of the workforce, the strikers had more allies, and the conflict was much more violent and genuinely threatening to the established system. But 1951 was the greatest civil disturbance between the Depression riots of 1932 and the Springbok tour protests of 1981. The contemporary notion that the dispute was the New Zealand campaign of the Cold War should be dismissed. But a moderate-right view might still be that the government took excessive but understandable action against a group of overaggressive militant unionists who were prepared to wreck the economy in pursuit of their own interests. Mild-left perspectives see the dispute as 'a struggle by conservatives to reassert complete political and economic dominance after a lengthy period of Labour rule'.[9] We need to acknowledge the merits of both these views, but go beyond them.

Despite his own attempts at reinventing history,[10] it does appear that Barnes, nicknamed 'The Bull', was almost pathologically bold, aggressive and stubborn. Whether or not the allegation that he sought revenge against the state for his unfair dismissal from the public service in 1932 has any substance, he led his men into an almost hopeless fight, and mishandled it once in. His efforts to gain allies and publicity were too little, too late, and in the bitter depths of the dispute he advocated the 'use of force against the police'. There was in fact one bombing incident, probably directed against property rather than life.[11] His support amongst rank-and-file watersiders was remarkably solid, yet union historians concede that he 'repaid their magnificent loyalty by leading them to defeat and destruction'.[12]

On the other hand, 'draconian' is too mild a word for the government's use of state power during the dispute. Only four years before, Holland had accused Fraser of 'totalitarianism and dictatorship' for keeping wartime emergency powers in peace.[13] In 1951, he used some of the powers Labour had bequeathed to him, and added others. Free speech was restricted; personal mail was opened; such actions as giving food to strikers' children were banned; the watersiders were falsely accused of being communist-inspired 'traitors'; and anti-communist hysteria was deliberately encouraged. In an 'almost hysterical' national radio broadcast, Holland made his claim that 'a very determined effort has been made to overthrow orderly government by force'. The armed forces manned the waterfront and the coalmines – losing two men killed to industrial accidents. Thousands of new 'specials' were recruited, though not used. The police used their batons freely against some protests and pickets; and employers were helped to victimise the mass of the watersiders, not just the leaders, after the conflict had ended. Walsh ruthlessly used the dispute to cripple his rivals, crusade against the communists he now hated, entrench his dominance of the union movement, and affirm his policy of incorporating it into the state system. The powerful, strangely out-of-control personalities of Barnes, Holland and Walsh naturally tend to dominate discussion of the conflict. No-one can say that New Zealand leaders were colourless in 1951. But underlying the clash of strong characters were deeper issues. Why was watersider support so narrow and yet so solid? Why was the anti-watersider movement so broad and so vehement, almost frenzied?

Barnes's personal motives do not explain the strength of his support among the watersiders, and among their fellow militants in the ships, mines and freezing works. The vast majority of wharfies 'stood firm' all 151 days, and survivors cherish the certificates proving it to this day. The personal and familial costs were considerable. Many were never able to return to waterside work. Furthering the personal feuds and aspirations of Jock Barnes or world-wide communist revolution was not their motive. The tight occupational subculture of the militant unions, noted in Chapter Four, was part of the explanation, and so, perhaps, was a desire to use their strategic position in the recolonial economy to defend and increase their share of prosperity. Private companies and farmers, they knew, were allowed, even encouraged, to exploit strategic position in their own interests. Why not the wharfies too? Profits flowing from a wool boom made such feelings particularly acute in 1950.

This is, I think, an important general explanation of the militancy of the strategic unions – watersiders, miners, freezing workers and seamen – who contributed the bulk of working days lost to industrial action between 1906 and 1951.[14] Strategic position not only gave them the strength to fight, but also an incentive. Not subject to farm-first ideology, they knew that an unfrozen, untransported lamb was as useless for export as no lamb at all. They were as vital to the recolonial economy as farmers or shippers, and, like farmers and shippers, they wanted their share of the profits. The share came in the form of paid leisure, control over their own work, and perhaps pilferage, as well as fairly high pay. As their critics noted, this probably did reduce the efficiency of their industries and the quality of services to the consumer. But the same could be said of some privileged businesses, such as shipping companies. Milking the milking system – exploiting the leverage luck, effort and the recolonial-controlled economy gave you in your own interests – was the name of the game. Why shouldn't workers join capitalists in playing it? This, perhaps, was the subtext of the militancy of strategic unions. They did not use it in their own defence, because it was selfish, though arguably no more selfish than the behaviour of businessmen and farmers. But the public had a deep-seated double-standard towards this. Farmers and businesses were allowed to use strategic position to their own advantage; unions were not. It was as though average New Zealanders resented privilege most when it accrued to people like them.

Resent it they did. Public antagonism to the watersiders was not an artificial construct of the government, though the government shared it, but a strand in modern folk culture. Wharfie jokes were legion: a wartime visitor said, 'In America, we bury our dead. In New Zealand, you give them a job on the waterfront.' An aerial photographer complained that his pictures of the Wellington waterfront had been ruined when one of the wharfies moved. A wharfie was said to have complained to his foreman that a tortoise had been following him around all day. The claim that 'few acknowledged dictators have possessed more effective control of the mass media than Holland did in 1951' is not strictly true. Anti-watersider bias in the press was awesomely unfair and consistent, but it was voluntary, not government-dictated. Press vitriol sometimes exceeded Holland's, as when an *Auckland Star* editorial suggested that the police should open fire on defiant watersiders.[15] Walsh and the FOL were not that far behind Holland and the press, and the attitude of employers, farmers, the National Party and some local bodies was right up with them. Some 30,000 men volunteered for Holland's Civil Emergency Organisation, the new specials.[16] National won a snap election soon after the strike, on the strength of its conduct during it. The watersiders and their allies were set up as enemies of populism, and pulled down, by forces wider than mere governments.

Anti-communist hysteria was, I suspect, subordinate to affronted populism in 1951, though it compounded and to some extent masked it. Real New Zealand communist influence in the union movement was sometimes significant, but never massive. The New Zealand Communist Party (CPNZ) was formed in 1919–21, preceded by Marxist discussion groups dating back to 1871, including the Petone Marxian Club of 1912.[17] Its membership and union influence grew in the 1930s with the Depression, and peaked in the 1940s after a setback stemming from the Hitler–Stalin Pact of 1940. Both membership and influence were battered in the 1950s and 1960s by internecine disputes, by the revelation of Stalin's excesses and by the Sino-Soviet split of 1960.[18] The New Zealand echo of this split left the rump of the CPNZ supporting China, and later Albania – a favour said to have been returned by Albania's voting for New Zealand's entry into the United Nations Security Council in 1994. A larger, more pro-Soviet, Socialist Unity Party (SUP) also emerged from the split in 1966, and it was this that resurrected communist influence in the union movement from the 1970s. By this time, communism was undemonising in the public mind; the millennialism of its revolutionary objective and its capacity for moderation in practice, if not theory, was becoming obvious in Western Europe; though the National Party was still jumping onto chairs and shrieking at the sight of a communist. Arguably, communists in the union movement were less insidious puppet masters than ingenuous activists, tricked into doing more than their share of the work by a cunning but lazy mainstream, who occasionally pretended to be partly converted to keep their Red workhorses happy. New Zealand communist groups were sometimes capable of ruthless concerted action, but more often against their colleagues than against capitalism. But this is mere history; in New Zealand's relationship with communism, it was the myth that counted more.

The demonisation of Marxism took off with the Russian Revolution of

1917. Exaggerating its threat to New Zealand and banging the drum of communist conspiracy became a mainstay of Reform and National Party election propaganda, from Massey's Bolsheviks in the 1920s to Muldoon's dancing Cossacks in the 1970s. (That Cossacks were traditionally anti-communist was presumably news to the relevant advertising agency.) Russia did have a few spies in New Zealand after World War Two, but so did America, and both did less damage than French spies. The willingness of the public to believe in communist bogeys varied. In 1935, it elected a government widely perceived as the most socialist outside Russia, re-electing it with an increased majority in 1938, which suggests that the grip of anti-communism was not yet great. The first Labour government had genuine ex-communists and militant socialists among its ministers; it officially preached an orderly transition to full socialism as late as 1951. But the 1940s were a period of transition, when Fraser and other Labour leaders, including Walsh, became increasingly anti-communist, almost rivalling National. Fraser was influenced by the incipient Cold War; by the Soviet seizure of Eastern Europe; and by a determination that 1930s appeasement should not be repeated. Labour reinvented its roots, playing down Marxism and syndicalism, and playing up the 'British socialism' of Richard Owen and William Morris. Whether the public cared much about the Marx–Morris debate is not clear; the main point is that anti-communism had become bipartisan. The new communist bogey was now more easily grafted onto the old bogey: Enemy of the People: 'These public enemies, as they were almost universally felt to be.'[19]

This indigenous merger may have been more important than inter-national anti-communism, which intensified around 1950 with the Korean War and the witch-hunts of Senator McCarthy in the United States. Full McCarthyism was not easy in New Zealand in 1949, with an ex-communist Minister of Labour who still publicly mantained that his government aimed at gradual but real socialism. Even under National, there were doubts about the un-British virulence of McCarthyism, and hesitations about attacking China in the Korean War. But, allied with old populism, anti-communism was able to make some headway, and to focus on the watersiders, despite the absence of hard evidence of communist direction. 'The surprising thing is that so little evidence was ever produced to substantiate such serious charges against the watersiders.'[20] But enemies of the people were always tried and sentenced in folklore, not court law. The spread and virulence of antagonism to the strikers can be exaggerated, but not easily. Some intellectuals were sickened by tinges of totalitarianism and popular frenzy, but they knew better than to say so loudly. Some workers felt the traditional sympathy for fellow workers and underdogs – the ban on help to watersiders' families was transgressed with the contempt it deserved. Labour's new leader, the fair-minded if undynamic Walter Nash, once stated that he was 'neither for or against' the watersiders. But he later admitted that this was the worst mistake of his political career.[21] It was not viable to be publicly neutral, let alone pro-watersider.

No government has the power to engender this strong and broad a current. Just as the 'strike' was no left-wing conspiracy, so the more powerful counterstrike was no right-wing one. Holland acted harshly and viciously, but most of the people approved, except to the extent that they wanted him to be more harsh and vicious still. A similar conflict could well have taken place under Fraser. Fraser described the watersiders as 'wreckers'; his colleague Bob Semple called them 'ratbags'. Barnes described his own opinion of Fraser as 'unprintable'.[22] Seeing something that Labour might have done too as a National Party conspiracy is unfair. There were analogies with early twentieth-century Sinophobia and other moral panics in this public paroxysm. Cherished ideologies sense threats, personalise them into a group of people, and attack the symbols. The ideologies threatened in 1951 are familiar enough: the populist compact, which banned overt or untraditional privilege, especially for people who were like us but not us; and recolonisation and its harmonies, against which the tides of history were turning.

Counterstrike rhetoric, while alleging communist conspiracy, did not preach the defence of one class against another, owners against workers. Instead, it played the old refrain of harmony between classes. The National Party preached the restoration of 'true harmony . . . a remarkable co-operative effort by all classes to live together'. The Police Offences Amendment Act of 1951 reaffirmed the view of the 1908 Crimes Act that sedition included 'promoting feelings of ill-will between classes'.[23] Holland proclaimed himself determined that 'Great Britain be not starved' through the actions of the watersiders. They responded by accusing Holland, 'the Senator from Fendalton', of being a puppet of the Americans, implying that it was he, not they, who had abandoned Britain. But 'nothing could shake the impression that the watersiders were "enemies of the people"'.[24] Walsh's attitude can be explained not only in terms of a personal desire for dominance, but also as a determination to suppress a mutiny against incorporation, or sectoral harmony, the unification of public, private and union sectors into one big happy state-bound family. We will see that he exacted a price for his support of the government.

The watersiders and their allies mounted a limited rebellion against incorporation, seeking advantage through the direct exercise of their power, their internal solidarity and strategic position. Various cultural forces – ridden and encouraged, but not created by the government – inflated the threat the watersiders represented, with 'enemy of the people' in the end taking precedence over 'communist conspiracy'. The populist compact, recolonisation and the tight society felt threatened – shaken by the unsuccessful but disturbing assaults of depression, Labour nationalism and the wartime strain on links with Britain; shaken afresh, if more vaguely, by the insecurities of the Cold War world, the decline of Britain, and portents of global, cultural and economic change. Focusing on a scapegoat enabled the system to reassert itself. The watersiders were crushed partly because they were genuine dissidents, but more because they were scapegoats. Moral, racial and social harmony clung on into the 1960s, as we shall see. It was the fourth, sectoral, harmony that benefited most directly from 1951.

A prominent National Party election promise in 1949 had been the abolition of compulsory unionism. This was supported by Barnes and militant unionists, and opposed by Walsh and the moderates, both on the grounds that voluntary unionism would increase the influence of the militants. Unenthusiastic, involuntary unionists tended to vote for moderate leaders. Employers' organisations favoured compulsory unionism for the same reasons. Walsh had established his credit with the National government during the Waterfront Dispute, and something of a special relationship with its Minister of Labour, 'Big Bill' Sullivan – another character in the Wild West cast of New Zealand industrial relations, circa 1951. This unholy alliance was able to drag the government back from its promise in 1952 and retain compulsory unionism. Doctrinaire abolitionism built up afresh in the National Party, and the second National government finally abolished compulsory unionism in 1962. But the Act was merely cosmetic. Compulsory unionism remained in most unions, intact in all but name.

Other National attempts to implement their philosophies of free enterprise, individualism and deregulation had a similar token or temporary quality. Economic deregulation appeared and disappeared in the early 1950s. Like the controlled economy, social security was left largely intact by National governments, though its direction changed. Like Labour's socialism, National's free capitalist individualism became largely empty rhetoric. Labour's alliance with the unions began to loosen; the FOL was not allowed to nominate the Minister of Labour in the second Labour government as it had been in the first, so shifted towards 'pressure group' status and away from party politics. Labour governments in 1957–60 and 1972–75 administered the controls, subsidies and tax shelters under which mutated New Zealand capitalism bloomed as enthusiastically as did National. The parties took turns at piloting the ship of sectoral harmony, which survived to 1984 while the other harmonies collapsed. The conflict of 1951, counterstrike more than strike, was the convulsive, broad-based defensive reflex of a threatened system. The watersiders were not exactly innocent victims – even the leading trade union historian compares them to the Jews of the Old Testament, 'a stiff-necked people'.[25] But they fought less to overthrow recolonisation than to secure what seemed to them a fairer share of its profits. Ultimately, they were crushed as scapegoats – symbols of dimly but widely scented winds of change. Populism, recolonialism and the tight society shored themselves up by the semi-ritual destruction of an enemy, by dancing around the bonfire on which Jock Fawkes burned.

Long Slow Booms

The industrial crisis of 1951 was a sharp defeat for New Zealand's hard left, communist or otherwise. It also ushered in a more gradual but equally profound defeat for the hard right. National's free-enterprise ideology and its antagonism to the mega-state were placed quietly on the shelf. In the 1950s and 1960s, under National governments except for Second Labour's brief spell in 1957–60, state spending not only maintained its 1949 level of 28 per cent of gross domestic product, but grew slightly. The compromise between recolonisation and the populist compact, renegotiated by First Labour in 1935–49, was maintained by First National under Holland and by Second National, which reigned from 1960 to 1972, mostly under Keith Holyoake. His own deputy, John Marshall, noted that Holyoake 'was a fluent speaker, but he never mastered the art of writing'.[26] He was no great reader either, like Sid Holland, and a later proposal to name the National Library after him aroused loud public laughter. But he was an even shrewder politician than Holland, and one more willing to buy continuity with limited change.[27]

Social retrospects on the 1950s and 1960s range from 'our country's golden age'[28] to the most boring time and place on earth. Economic perceptions are similarly, if less colourfully, contested. Most saw the postwar period as a boom. Some retrospective commentators saw in it the seeds of doom. The roots of the economic problems of the 1970s and 1980s, they argued, lay in the disappointing growth and diversification of the 1950s and 1960s. On the doom side of the argument, the economy remained extremely narrow, especially in the 1950s, with continued heavy reliance on a very few products and one market. Export manufacturing did not develop much, even from 1957, when the second Labour government tried to push it along. Imports grew at twice the rate of exports; balance of payment crises occurred sporadically, especially in election years; and inflation became entrenched, increasing farmers' costs much more than their returns. Above all, growth in gross domestic product per person was low relative to comparable countries – as low as 1 per cent a year on some estimates.[29]

On the boom side of the argument, there was substantial economic growth, reduced in per capita terms and in international relativities by various factors. The growth rates of some of the countries to which New Zealand was compared, such as France, West Germany and Japan, were boosted by a low starting point: namely, economic devastation in World War Two. If we had had a Hiroshima, we could have had high growth rates too. New Zealand's rates were sometimes reduced by taking a high starting point – the Korean War wool bonanza of 1950. Allowing for this, real per capita growth averaged closer to 2 per cent per annum than one, mid-1950s to mid-1970s. 'There is no doubt that the post-war economy produced growth that was comparable with any previous New Zealand experience.'[30] New Zealand also had its postwar 'baby boom'. Other countries did so too, but New Zealand's was proportionately bigger than most – Australia, France and Britain, for example.[31] Immigration, especially of British, Dutch and Pacific Islanders, was quite high, though less so than in Australia. These factors are discussed further elsewhere, but they meant that New Zealand's GDP had to go around more capitas, lowering its relative rate. In the light of all this, economic performance in the 1950s and 1960s was not at all bad – a slow boom but a long one.

One key to this was stage three of the 'grasslands revolution'. Farm output roughly doubled between 1945 and 1970. Some marginal land was brought into production, and some new farms were formed, notably through state rehabilitation schemes – this round of military settlers survived far better than their predecessors. But neither the number of farms nor their acreage changed very much. Increased output stemmed mainly from improved productivity per farm. The processes of mechanisation and electrification were completed. By 1960, the number of tractors and milking and shearing plants roughly equalled the number of relevant farms. Important new technical developments included improvements in stock breeds and stock-breeding techniques, such as artificial insemination. Welburn P. G. Butterman, a very well-endowed bull, achieved 110,000 inseminations. Such mega-sires helped achieve a 20 per cent increase in average butterfat production per cow between World War Two and the late 1960s.[32] New types of milking shed, the advent of milk tankers, improved roads and various other factors helped increase the average size of dairy herds to about 120, still often handled by a single, very hard-working family without permanent employees. Milk tankers had the incidental effects of increasing the size and decreasing the number of dairy factories, and of diminishing the pork industry. Many dairy farmers had fed pigs with waste products from cream separation on the farm, but tankers did away with the need for this.

Pasture and pest control also improved, thanks largely to the state and its scientists. The state-led war against the Germans and Japanese was replaced by a state-led war against rabbits from the late 1940s, with legislation establishing a Rabbit Destruction Council in 1947. It directed 185 rabbit boards by 1961. Possums lost their protected status in 1947, and were hunted, trapped and poisoned as pests. Deer were also treated as pests, with a government bounty on their heads, or ears. The strange trade of deer culling emerged. That people in some countries liked to eat deer seems to have occurred to nobody. Millions of pounds' worth of venison was left to rot, sacrificed to more traditional forms of protein. The discovery that cobalt was the missing element in 'bush-sick' soils, made in 1935, brought new acres into production after the war, notably in the Volcanic Plateau. Optimal strains of grass and clover were developed further, and powerful new insecticides were employed against pests from the 1950s.[33] Above all, aerial topdressing, pioneered in the 1940s and taking off in the 1950s, often with war-surplus planes and pilots, took fertiliser to the backblocks, greatly boosting the capacity of land to carry stock.

A second key to the long slow boom was the development of one or two new products and one or two new markets. A certain amount of export diversification took place. Traditional products found some new markets. Wool was particularly fortunate in this respect, thanks partly to the Korean War wool boom, and partly to New Zealand's dominant position in the international trade of strong wools, used in carpets and blankets. The development of new varieties of sheep reduced the need to mix New Zealand with imported wools, and allowed some expansion of local processing, while the threat of synthetics at first proved less dire than it seemed. With the direct and indirect help of the state, the protein industry expanded the export of beef and dairy products other than butter and cheese, notably casein and milk powder. This third arm of dairy exports first exceeded £10 million in the 1950s, and overtook cheese in the 1960s.[34] Casein sold in America and Japan; milk powder in southern Asia. Beef exports burgeoned in the 1950s, growing from 5 to 15 per cent of farm income by the late 1970s.[35] In 1954, most beef exports went to Britain; from 1959 most went to America, where prices were higher.[36]

These new products and markets supplemented the traditional British market; they did not replace it. In 1950, Britain took 66 per cent of New Zealand's exports. In 1965–66, it still took over half. By 1970, Britain took only 36 per cent of New Zealand exports. But it was still by far the leading market, taking more than twice the percentage of number two, the United States, and it was particularly important to the leading industry: protein. Its decline in export share had taken place in the context of greatly increased New Zealand output. With temporary fluctuations, New Zealand's exports to Britain climbed fairly consistently in terms of nominal value until

1972–73. The climb was fast from 1945 to 1954, when bulk purchasing ended, and slow thereafter – even so it went from $330 million in 1955 to $480 million in 1972. Taking into account inflation (the export price index moved up one-third), Britain between 1955 and 1972 was a stable market for New Zealand exports, rather than a declining one. New products and new markets supplied export growth in the New Zealand economy for the first time, but even in the early 1970s the British still supplied the base.

Despite the development of some new products and markets, the survival of the traditional products and market, and the huge boost in farm production, all was not well with the New Zealand export economy in the 1950s and 1960s. The doomsayers had a point. A decline of agriculture as a proportion of all economic activity (from about a third to an eighth of national income between the early 1950s and the mid-1970s)[37] was an international and long-term trend, stemming more from the expansion of service industries than the decline of farming. More importantly, farmers found their costs trebling while their returns only doubled. They themselves tended to explain this in terms of the greed of banks, wharfies and other parasites, with their excessive profits and wages. Economic historians explain it in terms of the superior price and demand elasticities of imports the farmers used over exports the farmers sold: prices and markets for imported manufactured goods tended to grow faster than those of exported primary products. The far greater difference, in both market and sophistication, between cars bought in 1920 and 1970 and frozen lambs sold in those years brings this point home.

A possible complementary explanation, discussed further in Chapter Fifteen, is that the new production, processing, transport, distribution and marketing systems required by new products and new markets involved establishment costs, were more competitive, and perhaps less easy and profitable than the well-worn grooves of the traditional British market. A formally and informally privileged niche in such a well-established market was naturally cheaper and easier than new markets, in which customers had to be expensively chased, products changed to suit them, and which were subject to the whims of protectionist governments. The new markets tended to be either not very reliable, usually because of the protection of their own farmers, or not very profitable. Protein was a product of medium volume and medium value, able to sustain the high cost of transport to distant markets. Wood products were high in volume and low in value per ton, and therefore less able to sustain these costs. Southern Asia could not pay as much for its milk powder as Britain could for its butter. Substantial diversification did occur from the 1950s, but it was towards less entrenched and less secure markets, with higher transactional costs.

As pressure on farm profits grew, the state was naturally drawn into the breach. We have seen that its pre-war and wartime role in agriculture was already substantial, and had been since the early days of the recolonial economy. Now, in the 1950s and 1960s, it expanded further, leading one economic historian to conclude that the notion of farming as private enterprise was 'political rhetoric not careful analysis'.[38] The scope of producer boards expanded; a Wool Board joined private wool buyers from 1944. In the 1950s, 'there was a deliberate attempt to bring all significant agricultural products within the purview of a body which enabled government and growers to co-operate in meeting marketing problems'. When bulk purchasing by Britain ended in 1954, elements of guaranteed pricing persisted under other names, such as 'deficiency payments' and, ultimately, 'supplementary minimum prices'. Producer boards received cheap loans from the Reserve Bank, at a quarter of the going rate; direct and indirect subsidies 'proliferated'. Fertilisers and other farm inputs were added to the subsidised list from the 1950s. Tax breaks developed from the 1960s, and direct subsidies expanded from 1973.

At first intended as temporary, such measures showed a tendency to entrench, to become integral to the public–private farming system. It would be unfair to suggest that farmers became civil servants. There is no doubt that the doubling of farm output was created partly by farmers' hard work and risk-taking, and by their traditional willingness to adopt new technology and techniques. Farmers rightly complained that their sector of the economy was less sheltered than manufacturing, the state sector, or service industries. But it is clearly quite wrong to suggest that it was unsheltered. It was increasingly sheltered by the state, and the state helped its expansion. Welburn P. G. Butterman belonged to the Dairy Board. All this cost money. Just as increased spending on social welfare had been caused by strains in the recolonial system from the 1930s, so too was increased spending on farmer welfare from the 1950s.

The costs of recolonisation also grew in other respects. After the disruptions of World War Two, the British were naturally eager to re-establish their own export markets for manufactured goods. New Zealand co-operated and bought British. The differential between the percentage of exports sold to Britain and the percentage of imports bought from Britain changed massively in Britain's favour. In 1940, New Zealand sent 90 per cent of its exports to Britain, and took 47 per cent of its imports from Britain – the percentage of imports had been no different in 1930. By 1950, however, the export/import figures were 66 and 61 per cent – from a discrepancy in New Zealand's favour of 43 per cent, to one of 5 per cent (not counting invisibles, which favoured Britain). For New Zealand, recolonisation was losing one of its special privileges – the right to export more than you imported. This stemmed as much from expanding New Zealand demand as from British preference, but increasing parity in trade with Britain decreased New Zealand's capacity to acquire new markets. Buying British obviously made it harder to say to new trading partners, 'We will buy from you if you buy from us.' Furthermore, as British economic historians themselves concede, many British manufactures were declining in quality, price and range in comparison with the competition. British-made Mini motorcars used 132 per cent more labour than Belgian-made Minis, and New Zealand bought 381,000 of the expensive British versions in the 1960s.[39] Buying British no longer meant buying better, if it ever had.

The Minis came in kitsets, to be assembled in New Zealand. The refurbished recolonial system allowed for growth in domestic manufacturing as well as export farming. In manufacturing, as we have seen, New Zealand was already significantly industrialised by the 1920s. Its leading subsector were 'mills', which processed a single raw material for export or local con-sumption. The 1920s added a new major category of factory – the assembly plant. Its earliest and most notable form was the car factory, the first of which was set up by Ford in Wellington in 1921.[40] Other car plants, also usually overseas-owned, followed, as did plants for assembling domestic whiteware and radios. The introduction of import and exchange controls in 1938, intended to help solve the humiliating foreign exchange and British debt crisis, had the secondary effect of boosting assembling. In the long term, it did not so much lower the import bill, as it was intended to do, but shifted imports from finished products to components.[41] Imports continued to grow, the British proportion rose too, but so did domestic manufacturing.

Import controls did mean that, in order to participate, overseas companies – mainly British but also Australian and American – had increasingly to set up in New Zealand. By 1965, a total of 165 companies had done so,[42] mainly in manufacturing and especially in meatworks and car plants, representing the leading manufacturing subsectors, milling and assembling. The assembl-ing subsector was further boosted by World War Two, as we have seen, and by increasing consumer demand stemming from rising expectations, per capita growth and the growth of capitas in the form of the baby boom. This was helped by the development of hire-purchasing arrangements and finance companies, the latter of which grew tenfold between 1955 and 1974.[43] Milling also continued to grow. Between them, the two subsectors doubled manu-facturing output by volume between 1935 and 1949, then almost tripled it between 1950 and 1970.[44] By this time, manufacturing employed over a quarter of the workforce, compared with 14 per cent in 1936.[45] Export manufacturing was not significant until the 1970s, but domestic manu-facturing was.

From 1945, both New Zealand and Britain sought to fully restore the economic recolonialism that had operated under storm sails through most of the war, apart from the brief period 1943–44 when Uncle Sam sat in for Mother. Adaptations, such as the development of assembling, were made, but, overall, the opportunity for postwar economic decolonisation was rejected. British tenders were given a 10 per cent advantage in postwar government contracts.[46] Sentiment, and a sense of gratitude to Old Britain for having fought the good fight and suffered for it, were important factors. An anti-British New Zealand government remained almost a contradiction in terms – certainly a contradiction in terms of trade. Despite supplementary diversification into beef and milk powder, America and Asia, both public and private sectors proved strangely reluctant to think beyond Britain. In 1966, the Director of the Overseas Trade Division of the Department of Industries and Commerce noted the extension of export markets but wrote, 'It is apparent, however, that in the absence of alternative markets of equivalent size New Zealand must always regard Britain as its main export market.'[47]

The cutural-economic matrix of recolonisation had its own resilience, and there were always the benefits for New Zealand: secure, established, massive markets for a tiny range of products, permitting concentration and economies of scale, avoiding the need for trendy packaging and advertising, and minimising the expensive hunt for new markets and products. What else but an enormously privileged and complacent export system could have got away without 'telescoping' – tucking the legs of frozen lambs inside their carcass and so saving 15 per cent on shipping space – until U-boats forced the change in World War Two?[48] For these and other reasons, recolonisation experienced its Indian summer in economics at least, its long slow end of the golden weather, and the summer was quite warm.

The long slow economic boom of the period 1945–72 was accompanied by an equally long but even slower boom in the role of the state. The state was already large at the beginning of the period. In 1948, owing to First Labour's welfare and warfare policies, and to the strong pre-existing tradition of state intervention, the New Zealand mega-state could be convincingly portrayed as Thomas Hobbes' 'Leviathan'.

> Infinite indeed are the services which the government . . . of New Zealand supplies its citizens. While it educates the children in its primary and secondary schools, it takes care of their teeth in its own dental clinics and distributes free milk and apples. It will lend you money to build a house of your own or allow you to rent one which it has constructed . . . It will give you insurance on your life and your property . . . It provides you with the services of the telephone, the telegraph, the mails, and a commercial bank. It will sell you coal which it has extracted from its own mines . . . It will

transport you on its railways, buses, or airplanes, and will invite you to spend a vacation in its own tourist hotels and holiday resorts. It will entertain, and possibly instruct, you with its broadcasts . . . Should you wish to erect a factory, import materials or manufactures from overseas, or send money abroad, you must obtain the state's permission. If you are a labourer, it fixes your minimum rate of wage, determines the hours and conditions of your work, and compels you to enrol in the appropriate trade union. If you are a farmer, it offers the assistance of its agricultural experts, buys certain of your products at prices it guarantees, and markets them . . . It plants forests, cuts its timber at its own sawmill, and sells it . . . Whenever you visit a doctor, it contributes a portion of the medical fees; and if you are unemployed, widowed, orphaned, aged, or totally invalided, it pays you a benefit . . . Finally, when you die, it will take its share of what you leave and will include your demise in the published statistics of its invaluable *Year Book* . . . Leviathan in New Zealand is a well-nigh universal provider.[49]

By 1949, Leviathan absorbed 28 per cent of gross domestic product. But increases in its cost, contrary to some legends, were modest thereafter until 1974. In the 1950s, the level was about 32 per cent, and until 1973, about 33 per cent.[50] Between 1949 and 1972, the number of core public servants increased from 51,000 to 72,000 – fewer than the population growth of the same period.[51] Growth in the cost of the state was well below that of the period 1974–84, and below that of some welfare-oriented European countries in the 1950s and 1960s. The relative stability in the cost of the state was due to economic growth and full employment, which kept the cost of social security down to about 7 per cent of GDP in the 1950s and 1960s. Cheapness did not mean that Leviathan was becoming less active, however.

There was further development in 'sectoral harmony': the alliance of workers, farmers and business with the state and – to some extent – with each other. Workers benefited from this, despite the signal defeat of 1951. Unemployment was virtually nonexistent, and real incomes per capita rose modestly to the late 1960s. There were pockets of poverty, but commentators tended to cry wolf about their scale. The number of days lost to strikes was low 1951–68. The mainstream union movement increased in strength, but also in moderation, and became increasingly closely allied to the state. As one left-winger noted in 1968, 'The unions have united the New Zealand working class, but at a cost of a subservience to the State unparalleled in any other country.'[52] Tom Skinner succeeded F. P. Walsh as leader of the Federation of Labour in 1962. 'Nobody would suggest that Skinner wielded the influence with a National Government that Walsh exerted under a Labour administration, but the Federation was, and still is, regularly consulted and listened to with respect.'[53] Indeed, National Party Prime Minister Keith Holyoake once sang 'The Red Flag' at a gathering of trade unionists.[54] The Public Service Association emerged as the uncrowned king of white-collar unions, but as much by working in tandem with their employers as by opposing them. Intensifying sectoral harmony also extended to farmers, as we have seen above, and to business, as we will see in Chapter Fourteen.

A second spurt of state activity in the 1950s and 1960s was a new, almost Vogellian spasm of development work: in transport, especially roading; in forestry; and in hydro-electric power. Public works expenditure, as a percentage of all government spending, was staggeringly high in this era. It peaked at 35 per cent in 1958, and exceeded 20 per cent in each year between 1949 and 1967. Compare this with less than 10 per cent in the early 1930s and the 1980s.[55] Tarsealed roads quadrupled from 5,500 miles in 1945 to 20,000 in 1965.[56] Motorways emerged in 1951, and the Auckland Harbour Bridge was opened in 1959. Only the cost of the last was repaid by tolls. Airports also sprouted, as did public buildings, especially school buildings.

State involvement in forestry was also high in the 1950s and 1960s, when state forests of exotic pines planted 30 years earlier began to mature. The industry did not become really significant in terms of exports until the 1970s, and is discussed mainly in Chapter Fifteen in relation to the economy of that era. The 1950s and 1960s was the golden age of giant hydro-electric power stations, built to meet a rapidly expanding domestic and industrial demand for electricity. The increase in demand ran at an annual rate of around 12 per cent between 1949 and 1972. At first, each island met its own demand, and by the end of the 1950s the capacity of northern lakes and rivers, especially the Waikato, was reaching their limit. The North and South Islands had each established their own 'grid' systems in the 1930s. The national grid came in 1964, with the laying of power cables across Cook Strait, and huge dams at Aviemore, Waitaki and Manapouri were built.[57]

This spasm of public works created camps and towns rather like those of progressive colonisation in the nineteenth century, strange frontier-like social entities with a tinge of the future as well as the past. During the construction of the Manapouri power station and its associated works, 1963–71, the 11,000-ton *Wanganella* was moored in Deep Cove, Fiordland, to house the workforce. Fourteen of the workers died in industrial accidents on the project, and the others comforted themselves with 183-proof bootleg liquor.[58] Other public works and timber towns were only somewhat more conventional than the *Wanganella*. Some, such as Turangi and Kawerau, became permanent, others rose and fell quickly. Roxburgh's construction camp sprang up from nothing in 1946, to a full town in 1953, and was nothing again by 1957. The new towns had no old people, few teenagers, some couples, and many single men. They were run by the Ministry of Works, known as

'Uncle MOW' – a play on 'Uncle Joe' Stalin. 'The Project Engineer is town boss, a sort of mayor, director, arbitrator and decision-maker.' Uncle MOW's engineering record was good; his social welfare record less good. Workers' families lived in 500-square-foot houses; managers' in 1,000-square-foot houses. 'Loneliness and apathy' and 'social disruption' were common, and ethnic diversity was considerable.[59] Maori and immigrants made up half the workers in some towns. This was the face of the future, but the future was not here quite yet.

Letting in Lolita?

The tight society had never been uncontested, as we have seen in earlier chapters, and this remained at least as true as ever during and after World War Two. Six o'clock closing remained a standing joke in Westland, and a blind eye was turned to gambling games in Returned Servicemen's clubs, especially on Anzac Day. 'Bottle stores', where takeaway liquor was legally sold, might have a choice of wines extending no further than red or white, sweet or very sweet, but they had an impressive range of flasks, half-bottles and quarter-bottles of spirits. These containers were designed to go into pockets and handbags for after-hours drinking in public places. Each little display of them represented a folk subversion of the liquor laws. After the war, a contested process of untightening was superimposed on the old subversions. The contest can be traced through the 1950s and 1960s in attitudes to the sacred weekend and other customs, and to gambling, drinking, censorship and sex.

Sundays untightened very gradually, and the process did not begin until 1965, when Sunday newspapers became legal. But it was not until 1980 that full Saturday shopping was legalised, and not until 1989 that full Sunday trading followed.[60] One delightful little custom of the tight society was 'the traditional compulsory dawn tea service'. In hotels and on overnight ferry services, you were woken by a strong cup of tea whether you liked it or not. The practice persisted on the ferries until 1972, and may have survived even longer in some hotels.[61]

In horse-racing, off-course betting through bookmakers had been banned since 1911. As noted in Chapter Five, juries were reluctant to convict book-makers; a conviction did not stop one being re-elected as mayor of Invercargill in 1948.[62] In 1949, finally recognising that it could not beat bookmaking, the state decided to nationalise it. The decision was endorsed in a national referendum that year, and legal off-course betting began. But it could only be done through the state Totalisator Agency Bureau – a very partial 'untightening'. In lotteries, the competition came not from private practitioners but from Australian state lotteries – the most famous 'Tattersalls', or 'Tats', represents the survival of the Tasman world in some spheres of folk culture. Limited lotteries with maximum prizes of £500 for charitable purposes were permitted between the wars. In 1932, a New Zealand 'Art Union' lottery was formalised, with a single contractor running it on behalf of the state. Again, the subtext was: if you can't beat it, nationalise it. But it was not until 1961, when the Golden Kiwi lottery replaced the Art Union, that the local state lottery began to compete effectively with the Australians. Moral evangelists responded with alarm. 'Instead of letting loose a harmless kiwi, we fear that our Government has liberated a marauding tiger!'[63]

The same referendum of 1949 that had supported off-course betting had condemned the demon drink to continued day-release, endorsing six o'clock closing by a huge majority. In the 1960s, restrictions on drinking began to ease at last – slowly. A few licences for restaurants and taverns became available from 1961; theatres could be licensed from 1969, airports from 1970, and cabarets from 1971. Above all, six o'clock closing expired in 1967, after another referendum reversed the 1949 result. You could now drink in bars until a daredevil 10 pm. There is some evidence that the two breweries favoured six o'clock closing and some of the associated restrictions. A cosy state-supported cartel with few demands for expensive innovation may have been more profitable, or at least more comfortable, than competition.[64] Beer remained watered down until 1980, when Australian brewers were allowed to compete with New Zealand's big two.[65]

The tight society made a stand on censorship in the 1950s and early 1960s. The Customs Department largely administered censorship, and filtered out such evil works as Dan Davin's novel *For the Rest of Our Lives*, Vladimir Nabokov's *Lolita*, and a wide swathe of Americana: Mickey Spillane, *Buck Rogers*, *Dick Tracy*, and the 1954 movie *The Wild One*, which New Zealanders were not allowed to see until 1977. Apollinaire's *Memoirs of a Young Rakehell* made it into New Zealand in 1962, but was 'restricted to persons professionally engaged in the study of abnormal psychology'. Comics were right out. 'Imports of children's books,' stated 1954 legislation, 'were to be restricted to the work of approved authors.'[66] Even the Lone Ranger was banned in 1956. 'It is unfortunate that he wears a mask, because in New Zealand it is an offence to do so in a public place.'[67] The establishment of an Indecent Publications Tribunal in 1963 was seen as a liberalising measure, and in the above context we should concede that this was true to some extent. But one founding member, a self-declared liberal, believed that 'Books, like firearms or motor vehicles, can be a source of danger to the untrained or unskilled user', raising the possiblity of being drunk in charge of a book. Still, after repeated appeals and applications, Nabokov's *Lolita* sneaked into paradise on a majority decision in 1965. In 1967, the film of James Joyce's *Ulysses* did likewise – but only to adult audiences segregated by gender. In the late 1960s, then, despite countercurrents of increasing strength, the tight society was alive and well and living in New Zealand. The same was true of recolonisation itself.

Between 1944 and 1954, New Zealand took a number of constitutional and foreign policy decisions that could be, and have been, taken for the beginnings of decolonisation. There was a degree of disconnection from Britain and a move towards the United States. New Zealand's first independent international treaty, the Canberra Pact of 1944, known to insiders as the 'Anzaxis', suggested a parallel move towards Australia. In 1947, New Zealand finally adopted the Statute of Westminster of 1931, which asserted the independence of the dominions. It was the last dominion to do so. A year later, a separate New Zealand citizenship was introduced and Kiwis were no longer British citizens. Between 1945 and 1949, Fraser and Nash played a modest but confident role on the world stage in the setting-up of the postwar United Nations Organisation. Between 1950 and 1953, in the Korean War, New Zealand contributed the services of six frigates and a peak of 1,550 ground troops to the American-dominated United Nations war effort. New Zealand declined to follow Britain in its recognition of Communist China in 1950. Australia, New Zealand and the United States – but not Britain – signed the ANZUS treaty of defensive alliance in 1951. Was this, finally, the birth of the national independence so often previously announced, a partial end to recolonisation? Repetitive though negatives may be getting, the answer has to be no.

The Canberra Pact of 1944, and the establishment of diplomatic representation in Australia in 1943, did not heal the rift over New Zealand leaving its troops in the Mediterranean, still less restore the Tasman world. Trans-Tasman relations quickly 'reverted to what they were before the "Anzaxis" came into being' – that is, bad. From 1946, New Zealand's leading diplomats, Carl Berendsen and Alister McIntosh, became 'more and more fed up with Australia', which they accused of 'a mild form of megalomania'. 'It is a great pity that we are so much victims of geography that in a sense we must play in a team with them.' 'It was never in our interests, and I doubt if it ever will be, to work in double harness with the Australians.'[68] In terms of trade as well as diplomacy, New Zealand did not work with Australia. Our closest neighbour, historically as well as geographically, took only 4.5 per cent of our exports as late as 1967.[69]

As for constitutional disconnection from Britain, government and public alike dismissed the adoption of the Statute of Westminster and New Zealand citizenship in 1947 as technical changes, forced by the other dominions.

Indeed, adopting the statute, announced Fraser, would 'strengthen the ties between ... New Zealand and the Mother-country'.[70] Kiwis became New Zealand citizens in 1948, but they remained 'British subjects'. As the relevant minister, Bill Parry, put it: '"British Nationality" comes first, and "New Zealand Citizenship" second'.[71] Where New Zealand foreign policy did diverge from Britain's, it did so in the tradition of 'loyal dissent'. Britain disliked its exclusion from the Canberra Pact and from ANZUS. Unusually 'tart telegrams' flew between Wellington and London, but Berendsen had no doubt that the two countries 'will slide normally back into their pleasant and amiable relationship'.[72] New Zealand felt that it was representing pan-British interests in the Pacific through these treaties. The refusal to recognise China in 1950 was also a Better British measure – what Britain should have done if it had been in its right mind. 'New Zealand alone had saved the Common-wealth from complete disgrace'.[73] When New Zealand Prime Minister Sidney Holland visited the White House three years later, he announced, 'I have come here to cement British–American relations.'[74]

ANZUS and the entry into the Korean War can be seen in a similar light. Holland was adamant that ANZUS 'was not incompatible with devotion to the mother country'. The new alliance was acceptable to the public, thought officials, only because Britain was also a close ally of the United States.[75] 'A fear of domination by America, even a dislike of Americans' existed among officials and politicians of both parties.[76] Holland was initially reluctant to involve New Zealand in Korea, but jumped in quickly once Britain decided to do so, beating Australia to the punch. His 'chief motivating force was probably an anachronistic desire to follow Britain'.[77] New Zealand fought in Korea under British command, as it had done in all its wars since 1899. New Zealand defence policy during the 1950s and early 1960s remained oriented to helping Britain. New Zealand was committed to supplying the usual division for service in the Middle East in wartime until 1955. Its commitment then shifted to South-east Asia but remained interlocked with British strategy. New Zealand's participation in the South-East Asian Treaty Organisation (SEATO) from 1954 was 'largely conditional on Britain's'.[78] From 1956, it helped Britain in an undeclared war in which there was no American involvement, the Malayan Emergency. Here, New Zealand units participated in operations against communists until 1966, losing 26 soldiers killed – not many fewer than the 41 killed in Korea.

In 1956, Britain and France involved themselves in the Suez Crisis, resisting by force Egyptian nationalisation of the Suez Canal. The United States disapproved of Britain's action, but New Zealand had no hesitation in backing it. Holland offered another New Zealand expeditionary force, and explained to the Americans that he would support Britain even if it was in the wrong.[79] When the chips were down, old links took precedence over new. Holland and his Minister of External Affairs, Frederick Doidge, were notoriously 'ardent imperialists', more British than the British. 'Mr Holland is all for sticking to the British through thick and thin, and so is Mr Doidge.'[80] Both were firmly of the view that the black Empire was theirs too. For them, as for many New Zealanders, 'Commonwealth interests' were code for 'pan-British interests'. 'We', thought New Zealand parliamentarians in 1947, were giving independence to India.[81] In 1950, Doidge attended a meeting of Commonwealth leaders at Colombo. 'In the presence of Nehru and other Commonwealth leaders [he] asked "was it not a fact that some Asian countries were politically immature and unfit to govern themselves?"'[82]

Doidge was unusual only in his clumsiness. The tendency to cling to recolonisation, despite winds of change, was fully bipartisan and extended beyond the government to the public. 'Both Labour and National stood for alignment with Britain on the great issues of the day.'[83] In 1961, 'the doctrine of "where Britain goes we go" is still firmly implanted in New Zealand hearts – no New Zealand government could ever ignore an attitude so firmly entrenched in our tradition'.[84] The Prime Minister, Labour's Walter Nash, was described in a secret American assessment as 'sentimentally pro-British and deeply devoted to the "mother country"'.[85] The assessment did not have to be secret. A general history published the same year correctly observed that, if Britain went to war again, New Zealand would have no hesitation in joining it. 'There might be a little more heart-searching than in 1939, but probably only a little.'[86] As late as 1969, Norman Kirk, leader of the Labour Party, a man with a reputation as a decoloniser, demonstrated the strength of recolonial tradition. 'Our people should realise that Britain is the only country in the world New Zealand can expect automatically and certainly to come to our aid if we were in military difficulties.'[87]

These attitudes accurately reflected majority public opinion. In late 1953, the new Queen of Britain and New Zealand, Elizabeth II, began the first visit to New Zealand by a reigning monarch. Her reception was hugely enthusiastic. 'Admiration has turned to wonder,' gushed journalist Pat Lawlor. 'A woman has sat at the keyboard of our thoughts and her charm has made music in our hearts.'[88] The monarch's birthday became a statutory holiday in 1952. At this time, New Zealanders were still more likely to give 'British' than 'New Zealander' when asked their nationality.[89] 'English influence dominates at all levels of New Zealand society,' observed a social commentator in 1966, '[it] is unnoticed because it is so dominant.'[90] 'The basic assumption that the connection will endure,' noted another, 'is scarcely ever questioned.'[91] When an arts council was established in 1963, it was called 'The Queen Elizabeth the Second Arts Council of New Zealand', and it retained this name until

1994. The national anthem, 'God Save the Queen', was played in cinemas until the early 1970s before every film, and New Zealanders stood up for it. When one-legged writer Maurice Duggan failed to stand, he was beaten over the head by an elderly woman with her handbag.[92]

It is possible to exaggerate the postwar reassertion of recolonisation. Britain's decline, America's rise and other tides in global history were against it. Forerunners of real decolonisation occurred with increasing frequency from 1965, when New Zealand sent a token body of troops to support the Americans in Vietnam. The Canberra Pact and ANZUS were indeed harbingers of change in the future. But they were false alarms in their present. Recolonisation survived the great global reshuffle after World War Two, just as it had survived earlier challenges since the 1920s. New Zealand in the 1960s remained a recolonial society. To this important extent, continuity outranked change in New Zealand history between the 1920s and the 1960s – indeed, between the 1880s and the 1960s. When the middle-aged adults of the year 2000 were children, and when the elders of today were in their middle years, New Zealand was still a colony – an informal colony, a privileged colony, a voluntary colony, but a colony all the same.

A People Without Songs?

INTRODUCTION

If, at a pub or party in Paris, London, Sydney or New York, you ask a white New Zealander to sing you a Pakeha folk song, you are in trouble. You may get a song about a sheila (young woman) in the railway station refreshment room at Taumaranui, 'on the Main Trunk line', but it will be sung self-consciously, as the caricature of a folk song rather than the thing itself. More likely, you will get an advertising jingle about cheese, or a Maori song, or nothing at all. The Pakeha, you might well be told, are a people without songs. Your informant will firmly believe this to be true, but will be quite wrong. One list records a hundred Pakeha folk songs whose words have survived in written form, and this can be only a fraction of the whole. 'It wasn't until the 1950s that the first serious search for the folk songs of the Pakeha began, a period of neglect long enough to account for the disappearance of many of the early songs from the oral tradition.'[1] There are Pakeha folk songs, it is just that the Pakeha have forgotten them.

Part Four explores some aspects of Pakeha cultural history. 'Culture' is a term that can mean many different things in many different contexts. In the rest of this book, it is sometimes used specifically, as in 'working-class culture', and sometimes in its broadest sense – almost everything that is not physical. Here in Part Four, it is usually used to mean the various lives of the mind, expressed in arts, folkways, and games. We focus on the recolonial period, 1880s–1960s, but culture can shift at different speed than other dimensions of history. The period 1890–1914 was a cultural epilogue to progressive colonisation, as well as a cultural prologue to recolonisation. In places, my analysis also stretches back before the 1880s, and forward beyond the 1960s. The story spills over boundaries in space as well as time, from New Zealand to Australia, to the pan-British world as a whole. You cannot stop short at borders in the hunt for Pakeha culture.

CHAPTER ELEVEN

The Expatriate Game

In 1906, aspirant author Charles Cleal hanged himself on a cross on the summit of Rangitoto, a hilly island in the Waitemata Harbour, Auckland. His book manuscript had been repeatedly rejected, ran his suicide note, 'and it is only by this extra-ordinary means that I can hope to get it published'.[1] Being an author in New Zealand was never an easy matter. A few years before poor Cleal's epiphany, a local lawyer told two famous Fabian visitors, Sidney and Beatrice Webb, that Auckland was 'a nondescript place with no intellectual circles'. Sport was 'the principal subject of conversation' and young people 'objected to intellectual pursuits'.[2] New Zealand's G. B. Shaw was a hurdler.

Visions of New Zealand as a cultural wasteland stretch back from the 1900s to the whole nineteenth century, and forward into the twentieth century. Katherine Mansfield, one of the world's half-dozen best short-story writers, was seen as a miraculous exception, and she left New Zealand as soon as she possibly could, aged about twenty, in 1908. The idea of the wasteland mixes inferiority and superiority complexes, accurate observation with recolonial myth. The tin-opening concept for this can of worms is *expatriation*. Elements of New Zealand culture were expatriated from cultural history on the grounds of their vulgarity, removed from respectable genealogy much as middle-class Australians once excised convict forebears. Other elements were retrospectively expatriated on grounds of questionable New Zealandness. The most culturally talented were often physical expatriates, or aimed their cultural product primarily at overseas markets, or both. Those who remained in New Zealand felt a strong sense of internal expatriation. Some were happy exiles, content to be provincial while hoping to visit London/Mecca. Others were unhappy exiles, aware that they were alienated from their own society, yet desperate to lead it out of the wasteland.

The first two sections of this chapter explore these various senses of expatriation, mainly in their literary dimension. We look first at a Neanderthal ancestor (and later at a Neanderthal cousin) that has been written out of the literary genealogy, and then at the internally expatriated literati of the period

1920s–60s. The third section broadens the definition of cultural production beyond art and letters, suggests that recolonial New Zealand had a surprising amount of it, and asks why.

Neanderthal Relatives

In literary history, colonial fiction and verse has long featured as a joke pre-history to the real thing. 'Before 1918,' announced Keith Sinclair, 'there were few New Zealand writers and very few of merit.'[3] With some recent exceptions, literary scholars pull few punches about its cringing colonialism or its lack of quality. Some allow for a 'false literary dawn' around 1900, but this was followed by 'the sinking back from a premature colonialism to a renewed cultural dependency – a reversion, in short, to provinciality'.[4] Two generally admirable recent compendia, the *Oxford History of New Zealand Literature* and the *Oxford Companion to New Zealand Literature*, question this view at some points but affirm it at others. Colonial New Zealand is still seen as a wasteland for fiction, and even the best of its poems are still dismissed as 'the typical late nineteenth-century medley of dreaminess and rant'.[5] One scholar seems tempted to generalise from the title of a 1910 poem, 'All Balls'.[6]

Someone needs to warn these literary historians about the dangers of 'presentism', of 'the condescension of posterity'. But they do have a point. The book often taken as New Zealand's first novel, Henry Butler Stoney's *Taranaki: A Tale of the War* (1861), raised only one interesting question, even for contemporaries. 'Is this the worst or only the second worst book we have ever met with?'[7] Alfred Domett, whose verse epic *Ranulf and Amohia*, according to one anthologist, made him 'incomparably the greatest' colonial poet to 1906, included one pithy phrase 'Dead Nun!' – intended to economically evoke horror at tragedy.[8] Stoney, Domett and the 'Dead Nun!' school will take future research students a lot of rescuing. Yet there is reason to believe that the vigour and vibrancy of colonial culture has been under-estimated.

Quantity was there even if quality was not. About 80 novels were published between 1860 and 1900, along with 150 volumes of verse – a further 47 were published by 1910.[9] The short story was already emerging as an indigenous art form – 150 by New Zealanders were published in one (Australian) journal during the 1890s.[10] The genre 'goldfields fiction' alone included 30 books published between 1860 and 1914. If we extend our definitions of New Zealandness in both time and space, such numbers multiply. Benjamin Farjeon produced three novels in the 1860s, as a New Zealand 'goldfields' writer, like George Chamier and Vincent Pyke, and then another 70 after he left New Zealand. Fergus Hume produced 137 racy novels from the 1880s. These were mainly set in England. Hume left Otago at the age of 26, and his novels were rejected as unwholesome by a tightening New Zealand society. 'Yet Hume and his contemporary readers united in perceiving him as a New Zealand writer.'[11]

Music, opera, and theatre were also lively, especially after the discovery of major goldfields in 1861. Much was performed by visiting professionals from overseas, but this masks an element of New Zealandness: a use of New Zealand actors, settings and scripts. 'Plays by New Zealand based authors . . . were a significant part of the 611 titles given 1,409 performances in Auckland's theatres in 1870–71.'[12] George Leitch's *Land of the Moa* (1895) featured 'an impressive reconstruction of the famous Pink and White Terraces . . . the lowest of which were strong enough to support actors and horses', three thermal pools, a geyser spouting 'rice and spangles', and a recreation of the Tarawera eruption. 'The eruption scene was not the only one to use pyrotechnic sensation: earlier in the play a bridge was blown up as the villain rode over it on his horse, in a scene that also used a real waterfall, a '"fount of fire", and an airborne flock of alarmed waterfowl'. The script of an earlier historical melodrama, by George Darrell, in which a coach and horses were driven across the stage, has not survived. Appropriately enough, it was entitled *The Pakeha*.[13]

Professional touring opera was extraordinarily vigorous from 1860. Lyster's Opera Company alone, between 1861 and 1880, was 'responsible for more opera productions in Australia and New Zealand than at any time since'.[14] The 1870s and 1880s were the golden age of opera in New Zealand, and many New Zealanders joined the touring troupes. Their repertoires included operas in English as well as Italian, and at the populist English end they blended into a tradition of vaudeville, music hall, black-and-white minstrel shows, circus and similar entertainments. From the 1870s, Harry Rickard and J. C. Williamson were important trans-Tasman promoters of shows of these kinds; P. R. Dix and the Fuller family were the leading New Zealand promoters. Vaudeville and its relatives remained strong until sidelined by cinema from the 1920s. Popular singers and songwriters, notably Charles Thatcher, and popular versifiers, notably Thomas Bracken, were also prolific.

Twentieth-century New Zealand high culture had little interest in this Neanderthal ancestor. Some reasons for this are obvious enough. It was often vulgar and sensationalist, and tended to blur cherished distinctions even when it was not. Colonial opera might have been a candidate for respectable lineage, but tarred itself with the brush of vaudeville. It was 'a remarkably egalitarian phenomenon' whose seats became cheaper over time. It was not sure if it was highbrow or lowbrow, and did not really care. It did not even keep its gloves entirely free of sport. A cricket prize-giving, and a personal appearance by the famous Australian bowler 'Demon' Spofforth, punctuated a performance of Donizetti's *Lucretia Borgia* in Christchurch in 1881.[15] Class crossing can be exaggerated. An élite colonial culture did exist. With all due respect to an eminent music historian, the notion that balls 'mixed together all elements of society' is balls.[16] But opera co-existed too happily with 'Klaer's Canine and Equine Hippodrome' to be quite respectable. Progressive colonial culture tended to be vulgar as well as vibrant, and its New Zealandness also seemed questionable.

As we have seen, an important homegrown element of Pakeha culture was a co-opted and adapted segment of Maori culture. But the cultural co-option of things Maori gathered force after the progressive colonial era peaked, in the 1880s, and really took off from the 1900s. Other borrowed components of colonial culture were more-or-less direct transplantations from the Pakeha homelands. Stories and poems contributed to the subtle persistence of Scottish and Irish New Zealand difference. An English genteel culture also transplanted successfully. Like genteel sport, it tended to be amateur and élitist, with the participants getting the entertainment as much as, or even more than, the audience. Even this had some flavour of New Zealand: the 'Wellington Mazurka', 'Waikato Waltz' and 'Pororangi Polka' all graced the dance floors of genteel balls between 1855 and 1880.[17]

Colonial culture also included a set of less derivative traditions – a set whose New Zealandness is not immediately obvious. A tradition of folk songs, verse ballads and capping yarns came to New Zealand with the first sailors and sealers, was reinforced by subsequent waves of male workers, and picked up local components, such as the Irish-colonial verse of Bracken's alter ego, Paddy Murphy. 'Goldfields culture', a motley assemblage of circus, theatre, opera, vaudeville, novels, folklore and ballads, was transposed upon this. This curious socio-culture bounced around the Pacific in the 1850s–70s, following the gold rushes in California, Victoria and New Zealand. Intersecting with both these traditions was a trans-Tasman culture, which did not see Australia and New Zealand as significantly different places.

An Australian literary nationalism is conventionally dated from the founding of the Sydney *Bulletin* in 1880, or from an increase in its literary content from 1896. There is a strong case for seeing the *Bulletin* as originally a Tasman, or Australasian, journal. Some 10 per cent of its content in the 1890s, including the 150 short stories mentioned above, was contributed by New Zealanders. This link persisted into the twentieth century. New Zealanders served as the *Bulletin*'s literary editor for 37 of the years between 1900 and 1960. After 1901, however, the Tasman world began to split in literature as in everything else. The 4,000 poems and 700 short stories published by New Zealanders in the *Bulletin* fell out of New Zealand literary history. The same was true of earlier and later strands of Tasman culture, such as colonial opera, theatre, the satirical songs of balladeer Charles Thatcher, the poems of Arthur Adams and David McKee Wright, and the novels of Jean Devanney. Like vulgarity, mixed origins discouraged the acceptance of colonial culture by its more precious posterity.

Questionable merit, respectability and origins were not the only causes of the disappearance of the Neanderthal ancestor. There were at least three other disconnections behind the amputation of a cultural past. One was a tendency to downplay the hinge period 1890–1914, or at least to link its cultural virtues forward, but its cultural 'vices' back. The 'virtues', or leading literary lights of this period, included novelists William Satchell and Edith Searle Grossman, poet Blanche Baughan, and Mansfield herself. It might be argued that these writers were as much an epilogue to progressive colonial culture as a prologue to recolonial culture. They sometimes deal in themes of potential unrealised, of promising flowerings now in doubt, which conform to the subtext if not the text of New Zealand history during the period. All four reflect a traumatic transition, and occasionally hint that the shift was from a promising future to a less promising one, as in Baughan's poem 'A Bush Section', quoted in Chapter Two. The current trend in the complex field of Mansfield studies seems to reassert her New Zealandness. Almost half her stories, 'a surprising number', were set in New Zealand, and she famously hoped 'to make our undiscovered country leap into the eyes of the Old World'.[18] Mansfield's work is said to have been a 'discourse of transition' between colony – New Zealand – and metropolis – Britain. Perhaps it was also a discourse of transition between two eras of New Zealand history.

A second possible disconnection is that between fiction and non-fiction. Much of the best New Zealand writing in the nineteenth century was non-fiction. Arthur Saunders Thomson and William Pember Reeves were, in literary terms, superior to most general historians of at least the first half of the twentieth century. In the writing of racy memoirs, E. J. Wakefield and Frederick Maning are recognised as authors of classics, but not *literary* classics. Yet, even in Britain, the nineteenth century was a time of some blurring between fact and fiction, not in the postmodernist sense, but in the sense of merging markets. T. B. Macaulay, for example, aimed his histories at novel buyers. This might have been still more true of colonial contexts, where people were not only more likely to buy 'local' histories and memoirs than local novels, but also more likely to write them. Whatever merits it may have in the present, the rigid fiction/non-fiction divide may be anachronistic when applied to New Zealand's literary past. Perhaps nineteenth-century non-fiction was another Neanderthal ancestor of twentieth-century fiction. If you are looking for the best New Zealand prose of the nineteenth century, you are more likely to find it in non-fiction than fiction.

The third disconnection was recolonisation's retrospective taming of its past, including its literary past. This wrote boastful, bombastic, vigorous progressive colonisation down or out, or at least tamed it into virtuous but dreary respectability. It also wrote out the surprising proto-nationalism of the 1870s and 1880s, when New Zealanders were readier to predict a future independent of Britain than they later became. The reputation of Thomas Bracken, colonial New Zealand's unofficial poet laureate, fell victim to this, as well as to his Australian connection and to his limited literary merit. Bracken's books included *Dear Old Bendigo*, and he was described as 'one whose country is Australasia'.[19] Though it might be true that 'his verse seldom goes beyond the predictable and the sentimental cliché' in terms of form, this is not so clear in terms of content. His most famous poem was the words to 'God Defend New Zealand', now the national anthem. Its five verses do not mention Britain once – or the King or Queen. New Zealand is unmistakeably a nation, a 'free land'. There is progressive colonial optimism in 'God's glorious plan' to make the country 'good and great', standing 'in the nations' van'.

Bracken published the song in 1875 as the 'National Anthem'. It was quickly demoted, and only partially recovered, to 'national song' in 1938, when the National Centenary Council, preparing for commemorations in 1940, gave it that status. But 'the Council was also unanimous in the opinion that the national song should be sung after the National Anthem, God Save the King'.[20] The use of capitals for the Anthem, but not for the song, added emphasis. It was not until 1977 – over a century after it was written – that 'God Defend New Zealand' became an official national anthem, and it still shares that status with 'God Save the Queen'. The years between the 1870s and the 1970s reflect a 'recolonial gap' in the story of New Zealand nationalism. You can hate the tune, which was chosen by three German musicians in Melbourne from a number of New Zealand offerings. You can find in the words 'the predictable and sentimental cliché', or the cloying hyper-piety of the day. But you cannot find cringing colonialism. The song was written in the 1870s; it is hard to imagine its being written in the first half of the twentieth century.

Waiting for Godwits

Waiting for Godot is a play by Samuel Beckett, in which two arid characters live out a sterile relationship while waiting for a saviour who never comes. Bar-tailed godwits are migrant birds that live in both New Zealand and the Northern Hemisphere. *The Godwits Fly* is a novel by the important New

Zealand woman writer Robin Hyde. It was published in 1938, a year before her suicide in London at the age of 33. Its themes include 'the dichotomy between being English and not English' and the 'dreary wasteland' of ordinary life in New Zealand. Like Hyde's life and death, this reflects the sense of alienation, of internal expatriation, that existed among the New Zealand literati between the 1920s and the 1960s. They, too, waited for a saviour, 'a child born in a marvellous year', in the words of leading poet Allen Curnow. He/she was thought to arrive a couple of times, in the forms of brilliant novelist Janet Frame and brilliant poet James K. Baxter, but never finally did. In the nineteenth century, New Zealand had a different attitude to Godot and to Godwits. Hyde's was not the birds' first appearance in New Zealand literature. In *My Simple Life in New Zealand*, published in 1908 and referring to about 1880, Adela Stewart notes a 'busy morning plucking godwits'.[21] This section seeks to unpick this little knot of metaphor and understand recolonial New Zealand literary culture, as well as its vexed relationship with its Neanderthal relatives.

Until the 1990s, you would have had to search the pages of New Zealand literary scholarship very hard to find Thomas Bracken or Fergus Hume. The Neanderthal ancestor was uniformly forgotten, and the first emergence of a New Zealand literature was dated to the 1920s at the earliest, with Mansfield as an inspired but disconnected prologue. The new literati included three types of expatriate: actual expatriates, living permanently abroad; happy internal exiles, content with provincialism; and unhappy internal exiles, agonising over their alienation from their own society.

One strand of actual literary expatriates – Arthur Adams, David McKee Wright, Jean Devanney – went to Australia, where the progressive fracturing of the Tasman world excised them from New Zealand literary history. Another strand went Home to Britain. Mansfield is the best-known example, matched by Frances Hodgkins, the leading New Zealand painter of the first half of the twentieth century. Current scholarship on Hodgkins sees her as a British rather than a New Zealand artist, but a central argument of this chapter is that the two were not mutually exclusive.[22] A great many other New Zealand writers spent at least part of their careers in Britain. Some held to the wasteland view of New Zealand culture, yet felt that it had virtually expelled them, and resented the fact. Others again, like postwar novelists James Courage and Dan Davin, lived in Britain but dreamed of New Zealand, in which they located their stories. Wrote Davin, after many years in Britain, 'I feel no wish to write about anything else but Nzers – indeed don't feel or don't feel in the same way about anything else – and all the time the old navel-cord is getting more shrivelled.'[23] Hodgkins was one of those who resented New Zealand's 'blank indifference' to her work.[24] When invited to contribute to a New Zealand collection, expatriate poet and eccentric Geoffrey de Montalk impolitely declined. 'Every month I spend in England, the New Zealand days seem more and more like a nightmare I had a long time ago, and am gradually forgetting . . . To Hell with New Zealand, those are my sentiments.'[25] The phenomenon of physical expatriation is discussed further in the next section, in a context wider than art and letters alone.

The second category of expatriates were the happy exiles, content with provincialism and occasional visits to the cultural capital, London. The producers of the anthology *Kowhai Gold* and other dross, they included writers and editors such as C. R. Allen, C. A. Marris, O. N. Gillespie, Pat Lawlor and Alan Mulgan. Like the Neanderthal colonials, these men accepted the transnationalism of New Zealand culture. But, unlike the colonials, they did not expect to contribute much to it or to help determine it. They were explicitly content with both subordinate and provincial roles. 'If we cannot evoke a literature out of Maori folklore and the romance of the pastoralist, and these two avenues are not so very alluring,' wrote Allen, 'let us not be ashamed to turn back . . . to the English tradition.'[26] Unsurprisingly, modern literary scholarship is not impressed by this group. Certainly, poets and writers such as Dick Harris and Ian Donnelly, whom the happy exiles praised as the greatest of their day, had a strong tendency never to be heard of again. But the happy exiles did contribute substantially to one interesting subgenre of New Zealand literature: tales of the great recolonial pilgrimage to Mother England.

Alan Mulgan's *Home: A Colonial's Adventure* was the classic example of this subgenre. Mulgan made his 'dutiful and happy pilgrimage' to Mecca in the late 1920s. Though an Ulsterman himself, he did not bother with Ireland, but wandered England 'half-dazed by the beauty', concentrating on London, 'a vast symphony in grey'. His afternoon tea on the train from Paddington was 'almost a piece of poetry', surely a first for British Rail. Watching England gather runs at cricket might be slow, but it 'was like watching a beautiful woman gather flowers'. When he hit his head on the low door of a pub, he comforted himself with the thought that a sight of the cute interior was 'worth a good many knocks'. One feels that if a London policeman had knocked Alan Mulgan down and urinated on him, Mulgan would have sprung up and shaken him gratefully by the hand.

Another pilgrim, Ian Donnelly (*The Joyous Pilgrimage*, 1935), a 'literary tramp from the colonies', specialised in meeting great English literary figures. Kipling, Shaw and H. G. Wells wisely declined such meetings. Donnelly proudly preserved their rejection letters, even though he was forced to hire a prostitute for someone to talk to – she was 'appallingly free in her language'. Donnelly, like many after him, noted a contrast in the British reception of

New Zealanders and 'bumptious' Australians. 'New Zealanders, on the other hand, are quiet, rather like country boys come to town, and trembling to hear brave tales from the lips of miraculous uncles.' These recolonial memoirs of pilgrimages Home are a cringing and cringe-inducing strand of New Zealand literature. But we have to understand them.

Mulgan believed that 'the English were the chosen people – perhaps I ought to say British'. But there were 'many Britons oversea as well as in Britain'. Old Britain was not without its faults. Caste was too rigid and there was a hint of decay – flaws against which New Zealand was the perfect South British insurance. Mulgan, Donnelly and their ilk saw themselves as shareholders in Old Britain. 'London was part of me, and I had become part of London,' wrote Donnelly. Mulgan saw Cockney guides in Westminster as degenerate modern Greeks in *his* Parthenon. 'It is a profound mistake,' he wrote, 'to suppose that overseas loyalty is incompatible with sharp criticism of England. The colonial is like a man who scolds his wife but will not allow anybody else to say a word against her.' Like William Lane before him, Mulgan was no eccentric, but the quintessence of Better Britonism. Before we dismiss him for this, we should note that he was the father of abler writer John Mulgan, author of the seminal novel *Man Alone* (1939). To some extent, John shared his father's views. New Zealand's relationship with Britain, he wrote, was 'stupid, irrational, and, in some melancholy way, satisfying to the heart. It has the texture of family relationships that can be full of internal bitterness but united against the outside world.'[27] If we want Mulgan junior as part of our cultural history, we also have to take Mulgan senior.

Our third category of expatriates were the unhappy internal exiles, also known as the 'literary nationalists'. Curnow defined their position: 'The condition of nationhood entails a degree of cultural self-reliance, along with some moral and imaginative identification of a people ... [and] some expression of this national identity in a country's art and letters.'[28] For reasons with which we can now sympathise, they were rebels against Alan Mulgan and company, who were the literary gatekeepers of the 1920s–40s. The point of origin of this self-aware, high-cultural literary nationalism is open to some dispute. One could date it back to the transitional figures of the 1900s, Mansfield, Satchell and Baughan. It tended to date its own origins to the 1920s at the earliest. Socialist poet Ron Mason began publishing in this decade.[29] A 1930s origin is more commonly asserted. In 1932, lively if short-lived literary journals, *Tomorrow* and *Phoenix*, emerged in Christchurch and Auckland, as did literary publishers, notably The Caxton Press of Christchurch. John Mulgan's *Man Alone* was published, though not yet widely read. A parallel development in New Zealand painting, featuring Colin McCahon, Toss Woollaston and Rita Angus among others, and also centred on

Christchurch, occurred at much the same time. One could also make a case for the later 1940s, when the important and long-lived journal *Landfall* was founded and some key collections were published.

These 'expatriate' literati, especially the first and third groups, unhappy external and internal exiles, shared a dire vision of New Zealand society. The most insightful saw this as a decline from an earlier, more promising, situation. Jane Mander felt that New Zealand had been 'a positively exciting country' on her departure in 1910. On her return in 1932, she found it afflicted with the 'awful disease' of puritanism and conformism – 'barren wastes of Victorian philistinism', 'brain-numbing, stimulus-stifling, soul-searing silence'. New Zealanders had become 'mentally and spiritually . . . one of the backward peoples of the earth'.[30] In 1924, poet Eileen Duggan noticed a similar shift.

> Five years ago New Zealand was a healthy rosy child peeping out from behind mother's apron. Now it is a simpering debutante, paying calls, and echoing Mother's phrases . . . At present the cry is Empire. The children have it week in, week out . . . I feel as if I want to stop every child in the street and say – 'this is your country – You can see it – touch it – love it. What do you know of Empire?'[31]

Eminent music historian John Thomson was later to endorse this vision.

> It is no accident that the 1920s and 1930s were in many respects the most artistically barren in New Zealand's history. The country seemed to have slipped into a cultural cul-de-sac dominated by the forces of conservatism and mediocrity. Many aspects of New Zealand life suffered in this way, including education.[32]

What Mander, Duggan and Thomson were observing was the advent of the height of recolonisation, of dominionism and the Great Tightening. They saw this transition as a downward shift in cultural terms, a promising future lapsed into wasteland. Most literary observers, however, lacked the sense of cultural shift, while they endorsed the sense of cultural wasteland, assuming that it had been there from the beginnings of European settlement. In 1944, Frank Sargeson, the leading literary nationalist in fiction writing, described his home town of Hamilton as 'The Grey Death, puritanism, wowserism gone most startlingly putrescent'.[33] Literary visions of the mainstream New Zealand society of the 1950s were not much better. Occasionally, literati such as Charles Brasch, editor of *Landfall*, noted countercurrents: 'quiet imaginative compassion from the simplest, plainest housewife or clerk, or a breath of generous interest in the voice of the prosy comfortable teacher'.[34] But for most of the literary nationalists, most of the time, there was no countercurrent in the wasteland except their own, and never had been. Society at large responded by ignoring New Zealand literature. 'Few people spoke of it, as if it were a shameful disease.'[35]

Diverse as they were, the literary nationalists therefore shared a common conundrum. They saw the mainstream of New Zealand society as sterile, materialist and dreary, the wasteland. But many rejected the traditional option of talented artists who felt this way: getting out, actual expatriation. Instead, they wished to remain in New Zealand and struggle to make the wasteland flower. The problem was that they were deeply alienated from the society they wished to fertilise. For its part, that society was not keen on being led from the putative wilderness by prophets who described it as 'The Grey Death'. The literati disliked mainstream society because it disliked them, and it disliked them because they disliked it. From the 1920s to the 1960s, and perhaps beyond, New Zealand's literati writhed in this unhappy trap.

Some writers were crushed by the trap of alienation, by the sense of being in exile both at home and at Home. Hyde and John Mulgan took Charles Cleal's way out. Others simply stopped writing fiction when the alienation and absence of reward became too much. Various routes of escape were attempted. One was to reject nationalism entirely and opt self-consciously for internationalism, notably Marxist internationalism.[36] The difficulty here was that successful literary internationalism requires both a larger locale and some enriching conversation between the general and the particular. If you dismiss the particular, you are talking to yourself; and if you do so in New Zealand, you are talking to a very lonely self. So Marxist poet Ron Mason found himself dumping 200 copies of his first collection off an Auckland wharf. When a socialist artist informed another poet, Rex Fairburn, that 'the New Zealand penis was not yet fully erect', Fairburn characteristically replied: 'True, but as a born New Zealander, why don't you try to hoist it up, instead of tossing off Russia?'[37]

Two groups, preconditioned to alienation, proved most adept at surviving the trap, though not necessarily at escaping from it. One was a strong strand of woman writers, including Mander, Frame and Sylvia Ashton-Warner. Mander stopped writing about New Zealand in 1925, and stopped writing entirely when she returned here in 1932, escaping as a person, but not as a New Zealand writer. Janet Frame, the leading New Zealand novelist of the twentieth century, used mental asylums and her writing as fire escapes from each other. News of the publication of her first book reached her doctors just in time for them to call off a planned lobotomy.[38] Ashton-Warner, an innovative teacher, published her first novel in 1958, at the age of 50. Her books featured twice in *Time* magazine's top ten novels, and one was made into a film starring Shirley Maclaine. But her own country doubted the New Zealandness, the highbrow status and the message of her work, and the response here was 'both muted and hostile'.[39] As with Frame, it was almost as though you were not allowed to be an overseas success *and* a New Zealand one.

Another groups of survivors was a talented cluster of homosexual men: Brasch, Sargeson, the brilliant critic Eric McCormick, and a few others. Their capacity to persist, their painfully grown thick skin, was crucial to New Zealand letters, 1930s–60s. The wealthy Brasch and the resilient Sargeson were active and generous mentors. Sargeson was also a master of a written Pakeha vernacular. But, while his characters were proletarian, his audience was intellectual, and he was in some ways alienated from both. 'I live in a community but am not of it.'[40] Brasch, Sargeson and McCormick did become the literary gatekeepers, 1940s–60s, but the gate led to a narrower road than they would have liked. Their impact on the general public was very limited. They simply did not *like* New Zealand society enough to be welcomed by it as redeemers.

Another reaction to the alienation trap was that of a masculine group led by poets Rex Fairburn and Denis Glover. One could also include the poet and historian Keith Sinclair – and perhaps the exiled novelist and publisher Dan Davin as an honorary member. These men were as hard-drinking and hard-partying – and often as good at doing practical things themselves – as any Kiwi bloke. They might be poets, but they were not pansies, and they could bloody well drink. Combined with a rejection of overt theorising, which they associated with Marxism and dogma, this enabled the group to partially evade the anti-intellectual reflex of New Zealand society. This 'blokerati' was therefore less alienated than its socialist, gay and female equivalents.

Fairburn, the dominant personality, tends now to be remembered more for his vices than his virtues. He was capable of intense irrational likes (for early fascism, for example) and dislikes (for Colin McCahon, for example). He was somewhat homophobic – 'I have no objection to pansies as persons' was the nicest thing he said about gays. He, Glover and Sinclair saw the Sargesonians as a something of a homosexual mafia, contributing to a 'prissiness' and 'preciousness' in postwar literature.[41] Sargeson responded by dismissing 'the beef, beer, and bombast school of the Colonial intellectual of the Glover school'.[42] But it is hard to dislike Fairburn, a man who went shopping with a wheelbarrow, did ballet in his underpants as a party trick, and set fire to the hairs on his chest to amuse children. At its best, his prose and poetry came close to the heart of the internal expatriate's dilemma. New Zealand was 'a Philistine community', but 'These people are my clansmen, my accomplices / I share the crime. This guilt is my reprieve.'[43]

The 'blokerati' may have come closest to bridging the gap between literary nationalism and its host society, but in the end they did not manage it. Their themes, like those of the other literati, were predominantly angry crusades against the tight mainstream, which they could chastise but not persuade – partly because they were so keen on chastising. The most successful was arguably Sinclair, who from 1959 broadened his appeal, and boosted a wider cultural nationalism by pretending it had long existed – an interesting strategy. But he did so as a historian, not a poet. In the 1960s, the blokerati were outflanked on the populist side by Barry Crump, discussed in the next chapter, and on the social redeemer side by James K. Baxter. Baxter, who arguably ranks in poetry with Frame in fiction, was a category-crossing figure: years of drunkenness followed by years of sobriety; homosexual episodes followed by considerable womanising. He died at the age of 46, in 1972, after becoming a long-haired symbol of 1960s counterculture and a founder of a new alliance between Pakeha intellectuals and Maori radicals. Baxter was suspected of being the 'marvellous child', the Godot, for which New Zealand culture had long been waiting. But in the end neither he, nor Fairburn, nor Sargeson nor Frame – nor any single individual – could fill this role. Yet there were godwits waiting to be plucked.

The most intriguing thing about the Neanderthal ancestor of Pakeha culture is the sense in which it never died. Instead, it grew to become far larger than its literary cousin. Just as the literary cousin rejected the shared ancestor, so it did the collateral line. It did so on similar grounds – questionable merit, lowbrow status and questionable New Zealandness. It did not know, and largely still does not know, what it was missing.

There has always been a sense in which national packaging falsifies history. The actual past, especially in culture, is no respecter of national boundaries. This book has provided two main examples hitherto, and applied them to cultural history in the preceding paragraphs. One is the Tasman world, which New Zealand shared equally with the colonies that became Australia. The other is recolonial blurring of aspects of British and New Zealand history, combined with recolonisation's tendency to reject its robust but vulgar colonial inheritance. To understand New Zealand literary and artistic culture, we have now to deal with a multinational entity that is still more vague, but just as real: an Anglophone, 'pan-British' or 'Britonnic' culture.

During the nineteenth century, a transnational culture emerged which had three main geographical bases: Old Britain, the neo-Britains (Canada, Australia, New Zealand) and the United States. A leading product of this Britonnic world was 'crew culture', the floating mass of male labour that staffed progressive colonisation as sailors, navvies, miners, lumbermen and the rest.

This flourished in the nineteenth century and declined in the twentieth, but left important cultural residues. One was a notion of (white male) 'national character': toughness, pragmatism, egalitarianism, ingenuity and so on. This was presented as distinct and distinguishing by each legatee nation, but was in fact almost exactly the same in all of them. In a strange way, Canada, Australia and New Zealand, and to some extent even the United States, each saw themselves as the Lone Apostle of Better Britonism, while gazing steadily past each other.

Another product of the Britonnic world, related to gold-rush culture and to crew culture itself, was a genre of late nineteenth- and twentieth-century pan-British popular fiction. Its subgenres ranged from detective stories, through various types of children's fiction, to light romances, culminating from the 1960s in the Mills & Boon novel. It also included war novels, the Western, and a related type of 'crew fiction', in which the hero was a wandering worker rather than a soldier or a gunslinger. His main enemy was not other Europeans or natives, but nature, inside and out. Obviously enough, the English language was a key vector, giving participating nations easy access to each other's book markets. But the genre could extend beyond the English language, as with the Westerns of Karl May, wildly popular in Germany. As the twentieth century wore on, pan-British fiction became still more international, perhaps piggy-backing on the globalisation of American culture. This pan-British genre and its international successor was the strange milieu in which the great bulk of recolonial New Zealand's literary output actually resided.

'Bulk' is no overstatement.[44] The 200-odd novels of Benjamin Farjeon and Fergus Hume were just the start. George Joseph's twenty 'sex-and-violence thrillers' and 1,000 short stories of the 1930s–50s carried on their tradition. Women increasingly took the lead in this New Zealand, yet transnational, popular literature. Edith Lyttleton, writing as G. B. Lancaster, became a 'voice of the crews'.[45] Her fourteen or so books and numerous stories, published between 1904 and 1943, were set variously in New Zealand, Australia, Canada, the United States and England. Her 'earlier male-centred fiction' tended to 'idealise' the colonising process. Three of her novels were made into Hollywood silent movies. Two other New Zealand women writers, Louisa Baker and Isabel Peacocke, produced 55 more pan-British romances and children's books between them at roughly the same time. Between the 1920s and the 1960s, another group of women continued the New Zealand/pan-British literary tradition. They included Rosemary Rees, Nellie Scanlan, Dulce Carman, Dorothy Quentin, Mavis Winder and Mary Scott, who published 210 novels among them.

Better known than all these was Ngaio Marsh, one of the world's best writers of detective fiction, who produced 31 novels and sold a couple of million copies worldwide while living mostly in Christchurch. Lesser New Zealand lights in similar subgenres included Dorothy Eden (40 novels) and Elizabeth Messenger (ten). As they had in dairy farming, men came to the party once they scented money. The most notable of between six and a dozen New Zealand male thriller writers, from the 1960s, was Colin Peel, who produced twenty internationally successful novels. But women finished the twentieth century as they had started it – well in the lead. A new echelon, led by Anne Holden and Yvonne Kalman, produced about 40 novels for a market now increasingly extending beyond English-speaking countries – Holden's *The Witnesses* sold 250,000 copies in East Germany. From the 1960s, this group was joined on international bestseller lists by a dozen New Zealand Mills & Boon writers, all female. Led by Essie Summers, whose 50 or so romances set in New Zealand and England sold seventeen million copies, the New Zealand branch of Mills & Boon has produced between 200 and 300 titles. New Zealanders have also been active producers of children's literature. In his youth in the 1930s, John Marshall, a future prime minister, wrote 50 children's stories, *The Adventures of Dr Duffer*, later published as books. But again, women dominated. Peacocke, Edith Howes, Mona Tracey, Phyllis Garrard, and Joyce West wrote about a hundred international children's books mainly in the first half of the twentieth century.[46] A larger group, led by Joy Cowley, Lynley Dodd and Margaret Mahy capped this with five hundred or so in the second half.[47]

The motley but massive canon of New Zealand/pan-British/international popular fiction appears to total some 1,500 titles. In the forms of light romance and children's fiction in particular, it is at least as active in the present as it was in the past. It is one of the few branches of New Zealand history that *did* progress, onward and upward, through the great divides of recolonisation and decolonisation. One could arguably extend it to film and television. One example is the New Zealand-made and New Zealand-led American television series, *Xena Warrior Princess*. Its special effects might have surprised the early authors of New Zealand popular fiction, but neither its ruthless populism nor its feminist message would have done so. Another intriguing example is J. R. R. Tolkien's *Lord of the Rings*, steeped in Anglo-Saxon folklore as well as fantasy, which was filmed in New Zealand on a massive scale, by New Zealand writer and director, Peter Jackson. It is not the first time that Better Britain has been entrusted with the reworking of a great British legend.

The integration of the popular tradition with its smaller literary cousin, and of both with their pasts, offers exciting prospects. Rediscovering an immensely vigorous cultural past can only be good for the cultural future. Mills & Boon may not be everyone's cup of latte, but Ngaio Marsh, Margaret

Mahy and Peter Jackson are a club worth joining, or at least worth recognising as a club. However, not all the implications of a New Zealand, yet trans-national, cultural history are entirely comfortable. Some of the authors of New Zealand's huge output of popular fiction lived in New Zealand, some lived overseas (mainly Britain) and some did both. Especially in the first half of the century, their books were set mainly overseas. But a significant and growing minority were set in New Zealand, while being aimed primarily at the 'overseas market' – at first pan-British, later merging into international. One British publisher spoke of the 'Maoriland romance' as a subgenre in itself. New Zealand, as it was known to the world from these books, was often an idealised, even sentimentalised place. This developed a motif as old as the historians Gibbon and Macaulay, New Zealand as Britain's little 'Other'. It was a place of safe otherness, where simple virtues were preserved. New Zealand has long played Shire to the West's Middle-earth.

Cultural Overproduction?

Cultural maturity may well stem from the interaction between an innovative high culture and a vigorous low culture, and from a conscious challenging of the line between them. New Zealand has in fact long possessed the basic ingredients. The godwits have always been here. But the two strands remained too disconnected for cultural sparks to fly. The problem was that recolonial literary culture declined to acknowledge, or interact with, its Neanderthal relatives, notably the New Zealand strand of pan-British popular fiction. Instead, it either complacently accepted provincial subordinacy, or rejected transnationalism and populism, essential components of New Zealand's hybrid culture.

Recolonial New Zealand was not a cultural wasteland. Its culture was active, but transnational as well as national, living like the godwit in two hemispheres – and on two 'brows', high and low. Indeed, one could invert the wasteland image and suggest that, in some spheres, New Zealand culture was peculiarly productive. Fifteen hundred titles contributed to pan-British and international popular fiction are big numbers for a small country. One could extend this picture beyond literature. New Zealand playwrights Merton Hodge and Roger Hall were names to conjure with in London's West End, in the 1930s and 1970s respectively. New Zealand's first Oscar winner, in 1961, was Noni Wright, a British Broadcasting Corporation documentary director, who also won ten first prizes at Asian film festivals. As in popular fiction, clusterings of expatriate New Zealand talent occurred in opera singing, cartooning and publishing. A recent study suggests that, from the late nineteenth century, almost 60 New Zealanders have become international opera singers. Malvina Major, Donald McIntyre and Kiri Te Kanawa are only the best known and most recent of a long list of names.[48] There is also a line of internationally successful New Zealand cartoonists, including David Low, Kim Casali and Murray Ball.[49] As for publishing:

> For many years there was a notorious 'New Zealand mafia' at Oxford University Press – Kenneth Sisam, John Mulgan, Dan Davin, Robert Burchfield, and others less renowned. Oxford (in Oxford) after the Second World War counted almost as a New Zealand publisher. As late as the 1960s, the local manager complained that there was no point in his developing a local list since anything really good would be snaffled by Clarendon. For a New Zealand scholar the imprint of the Clarendon Press, Oxford's academic arm, was the ultimate accolade.[50]

One could extend the picture still further, beyond artistic culture. In discussing World War Two, we have seen that a staggering number of New Zealanders, including a dozen air marshals, achieved high rank in the RAF. The line begins in World War One, peaks in the early 1960s, and continues to the present.[51] New Zealanders were prominent in British reconstructive surgery and other branches of medicine. Eminent names include Sir Harold Gillies, Sir Archibald McIndoe and Sir Robert Macintosh. The expatriate game was very widely played by recolonial New Zealanders. In the 1930s, 'one retired [New Zealand] headmaster met in England nearly the whole of his top form of a few years earlier'. A New Zealand architecture professor dined in London with twenty of his old students. There was a ten-episode radio series made in 1940 entitled *New Zealand Brains Abroad*.[52] Some of this expatriate talent aimed at pan-British markets, Australia, Canada and the United States, equally with Old Britain. Some aimed at still more international markets. Some expatriates lived in Australia or, after World War Two, in the United States. But most lived in, or focused on, Britain, especially London, which, with the universities of Oxford and Cambridge, did indeed operate as the cultural capital of New Zealand. An article in the *Encyclopedia of New Zealand* of 1966 listed about 350 eminent New Zealand expatriates. Twenty-seven lived in the United States, 24 in Australia, and about 180 in Britain – with a further 90 or so in the black Commonwealth, where they formed part of the rearguard of the *British* colonial élite.[53] In 1990, an Oxford magazine featured obituaries of three of the university's great professors. Two were New Zealanders, including the country's most famous historian, Sir Ronald Syme, whose book *Colonial Elites* was about ancient Rome, not New Zealand.[54]

Yet New Zealand had good access to the cultural output its expatriates helped create – brains out, books back. And there is an obvious positive side to the possibility that New Zealand was a site of what we might call 'cultural overproduction'. Such a claim could easily smack of empty nationalist boasting. Yet the above paragraphs suggest it is not without evidence. A dozen air marshals and 1,500 works of popular fiction was more than New Zealand's fair share – New Zealanders amounted to about 3 per cent of the joint New Zealand–British population in 1940, and about 2 per cent of the pan-British population, including Canada and Australia but not the United States. Cultural overproduction seems to me to be a real phenomenon, and one that requires a preliminary attempt at explanation.

We should concede that a desperate desire to escape from the tight society is one possible explanation. Talented New Zealanders might have fled to high scholarship, and therefore London and Oxbridge, as one of the few routes of escape, like talented American Blacks into basketball. Another possibility is that, if you could manage to flower intellectually in the wasteland, you were a hardy plant. 'The Grey Death' may have acted as high altitude does for Kenyan runners – if you can breathe deep here, you can breathe deep anywhere. Such explanations are temptingly unflattering but not fully convincing. A possible contributor to the mass of female talent in literature and opera is a 'woman bonus', which had long been important to the high quality of New Zealand schoolteaching. In a society that gives female talent very limited options, women not content with traditional roles naturally concentrate on those few opportunities that do exist. This helps explain the overproduction of writers and singers. What may help explain the scientists, publishers and air marshals is the Kiwi mafia factor, the tendency of like to attract like through mentoring and national nepotism. Both these factors may have contributed to New Zealand's impressive succession of woman writers.[55]

My own best guess is that cultural overproduction stemmed mainly from the recolonial system itself, and from an element of self-fulfilment in the myth of New Zealanders as 'Better Britons'. We saw in Chapter Two that the recolonial relationship gave white colonists a big advantage over black in the transfer of technological infrastructure, as against technology itself – the schools that trained the engineers, as against the engines themselves. Though New Zealand began to rely more on British factories for equipment after the 1900s, the cultural infrastructure remained in place, producing more and better engineers and scientists than the narrowing recolonial economy itself could use. This was not just a matter of education systems, but of the cultural attitudes that led New Zealanders to see themselves as metropolitan, with metropolitan career options, rather than colonial. New Zealand was systemically inclined to produce talent surplus to local requirements. It was systemically inclined to pump some of this talent, along with the protein, into London, where both were well received.

Expatriation and cultural overproduction were games also played in science. Recolonial New Zealand science, too, had a 'Neanderthal ancestor', a highbrow–lowbrow divide, and 'internal' and external expatriates. The Neanderthal ancestor was a dynamic nineteenth-century interaction between New Zealand natives and nature and post-Enlightenment science, in this case pan-European rather than pan-British. Charles Darwin's visit to New Zealand in 1835–36, for example, had its influence on his theory of evolution.[56] Applied science was the equivalent of lowbrow literature, theoretical science the equivalent of highbrow, and New Zealand was surprisingly strong in both. External scientific expatriates flowed to Britain as freely as writers. The most notable was physicist Ernest Rutherford, who split the atom and features in any short list of the greatest scientists of the twentieth century. Though Rutherford lived most of his adult life in Britain and Canada, his New Zealand upbringing and his three University of New Zealand degrees were important to his science. 'Even when at the top of his profession Rutherford still thought of himself as a New Zealander.'[57] Like Mansfield, Rutherford was not some solitary miracle but the flagship of a fleet. A New Zealand contemporary, chemist Joseph Mellors, moved to Britain and contributed massively to the development of alloys for artillery shells during World War One.[58] After Rutherford and Mellor, 32 more New Zealanders, 1937–94, became Fellows of the Royal Society, the ultimate accolade of British science.[59] They clustered not only in plant and soil sciences, as one might expect, but also in chemistry and physics. From the 1940s, as scientific leadership shifted away from Britain, the flow was to some extent diverted to the United States, where several New Zealand scientists achieved great eminence.

The internal expatriates were leading New Zealand-based scientists who had transnational reputations, networks and outputs. New Zealand exported applied science, as well as imported it. In such fields as agriculture, this was commendable but unsurprising. More surprisingly, during World War Two, New Zealand scientists punched well above their weight in Allied radar and atomic bomb programmes. 'The radar programme had a brief and glorious history in DSIR . . . With the agility of a small operation building short production runs, [it] was briefly able to outpace the American mass-production machine in delivering new models of radar to the Allied forces in the South Pacific.'[60] New Zealand scientists contributed disproportionately to Anglo-American atomic projects during and after World War Two. Six New Zealander scientists were involved in the Montreal Project alone – more than either the French or the Australians.[61] By 1940, a government publication could boast that 'in proportion to their numbers, New Zealanders have done more for the progress of modern science than any other people'.[62] Even discounting by half for parochial exaggeration, this seems a little strange for an isolated, sparsely populated country with a pasture-based economy, whose European settlement was only 68 years old when Rutherford won the Nobel Prize.

In contrast to literature, science valued its Neanderthal ancestor, and relations between its two 'brows' were quite good. Relations between external and internal orientations were also good – more like those in popular fiction than those in high literature. New Zealand culture was hybrid, existing both inside and outside New Zealand, and on both brows. It was indigenous but also part of a transnational network. The English language was one vector of the network, which could lead to America as well as Britain. The recolonial system was the other vector, and it led to Britain alone. I suspect that it was this intriguing hybridity that produced cultural overproduction.

Better British mythology, on the battle and rugby fields, had some capacity to make itself true. When Better Britons went to Old Britain to build careers, they sometimes carried an overt cultural cringe. But they could also see themselves as returning shareholders in, not visitors to, Old British culture. Some nurtured the conviction that, if anyone could beat the Old British at their own games – even the subtle games of Bloomsbury and the Cavendish Laboratory – it would be Better Britons. More surprisingly, the Old British sometimes seemed to agree. New Zealanders appear to have had almost a privileged access to the upper reaches of the British job market. They were believed to work hard, to be rich in initiative and ingenuity, and to cross class easily. This view persisted to 1995, in the *Sunday Times*, a major British newspaper.

> In a subtle, quiet, subfusc sort of way, New Zealanders have become our favourite, most admired people. New Zealanders in Britain are in unquenchable demand; the positive discrimination in their favour borders on the racist. In New Zealanders, it appears, we see a uniquely appealing picture of go-ahead Aussie can-do-ness, old-fashioned Scottish rectitude and clear-eyed Canadian freshness.[63]

In the early 1990s, New Zealander Bryan Gould came quite close to becoming leader of the British Labour Party and, therefore, to being Prime Minister of Britain. His failure robbed this story of the perfect ending. It is, to some extent, a story of *reverse* colonialism, and its legacies in the present are not all bad.

CHAPTER TWELVE

Life During History

When we think of New Zealand folk culture, we sometimes visualise people in funny hats dancing slowly around maypoles. We associate real folk culture or folklore with the far past, with ethnic minorities and with non-Western countries. In fact, folk culture is all around us, like air, invisible through sheer familiarity. The few New Zealand studies of the subject either postmodernise it into forms unrecognisable to most of us, or trivialise it into twee nostalgism – 'Boats and Blokes', 'Blokes and Sheds', 'Great Longdrops I Have Known'. Both approaches do have their virtues, but in the end folk culture is too important to be left entirely to postmodernism or nostalgism. Another problem is that much Pakeha folk culture seems also to belong to someone else, notably our Big Four Others: Old Britons, Australians, Americans and, last but not least, Maori. We can draw a certain amount of comfort from the fact that what we think of as theirs is ours too. Much of what we ascribe to Britain and America is in fact 'global culture', just like much of what Maori think of as Pakeha culture. In reality, both Maori and Pakeha have as much right to it as any other people. Pakeha – and those Maori who wish to acknowledge their European links – are also shareholders in what the last chapter described as Britonnic or pan-British culture, and indeed in Old British culture itself. It is just as appropriate for New Zealand archaeologists to sift through English sites for the prehistory of Pakeha culture as it is for them to sift through Pacific Island sites for Maori prehistory. Perhaps the maypoles *are* part of our folklore after all.

We can also draw comfort, perhaps, from the strong possibility that there is a unique dimension to Pakeha folk culture, as well as a shared one. It may only be subtly different from Australian, but it is – and has long been – different enough from Old British to shock Old Britons expecting 'the Britain of the South'. After World War Two, as we shall see, a number of Old Britons put the matter to the test by migrating to small New Zealand communities. For Londoners resettled in Putaruru, the notion that New Zealand was just another England did not last long. How were you to know that 'tramping in

346

the bush' meant hiking in the woods? You might hear 70 different colloquialisms for sheep and almost as many for sheepdogs, wonder why people laughed when you took an empty plate to a social function as instructed, and be kicked out of the pub at 6 pm while still wondering what 'Giz a chug' meant. (It means 'Please give me a two-pint jug of beer'.) In 1988, a government *Guidebook for New Settlers* tried gallantly to save new immigrants similar troubles. 'BYO', 'shouts', 'rounds' and 'going Dutch' were defined, as were 'pot-luck dinners'. They were warned that 'some New Zealanders may not be the open people you might expect', and that 'belching and breaking wind are not acceptable in New Zealand'. But the guidebook did not stretch to matters such as the nature of friendship, gender behaviour at parties, attitudes to work, and a persistent distinctiveness in New Zealand childhood.[1]

The chapter takes our customary quick cruise through a complicated subject, in this case Pakeha folkways. It does so by looking at some of the places in which it was practised: home and garden; shops, halls and churches; pubs and workplaces. The chapter focuses first on the 1920s–60s, the 'classic' period of Pakeha culture, during which the exemplary paradise relaxed into the 'Quarter-acre, Half-gallon, Pavlova Paradise'.[2] It then turns to the chrysalis phase of being Pakeha – childhood. Here, the chronological span is longer. We reach back into the murky depths of wild colonial childhood in the nineteenth century, and try to understand its partial taming in the twentieth.

Pakeha Folkways

If, heaven forbid, you were to place all New Zealand historians on the top of Mount Victoria in Wellington or Mount Eden in Auckland and ask them to name the most historically important building they could see, one at least would plump for the most common. Under the colourful patchwork of roofs that fills out the view between landmarks is New Zealand social history's most central artefact, the common-and-garden Kiwi House.

Between 1921 and 1971, the number of inhabited dwellings in New Zealand rose from 260,000 to 800,000. Numbers at the top and bottom extremes of the housing range, like the income range, were small. In 1921, only 4 per cent of 'houses' were huts of one room, in 1971 the figure was less than 1 per cent. Large houses of nine rooms or more also amounted to about 4 per cent of the total in 1921, and about 1 per cent in 1971. Throughout, the dominant type was a single-storeyed villa or bungalow with its own plot of land and three bedrooms. About 72 per cent of all houses in the 1920s and 75 per cent in the 1960s had between four and six rooms.[3] Apart from the bedrooms, the typical house might have a front room, known as the living room or lounge, and a large kitchen or a small kitchen with adjoining dining area at the back of the house. The kitchen was originally a detached or semi-detached building, because of the risk of fire. There would also be a detached laundry (or 'wash house'), a bathroom (at first not including a lavatory), a shed in the back garden and, increasingly, a garage. A frequent variant was the open porch, in which children sometimes slept for fear of tuberculosis, since closed in to make a 'sunroom'. The lavatory would have begun life deep in the back garden. Initially, it would have been a 'long drop' in the country, with a 'night-soil man' clearing it regularly and discreetly in the towns. Its smell might be concealed by a datura or 'lavatory tree'.[4] As sewage systems developed, it would have crept demurely up the garden to a detached position beside the laundry, finally making it into the house itself after World War Two.

Modern appliances moved unevenly into the Kiwi House. Telephones climbed from 81,000 in 1920 to 157,000 in 1930 – already equivalent to about half the number of occupied dwellings. The number of telephones exceeded the number of dwellings by the 1960s. Radio (and, a little more slowly, motor vehicles) followed a similar pattern.[5] Electric lighting was also common before World War Two, but whiteware (electric stoves and refrigerators) was rare until the 1950s. The meat safe, the pantry and the external delivery boxes for milk, bread and meat that you see in some older houses were displaced by the fridge, the woodpile by electric or gas cooking and heating. A survey of 450 'typical' dairy farmers' houses around 1940 found that nearly all were wooden, with most having four or five major rooms. The great majority had radios, motorcars and electric lighting, and 63 per cent had telephones. But only a quarter had electric stoves or electric water heating, and only 2 per cent had mains sewerage. The rest made do with field drains, septic tanks and 'cess pits' – the official name of the long-drop toilet.[6]

The plot of land, or 'section', traditionally extended to a quarter-acre, or 1,000 square metres. Overseas visitors are still struck by the persistence of these large sections and detached houses, even in large cities and poorer suburbs. The insistence on detached houses accounts for the geographical growth of Auckland, which is physically the size of cities several times its population. Many houses were oriented to the street, not the sun, and were quite open to it. 'They faced with their important rooms to the street regardless of where the sunny aspect might be.'[7] Fences, borders and hedges were token boundaries, not obstacles. The front garden and its path to the door were kept neat; growing fruit and vegetables and other economic activities took place in the back garden, though grass was the predominant plant. Even *Flower Gardening in New Zealand* (1919) instructed that 'the person with a quarter acre section should have as much grass as possible'.[8]

The Kiwi House exemplifies a number of themes that will recur in this chapter. One is the internalising of mores of the tight society. The three bedrooms are there, even in poorer homes, because male and female children had to sleep separately for moral reasons. The neatness of the front section and front porch, or verandah, was a tribute to social pressure: 'women competed to have the cleanest, whitest verandah floors'.[9] The president of the Christchurch Beautifying Society, founded in 1897, announced that 'a man who did not keep his garden tidy would be shamed into doing so'.[10] Such organisations helped stimulate a shift, 1930s–50s, from the hedged or high-fenced section, to a more exhibitionist approach – 'it was *public spirited* to expose one's garden to public view'.[11] More prosaically, tarseal reduced the need for a high barrier against road and footpath dust.[12] Most strikingly of all, the largest and best room in the house, the lounge or front room, was seldom used but kept inviolate for special occasions like visits from the local minister or priest. The ornaments on the mantle, and the mass-produced painting – a black horse and a white horse frightened by lightning was a 1930s favourite – and the covers on the sofa cushions were features of the parlour-shrine to respectability.[13] Front rooms were domesticity's temples, and a roast meal on Sunday was its sacred hour. They remained important family rituals even among those who did not take the religious aspects of the Sabbath very seriously. Kitchens were the focus of the house, not only for warmth and convenience, but also because of the sacrifice of the lounge to ritual purposes. On the other hand, close search would show that the tight society was not entirely uncontested. It might yield evidence of home-brew in the garden shed, comics in the children's bedrooms, and empty bottles of (brandy-based) Lane's Emulsion at the back of grandma's wardrobe.

One can read other kinds of history in the Kiwi House, including recolonisation. The Californian bungalow contested with the villa and cottage from 1910, and orange Marseilles roof tiles appeared by 1902, but there was a shift back to English styles in the 1930s. This applied to fixtures and fittings, which, like motorcars, were more American in the 1920s than the 1930s – the Ottawa Agreement of 1932 again.[14] The Kiwi House was quite rigidly gendered, its garden even more so. In the cities, the front garden, producing flowers, belonged to the woman of the house; the back garden, producing vegetables, to the man. On farms, women did both the vegetable and the flower gardening.[15] Women did virtually all the housework, strictly defined – even today they do twice as much as men, and three times as much childcare. But men contributed not only through wage packets, but also through a camouflaged category of male 'housework': repairs and maintenance of property and appliances, lawn mowing, vegetable growing, wood chopping. The backyard shed was a male domain, treasured in nostalgic literature today.

These bloke museums were full of things kept ostensibly because they might 'come in handy', but often because they had some resonance in memory. There is no doubting the male dominance of the tight society, but it needs noting that the home may be the site where this applied least. After all, it was the husband who had the shed, and the wife who had the house.

From 1911, most Kiwi houses were in towns and cities, yet even in these a kind of urban ruralism can be detected. Shingle roofing, bay windows and other design features of urban houses 'suggest rusticity'.[16] Backyard production was common, including vegetables, fruit, and poultry – half of which were still located in backyards in the 1960s, mainly for eggs rather than meat.[17] The mass poultry farming that then developed was not good for the birds, but it did reduce the smell of backyards and made chicken a routine meat rather than a Sunday luxury. Urban ruralism could still be detected in male popular culture in the 1960s, 1970s and 1980s, whose stock figures tended to be farmers or bushmen: Barry Crump's 'Good Keen Man'; John Clarke's comic television persona Fred Dagg: and Murray Ball's Wal in the cartoon series *Footrot Flats*. Interestingly, female equivalents – Ginette McDonald's 'Lynn of Tawa' and the Topp Twins – tend to be more recent and more urban.

Moving out from the house, along the Kiwi's customary trails (typically dusty and metalled before World War Two, and tarsealed with footpaths thereafter) we trace our way up the networks and foci of local community. Communities were more stable in the first half of the twentieth century than in the half-centuries before and after. In 1939, 80 per cent of soldier recruits from Otago and Southland had never been out of the South Island, and over 50 per cent had never left their home province.[18] The networks included roads, radios and telephones, and the more subtle wirings of human relationships and interactions. There was a preference for domestic technology, which enhanced the capacity to interact: telephones and cars came before fridges and stoves. 'Main Street' was 'the centre of community', with rail and bus stations, public park, shops, churches and their state-equivalent, the post office, which handled a wide range of business, including banking, as well as the mail.[19] The postmaster was the local representative of the state, just as clergymen stood in for God. If the community was large enough, there might also be a town hall, municipal offices, public library, police station, an RSA club and a public swimming pool. There might also be a cinema and a pub or two, but in the bigger cities these tended to shift 'into town' – into the city centre.

Churches, and the sports and youth groups increasingly associated with them, remained a key site of Pakeha culture, but in diminishing degree. Between 1926 and 1966, religious adherence in the main Protestant denominations fell slowly but steadily – Anglican from 40.9 to 33.7 per cent of the population; Presbyterian from 23.5 to 21.8 per cent; and Methodist from 8.9 to 7 per cent. Only the Catholic Church held steady and even grew a little, to almost 16 per cent.[20] Along with Catholics, women and rural people tended to be more religious, and some denied that churchgoing was decreasing.[21] In fact, in the big cities at least, the situation was even worse than the adherence figures suggested. 'A survey . . . of church attendance on Sunday, July 17, 1949, in Auckland city, showed that approximately 4% of the Anglicans, 32% of the Presbyterians, 26% of the Methodists, and 75% of the Catholics worshipped that day.' A similar survey of 1962 Christchurch put attendance at 11 per cent of Anglicans, 18 per cent of Presbyterians, 25 per cent of Methodists and 68 per cent of Catholics.[22] Except for the Catholics, these figures were even worse than those of 1926. The crisis in churchgoing came to a head in the late 1960s and is discussed in a later chapter.

Another site of Pakeha culture was the shop. Every small town, suburb or urban neighbourhood had its cluster of retailers: grocer, greengrocer, dairy, butcher, draper, women's hairdresser, hardware store, barber and tobacconist, and perhaps fish-and-chip shop. In the larger cities, these clusters were more numerous than formal suburbs, especially before cars became pervasive, and authority would try to impose a sub-suburban name. But to locals they were simply known as 'the shops'. The greengrocer, or fruiterer, would probably be Chinese or Indian; the fishmonger Greek or Dalmatian. The dominant gender of shoppers, except at the barber's, was female. The local shopping centres were typically accessed on foot and were therefore quite numerous. They were supplemented by mail-order retailing, travelling salesmen and occasional trips to town. The range of shops and services available locally diminished with the rise of the motorcar from the 1920s, which enabled people to 'go into town' more readily. The mass advent of the supermarket in the 1960s was another blow to local retailing.

From the 1920s, shopping in town increasingly involved department stores.[23] One chain alone – Farmers – opened 46 branches in the upper North Island in that decade.[24] It was entirely appropriate that recolonial New Zealand's largest urban retail chain be called 'Farmers'. Hire purchase arrived in the 1920s, but remained heavily state-regulated until 1983. Perhaps for this reason, perhaps because New Zealanders were more careful with their money, the local rate of hire purchase was only 40 per cent that in Australia and 12.5 per cent that in the United States in 1965 – when poverty was not an issue.[25] There was a related rise of newspaper and magazine advertising, mostly aimed at women. Men did shop occasionally, but it was seen as a threateningly feminising activity. Male-oriented sections of department stores were located close to the street, to allow for discreet entry and rapid exit.

Male-oriented advertising emphasised sport and smoking to compensate for what was thought to be the inherent effeminacy of shopping.

Fashion and clothing were commodified and romanticised. Middle-class men – and working-class men on formal occasions – stuck to their suits and hats. Better Britonism applied here, too. 'The makers of men's suits prospered because the cheap reach-me-downs from England were not made to fit the average New Zealander, who was broader in the shoulders than the average Englishman.'[26] Male hat-wearing is said to have diminished with the televised example of US President John Kennedy in 1960. Women could draw on new fabrics – rayon from 1921 and nylon from 1935 – and shorts and trousers for women did appear in the 1930s. But they, and stockingless legs with skirts, where not fully legitimised until forced into fashion by the exigencies of World War Two.[27] Stereotypes about romantic marriage and appropriate behaviour and appearance abounded in retail advertising, but it also left no room for doubt about which gender did the shopping. Postwar developments in female gendered culture and women's work are discussed mainly in Chapter Seventeen.

Waged-workplaces were primarily a male domain until the 1960s. Attitudes to work in the classic age of the Pakeha, 1920s–60s, show clear descent from colonial populism. This valued opportunities to adopt selected and adapted features of higher class cultures: having leisure; playing sport; hunting, shooting and fishing; eating prime roasts of meat; owning houses and horses (whose twentieth-century equivalent was the car). Overseas observers and irritated local reformers alike noticed an attitude of 'relaxed ease' in the workforce. The 'glide time' syndrome, whereby public servants came to work late or left early, was sometimes extended to arriving late and leaving early, and sharp practice was quite rife. Some state-sector examples are cited in Chapter Fourteen, but the tendency extended beyond the state: it was a feature of classic Pakeha folk culture. Petty pilfering was one form. In the early 1970s, a student working weekends at a petrol station was encouraged by co-workers to join them in taking petrol, cigarettes and sweets. He eventually succumbed, and one day was called into the office by the owner. He expected an embarrassing end to a promising career, but was instead congratulated for the greatly increased take on his shift. He had pilfered too moderately. 'Glide time' was also worked in the private sector, as on a building site where the labourers went to the pub whenever the boss was absent. A car-assembly plant, Ford at Seaview, dealt with lateness and absenteeism by paying part of weekly wages as a 'bonus', the whole of which was docked if a worker was more than four minutes late on a single day. The factory was generally highly supervised and regimented, with a strict ten minutes for morning and afternoon tea. Workers took revenge by 'spelling' during less regimented and more highly paid Saturday morning work. Workers spent about half their time sleeping in the cab of a brand-new truck. Take that, Fordism.

Yet New Zealanders could also work very hard when they chose to. Subunits in and out of the state sector could be very hard-working, depending on the extent to which workers identified with their tasks. Even glide-timers would rush home from their afternoon sleep to slave away for nothing on their homes, cars or sections. An earnest American visitor in the 1950s was bewildered by New Zealand attitudes to work. 'Why do New Zealanders, by American standards, display so little ambition, enterprise and initiative in pursuing a livelihood while exhibiting almost unbelievable energy, enthusiasm and resourcefulness in such pursuits as sport, gardening, and "do it yourself" projects?'[28] New Zealanders in Britain and Australia had reputations as hard workers – or perhaps as less lazy workers. The subtext here, it seems to me, was a populist insistence that there was life outside work. Unions had always defended time as well as money. There was a sense in which you were paid not for your work but for the deprivation of free time. Overtime, extra money for the same work outside normal hours, symbolises this. Employers were compensated to some extent by the expertise of a stable workforce, culturally oriented to being technically adept and in some degree self-managing. The ratio of managers to workers in the 1950s was a fifth that of the 1990s.[29] This may be behind the apparent paradox of a complacent workforce and an efficient economy, discussed further in Chapter Fifteen.

The managerial and owner-operator equivalent of glide time and pilfering was tax evasion, a traditional Pakeha art. Worker folklore may exaggerate this a little. One farm labourer was firmly convinced that his employer wrote off his liquor bill as sheep dip. But there was some fire under the smoke of urban legend. In the decades before 1984, tax rates reached up to 66 per cent, and those who could took their remuneration in forms other than wages. A senior executive might get one car for himself and another for his spouse. Only the former was arguably justifiable as a work-related expense. 'Perks' could exceed salary in a remuneration package. Rural tax evasion and avoidance had a gentler, older, rhythm. Domestic purchases went down as farm expenses; farm subsidies became household subsidies. No self-respecting farmer would pay normal prices for his petrol, even if he drew the line at drinking sheep dip. To avoid death duty, farmers would gradually sell their farms to their heirs, in chunks whose size was determined by the level above which gift duty was charged. None of their peers thought the worse of them, and the same was true of pilfering and glide-timing workers, as long as all these activities met the informal rules. Legal or formal offences were not social or informal offences, and the same was sometimes true in spheres other than work and tax. Other examples of legal crimes that were not considered social crimes include drunken driving, evading liquor-purchasing laws, bookmaking and, from the later 1960s, marijuana smoking. This demonstrates the limits of the tight society. It would be quite hard to find an adult male New Zealander who has never broken the law.

Another key site of male culture was the pub, and its cousins the RSA, the workingmen's club, TAB and the racecourse. The delights of the 'six o'clock swill' have been noted in Chapter Five, and there were other pub rituals: the free counter lunch (ended for financial reasons in 1939)[30]; the shouting of rounds (which recovered from its brief banning during World War One); and the radio racing commentary, which developed from the 1930s, immortalised by Rex Fairburn.

> They stood stock-still, their heads bowed in reverence, each holding a glass ... the voice of the priest was heard intoning the service. His nasal monotone, which was amplified to fill every cranny of the building, rose in a slow crescendo, to a crisis of religious emotion, and then sank again quickly ... Glasses were applied to the lips in an act of devotion ... The intense concentration of all present while the service was in progress, and the animated discussion of it that followed were strong evidence of the devoutness of these New Zealanders.[31]

There were no women at this religious service. The male culture that sloshed between workplace and pub was an interesting beast, with an ancient lineage, its own literature and both dark and light sides. Its archetype was the 'Kiwi Bloke', or 'Kiwi Joker', a man's man, bonded to other men through 'mateship' – an intense but sometimes restricted and ephemeral comradeship. The Bloke was typically single – or married but behaving as single, without the inhibiting presence of wives. The Bloke approached women either sentimentally, romantically in theory but often with crippling shyness in practice, or instrumentally, as sources of sex and housework rather than friendship. Moral evangelism's cult of domesticity, though mainly studied in terms of motherhood, was also an attempt to domesticate the Bloke into the Good Breadwinner, the Family Man. The 'Family Bloke' still doesn't sound right. The Bloke fought a losing battle against the Family Man in the twentieth century. The percentage of men 'never married' halved between the 1910s and the 1960s. The married Bloke salved this wound by whingeing about 'pushful wives': 'materialistic spendthrifts', 'talkative nags' and 'moralist prudes'.[32] But the Bloke survived in his citadels: bachelorhood, the pub and the bush.

The modern quintessence of the bush version of the Kiwi Bloke was the deer hunter, or 'culler', the new face of an old folk hero. Deer culling originated in 1930, when the legal protection for deer was removed, and they officially became pests. The Department of Internal Affairs employed varying numbers of cullers to 1956, when the Forest Service took over. In 1967, it employed 120 cullers, and the total bag of deer between 1930 and 1970 has been estimated at six million. By the 1960s, however, cullers used helicopters and the classic age of the deer-culler/bushman was over.[33] It was this occupation that supplied the definitive voice of the Kiwi Bloke: Barry Crump, an uneducated young culler whose books sold over a million copies in New Zealand, beginning with *A Good Keen Man* in 1960. Crump had predecessors and successors, but the best known, such as Frank Anthony, John Clarke and Murray Ball, were actually only indirectly related. Their characters were comic farmers, gently parodied; Crump's were bushmen, and they were exalted as well as parodied. His deer-cullers, and the new North Island timber towns in which they had their payday binges – 'wild places full of hard men and women in the 1950s' – were residual examples of crew culture.

> The deer-cullers live the sailors' life – months away, lost on the deep ocean of forest, and then ashore for brief periods and into town with their pay cheque . . . to drink it all up in the pub and tell some boastful yarns about their bush exploits, make the acquaintance of some of the local ladies.[34]

Crump's most successful books were actually 'capping yarn' cycles, the characteristic oral literature of crew culture, first noted in New Zealand in 1773.[35] They drew on stories shared orally as much as his own experience. As a result, Crump's output after 1960–61 was both more sporadic and less popular than when his repertoire of unpublished oral stories had been fully stocked – even though some of his later books were actually better written. His publisher constantly complained that his books were too short, and tried to cover this up with large type and illustrative drawings. But the fact was that capping-yarn cycles were not the same length as novels. Crump's real predecessors were never published.[36]

Crump's writing and life epitomised the light and dark sides of the Kiwi Bloke. Male mateship has its good points: undemanding friendship; laughter; the psychological sauna of the pub, the hunt and the sports game. Crump's bloke had immense practical competence, disregard of material possessions, an ability to survive in tough conditions, a willingness to try anything, even if it was unconventional, and a rough-hewn wisdom and wry wit. The wit and wisdom, which require an audience, co-existed somehow with a liking for solitude and a dislike for the city. Crump was 'a sort of loner who prefers to have someone else around'.[37] Blokes also had a propensity to binge drinking, violence towards both men and women, misogyny and the use of physical escape – 'shooting through' – as the solution to all problems. The Kiwi Bloke 'eats roots, shoots and leaves'. Crump liked all children but his own, perhaps because they reminded him of mortality and the lurking threat of the Family Man.

Why were Crump's books so staggeringly popular in the 1960s? Australian historians have debated the role of the 'Australian legend' of the bushman motif in their culture. Some argue that, from the 1890s, urban intellectuals used it to construct a nationalist Australian archetype, independent of their version of recolonial culture. Crump, perhaps, was expressing a hitherto-oral version of something similar. But he was doing it much later, he was doing it himself and he was appealing to popular culture rather than the literati. Just as Australia's Henry Lawson did time in New Zealand, Crump did time in Australia – crocodile hunting among other things in the rough and tough Queensland settlement of Cooktown. Crump and Cooktown got on very well with each other. Crump could match his Aussie mates in bush skills, bullshit and bombast, and even in misogyny. But the fit was not perfect – it was that of cousins, not identical twins.

In any case, for New Zealanders in the 1960s, as doom clouds gathered over the recolonial system, Crump and his Kiwi Bloke reasserted a traditional New Zealand *distinctiveness* – a New Zealandness very different from Britishness, and even somewhat different from Better Britonism, into which the Family Man and Farmer Backbone fitted more easily. Crump's Kiwi Bloke pre-dated these archetypes by a long way. Frank Sargeson picked this up, simply after meeting Crump and before the latter had published anything. 'You know, that man's a living anachronism. He's like an echo of our past.'[38] The Pakeha cultural strand represented by Crump, his Kiwi Bloke, and their yarns survived the recolonial system, adapted to it, and compromised with it, but were not a creature of it. The first suggestions that Crump should read his *Good Keen Man* on the radio were turned down in the early 1960s on the grounds that his accent was too broadly Kiwi.[39]

The Wild Child and Its Taming

Between 1934 and 1954, New Zealand children grew substantially in height and weight. Five-year-old boys were 1.7 kilograms heavier, girls 1 kilogram heavier – babies boomed in size as well as number. Fifteen-year-olds grew an astonishing 12 kilograms for boys and 7.5 kilograms for girls.[40] This must surely have been due to earlier maturity as well as improved nutrition. Even before 1934, a 1927 survey had showed that New Zealand children were bigger and heavier than Old British ones.[41] To this day, a visit to Britain by a mature New Zealander seems to increase their relative size by about 10 per cent. New Zealanders did become Bigger Britons, if not better ones.

Modern New Zealand children are physically well developed. But this is not yet true of their history.[42] Some use has been made of two models from the international literature, which at their simplest can be described as the Chattel Child of the nineteenth century and the Cherished Child of the twentieth.[43] The Chattel Child was repressed, overworked and often short-lived, and comprehensively subject to parental control. For nineteenth-century working-class children, the argument is, prevailing attitudes and economic conditions combined to create a childhood based on work and obedience with little in the way of overt affection. Parenting was stern and cold, and sometimes harshly oppressive. From the founding of compulsory education in 1877, with the pace picking up from 1900, the Chattel Child was progressively replaced by the Cherished Child. The change was accompanied by a huge improvement in children's health, education and general wellbeing. In the first half of the century, the child was 'cherished' by society at large, as a crucial form of 'social capital', the soldiers and citizens, wives and mothers of the future. From about 1945, the child was overtly cherished by the family as well, as a 'psychological being'. Adoption replaced orphanages, the carrot replaced the stick, and Dr Spock replaced Dr Truby King.

The Chattel Child certainly existed in nineteenth-century New Zealand, a society not given to sparing the rod and with a considerable demand for child labour. But I doubt that it was dominant. The Chattel Child idea buys in to what I suspect is an exaggerated international picture of childhood as nightmare before the advent of benign modernity. Children were at best 'luxury objects' or 'superior pets'; at worst 'not even regarded as human'. Parents, claims one scholar, 'routinely resolved their anxieties about taking care of their children by killing them'. Infant mortality rates of 60 per cent by the age of two have been suggested. There was 'a lack of toleration for any assertion of the autonomy of the child'.[44]

The New Zealand Chattel Child seems to echo this lurid historiography, and there is all too large a kernel of truth in it. One eighteenth-century British baby, ten months old, was whipped regularly for frolicking in bed. There was a persisting concept that saw the baby as proto-human chrysalis, to be kept quiet with tight swaddling clothes and extract of opium until it opened into a Little Adult, who worked, prayed, drank and dressed like everybody else. There was also the old Puritan concept of Devil Child, steeped in Original Sin, on whom the rod should not be spared. 'Iniquity is co-natural to infants', and parents had to 'break their wills'. The notion of children as natural savages who had to be tamed was quite widespread. 'It has been said that every child is born a little savage and has to be civilized,' remarked one expert, 'the process of civilization has not got very far with some.'[45] There was even a racial theory that argued that the foetus replicated the stages of evolution – polyp, prawn, primate, baby – making premature birth a horrifying business.[46] From the 1980s, however, overseas scholars such as Linda Pollock and Christina Hardyment have argued that the horror stories are exaggerated. 'The countless records of loving parents from Genesis onwards are ignored in favour of the sensational.'[47]

Behind some of the horror stories concerning childhood is the view that high infant mortality made parents reluctant to invest affection in what might be an ephemeral life. British scholars now discount this, and it seems to me that notions of 'the little angel only lent' might encourage parental affection rather than discourage it. The New Zealand evidence is that infant death caused great grief. Women's diaries, letters and memoirs interrupt their cheery tone for a grim chapter on 'death comes to our new home'.[48] It is true that, in Britain, the prospect of death was used to discipline children. 'The spectre of death was constantly used to frighten the young reader or listener into good behaviour.'[49] The logic was religious – children needed to abjure sin as soon as possible to have a chance of getting to heaven. Perhaps this did increase parental control over children. In New Zealand, however, though migrant children passed through a funnel of high mortality in the form of the voyage out, both religion, as measured by church attendance, and infant mortality were lower than in Britain. If the pairing of religion and infant death was important to parental control in Britain, then it must have had less effect in New Zealand.

Some adults in nineteenth-century New Zealand did believe that their children were wilder than British contemporaries. 'Even quite little things are pert and independent,' wrote Lady Barker, 'and give me the idea of being very much spoiled.'[50] In 1896, an Otago clergyman preached 'Obedience! OBEDIENCE! OBEDIENCE!' for children. 'It should be taught this lesson in unconscious years, and have formed the habit of obedience . . . long before it can reason.' This was the only way to overcome the innate 'evil tendencies and weaknesses' apparent everywhere.[51] A parliamentary inquiry in 1897 was told that young people in New Zealand were 'less moral than in England'.[52] Other observers felt that, at least below the upper classes, nineteenth-century New Zealand children were a wild bunch, and parents of tame children feared seduction by wildness.[53] Missionaries and settlers were anxious about the reverse conversion of their children into wildness by Maori schoolmates and playmates. This was not simple racism but a tacit concession that free Maori childhood might well prove more attractive to Pakeha children than parentally approved models.[54]

It can be argued that such perceptions reflect moral panic rather than actuality. But I think there is enough probability and evidence for a Wild Child model to displace the Chattel Child model for nineteenth-century New

Zealand, at least as a working hypothesis. One problem with the Chattel Child model is that it does not deconstruct the concept of parental control. While there is evidence of strict control in nineteenth-century New Zealand, it may have been sporadic and limited, aimed more at children's external world than their internal world. Children might be severely punished for not doing chores, being rude to parents, especially in public, for breaking or dirtying things, and for not being mannerly at mealtimes, but if they met this set of requirements, they were left to themselves. Control might be more coercive than in the twentieth century, but it was also less comprehensive. Parents rode shotgun on their offspring herds, ensuring that they did not stray into a quite limited set of transgressions, but without huge concern about what went on *inside* the herd – in part simply because the herds were bigger, and because there were fewer tools of indoctrination. There was clearly less adult control of children's play and socialisation in the nineteenth than in the twentieth century.

It is true that, below the top socio-economic classes, children's labour was more important in the nineteenth than in the twentieth centuries. Fathers' wages were often irregular, and women and children were key contributors to a family package of economic activities. Children helped with housework, farm work and in small businesses; they tended the cows, pigs and chickens, which were common even in non-farm households; they gathered firewood. They helped with the care of younger children. In towns, they sometimes performed regular or irregular work for cash, such as selling newspapers and running errands, or scavenged for scrap metal, bottles and rags to sell. In the country – and in small towns and the sub-rural fringe of large towns – they hunted, fished and gathered wild foods. Yet I think we need to qualify the notion of the child worker.

For one thing, scavenging and gathering activities merged easily with play. Such hunt pursuits were a key characteristic of colonial childhood; they went on without direct parental supervision; they typically involved two or more children; and they were as much play as work, perhaps more. Work closer to home was normally intermittent rather than constant. It was known as 'chores', and the very term implies something much less than a long day's work. 'Finish your chores and then you can go out and play.' Family work responsibilities varied according to age and order in the family. Young children, aged between, say, three and seven, old enough to be mobile but too young to be effective workers, were presumably more exempt. The eldest daughter and son had most working responsibilities – the former were sometimes virtually surrogate mothers. Younger siblings had things sweeter.[55] It may be that the Wild Child model applies especially to the younger halves of colonial families, who would not have existed at all in the twentieth century.

Several other considerations also count against the Chattel Child model. They suggest that nineteenth-century New Zealand was more prone to wild childhood than either of its two baselines for comparison: nineteenth-century Britain and twentieth-century New Zealand. The sheer number of nineteenth century Pakeha children must have reduced the potential for parental control and increased the potential for children's autonomy. Twentieth-century New Zealand families (until the 1950s) were less than half the size of nineteenth-century ones. In the 1870s, the average number of children was about seven; in the 1920s, about three. Lower-class families were larger still. One group of working-class mothers in colonial Canterbury averaged 9.3 children.[56] Colonial parents had at most half the time for child control as their twentieth-century successors. Colonial children were much more likely to have been brought up by an elder sibling than were their successors, and had twice the number of potential playmates per policing parent.

Second, even the settled districts of nineteenth-century New Zealand contained much more 'wilderness' than their nineteenth-century British or twentieth-century New Zealand equivalents. Even in large towns, houses or clusters of houses were interspersed with empty sections, patches of bush, gullies and creeks. If children did manage to get away and play, there was more space available for them to do so, free from prying eyes. Here, hunt pursuits took place that were child-led but could merge work and play. New Zealand's lack of dangerous animals such as snakes may have made such pursuits more common than in other settlement colonies in Africa, America and Australia, where immigrants unused to the relative timidity of wild animals tended to exaggerate nature's peril. Prey included rabbits, birds and, later, possums and wasps, for skins, meat and bounties as well as fun. One boy made £1 a week from rabbiting in the 1880s.[57] Fishing, eeling, collecting shellfish and freshwater crayfish were also common, as was gathering wild plants. Unpoliced spaces included beaches, orchards, paddocks, abandoned houses and huts, as well as bush and the long, winding route between home and school. They were the sites of wild New Zealand childhood.

Third, even after 1877, colonial schooling was far from universal. According to one estimate, about 30 per cent of school-aged (six- to fifteen-year-old) children attended school in 1858.[58] By 1871, the figure was 54 per cent. It can be argued that these figures were quite high for a new society, where a school system had to be built from scratch and where settlement was often only loosely clustered. But, in contrast to the twentieth century, they mean schooling reached a bare majority of children by 1871, and fewer before that. Even after the introduction of 'compulsory education', around a quarter of children failed to attend. The attendance rate was 72 per cent in 1878 and 79 per cent in 1888, and did not really become anything like universal until about 1910.[59] What is more, colonial schools were more closely focused on the classroom than in the twentieth century. They seldom organised sports or social activities outside school hours; teachers stayed out of the schoolyard at lunchtime; and routes to and from school were also unpoliced. If parents did not constantly control children, the agencies for social or public control were fewer and weaker. Schooling had less wide and tight a grip; there were few youth organisations, little organised sport, and less indoctrinating children's literature. In short, there were more children to be wild with, more places to be wild in, and fewer means of controlling wildness. This does not prove that the Wild Child existed, of course, but it is not a bad start.

Direct evidence of wilder, or at least more autonomous, childhood, is to be found in the nature of children's play in the nineteenth century. The oral research of Brian Sutton-Smith, carried out in the 1940s, and recording memories reaching back to the 1840s, shows that the list of remembered children's folk games was far longer for the South Island than the North.[60] The South grew much less fast from the 1880s, and so maintained more continuity of transmission. Some ancient games, such as 'Bar the Door' (also known as 'King Caesar' and by several other names) knucklebones and being chased by a 'He' or an 'It', survived. Their status as folklore is camouflaged by their familiarity. Some games and rhymes inculcated adult norms, such as gender roles, and would therefore have been parentally approved, perhaps even parentally transmitted. Other amusements were more neutral, or even heathen and subversive. They are unlikely to have been parentally transmitted, but would have been passed on from child to child. This independent transmission implies a degree of independent children's culture, or subculture, capable of reproducing itself. The number of folk games played was much greater in the nineteenth century than in the twentieth. This in turn implies that children's culture was more autonomous early than late. There was admittedly a great growth of alternative amusements in the twentieth century, which may have led to children voluntarily abandoning their folk games. But many of these alternative amusements were adult-led.

Below the élite, the commercial toys available until the 1900s were few, simple and interactive – adjuncts for games rather than games in themselves. Knucklebones, for example, were to be had free from the butcher. You got your iron hoop for ninepence from a blacksmith, not a toy shop. Marbles were among the most expensive and therefore most cherished. The word 'bonzer', meaning excellent, derives from the name of a large marble.[61] Some toys, such as slingshots ('shanghais') and rag dolls, were home-made. Children tended to make their own games and their own fun, and some resented this in retrospect. 'One of the outstanding recollections is that practically *nothing* was provided to help us in our play.'[62] Others leached the fun out of their memories in the 'We had it much tougher in my day' oral tradition. In 1913, a writer commented sourly that, in his childhood, 'the modern feverish thirst for excitement and amusements was unknown . . . Young folks helped their parents in the housework and never felt the lack of picture shows and skating rinks.'[63] But fun there was, some remembered it, and it was available in some degree at least to girls as well as boys. 'We had more freedom,' recalled one woman of hunt pursuits in her childhood. 'It seemed like one long picnic,' remembered another. Colonial childhood involved 'a vigorous autonomy, a passionate excitement, and a furtive rebelliousness all at the same time'.[64]

Wild childhood had its less attractive side. 'Another common practice was inflating frogs with a straw, which were then floated on water or stoned.'[65] Mocking epileptics and harassing outsiders such as Chinese and Dalmatians was also popular. Tossing packets of gunpowder down lonely old men's chimneys was a great favourite.[66] Whether racialism was adopted from adults, or self-generated by children towards those who seemed different, is a moot point. Maori were less ideologically committed to racialism than Pakeha, yet petty persecution was practised by them as well. Two five-year-old Dalmatian girls going to school in Northland in 1913 were beaten for being different by older Maori school fellows.[67] Gangs were formed, and developed secret languages and initiation ceremonies, the later usually involving urine – that of your seniors, a horse, or your own, urinated into your own cap. An alternative ritual, in the Hutt Valley in 1900, was as follows. 'We would take the boys' and sometimes the girls' trousers [sic] down and spit on their privates.'[68] Kids will be kids.

There were stories of 'open warfare' between pupils and teachers – 'tales of flagellating teachers were legion'. A Takaka district legend dating from around 1900 tells of a four-year-old who was strapped 144 times by a sadistic teacher and died from the effects. This is probably untrue – 144 is a suspiciously ritual figure – but the existence of the legend hardly indicates much love of teachers. Several of Sutton-Smith's informants had memories of thrashed children rebelling, breaking the teacher's cane and walking out of school forever. They themselves never did this, but the prominence of the memory suggests they may have wished to. Documented rebellions included a riot at Mount Cook School in Wellington around 1880 in which a master had his arm broken, the principal was flogged with his own cane, and the police had to be called in. There was also a school riot in Christchurch in 1906 in which a principal was pelted with inkpots and slates, and then 'rushed' and 'downed'. Six pupils were expelled.

Milder forms of resistance included nailing fish under the teacher's desk; 'exploding gunpowder in the classroom'; and tacking a sign reading 'Mac is an Ass' to Mr McLeod's coat-tails. Pranks expressing contempt for the conventions being inculcated included arranging pegs to poke like a penis through wall charts; 'putting pins into other children'; converting 'far' to 'fart' in class songs, and a whole host of other jolly little japes. It may be of some comfort to modern teachers to know that today's class prankster has an ancient lineage. Truancy was an endemic problem, sometimes but not always associated with the need for children's labour. Uncovenanted holidays sometimes echoed the 'Saint Monday' customs of early nineteenth-century Britain. 'Seventy pupils succumbed to the attraction of the Fire Brigade procession,' read an 1895 school logbook; 'Fifty pupils absent at the races,' noted another, three years later.

Some folk games, such as 'Crowning' and 'Punch King', were very violent. Individual and group fights, often ritualised, were common. 'Individual fights were almost a daily experience' among boys on way to one school around 1870. 'Most schools . . . had a regular fighting pit.' Fights were sometimes 'arranged by the school bullies' – positions almost as regular as teachers, though informal. 'Small boys were made to fight for sport.' A teacher at Kaikohe in 1890 learned 'during the course of an incredulous investigation that every boy had to fight twice a week to retain respectability. Opponents were selected by a committee, and the fights took place on Wednesdays and Fridays.' There are other instances of organised or semi-ritual fights, including a few involving girls. Child-led group formation and rivalry, Us-ing and Them-ing, was sometimes associated with fighting. In Wellington in the1840s, Thorndon 'Sharps' and Te Aro 'Flats' engaged in ritual fights with real animosity. These home-made groups were common: 'Home Gully' versus 'Wet Gully'; 'This Valley' versus 'Church Valley', 'Reds' versus 'Blues'. When the adult community provided no factions, children created them.

Wild children had allies among other subcultures that diverged from official norms. Like crew culture, children's culture had strong sanctions against informing. 'Tell-tale tit / Your tongue shall be slit / And all the little puppy dogs shall have a little bit.' Both cultures were quite powerful in imposing norms, even on newcomers. 'Most of the play on school playgrounds was made compulsory by one's peers.' In both, there was an ambiguous, two-faced, element. The child had one persona inside house or classroom, and when engaged with adults, and another outside. Direct connection may have contributed to these similarities. Children acquired tobacco and new swear words from nomadic male workers, and admired their devil-may-care attitudes. But the fact that both children's and male cultures involved 'prefabricated communities' was probably more important.[69] Prefabricated communities have interchangeable parts in the form of individuals; a member of one group slots easily into another. Children could slot into a new school or urban street scene that had some familiarity, like sailors in new ships or labourers in new gangs. As with crews, children's prefabricated community had to impose its norms crudely and quickly, shield itself from outside sanctions with taboos against tale-bearing, and survive the solvent effects of colonial transience.

Wild colonial children were never the whole story, even in the depths of the nineteenth century. Parents did dominate child–adult relations – it was children's internal world that was wilder. Higher-class children were more decorous and controlled from the outset. But I suspect that a somewhat wilder childhood was a widespread experience. Recovering this is step one of an historical revision process. Factoring it back in to the mainstream of history is step two. It may be that wild colonial childhood helps explain two curious features of Pakeha history, outlined earlier in this book. One is the contribution of what we can now call 'wild childhood' to the emergence of the tight working class in 1912–13. This was noted in Chapter Four. The other is the possible role of wild childhood in populist feminism.

Although gender divisions existed even at the most informal levels, and increased with age, colonial childhood was at least a little gender-contested. Boys were quite likely to be brought up by older sisters, to have young women teach them at primary school, and to have girls as the brightest pupils in the class. They also played with girls, if only because families, small schools and communities lacked the numbers for separate group play. A missionary found her five-year-old son too 'fond of playing with the little girls, and such an admirer of everything they do'. Little Henry had to be taken in hand and taught to be a boy. Girls had to be literally constricted into girlhood through the ritual adoption of restrictive clothing. 'A common complaint among young girls at this time, forced into adult styles of clothing, was that they could not move their arms.'[70] Girls engaged in hunt pursuits for a period of their lives, and even in fighting and 'male' sports such as rugby and cricket. This persisted in small rural schools as late as the 1920s, when Sister Pauline O'Regan became one of the few future nuns to boast a rugby injury.[71] Infancy is often thought of as ungendered; there can also be a less gendered period of childhood, around ages two to ten, and this might have been unusually true of colonial New Zealand. This was a matter of degree, and it should not be exaggerated. Today's informal children's culture teaches gender roles whether parents and teachers like it or not, and no doubt it did then too. Gender divisions in informal games increased with age. Many girls' activities stressed marriage, homemaking and other values prized by adults; girls teaching themselves to be girls. Girls played 'Houses', 'Shops' and 'Dress-ups'. But girls also liked to play at being cats when no adult was watching, and they, too, participated in the initiation rituals and hunt pursuits of wild colonial childhood.[72] Might this little tinge of extra independence have contributed to New Zealand populist feminism, and therefore to the mass support for suffrage, to women's entry into uncovenanted work, and to the Great Mothers' Mutiny?

Wild childhood, of course, was very offensive to moral evangelism, which might tolerate the odd burst frog but drew the line well above spitting on privates. A whole series of measures from 1877 can be seen as an amorphous but vaguely unified effort to control wild childhood, to civilise the savage within. This important dimension of the crusade for moral harmony tried to convert the Wild Child into the Tame Child, a being much more useful to themselves and to society.

The introduction of the state education system in 1877 was an important first practical step. Attendance regulations and policing was progressively tightened to the 1900s, when the great majority of children were caught in the school net. Schools expanded from the 1890s, into organised sport, military drill and physical education.[73] In the late nineteenth century, playgrounds proliferated – fenced areas in which play could be contained and policed, spaces where unruly youth could be paraded and drilled. In larger, mainly urban, schools they were rigidly gendered by high fences. 'We grew up like two races apart. Consequently on the few occasions we did meet we were absolutely at a loss.' Playgrounds were often policed by child collaborators, monitors and prefects, who also began to proliferate. 'By 1908,' writes Sutton-Smith, 'most of the dangerous games had already disappeared, at least from the playground.' The playground had been 'domesticated'.[74] The cult of domesticity, with Truby King and Plunket at its centre, sought increasingly to structure motherhood and infancy, with spin-off implications for childhood. Plunket instructed, for example, that 'mental precocity, called smartness should be regarded as danger signals, and call for repression rather than encouragement'. Child welfare legislation restrained children, as well as protected them. Indoctrinating literature burgeoned, with School Journals and textbooks preaching patriotism and civic virtue from the 1900s.

Youth movements were important agencies of taming. Some, notably the Young Men's Christian Association and the Boys' Brigade, were religious. These organisations were established in New Zealand in 1855 and 1886 respectively, (female wings in 1878 and 1928), in each case some years after their founding in Britain. Less religious but more numerous were the Boy Scouts, established in New Zealand in 1908, the same year as their British origin. It quickly mushroomed to 15,000 boys by 1911. New Zealand Boy Scouting had its ups and downs, such as a demarcation dispute with compulsory military training in 1912, and a recolonial reassertion of the

British mother organisation's authority in 1923. Between that year and 1953, 'the New Zealand organisation was a branch of the Boy Scouts Association of the United Kingdom'.[75] But, in the long term, New Zealand Scouting flourished, especially after World War Two, and had 40,000 members by 1958. Its sister organisation, the Girl Guides movement, began in the same year and flourished likewise. By the early 1960s, the Scouts and Guides, and the Boys' Brigade and Girls' Life Brigade included 106,000 children. In short, the broad pattern for Scouting, and to some extent other youth organisations, was one of an explosive start in 1908–18, followed by problems and stasis in the 1920s and 1930s, and then by renewed strong growth from World War Two to the 1960s.

Founded by Boer War hero Robert Baden-Powell, Scouting preached military preparedness and moral and social harmony. 'It was part of Baden-Powell's talent that he could sell the virtues of submission to authority and self-sacrificing teamwork,' writes one biographer, 'unquestioning obedience to properly structured authority; happy acceptance of one's social and economic position in life; and an unwavering, uncritical patriotism.'[76] In his own words, B-P liked steamships: 'pounding out their work, all in order and exactly in agreement with each other . . . almost like gigantic boy Scouts', and bees. 'They are quite a model community for they respect their queen and kill their unemployed.' He also shared New Zealand moral evangelism's concern about masturbation. 'A very large number of the lunatics in our asylums have made themselves mad by indulging in this vice although at one time they were sensible cheery boys just like you.'[77] Like Frederic Truby King, Baden-Powell would wholeheartedly have agreed with a sentence written to the latter by Benito Mussolini: 'Our future is in the hands of the boys.'

Early Boy Scouting then, was a natural ally for dominionism and the Great Tightening in New Zealand, and this accounts for its initial explosive growth. The recolonial Tame Child took to its disciplines readily, but the colonial Wild Child did not, and both often co-existed in the same young skin. Too overbearing a militarism and moralism may help explain drops in Scout numbers in the 1920s and 1930s. My guess is that there was another strand in Scouting, which compromised with wild childhood by legitimating play. In 1909, a girl and her two brothers started their own Scout troop, for both sexes, with its own Scouts' Law: 'A scout always slams doors.' 'Our favourite game was stalking happy couples in the Mt Hobson reserve.'[78] Bush skills and collective fantasy had always been a part of Scouting. From World War Two, the compromising strand took the lead from the militarist and moralist strand, leading to renewed growth in numbers. We will see in the next chapter that a similar kind of compromise occurred in organised sport, and there were others.

Another key child-tamer was the commercialisation of childhood, which in the twentieth century became a major adult industry. Cheap mass-produced toys, sometimes mechanical, made their appearance from the 1890s, with a boost from the advent of chain stores in the 1920s. Expensive solid-metal toy soldiers had long been available to the affluent; now they were joined by cheaper hollow varieties, featuring the British army. Mass-produced child dolls displaced hand-made lady dolls.[79] Children had always had toys, of course, but earlier they had been more home-made, child-made, or tools for making play, such as knives, spades and iron hoops, rather than games in themselves. Collecting fads, for such things as postage stamps and cigarette cards, appear to have increased, as does pocket money. Pocket money may indicate improved parental attitudes towards children, but it also adds a control carrot to the various sticks. Cinema, regularly available in the main centres from 1909, was another carrot, as were sweets. The range of these available increased greatly between the 1880s and 1910s, and continued to increase thereafter.[80] Commercialisation bribed children rather than coerced them. It was adult-controlled, and in some respects augmented adult control of children. But, like Scouting, it was found to work best when it compromised with what children themselves wanted.

Wild childhood had its vices, and tamed childhood its virtues. We must beware of overreacting to the Chattel Child and other horror childhood models; of inventing lost freedoms to be nostalgic about; and of over-romanticising the underdog. Tamed childhood reduced the control of bullies and larger children over younger, though it increased control by adults. Twentieth-century children had more toys and more entertainment, even if it was made for them by adults, and they could pick and choose between adult offerings – often choosing those the parents liked least. They were also healthier and better educated. The difference between nineteenth- and twentieth-century childhoods was far from total; it was a matter of degree. When I first publicly discussed the hypothesis, in 1995, I believed that the Wild Child was mainly a denizen of the nineteenth century, with substantial residues to about 1920, and only minor residues thereafter. But the hypothesis prompted people to recount anecdotes from their own wild childhoods, 1920s–60s. They were a little tamer than my nineteenth-century examples, but not much – I was even informed of a residual case of frog-bursting. Even urban New Zealand was considered a safe place for children to wander alone in until the 1960s, and it still had considerable unpoliced space – the reserve, the empty section, the bush, the beach. Taming, it seems, was substantial but incomplete, and wild childhood persisted deep into the twentieth century. Like the Kiwi Bloke, it was an unofficial but distinctive strand of Pakeha popular culture.

CHAPTER THIRTEEN

Games People Play

Apart from history, there are only two spheres in which New Zealand has been a world superpower. One is the export of protein. The other is sport. New Zealanders held four professional world boxing titles in the 1890s; in the 1900s both their rugby union and league teams had the best of test series against both Britain and Australia. Small provinces had staggering records against touring rugby union sides: Taranaki beat Britain in 1888; Southland recorded eighteen wins against international sides between 1896 and 1979, including eight out of ten encounters with Australia. The national rugby league team won half its matches against the powerful Australians between 1908 and 1956. Professional athletics was quite strong as early as the 1870s. The walker F. S. Hewitt held a rather dubious world record in 1871 for the 880 yards. New Zealand's G. B. Shaw was British hurdling champion over 120 yards four successive times in the 1890s, and world record-holder over 440 in 1891. Sprinter J. H. Hempton equalled the world 100-yard record in 1892. Jack Lovelock, Murray Halberg, Peter Snell and John Walker made New Zealand strong in middle-distance running from the 1930s to the 1980s.

New Zealand women runners unofficially broke the world 100-yard record three times in the 1920s. The women's netball team became almost as internationally dominant as the All Blacks from the 1960s. Women long-distance runners won many international competitions in the 1980s and 1990s; 1952 Olympic long-jump champion Yvette Williams was New Zealand's 'athlete of the century'. New Zealand was periodically an Olympic force to be reckoned with in rowing, running, jumping, hockey, cycling, canoeing, equestrian events, swimming, shooting and yachting, in all of which it has taken gold medals. The country won ten golds at the 1984 Olympics, a remarkable achievement despite boycotts. The country is spasmodically strong in golf and skiing; always strong in lawn bowls and yachting. In 1953, a New Zealander, Edmund Hillary, was the first person to climb the world's highest mountain. His rewards eventually included appointment as ambassador to India. Sprinter Arthur Porritt, in 1924 New Zealand's first Olympic medallist, naturally became governor-general. New Zealand was world croquet champion in 1950.

Even cricket and soccer, the Cinderellas of New Zealand international sport, had flashes of glory early and late. The Canterbury cricket team beat Australia in 1878, despite a bag of 9–17 by 'Demon' Spofforth, and also beat an MCC side in 1906–07. Nelson beat Australia in 1881, and New Zealand has sometimes been competitive with the best since the 1970s. New Zealand soccer beat Australia two tests to one on its first international tour in 1922. It qualified for the World Cup finals in 1982, before lapsing back into mediocrity through maladministration, television indifference and its special role as a King Country of recolonisation, a retirement home for second-rate English players and coaches. Anthony Wilding, arguably New Zealand's greatest-ever sportsman, won ten Wimbledon titles at tennis between 1907 and 1914, including the singles four times in succession, 1910–13, and was half the Australasian team that won the Davis Cup four times between 1907 and 1914. This, combined with his personal qualities, his degree from Cambridge and his death at Ypres in 1915 as a captain in the (British) Royal Marines, made him the quintessential New Zealand gentleman. Proportionally, New Zealand's Olympic record exceeds even Australia's, another great sporting nation. It has been estimated that, between 1948 and 2000, New Zealand won 7.3 Olympic golds per million people, compared with Australia's 4.6.[1] This may not be the best national sporting record in the world, but in proportion to population it must come very close.

Why have New Zealanders been so good at sport? It happened early; indeed, the ratio of international success declined as other countries caught up and New Zealanders concentrated on fewer codes. One factor almost too simple to believe may be high-protein diets. As noted in the previous chapter, New Zealanders were bigger and stronger younger than most other people, perhaps almost as much in reality as in racial rhetoric. Other neo-Europes ate as much meat; few consumed as much in the way of dairy products. In 1927, the newspaper headline 'A SUPERIOR RACE' triumphantly announced the physical superiority of New Zealand children aged ten to fourteen over the other neo-Britains, except the fellow fatties of Toronto.[2] In sports where bulk counted and Toronto did not play, such as rugby and netball, New Zealand does appear to have had a nurtural edge.

Britishness, gentility and egalitarianism were also important. Britain, especially England, was the first place to organise, codify and proselytise sport. It was the place of origin of *Homo ludens* as well industrialisation. From the 1880s, New Zealand sought to be the most British of neo-Britains. Before this, the special relationship of New Zealand with gentility, especially marginal gentility, played a key role in the rapid introduction and organisation of many sports. The New Zealand Athletics Association founded in 1887, for example, is among the oldest in the world. Aspiring gentility found the playing field a good place to prove itself, and this attitude stayed with secondary schools even when their catchment spread to the middle classes from the 1900s. At the same time, the downward percolation of aspects of gentility and the strength of populism ensured an unusually wide participation in sport. This was probably a general neo-British phenomenon. The gentlemen of England played the gentlemen *and* workers of Empire, and often lost to the larger pool of talent. If moral evangelism was indeed a little more successful in New Zealand than elsewhere, this, too, may help explain its per capita advantage in sport, once the evangelists took organised games under their wing. But it may be that another dimension of influences was as important as all these factors. Sport in New Zealand was a means of expressing various collective identities that otherwise found it difficult to achieve recognition. This, together with the interplay of gentility, moral evangelism, gender and populism, are themes of this chapter.

The increasing importance of technology, money and numbers at the highest levels of sport may stem the flow of international success in the twenty-first century, but from the 1890s to the 1990s New Zealand was arguably *the* sporting country, in participation as well as success rates. In 1987, participation in major competitive sports was equivalent to two-thirds of the population, men, women and children, old and young, black and white. New Zealand rugby union ranks in socio-cultural resonance with soccer in Latin America and cockfights in Bali. New Zealand should be a world capital of the historical study of sport. It is not – almost as though sport is a religion too important for scholars to tamper with. Until recently, 'scholarly neglect' was something of an understatement. Of about 663 books published on New Zealand rugby between 1877 and 1985, virtually none attempts analytical social history. This appears to be largely true of other sports and of sport in general. The situation is rather like that of military, religious and local history, which narrow-minded academic historians avoid, and other writers embrace with narrow-minded fervour. The literature is vast, and some of it is good on its own terms; but those terms seem to preclude engaging with history as a whole. The situation has improved recently, but it remains fair to say that 'the historical analysis of New Zealand sport is still in its infancy'.[3] What follows is yet another inadequate attempt to guess into a gap – the gap where the history of New Zealand's interaction with sport should be.

Sporting Society

There is a sense in which class cultures form a circle rather than a hierarchy. The circle joins at the leisures and pleasures of rowdy lowest-class disrepute and raffish gentility, including drinking, prostitution, gambling and sport. The gentry, and middle-class respectables who adopted aspects of their culture, fished and hunted, making a game of what their ancestors had done for a living. This symbolised leisure and affluence, inculcated what were thought to be desirable qualities, and was also fun. For much of the nineteenth century, hunting, shooting and fishing were still the quintessential sports, and as late as 1904, books entitled *Sport in New Zealand* were likely to be about these pursuits.[4] In New Zealand, the gentry quickly lost their monopoly of these activities. Pig-hunting, duck-shooting and, eventually, even trout fishing and deerstalking were available to at least the rural masses. Democratisation was not complete. Well into the twentieth century, hosts of the Waikato Hounds, forced to chase hares by the absence of foxes, provided the traditional repast only to the social élite. The non-élite went home hungry, but at least they were there. Indeed, they were there as early as 1878, when 150 people at frontier Cambridge joined a hunt, well in excess of the number of available gentry. There were no kills because the dogs were distracted by the abundance of hares.[5] An important distinction between Old and New Britains was, and still is, that even workers can hunt, shoot and fish in the latter. The classes forget or at least conceal their differences and happily kill animals together.

This was a valued right and, combined with genteel sponsorship, it meant that moral evangelism had little to say to the traditional hunt sports, although morally and physically uplifting activities such as tramping and mountaineering did in a sense compete with them. These 'rational recreations' are discussed in a different context in Chapter Eighteen. Horse-racing was also protected from the reforming middle by the high-low alliance. Genteel presidents of racing clubs persisted well into the twentieth century; and the races flourished. The associated gambling was progressively and heavily regulated from 1881, but it was not eliminated.

Traditional blood sports associated more with the disreputable than the gentry fared less well, although it is not clear whether this was due to moral evangelism, a broader 'rise of refinement', or other factors. Dog-fighting, cock-fighting, and boar-baiting do seem to have made the jump to New Zealand – like foxes, bears and badgers were saved by their absence – but either they did not survive very long or remained well hidden. The same could be true of bare-knuckle boxing. This was common among crewmen in the 1860s, and was associated with heavy gambling. A London exponent of the art, Jem Mace, fought and taught in New Zealand around 1880, but he may have worn gloves. Prizefighting, a partly genteel but mainly populist spectator sport, was more enduring. It dates from 1862, and in the 1890s New Zealand had two world champions – one of whom, Timaru blacksmith Robert

Fitzsimmons, gained the world titles for heavy, light-heavy and middle weights.[6] Muscular morality, like its Christian ally, licensed gloved boxing, though it preferred and even evangelised the amateur version. Boxing, like billiards, was disassociated from gambling to some extent and became more respectable from the 1920s. The populist *Truth* correspondingly lost interest in both. From the 1960s, boxing increasingly became the domain of black outgroups, as in Britain and the United States. In New Zealand black boxers are mainly Pacific Islanders, not Maori, and they dominate the sport. Some are very muscular Christians, punching hard for Jesus.

Swimming was a problem for moral crusaders. Teaching and encouraging swimming was obviously a good thing because it lowered the death rate from drowning, the nineteenth-century New Zealand death. New Zealand has just about the world's highest ratio of coastline and riverside per person. Moreover, fads, science and even some versions of moralism increasingly associated sun and sea with good health. But swimming normally involved the removal of clothes, and such semi-civilised activities as playing about in the surf. Swimming had therefore to be accommodated and even encouraged, but also tamed, or gloved. Local ordinances, segregating the sexes and insisting on knee- or even ankle-length bathing costumes in public swimming places, did part of the job, and social attitudes did the rest. 'There was a prejudice against feminine participation in swimming carnivals.'[7] The vestigial skirts on women's swimsuits in the 1960s were physical residues of moral evangelism, functionless survivals like the tuatara's third eye.[8] As in Britain, public nude swimming was not quite stamped out. As late as the 1930s, *Truth* was indignantly exposing exposure at Wellington's Oriental Bay.[9] Surfing appears to have transformed itself from a disreputable and subversive activity to a socially-approved one around 1900. Surfers turned themselves into 'surf lifesaving clubs', a legitimate and even charitable organised sport; poachers into beach police. The modern sport of surfboarding, subversive and counter-cultural on its introduction from America in the 1960s, may be in the process of performing the same feat.[10]

Two clusters of genteel sport became organised and nationalised in the late nineteenth century. One, largely for men only, included cricket, rowing and athletics. Cricket was played in New Zealand in the 1830s. William Williams ordered a set of gear from England in 1833, and Charles Darwin watched a match in 1835.[11] Genteel cricket clubs formed in the 1840s; they were especially strong in Nelson and Canterbury, among the most English regions. Rowing clubs date from 1866; athletics from 1875. These sports came to be associated with a cult of muscular, athletic and Christian gentility that peaked in Britain about 1900, and was in turn linked to racial vigour, imperial greatness and provision of the leadership thought to be essential to both.[12]

The second cluster included sports played by both males and females: golf, croquet, tennis and hockey, whose organised forms date from about 1870, 1872, 1881 and 1890 respectively. Tennis was the quintessential court sport: it came from royal courts, was played on courts and was important in marital courting. It was seen as refined, perhaps over-refined. Working-class male culture came to associate it with effeminacy and the writing of poetry. These sports, along with most others, formed national associations between the 1880s and 1900s.[13]

Of all these sports, cricket came to seen as the most quintessentially English and genteel. The English game was run by aristocratic committees of the Marylebone Cricket Club (MCC) until 1968, a gang whose home turf is not called Lord's for nothing. The intriguing thing is that the sport was never socially exclusive in the strict sense, but incorporated class divisions – genteel batsmen and decent bowlers, Amateurs and Professionals, Gentlemen and Players, with different dressing rooms to 1939. In England, gentlemen led the game until the recent past; the national XI had its first professional captain since the 1880s in 1952.[14] This was a little less true of New Zealand. The colonial gentry ran the game in the nineteenth century, but the semi-professional bowler Alex Downes, an industrial craftsman by trade, was captain of Otago in 1910.[15] New Zealand cricket was not big or rich enough for full professionalism, and this presumably joined with colonial populism, egalitarianism and the gradual twentieth-century decline of the gentry to lower class barriers. Cricketing leaders in New Zealand were more cross-class than in England, and the wider pool should theoretically have provided better captains, but this was not so as far as teams as a whole were concerned. Cricket's grip on the New Zealand masses does not appear to have matched that in Australia or the West Indies. It did match England's, but England was bigger. This is one factor behind New Zealand's awesome lack of success in international cricket – no test victories at all until 1956, and not a lot until the 1980s. Other factors include climate, increasing displacement in public esteem by rugby union, and a recolonial tendency to look to England rather than to Australia for cricketing models.[16] For England, the incorporation of the lower orders into cricket, separately dressed or not, provided some insurance against defeat by the cross-class teams of Empire. For New Zealand, cricket could not be the national game, because we did not win enough.

In New Zealand as elsewhere, cricket and other genteel sports became tools of moral evangelism. It used them to inculcate team spirit and other desirable virtues such as 'manliness' and 'character', and in turn helped spread them from élite to non-élite, civilising the worker and taming wild colonial children. As in England, moral evangelists 'advocated taking sport to the masses with an enthusiasm equalled only by their missionary zeal overseas'.[17]

Church organisations and secondary schools were important vehicles of the spreading. Wellington cricket clubs included the 'Wesleyan Rising Stars' as early as 1874, and school principals such as J. P. Firth of Wellington College were important in disseminating cricket and other approved sports, especially during the great spasms of secondary school growth in the 1900s, 1920s and 1950s.[18] Sport also came to be linked with allies of moral evangelism: racialism and militarism. It was thought to enhance racial and warlike virtues as well as individual and social ones.

The marriage between moral evangelism and its allies, on the one hand, and organised sport on the other, was not instant or automatic. The shift appears to centre around 1900, rather later than many sources imply. In the 1890s, for example, policemen's involvement in sport was discouraged as disreputable; in the 1900s the police authorities began to look on 'manly' and 'amateur' sports with more favour.[19] In Hastings, rugby and other organised sports emerged from 1878; but the pattern was one of limited, largely genteel participation and spasms of enthusiasm followed by collapse. Rugby itself had to be 'resuscitated' in 1897. 'By 1905 a number of prominent tradespeople were convinced that football and cricket would keep young men "from hanging about the streets with their hands in their pockets". Until this time organised sport in Hastings had been largely the prerogative of sheep farmers and their sons and a few privileged towns people.'[20]

New Zealand sport was organised before 1900, but it was poorly organised, fragmentary and class-culturally contested. Many sports had dual origins: recent-genteel and ancient-disreputable. The latter aspect had to be tamed, converted and preferably forgotten. The disreputable parents of modern sport tend to be written out of sporting history, but sometimes their legacies persisted, like the heathen festival of Easter in Christianity. This case is made in more detail in the next section. But it is obvious enough in boxing, where the bare and dangerous fist lurks behind the padded glove. Many other sports had populist or even disreputable parents as well as genteel ones: hockey had shinty; tennis had rounders; athletics had picnic foot races; rowing had whaleboat races and carnival-like regattas. Even genteel cricket has skeletons in its closet. In the 1860s and 1870s, professional English sides were toured through Australia and New Zealand as public spectacles, fairground affairs, and heavy gambling was associated with the game – until the 1880s in New Zealand. In 1867–68, this contact process boomeranged back to England when an Australian Aboriginal team toured, giving cultural performances on the side – a dog was almost cut in two by a stray boomerang at the Oval, no doubt the last fate it expected.[21] Codification was incomplete – strong XIs played weak XXIIs, and round-arm, overarm and underarm bowling co-existed to the 1890s. This chaotic past, populist as well as genteel, had to be cleaned up in myth and actuality. Like boxing, most sports had to be gloved before they were of use to reforming society. Sport came from both the top and the bottom; what occurred between the 1880s and the 1920s was a middling process. It had mixed consequences for women.

Golf, croquet and tennis became organised early in the history of New Zealand sport, and gentlewomen were prominent in them. Women also featured large in cycling and swimming. But women's cycling was the domain of 'lady cyclists' to the 1910s, when it became less fashionable and more common.[22] Women's cycling does not seem to have become competitive; swimming did, in schools, by 1898 – in neck-to-ankle costumes, with male spectators excluded, and over a maximum distance of 50 yards. The key here was probably state support, perhaps motivated by water-safety considerations: swimming became officially bisexual because drowning was. 'By comparison with world standards, our women swimmers have a higher level of performance than the men.'[23] Leading swimmers of the 1920s included Gwitha Shand and Violet Walrond. In 1920, aged fifteen, the latter became New Zealand's first female Olympian, coming fifth in the 100-metre finals. She won many national and international swimming races, and at seventeen looked poised for more. But Walrond then retired from competitive swimming on the instructions of her father and coach. Competitive sport and public acclaim might be acceptable for girls but not for ladies.[24]

In team sports, there were unsuccessful female efforts to invade cricket, rowing and even rugby between 1886 and 1916. Women successfully entered hockey from 1889, and a national association was formed in 1908. Hockey is quite a dangerous sport, and some considered it 'too strenuous and unladylike for girls'.[25] But it became very popular at girls' secondary schools even so. Women's outdoor basketball, or netball, was introduced to New Zealand certainly by 1906, and perhaps in 1902.[26] Netball, theoretically a non-contact sport, was considered more ladylike than hockey, and was enlisted by moral evangelism. Some sources say it grew rapidly from the outset; others, more convincingly, date its burgeoning from 1926, 'the real beginning of New Zealand basketball'.[27] In 1924, there were 127 teams affiliated to the new national association, which implies little more than 1,000 players.[28] By 1954, there were 2,381 teams, and 11,000 in 1992, with 106,000 players.[29] The upsurge dates, I suspect, from the introduction of formal competition in the 1920s, hitherto considered unladylike. Ladies might not like competition, but populist feminism did. As in other spheres, moral evangelism had to compromise with populism to attract even a fraction of the masses.

A women-only team sport emerged in the 1920s or 1930s – the time and type of origin is uncertain. This was 'marching girls', the only New Zealand-originated sport, a favourite subject for leers and sneers. It has recently been pointed out that the sport had real benefits for participants in physical self-confidence, and that it did not discriminate for appearance. On the other hand, the administration of the sport was male-dominated from the formation of the national association in 1932 until 1959, and it was extremely militaristic – teams were called 'Brigadiers', 'Grenadiers' and 'Hussars'. It 'appeals to girls who might not be attracted to messier or more strenuous activities'.[30]

Overall, the successes of the female sporting pioneers were impressive; women's sport did make some gains and improve the quality of life for some women. In the 1890s and 1900s, for reasons discussed in earlier chapters, feminism, populist feminism, and their allies were quite strong in New Zealand. It was possible to hope that women might achieve some physical as well as political and economic emancipation. W. P. Reeves claimed that modern bicycles in the 1890s did more to free women than the vote,[31] and verses written in 1892 revealed similar sentiments.

> They tell me 'twas the fashion,
> O, long and long ago,
> For girls to look like lilies white,
> And sit at home and sew . . .
>
> Today the times have altered,
> And pretty Kate and Nell
> Are playing merry tennis –
> In sooth they do it well.
> They ride across the country,
> They climb the mountain side,
> And with oars that feather lightly
> Along the rivers glide.[32]

Yet the author of these lines might have been disappointed by the state of women's sport relative to men's in the next half-century. Women's sport made absolute gains, but it took much longer than men's in breaking out of its higher-class base, and it was less successful in achieving public support, mass participation and social and cultural centrality.

One of the few studies of women and sport concludes that the former did not see the latter as a means of 'any kind of role reversal with men. They simply enjoyed the novelty of physical exercise and believed that playing sport would make them healthier and fitter companions for husbands and children.' No doubt this was true at the level of intention, but sportswomen were 'perceived as a threat to the very structure of Victorian society'.[33] Victorian society had a point. Sport, like social drinking, asserts that there is life outside work and familial roles. It licenses fun and single-sex activity and bonding, and it does inculcate self-confidence. Moreover, it annexes familial leisure. Family members playing sport in their time off work are not performing tasks at home. In the nineteenth century, decent families, as against young singles, had little leisure for sport. As a family surplus of time emerged, the question arose of who should have it. Women may have made a bid for a share in decades around 1900, but if they did they were knocked back. Sport was clearly important for male culture in the twentieth century, and husbands and boys living at home had the leisure for it because their wives, mothers and sisters did not. For the lower classes, there was a tension between the rise of men's and women's sport over who would annex the new familial leisure, and it was male sport that won out. In 1924, males had about five times the sporting participation rates of females.[34]

Gender-contested leisure time was important for those who did not have servants. Only gentlewomen would have found physical exercise a novelty; housekeeping before the spread of domestic technology was comparable in physical effort to weightlifting. The present writer learned about the upper-body strength of old working-class New Zealand women when he once tried to relieve his grandmother of a very full coal scuttle. The notion of physical exercise as 'a novelty' hints that women's sport remained more élitist than men's, and this seems to have been true. Only four of fourteen substantial sports surveyed in 1924 had significant female memberships. They were tennis (41.5 per cent female), golf (42 per cent), croquet (98.5 per cent) and hockey (52 per cent).[35] Except for hockey, these were very genteel and respectable sports. Netball, it seems, did not yet make the top fourteen. Females were expected to abandon team sports at marriage to a much greater extent than men. Married netballers and hockey-players were rare until the 1970s. This was less true of tennis, croquet and golf players. Ladies and girls played sport before World War Two; generally speaking, women did not.

Women's sport was a four-cornered interplay between moralism, racialism, feminism and populism, with male and female populisms clashing as well. It can be argued that feminists used moralist rhetoric to subvert moralism. While such things as physical education for girls in schools were 'ostensibly aimed at race revitalisation', they were actually a 'convenient rationale for allowing girls the kind of physical freedom enjoyed by boys'.[36] This case is attractive but unconvincing. It is true that sport was said by some to improve women as scientific and race mothers; but it was said by others to ruin them, and overall official opinion appears to have tended towards the latter view. Physical education activities in schools, including swimming and group exercises, were licensed and encouraged, as was a moderate degree of participation in some team sports. But the options, like the clothing, were restricted, public and state support even for girls' sport was limited, and for women's sport it was weak. Sport was an area where authority could make its opinion count through the provision of facilities. Some girls' schools had strong sporting traditions, but boy's sport was clearly privileged in relation to them. At two pairs of boys' and girls' secondary schools in Auckland and Wellington in the 1900s, the boys' school had 31 times the sports funding and 28 times the playground space of the girls'.[37] The movement of young men from sport to France during World War One encouraged women's and children's sport to some degree, 'but it did not initiate a significant change in attitudes to women's involvement in sport'.[38]

Women's team sport was more dependent on sponsoring institutions – schools, teachers' colleges, and church organisations such as the Young Women's Christian Association; it was less deeply rooted in local communities. Sport became an increasingly important part of idealised New Zealandness between the 1880s and the 1920s; and their secondary role in sport made women more marginal in it. This combined with the cult of domesticity, a reassertion of limiting ideas of femininity, and perhaps with the puritanical element of moralism. Muscular female physiques were frowned upon; and my impression is that this was one of the formal views that did succeed in sinking its teeth deep into the informal public mind. The shift to less restrictive clothing was slower than the rise of organised sport. New Zealand women got the vote well before their English sisters; they got running shorts well after them.[39] There is, I think, an element of unleashing and backlash here. Another factor is that women were left out of New Zealand's great game.

Representative Rugby

New Zealanders whose memories stretch back to 1956 may remember that the country went to war in that year – not with the Egyptians over Suez, although that came quite close, but with the South African rugby union team. That the All Blacks should beat the Springboks in this series was a national obsession. The trigger was the 'national humiliation' of defeat, by four test matches to nil, in the previous test series of 1949, but the causes of obsession went deeper than this. Not all the people shared in it; some women and some immigrants ignored it, and intellectuals struggled to avoid seduction. But very many people did participate in a frenzy not far short of group hysteria. A recent history has concluded that 'a great national crusade arose spontaneously', not through media hyberbole.[40] Even traditional rugby history concedes that 'the whole country was worked up to the point where reason seemed to have fled and the sole ambition was revenge'.[41] New Zealand 'lost its sense of proportion on the tour'.[42] The South Africans, rugby fanatics themselves, were shocked by New Zealand's white-hot will to win. Their coach

Danie Craven, Godfather of South African rugby, a man with 'three tongues in his cheek' and the world-record in excuses for losing – eighteen – did get this right. 'You're wonderful until it comes to winning or losing,' he told New Zealand, 'and then, by God, its only one thing and that's winning.' New Zealanders in the 1950s were literally willing to put themselves on the rack for success in rugby. An aspiring but short Waikato lock forward in the 1950s had himself stretched regularly by physiotherapists in the hope of gaining height and making the All Blacks.[43]

From medieval times, the peoples of Britain played a ball game sometimes known as folk football. This is a misnomer because you were allowed to throw the ball and hit it with sticks as well as kick it. Some players rode horses, and polo, hockey and basketball as well as the various denominations of football can probably trace descent from this great amorphous ancestor, like mammals from some amphibian progenitor. Folk ball was very much a people's game, played by uneven communal 'teams' of up to 2,000, and feared by authority for its violence and potential for disorder. English monarchs banned it at least 30 times between 1314 and 1667, and as late as the early nineteenth century there was an East Anglian 'camp ball' match in which nine people were said to have been killed.[44] Clearly, folk ball was a natural enemy of moral evangelism, and, superficially at least, it largely disappeared in Victorian Britain with the general decline of rowdiness. Its demise stemmed from two broad sources: suppression and voluntary rejection, involving greater social control and taming into organised, codified and restrained team sports, in which mortal injury was not countenanced, at least in theory.

The second development started from the top: from the great public schools taken over by the aristocracy, titled and untitled, in the eighteenth century, such as Eton and Harrow. Codified soccer – 'Eton Rules football'– was their game, initially a *more* élite sport than rugby. The old public schools and universities dominated the Football Association, formed in 1863, and the FA Cup, from its inauguration in 1872 to 1883, when the weavers and tradesmen of Blackburn Olympic had the temerity to beat Old Etonians. Genteel soccer was willing to play the lower orders, but not to be consistently beaten by them. It opposed, then compromised with, the rise of professionalism in the 1880s, and retreated into its own amateur competitions. Rugby, the variant of football played in the 1840s at Rugby School and immortalised in *Tom Brown's School Days*, codified itself a little later than soccer, founding its union in 1871. It was the product of newer, less socially secure, public schools, although they were still genteel. Especially in south-east England, it was associated with aspirant gentility, notably the newer professions such as medicine and the more genteel business occupations such as banking. It was therefore more rigid in its defence of the central principles of genteel sport:

amateurism, 'sportsmanship', non-commercialism, an emphasis on player control, playing rather than winning, and the interests of players over spectators. A fifteen-minute 'scrimmage' in which you could not see the ball from the sideline was no problem in rugby. This rigidity led to the 'Great Schism', the secession of the Northern Union, later known as the Rugby League, in 1895. League was run by the industrial middle class but increasingly played and watched by workers. It was more tolerant of professionalism and commercialism.[45]

Among rugby union's defence mechanisms was the 'reductionist origin myth' that the game was invented in 1823 when William Webb Ellis picked up the ball and ran with it. Scholars now suggest that this story was invented in the 1880s. They also note the taming capacities of tamed sport, inculcating regulation, team spirit and self-restraint in the 'semi-savage' masses. Soccer was an extremely restrained game, in the sense that it forbade the use of the human's main instrument, the hands, like non-swimming fish. What they do not seem to note as clearly is, first, that rugby, in terms of participation, was less restrained, more violent and more collectivist than soccer – more akin to folk ball. *Supporting* soccer could be as unrestrained, communal and violent an activity as supporting rugby, or even more so, but *playing* it was not. Rugby was conceivably more attractive to a colonial populist culture that emphasised playing sport as much as watching it. Second, the early history of British organised sport seems to suggest that sport as means of expressing collective identity was strongest where formal identity was weakest. The public of the industrial and fast-growing north embraced league partly for its greater egalitarianism than union, but also perhaps because their newly large towns had few other means of communal self-expression. Wales provides a still more clear-cut example. Rugby union took over Wales quickly and deeply in the 1890s, just as the Methodist religion had done before it. Like Methodism, rugby in Wales burst the class boundaries of the English versions and became cross-class. Both religion and sport, perhaps, acted as proxies for an otherwise suppressed Welsh nationalism.[46]

This potted British prehistory of New Zealand sport gives us some clues about the rise of rugby in New Zealand. Types of football, which rugby books sometimes annex as proto-rugby, were played in the 1860s and 1870s. Rugby was brought to public-school equivalents like Christ's College and Nelson College by the old boys of English public schools. This myth of origin gives New Zealand rugby the correct bloodlines, and there is substantial truth in it. Both rugby and New Zealand were sites in which marginal gentility sought to assert and entrench itself. The aspiring and insecure New Zealand gentry opted for the matching sport. But this was not enough to entrench rugby as the 'national game', a label in somewhat premature use in the 1880s.[47] Prior to this, rugby was rather loose in its own habits. It was in roughly equal competition with other football codes, and football itself was only one of many roughly equal sports, which between them engaged only a fairly small minority of the population. Rugby history tends to write its dominance back into what was actually a contested and chaotic past. 'During the 1870s the sport suffered from misinterpretation of the rules, lack of attendance, shortage of players, and failure to start matches on time.'[48] A rugby game at Otago Boys' High School in 1871 'lasted about seven hours and was played on two successive Saturdays'. The balls played with before 1880 were sometimes suspiciously round; and Australian Rules was also a force in the 1870s. Christchurch Football Club, founded in 1863, did not adopt rugby rules until 1876. Rugby did not gain ascendancy over Australian Rules in Southland until 1879.[49] 'The formative years of New Zealand rugby were times of inordinate chaos.'[50] As late as 1900, it is not clear whether a game in which New Zealand troops at the Boer War beat a Canadian team was rugby or soccer.[51] There were four rugby clubs in Otago in the late 1870s, compared with five curling clubs in 1883.[52] The 78 rugby clubs in the whole country in 1879 mushroomed to 700 in 1890, though most consisted of only one team. Rugby achieved prominence in the 1880s; precedence in 1890–1910, and dominance by the 1920s. In 1924, it was incontestably the national game in fact as well as slogans, with twice as many club members as the next most important sport (tennis) and four times as many as soccer and league combined.[53]

The intersections between New Zealand, rugby union and marginal gentility were important to the rise of the sport, but represented only one of four prime causes. The others were populism, moral evangelism and recolonisation itself. The populist contribution, which has largely been laundered out of, or glossed over in, the official version, came mainly from crews and children. An old characteristic of crew culture was the eclectic enjoyment of sport, genteel or disreputable, played, watched or betted on. Goldminers in the 1860s played anything that moved, allegedly including quoits at £100 a side.[54] Crews were disproportionately young, male and team-like. Sojourning soldiers and sailors had access to genteel codes through their officers, and they were important in introducing cricket, boxing and football to New Zealand. Other crews also liked their sport; rugby became their favourite, and they were able to give it a push before they sank with the decline of progressive colonisation. The Armed Constabulary garrisons, lumbermen and other crew combined with closely concentrated dairy farming and with competing small communities to give Taranaki a headstart in rugby. This led to the triumph against an Anglo-Scottish team in 1888, and to a disportionately large number of All Blacks. Miners, navvies and timber and flax workers also played rugby. In the 1880s, rugby clubs included 'Thames Rough and Ready', 'Helensville Kauri Rickers' and 'Mabel Bush Sawmillers'. Rugby books ritually claim that 'history reveals that the game in the centres and cities followed some way behind the country'.[55] It is true that dairy farming was one stimulant of rugby but, outside Taranaki, dairying was not big until after 1900. There are signs that the camps and towns were at least equally important in the rise of rugby, which after all needs at least 30 males living within easy reach of each other. Town rugby stemmed not only from public schools and genteel clubs, but also from lower-class children.

The last chapter suggested that there were links between children's and crew culture, and some sharing of attitudes to sport bears this out. Children were also the bridge by which folk sports made their way to New Zealand. This does not feature in most sports books, but is demonstrated by the research of Sutton-Smith.[56] As early as the 1840s, children played rounders, tamed into tennis; shinty, a very rough game played with iron-shod staves, tamed into hockey; and folk ball, tamed into rugby. They organised their own teams, and some of these became rugby clubs. New Plymouth boys 'used to assemble in the evenings on the moonlight nights in various localities and play scratch games among themselves'. Their informal teams were known as 'Moonlighters', 'Irishtown', 'Starlighters' and 'Pirates' (a favourite name countrywide), and later became the constituencies of formal clubs. 'It is strange to note that although such intense enthusiasm existed among the boys of the town during these years the standard of the game with the senior clubs was at a low ebb.'[57] A similar development stimulated Invercargill rugby, which was initially almost synonymous with Southland rugby.

Relative egalitarianism and the expression of communal identity, discussed below, encouraged crews and youths to turn to genteel sports such as rugby, or at least to clothe their folk sports in the new genteel codes. But I think they were also attracted to rugby because it was relatively unrestrained, collectivist, and violent. The same factors at first put moral evangelism off rugby. It eventually turned to this sport, from the 1900s, as a means of social control and inculcating approved virtues, but this was in some degree a concession of defeat, and the moralising crusade initially seems to have preferred other sports. Reading between the lines of the rugby books, I get the impression of a three-cornered contest, 1880s–1920s, between genteel, moralist and populist rugby, with victory going wherever two opposed one. Gentility and moralism allied against rowdiness and full professionalism. Populism and moralism allied against social exclusiveness and in favour of improving the game as a spectacle. Muscular gentility and populism allied in favour of robustness, including a persistent degree of violence.

In 1877, a coroner commenting on one of a substantial series of football fatalities considered that 'the game of football was only worthy of savages'.[58] Others agreed, and the Welsh jest in *Hints to Rugby Players*, 'Hint One: Make your will', applied as forcibly to New Zealand. The rugby authorities had to work very hard to overcome its reputation as a brutal and disreputable sport, comparable to bull-baiting and cockfighting, and much more dangerous for humans. This would hardly have been necessary if the sport was of solely genteel origin. Muscular Christian gentility licensed restrained and 'manly' violence; it did not license riot and disrepute. Success in cleaning up rugby was slower and less complete than official legend allows. In 1892, spectators rushed the ground at a match in Gore, supporting a team composed largely of crewmen from the surrounding flax and timber mills. 'They assisted the Gore forwards in the scrums and picked up the ball to prevent the Pirates from scoring.'[59] Twelve players were severely injured in a Christchurch club match in 1896.

The unions sought to contain violence, clamped down on endemic betting, and in Auckland adopted the desperation measure of allowing women into matches free of charge, to raise the tone and 'discourage any kind of uncivilised behaviour'.[60] The formation of the New Zealand Rugby Football Union (NZRFU) itself, in 1892, can be seen as part of the clean-up campaign. It may be that these efforts had only limited success in the 1880s and 1890s, when there was a possibility of populist takeover and genteel withdrawal. The elements that left to rugby league in Britain were still present in the New Zealand game. University rugby, a stronghold of the genteel game in Britain and twentieth-century New Zealand, was very weak in this period. Canterbury University came last in the Christchurch club competition of 1893, despite the best efforts of Ernest Rutherford, and collapsed in 1897, before reviving in 1900 – the process euphemistically known in institutional history as 'going into recess'.[61]

Rugby history tends to read back the successes of the twentieth century into the nineteenth. But in the struggle to tame the game, the tide appears to have turned in the 1900s, as it did in sport in general. The surge in secondary schooling could have been an important factor in entrenching rugby's precedence from the 1900s. It may have been the major boys' secondary school sport before this, but there were not many boys at secondary school. The stamp of approval from the state and the moralising crusade also became unambiguous in this decade, but such 'top down' factors do not wholly explain rugby's success. The cross-class character of rugby preceded the twentieth-century penetration of secondary schooling into the lower classes. It also preceded the wholehearted adoption of the game by moral evangelism. Rugby's broad social grip was not taken by the top to the bottom, a gospel to the heathen, but came from top *and* bottom, and it continued to bear the stamp of both its origins.

Overtly populist rugby died hard, and covertly it did not die at all. Some clubs, and even whole unions, did not affiliate to the NZRFU, so evading its clean-up campaign. The Thames Valley 'Goldfields Union' held out until 1922.[62] The social activities associated with rugby are still more populist than moralist. Rugby was introduced into some mining regions of Britain to 'retard the drinking habits' of the workers, and this was a moralist motive in New Zealand, too.[63] In this respect, rugby has been a spectacular failure, and the campaign to limit violence was not a great success either. As late as 1917, eight players were knocked unconscious in another Christchurch club game, where teams 'played the man instead of the ball with a ferocity that would have been more appropriately employed against the ravagers of Belgium'.[64] Maori, Irish and worker teams were prominent in some particularly violent matches. English and Australian observers of New Zealand rugby – and rugby is the aspect of New Zealand society that receives most attention from those countries – regularly noted the ruthlessness of New Zealand play. This is a recurrent theme from the 1880s to the 1980s. Such comments are traditionally attributed to the whingeing of poor losers, but they are also a theme of such central New Zealand rugby books as Gordon Slatter's *On the Ball*. New Zealand rugby *was* relatively ruthless, hard, serious and even brutal, character-ised by the will to win, with little in the way of prisoners taken. There were an estimated 18,000 rugby injuries in the 1967 season.[65] In 1991, a player was suspended for one season for biting off an opponent's ear.[66] There was nothing genteel about this. The 10,000 scrums that pack down every winter Saturday are sixteen-bum salutes to a dual tradition, rough and tough populism as well as muscular gentility; ancient folk ball, crews and wild children as well as William Webb Ellis.

Having said all this, it is still possible to exaggerate the pervasiveness of participation in rugby. In 1924, the number of members of club and school teams was equivalent to about 20 per cent of the male population aged ten to 29 – large but far from universal. Horse-racing coverage overwhelmed rugby in *Truth* in the early 1920s; billiards, boxing and even soccer and hockey contested the minor placings with it. The organ of populism was more interested in pre-match 'high jinks' – a sporting euphemism for drinking, pranks, and sex – before the first test against the touring South Africans in 1921 than in the match itself.[67] From the late 1900s, rugby league proved attractive to some workers. League's rise is usually linked to the 'All Golds' victorious tour of Britain in 1908. The team was drawn from heretic union players, including several 1905 All Blacks. But a league match was played in Wellington prior to this, in 1907, attended by 7,000 people, and the rise of the rival code dates back to about 1906.[68] It is tempting to associate its sudden popularity in Wellington and Auckland with the simultaneous rise of working-class consciousness. Certainly, league sometimes operated as a denomination of dissent, like Catholicism among Maori in the mid-nineteenth century. On occasion, clubs in dispute with the rugby unions turned en masse to league, which quickly developed a 'reputation for flouting authority' and 'appeared to respond more slowly to the war crisis than rugby union'. It evangelised working-class Westland during World War One even faster than Methodism and union did in Wales. Conversely, the association with dissent 'nearly destroyed' league in Christchurch during the war.[69] Union was sometimes defensively paranoid about league but was never seriously threatened by it – at least until the rise of televised 'Aussie league' in the 1980s, a part of the recent revival of the Tasman world. What protected, entrenched and increased the dominance of union, and magnified its importance well beyond the numbers participating, was its role in collective identity.

Among the smallest and least formal of groups in colonial society were the children's gangs and proto-rugby clubs noted above. These split the people of a single locality, as though new, fast-growing or changing communities have a natural demand for division, making their own Us and Them perhaps as some kind of response to change trauma. Sport seems often to clothe these informal factions, perhaps all the more intensely because they *are* informal and cannot be expressed in other ways. The Reds and Blues, Stars and Pirates of colonial New Zealand may have analogies as far apart as the chariot-race fans of old Constantinople, and the Australian Rules barrackers of new Melbourne. Some intra-community sporting divisions persisted and developed, and naturally this was especially true in the cities and larger towns. Most rugby clubs in multi-club towns appear to have been based on particular suburbs and the old boys of particular schools. In smaller communities, there may have been a trend, circa 1900, towards a single rugby club as transport improved, transience declined, and growth slowed. As elsewhere, people came to link the prestige and morale of the town to its achievements in the leading sport – one thinks of an FA Cup win boosting birth rates in English Sunderland in the 1970s. There was perhaps an element of substitution for colonial town boosterism. Striving to win the subregional rugby championship acted as a recolonial replacement for striving to become the London of the south. Amateurism combined with the continued limitations of transport to make national or even regional regular club competitions rare. This may have helped rural rugby. National club competitions naturally privilege city clubs. There was more room for farm-first mythology in the Southland and Taranaki representative teams than there would have been in the Invercargill Knights or the New Plymouth Raiders.

Regional rivalries were mainly expressed by representative teams rather than champion clubs. Full-scale regional rugby competitions are a relatively recent innovation – they were long thought to smack of professionalism. But regions played international tourists, toured themselves, had regular fixtures with rivals and competed for a challenge trophy, the Ranfurly Shield. A converted soccer trophy donated by a governor-general in 1901, the Shield was a stamp of official approval for rugby.[70] There was no state religion, but there was now a state sport. The Ranfurly Shield quickly became a central symbol of New Zealand regionalism, with contesting regions subject to intense 'Shield fever' and Shield challenges watched by huge crowds. Representative rugby was among the most important, perhaps even the most important, expressions of a New Zealand regionalism that had few other outlets. After the abolition of the provinces, local government was so fragmented into counties and boroughs that regionalism had a very limited formal existence. As in Wales, rugby acted as proxy for suppressed collective identities. The pattern in the formation of regional unions seems to reflect this.

From the mid-1870s to the 1880s, rugby unions expanded until they converged with the old provincial boundaries. Thereafter, while rugby probably remained the sphere in which the term 'province' persisted most, unions split to reflect the existence of outregions and natural shifts in regionalisation. The concepts 'Manawatu' and 'Manawatu rugby' had a strong correlation, with the incorporation and separation of Horowhenua perhaps mirroring the economic oscillation of that border region between Wellington, Manawatu and autonomy. Northland, or 'North Auckland', where unifying rail links remained sparse between the wars, had five separate rugby unions until 1922.[71] To this day, 'Northlander' does not imply the cohesion of 'Westlander' or 'Southlander'; subregions such as Hokianga and the Far North remain important; and such unity as this diverse region did develop owed something to the North Auckland rugby team. The history of New Zealand regionalism is probably better mapped through rugby unions than through official divisions such as land districts. 'Shield fever' suggests these informal regionalisms could be quite intensely felt, perhaps all the more because they lacked much formal expression.

Rugby provided an obvious metaphor for pluralist unity.[72] Clubs competed fervently, their best players uniting into regional and then island teams (for the annual North v. South match) and competing quite bitterly at these levels too. All then united into the national team. International success, which came as early as the 1880s, clearly helped in rugby's becoming the 'national game'. New Zealand national teams were first officially formed in the 1890s, and were confirmed as symbols of the nation by a triumphant All Black tour of Britain in 1905, in which a New Zealand team won 34 games and lost one, scoring 976 points in total, with only 59 scored against it.[73]

Seddon, of course, was among the first to realise that this was happening. He officially received a returning team in 1893, and turned subsequent triumphs into something close to state celebrations, leading newpapers to describe him as the 'Minister for Football'.[74] But other sports, such as boxing and athletics in the 1890s, and rugby league and tennis in the 1900s, also enjoyed success in international competition, and other factors helped rugby overcome their challenge. Its populist roots, its base as a local and regional expression of identity, its pluralist unity motif, and the fact that it was played more widely than other sports – throughout the nation as well as by the nation – were also important, as were wider historical trends. Rugby incorporated the notions of New Zealand military excellence, and racial homogeneity and superiority; it reflected and reinforced a twentieth-century reassertion of masculinity. It also reflected modern New Zealand history's master variable: recolonisation.

Cricket is the most English of games; rugby, one of the very few things that unite even Ireland, is the most British. 'The game of all games that calls for all the qualities that go to make a true Briton.'[75] There was an innovative strand in New Zealand rugby that might have produced a unique variant. But equivalents to Australian, American and Irish Rules football did not develop in New Zealand. A leading rugby historian bemoaned the fact that New Zealand had been 'the plagiarists of Rugby for too long'. It invented the 2-3-2 scrum and the wing-forward, refinements said to have speeded up and improved the game, then abandoned them under English pressure – 'but another example of New Zealand subservience to the Mother country'.[76] If there was an embryonic New Zealand Rules in the wing-forward and the 2-3-2 scrum, it was aborted by recolonisation. It was essential that Better Britain should beat Old Britain, especially at its own game. It was also essential that Better Britain should play Britain's game, rather than its own.

Like the Better British image in general, Old British acknowledgement of New Zealand rugby superiority ricocheted back to sender. The 1905 All Black tour had massive newspaper coverage in Britain, and record-breaking attendances at matches. All Black motifs were used in English advertisements rather like Maori motifs in Pakeha advertisements. The All Black victories were used by Old British commentators to point up an alleged moral and physical degeneration in the local manhood, first revealed by the Boer War of 1899–1902. There was an element of the Noble Savage technique here: using a benign 'Other' to critique flaws in one's own society, and to advocate their repair. British acknowledgement of New Zealand superiority was remarkably widespread, but it was not universal. The 1905 All Blacks did lose one match – against Wales – in 'the Gallipoli of New Zealand sport'.[77] After it, London's *Punch*, in a satire of the usual British self-flagellation over

All Black victories, suggested that the New Zealanders had 'become a race weakened by the enervating effects of the geysers', Premier Seddon's example of 'national obesity', and women's suffrage. 'When the women of a nation become men, the men are apt to become women.'[78] In New Zealand, this was not a joking matter, and *Punch*'s comments were culled out. New Zealand's use of its Old British mirror was selective.

By the end of the 1920s, even *Truth* had succumbed to rugby with the fanaticism of a convert, discussing it in a 'reverential language which saw rugby as some type of pseudo-religious activity'. The organ of populism had to concede that rugby had become part of the essence of Better Britain, proving both Britishness and superiority with every victory over fellow dominions and mother countries. Rugby continued to be used, certainly to the 1960s and arguably to 1981, to powerfully assert a strong and distinctive New Zealand collective identity. It was asserted against South Africa, Australia and even France, as well as against Old Britain. But the collective identity was not fully independent nationalism. How better to prove Better Britishness than by being better than Britain at the most British of games?

PART
5

Beyond Better Britain 1960s–2000

INTRODUCTION

In discussing the 'New Zealand Empire' in Chapter Seven, I did not mention its biggest bit: the Ross Dependency in Antarctica. At 440,000 square kilometres, the Dependency is much larger than New Zealand itself, and that is not counting 330,000 kilometres of ice shelf. New Zealand has nominally controlled this vast frozen tract since 1923, courtesy of Britain, but did not do much with it until 1957, when it set up a base at Cape Adare, later shifted to Scott Base in McMurdo Sound. A skeleton crew winters over at Scott Base, and a small stream of scientists visit annually (403 in late 1989 alone)[1], but otherwise New Zealand's biggest domain is uninhabited. The Ross Dependency is preserved from exploitation by its harsh climate and the Antarctic Treaty of 1959. But in the late 1970s, airline operators and tourists decided there was no harm in going to have a look. On 28 November 1979, one of these sightseeing flights, Air New Zealand's Flight 901, struck Mount Erebus, killing all 257 people aboard.

The Erebus disaster had its season of pain and fame, including a television mini-series and several books.[2] An investigating justice, Peter Mahon, accused Air New Zealand of 'an orchestrated litany of lies' in covering up the roots of the accident, which he argued lay more in Air New Zealand's procedures than in climatic conditions or pilot error. His view was rejected by the Court of Appeal, but opinion has since swung back in Mahon's favour. His 1981 report was finally tabled in Parliament in 1999, to praise from all sides of the house. This was little comfort to Mahon, who died in 1986. Like the Tarawera eruption of 1886 and the Napier earthquake of 1931, Erebus was a disaster great enough to fix itself in the minds of New Zealanders living at the time. Like them, it was a point where private and public histories intersect, and helps us mark out the advent of a new era.

This new era happens to include the present, and problems face historians when they encounter their own present. For one thing, we prefer subjects who are safely dead. In several New Zealand general histories, biting comments about politicians suddenly diminish once the politicians can bite back, and alienating living reviewers is even more dangerous. There can also be problems with impartiality, most innocently in the tendency to promote one's own present to decisive moment in history. Everyone is an expert, and existing studies include too much non-historical literature and too little historical literature. But the main problem with the history of the present is simply that we do not know what happens next. History needs retrospect, and the present does not have it. The reader should be warned of these dangers. But, for this history to be whole, the risks of contemporary history must be accepted. The following chapters claim that the recent past was a greater watershed than the 1930s or the 1890s; that it ranks with the 1880s in opening a new epoch of modern New Zealand history. They also argue that the role of government-led reform in this big shift is overestimated; that New Zealand did not reach full independence until the late twentieth century, and that it did so then only because it had to.

On 29 May 1953, New Zealand was on top of the world. An Auckland beekeeper, Edmund Hillary, became the first man to climb Mount Everest, the world's highest mountain. New Zealand chests swelled with pride. Hillary, announced the Acting Prime Minister, Keith Holyoake, 'has put the British race and New Zealand at the top of the world. And what a magnificent coronation present for the Queen.'[3] Forty-two years later, in 1995, New Zealand won the world's leading yachting trophy, the America's Cup. There was a comparable upsurge of New Zealand pride. Like Hillary, yachtsman Peter Blake became an exceptionally young knight. Britain and the Queen were not mentioned. In the 1950s, New Zealanders saw themselves as Britons too. In the 1990s, this was no longer true.

There were forerunners of this decolonisation of collective identity in the 1950s, and residues of its opposite in the 1990s. In 1953, Hillary had climbed Everest as a member of a British team. In 1958, however, he led a New Zealand Antarctic expedition that co-operated in theory but competed in practice with a British expedition led by Vivian Fuchs. In 1995, Blake's knighthood came in theory from the Queen, still New Zealand's nominal fount of all honour. New Zealand's head of state and its ultimate court of appeal (the Privy Council) still reside 12,000 miles away. But, while these and other residues are significant, and while a mature relationship with Britain could still be an important part of New Zealand's future, collective identity has shifted away from 'New Zealanders and Better Britons' towards 'New Zealanders' alone.

Right up to the 1960s, though there was arguably writing on various walls, the recolonial relationship with Britain had survived challenges and was still going strong. Britain was still the major source of imports, export receipts, investment, technology, culture and immigrants. The cars in the street were British, as were the postage stamps and the governor-general. As we have seen, the foreign policy of both parties could still be summed up as 'Where Britain goes, we go', and Britain still took over half of New Zealand's exports. The Australian connection remained largely dormant, especially in terms of trade. The American alliance was increasing in importance but was still seen as supplementary. Recolonisation, the four harmonies and the protein industry still dominated internal politics and economics. By year 2000, though residues remained, recolonisation was closer to gone than going. The American alliance had grown quickly in importance from 1965, only to bite the dust in 1985, while the Tasman world had revived. The British alliance weakened from the early 1970s and virtually disappeared in the late 1980s. Furthermore, Britain was no longer the destination of most exports, nor even one of the top three, nor the source of most imports or even immigrants. It was no longer Home.

This massive transformation had cultural, social, ethnic and gendered dimensions, discussed mainly in Part Six. In economics, politics, technology, international relations and trade, the changes were also revolutionary, and these are the subjects of Part Five. Chapter Fourteen investigates one explanation of change – the '1984 thesis' – and explores dramatic developments in New Zealand politics and the state, mainly 1972–96. Chapter Fifteen investigates another explanation – the '1973 thesis' – and examines New Zealand's relationships with the world in recent times.

CHAPTER FOURTEEN

1984 and All That

If called upon to explain the comprehensive transformation of New Zealand between the 1960s and the 1990s, the words '1984' would occur to many. In that year, the reforming fourth Labour government was elected. It proceeded to comprehensively restructure the New Zealand state and economy, in the direction known as 'New Right', 'neo-liberal' or 'free market'. Its policies were continued, initially with enthusiasm, by the fourth National government of 1990–99. Between 1984 and 1993, these policies massively deregulated the economy, reformed the money system and sold off $13 billion worth of state assets – or at least sold off state assets for $13 billion. This book evaluates the great restructuring not only in terms of its effectiveness but also in terms of its responsibility for the great changes outlined above. Most analysts, whether critics or defenders of restructuring, accord it great centrality. Are they correct? Was 1984 the big turning point in recent New Zealand history?

My attempt to answer this question begins with an account of the period 1972–84, when the context for restructuring was created. This period can also be seen as one in which the recolonial system mounted its 'last stand', its rearguard led by Robert Muldoon. This stand was gallant in its way, but unsuccessful, and a process of unacknowledged decolonisation took place despite it. Post-1984 governments may have hastened the pace of this change in some respects and helped crystallise it in others. But they did not cause it, nor even fully recognise it. History has no single current, but its tides are usually too big for a few politicians to turn. With fingers and sledgehammers, Muldoon and his successors defended and attacked dykes that were already crumbling.

Recolonisation's Last Stand

In 1972, amid considerable rejoicing in some circles, the twelve-year reign of Second National came to an end. The third Labour government, elected in a landslide, was a compromise between old and new guards. The new guard represented a coming force in New Zealand politics and society, left-leaning university-educated professionals, products of a massive expansion of tertiary education in the 1960s. But these middle-class Labourites were young and they featured mainly on the backbench of the new government. The top positions were still in the grip of the old guard, traditional Labour politicians, men with blue-collar, often unionist, backgrounds. The Prime Minister and Deputy Prime Minister, Norman Kirk and Hugh Watt, did not have a tertiary qualification between them. In a nice recolonial irony, a minister of similar background, Sir Basil Arthur, happened to be a hereditary baronet.

Kirk, a huge, humane, intelligent but rather obsessive and solitary man, is still something of an enigma. He died after less than two years in office. Tragic though it is in its present, premature death is good for a politician's reputation with posterity. For supporters, 'Big Norm' was a new Micky Savage. For opponents, he was a 'brutal' debater who led New Zealand politics to new lows, forcing National to turn to a leader equally tough and ruthless – Robert Muldoon – as counter-Kirk. From an historical perspective, Kirk and his government seem to have been bewildered by major externally driven change. They took some initiatives in education, welfare and diplomacy, but these did not gel into a coherent strategy to cope with new circumstances.

Despite Kirk's premature death, it was widely believed that Labour's large majority of 1972 would take at least two elections to corrode. 'Nearly everyone saw Labour's young team as invincible.'[1] But the tidal shift of the 1970s was internal as well as external, and in electoral behaviour, as in much else, the game had changed. The third National government, led by Robert Muldoon, entered power in 1975 with the same large majority as Third Labour had enjoyed in 1972. This unprecedented electoral somersault was part of a vague but broad sense of tides turning in the 1970s, attested to by contemporaries and historians alike. There was 'a prevailing uneasiness in society at large'.[2] 'Many people sensed during the 1970s that something was wrong with New Zealand's economy, and there was a widespread general mood for change despite uncertainty as to what precisely should be done.'[3]

Despite the new volatility of the electorate, the third National government managed to remain in power until 1984. Labour actually scored more votes in the 1978 and 1981 elections, but their uneven spread gave National slightly more MPs. Muldoon was an appropriate commander of recolonisation's last stand. Deeply attached to Britain, suspicious of Americans and Australians let alone Asians and Africans, he was fully and explicitly committed to keeping New Zealand the way it was, and doing so his way. He was the first New Zealand politician to effectively exploit the new medium of television, and he used it to berate populist enemies: financiers, foreigners, immigrants and Reds-under-the-bed. An extremely intelligent man himself, Muldoon invited and reciprocated the hostility of intellectuals and radicals, so strengthening his grip on the populist mantle. This technique had previously been used by Seddon, Massey, Holland and Holyoake. If leftist stirrers and intellectual pointy-heads hate you, thought populist New Zealand, you must be a good bloke. Despite this, Muldoon was suspicious of the New Right more-market economic thinking that was becoming fashionable from the late 1970s, and was genuinely committed to the populist compact, sectoral harmony and the full-employment welfare state. But there was no surer way to enrage him than to acclaim him as a hero of the left. In latter life, he expressed bitter contempt for most of his parliamentary colleagues on both left and right. In 1990, he suggested that they be sold off as pet food, in the last asset sale, if this was not too unfair to pets.[4]

That Muldoon managed to generate real fear and hatred in his opponents, both within and without his own party, is an intriguing mystery. After his fall from power in 1984, and even more after his death in 1992, retrospective heroes emerged from the woodwork claiming they had never been frightened of him, but on the contrary had stood up to him. Overreacting to this contemptible chorus, a recent scholarly biography of Muldoon fails fully to explain why he seemed genuinely frightening in his days of power.[5] One reason – that the New Zealand system permitted a strong prime minister to dominate Cabinet, which dominated the government caucus, which dominated Parliament – applies equally to other strong prime ministers. Muldoon's extra role as finance minister, the keeper of everybody's purse-strings, certainly tightened his grip. But another factor, I suspect, was a certain mad-dog quality in Muldoon, including an inability to distinguish the significant from the trivial. He wasted his time writing insulting answers to insulting letters, and sending threatening telegrams to university lecturers who criticised him in their courses. He lashed out at protesters (on one occasion literally), parliamentary opponents and American presidents with the same vigour and disregard of consequences. New Zealand's totalitarianism, which was beginning to crumble anyway, had never been of the kind that allowed the Leader to send opponents to gulags or have them shot. But Muldoon could and would destroy your career if you crossed him, as promising politicians Colin Moyle, Brian Talboys and Jim McLay discovered to their cost. Two of these, not coincidentally, were Muldoon's own deputies.

In essence, Third Labour and Third National faced an unravelling of the traditional system. A sharp recession in 1967–68 is sometimes seen as the beginning of the end, but the big shift really came from 1973, apparently triggered by two external events. One was the 'oil shock', which nominally quadrupled New Zealand's petroleum bill, and the other was Britain's joining the European Economic Community, which shifted the decline of New Zealand's British market from gradual and relative to rapid and absolute. Both events are discussed further in the next chapter. As import costs rose and export receipts fell, New Zealand's terms of trade deteriorated by over 40 per cent in the mid-1970s – similar to the decline during the Great Depression. It became increasingly difficult to balance the political economy's three core elements: the populist compact, the four harmonies and recolonisation.

As we have seen, the populist compact of the nineteenth century had been refurbished since World War One in two main ways. Massey had converted the populist demand for access to 'independencies', such as farms, into demand for access to post-primary education and home-ownership. First Labour had added a layer centred on full employment and social welfare. Third Labour paid due attention to the Massey version. Spending on education increased. Indeed, as a percentage of total government expenditure, it was higher than for the rest of the twentieth century.[6] The number of students in tertiary education continued to grow – a belated New Zealand engagement with a First World trend. But after 1975, the new students were to be increasingly funded at less than First World rates. Third Labour did represent the end of the golden weather in education at least. The government also paid great attention to housing. Under it, between a third and a half of new houses were financed by the state in some way.[7] Muldoon restrained growth in spending in both these areas, most readily in education – an important change discussed further below. He was less comfortable with reduced financial assistance for housing, but he managed it. 'Housing was one area in which the Muldoon government moved decisively to reduce the role of the state.'[8] People still bought their own homes with the help of private-sector mortgages, but it cost them an increasing proportion of their incomes.

Third Labour and Third National diverged on housing and education, but they were united on the need to maintain other elements of the traditional system. Ironically, Muldoon rejected the right-wing version of the populist compact, centred on access to housing and education, but was at one with Kirk on the left-wing version, centred on social welfare and full employment. Demography was behind two great problems looming on the welfare horizon. One was the increasing number of single-parent families, which needed state help to provide their children with anything like the equal opportunity promised by the populist compact. An emergency benefit for such families was introduced by Second National in 1968. Third Labour extended it to virtually all solo parents, and, grudgingly, Third National kept the domestic purposes benefit in place. The DPB was to become a favourite target of anti-welfare rhetoric, but its cost was dwarfed by the expansion of the number of older people entitled to superannuation, the second great welfare problem. Third Labour courageously attempted a long-term solution to this in the form of a contributory superannuation scheme. Muldoon countered with a universal non-contributory scheme, described by Keith Sinclair as 'the biggest election bribe in New Zealand history'.[9] The cost of superannuation rocketed from $200 million in 1972 (including the old age pension) to $2.5 billion in 1984.[10] Muldoon's scheme was staggeringly reckless, but it must be said that any government would have had to cope with the demographic fact of longer lives.

For Third Labour, Third National and the voters alike, unemployment was public enemy number one in the 1970s. This is remarkable, given the jobless remained less than 1 per cent of the workforce until 1978. It was as though an unspoken general agreement existed that saw rising unemployment as a harbinger of socio-economic doom even when its levels were very modest by the standards of the 1930s or 1990s. From 1978, however, unemployment became a real problem as a well as a symbolic one. Muldoon tackled it as aggressively as Kirk would have done: trimming but essentially maintaining the key import controls to protect manufacturing, creating job schemes and propping up farming, whose highs and lows were traditionally supposed to flow through to other sectors. External hammer blows to the economy, discussed below, meant that unemployment continued to rise despite this, from 0.4 per cent in 1972 to 6 per cent in 1984.

Like the populist compact, moral, racial and even social harmony began to fray in the 1970s. Muldoon was far less comfortable with this than Kirk, and the two took opposite positions on such issues as alternative lifestyle communities, Pacific Island immigration, Maori land rights and sporting contacts with South Africa. They swapped places on homosexual law reform, which Muldoon supported but Kirk did not. These issues are discussed in later chapters. Third National and Third Labour reconverged on sectoral harmony, which both strongly favoured. Apart from a decline in the size of the economic cake to be shared, two factors triggered an increasing amount of industrial friction. In 1968, the Arbitration Court announced a nil wage order and, although the decision was soon reversed, the traditional arbitration system came close to effective collapse. High inflation, which settled in for a long stay in 1971, encouraged, and was encouraged by, a continuing spiral of wage and price increases. But sectoral harmony did not collapse yet, because all sectors were keen on maintaining it. The reversal of the Arbitration Court's decision in 1968 was brought about by an unholy alliance between business and unions. Muldoon's bark was much worse than his bite with regard to unions. The number of working days lost to industrial disputes increased substantially in comparison with the 1960s, but remained modest compared with 1985–86. Sectoral harmony staggered on, but it became more ad hoc and less systemic, relying increasingly on such things as the gin-and-tonics Muldoon shared with Federation of Labour president Tom Skinner on Sunday mornings.[11]

Third Labour's and Third National's handling of international issues may also have been more similar than they seemed at first sight. Norman Kirk was keenly interested in foreign affairs, and he took a number of measures in the direction of independence. A small New Zealand contingent had been in Vietnam since 1965, fighting alongside the Americans and against the North Vietnamese and Vietcong. This was the first war New Zealand had fought without Britain since Pakeha–Maori conflict ended in 1872. But it was a transfer of dependence to America rather than an act of independence – a matter discussed further in the next chapter. Kirk withdrew completely from Vietnam in 1972 – combat troops had already been withdrawn by the National government the previous year. Kirk left New Zealand troops in Singapore, as a kind of token replacement for British withdrawal.[12] Communist China was recognised in 1973, but Britain had long since taken this measure. Overseas aid was increased, relations with Black Africa were improved, and New Zealand's sparse network of diplomatic posts was extended into the Middle East and elsewhere. Most spectacularly, a warship, equipped with a Cabinet minister, was sent into the French Pacific to ram home New Zealand's objection to nuclear tests.

But Kirk and Third Labour still held strongly to the British connection and to its increasingly important supplement, the ANZUS alliance with Australia and the United States. Its main effort in international relations, like that of the National governments before and after it, was the desperate struggle to preserve the British market. One commentator observed at the time that Third Labour 'was not nearly so innovative in the field of foreign relations as its spokesmen once proclaimed, and indeed still protest. Without the French to blast off at, Mr Kirk and his men would appear quietly and, I'm sure, efficiently orthodox.'[13] This may overstate the situation. Third Labour did mark a shift in the mood of New Zealand's international relations. But it was as yet more a matter of form than content.

In any case, Muldoon quickly reversed any independent trend in Labour's foreign policy. 'Muldoon was probably the last New Zealand prime minister to attach more importance to the relationship with Britain than his officials believed it was really worth in practice.' But it was Muldoon's view that counted, and his advisers were dismissed as 'a bunch of prima donnas and socialists'.[14] In 1982, the Falklands War broke out between Britain and Argentina, and the incident with which this book began occurred. It has been suggested that Muldoon's support for Britain in this war was cynically aimed at retaining access to the British market. No doubt there was an element of this ancient strategy in this last New Zealand backing of Britain. But Muldoon's commitment to Britain was genuine – and recolonial. 'No European Economic Community and no British or New Zealand government,' he wrote in 1974, 'will break the ties that bind us to the lands from which we came.'[15] 'There can be no doubt,' writes his biographer, 'that Muldoon genuinely wanted to align New Zealand with Britain over the Falklands issue.'[16] His aggressive attempt to 'humiliate' the Argentine ambassador was not designed to increase butter sales. For all his faults, Muldoon was neither a fool nor a lickspittle. He was simply the last of the Better Britons.

Third Labour and Third National converged more obviously in their economic response to the decline of the recolonial system. One shared feature was a sharp increase in state support for the farming sector. This had long been substantial, but from 1973 – arguably from 1967 – there was a change in kind as well as degree. All governments of the 1970s managed firmly to convince themselves that the decline in terms of trade was a temporary recession of a kind that had happened before. They therefore sought to encourage farmers to maintain, even increase, the production of goods that were becoming increasingly difficult to sell profitably. They did so through the usual raft of tax breaks, cheap loans and indirect subsidies, but also through an increasing use of direct subsidy, of which the most notorious was the 'supplementary minimum price' (SMP) scheme. Kirk had dubbed a precursor of this 'the family benefit for sheep'. But his government, too, rapidly increased state support for the farming sector, though Muldoon went faster and further.[17]

The basic approach of both National and Labour governments to the economic crisis of the 1970s was to try to grow the state as 'scar tissue' over widening wounds in the old system. Muldoon did take two small steps away from this path, but then took a large step up it, well beyond Labour. One step away was some cautious deregulation of the economy, in 1976–77 and 1982–83. These look limited in retrospect, even though they were coupled with a move towards closer economic relations with Australia in 1983. This move was one of the few policies Muldoon's ministers managed to push past him, despite his disinterest, if not opposition. The agreement was 'concluded despite [Muldoon] rather than because of him',[18] but it was to become significant after 1984. Muldoon's second small step away from the mega-state solution was to retrench, vigorously but briefly. Under Third Labour, state spending had rocketed from 30 per cent of GNP (only slightly above its 1949 level) to 42 per cent. Muldoon managed to bring it back to 35 per cent in 1976–77.[19] But he was unable to stop spending ballooning back up to its 1975 level by 1984.

Muldoon's boldest step down the path of increased state spending became known as 'Think Big'. Commencing in 1979, this programme sought to develop New Zealand energy resources and use them to boost or create large export or import-substitution heavy industries. One cluster of Think Big projects was based on the Maui natural gas field in Taranaki, which came on stream in 1979. The gas was used to produce petrol substitutes (liquid petroleum gas and compressed natural gas) and synthetic petrol (at Motunui), and to power ammonia-urea fertiliser and methanol plants. Other projects included a massive expansion of the Marsden Point oil refinery and of the New Zealand steel and aluminium industries. The idea was that Think Big would halve New Zealand's petrol imports, dig the New Zealand economy out of its 1970s hole and directly and indirectly create 410,000 jobs. Only the first of these objectives was achieved. Most of these projects were largely state-implemented as well as state-led. Their eventual cost to the taxpayer is variously estimated at between $7 billion and $11 billion, with the latter figure the more convincing.[20]

'Think Big' was not new. A desire for full industrialisation, as a symbol of economic maturity, dates back to the 1880s, as we saw in Chapter Two. The second Labour government and its leading economic adviser, William Sutch, had attempted something comparable in 1957–60.[21] The second National government had inherited some of these projects, such as a steel mill, which opened in 1965, and an aluminium smelter, which opened in 1971. It had also continued with the big hydro-electric and forestry projects of the 1950s. State-led efforts to reorient the New Zealand economy should not be dismissed out of hand. Arguably, the hydro and forestry initiatives were appropriately tailored to New Zealand's needs. But the Sutch and Muldoon spasms of Think Big were not. Sutch appears to have used an old British model of industrialisation, involving cotton and metal industries that imported raw materials from overseas and in which New Zealand's chances of competitive efficiencies of scale were slim. Some of Muldoon's projects had similar failings. Added to this was a curious paradox. Muldoon, among others, was firmly convinced that the economic 'recession' was temporary. Yet he was equally firmly convinced that the high price of oil, resulting from the initial shock of 1973 and a second shock in 1979, was permanent. Both assumptions proved to be wildly wrong. But the point here is not so much the failure of forecasts, to which all economists are subject, but the fact that the two forecasts were contradictory. Muldoon and his advisers believed that cyclical laws of supply and demand would right the situation for New Zealand's pastoral exports but not for its oil imports. Think Big, perhaps, was a proxy for things less rational than careful economic forecasts: a sense of change that needed shape, a sense of emergency 'akin to a wartime crisis', and a sense of inappropriate dependence on the oil-exporting countries. Depending on Britain was one thing; depending on a bunch of Arabs was another.

There is a certain amount of evidence of political expediency in the timing and structuring of some Thing Big projects. It was, perhaps, not only 'Think Big' but also 'Think Votes'. Muldoon did have his principles, notably a philosophical as well as pragmatic commitment to the way we were. But he was also a master politician, like Holland and Holyoake before him and Jim Bolger after him. Each of these National Party prime ministers, unlike any Labour Party prime minister, managed to win at least three elections. In the half-century between 1949 and 1999, National was in power for 38 of 50 years, and between 1949 and 1984 the discrepancy was even greater. Yet it was a truism among political scientists that, for most of this period, there was no great fundamental difference in policy or practice between the two parties. Each supported the recolonial system and its internal corollaries. Each claimed the populist mantle by asserting that it represented all sections of the community, not just a single class. The divide between Labour's state socialism and National's capitalist individualism was more rhetorical than real. Why then did National win so often? Was it somehow 'born to rule'? How did it become later twentieth-century New Zealand's default government?

The National Party had emerged from defeated Reform and the wreckage of the Liberals in 1936. Like its predecessor, Reform, it had two main philosphical strands: 'patrician' and 'popular' conservatisms.[22] To be successful in New Zealand, it was always the latter that had to take the lead. Popular conservatism was also more comfortable than the patrician variety about accepting the welfare state. Though farming and business made up the core of its support, this helped National to put together a much wider electoral alliance, involving the white-collar and small-business middle classes of both town and country, and elements of the rural and even urban working class. The populist compact, and the opportunity for class promotion that it promised, helped here too. People often voted on the basis of what they hoped to be, not what they actually were – aspiration voting. Hence Labour's difficulty in mobilising the whole of its 'natural constituency', the working class, who themselves made up a narrow majority of the population.

National was also favoured by the widespread sense that farming was the 'backbone' of the economy, even the nation. Curiously enough, farmer governments were seen as less sectional, less contrary to the populist compact, than worker governments. Between 1936 and 1986, 40 per cent of National's

MPs were farmers – hugely in excess of their share of the population.[23] Farmers directly represented a quite small minority of the electorate. They themselves were usually a minority, though a large one, even in rural electorates. But aspiration voting gained the support of the likes of rural labourers and sharemilkers. The backbone syndrome broadened support still further. Labour also tried hard to claim the populist mantle. From Savage to Kirk, its 'leaders have played down class divisions within society and stressed national unity'.[24] But somehow farmer governments were more convincing.

Another possible explanation for National's dominance of government in the second half of the twentieth century is conspiracy, corruption and undemocratic support from business interests, notably the newspapers. To some extent, this was the left's equivalent to the right's 'Reds-under-the-bed' conspiracy theories, with the CIA playing the KGB as sinister external puppet master. There were rumours that American intelligence agencies contributed to Third Labour's defeat in 1975, and even to the death of Kirk. Whether ugly Americans lurked in the background or not, National was explicitly accused of some 'dirty tricks' in this election. They were traced to 'some dubious characters on the fringes of the Wellington National party . . . [who were] in and out of property speculation, car dealing, massage parlours and nude parties'.[25] Associating National and nude parties does not seem intrinsically convincing. The same could be said of allegations of overt corruption, such as bribery, but in fact such allegations were scarcely ever made. Like the public service and Labour governments, National governments appear to have been virtually free of the odour of overt corruption. Here was one benign legacy from the tight society.

Yet the notion that various dice were systemically loaded in National's favour cannot wholly be dismissed. Media analysts are in general agreement that the daily newspapers were almost universally biased towards National, at least until the 1970s. The tiny *Grey River Argus*, which expired in 1966, 'was for many years the only Labour supporting daily in the country'.[26] State-owned radio, from 1935, and television, from 1960, counteracted this to some extent. There was also a low-grade, quintessentially Kiwi, semi-corruption, colloquially known as 'looking after your mates'. The New Zealand government had over 4,000 appointments to boards and the like in its gift. One National prime minister, John Marshall, conceded that 'governments of whatever colour tend to appoint their own supporters'. He claimed that he himself was an exception, which may help explain why he remained prime minister for less than a year.[27] Labour might, as Marshall suggested, have done the same if it had the chance, but it had fewer chances. For Labour Party stalwarts, there were first prizes only: gaining the nomination and entering Parliament. For National Party stalwarts, there were also attractive second prizes in the form of cherished appointments among other things. In 1964, National Party electorates averaged £42,000 in community grants from the government-controlled Lotteries Board. Labour electorates – which were generally poorer – averaged £13,000. Does one have to be a conspiracy theorist to find this fact hard to explain away?[28]

Larger and better grass-roots party organisation may also have contributed to National's lengthy reigns. This seems surprising, given that Labour was first in the field of mass party organisation. Its membership increased sixfold between 1935 and 1938, to 51,000.[29] But it was quickly matched by National, which had 1,000 branches and 100,000 members in 1938, only two years after its establishment.[30] Labour had union funding and support as well, and many National Party members were not very active politically. But they were active socially, organising dances, theatrical evenings and debutantes' balls as well as discussion meetings and guest speakers. By 1960, the National Party had 246,000 members and has been described as a very effective 'matrimonial agency' if nothing else. A drop in membership in the 1970s has been attributed to the emergence of alternative forms of entertainment.[31] Before this, believe it or not, the National Party was in some districts the best fun available. Labour's membership declined drastically in the 1960s, to 13,000 in 1969. Just how important this was electorally is difficult to say. But if it was important at all, it was National that had the numbers.

In the end, it could be political demography that best explains National's high success ratio, 1949–99. National voters were well spread, whereas Labour's natural constituency, the working class, was not only shrinking relative to other classes, but also continuing to concentrate in small urban electorates. Labour tended to win these with big margins, but lost more electorates with narrower margins. There was a case for aiming Labour policies more at the middle class, even at the risk of losing some of its 'surplus' working-class support. The Labour leadership was becoming more middle class anyway. The 1960s inclined a 'post-materialist' generation of university-educated professionals to pick their party on issues such as Vietnam, nuclear weapons, feminism and environmentalism rather than on the economic advantage of their class. Professionals such as lawyers and teachers provided a quarter of Labour MPs in 1957; three-quarters in 1984.[32] For Labour, voter 'misalignment' was most chastening in 1978 and 1981, when it won more votes but fewer seats than National. This was the most frustrating result possible, and it happened twice in succession. The need to spread the Labour vote to the middle class, as well as increase it overall, was a factor in the 1984 revolution in Labour policy – and, according to some, in revolution in New Zealand history as a whole.

Right Turn

Between 1984 and 1993, a series of dramatic government-led changes took place in the New Zealand political economy. The intense spasm of reform was triggered by the political demise of Robert Muldoon, who in June 1984 surprised all pundits by calling a snap election. Muldoon himself claimed the decision was forced on him by an MP of his own party whose willingness to vote with the Opposition threatened his narrow majority. Others attributed the decision to a moment of drink- or diabetes-induced madness on Muldoon's part. Another explanation, that Muldoon realised the country faced an economic crisis even he could not handle, is not very likely. Muldoon was not known for awareness of his own limitations. Whatever the case with the little mystery of its causes, the snap election not only gifted Labour victory, helped by a substantial third-party vote, but also enabled it to win without declaring a clear-cut economic programme.

Labour had scarcely begun celebrating its return from nine years in the political wilderness when it discovered a sting in Muldoon's tail. One Labour leader had foreshadowed an intention to substantially devalue the New Zealand dollar. Others denied it, but the need to devalue was as obvious to speculators as it was to most economic experts except Muldoon. Hundreds of millions of dollars fled the country to other currencies, their owners or borrowers hoping to profit by buying back in after devaluation. Both the incoming government and the public service experts asked Muldoon to devalue by 20 per cent immediately, as his last act as prime minister, to stop the flow. Against constitutional convention, he refused, or at least appeared to refuse.[33] King Rob was thought to have booby-trapped the command bunker before vacating it. After a couple of hectic days, Muldoon was forced to devalue by his own Cabinet, but not before speculators had set themselves up for a 20 per cent profit. This foreign-exchange crisis of July 1984 generated a sense of urgency in the first months of the Labour government, to which the pace and scale of the reforms it introduced is often attributed. Incoming Prime Minister David Lange went so far as to attribute their whole trajectory to Muldoon and the foreign-exchange crisis, but this is unconvincing.

Lange, a relative latecomer to Parliament, was clever and quick-witted to the point of brilliance, but without experience or a solid base of personal support. Until 1988, the government was in fact dominated by Roger Douglas, Minister of Finance. Even his mother would concede that, as a public speaker, Douglas was charisma-free. But Douglas had one characteristic exceptional in politicians: a preparedness to sacrifice his own political career to implement his programme. In addition to this, his lobbying skills were low profile but substantial, and his programme – more market, less state – was nothing if not coherent.

Douglas's policy involved the reduction and reorganisation of the state sector; deregulation of the economy, and comprehensive commitment to the free market. The policy became known as 'Rogernomics', after the 'Thatchernomic' and 'Reaganomic' policies sporadically applied before 1984 by British Prime Minister Margaret Thatcher and American President Ronald Reagan. As this indicates, Rogernomics was by no means new. Its rapid and comprehensive application to New Zealand, however, was new. Indeed, it was arguably revolutionary. Among critics at least, the term 'New Right revolution' is gaining popularity as a description of the changes made between 1984 and 1993.

At first, energy pent up under Muldoon and a global recovery led to a substantial if speculative boom. From 1984 to 1987, Fourth Labour found itself presiding over a volatile but generally buoyant economy. Inflation was rampant, peaking at 20.4 per cent in June 1987, and farmers, the first 'beneficiaries' of Douglas's removal of state benefits, were in the doldrums. Their net incomes declined by a third.[34] But other sectors boomed, including consumer goods, property, financial services, investment companies and, above all, the share market, which tripled in value, 1984–87. Labour won the August 1987 election, increasing its share of the vote from 43 to 48 per cent. Losses in working-class electorates were more than compensated for by gains in middle-class ones.[35] This was Labour's first back-to-back victory for 41 years. Two months later, however, the nascent new golden age began to unravel when the world's share markets collapsed on 'Black Tuesday', 21 October 1987. New Zealand share values dropped $10 billion in a single day, and continued to fall. The market, valued at $50 billion in 1987 before the crash, dropped to a low point of $14.5 billion in January 1991. Company bankruptcies climbed from 300 a year at the beginning of the 1980s to 2,000 a year at the end.[36]

The 1980s boom and bust of the New Zealand share market naturally engendered something of a witch-hunt. High-flyers such as Allan Hawkins of Equiticorp, who was bankrupted and imprisoned, crashed to earth, to a chorus of satisfaction from those who had previously worshipped them. Some deserved their fall. Shoddy practice in stockbroking firms, 'insider trading' and unprofessional and even illegal conduct in investment corporates was common. Burned shareholders reserved their most intense rage for villains close to home, but impersonal global forces also received their share of blame. It is true that New Zealand shared in a global crash in 1987, triggered as in 1929 by Wall Street. But there were some exceptional features in the local example.

First, as many commentators have observed, the New Zealand share market rose higher, fell further and stayed down for longer than those in comparable countries. New Zealand share-trading volumes boomed 100 per cent in the year preceding Black Tuesday. In Australia, Britain and the United States the figure was between 20 per cent and 30 per cent. 'The New Zealand market's performance in the year following the crash was the worst in the world.' There was no hint of recovery until 1991, with the successful public float of Telecom shares, and the market had arguably still not fully recovered as late as 2000.[37] Second, though the free market's first ventures had hardly been edifying, the government did not react much. Rogernomic reforms proceeded majestically through the debris of the crash. From 1988, they were without Roger himself, but this had nothing to do with the crash. Douglas was forced out by Lange, who had developed hesitations about the social impact of a proposed new round of reform involving a flat tax of only 23 per cent. The New Right revolution took little account of the present, let alone the past, in its quest to reforge the future.

Third, the boom and bust reached deep into the lives of many, not just a few speculators. The corporate cowboys were false prophets, condemned by the followers who had raised them up, but they were popular at their peak. No fewer than 900,000 New Zealanders are estimated to have owned shares – about 40 per cent of the adult population. 'It was almost evangelical.'[38] Virtually every adult New Zealander could tell you a story about somebody like the 28-year-old Wellington panel-beater who was a paper millionaire one day and owed $50,000 the next. 'Joining a share club or attending an investment seminar had become as common as buying a lottery ticket or going to the races.'[39]

The boom was a mass movement, and it was a curiously nationalist one. It may have been encouraged by a sense of release from Muldoon and the recolonial system, a strange nationalist euphoria or hysteria reflected in share-buying. The boom market suffered a substantial blip in early 1987, when the New Zealand yacht *KZ7* lost its America's Cup challenge in Perth. 'Remarkably, a twelve-metre plastic boat had carved 3 per cent off the share market's value.'[40] 'Corporate cowboy' attitudes clearly infected some more than others and, as in the 1880s, it tended to be those with the most New Zealand in them who were most infected.[41] By March 1989, the Bank of New Zealand had appointed receivers to 264 companies. Its competitors, Westpac, ANZ and the (British-owned) National Bank, were far less exposed, with 73, 47 and 23 receiverships respectively. The BNZ required expensive rescue operations from the state, just as it had a century before. Its subsequent sale to overseas interests means at least that this is one problem we will not have again. The number of shareholders in one of the most famous companies,

Brierley, rocketed from 12,000 in 1982 to 182,000 in 1988 – equivalent to 5 per cent of the total population. 'The shareholding of Brierley at the time of the boom relative to the population was way ahead of similar experience in any other country.'[42] Neither global trends nor rational actor models can explain New Zealand's particular experience of the 1980s share boom and bust. Like the electoral somersault of 1975 and the paradoxical reasoning behind the Think Big projects, it is evidence of mass change trauma and a widespread, but strangely repressed or mutated, surge of nationalism.

After the crash, Lange had at first reined in, then replaced Douglas as finance minister in 1988. Douglas was re-elected to Cabinet the following year by bewildered colleagues who wanted the best of both worlds. Unable to accept this, Lange himself resigned. The Labour government, now in disarray, went through two more prime ministers before going down to heavy defeat in the general election of 1990. Political changes did not greatly affect the direction of economic reform. Rogernomics survived Roger Douglas, and indeed survived Labour. The fourth National government, led until 1997 by Jim Bolger, spent 1990–93 implementing its predecessor's policy even more enthusiastically – and expanded it from economics to industrial relations, social welfare and political reform. Notably, it cut $1.6 billion from welfare spending.[43] The narrowness of National's victory in the 1993 election diminished enthusiasm somewhat, and its Douglas clone, Ruth Richardson, who had trumped 'Rogernomics' with 'Ruthanasia', was dismissed as finance minister. But the broad trajectory of government economic policy held good from 1984 to 1996. The introduction, by referendum, of proportional representation into Parliament for the election of 1996 can be seen as the last of the great reforms of the era or, alternatively, as a response to them – the voters' revenge on politicians they had come to distrust. It was arguably the greatest change to the electoral system since women's suffrage in 1893. For the first time since the 1920s, parties other than the 'big two' became forces in parliamentary politics. But this did not immediately affect the National Party's dominance of government, which persisted until 1999.

The range of reforms that made up the New Right revolution was substantial. Economic changes proceeded on three main fronts: financial deregulation and reform; state-sector reorganisation and reduction; and the ending of state support for industry. There was a comprehensive removal of controls on such things as foreign-exchange transactions, interest rates, overseas investment, banks and other financial institutions, and the share market. After the 20 per cent devaluation of 1984, the New Zealand dollar floated free from 1985. Over the next fifteen years it sank, swam, then sank and sank again. Tax reform began the same year, followed by the introduction of a goods and services tax (GST) in 1986. Income tax was reduced and simplified – a process completed by further measures in 1989. This shift towards taxing spending reversed a trend towards taxing income that had been in place since World War One. Even defenders acknowledged that this was a 'regressive' move, in that it benefited the rich more than the poor. But they argued that the closing of tax loopholes to which the rich had best access ameliorated this, and that increases in welfare benefits could compensate for it.

Another historic fiscal measure was the Reserve Bank Act of 1989. This charged the Governor of the Reserve Bank with control of the money supply through interest rates, making him to some extent independent of the elected government. This measure was not only designed to be 'politician-proof' but also to be narrowly focused on minimising inflation – since 1936 the Reserve Bank had been expected also to take account of other economic and even social factors, such as unemployment. The new role of the bank meant that the financial reforms were not so much total deregulation as mono-regulation, but by an agency partly insulated from government.[44] Both fans and critics of the Act need to distinguish between the principle of insulation from politics and the principle of narrow focus.

Change in the state sector was just as radical. One measure was the introduction of 'user pays', a major extension of part-charges for government services that was designed to discipline their use as well as to increase revenue. The very poor were sometimes protected from this by special provisions; the fairly poor were not. Like tax changes, this was regressive, impacting hardest on those least able to pay. The main reorganisations were the separation of the policy-advice and service-delivery functions of government departments; the splitting-up of giant departments such as the Post Office (which became Telecom, Postbank and New Zealand Post); and 'corporatisation', the restructuring of government service-delivery organisations on private-sector, market-oriented principles. Permanent secretaries became chief executive officers, with more pay, more accountability to their employers and more power over their employees. Critics might suggest that the pay and the power were less theoretical than the accountability. Some two dozen organisations were corporatised in 1987–88. 'The Labour government applied the corporatisation formula to almost every state activity with a conceivably commercial function . . . the early corporatisation policy was implemented virtually without debate. The public service was widely perceived as inefficient, privileged, and in need of a good shake-up, and no alternative models were being promoted.'[45]

The state sector was not only reformed but also reduced, for the first time since the immediate aftermath of World War One. The newly market-oriented 'state-owned enterprises' shed staff in thousands. There was 'a decrease in state employment of about 80,000, including 29 per cent in the core public service'.[46] Most dramatic of all was 'privatisation' or 'asset sales': the selling of state-owned organisations and resources to the private sector. By 1990, eighteen organisations had been sold, ranging from minnows like the Health Computing Service, which sold for $4.25 million in 1988, to giants like Telecom, sold for $4.25 billion in 1990. Raw resources, such as broad-casting frequencies and forestry and fishing rights, were sold off as well as government businesses. Asset sales were continued by Fourth National after 1990. By the end of 1994, returns from sales totalled $13 billion – not quite enough, taking account of inflation, to pay off the debt for Think Big.[47]

The third front of Fourth Labour's economic reforms was the removal of support for industry, the complex web of subsidies, tax breaks, government-supplied services and protective border controls built up by almost a century of recolonial government. Supplementary minimum prices for farmers were among the first to go, in 1984, followed by various tax concessions for agriculture in 1985, and cheap credit for producer boards by 1988. Monopoly rights and restrictions in the transport sector were removed, and export incentives and import controls were phased out, completing processes hesitantly begun by Muldoon around 1980. Tariffs were reduced and earmarked for eventual extinction. New Zealand's borders opened up to overseas goods as they had to overseas money. Complaints that New Zealand's competitors – in the shipbuilding industry, for example – were still state-supported went unheeded. New Zealand's adoption of free trade was unilateral.

If economic measures had not overshadowed them, Fourth Labour's reforms on other fronts would also have seemed substantial. Local and regional government underwent its greatest-ever reshuffle since the abolition of the provinces in 1876. Immigration restrictions were loosened; the deregulation of retail trading hours was completed; liquor licensing was opened up massively. Homosexuality was legalised in 1986. The Waitangi Tribunal was given teeth in 1985, when its capacity to hear Maori grievances was made retrospective to 1840. In international relations, old alliances collapsed and New Zealand's anti-nuclear sentiment greatly strengthened. The implications of these measures are discussed in later chapters.

The fourth National government, which came to power in 1990, is sometimes said to have been a major contributor to the New Right revolution, with extreme marketeer Ruth Richardson building on Douglas's start. Authoritative listings of the reforms suggest that this was not true on the economic front. Even by 1998, economic reform measures initiated by Labour outnumbered those initiated by National about three to one.[48] The New Right revolution was more Rogernomics than Ruthanasia. But Fourth National did entrench the revolution by making it bipartisan, and extended it or replicated it on the social front. It cut welfare spending, extended Labour's policy of 'user pays', and attempted to corporatise hospitals and semi-corporatise schools through 'bulk funding'. Its highest-profile measure was in industrial relations, where its Employment Contracts Act of 1991 left no institutional place for trade unions. Union membership halved from 45 per cent of the workforce in 1989 to 23 per cent in 1994.[49]

What caused the New Right revolution? It was, from most perspectives, a surprising phenomenon. It was initiated by a Labour government wholly against the grain of its traditions, and – until 1987 at least – without a mandate from the electorate. A leading economic historian, writing in 1982, had the misfortune to state that 'a Thatcherite solution to New Zealand's inflation problem is simply "not on"'.[50] In July 1984, it was still possible for another well-informed observer to conclude that Douglas's ideas, as published in a book in 1980, 'have not received widespread support'.[51] Yet not only was Douglas able to implement his programme himself between 1984 and 1987, but he also saw it continued by his successors from 1987 to 1993.

Various explanations of this sharp right turn have been offered. One centres on conspiracy, alleging a 'hijack' or 'coup' by the 'Rogernomes'. This is one context in which conspiracy theory is not automatically to be dismissed, although it must be noted that the 'conspirators' conspired according to their perception of the public good. A network does seem to have formed, consisting of small groups of politicians, centred around Roger Douglas; officials, centred around the Treasury; and businessmen, centred around the Business Roundtable – a coterie of business leaders that emerged in 1976 but was not formally established until 1984. In the 1970s and early 1980s, these groups began to have doubts about the trajectory of the New Zealand economy and to posit a radical more-market solution to its problems. The doubts were widely shared; the preferred solution less so. It was influenced by various more-market theories, notably those of Milton Friedman and the 'Chicago School', where a few of the 'conspirators' had been educated. Douglas himself was a relatively late convert, and Treasury is sometimes portrayed as the real villain of the piece, with Douglas as its puppet.

It is true that Treasury had come out on top in a shadowy inter-departmental struggle for pre-eminence. It played tortoise to hares such as Defence, Works and Foreign Affairs, and beat off the later challenges of the Prime Minister's Department and the State Services Commission. Treasury outgunned alternative sources of economic advice in sheer numbers of economists. It increasingly dominated the economic options placed before the politicians, and the number of options was increasingly reduced towards one. A 'conspiracy' of Treasury, Douglas and company, and the Business Roundtable might explain the consistent and powerful advocacy of a coherent more-market programme by potentially influential groups. What it does not explain is the acceptance of this radically un-Labourite programme by the Labour Cabinet and caucus, by the electorate in 1987, and by the National Party in 1990. Nor can it explain the fact that public criticism and protest was curiously muted. The mystery is not that Rogernomics was offered, but that it was accepted without very much of a fight.

One factor here was the political skill of Douglas himself. He realised that his programme had to be broad and fast to outflank and outpace backlashes. The breadth meant, in Douglas's own words, that 'individual groups lose their privileges but simultaneously they no longer have to carry the cost of paying for the privileges of other groups'. The speed meant that 'the fire of opponents is much less accurate if they have to shoot at a rapidly moving target'.[52] What is somewhat disturbing here is the possibility that the breadth and pace of change were set by the political needs of implementation, not economic or social desirability. Douglas was no doubt helped by the New Zealand political system's notorious shortage of checks and balances. In a small Parliament, a majority in Cabinet could dominate both the government caucus and the House as a whole. But Rogernomics was often supported by a majority of the Labour caucus as well as of Cabinet – in the vote on GST, for example – and, as 1990–93 was to prove, it was also supported by National.

A second explanation for the great right turn was a global shift away from 'neo-Keynesian' interventionist economics and towards more-market economics. On this theory, New Zealand merely participated in a worldwide change. There is obviously some truth in this, but it does not explain the extremism of the New Zealand experience. Under Muldoon, the country was exceptionally Keynesian, or interventionist. Under Douglas and Richardson, it somersaulted to the opposite extreme. 'New Zealand arguably presents the extreme case of policy reform and public sector reorganization among the developed countries in terms of the extent and speed of policy and institutional changes.'[53] 'Economic restructuring was far more radical in New Zealand than in other democracies.'[54] Not for the first time, a world fad became a New Zealand fetish.

Yet another explanation is simply that 'there is no alternative', a phrase repeated so frequently that it has developed its own acronym, TINA. This was clearly untrue, in its most literal sense at least. Other alternatives were known to exist, but had been discredited by Muldoon in 1975–84. In his desperate writhings against the forces of economic decolonisation, Muldoon, as we have seen, had tried the increasingly hands-on state management of the recolonial system, the grand scheme of Think Big and even some gestures towards gradual and moderate liberalisation of the economy. In doing so, he managed to taint all three options. There was irony here: Muldoon's policy failings, his autocratic personal approach and his right-wing attitudes to social and political issues smeared his left-wing economic practice even in the eyes of the left. There was also an element of demonisation and the construction of a unifying ogre. Shared dislike of Muldoon was the one bond between New Left and New Right. Muldoon had pulled the old house down, and there was 'no alternative' but to join Roger Douglas in rebuilding by gain through pain. Early Rogernomics inverted Muldoonism like a mirror image: left-wing economics and right-wing everything else turned into the reverse.

An alternative that survived Muldoon was one that many members of the Labour Party actually thought they were implementing in 1984–87: New Right economics powering New Left political and social policies. Whether the two are actually compatible is a matter of debate. But, illusory or not, the right/left alternative was crucial in generating Labour support for the first phase of Rogernomics. It was not so much that Labour's left was diverted or bought off by such things as the anti-nuclear policy, but that they and others believed they could ride the whirlwind. TINA's power actually derived from its tapping-in to a widely shared sense that the time had come for major change. Change *was* inevitable, but it does not follow that Rogernomics was inevitably the shape it had to take. There was widespread agreement that 'the economy was in such serious difficulty that major, deep, and temporarily painful surgery was needed'.[55] The question was, which leg?

Post-Restructuralism: An Audit

The long-term objectives of the 1984 restructurers were clear enough. They wished to destroy the belief that New Zealand could fully insulate itself from the world economy, and make it sufficiently robust, flexible and resilient to engage successfully in that economy. The means to this end were deregulation, asset sales and a more-market orientation, which were to make the New Zealand economy more efficient, more competitive, both internally and externally, and to restore growth. How far have these goals been reached? Fifteen years out, it is still early for historians to address this question, and it is tempting to resort to the traditional escape clause: 'The jury is still out.' But the restructurers themselves insisted on accountability, and, despite acknowledged risks, it would seem a pity to deny them this.

Debate on the success of the big right turn, as one would expect, has been intense, but it tends to be partisan, polarised and unhistorical. From the left, we have vehement and comprehensive criticism. Some even suggest that there was no problem at all in 1984, which flies in the face of the facts. From the New Right, we have a litany of self-praise from the restructurers themselves, and a similar paean from 'overseas experts' who are in fact preachers of the same more-market religion. Evangelists from the same church are seldom reliable assessors of each other. Where fans and critics tend to converge is on the historical *decisiveness* of the 1984 restructuring. For good or ill, they believe, it was the great 'turning point' in recent New Zealand history. What we have here is two questions: how far was restructuring successful in terms of its own objectives, and what is its status as an engine of historical change?

Over-regulation in late recolonial New Zealand seems hard to deny. After 1945, though 133 sets of wartime regulations were abolished, 362 were kept. The reader may recall from Chapter Five the regulation banning the mating of horses and cattle within sight of public roads. Even when I dated this to about 1900, it raised a laugh in lectures. I subsequently found that, according to John Marshall, who was then Attorney-General, the rule remained on the books in the 1950s.[56] A regulation banning cats in dairies was not repealed until 1975.[57] Another classic is that one was not able to buy margarine, that economically subversive substance, without a doctor's prescription until the mid-1970s. Decision-making could not be described as devolved in recolonial New Zealand. In 1948, there was a 'standing regulation in cabinet that a minister must obtain the agreement of his colleagues before he can authorize expenditure on any item over £250'.[58]

There was, surely, an element of 'regulomania' and overcentralisation here, just as the restructurers claimed. It also seems hard to deny that the swathe they cut in the rulebooks improved elements of the quality of life in New Zealand – if you had money to buy. As imports flowed in through the dismantling barriers, the range and quality of consumer goods improved substantially, and some prices dropped in real terms – of cars and televisions, for example. Restaurants, bars, cafés, clubs and holiday resorts improved and proliferated. Nightlife on Main Street is one of the triumphs of restructuring. The average experience of services such as air travel and taxis *was* enhanced by competition. Your taxi driver may not be able to find his way, but at least you can find him, unlike in the 1970s. These positives should be conceded, but they also need to be qualified in several ways.

First, the trend towards deregulation began before 1984. Critics of restructuring are at pains to point this out, and they may overstate the case. The year 1984 did mark a major increase in the pace and extent of both economic deregulation and social 'untightening'. But it remains true that the process began before, symbolised by the demise of six o'clock closing in 1967, and that the 1984 restructuring cannot therefore wholly explain it. Second, while complacent attitudes to work and business were undoubtedly given a shake-up, it is not clear that deregulation in general and deregulation of the labour market in particular, delivered net benefits to most New Zealanders. Third, deregulation was sometimes overdone. For example, the absence of internationally normal restraints on the stock market, combined with the inexperience of many participants, contributed to the extra penalty New Zealand suffered from the 1987 global crash. This was a product of the evangelical element in Rogernomics; doctrine was applied, ready or not, appropriate or not. Finally, increased competition and resulting consumer benefits did not occur in all sectors of the economy. In some areas, public regulation went but private regulation may have remained.

New Zealand has long been prone to cartelism in certain sectors of the economy. In 1920, the Secretary for Industry and Commerce wrote: 'competition seldom, if ever works freely . . . Businesses themselves are showing a very prevalent tendency to combine and agree for the purpose of eliminating many of the important features of competition.'[59] Companies, more often two or a few than one alone, establish informal 'oligopolistic' or cartel arrangements by which they set prices and share artificially high profits at the expense of the consumer and, arguably, of national economic efficiency. Between the wars, conspiracy theories about Auckland cartelism, involving the shadowy 'Kelly Gang' and a network centred on wealthy brewer Sir Ernest Davis, were lurid and exaggerated. But they did have a kernel of truth.[60] Sectoral harmony combined with state regulationism to facilitate cartelism at least as much as it controlled it. Even before the advent of First Labour and its stimulus of sectoral harmony, businesses were willing to consider alliances with the state as well as with each other. In 1934, a business leader noted 'a tendency towards State control', in which businesses 'should themselves participate'.[61] By the 1960s, monopoly and duopoly snuggled down in the bed of regulation, exerted pressure on politicians, and solved their problems by meeting officials in Wellington. 'To suggest that firms are presently operating in a competitive environment,' wrote one business analyst in 1973, 'would be to ignore the facts.'[62]

The classic duopoly was the beer industry, which was completely controlled by New Zealand Breweries (later Lion) and Dominion Breweries from 1970, and dominated by them since their formation in 1923 and 1930 respectively. 'The disappearance of smaller firms . . . was not only the result of competition from the bigger and more efficient brewers: it was also a consequence of the discriminatory ways in which successive governments chose to levy excise duties and institute and operate a system of price controls.'[63] A classic monopoly was Wattie's, selling canned and frozen fruit and vegetables.

'[Wattie's] competition in New Zealand was minimal. Potential offshore competitors were kept out by high tariffs and import licensing ... The country simply wasn't big enough to justify a second large food processor ... Overall, in many fields Wattie's had a virtual local monopoly ... We lobbied extensively to protect ourselves from imports. More and more, we took on the appearance of a State Owned Enterprise whose business success was determined by how well we managed Wellington.[64]

Deregulation put an end to elements of this cosy game. It spelled doom for what might be called *systemic* cartelism, the type most enhanced by sectoral harmony. This could be rated among restructuring's successes. But to some extent it replaced public monopoly with virtual private monopoly, as in the case of Telecom. It is not clear that efforts to ameliorate this situation through anti-monopolistic legislation, such as the 1986 Commerce Act and the encouragement of competition, have yet been successful.[65] Further, there were other, longer-standing and even deeper-seated, causes of monopolistic practices than systemic cartelism – an *endemic* cartelism. Since the 1860s, New Zealand had been a small yet homogenous economy – too small and homogenous, perhaps, for competition ever to work as it should in theory. Business élites tended to be quite cohesive, interacting both socially and through interlocking directorates. Even before the post-1935 heyday of sectoral harmony, companies had found co-operating on price more profitable than competing on sales. The small size of the country made it easy to snuggle up to each other, as well as to the state.

The solution to this problem of endemic cartelism, thought the 1984 restructurers, was to inject competition from abroad. Overseas takeovers tripled in 1984–88 compared with the previous five years.[66] But, though the scale increased, New Zealand had long been a transnational economy. In many crucial sectors, such as shipping, banking, meat processing and petroleum, overseas ownership was high well before 1984. This had not prevented the tendency to cartelism. Overseas companies also found that the small New Zealand market was better exploited through high profits than high sales. Sometimes with local partners, and sometimes without, they, too, formed unofficial cartels.

Ironically enough, the first government ownership of businesses in New Zealand was designed to combat this internal and external endemic cartelism. State ownership dates from the 1860s, when central government set up the Post Office Savings Bank and the Government Life Insurance Office. This was not justified on grounds of socialistic principle, or by a belief that if the state did not provide these services no-one would, but on grounds of deficient competition. The state did not nationalise whole industries but acquired one of several large companies to force down prices. In life insurance, for example, private companies based their life tables on the aged population of Britain, applied them to the youthful colonies and pocketed the difference.[67] The state intervened because the New Zealand market was so small, and so prone to cartelism, that competition failed to generate efficiency and protection for the consumer. In short, competitive capitalism, whatever its merits in a large economy, did not work properly in New Zealand. This was not some claim of rhetorical radicalism, but a basic truth recognised consistently and repeatedly by governments of every shade of political opinion, in practice rather than preaching, from the 1860s until 1984.

It has been suggested that 'there are direct links between the deregulatory policies of the Fourth Labour Government [and] the strengthening of the market power of large companies'.[68] This seems unfair. The effect of deregulation on internal competition appears, on the whole, to have been more positive than negative. Cartelism is not as widespread, secure or state-assisted as it was before 1984. Restructuring did not cause, or even increase, New Zealand's long-standing propensity to cartelism. But it did not eliminate it either, at least partly because it focused on the medium-term systemic variant rather than on the long-term endemic one. A measure of cartelism in a particular industry is its speed of response to exogenous price changes – in the overseas price of oil, for example, or the Reserve Bank setting of basic interest rates. In fully competitive industries, price decreases should be passed on to the consumer quickly, and price increases should be passed on slowly. The opposite is often the case, in the banking and oil industries at least, although these industries are now sometimes intensely competitive in other respects. This suggests that endemic cartelism is still alive and well in post-restructural New Zealand. The fully free market has yet to arrive. Paradoxically enough, history suggests that it requires a (sparing and intelligent) use of the state to thrive in local conditions.

A key target of restructuring was Leviathan: the late recolonial mega-state, which was absorbing about 42 per cent of GDP in 1984. Here again, we tend to be caught between polarised extremes of debate: state expansion was either all good or all bad. It may be useful to distinguish between four kinds of state expansion: 'bloat', 'mutation', 'scar tissue' and 'adaptive growth'. Simple 'bloat' – plain inefficiency and growth for its own sake – is difficult to defend. Over-regulation was one form, where the promulgation and enforcement of unnecessary rules generates unnecessary costs. Overstaffing, notably in state-owned enterprises such as New Zealand Rail, was another notorious form. It is sometimes defended as a job-creation scheme, but creating jobs by seeding new industries would seem a more sensible use of public funds than double-manning railways. Restructuring attacked bloat through corporatisation, and even left-wing critics concede that this did lead to efficiency gains.[69] The marketeers' claim that privatisation necessarily followed from corporatisation is more contestable. So is the timing of asset sales, most of which took place in a buyers' market. But, on the whole, restructuring had considerable success in its attack on 'bloat'.

Mutation, also known as 'interest-group capture', was a more problematic type of state expansion. It occurs when state spending is channelled away from its intended target to unintended targets. 'Interest-group capture', via 'public-choice theory', is sometimes converted into 'provider capture'. This implies not only that state servants are motivated mainly by the desire to preserve and enhance their own jobs, but also that they succeed in harnessing the state sector to this purpose. Anecdotes of provider capture are legion, and I may as well add a couple of my own. In the mid-1970s, a senior manager of state-owned television made a snap inspection of a set workshop where about twenty people were supposed to be working. He found only one actually at work, and called the rest together for a severe dressing-down, pointing to the sole worker as the example to follow. That worker was in fact using public time and public materials to make furniture for his own home.[70] Ten years later, a Wellington physiotherapist's rooms were brimming over with patients who were given perfunctory treatments and encouraged to return for numerous repeat visits. The same therapist even worked two or three rooms in the same treatment period. There was panic when one patient revealed that he might not be eligible for state-paid treatment through the Accident Compensation scheme. All were well aware that no-one paying their own money would tolerate the situation for a moment.[71] To cite a more widely known anecdote, in the 1970s milk subsidy reached the point where farmers sold it for 6.5 cents a pint, while it retailed for 4 cents. Farmers profited by buying bottled milk back as stockfeed.[72] There *was* a widespread addiction to, or at least acceptance of, milking the milking system. But, as the last two examples suggest, this was prevalent outside the state sector as well as within it. Business, farmers and strategic unions were pretty good at harnessing the state too – 'private-choice theory'. This was a feature of recolonial society, not of the state alone.

'Middle-class capture' is another variant of mutation. Emphasis on interest groups or pressure groups has long been a staple of New Zealand political studies, which sometimes expressed vague hopes that everyone was represented by a pressure group and that their pressure for benefits on the state system is somehow proportionate to their numbers. The obvious counter-argument is that pressure groups are likely to be unequally resourced – in the capacity to hire full-time lobbyists in Wellington, for example – and, therefore, unequally successful. The test of whether interest group capture of the New Zealand state did in fact take place is simple enough in principle: Was there a shift in benefits from the most needy to the most influential? The answer is a qualified 'yes', but with the qualifications as important as the affirmative.

Historian David Thompson suggests that one lucky interest group who captured disproportionate benefits from the state was a whole generation, working class and middle class alike: that born between 1920 and 1945. Thompson argues convincingly that the young adults of the 1950s and 1960s did far better than their parents and children in the benefits they derived from the state in general and the welfare state in particular. When they were young, the welfare state favoured them with family benefits that had real value, cheap housing loans, free education for their children even at tertiary levels, tax exemptions for dependents, and comprehensive health care, as well as full employment. He estimates that benefits received, less tax paid, boosted family incomes by about a third. As the 'lucky generation' aged in the 1970s and 1980s, so did the orientation of the welfare state. Its benefits shifted from the young, whose housing and family benefits and tax exemptions went down, to the old, whose superannuation went up. The elderly's share of government welfare expenditure doubled between 1971 and 1986 – very much more than the increase in their share of the population – while universal benefits increasingly gave way to means-tested ones for the young. Despite the fact that the rapidly growing domestic purposes and unemployment benefits went mainly to the young, their share of welfare spending stayed static.

The young adults of 1950 and the ageing of 1980, of course, were the very same people. The prime benefits of the welfare state, therefore, tracked the same people through their lives. Their successors, while still paying for them through increasing taxes, faced the crumbling of the costly system when their own turn came. Though Thompson uses the rhetoric of conspiracy theory, preferring the label 'selfish' to 'lucky' generation, he stops short of suggesting some deliberate plot. But the ad hoc pursuit of sectional interest can have the same effect.[73] Thompson is perhaps less than fair in some respects. The childhood and youth of the lucky generation, 1920–45, were in fact marred by depression and war. Their generation was half the size of the succeeding one – there were roughly twice as many births 1945–70 as in the preceding 25 years[74] – and generosity to them was therefore more affordable. Some of the lucky generation's privileges were shared by their children, the 'unlucky generation', and the generation of 1970–95 was in this and other respects unluckier still. But Thompson's thesis does appear to have considerable validity: there was a shift in emphasis in the welfare state from young to old, dating from around 1970, which tended to benefit the same group in different phases of their lives. The good news is that the lucky generation's gains went to both rich and poor, working class and middle class, and to some extent to their children as well. If your state is to be 'captured' by interest groups, then it is better that they should encompass a majority of the population.

Business, farming, state servants and unions were also interest groups that secured significant benefits from the state, as noted above. Like the lucky generation, with whom they obviously intersected, they probably encompassed a majority of the population between them. Significant groups such as Maori, single women, and workers in weak-union industries such as retailing benefited less than average. But 'no section of the community failed to tap into New Zealand's benevolent state'.[75] Interest-group capture of the late recolonial state was to some extent a reality. It was by no means fully equitable, but it was so broad-based that it strengthened, rather than weakened, the populist compact and the wide acceptability of the mega-state. This, after all, was the essence of sectoral harmony. It highlights the fact that the state was not some fully separate entity but part of a system that closely integrated several sectors. The dreary old theory of self-balancing pressure groups, familiar to many from POLS 101, appears to have had something to it after all. Public-choice theory, on the other hand, needs capture by a *minority* interest group to generate the privileges and inequities it alleges, and this does not appear to have happened. Mutation existed in the state, but it was arguably relatively benign, extending privileges to most sections of society. From a practical and populist, rather than theoretical, viewpoint, the restructurers were only entitled to attack it if doing so increased overall social efficiency and supplied replacement benefits to the majority of New Zealanders.

An obvious argument against even this relatively benign mutation is that it progressively increases the cost of the state. Yet the fact is that state spending, as a proportion of gross national product, did not increase much between 1949 and 1973 – a period during which interest-group capture should have been already in full swing. State spending hovered around 30 per cent of gross domestic product throughout that whole period, then rocketed up to over 40 per cent. In short, 'mutation', or interest-group capture, cannot explain the growth of the state from big to very big after 1973. As we have seen, Muldoon's efforts to control it failed, and so, at first, did those of the restructurers. The 40 per cent mega-state remained in place between 1984 and 1990, and only began to shrink – slowly – in the 1990s. In 1999, it stood at 36 per cent, still well above pre-1973 levels. The reason for this growth was not so much bloat or mutation, but 'scarring': the growing of a state callus over socio-economic wounds, but not the curing of such wounds.

One wound was the problem of superannuation, stemming from the growing number of elderly, and boosted by the diminishing number of children, or future taxpayers. Third Labour's attempt to address this problem, with a contributory superannuation scheme, was reversed by Muldoon. Superannuation took a rapidly increasing share of state spending. Other types of scar tissue stemmed from the collapse of the recolonial economic system, in and around the early 1970s. Both Third Labour and Third National, as we have seen, developed a complex and expensive system of support for the economy, especially agriculture, in the hope that this problem would somehow go away – papering over the problem rather than solving it. Substantial unemployment also dates from this period, another increasingly expensive form of scar tissue. Finally, there was a big expansion of overseas public debt between 1975 and 1987, growing at rates of between 12 and 33 per cent per year to about 50 per cent of GDP.[76]

The restructurers attacked the industry-support and debt elements of scar tissue with some success. Industrial support was almost eliminated, and public debt fell from nearly 50 per cent in the late 1980s to 20 per cent in 1999. But this was essentially a transfer of overseas debt from public to private sectors. Total overseas debt grew from 47 per cent of GNP in 1983 to 70 per cent in 1990, and to 103 per cent in 1999.[77] One could argue that this transfer of debt was an improvement from the point of view of the taxpayer, but the same is not necessarily true for the economy as a whole. 'The international credit rating agencies hardly make a distinction between a nation's public and private debts in assessing its credit worthiness . . . The ownership of a country's debt is therefore of less relevance than its ability to service and repay the debt from its regular foreign exchange earnings.'[78] And the restructurers did not successfully address the two other forms of scarring: superannuation and unemployment. It was the increase in these areas that doubled social security payments from about 20 to about 40 per cent of state spending between 1970 and 1990.[79]

The final form of state expansion was adaptive growth: extending the state sector to meet new or expanding agreed needs, or to make successful long-term adjustments to long-term changes. Such spending is more common than critics of Leviathan allow, notably in such areas as health, education, and research and development. One historian writes of major 'blowouts' in health and education spending before 1984, and attributes them partly to the 'special pleading' of teachers and health professionals.[80] This is surely unfair. Costs increased, first, because the number of people seeking health care and education – people whom government and public agreed were entitled to it – increased. Costs went up, second, because health care and education became more sophisticated – in technology, for example – and therefore more expensive. This is a reason why economic growth is necessary – needs do not stay static. You cannot blame teachers for the need for computers in schools, or nurses for the availability of chemotherapy. You can certainly argue that we cannot afford such increasing costs indefinitely, but you cannot reasonably blame them on the messengers.

The restructurers of 1984–93 joined the Muldoon government of 1975–84 in an educational horror story that appears to have gone largely unnoticed. Between 1945 and 1975, primary schooling expanded to cope with the baby-boomers, secondary education became universal and tertiary education began the transition from the privilege of a small élite to a middle-class norm. The number of tertiary students increased from less than 10,000 to over 50,000, and a new type of tertiary institution emerged – the polytechnic. As one would expect in these circumstances, the proportion of government spending devoted to education went up markedly in these years, from 10.5 to 17.5 per cent. This university boom of the 1960s and early 1970s is well known. What seems less recognised is that, over the next twenty years, as New Zealand made the painful shift from a semi-skilled workforce to a skilled workforce, tertiary student numbers expanded at a similar rate: from 50,000 or so in 1975 to 210,000 in 1995. But government education funding did not expand to match. On the contrary, between 1975 and 1985, it declined sharply as a proportion of total spending, from 17.5 to 10.8 per cent. It picked up thereafter, to 15.6 per cent in 1995–96 – still well below the 1975 level despite the quadrupling of tertiary students.[81] Bear in mind that we are not talking about *absolute* levels of education funding, or even funding per student, but funding as a proportion of government spending. This measure accommodates any general need for fiscal restraint, or any fall in revenue. It indicates the priority governments give education in spending what money they do have.

There was some decline in primary and secondary school populations, owing to demographics, from about 740,000 in 1975 to 670,000 in 1995, but nowhere near enough to compensate for the extra 160,000 tertiary students. Significant fees were introduced only in 1992, and still constitute only a small proportion of tertiary funding. Thus, the second great expansion of tertiary education, 1975–95, was largely unfunded, with obvious implications for quality. At worst, in 1985, education received 10.8 per cent of government spending – less than in any year of the Great Depression of the 1930s, even though the tertiary sector had scarcely existed then. Despite rhetoric about the knowledge economy and the need for skills, post-1975 governments have coped with the economic drought by eating the educational seed corn. This conclusion is independent of the question of whether the tertiary sector is efficient or not. If it is inefficient, you reform it; you do not slowly strangle it.

A similar story could probably be told about the public funding of research and development, which dropped dramatically in real terms under the fourth Labour government and is still internationally low. Gallant efforts to reverse the trend, by David Lange in education in the late 1980s and by Simon Upton in science funding in the mid-1990s, were too little, too late.

The 1984 restructuring did not bring a fully competitive market to New Zealand, because it neglected endemic causes of cartelism in favour of systemic, or regulatory, ones. It hacked at the healthy bits of Leviathan with as much vigour as at the unhealthy. Indeed, it failed to distinguish between the two, or to recognise the ambiguities of 'mutation' and 'scar tissue'. We will see in later chapters that restructuring produced many types of social cost as well. All this might have been forgivable if restructuring had delivered economic growth, as it promised it would. It did not.

As we have seen in Chapter Ten, broad growth statistics can be controversial and contestable, and the 'before and after' snapshots of restructuring are no exception. Fans of the 1984 restructuring play down growth levels in the 1960s and 1970s; critics play them up; and then the two reverse positions for the 1980s and 1990s. In the mid-1990s, there was a spasm of promising growth in gross domestic product, but a variety of sources suggest that the overall picture is less good. Growth in per capita GNP in the 1945–73 period was, as we have seen, moderately high, usually over 2 per cent. The actual downward shift in growth patterns appears to date from 1973 but it was not reversed by 1984. From 1973 to 1990, growth per capita was below 2 per cent in all but four years, despite the slowing-down of population growth.[82] GNP in constant 1983 dollars increased about 130 per cent between 1956 and 1976 (from $13 to $29.5 billion), but only about 35 per cent (to just over $40 billion) between 1976 and 1996.[83] Another estimate puts economic growth per capita in the first period at 2 per cent, and in the second period at 1.05 per cent.[84] Even a commentator who favoured the New Right revolution had to concede, in 1993, that 'after nine painful years of restructuring . . . our GDP is where it was when the revolution began'.[85] The broad impression of moderate growth to the mid-1970s, and low growth thereafter, appears to stand up.

The 1984 restructurers did not solve the problem of low economic growth. Nor did they fully solve the propensity to cartelism or the post-1973 surge in the costs of the state. But they did not cause these problems either. Indeed, they bravely and systematically sought to solve them, which is more than anyone else did. They failed – partly because some problems were intractable, but also because others were misdiagnosed. The restructurers believed that the crying need was to supply new *form*, whereas there was also a need for new *content*. The roots of the misdiagnosis were a widespread reluctance to face the facts of the recolonial system, an embarrassingly persistent neo-colonialism, and therefore to face up to the implications of its collapse. As an engine of fundamental change, the New Right revolution has been overhyped. It is something of a 'blue herring'. Its architects freed up the fiddle market while Rome burned, restructured the stable door after the horse had bolted. The big shift in recent New Zealand history was not restructuring in and around 1984, but decolonisation in and around 1973. It is to this real big shift that we now turn.

CHAPTER FIFTEEN

Rainbow's End

Debunking myths can too easily extend to denying their kernel of truth. The restructuring of 1984–93 was by no means insignificant in recent New Zealand history. It radically changed the form, though not the content, of the economy; and form can be important. It speeded up social untightening and other processes of change. It may have alleviated the slowing of growth, or it may have worsened it, and it certainly worsened unemployment and the erosion of education. But, just as it cannot be blamed for causing slow growth and unemployment, so it cannot be credited with causing the main shifts of the last four decades of the century. In the end, though it was not entirely displaced, restructuring was outranked by decolonisation as the main engine of change.

The process of decolonisation can be dated broadly to the years 1965–88, and more narrowly to 1973–85. If a single year has to be chosen as the turning point, it would have to be 1973, when Mother Britain ran off and joined the Franco-German commune known as the European Economic Community (EEC). But 1973, like 1984, was even more symbolic than substantial. It was not a complete watershed but the representative of quite a long and complex process. Decolonisation was a product of four interacting sets of historical forces, two largely internal and two largely external. One internal set centred on the great Maori resurgence after 1945, which, with a renewal of immigration, helped to cause something of an ethnic revolution and to challenge traditional notions of unitarian New Zealandness. Another was the rise of Pakeha groups, notably women, graduates and youths, to a new political and social significance. These internal change agents are explored in Part Six. The external change agents are the subjects of this chapter.

One of these agents can be loosely – and to some extent deceptively – known as 'globalisation'. In recent New Zealand history, it took the form of the opening of new gateways between New Zealand and the world. The other was the transformation of New Zealand's main international relationships: disconnection from Britain, the rise and fall of the American alliance, and reconnection with Australia. Each of these relationships had economic, cultural and security dimensions. The most important change was the disconnection from Britain, and the most clear-cut feature of this was economic. Between 1965 and 1989, the proportion of New Zealand's exports taken by Britain dropped from over 50 to 7 per cent – a revolution in terms of trade. Yet this transformation, unlike that symbolised by 1984, has had a curiously muted impact on both scholarly analysis and public discourse. Somehow, New Zealand decolonised without fully realising it, and this contributed substantially to the misdiagnosis of its problems and the mismanagement of transition.

Exit Britain, Enter World

Although globilisation is often seen as a thing of the present, future and recent past, it is an ancient process, if it is defined as the formation of widespread transnational networks. New forms of transport and communications, such as sailing ships and literacy, formed new networks across the globe, even if they did not embrace the whole of it. If things or thoughts, such as guns, Christianity or the phonetic alphabet – all of which were Asian in origin – were considered desirable, they could disseminate widely and rapidly through the network. Global networks were sometimes dominated by the nation or nations that placed themselves closest to the centre of the network and became the clearing houses of international exchange. Western Europe in the seventeenth to nineteenth centuries, and the United States in the twentieth, are cases in point. But anything could flow through the gateways that globalisation created, including both cultural hegemony and new means of resistance to it, McDonald's and Black Power.

The four key technological changes behind the increasing speed and pervasiveness of globalisation in the second half of the twentieth century were in the linked areas of mass media, transport, communications and information. These opened four new gateways between New Zealand and the world – gateways harder to police and control than the old. The new mass-media gateway was television, which arrived in New Zealand in 1960, internationally late. It had been available in Britain and the United States since the 1930s, and introduction was considered by the New Zealand government in 1949. But, probably because the tight society considered it an unnecessary and vaguely effete luxury, nothing was done during the 1950s except for some closed-circuit demonstration transmissions. When television finally did come, to the four main centres in 1960–62, it broadcast for only two to four hours a day, with advertising allowed only on alternate nights.[1] But it was enthusiastically embraced by the public, who had purchased half a million expensive sets by 1966. By 1970, television was available in 77 per cent of New Zealand homes, compared with 71 per cent in Australia.[2] A capacity to broadcast nationally came in 1969 – an important development that enabled all New Zealanders to see and hear the same thing at the same time.[3] Colour television arrived in 1973, a second channel in 1975, videos in the 1980s, the first private channel in 1989, and subscriber television in the 1990s, by which time 98 per cent of homes had television sets.[4]

Less vaunted but arguably even more significant than television was the opening of the second new gateway: the advent of the jet aircraft. Scheduled and regular international air services began in New Zealand in 1939, by the British carrier Imperial Airways, which 'encountered none of the problems of nationalism which had bedevilled it in India and Australia'.[5] However, the New Zealand government did insist the first flying boat have the hyphens removed from the *Ao-tea-roa* painted on it, and in 1940 joined the British and Australians in establishing Tasman Empire Airways Limited (TEAL). A Pan-American service began in 1940, but was aborted by Pearl Harbor in 1941, and the nascent commercial services all languished during the war. Even after it, they remained reliant on flying boats of inferior British makes, with limited range and carrying capacity. Unlike the Australians, 'the New Zealand government ... was not prepared to offend Britain by buying American aircraft'.[6] Harbour boards interested themselves in air traffic because, owing to the initial dominance of flying boats, seaports and 'airports' could be the same thing. For New Zealand at least, international air travel remained a short-hop, minority activity until the 1960s. The total number of international passenger flights was still only 92,000 in 1960.[7]

A jet aircraft first visited New Zealand in 1946, and the air force had them by 1951. But the government appears to have been as slow to embrace them as it was to embrace television – almost as though new portals into paradise were considered undesirable. However, scheduled jet services did arrive in 1963. The government changed the name of TEAL, whose Australian shareholding it had bought out in 1961, to Air New Zealand in 1965, and opened the first real international airport, at Mangere, Auckland, in 1966. International passenger flights in and out of New Zealand increased sixfold from 92,000 in 1960 to 554,000 in 1970. The new jet gate creaked wider open with the advent of the wide-bodied jet in 1973 – again despite some official reluctance. By 1974, flights were twice the 1970 level, at 1,117,000 – the age of mass jet travel had arrived. It was getting very difficult to keep the world out of New Zealand, and New Zealanders out of the world. Ten years later, the figure was closing on three million, a thirtyfold increase in 25 years.[8]

The third new global gateway was in communications. Interpersonal communications had first been separated from transport by telegraph in the mid-nineteenth century. Radio-telephone links with Australia and Britain were established in 1931, but international toll calls were extremely expensive until the advent of microwave transmission in 1960 and satellite transmission in 1965.[9] First telex, then facsimile machines subsequently trumped airmail in the transmission of written words. In the 1990s, electronic mail began replacing the lot. Instant international communication became cheap, easy and available to the masses – or at least the middle-class masses. The cost of instantly sending a page of print from New Zealand to London fell from $1,315 in 1938, by telegraph, or $438 by phone, to $2.95 by phone in the year 2000, or 59 cents by fax, or less than a cent by e-mail.[10] Moreover, state-of the-art communications were no longer with London only, but with much of the world.

Information technology also revolutionised at increasing pace, our fourth and final new gateway. The first computer, a primitive International Business Machines giant, arrived in New Zealand in 1960 – used, appropriately enough, by Treasury to work out the pay of state servants. Personal computers appeared here in the late 1970s, and New Zealanders engaged with them eagerly, despite the fact that the third Labour government had imposed a 40 per cent sales tax on them, 'largely for fear of job erosion'. By 1985, when 12,000 people were employed as data processors, there were claims that 'New Zealand has gained pre-eminence in advanced programming techniques'.[11] By 1998, over a third of New Zealand homes had computers. The Internet, literally a global information network, arrived in 1986, and took off from 1989. By 1998, New Zealand had over half a million users; by 2000, it had over one million. It ranks about seventh in the world in the rate of Internet access.[12]

Together, these four new gateways went a long way towards eliminating what had hitherto been one of the most central characteristics of New Zealand history: isolation and insulation from the rest of the world, except Britain. Each gateway represented the opening of a new path between New Zealand and the world, along which both saints and serpents could enter paradise unchecked. One dark secret, revealed early by overseas television programmes and overseas visits, was that other people were allowed to drink in bars even at night. In the long run, such revelations probably spelled doom for the tight society. But they did not necessarily spell doom for recolonisation, at least until the 1970s. You could learn about the sinful pleasures of night-time drinking as easily from Coronation Street as from American programmes. It is true that America was central to most of the new technologies. It dominated the manufacture of jet aircraft and television programmes, and later of telecommunications and computers. This raised the spectre of 'Americanisation' as the new shape of global culture. But, if it existed, this spectre was as dangerous to Britain itself as to New Zealand.

'Cultural colonisation' by America was more general and less intense than the recolonial relationship with Britain, and did not automatically displace it. Indeed, it looked at first as if the new gateways might even help sustain the British connection. Britain initially contested American dominance of the small New Zealand screen rather more successfully than it had done with the big screen. In 1967, 35 per cent of television programmes were British, as against 30 per cent American.[13] In 1966, popular music playing in New Zealand was more British than American – the two were still roughly even in 1985.[14] The new hordes of flying Kiwis chose London as their long-range destination, not New York or Los Angeles.[15] The first satellite telephone link, in 1965 'allowed a connection with Britain' – where else? – as did the first satellite television link.[16] 'In February 1973 the first live colour TV show was transmitted from New Zealand when Harry Secombe, on camera in Auckland, appeared on Cilla Black's programme in Britain.'[17] The highest proportion of long-range toll calls still went to Britain in 1981.[18] The new gateways were not the villains behind the collapse of recolonisation. What was?

At some point between 1956 and 1973, Britain's two-century career as a global superpower came to an end. With hindsight, the Suez Crisis of 1956, when Britain learned the hard way that it could no longer take major global initiatives without the consent of the United States, was the beginning of the end. The end, however, was not fully obvious until the early 1970s. The marathon withdrawal from Empire, begun in 1947 with the independence and partition of the Indian subcontinent, entered the home stretch in 1968, when Britain announced its intention to withdraw its armed forces from the Middle East and the Far East within the next few years. Where possible, Britain left both regions in the hands of regimes it fondly hoped would be favourable to it, but by 1973 it was no longer a significant power in either.[19]

New Zealand shared the death agonies of an empire in which it saw itself as a shareholder. The experience was less acute than in Britain itself, but it was not wholly vicarious. For one thing, the expatriate game was still in full flow. Around 1960, at least two dozen New Zealanders held senior positions in the British colonial service, clustering in Fiji and Hong Kong, but also including the governors of the Bahamas and Western Nigeria.[20] As we have seen, New Zealand was even more strongly represented in the British armed forces, especially the RAF. The withdrawal from Empire was sometimes led by Better Britons. More significantly for the future, Britain's withdrawal from the Middle East helped pave the way for the oil shocks of 1973 and 1979 – an economic blow for New Zealand as for many other oil-importing countries.

The Middle East had become a major supplier of oil to the world, including New Zealand, after World War Two. In the 1950s and 1960s, Britain had used its strategic position in the region to help keep oil prices low, production high and profits flowing to European companies rather than the oil-producing countries themselves. New Zealand was a collateral beneficiary of this arrangement. Between 1938 and 1960, the price of petrol in New Zealand rose at about half the rate of the general price index – an indirect benefit of the recolonial system.[21] Wellington's abandonment of electric trams in 1964 is an example of New Zealand's confidence in the continuing inflow of cheap oil. As Britain's influence in the Middle East declined, and was only partially replaced by that of the United States, Arab producing countries were able to assert control of the oil flow, and boost prices. They did so in 1973, during a war with Israel, and they did so again in 1979–80, after the Iranian Revolution replaced an (initially British-backed) monarchy.

New Zealand politicians and many analysts blamed the economic woes of the 1970s squarely on the oil shocks, which they seem to have seen as some random global accident. The shocks did indeed boost New Zealand's import bill but, like the emphasis on the downturn of commodity prices in 1967, they helped conceal the fact that decolonisation was a more fundamental cause of change. For one thing, the extent of the price increase is often wildly exaggerated. The first oil shock nominally quadrupled the wholesale price of oil, while the second increased prices to ten times their 1973 amount.[22] These are extremely deceptive statistics for New Zealand at least. This was a time of very high inflation, and the retail cost of petrol in real terms actually never more than doubled – bad, but nothing like a tenfold increase.[23] For another thing, the shocks were temporary. Oil prices fell in the mid-1980s almost as dramatically as they had risen, and remained low into the 1990s. Third, Britain itself had discovered oil in the North Sea in 1970, and by 1981 had become a net exporter. If the recolonial relationship had held up, New Zealand, too, might have benefited from this. Finally, the oil shocks themselves only became possible on the scale they occurred because of Britain's withdrawal from Empire. In the 1950s and 1960s, when the British still had a strong presence in the Middle East, this would not have happened, at least to the degree that it did. New Zealand commentators have consistently missed the point that the oil shocks of the 1970s were a decolonising phenomenon, partly an indirect consequence of the decline of British power. Furthermore, their effect in New Zealand has been overstated – an important contributor to the *understating* of decolonisation.

Between the early 1950s and the early 1970s, for various reasons, Britain's share of world manufactured exports plummeted, from 21 to 9 per cent.[24] As a consequence of this, and the rise of the American dollar as the dominant international currency, the 'sterling area' became increasingly difficult to maintain. The sterling area, formally established in 1931, was a group of countries that did most of their trade through London and held their reserves in British currency. It included such countries as Argentina and Denmark, but intersected substantially with the recolonial and imperial economic systems, the white Empire and the black. The sterling system was tightened from 1939 and provided some shelter for increasingly uncompetitive British manufactured exports thereafter. But it began to crumble rapidly in 1967, triggered by a devaluation of the pound, and was gone by 1972.[25] The sterling area, like the Ottawa Agreement, represented a 1930s turn by the British economy away from the world and towards the Empire. Its demise represented a turn away from the Empire.

Britain's turning away from Empire was coupled with a turn towards Europe. In 1947, as India celebrated its independence, war-torn nations of continental Europe began discussing economic integration. In 1957, France, West Germany, Italy, Belgium, the Netherlands and Luxembourg formed the European Economic Community. The British, or at least their government, soon showed interest in joining up too, and tried to do so from 1961. Almost as though he was a New Zealand secret agent, President Charles de Gaulle of France vetoed this attempt, and another in 1967, but the writing was on the wall. On 1 January 1973, a black-letter day in New Zealand history, Britain joined the EEC. We will see that desperate diplomatic offensives by New Zealand reduced the pain of parting by retaining some access for protein. But Britain's relative share of New Zealand's exports, declining slowly since 1950, suddenly halved in the 1970s. This was external shock indeed.

The EEC was in some respects the nemesis of the New Zealand–British recolonial system. By joining it, Britain would buy in to the Common Agricultural Policy, which heavily subsidised Community farms. Added to this, free trade between EEC countries would inevitably displace New Zealand products in the British markets, as protein exporters like the Netherlands, France and Ireland took revenge for New Zealand's long era of pre-eminence. But the EEC was far from the whole story, which in fact extended deep into British cultural and economic history. Slow population growth and relative economic decline in Britain can be dated back to World War One or before. But the decline was relative to other rapidly industrialising countries, not absolute. Slow British growth was not in itself the key long-term threat to the recolonial system. The real problems were, first, a trend towards the revival of British domestic agriculture and, second, 'polysaturation' – the ending of the trend to increased consumption of New Zealand protein among British consumers.

This growth of the British market for New Zealand protein had always been less a matter of simply eating more than of the expansion of the British middle class and its eating habits. As the middle class grew, and the eating habits of higher classes were adopted even by some workers, people ate less low-status grain and more high-status protein. As we have seen, they also shifted from low-grade protein, such as lard and sausages, to high-grade, butter and prime cuts of meat – and from bare floors to carpets. 'Polysaturation', the natural end of this process, may have been settling in from the late 1930s, but there was a countervailing surge in consumption after 1945 – a recovery from, and reaction to, wartime shortages. By the middle 1960s, even this late spurt had been exhausted. 'The demand for food and for furniture was seen to have been largely sated by 1965.'[26] Meat consumption stabilised and butter consumption dropped. This was exacerbated by shifts in consumer preference away from butter towards margarine – and later from red to white meats. French chemist Hippolyte Mège-Mouriès, the villain who invented margarine in the 1860s, ranks with the originators of the U-boat in recolonial New Zealand's pantheon of demons. Though New Zealand dairy exporters long had nightmares about margarine, it was not a huge threat until the postwar period, when some fool discovered the fact that its polyunsaturated fat did less damage to arteries than butter did.

On top of all this, the British government made its greatest-ever effort to boost domestic agriculture, and it had some success. 'Output grew more rapidly between 1945 and 1965 than in any period before or since.'[27] The wartime policy of 'higher production at all costs' continued, and by 1952 agricultural production was 50 per cent higher than in 1939. A massive and complex system of government subsidies was introduced in 1947, and maintained by successive governments. The 'heavy programme of investment' in farming from this date 'reflected the confidence of farmers in a continuing policy of agricultural support from the government'.[28] From 1973, the EEC's Common Agricultural Policy merely added new layers to the system of British farm subsidy already in place. We can guess that the U-boat lay behind this state intervention in agriculture. Recolonisation required that Britain be confident in the security of the sea lanes that fed it. This confidence had recovered after World War One, but could not survive the much heavier losses to U-boats of World War Two. Another factor was a revival of what might be called 'cultural ruralism', in Britain and elsewhere. The diversity of small-scale agricultural production, and the village life associated with it, was increasingly linked to national character and identity. Europeans wanted a living countryside, even if it was economically inefficient. Both cultural ruralism and the U-boat were bad news for distant town-supply districts.

Britain did not join the EEC until 1973, and painstakingly negotiated transitional provisions meant the New Zealand economy did not feel the full effects of this for about ten years. Yet the imminent demise of recolonisation was, surely, obvious well before this. The long-sighted had feared that the British market could not grow indefinitely since the early 1930s. The revival of British agriculture was clearly foreshadowed in 1947, Britain's intention to enter the EEC was suspected from 1959, and was plain from 1961. The decline of protein consumption was clear by 1965. Yet New Zealand devoted its efforts less to adapting to the inevitable than to resisting or evading it.

Are You My Mother?

Between 1961, when Britain first announced its intention to join the European Community, and 1988, New Zealand conducted a long and intensive diplomatic and political campaign to preserve the economic basis of the recolonial system: privileged access for its protein products. 'All the interests in New Zealand that were likely to be affected combined in a massive effort to ensure that New Zealand's need for special trading arrangements was known and as far as possible understood in Britain.'[29] These writhings of recolonisation *in extremis* tell us quite a lot about it. An overseas analysis of the process, by Juliet Lodge, does not make pleasant reading for New Zealanders.[30] New Zealand negotiators specialised in

> emphasising weakness . . . dependency, and vulnerability . . . New Zealand politicians have implied, even as late as the early 1970s, that New Zealand foreign policy-makers took their cue from Britain; that NZ foreign policy behaviour was not independently determined . . . While some also resent New Zealand's continuing dependence, policy makers have deliberately sought to ensure its persistence . . . New Zealand protected its interests not by wholesale market diversification but by reaffirming and entrenching its dependence . . . The NZ strategy was . . . to play up the idea of weakness: to portray NZ as a small, weak state . . . There is a feeling in the European Community that . . . New Zealand has not come to terms with the reality of the EC, and tends to invoke sentiment in a manner appropriate to the 1950s not the 1980s.

These words are harsh but true. Two consistent features of the New Zealand effort were unabashed appeals to sympathy and sentiment. New Zealand negotiators regularly sought to evoke British and European pity by pro-claiming small size, economic fragility and utter dependence on the British market. New Zealand was, and should remain, 'Britain's other farm', in the words of John Marshall, New Zealand's chief negotiator during eleven trips to Britain between 1961 and 1971.[31] New Zealand also evoked sentiment along two ancient lines: 'We are your kith and kin,' and 'We died for you in two world wars.' For a while, this triple assault on British consciences worked surprisingly well. During their first attempt to enter the EEC in 1961, the

British agreed not to join unless New Zealand received satisfactory 'special arrangements'. When Britain did negotiate entry, in 1971, special arrangements for New Zealand were indeed included, notably 'Protocol 18'. Repeatedly renegotiated, they provided much-reduced but significant access until about 1988, and residual access to the present.[32]

This degree of success mystifies Lodge, who does not grasp the depth and reciprocity of the recolonial relationship.[33] Some British politicians apparently even believed that New Zealand could have turned the scale in the 1972 vote on entry, through a direct appeal to the British press, parliament and public. If true, this is an indicator of New Zealand's remarkable status in Britain – more like a virtual Scotland than a distant neo-colony. It seems New Zealand did attempt the direct appeal, thinly veiled. In 1971, a British journalist accused Marshall of 'interfering in the affairs of a sovereign state'.[34] In 1977, Robert Muldoon condemned the Common Agricultural Policy as 'a thoroughly bad thing . . . one of the greatest political tricks of all time', and predicted the European Community's disintegration.[35] In 1983, Muldoon followed his Falklands effort with another article in *The Times*, on the Common Agricultural Policy: 'Can Ties of Blood Survive These Selfish Policies?'[36]

New Zealand's crusade for special arrangements had its pathetic elements, but it was in some respects a sterling effort. New Zealand embassies in continental Europe proliferated from 1961, and some profitable relationships were developed – often by officials, who tended to be more realistic than politicians. France, and later Ireland, showed little sympathy, but countries such as Belgium and Italy gave New Zealand a good hearing. The campaign to continue special arrangements after 1977 had a sympathetic supporter in Margaret Thatcher, Prime Minister of Britain from 1978. It developed a certain robustness under Muldoon, who demanded Better British privileges rather than begged for them. The campaign is sometimes portrayed as very effective. But New Zealand sought permanent and substantial special arrangements, while it got temporary and decreasing ones. A process that saw Britain's share of New Zealand exports drop from over 50 to 7 per cent in 25 years can hardly be acclaimed as a trading triumph. The special arrangements anaesthetised the New Zealand town-supply district's amputation from its town – and perhaps thereby helped camouflage it. It did not prevent it or even slow it down very much. It 'absorbed much political and diplomatic effort'[37] that might have been better employed developing alternative relationships. But the scale and character of New Zealand's crusade do confirm the strength and persistence of recolonialism to the 1970s. The determined rearguard action finally came to an end in 1988, when the British withdrew their customary support for New Zealand in renegotiating its 'special arrangements' with the European Community. Something had 'damaged the family atmosphere'[38] in residual New Zealand–British relations, and this was the final nail in recolonisation's coffin.

The factor that 'damaged the family atmosphere' was the comprehensive and possibly permanent breakdown of New Zealand's traditional military alliances. This dated from 1984–86, and stemmed from a sudden intensification of New Zealand anti-nuclear sentiment. The British military alliance was as much shattered as the American,[39] and in this sense the term 'ANZUS crisis' is a misnomer, because Britain was never a member of ANZUS. It remains true that, since the mid-1960s, America had increasingly become New Zealand's main military ally. This was arguably a transfer of dependence from Britain to America in terms of security, but it proved relatively short-lived and was not matched by comparable levels of economic or cultural dependence. Culturally, the particular British connection still outranked the general American connection in the 1970s. New Zealand's postgraduate students began to look to America as well as Britain for their higher degrees from the 1950s, but more still went to Britain. As late as 1977, a New Zealand student who had won scholarships to both British and American universities was automatically withdrawn from the latter by University Grants Committee officials – without his consent. The grounds, presumably, were that no decent Kiwi lad could possibly prefer Harvard to Oxford. In economics, trade relations with America never reached anything like the scale, intensity or reliability of the recolonial link to Britain. Even so, between 1965 and 1985 New Zealand was part of the American-led team in international relations, including their nuclear dimension.

To the early 1960s, New Zealand had a strong record of active co-operation with the British – and, through them, the American – development of nuclear weapons. While US Secretary of State Henry Kissinger might dismiss New Zealand as 'a dagger pointed at the heart of Antarctica',[40] it had played a surprisingly significant part in the genealogy of the Big Bomb, noted in Chapter Eleven. Nuclear-power facilities in New Zealand itself were considered in the 1950s.[41] New Zealand warships also participated in British nuclear tests in the Pacific and in Australia in that decade. In 1960, New Zealand was far from an obvious pick for the world's most anti-nuclear country. Such anti-nuclear sentiment as did exist was not associated with nationalism. New Zealand's first anti-nuclear group, formed in 1959, was merely a small offshoot of the British left's Campaign for Nuclear Disarmament.

From the early 1960s, however, the New Zealand anti-nuclear movement began to gather strength, helped by the fact that the most active nuclear power in the Pacific was France, an easier target for traditional New Zealand sentiment than Britain or even America. After losing Algeria in 1963, the French began preparations for testing their nuclear weapons in their Pacific colony of French Polynesia, centred on Tahiti. Testing began in 1966. Along with other nations, New Zealand protested; even right-wing governments were prepared to join in against the French; and protests took on a harder edge with the advent of the third Labour government and the formation of Greenpeace New Zealand, a very activist environmental protest group, in 1972. That year, Greenpeace dispatched a protest vessel to the French nuclear testing site of Mururoa Island. It was rammed by a French warship, and New Zealand sentiment intensified. The following year, the Kirk government sent a warship of its own – a dramatic gesture. As international pressure increased, the French responded by taking their tests underground in 1974. But they kept testing and New Zealanders kept protesting.

Government and protesters could agree on France, but Britain and America were not so easy a matter for the former. Both the British and the Americans had long been visiting New Zealand ports with warships that they refused to 'confirm or deny' were nuclear-armed. Some almost certainly were, and some were certainly nuclear-powered, though not many. 'The United States Navy visited New Zealand ports 148 times from 1960 to 1984. Only ten of the U.S. Naval vessels were nuclear-powered during that time and constituted only thirteen of the total number of visits.'[42] The 'neither confirm nor deny' policy meant that a ban on nuclear-armed warships effectively meant a ban on all warships, British or American. The Nash Labour government of 1957–60 favoured ship visits, but thereafter the Labour Party became increasingly anti-nuclear. Until 1984, the parliamentary leadership struggled to restrain this sentiment and stop it short of threatening the British and American alliances by completely banning ship visits. The Holyoake government paid lip-service to the anti-nuclear movement from 1964,[43] but the Muldoon government of 1975–84 actively sought ship visits, to the rage of the growing anti-nuclear movement. Visiting warships were greeted with intense protests and even non-violent resistance in various forms.

From 1984, pressure mounted on the restructuring Labour government to ban all nuclear visits. It is reasonable to suggest that a left-wing position on the nuclear issue acted, consciously or unconsciously, as a sort of trade-off for a new right position on economics. Prime Minister Lange himself appears to have wanted to arrange some kind of compromise, and the Americans believed that he did so. The USS *Buchanan* was selected for the visit – a vessel that was not nuclear-powered and was highly unlikely to carry nuclear weapons.[44] But, if he made some deal, Lange was forced to renege by his own party, and in January 1985 the Labour government 'crossed the

Rubicon' by refusing permission for the *Buchanan*'s visit.[45] Negotiations continued until 1986, but failed, and New Zealand's participation in ANZUS ceased. Enshrining the nuclear ban in legislation in 1987, majority support for this move, which was clear from polls in 1989, and the fourth National government's consequent acceptance of the ban in 1990, spelled the long-term end of the American – and British – military alliances.

The internationally exceptional scale and success of the New Zealand anti-nuclear movement means that it cannot be explained simply as part of a global trend. A more promising explanation is that of diminishing threat-perception, developing from about 1960. New Zealand had the world's widest moat, and prospective nuclear war was in any case increasingly looking like assured mutual destruction. New Zealand, then, had less need for military alliances. This was no doubt a factor, but the anti-nuclear movement in New Zealand actually surged from 1979, when the Cold War, in remission since the American withdrawal from Vietnam in 1973, hotted up again with the Soviet invasion of Afghanistan and US President Ronald Reagan's hard line. Moreover, diminishing threat-perception actually extended from the protest movement to even conservative New Zealand governments, and did not necessarily result in a greater willingness to ban allied warship visits.

Government threat-perception is perhaps best measured not by official rhetoric but by the extent to which governments put their money where their mouths were. Between 1945 and 1957, Fraser and Holland, who remembered all too well being ambushed by the Japanese threat in 1942, took the Soviet danger seriously. In these years, which were mostly peaceful, between 10 and 15 per cent of government spending went on defence. As late as 1963, the figure was a substantial 10 per cent. Under Holyoake and Kirk, however, it halved to 5.5 per cent by 1975. Under Muldoon, it dropped still further to 4.7 per cent in 1983–84.[46] The level in 1980 was one-sixth of United States spending per capita and less than half of Australia's.[47] The intriguing thing about this is that, while Muldoon in particular talked the talk about full membership of the Western alliance, he did not walk the walk. Yet he not simply accepted but actively sought visits by American nuclear warships. In 1977, he asked the American admiral commanding in the Pacific to send a ship. 'The Admiral was taken aback and replied: "But I have no plans at present for sending any ships to New Zealand." "Send them," said Muldoon. "I want them."'[48]

Muldoon, it seems, wanted to maintain the traditional alliances for reasons other than fear of some real security threat. For him, perhaps, they were rocks to cling to in changing times. As we will see in the following chapters, he took comparable positions on other issues, including the South African rugby tour of 1981 and Maori protest at Bastion Point in 1978. What he was doing in all cases, it seems to me, was placing himself at the head of a traditonalist populist 'backlash', sometimes described as 'Rob's Mob'. This group came from the middle ground of public opinion, which might vote for either major party every three years, and was normally apolitical. It included traditionalist elements of the working class and lower middle class. Its engagement with Muldoon aroused as much concern among the patrician right and the New Right as it did on the left. Its backing gave the Muldoon position on the need to maintain the traditional alliances a narrow majority of public support – until 1985–86, when part of the populist middle ground suddenly turned left.

The success of the New Zealand anti-nuclear movement in 1985–86 has been misattributed to 'a kind of highjacking of the peace movement by a radical left movement'.[49] In fact the movement developed in three steps. In the 1960s, it was a small, left-wing and somewhat derivative group of groups with a modest minority of public support. Between 1972 and 1984, it broadened very considerably to about 400 groups, with support embracing much of the educated middle class and especially strong among women.[50] It was helped in this by its identification with environmental concerns, centred on the risk of nuclear accidents, as well as with anti-war sentiment. Middle-class environmentalists could not yet be mistaken for frothing radicals. By 1984, a majority of the public favoured banning nuclear-ship visits, but those that were prepared to do so even at the cost of the ANZUS alliance remained a minority – a not-untypical populist desire to have things both ways.[51] From 1985, however this began to change and the anti-nuclear position became increasingly bound up with an upsurge in nationalism. The trigger incident was the sinking of the *Rainbow Warrior* in Auckland Harbour by French secret service agents.

The British and French have been caricaturing each other for several centuries. A modern example is the *Pink Panther* series of films starring Peter Sellers as the bumbling Inspector Clouseau. In July 1985, five months after the New Zealand government had banned the visit of the *Buchanan*, fiction became fact. A dozen French agents mounted a covert operation in Auckland, New Zealand, with all the skill and panache of Inspector Clouseau. They did succeed in their objective, which was to sink the *Rainbow Warrior*, mother-ship of a flotilla bound for Mururoa Island to protest at more French tests. But some of the agents also succeeded in getting caught after they bombed the ship, and in leaving ample evidence of their activities, including the sexual liaisons with local women apparently *de rigueur* for spies. 'The operation,' writes an historian of the French secret services, 'was so ill conceived, so amateurish, that New Zealand police, hardly more than a country con-stabulary but able to break the case in an eyelash, suspected at first it must be a frame-up.'[52] 'It left a trail so Gallic,' admitted one French agent, 'that the only missing clues were a baguette bread loaf, a black beret and a bottle of Beaujolais.'[53] The affair had its less funny side. A member of the Greenpeace anti-nuclear organisation, Portuguese photographer Fernando Pereira, was killed in the *Rainbow Warrior* explosion. The French government of President François Mitterand at first adamantly denied, but was later forced to admit, its involvement.

This was technically an act of war against New Zealand, but the response of its major allies was disappointing to say the least. Australia alone roundly condemned the attack, despite its strong opposition to New Zealand's new anti-nuclear policy. The British and American responses were very different. While no-one was asking them to take active measures against France, New Zealanders were shocked 'by the unwillingness of both allied governments to condemn the bombing, even when it was acknowledged to have been the work of the French government'.[54] 'The British government was noticeably lukewarm in its response, despite the fact that the *Rainbow Warrior* was a British-registered ship.'[55] 'In the United States President Reagan's officials sharply rejected calls to condemn the French action.' In an article entitled 'Mitterand's Finest Hour', the *Wall Street Journal* 'stated bluntly that the French government had its priorities straight if it was involved in sinking the Greenpeace ship'.[56]

New Zealand opinion hardened in response to its allies' lack of response. This was not immediately obvious from the polls of 1985–86, when the public preference was still to have things both ways. The French government's involvement took some time to establish beyond doubt, and negotiations with the Americans over ANZUS did not finally break down until late 1986. It was not until 1989 that polls showed clearly that a majority of New Zealanders were prepared to sacrifice the traditional alliances for the anti-nuclear policy.[57] Yet it seems likely that the crucial shift dated from the sinking of the *Rainbow Warrior* and the allied non-reactions to it, when affronted new nationalism began to contest with traditionalism in the minds of the populist middle ground.

A leading diplomatic historian has asked, 'Was the ANZUS crisis New Zealand's war of independence?'[58] My answer is yes, with the sinking of the *Rainbow Warrior* as the Boston Tea Party, but in a strange mutated way. The crisis interacted decisively with an upsurge in New Zealand nationalism, but this was inchoate, contested and suppressed by the prevailing belief that independence had come long before. One form was a gradual disconnection from Britain in mass attitudes. Somewhere between the 1960s and the 1980s, a prospective attack on Canterbury, Kent, ceased to seem similar to an attack on Canterbury, South Island. This was related to economic disconnection, which is much more easily measurable. New Zealand's trade lifelines were spreading and multiplying, as we shall see in the next section. They now ran to prospective enemies as to allies, and the enemies were less and less convincingly prospective. These factors merged with socio-cultural changes from within New Zealand, which produced new, liberal and influential groups. This complex process is discussed further in Part Six. But, combined with the British disconnection, it created the 'lash' to which Rob's Mob 'backlashed'. Even some members of Greenpeace New Zealand, middle class and committed internationalists, resented the 'international takeover' of their office by overseas activists after the *Rainbow Warrior* sinking. 'Suddenly the crowded office was full of Americans and Europeans, and suddenly it was no longer ours.'[59] The liberal 'lash' and the traditonal populist 'backlash' were both nationalist responses to decolonisation. As a target for nationalist sentiment, France was in some respects a proxy for the United States, which was in turn a proxy for Britain. It was not only ANZUS that went down with the *Rainbow Warrior*, but also the remnants of the British alliance. New Zealand now had only one ally left: Australia.

From the 1880s, as we saw in Chapter One, the recolonial connection with Britain had gradually displaced the old, Australasian, 'Tasman world'. The Tasman Sea widened increasingly after Australian federation, and New Zealand non-federation, in 1901. The various components of the Australia–New Zealand relationship diminished at varying speeds – quite fast in economics, politics and the writing of history; more slowly in sport, where the two countries shared an Olympic team until 1919; and more slowly still in such spheres as unionism, radicalism, and literature. Connections persist in such things as migration, banking and popular culture. But even in these spheres there is a strange element of mutual plagiarism. Australian influences have to have their labels ripped off before being fully popularised in New Zealand, and vice versa. The rift between neighbours was camouflaged by these residual connections, by shared membership of the British Empire and Commonwealth, and by the legend of Anzac, which nominally united Australia and New Zealand. We have seen that the Anzac alliance was not that close in the Second World War, and in any case this relationship was restricted to wartime.

The root of the rift was the development of similar but separate recolonial relationships with Britain. Australia, too, underwent 'recolonisation' from the late nineteenth century, though those of its historians who realise this do not use the name or, perhaps, grasp the full implications. The Australia–New Zealand–British relationship was both horizontal and vertical in the nineteenth century. Horizontally, it connected Australia and New Zealand, then stretched vertically from a shared Australasia to Britain. In the twentieth century, it split into two separate vertical relationships: Australian–British and New Zealand–British. Because Australia was bigger, and somewhat less export-dependent and economically narrow, and perhaps because of its larger Catholic Irish population as well, its recolonial connection with Britain was always a little less intense than New Zealand's. Decolonisation, and a parallel social untightening, began earlier in Australia – but not by much. About a third of Australia's exports went to Britain in the early 1960s, compared with half of New Zealand's. Australia received no 'special arrangements' with the EEC, and its trade with Britain reached relative insignificance in the late 1970s, ten years before New Zealand's. Australia also decolonised demographically faster than New Zealand. There was huge Southern European immigration in the 1950s and 1960s, and East Asian immigration in the 1970s and 1980s. The former was never matched in New Zealand, and the latter did not occur until the 1990s. Australia adopted the Statute of Westminster in 1942, five years before New Zealand, and obtained television in 1956, four years before. Those Tasmanian hedonists got rid of six o'clock closing of pubs in 1937, and New South Wales in 1954, but South Australia waited until 1967, the same year as their Wakefieldian cousins in New Zealand.[60]

The decline of recolonisation on both sides of the Tasman led to a revival of the Tasman world. This began formally with the New Zealand and Australian Free Trade Agreement (NAFTA) of 1965, but was not really reflected in flows of trade until a few years later. The proportion of New Zealand exports to Australia rose from 4.5 per cent in 1967 – the same level it had been since 1920 – to about 8 per cent in 1970, 12 per cent in 1980, and to 20 per cent in the 1990s, by which time Australia was New Zealand's biggest trading partner.[61] The expansion actually began before the Closer Economic Relations agreement of 1983, though this did provide another boost. CER was originally an Australian initiative, but New Zealand became increasingly enthusiastic about it.[62] After the demise of the British military alliance in the early 1970s and the American alliance in the mid-1980s, Australian and New Zealand relations in defence also tightened. The number of New Zealand servicemen training in Australia, for example, rocketed from 58 to 415 between 1976 and 1986.[63] Australia was now the only ally New Zealand had left. Much as Australia might dislike aspects of New Zealand's foreign policy, the addition of about 20 per cent to its defence and economic resources was not to be sneezed at. The recent tightening of economic and defence relations has led experts to assert that the Australian–New Zealand connection is the closest of any two countries in the world. This is true to a significant degree. Few other pairs of peoples share so many professional associations, merge military units so readily or fit so easily into each other's lifestyles when visiting or migrating. Yet, under the surface, all is not yet well in the trans-Tasman remarriage.

The pea under the mattress is not the occasional Australian denunciation of 'Kiwi bludgers' – New Zealand migrants on Australian social welfare – or the thriving genre of trans-Tasman jokes. The former inverts nineteenth-century New Zealand feelings about Australian migrants, and ignores the fact that Kiwis in Australia, who now number about 400,000,[64] have better employment records than the native-born population. The jokes usually have the flavour of sibling joshing and can be seen as a valuable part of Tasman culture. But occasionally they take on a nastier edge. When they do, they merge with a surprising degree of mutual disregard and mutual neglect between the world's best neighbours. In the 1900s, Edward Tregear, Secretary of Labour and an important architect of New Zealand's arbitration system, which was also of interest to Australia, visited Melbourne. He offered local newspapers an article on labour relations in New Zealand. It was rejected. When he asked why, he was told, 'You are too microscopically small for us.'[65] Such attitudes appear to persist into the present, at least among Australian politicians. 'In the words of a senior Australian politician, "Australians don't care a —— about New Zealanders, and they resent us for it." '[66]

New Zealanders reciprocate this attitude. In 1984, a survey indicated that 71 per cent of New Zealanders disliked something about Australians. Anti-Australianism has recurring spasms of popularity in New Zealand television advertisements. Dame Edna Everidge, a comic icon of Australian cultural nationalism, returned the favour in the form of her silent sidekick Madge, a New Zealander. Only 36 per cent of Australians disliked something about New Zealanders, but this was more a function of ignorance than benignity: 73 per cent of Australians 'knew little or nothing about New Zealand', not even the name of its capital city. The surveyed Australians managed to remain ignorant despite the fact that 40 per cent of them had friends or relatives in New Zealand. It must have been quite hard work. Presumably their letters were marked 'Poste Restante, New Zealand'. New Zealand is indeed less important to Australia than the reverse. But, in terms of trade and of population and economic size, it is at least twice as important to Australia as Australia is to the United States.

This curious mutual neglect also extends to writers and historians, though more by omission than commission. As an Australian literary historian has noted:

Cultural exchanges between the two countries are now probably weaker than a century ago . . . Two countries that a century ago almost federated are now in crucial respects at a greater cultural distance than at any time since European settlement to the detriment of both.[67]

The situation is at least as bad in the study of history, where the two countries' mutual neglect is awe-inspiring. James Cowan, a leading New Zealand historian of the early twentieth century, matched Melbourne's rejection of Tregear in 1901. New Zealand, wrote Cowan, 'has a history. Australia has none.'[68] Studies of one shore of the nineteenth-century Tasman world still manage somehow to ignore the other. This misrepresents a shared past and also deprives historians of a rare opportunity to use each other's history as a control group, or reference point. Such control groups can be crucial to scientific inquiry. Historians' debates about male culture, indigenous resistance, women's history and attitudes to the state, along with many other things, would benefit greatly from Tasman comparisons. In theory, historians should give their eye-teeth for an intriguing shadow-self, an instructively distorted mirror image. Yet, generally speaking, Australian and New Zealand historians prefer to look past each other.

In doing so, we not only pass up rich comparative opportunities, but also reinvent our own national histories. New Zealand and Australia, after 1901, required separateness and difference in the present, so they invented it in the past. For the nineteenth century, to an important extent, a wholly separate history of New Zealand and a separate whole history of Australia are gigantic myths, which helped make themselves true in the twentieth century. New collective identities need negative definitions, Madges for Dame Ednas, especially those that assuage one's own perceived inadequacies. Until the mid-twentieth century, Australia was small in population and very dependent on sheep and Britain; but less small and dependent than New Zealand. New Zealand had some convict stock and a great deal of racialism and frontier wildness; but less of all three than Australia. Just about the only thing the six Australian states in 1901 had in common, which New Zealand did not share, was that they were not New Zealand. A principal definition of New Zealanders was that they were the Australasians who were not Australians. Do we still need our mild antagonisms and our dismissals of shared history to maintain our collective identities?

Terms of Trade

New Zealand economic analysis sometimes seems to have a fetish about growth and exports. It has been suggested that New Zealand does not need much of either, and that it could – maybe even should – accept a low-growth, low-export future.[69] The case for export-led growth, however, remains strong.

New Zealanders want some goods and services that they cannot produce themselves, and must therefore trade for them. Populations grow, and therefore economies must. Expectations rise, and this is not necessarily a matter of mere greed. New medical equipment and drugs, for example, do more and therefore sometimes cost more. Exports and growth remain central in New Zealand's past and – in the medium term at least – its future. This section traces the response to decolonisation and its harbingers in the export economy in the second half of the twentieth century.

During the 1950s and 1960s, the traditional British market ceased to be able to deliver growth to the New Zealand economy. In very broad terms, it remained static between the early 1950s and 1973, at over 500,000 tonnes of protein products, and 60,000–80,000 tonnes of wool. It was still the basis, the meat and butter, of New Zealand's export market but, from the end of wartime bulk purchasing by the British government in the early 1950s, exporters increasingly had to look elsewhere for the extras. This led to the beginning of the main good news of recent New Zealand economic history, a process known as 'diversification': an apparently successful hunt for new markets and new products, 1950s–90s.

The first stage of this process reduced Britain's share of New Zealand exports from two-thirds in 1950 to less than two-fifths in 1970. The year 1965 was the last in which Britain took more than half of New Zealand's exports, a watershed indeed. From 1965, for the first time, it mattered more to New Zealand if the rest of the world disappeared than if Britain did. Yet Britain remained far and away the leading market, especially for the leading industry, protein. A shift from the *relative* decline to the *absolute* decline of the British market took place in and around 1973, when Britain joined the EEC. In only two years, between 1972 and 1974, protein exports to Britain fell from 515,000 to 387,000 tonnes, and continued to fall. New Zealand put enormous diplomatic effort into negotiating transitional arrangements, as we have seen, but this only slowed the decline. By 1980, Britain took only 14 per cent of New Zealand's exports. The figure was 7 per cent by 1989, and has remained at or below that modest level.

The pattern, then, is not one of steady decline of the British market 1950–90, as most economic history would have it, but of moderate (and relative) decline 1950–70 (from 66 to 36 per cent), followed by steep (and absolute) decline 1970–90 (36 to 7 per cent). The decisive drop came in the 1970s. Diversification has therefore to be divided into two types. *Supplementary* diversification augmented the major market, Britain, because it had ceased to grow. *Replacement* diversification sought to substitute for it, because it had begun to shrink – fast. The two types of diversification sometimes intersected in time and industry, but the distinction is important. Supplementary diversification tended towards new markets and old products, or adaptations of old products. Replacement diversification tended to new products.

The major form of supplementary diversification, noted in Chapter Nine, was the extension of the traditional protein industry into beef, milk powder and casein, aimed initially at Britain but increasingly, from the late 1950s, at the United States and Japan. Yet, initially, there was something curiously casual, even half-hearted, about New Zealand's 'drive' to open up these markets. 'The demands from the US and Japan were spontaneous diversifications springing from the importing countries and not originated by exporters. They occurred before . . . the Meat Board or the Government had recognised the need to diversify.'[70] New Zealand had appointed a trade representative in Japan in 1947, but only because everyone else had, and trade was minimal for the next ten years.[71] No ships at all ran between the two countries before 1952, and for the next five years carriage was restricted to occasional 'tramp' steamers and Japanese whalers doubling as freighters on the journey home. In 1957 there were still 'no shipping services to Japan'. But in that year, New Zealand meat exporters 'suddenly experienced a most welcome inquiry from Japan for beef or mutton'. The big British–New Zealand meat companies, Vestey's and Borthwick's, decided to send emissaries to Tokyo. In one case, the decision was made by executives strolling in Smithfield, London, capital of the New Zealand–British meat industry. The emissary, a New Zealander, was ludicrously unprepared. He spoke no Japanese, had no interpreter, no contacts and no pre-arranged appointments. 'How do you direct a taxi when you cannot speak the language, or ask a policeman? How do you find your way back to the hotel if you venture out? No one had thought of these problems in London.'[72] As late as 1965, experts were pleading with exporters to sell the Japanese what they wanted to buy, and not necessarily what New Zealand traditionally sold.[73] Japan took less than 3 per cent of New Zealand's exports in 1960.

Before the Second World War, the United States had been a spasmodically significant market for New Zealand beef. During the war, as we have seen, economic as well as military relations with America intensified greatly. After the war, however, the potential new trade relationship was shouldered aside by the re-establishment of the recolonial system. In 1954, the United States took only 500 tons of New Zealand beef, while Britain took 48,000 tons. In 1955, a medium-sized New Zealand meat company, Hellaby's, became interested in exporting beef to the United States. It discovered 'one fatal hitch. No shipping company was interested in providing refrigerated service from New Zealand to American ports. The trade was lost by default.'[74] Hellaby's later hired its own ship and, with other companies, managed to revive the

American trade by 1959, when the United States took 62,000 tons of New Zealand beef. The government established a marketing company in the United States in 1960. Over the 1960s, beef production doubled, with the United States as its major market. But New Zealand beef did not establish itself as a high-value branded product. It tended to go into hamburgers rather than be sold as cuts. On top of this, spasms of protectionism made the United States an unreliable and limited market.[75] It took 10 per cent of New Zealand exports in 1960, and 13 per cent in 1970, but remained at about this level in the 1980s and 1990s. It was more a supplementary market than a replacement one.

The development of casein and milk-powder exports was at first sight the most remarkable of these early diversifications. In fact, the export of these products was an old game, but one that had hitherto not been played very hard. Milk-powder exports began with Glaxo in the 1900s, grew during World War One, and thereafter basically tracked the fortunes of this single company until after World War Two. Casein was a milk by-product used in food, paints, plastics and, after 1935, in synthetic fibres. Exports of casein dated from 1920 but, like milk powder, remained modest until after the war. Britain, as usual, took most of these products at first, but it quickly became clear that both had global markets: casein in developed countries for its industrial uses, and milk powder in less developed countries as a substitute for fresh dairy products. Between 1948 and 1960, exports of the two rose from 30,000 to 90,000 tons. This still amounted to only 2 or 3 per cent of export receipts. In the 1960s, however, as portents of doom appeared over the British market, casein and milk powder entered a second, even greater, spurt of growth, involving many more markets, notably in South-east Asia. Between 1960 and 1973–74, production of milk powder and casein rose from 90,000 to 300,000 tons. This amounted to about 10 per cent of exports receipts – and the two products remain at about this level. Indeed, the New Zealand dairy industry is now more a matter of milk powder and casein than butter and cheese. In short, New Zealand does not appear to have been hugely interested in extending the market for these promising products until it had to be. In their moderate-growth phase, to the 1950s, they were supplementary diver-sifications. In their high-growth phase, from the 1960s, they were replacements.[76]

Since the 1850s, the long-distance stayer of the New Zealand economy had been wool, though driven into second place in a two-industry race first by gold, and then by protein. In the 1950s, high demand and high prices seemed likely to restore wool to its former glory. Demand and prices fluctuated in the 1960s – sharply downwards in 1967–68 – but production continued to grow. In 1969, it could still be said that 'wool is king and likely to remain so'.[77] In 1972–74, as with protein, there was a sharp drop in exports, from 334,000 to 240,000 tonnes. Subsidy, notably supplementary minimum prices, then pushed production back up, to 373,000 tonnes in 1985. Sheep numbers grew from 55 million in the mid-1970s to 70 million by 1982, a huge growth unjustified by demand.[78] Tens of millions of sheep that would not otherwise have existed owe their short lives to Robert Muldoon, who was a sheep-god if nothing else. After the removal of subsidies in 1984, decline set in again. By 1999, wool production was less than half its 1985 level. Wool, which provided a quarter of New Zealand's exports as recently as 1967, had plummeted to a measly 3.8 per cent.[79] It was no longer king and, barring a new ice age, never more will be so.

Wool had long been less dependent on the British market than protein, and therefore suffered somewhat less from the relative and absolute declines of that market. Another factor of equal importance in its fall from grace was increasing competition from synthetic fibres (perhaps including those made partly from New Zealand casein). There was also an inherent volatility stemming from the fact that the countries that now wanted wool, such as China and Russia, were less able to pay for it. Finally, there was a succession of droughts that hit sheep country particularly hard. But the collapse of recolonisation contributed here too. Britain was not totally dominant, as in protein, but it was still the leading market for New Zealand wool until 1973. Its take then fell sharply: from 60,000 tons in the early 1970s, to 40,000 in the early 1980s, to 20,000 in the early 1990s. New Zealand's British market for wool had long been well *supplemented*, and the supplements remain, but it was not *replaced*.

The new emphasis on beef, casein and milk powder was an adaptation of the protein industry rather than a set of wholly new industries. Each had been exported in small quantities for a long time. Shifting a farm from sheep to beef cattle or a dairy factory from cheese to milk powder was neither quick nor easy, but it was vastly quicker and easier than shifting to horticulture or forestry. New Zealand pastoral production had long had flexibility within its limits. It was able to switch quickly from cheese to butter and back during World War Two, for example. The switch to the new dairy products was also made with impressive smoothness on the farm and in the dairy factories, although not necessarily in distribution and marketing. Dairy farmers had long sold their bobby calves as meat, and some sheep farmers had long run beef cattle on the side, so the shift to beef was also quite smooth.

There were also more radical adaptations of pastoral farming. Goat farming, for fine mohair, cashmere and angora wools, and even ostrich farming for meat, developed in the 1980s and 1990s. Because of the particular volatility of the world fibre market, goat farming proved somewhat disappointing. Goat numbers dropped by two-thirds between 1991 and 1996, to fewer than 300,000 animals. More important was deer farming, which developed a remarkable dual market, enhancing sex as well as diet. Antler velvet was used as an ingredient in aphrodisiacs and other medications in China and Hong Kong, while venison was popular in countries such as Germany. These were not new industries; they were either revived or activated from long-standing latency. Goat and ostrich farming had been tried in the nineteenth century, and New Zealand had long been rich in wild deer, to the point where they were culled as pests. Wild venison was occasionally exported in the 1950s, and velvet began selling in Hong Kong in 1962.[80] But the first deer farm was not established until 1970, and the number of deer was still only 100,000 in 1980. As in the nineteenth century, there was a 'rush phase' in deer farming, as in goats, with existing farms stocking new ones at high prices. Deer numbers rose to over a million in the 1990s, but they still provide less than 1 per cent of exports.[81]

The broad pattern in the volume of pastoral exports is one of good growth to 1970, a sharp fall in the early 1970s, some recovery in the later 1970s, and stasis in the 1980s. In the 1990s, the pattern began to diverge sharply by product. Dairy products grew strongly as their markets globalised still further; meat was static; and wool declined in both volume and value. Pastoralism, traditionally the main engine of the New Zealand economy, scarcely broke even in the last three decades of the twentieth century, let alone supplied growth. Pastoral products, which had accounted for about 90 per cent of exports in 1950, provided only a third at the end of century.[82] Despite efforts to supplement markets and adapt products, New Zealand's brilliant career as a one-industry economy, a pastoral town-supply district, was over.

To the 1960s, the New Zealand export economy was still a one-legged animal, overwhelmingly dependent on pastoral industries, old and new. From the 1960s, it transformed itself into a four-legged beast. The three new limbs were non-pastoral primary industries (forestry, fish and horticulture), manufactured exports, and the export of services, notably tourism.

The major non-pastoral new primary industries were the three Fs: forestry, fishing and fruit (including vegetables and viticulture). Forestry consisted essentially in the export of radiata pine and its products. The planting of these Californian trees on a large scale began in the 1920s – prompted, ironically enough, by Britain, which had experienced acute timber shortages during World War One.[83] Planting continued in the 1930s, especially in and around the Bay of Plenty, and the trees began maturing in 1952. A second bout of planting occurred in the 1970s and 1980s. The state initially took the lead, in both planting and processing. Timber towns emerged and Tauranga grew rapidly as a timber port. Private companies also entered the industry, drawing even with the state in the 1970s and taking over leadership in the 1980s. The main products were pulp and paper, which went mainly to Australia, and raw or rough-cut logs, which went mainly to Japan. Forestry was being vaunted as a coming industry as early as the 1950s. But the export of forestry products was virtually non-existent in 1950, and reached only 2.5 per cent of exports by 1958 and 4 per cent by 1967. This share doubled over the next decade, however, to 8 per cent, and fluctuated between that figure and 12 per cent through the 1980s and 1990s.[84] Using 5 per cent of total exports as the threshold for a really major export industry, forestry reached this status, for the first time since the kauri-exporting days of the early twentieth century, in the 1970s – not before.

In 1885, Robert Stout asserted that potentially 'the fishing industry is as important as the agricultural and pastoral industry'. New Zealand certainly had abundant resources of fish, but Stout proved as poor a prophet as he was a politician. From the decline of whaling in the 1850s until the 1970s, New Zealand fishing was the classic 'Cinderella industry', and was frequently described as such.[85] This was true of domestic commercial consumption, let alone exporting. Fishing was primarily a sport, not a business. In general, if you could not catch your own, you went without. It is still not possible to buy one of New Zealand's numerous trout, which the tight society always maintained should be left for anglers. Fish markets in Auckland and Wellington closed in the 1920s.[86] A small industry, with Dalmatians, Greeks and Italians prominent, struggled along, providing fish to the mainstream population only as a cheap meat of last resort or as a takeaway convenience food in the form of fish and chips. Bluff oysters, crayfish and whitebait were valued as rare or seasonal treats. But per capita consumption of fish and shellfish was small, at 14 pounds per year to 1969. Per capita consumption of red meat, on the other hand, averaged about 200 pounds a year, with pork and poultry on top of that.[87]

As for the exporting of fish, two commissions of inquiry, in 1937 and 1956 'found no evidence to suggest that they [the fisheries] could be substantially upgraded to contribute to export earnings'.[88] In 1963–64, the government attempted to stimulate the industry by setting up an industry board, but immediate success was limited, with one exception. This was the Chatham Island crayfishing boom of the 1960s, which exported frozen crayfish tails to the American market as rock lobster. The boom was intriguingly reminiscent of nineteenth-century rushes, with high rewards, sharp practice, little regard for locals or environment, and a quick exhaustion of the resource. Deer culling and crayfish rushing were twentieth-century

New Zealand's Wild West industries, along with the sharemarket boom of the 1980s. The Chathams boom peaked in 1968–69. Apart from crayfish tails, which yielded $14 million, export receipts from fish in 1969 were a miserable $2 million. In 1965, including crayfish, it had been $5 million.[89] Fish exports remained modest to the mid-1970s, at between $17 million and $25 million a year, but began to climb with the establishment of the 200-mile New Zealand 'External Economic Zone' in 1978 – to $130 million in 1980. In the 1980s, deep-sea orange roughy joined hoki as a major finfish export, and fish farming of mussels and oysters emerged. Total exports exceeded $1 billion in the 1990s, when the industry cracked the 5 per cent threshold.

Horticulture is New Zealand's oldest type of farming, dating from the cultivation of East Polynesian tubers – kumara, taro and yam – by the first settlers in or around the eleventh century. Apples, carried to Britain in cool storage on the great meatships from 1899, were the only long-term horticultural export of any significance until the 1970s, sitting at around 1 per cent of total exports by value. The export of New Zealand grass seed to Australia and Britain was intriguing, but even more minor. Commercial vegetable production commenced on a large scale with Wattie's Canneries in Hawke's Bay in the 1930s.[90] In World War Two, it produced for a temporary export market – American troops in the Pacific. Exports of fresh, frozen and canned vegetables, mainly to Australia, continued at modest levels. In the late 1950s, the whole sector contributed about 2 per cent of export receipts. The level was no different in 1971. During the 1970s and 1980s, however, the trade boomed towards the $1 billion mark and exceeded 5 per cent of export receipts. By 1999, the figures were $1.5 billion and 7 per cent. Fruit, like fish and, to a lesser extent, forestry, was a replacement industry, its great growth, though not its prehistory, dating from decolonisation in and around 1973. Two horticultural products in particular, kiwifruit and wine, can be used to illustrate themes in this process: the tardiness of replacement diversification, and the 'recolonial gap'.

The big contributor to the New Zealand fruit rush was a wild Chinese plant known as the monkey peach, or Chinese gooseberry, later rechristened the kiwifruit. In 1903, Isabel Fraser, principal of Wanganui Girls' College, visited her sister, a mission nurse, in China. She brought back the original seedlings, but they were used mainly as garden creepers until the 1920s. Commercial planting began in the 1930s with the advent of the improved 'Hayward' variety. Experimental exports were made in 1952, to Britain, and in 1964, to the United States, but exports did not even exceed domestic consumption until – you guessed it – the mid-1970s. Kiwifruit boomed thereafter into a major industry. Production, now predominantly for export, increased 25-fold between 1978 and 1988, to 230,000 tonnes. Overexcitement in this rush phase, and the export of seedlings to competing producers overseas, reduced prices and the bubble of green gold burst to some extent around 1990. But kiwifruit remained alongside apples as the leading horticultural export. What is interesting about this is that the main preconditions for kiwifruit export were available well before the export boom of the later 1970s and 1980s. It was known that the fruit stored well for four months or more, even without cool storage, from 1926. The optimal variety had been developed by the 1930s. The kiwifruit name and the overseas market had shown promise by the early 1960s – an American mail-order fruit supplier adopted it as 'fruit of the month' in 1964. But again, nothing much happened until after the mid-1970s.[91]

Grape growing in New Zealand dates from 1819, and the making of wine from the 1830s. James Busby, the British Resident in New Zealand from 1833 to 1840, was an important pioneer in both the Australian and New Zealand wine industries. His house at Waitangi should be sacred to wine as well as treaties, as the first place where, in 1840, a Frenchman passed judgement on New Zealand wine: 'very sparkling and delicious to taste'.[92] Other pioneers include the Marist Brothers of Mission Vineyards in Hawke's Bay, and the Spanish winemaker Joseph Soler of Wanganui. Soler's wines won a large number of international awards in the 1870s and 1880s. From the 1890s, these pioneers were joined by Dalmatian winemakers moving south from the gumfields to the outskirts of Auckland. In the 1890s and 1900s, the Liberal government attempted to give a boost to the industry by bringing in an adviser, Romeo Bragato, and establishing state vineyards. Suddenly, however, the bottom fell out of a promising industry. State support faded from the late 1900s and the industry experienced lean times until the 1960s. One factor in this was clearly the drive for moral harmony, in the form of the prohibition movement. But there was also a collapse of state and public interest in wine as an import-replacement or export industry. Between 1909 and 1923, the area growing grapes dropped from 668 to 179 acres. When the state winery at Te Kauwhata was put up for auction in 1933, there were no bidders. Wine production in the 1950s ran at about a 30th of 1990s levels, when significant wine exports at last began – more than a century after Soler's international successes.[93] Quality New Zealand winemaking is not a new industry, it is a revived one. It experienced a long 'recolonial gap', roughly 1900s–60s, and it was by no means the only industry to do so.

In the 1880s, the New Zealand economy had undergone its previous bout of traumatic transformation, from the progressive colonial system to the recolonial one. Then it had been rescued by a technological knight in icy armour: refrigeration. The rescue was not immediately apparent, and there was much work to be done on New Zealand production and British distribution, but it was refrigeration that opened the gate to the protein industry. Has there been a modern equivalent of refrigeration, a technological 'Get Out of Jail' card, for the New Zealand economy of the late twentieth century? There have been important technical improvements of various kinds in various of the industries mentioned hitherto. Advances in the vacuum packaging of meat, for example, were quite dramatic,[94] but as yet nothing to match the big seaborne fridge. The Internet is one possible technological saviour, in that it eliminates New Zealand's disadvantage of distance in communications and information, and permits it to compete on even terms in the creation of knowledge-based services. The closest thing to a modern equivalent of refrigeration is not the Internet, however, but the wide-bodied jet.

Until the 1960s, for all the hype about scenic wonderlands and all the government intervention, overseas tourism was a very minor industry. The number of overseas visitors a year was 12,000 or fewer until the 1920s, reached 17,000 in 1935, and was still only 36,000 in 1960. From 1963, numbers rose with jet services, reaching 154,000 in 1970, 445,000 in 1980, 933,000 in 1990, and 1,550,000 in 1997 – roughly a 50-fold expansion in 37 years. In 1999, the official estimate of income from overseas tourism, excluding international airfares (which often went to Air New Zealand), was $3.6 billion, equivalent to over 15 per cent of merchandise exports. Other estimates are higher.[95] Tourism now vies annually with dairy products to be New Zealand's biggest earner of overseas funds.

Overseas tourism seems to be the great success story of the decolonising economy, and to a considerable extent it is. Adventure tourism has developed a special Kiwi flavour, with commercial jet-boating from 1965, white-water rafting from 1974, and bungy jumping from 1988.[96] Whales became a valuable commodity for the first time since the nineteenth century, with whale watching at Kaikoura attracting 140,000 tourists in 1995.[97] 'Backpackers', a relatively unintrusive type of tourist, became prominent, contributing over 20 per cent of tourist revenue in 1993.[98] Yet even in tourism it is not clear that development has been as complete, as rapid or as decolonial as it might have been. Many New Zealanders have hesitations about tourism, as though it is an optional extra rather than one of the four legs of the export economy, and despite the fact that tourist numbers relative to host population are still quite low compared with global tourism hotspots such as Greece or Florida. New Zealand had almost as many overseas tourists as Australia in 1965, but only half as many in 1985, and just over a third as many in 1995.[99] The main tourist route is still Auckland–Rotorua–Christchurch–Queenstown, with the two big cities more access points than attractions in themselves. One expert describes government tourism policy as 'ad hoc and incremental . . . The tourism portfolio never ranked very high'.[100] When one politician did take an interest in boosting the industry in 1977, he found that operators preferred things as they were. 'I found myself out on my own facing private-sector reluctance.'[101] Between 1969 and 1978, the number of hotel rooms increased from 10,000 to 15,000, or 5.3 per cent per year, well below the levels required by increasing tourist numbers.[102]

Moreover, experts and the industry itself are still united in the belief that it is New Zealand nature alone, and not culture as well, that attracts overseas tourists, and always will. 'Natural heritage is unrivalled in its status as New Zealand's most lucrative tourist commodity.'[103]

> Maori culture is of interest to many visitors but the relatively short history of European settlement has meant that the country lacks the historical resources of many 'old world' destinations while the small population base and city size have constrained the development of urban attractions and entertainment.[104]

The same attitude is all too clear in the national tourism organisation's strategy as recently as 1999.

If this book and its predecessor, *Making Peoples*, prove nothing else, they prove that New Zealand, too, has 'historical resources'. As for urban attractions, these are no longer lacking in Wellington, for example. Its arts festival and professional theatre are internationally competitive, and fieldwork suggests that the less formal entertainment in Courtenay Place on a Friday night compares quite favourably with that in Soho or Kings Cross. If tourism is 'commodified difference', then New Zealand has plenty of cultural as well as natural difference. The 'great nature, pity about the culture' assumption is a recolonial one, and it persists in tourism, otherwise a decolonial industry, to the present.

In 1999, the three Fs – forestry, fishing and fruit – together supplied 23 per cent of New Zealand's merchandise exports, compared with the modern, modest, protein industry's 33 per cent. Tourism and other services exports together were also in this league. The final new export leg was the long-awaited growth of manufactured exports, from 4 per cent in 1970 to over 20 per cent in 1990, and to 29 per cent in 1989.[105] There were three major elements to this very respectable growth: Think Big, the new Australian market and an increase in 'adding value' through the further processing of primary exports. Exports from the major Think Big projects were mineral fuels (2 per cent of exports in 1999), iron and steel (2 per cent) and aluminium (4.2 per cent), a total of over 8 per cent of exports.[106] These 'manufactures' were not always very highly processed in New Zealand – iron and steel, for example, left mostly in raw form. Import substitution in mineral fuels, in which New Zealand had been 30–50 per cent self-sufficient since the mid-1980s, could be added to the total. But this was arguably more a cost than a benefit given the low global price of oil between the mid-1980s and the late 1990s. Some 8 per cent of exports after twenty years was hardly what the architects of Think Big had hoped for, and there is still no sign of the 410,000 jobs. One cannot help but think that 11 billion 1980 dollars of public money could have boosted exports more if invested in other ways. Adding value through further processing had long been a Holy Grail of New Zealand economic reformers. It applied mainly to primary products and could therefore be associated as much with primary industry as with manufacturing. Adding value is not easy to measure, but is likely to have contributed substantially to the growth of manufactured exports, particularly in the 1970s.

Trade with Australia burgeoned from the late 1960s, as we have seen, and manufactured exports were a significant part of it. By the late 1980s, the trade amounted to a partial merging of the two countries into the same domestic market. Australian and New Zealand businesses set up in each other's markets and invested in each other's companies as the Tasman world revived. There was a certain amount of rationalisation – the same chewing-gum company produced stick gum in Australia and bubble gum in New Zealand – and a certain amount of complementarity. The two countries met needs for each other that, by nature, they could not themselves fully supply – wood to Australia, oil to New Zealand. There were developments in the New Zealand export of machinery and equipment – about 10 per cent of all exports in 1999 – about half of which went to Australia. For the first time since World War Two, New Zealand-made machines crossed the seas in bulk. Such exports received considerable stimulation from the devaluations of the New Zealand dollar in the mid-1980s.

However, the promise of the Australian and other new markets for manufactured exports has to be set against the decline of domestic manufacturing. The removal of import controls and the big reduction in tariffs from 1984 hit domestic manufacture harder than export manufacture. But the former was often the base for the latter, and it was a shrinking base from 1984 as the barriers to overseas competition were removed. Even manufactured exports actually dropped in the early years of restructuring, and did not recover their 1984 level until 1990. 'The loss of market share and the failure to increase exports are suggestive of decline rather than restructuring.'[107] Many domestic manufacturing industries shrank dramatically, while the motor-vehicle-assembly industry, once large, disappeared completely in 1998. Sometimes, increased exports compensated for decreased domestic sales, but only partly. In the clothing industry, for example, exports climbed from $49 million in 1989 to $185 million in 1997, but imports climbed from $129 million to $616 million – a huge net loss in sales by local producers. Restructuring not only seems to have increased the drift north of manufacturers to Auckland, but also superimposed a drift further north, to Fiji, where labour costs were lower, and a drift west, to Australia, where more consumers were concentrated.

It may be that the restructurers were not wholly responsible for the collapse of domestic manufacturing, which was showing signs of decline before 1984. Despite protection, it was harder to compete with cheap Japanese goods than with expensive British ones. Consumers benefited, and one does not have to be a free-marketeer to see the system of old tariffs and import controls as unduly cumbersome. But it is also true that restructuring was not responsible for the main growth of manufactured exports. The big jump, from 4 per cent to 16 per cent of all exports, a 300 per cent increase, occurred in the 1970s. The 1980s contributed only a 25 per cent increase, and the 1990s a 50 per cent increase. As with the other legs of the new economy, the restructuring of content, to the extent that it existed, actually pre-dated the restructuring of form.

New Zealand businesses themselves sometimes showed a curious reluctance to seize the opportunities of the new four-legged economy. We have seen that primary exporters hesitated about the Japanese and American markets in the 1950s, and tourism operators about ambitious new developments in the 1970s. The state had to take the lead in Think Big. New Zealand businesses dragged their feet about plunging into the Australian market. John Marshall claimed that after the NAFTA agreement of 1965, 'I had to drag our manufacturers kicking and squealing' into the Australian market.[108] Most manufacturers lobbied against CER in the early 1980s. Neither the Kirk government, nor Muldoon himself showed much interest.[109] Value-adding was remarkably slow, given the seemingly obvious advantages and the vigour with which it was preached. As late as the mid-1980s, in the meat-freezing industry 'a "carcass for consignment" mentality slowed moves into further processing despite farmer, union and government calls for such developments'.[110] This indicates the deep entrenchment, in attitudes as well as the structure of industry, of the recolonial economy. But it is not entirely fair to dismiss the reluctant as dinosaurs. They proved to have a point. The hard fact is that the sophisticated new quadruped cannot seem to run as fast as the primitive monopod could hop.

The one-legged economic tortoise of the third quarter of the twentieth century beat the four-legged economic hare of the fourth quarter. Why was this so? Some fans of the 1984 restructuring admit the low growth but urge us to wait a little longer. These disappointing outcomes, claimed the OECD economic surveys in 1999, 'probably reflect the long time it takes for economic behaviour to change and adjust to new policies'.[111] It is about fifteen years out from the 1984 restructuring of form, and about 25 years from the earlier restructuring of content, the transformation from monopod to quadruped. How long do the two restructurings get before they are judged? The explanation for the disappointing growth of the past twenty or thirty years offered here focuses on inappropriate investment; an erosion of 'social capital' and transactional advantages; and the fact that a widespread but vague sense of change was not matched by widespread and accurate analysis of its nature.

Most economic analysts, right and left, would probably agree that domestic investment has been inadequate in recent decades. The Reserve Bank's explanation is that New Zealanders have been poor savers and addicted to debt, partly because of persistently high inflationary expectations, notably in property, despite the recent reality of low inflation. This, coupled with the reduction of state controls, has led to an increased reliance on overseas investment for new developments. The notion that this is somehow necessarily evil is contestable. New Zealand has long had substantial overseas investment, it is just that it now has even more, and that it comes from Asia and America as well as Britain and Australia. But it remains true that overseas direct investment, like overseas borrowing, is second-best. Profits or interest repatriated overseas obviously have less growth impact on the domestic economy than those that remain in the country. It is no use crying over spilled investments, but we can ask whether domestic investment was available in the period since 1970, and whether there were areas in which it could have been better spent than it was. This, of course, is being wise after the event, but that is in the nature of the historian's trade.

There were at least three major potential sources of investment. One was Think Big, which absorbed $11 billion dollars of public money in the 1980s for a disappointing yield of 8 per cent of exports 20 years later. Another was the funded superannuation scheme of 1975 – Roger Douglas's indisputably good idea – which would have provided a large fund for investment as well as lowered the costs of social welfare. A third was the 'New Zealand crash penalty' of 1987 – the difference between the New Zealand share market's loss and the average international loss. A debatable fourth source might be the 'asset-sale penalty' – the difference between what was received and what might have been received if sales had been better handled and/or spread over a longer period. Even without this, the other potential sources between them indicate that money was there. Where could it have been better spent?

Pundits galore have noted the promise of 'knowledge-based industries'. Yet progress has so far been modest in terms of exports. Information technology is an obvious example. Here, New Zealand has certain cultural and natural advantages. Cultural advantages include the tendency to the quick uptake of new technologies, and the tendency to 'cultural overproduction'. A natural advantage is the Antipodean factor. New Zealanders are awake when most of the wealthy world is asleep, and could utilise this fact to provide such things as banking, news and stockbroking services. The actual export of information technology – tending, contrary to predictions, to hardware rather than software and services – is still modest, at $479 million, or about 2 per cent of exports in 1998.[112] Another field of promise as yet unfulfilled is the provision of educational services to overseas students, here or abroad. New Zealand has clear advantages here, too. English is the nearest thing to a global language, and the demand for tertiary education using it as a medium is high – in Asia, for example. New Zealand has the lowest living costs and educational costs of the English-speaking countries. Yet the 'export' of this service also remains low – at $415 million, again less than 2 per cent of exports in 1999.[113]

The knowledge-based approach, extended to history and culture, could also enhance existing big export industries. Complementing nature-based tourism with culture-based tourism is one possibility, noted above. Another is the use of history to predict demand for exports. New Zealand's recolonial protein industry stemmed from second-phase industrialisation in Britain, the consequent and predictable growth of the middle class, and its predictable adoption of predictably adapted élite consumption patterns. New Zealand plugged into, and reinforced, this trend by producing 'mass luxuries' – butter to replace lard; prime roasts to replace inferior meat or no meat at all; and carpets to replace bare floors. Second-phase industrialisation is now occurring in other potential markets, such as China, and is likely to follow the same pattern. But how much New Zealand awareness or research is there into the consumer history of China?

Knowledge-based industries have as yet not delivered on their promise. One reason is gross underinvestment in education and research. Another, perhaps, is the paucity of coherent strategies and leadership. A recent analysis suggests this is a problem in the information-technology industry, for example. 'The possibility of steering a middle path between the two extremes of laissez-faire and full-fledged government support for the IT industry does not seem to have been considered,' noted one industry commentator in 1996.[114] Yet co-operative and co-ordinated approach for the IT industry had been advocated since 1985.[115] Whether such leadership comes from the state, from an industry-wide collective approach (an ancient tradition in primary industries) or from one or two big entrepreneurial companies is not the issue here. There have been laudable efforts in this direction, notably the state-initiated Foresight Project of the late 1990s. But this and similar efforts have yet to yield major export results in knowledge-based industries.

The second set of explanations of slow growth centre on the concepts of 'social capital' and 'transaction costs'. These concepts, which have an overseas academic origin, are emphasised in two recent works: the memoirs of Jim Bolger, Prime Minister 1990–97, and a scathing attack on the 'failed revolution' of 1984–93 by academic economist Tim Hazledine. When two such disparate commentators stress the same ideas, it is time to take notice. 'Transaction costs' are the less obvious expenses of economic interaction, such as legal and banking fees, recruitment expenses, inventory costs and the like. They can also take less tangible forms, such as the speed with which a deal can be made because of common ground among the parties. The idea can usefully be extended to management, research and development, packaging, transport, market research, public relations and advertising. 'Social capital' indicates a socio-economy's capacity to limit such costs through established and effective but informal means, often semi-tangible: ways of co-operating and co-ordinating; ways of doing and discovering things; mutual trust; shared values and attitudes.

Bolger – rather late in the day, it has to be said – rightly advocates the need 'to develop the "social capital of the nation"'.[116] Hazledine argues that pre-1984 New Zealand was rich in social capital, but that restructuring has ravaged it, leading to an immense increase in transactional costs. For example, he states that the ratio of managers to workers in New Zealand rose from 1 to 20 in 1956, to 1 to 9 in 1981, to 1 to 4 in 1996.[117] Hazledine's general picture of declining social capital and rising transactional costs is convincing, and this does help explain disappointing growth to some extent. But he paints too bright a picture of New Zealand in 1984, and blames all ills on the subsequent restructuring. His own management example shows that decline set in well before that – the increase in manager-to-worker ratios was greater 1956–81 than 1981–96.

The question of whether formal restructuring alleviated or exacerbated the problem is less important than the fact that it neither caused nor cured it. Moreover, both Bolger and Hazledine focus on social capital and transaction costs *within* New Zealand, which does not necessarily explain disappointing export-driven growth. Both miss the fact that, to the 1970s, New Zealand was only one end of what was in some respects a single cultural-economic system, the other end being Britain. This recolonial unity provided shared social capital and therefore lowered the transaction costs of the trade between Britain and New Zealand. Because the new markets that replaced Britain after 1973 did not share this type of system with New Zeraland, transaction costs in trading with them were higher. Export *volume* held up, and even grew, but export *profitability* did not.

During both supplementary and replacement diversification, the British market was replaced in quantity but not in 'quality' – reliability, ease and profitability. The key reason for this was that the British–New Zealand trade relationship was 'thick' rather than 'thin': broad-based, secure, closely integrated and complementary rather than competitive. We need to remind ourselves of just how close the integration was. A study of Glaxo, by an eminent British business historian, unconsciously takes on the organisational culture of its informants. When talking of the period to the 1940s, when Glaxo was still very much New Zealand–British, it refers to 'international' and 'overseas' as being outside *both* Britain and New Zealand, as though the two were actually physically connected by the invisible protein bridge.[118] Between 1927 and 1967, a New Zealand advertising agency had five offices: in Auckland, Wellington, Christchurch, Dunedin and London.[119] When you look at the substantial older buildings of Smithfield and Tooley Street, you are looking at New Zealand historical artefacts as well as British ones. New Zealand production and London consumption specialised to suit each other, and grew together.

All this meant that, as we have seen, New Zealand exporters to Britain did not have to worry much about new products, new packaging, market research or marketing – or transport or infrastructure. The protein ships were cartel-dominated, but they were also safe, fairly efficient and secure. Infrastructure at both ends of the system was well established and changed quite slowly, minimising the need for reinvestment. The amounts proudly announced to have been spent on advertising were ludicrously low. The New Zealand Meat Board's advertising spending in Britain was £3,000 in 1926, and peaked at £34,000 in 1939.[120] The real publicity was the image of New Zealand as the Britain of the South. Economic relations were underpinned by cultural relations. New Zealand's image in Britain was everybody's business, not that of exporters alone. New Zealand products were branded, implicitly as Better British, explicitly as New Zealand. A *transnational* social capital existed, and transaction costs were consequently low.

After 1973, New Zealand's new markets seldom matched this. Some were poor and politically unstable. Others were periodically closed to protect their own farmers. Others again had the temerity to want what they wanted, not what New Zealand was accustomed to selling. In any case, milk powder to the Philippines just did not match butter to London, and beef to the United States did not match lamb to London either. New Zealand beef was unbranded and expendable, a nameless ingredient in American hamburgers, unlike the branded and valued lamb roasts on English dinner tables. Trade relations tended to be thin not thick, lacking social capital and cultural buttressing, and with higher tangible and intangible transaction costs. Hence the fact that growth in exports generated more overall economic growth before 1973 than after.

This is an explanation of the low economic growth of recent years. It is not an argument for a return to the past. The recolonial relationship is gone beyond recall and, in many respects, that is a good thing. But there are leaves to be taken from recolonisation's book. New Zealand need not be permanently content with 'town-supply district' status, and cannot and should not merely swap one town for another. But most exports are still primary products, old and new, and these are bought principally by people in towns – big towns. The trick is partly to supply more than one town, to divide and avoid being ruled. But it is also important to develop 'thicker' relationships with these prime export destinations, more like that of the old New Zealand–British protein bridge. The relationships need to be specialised and dedicated, so that New Zealand's limited resources do not disappear in the mass of the market. They need to be broad-based, carefully and systematically developed and researched, and culturally buttressed in order to lower transaction costs and permit branding. New Zealand should not sell lamb and ski-slopes, it should sell *New Zealand* lamb and *New Zealand* ski-slopes. For this to work, buyers have to have some idea of what New Zealand is.

Behind inappropriate investment and increasing transactions costs in exporting lies a failure to understand the great change in recent New Zealand history. The actual nature of that change was not restructuring and the problems at which it was directed, but the collapse of recolonisation and the advent of decolonisation. The town-supply district lost its town but failed fully to notice it. Why this was so is more a cultural question than an economic one, and it is reserved for a later chapter. But the misdiagnosis of change led to a failure to optimally manage it, to the misdiagnosis of economic problems and, therefore, to poor economic growth in the recent past.

Coming In, Coming Out

INTRODUCTION

If, by courtesy of some time machine, New Zealanders had been transposed from 1960 to the year 2000, or vice versa, they would have encountered a land transformed. In 1960, New Zealand was a tight society, in which the four harmonies still ruled. It was homogenous, conformist, masculist, egalitarian and monocultural, subject to heavy formal and informal regulation. There were no licensed restaurants, little weekend shopping, one supermarket (opened in Auckland in 1958) and a very limited range of goods and foods to buy in the shops and unlicensed restaurants that did exist. Most forms of gambling on anything other than horses, drinking in pubs after 6 pm, and Sunday newspapers were banned by law. School milk was free, but you had to drink it; compulsory military service had just been reintroduced; and a New Zealand folk motto was 'What will the neighbours say?'. In early 1960, there was no television, no radio stations other than those run by the state, and only four New Zealand feature films had been made in the previous twenty years. The cars on the street were very old and very British, and Vladimir Nabokov's novel *Lolita* had just been banned.

By the year 2000, New Zealand, for better and for worse, was one of the least regulated societies in the world, economically even more than socially. There were a dozen television channels, numerous private radio stations, and 120 New Zealand feature films had been made in the previous twenty years.[1] There were innumerable licensed restaurants, bars and cafés, and pervasive supermarket shopping, on Sunday, Saturday and the rest of the week. There were also Sunday papers and Sunday sport. The cars were now modern and Japanese; and a New Zealand academic had recently completed the definitive biography of Nabokov, whose work he would not have been able to legally read a generation before. The bars still closed at six o'clock, but am, not pm.

In 1960, most Aucklanders could scarcely bring themselves to say 'homosexual'; by 2000 they lined the streets in thousands to watch the 'Hero Parade' redefine the Queen City. The 'woman's place' in 1960 was still predominantly the home. By 2000, most women spent considerable time in the workforce, or at least on benefits waiting for a job. A mass female invasion of traditionally male professions was occurring quietly in tertiary education, which had mushroomed from 15,000 well-funded students in 1960 to 220,000 underfunded students in 2000. In 1960, women were insignificant in Parliament and local body politics. In 2000, though they remained under-represented, they were very much less so. Both major political parties were led by women, one of them the Prime Minister. The Chief Justice, the Governor-General designate and the head of the largest corporation (Telecom) were all women, too. On the other hand, more women face poverty and violence than they did in 1960, and mass entry into the modern workforce was a mixed blessing. Young people, who in 1960 were still largely seen and not heard, had also become more prominent. Mass tertiary education gave youth culture a whole new site, and global culture aimed young. But the youth-suicide rate had increased sixfold for girls and threefold for boys, the latter from a much higher base.[2]

In 1960, though their great urban migration was under way, Maori were still not seen or heard very much. The assimilationist Hunn Report was being written, and as late as 1972 a political commentator could argue that Maori leaders made Uncle Tom look like Eldridge Cleaver.[3] Today, some make Eldridge Cleaver look like Uncle Tom. Maori are culturally and politically – though not yet economically – resurgent. There are three times as many of them as there were in 1960, and their centrality in public discourse has increased massively. Ethnicity in general is another difference that has 'come out'. In 1960, New Zealand immigration policy heavily favoured Northern Europeans, with the exception of presumed guest workers from the Pacific. The claim that New Zealand was '98.5 per cent' British could still be heard. Today, there is considerable ethnic diversity, especially in Auckland, where almost 10 per cent of the population is Asian, 13 per cent Pacific Island, and 12 per cent Maori. The human face of Queen Street would have been quite hard to recognise, and the campus at the top of the hill would have been harder still. Some 30 per cent of University of Auckland students are now Asian – a change the students of 1960 would have found simply unimaginable.

As we have seen, economic change was also very substantial, but it was not very profitable. In the twenty years before 1960, New Zealand's per capita growth in real terms was healthy. In the twenty years before 2000, it was not. Unemployment was the human face of slow growth. Unemployment was not unknown in 1960, on the contrary he was very well known because there was only one of him in each district. The unemployment rate in 1960 was 0.8 per cent. By 1999, it was 9.8 per cent, having peaked at 12.5 per cent in 1991.[4] Income distribution had become less equal, with high incomes getting higher, and low and middle incomes getting lower. Crime, poverty and ethnic and social tensions had also rocketed. Violent offences had leaped from under 4,000 in 1960 to over 40,000 in 1999.[5] There had also been big shifts in collective identity. In 1960, most Pakeha New Zealanders had little doubt who they were. They were Better Britons: a distinctive Kiwi branch of the British tree, a species of the genus *Briton* whose superiority to the original was demonstrated in war, sport and the climbing of mountains. By 2000, an identity crisis had developed among Pakeha. While Maori were becoming increasingly assertive and other ethnicities were more prominent, too, some people are hard put to say what Pakeha culture is, or even if there is any. Paradise has been reforged a second time, but it is not so clear that all is well in it.

A domestic process of decolonisation – a 'coming-out' of difference and dissent, and a 'coming-in' of new influences and new migrations – created the great changes of the period 1960–2000. It interacted very closely with external decolonisation: the disconnection from Britain, and the opening-up to the world. But the internal process was not always subordinate to the external. Some of the new influences and migrations that 'came in' did so from *within* New Zealand. Some of the differences that 'came out' were both indigenous and old, existing hitherto on the margins of the tight society but now taking their chance of a place in the sun. The final part of this book explores this multifaceted process of social and cultural change.

CHAPTER SIXTEEN

Resurgent Maori

In the mid-1990s, the National government's Minister of Justice, Doug Graham, and Prime Minister, Jim Bolger, tried very hard to give away one billion dollars to Maori tribes in partial recompense for wrongs done to them in the past. Graham was a patrician Auckland lawyer; Bolger a King Country farmer. If, at any time during the first nine decades of the twentieth century, you had told someone that this was going to happen, you would have been taken away by men in white coats. Yet happen it did, and it was only a small part of a massive Maori resurgence in the second half of the twentieth century.

Around 1900, the Maori people were only 45,000 strong, about 5 per cent of the total population. Their independence was gone along with their best lands and their national influence. A tiny, isolated minority in their own country, they were widely thought to be dying out. As we saw in Chapter Six, various myths and realities, developments and initiatives combined to disappoint the doomsayers. Maori survived, culturally as well as physically. But even in the 1930s, with Apirana Ngata's brilliant strategy of subversive co-operation in full swing, Maori remained marginal. Their numbers had doubled since the 1890s nadir, but their proportion of the total population had improved only a little – to about 6 per cent. With the Depression counteracting land development, most were still poor. Maori were over 80 per cent rural and derived their living from primary industries, which employed 76 per cent of the male Maori workforce in 1926. Some had Pakeha bosses, but much employment was casual or seasonal, and the Maori economy was still 'semi-independent' and marginal. Because most Pakeha were already town-dwellers in the 1930s, only a minority had Maori acquaintances or workmates, let alone friends. 'Most Pakehas . . . scarcely ever saw Maoris, let alone knew any.'[1] Though Ngata and his ilk operated persistently and cleverly in the Pakeha political arena, they did so largely behind the scenes, except in war, sport and commemoration. Other Maori issues were far from prominent in the mass media in the 1930s. A Maori timber worker made the headlines in 1933 by amputating his own leg with a small knife after an accident, but that was about it.[2]

By the year 2000, the Maori population had exploded to nearly 600,000, over 15 per cent of the total population, an awesome rate of increase not dissimilar to that of progressive colonial Pakeha in the nineteenth century. A staggering 83 per cent of Maori now lived in cities or towns, and most who had jobs now worked in secondary and tertiary industries. Maori had urbanised and industrialised with great rapidity. Maori issues can no longer be avoided by Pakeha. Maori are central in New Zealand media and politics, though partly for ambiguous reasons. Maori socio-economic disadvantage, high crime and protest are now national issues. This massive transition was the fifth great revolution of Maori history, after the adaptations to Aotearoa itself, to the demise of big game, and to European contact and conquest. New Zealand is still in the middle of it.

Revenge of the Cradle

While Maori leaders and the enlightened minority of Pakeha leaders deserve some credit, the real root of the Maori resurgence of the later twentieth century was demographic: a massive population explosion rarely equalled anywhere. This is sometimes thought to have stemmed from a baby boom – a spasm of high birth rates in the 1950s and 1960s similar to, but even bigger than, that among Pakeha. Maori birth rates in these decades were indeed very high – high even compared with Pakeha boom rates of 26 per 1,000. But Maori had long had high birth rates. A leading demographer estimates rates of between 42 and 47 per 1,000 over the whole period 1901–62.[3] What happened in mid-century was less a baby boom than a death bust – a sharp decrease in Maori mortality. It was even greater than the mortality decline dating from the 1890s, discussed in Chapter Six. The early transition doubled the Maori population between 1891 and 1936; the later transition, which appears to date from the late 1930s, increased it fivefold 1936–86.

What caused this huge and influential reduction in Maori mortality? As with other health advances, potential heroes range from great leaps forward in medical science or public health, through gradual improvements in living conditions or immunity, to individual Pakeha heroes who implemented reform, such as the Health Department's Dr Harry Turbott, 'the individual most responsible for lifting standards of Maori health'.[4] As we have seen, improved immunity was probably the key factor in the first mortality transition, but it does not explain the second. One possibility is that Maori were at last substantially incorporated into the public health and welfare systems, which were themselves improving in effectiveness because of increased government support from 1935. This is certainly true to some extent, most notably after 1945. But there is a chicken–egg element here: access to health services improved with urban migration, which was stimulated by population growth, which was stimulated by better access to health services.

According to Pakeha experts in the 1930s, the chief causes of Maori health problems were inadequate and overcrowded housing, poor hygiene and the lack of sewage systems and clean water supplies. The case was made most strongly in 1933, in Turbott's survey of 2,000 Maori in the isolated and rural district of Waiapu on the East Coast. We should treat the first pair of factors, housing and hygiene, with some suspicion. Pakeha had long been prone to blame Maori disease on their 'uncivilised' customs and practices. In fact, Turbott found that less than 10 per cent of the houses surveyed were actually dirty. 'Some of the huts, even with earth floors, were scrupulously clean. Clothes [and] bedclothes are frequently washed.' Personal hygiene 'was no more deficient than in the average European community', though this was not necessarily saying much.[5] As for overcrowding, this is more likely to have postdated urbanisation and the population explosion than to have pre-dated it. It is true that Maori in the 1930s were unaccustomed to modern toilets. Whina Cooper 'never forgot the puzzlement and then the joy of one elderly kaumatua who received a wooden toilet seat among the materials supplied for his unit home. [He said] that he had not only been supplied with a house, he had also been given a frame in which to hang his portrait.'[6] Yet Maori custom laid great stress on the proper disposal of human wastes, with latrines well separated from cooking and living spaces, and manure, human or animal, never used to fertilise crops. It is not easy to believe that 'faeces being broadcast' on the ground close by dwellings, as reported by Turbott, was common.[7] But it remains true that Maori sewage systems and water supplies in the 1930s were even worse than those of rural Pakeha.

The solution, believed Turbott and others, was a mass improvement in Maori housing, and it is widely believed that such a thing did occur from 1935, when the first Labour government began its state housing and welfare programmes. Maori are generally thought to have participated fully in these from the outset, but recent studies suggest that this is not true. In social welfare in general, and housing in particular, 'Labour's rhetoric of equality brought little change in . . . practice.'[8] In was not until the end of World War Two that, for reasons discussed below, Maori began to participate equally in state welfare and housing schemes. Indeed, it was not until the late 1950s that state housing had substantial impact on Maori needs. Tuberculosis (TB), long a major killer of Maori, plummeted in the 1950s – it appears to have actually increased between 1936 and 1945.[9] At first sight, this supports the view that 'in all probability the main factor leading to high tuberculosis rates in Maori communities was poor housing conditions'.[10] But improved nutrition, improved detection of infectious cases through X-rays and skin tests, and vaccinations were also factors in the defeat of Maori tuberculosis. BCC (Bacillus Calmette-Guérin) vaccine was developed in the 1920s, but took a long time to be accepted in New Zealand. Ngata, whose own daughter died of TB, advocated its use in 1938, 'but his pleas were effectively ignored'.[11] In 1949, however, it was introduced and 'swiftly proved its worth'. By the 1960s, though still far higher than Pakeha rates, tuberculosis was no longer a significant cause of Maori death. 'Consumption', the strange and frightening shadow that had hung so long over both Maori and Pakeha, had finally dissipated.

Apart from tuberculosis, the major killers of Maori were respiratory diseases, typhoid and infant death from various causes. All three dropped substantially between 1936 and 1945 – *before* state-led improvements in Maori housing. Insanitary water supplies causing typhoid may have been one problem that the state and Pakeha health heroes did help solve. Turbott claimed that he obtained £40,000 from Peter Fraser, spent it on rainwater tanks and privies, and so reduced Maori typhoid from 39 times the Pakeha rate in 1936 to parity in 1940. This is certainly exaggerated, but the incidence of typhoid among Maori did decline dramatically from 14.2 to 2.6 per 10,000 between 1932 and 1948.[12] Increased Maori willingness to install rainwater tanks and to boil drinking water may also have been factors. The drop in Maori infant mortality, which halved between the 1930s and the 1950s, can easily be attributed to the increased hospitalisation of Maori mothers during birth. In 1937, only 17 per cent of Maori births took place in hospital. By 1962, the figure was 95 per cent.[13] But the big drop in infant deaths must have begun before hospitalisation had progressed far. Furthermore, it occurred in the ages one month to twelve months, not in the first month of life when the hospitalisation of birth might have been expected to have most effect.[14]

Better housing, better access to public health services, and individuals such as Turbott were important to the Maori death bust. But I suspect there were also two clusters of unsung, or less-sung, heroes. One was a substantial improvement in Maori cash incomes, dating especially from 1935, for reasons discussed below. Its key contribution to health may have been through better or more regular nutrition. Subsistence economics might have been able to feed Maori most of the time without the need for much cash. But there were periods when food was short: during the illness of breadwinners; during winter; or after traditional group hospitality had exhausted reserves. Cash was in effect an emergency reserve against the lean times of subsistence economics, and infant health could not afford lean times. Turbott found that about a quarter of Maori in his East Coast sample were undernourished in

1933,[15] and according to Te Puea the Maori of this area were unusually well-off. Improved cash incomes may have combined with better access to milk for children. This was provided in Native Schools even before nationwide introduction of the free milk in schools scheme in 1937. From 1929, Ngata's land-development schemes, which primarily encouraged dairy farming, were also improving the Maori milk supply.

The other unsung factor in the Maori death bust may have been the gradual spread among Maori of a new health creed. This did not necessarily involve the abandonment of traditional medicines and attitudes but, rather, added to them, much as Christianity had done in the nineteenth century. The new creed encouraged such things as the boiling of water, regular milk for children, the breastfeeding of babies, and the use of medical services, even the dreaded hospitals. Pakeha had been preaching a health creed to Maori since the early days of missionary activity, from 1814. But it was not until late in the nineteenth century that medical science gave them much useful to preach. James Pope's *Health for the Maori*, published in 1884, was the early bible, and it had some influence. The cause was taken up by the Young Maori movement, with Pomare and Buck preaching their own versions of Pope's creed. At least in the case of Buck, 'their versions' were less patronising and moralising, and more adapted to Maori beliefs. Buck used traditional Maori medicine as well as 'Western' versions.[16] Buck and Pomare teamed up again in the 1920s, the former as Director of Maori Hygiene, 1921–27, the latter as Minister of Health, 1923–26. They continued to evangelise and, since both now had greater mana and experience, may well have done so more successfully than in the 1900s.

With the help of the new Department of Public Health, Pomare had introduced a nursing service for Maori districts in 1909. State commitment to this fluctuated, but 63 nurses served in it by 1930. Their mission was officially described in 1911 as being 'to preach and show by practical example the gospel of cleanliness and proper sanitation'.[17] Nurses who ignored Maori practices had little success; those who compromised and did such things as employ Maori assistants were influential. The most influential district nurse of all was Robina Cameron, who was appointed to the Rotorua district in 1931. 'Kamerana' initiated a network of women's health committees among the Arawa confederation. It spread rapidly and became a national organisation in 1937 – the Women's Health League – with 165 branches by 1950.[18] It was subsequently overshadowed by the Maori Women's Welfare League, established in 1951, which did not share its hesitations about government sponsorship. But the earlier league's rapid and early growth, and the way it reconciled 'Maori values and beliefs with principles of public health', meant its contribution to the mortality transition of 1936–45 may have been significant.[19]

Another agency of health evangelism was the Native School system. There were 250 Native School teachers in 1918, compared with eighteen district nurses at that time, and sheer numbers may have made the teachers important.[20] Doses of cod-liver oil and strappings for dirty fingernails were not necessarily very helpful, and there were times when the superiority of modern medicine was far from clear. In the 1950s, a teacher warred with a Maori grandmother over the treatment of a boil on a child's bottom, daily replacing the other's poultice with their own. 'I suppose now we could say that that child's bottom represented a site of cultural struggle.'[21] But nursing by teachers during epidemics, free school milk from the 1930s, and some, though not all, of the attitudes to health drummed into children were useful. Respected Maori leaders also preached the new health creed. Te Puea was an important Maori evangelist, and T. W. Ratana may have been one as well. Like Christianity before it, the new health creed failed to catch on with Maori when it failed to compromise with them, and succeeded when it did.

From the 1960s, Maori birth rates began to drop until, by the end of the century, they were only slightly above both Pakeha rates and replacement levels. The echo effects of earlier transitions, as a numerous generation reached the age of parenthood, kept Maori population growth up. But the rate of increase slowed, and Pakeha fears about being swamped in reverse are misplaced. The Maori proportion of the population is likely to stabilise in the early decades of the twenty-first century, at around 20 per cent. Maori mortality rates continued to decline. By the end of the twentieth century, death rates among Maori children aged one to fourteen years were actually lower than non-Maori rates.[22] In other age groups, Maori death rates remained higher, and Maori are still disadvantaged relative to Pakeha in terms of health. But the broad picture is one of massive improvement. This great mortality transition is of more than academic interest. It was more important than Pakeha enlightenment or radical Maori activism in generating the Maori resurgence of the later twentieth century. It created the dominant fact of modern Maori history: in the year 2000, there were twelve times as many Maori as there had been a century before.

From the 1930s, Maori shifted more as well as died much less. Some of the shifts were from one rural abode to another. Most were to town. In 1936 Maori were 83 per cent rural and 17 per cent urban. Many of these 'urban' Maori were actually members of subrural communities who had been engulfed or encapsulated by the growth of neighbouring Pakeha cities. By 1945, there was a substantial increase in the urban proportion to 26 per cent. By 1966, Maori were 62 per cent urban; by 1986, 83 per cent. The figure then stabilised, but a complete inversion of urban–rural proportions had occurred in 50 years. Around 1960, the Maori became a predominantly urban people. Maori inter-regional migration had long been higher than Pakeha.[23] Shifting for economic, social and religious reasons (to Parihaka and Ratana Pa, for example) was a long-standing Maori practice. It tended, however, to be temporary, tribally organised and to avoid cities. The new migration, on the other hand, went especially to the big cities, above all Auckland, and was seldom tribally organised. In the 1950s, the largest single category of Maori urban migrants were young single people, with a shift towards nuclear families in the mid-1960s. The scale was huge. Though the non-Maori population of Auckland grew fast, the Maori proportion grew even faster, from 2 per cent in 1945 to 11 per cent in 1986.[24]

Maori urban migration is generally thought to have been triggered by World War Two. Young Maori were encouraged by the state and their own war-effort organisation, discussed below, to fill urban jobs on the expectation that they would return to their rural homes once the war ended. But there are signs that the big take-off in urban migration did not occur until about 1950. Auckland's Maori population grew at an annual average of 18.7 per cent between the 1936 and 1945 censuses, probably with a heavy loading towards the second half of the period. But growth then dropped quite dramatically to 10.8 per cent between 1945 and 1951, before taking off again in the 1950s. It peaked in the early 1960s when, despite continued high birth rates and plummeting death rates the *rural* Maori population actually dropped 14 per cent. Net urban migration continued less strongly through the 1970s, before dropping back towards stability in the 1980s, owing to reverse migration – Maori city-dwellers responding to economic recession by going home. The World War Two 'false start' tends to confirm that it was falling death rates and the resulting population explosion that caused urbanisation – not the other way around. It was not so much deterioration in the rural Maori economy or housing situation as the fact that there were now far more mouths to feed and bodies to house.

The great Maori urban migration has some features that echoed those of overseas immigrants in the twentieth century, and some that were more similar to the great Pakeha migration of the nineteenth century. The 'push' from the country stemmed largely from population growth, but also from changing aspirations among the young. Young women were intriguingly prominent in the early migration. 'Until 1956 it seems that Maori female migrants heavily outnumbered men.'[25] Like their brothers, they are said to have been influenced by a desire to 'shake off the hampering authority and conventions of their elders'.[26] This may be another example of women's tendency to use major contextual change to loosen constraints placed on them. Bright city lights joined escape and jobs as motives but, as with many nineteenth-century Pakeha, social promotion did not. While some Maori migrants made their way into white-collar occupations, notably teaching, most did not, and they did not want to. During a transitional period of a year or two, the young migrant would shuffle jobs and residences before 'settling down', marrying and moving from unskilled short-term jobs to semi-skilled long-term jobs. Housing was poor, especially in the transition period – restricted to inner-city slums where multiple occupancy was the only way to cope with exorbitant rents. Once it had belatedly accepted that Maori urbanisation was inevitable, in the late 1950s, the state at last made a major effort to house Maori through state houses, state advances, and loans and savings schemes run by the Maori Department. In 1961, 44 per cent of Maori houses generally still had no flush toilet, and 30 per cent had no hot water, but many of these were in the country.[27] The urban situation improved further in the 1960s, though Maori housing remained – and remains – much more overcrowded than Pakeha. Despite some efforts at 'pepper-potting' – scattering Maori houses among Pakeha homes – suburbs not far short of Maori ghettoes emerged. In some cases, the effect was reinforced by 'white flight' in a cause–effect spiral. In 1965, 65 per cent of Otara schoolchildren were Pakeha. In 1980, the figure was 12 per cent.[28]

Population explosion and urbanisation were traumatic for many Maori. They made Ngata's land-development schemes almost irrelevant and devastated some ancient Maori communities. They dumped a whole new people in the northern cities and contributed to massive increases in Maori social dislocation and Maori crime. But this undoubted bad news camouflages a substantial upturn in Maori economic fortunes, supercharged by urban-isation but perhaps not started by it. From 1935, Labour put more money into public works, and the Depression began to lift. Between 1939 and 1945, war, for all its evils, provided Maori with 27,000 brand-new paying jobs in the armed forces and in war industries. After the war, there was expansion in housing, forestry and hydro-electric facilities. There was also expansion in the assembly of imported components into consumer goods. Though new and seemingly modern, these industries had a big appetite for 'unskilled' or 'semi-skilled' labour – jobs that did not require much in the way of formal educational qualifications or training. Never before had Maori had so much access to so many jobs.

There is some evidence of 'occupational clustering' like that of overseas immigrant groups. In the 1960s, three-quarters of the men of Ngati Whatua of Orakei were said to have worked for the Auckland City Council. The beer tankers of one of the two large breweries were 'almost all driven by Maori'.[29] The favoured Maori occupations in the country included forestry. In the city they included manufacturing (such as freezing works for men and clothing factories for women), construction and transport. These jobs were nominally 'unskilled', but the male ones at least were not low-paid. 'In 1961, the average income of Maori males was 89.8% of that of non-Maori males.'[30] Historians sometimes cite such figures to demonstrate persisting Maori disadvantage, but they surely represent a massive improvement on the situation 30 years before. Added to this, Maori from 1945 at last became fully eligible for the benefits of the welfare state. These were quite generous at the time, and you did not have to be unemployed or sick to get them. In the 1950s, the family benefit must have been a real boost to large Maori families, increasing incomes by around 50 per cent. In terms of cash if nothing else, the period 1945–75 was something of a golden age for Maori. The era of Maori protest and activism that began around 1970 did so at a time when Maori were economically better off than they had been for a century.

The trouble was that Maori workers were in sectors particularly vulnerable to the kinds of economic changes that occurred from 1973. One change, known to experts as 'upskilling', was a shift in the labour market from unskilled to skilled, and from blue collar to white collar. Still more important was the general economic downturn that marked the end of the recolonial system. As growth slowed to a halt, unskilled workers were first to the wall, and Maori were disproportionately represented among them. The family benefit eroded into insignificance at the same time. The economic king-hit clearly suffered by Maori in recent times tends to be attributed to the restructurings of 1984. In fact, its beginnings clearly pre-date 1984. In the 1960s, Maori unemployment, while higher than Pakeha, was not very significant – 1.2 per cent in Auckland.[31] From the mid-1970s, it grew in leaps and bounds, at far higher rates than Pakeha. In 1976, young Maori women workers (aged 15–29 years) already had between three and four times the unemployment rate of their Pakeha equivalents.[32] In 1981, overall Maori unemployment was 14.1 per cent, compared with 3.7 per cent for Pakeha.[33] Just as Maori had carried the economic can for Pakeha colonisation in the nineteenth century, so they carried the can for decolonisation from 1973. But 1984 certainly worsened the situation. Between 1986 and 1989, the general Maori unemployment rate jumped to close on 20 per cent. 'In effect, about one fifth of the Maori working age population lost their jobs in the two years from March 1987 to March 1989.'[34] Unemployment was proportionately about four times as bad for Maori as for Pakeha, and these figures may not tell the whole story, because many Maori gave up registering as available for work and were therefore excluded from unemployment statistics. In some Maori districts in 1991, the proportion 'not available for work' reached 49 per cent.[35] The streets of Auckland were no longer paved with jobs.

The Treaty Strikes Back

Maori history experienced a much sharper shift in the middle of the twentieth century than did the rest of New Zealand history. The Maori population increased, urbanised and industrialised very rapidly. Change trauma was great, but the money was good. Then, in the 1970s, Maori history began to reconverge with New Zealand history in general. On the one hand, a partial Maori 'decolonisation' took place, with a huge increase in Maori activism, radicalism and political and cultural self-assertion. Pakeha were somewhat readier to listen to it, partly because they themselves were decolonising and liberalising to some extent, and partly because a large and urbanised Maori population was less easily ignored than a small and rural one. On the other hand, economic change and economic downturn from the mid-1970s hit Maori especially hard. A socio-economy that had said to young Maori, 'Leave school as early as you can, we need you in one of our high-paying though unskilled jobs,' suddenly changed its mind. The upturn in activism and the downturn in economic fortunes were not necessarily directly connected. But economic upturn, like that experienced by Maori between the late 1930s and the early 1970s, generates increased expectations and aspirations. A subsequent downturn creates fertile ground for activism, as it did for the Pakeha working class in the 1900s. These, then, were the main economic and demographic undercurrents of modern Maori history. How did Maori – and Pakeha – respond to them? We look first at political responses of various kinds, including protest, then turn to social responses to the tides of change.

Apirana Ngata had been forced from government in 1934, and lost his parliamentary seat to a Ratana-Labour candidate in 1943. Ratana now held all four Maori seats, and it was these MPs, led by the low-key but able Paraire Paikea, who took over leadership of Ngata's 'engagement' strategy. Ngata may never have fully reconciled himself to this before his death in 1950. But in the longer view, the initial Ratana performance did him proud. It took the form of the remarkable Maori War Effort Organisation (MWEO). Informal organisation began with the outbreak of war in 1939, and the formal organisation dates from 1942. Both were led by Paikea until his own premature death in 1943, and then by his deputy Eruera Tirakatene. Despite the Ratana movement's hesitations about tribalism, the MWEO compromised comprehensively with it, setting up 315 tribal committees and 41 executive committees. Though some Pakeha did not like the facts, the MWEO was Maori-led and had considerable autonomy.[36]

A principal activity was recruitment, and such a voluntary flow was maintained that Maori were able to persuade the government not to apply conscription to them. Some 17,000 Maori served in uniform, from a Maori population of only 95,000 in 1943. The old kupapa tribes again contributed disproportionately – Ngati Porou, for example, appear to have sent about double their share.[37] Few of their fit men of military age can have been left at home. But, as the high overall number of recruits indicates, traditional 'disengagers', such as Tainui, also contributed. This was still more true of another form of mobilisation: 'manpowering' into war work in industry, which the MWEO also handled. The organisation encouraged food production and gifts for the troops as well, and began to move into welfare and housing. The MWEO was very successful. It supervised what must be one of the most comprehensive mobilisations anywhere in World War Two: 17,000 male military recruits and 10,000 war workers, male and female, or about 30 per cent of the whole Maori population. The achievements of the Maori Battalion in the field, where it became something very close to the élite unit of the Second New Zealand Division, were even greater and more prominent than in World War One. It was these factors that finally induced the Pakeha state to give Maori equal access to welfare benefits, postwar rehabilitation and, to some extent, housing. By 1945, Ngata's strategy, though now without the man himself, had chalked up another victory. It was, however, to be the last for some time.

The postwar era opened very promisingly for Maori. Incomes were on the rise, urbanisation had yet to bite fully and a proven organisation existed that may well have been capable of orchestrating a comprehensive and autonomous Maori reformation, a culmination of the trend to 'benign segregation'. The Ratana MPs, and many other Maori, wanted to keep the war effort organisation in place, and adapt it to meet the challenges of peace. After the election of 1946, the four Maori seats held the balance of power. But a backlash was building. The press portrayed the Labour government as being a puppet on the string of the 'Maori mandate'. The Department of Native Affairs, whose name was changed to Maori Affairs in 1947, had always looked askance at the MWEO, which it feared – perhaps rightly – was usurping its functions. More Pakeha-dominated than in Ngata's day, the department's attitude was 'unimaginative' and 'unhelpful'.[38] Paikea and Tirakatene were superb organisers of Maoridom, but they lacked Ngata's awareness of the murky depths of Pakeha politics and ideology. Urbanisation, once fully under way from about 1950, did raise genuine questions about Ngata's engagement strategy, which had always envisaged that Maori would remain primarily a rural people. On top of all this, Maori parliamentary power suddenly disappeared in the 1949 election. Maori had put all their eggs in the Labour basket, and it was National that dominated politics between 1949 and 1984. The Maori technique of having a political bet each way pre-dated even the Young Maori movement, and goes back to the New Zealand Wars, when some tribes deliberately split themselves into pro- and anti-government groups. It had been a subtext of Maori parliamentary politics for the whole first half of the twentieth century, during which each major political party had included senior Maori leaders. In 1949, it lapsed, and this left Maori less able to resist an assimilationist backlash in the 1950s and 1960s.

Assimilationism's last stand began in 1945 with the dismantling of the MWEO and the incorporation of some of its structures and personnel into the Native Department. It climaxed in the 1960s, with the Hunn Report and the disestablishment of the Maori Schools system, completed in 1969. The Hunn Report needs to be seen in the context of its times. Produced by leading public servant J. K. Hunn in 1960 (and published in 1961), the report was commissioned by Labour Prime Minister Walter Nash.[39] It attempted to address the genuine new problems created by the Maori population explosion and by mass urbanisation. The renewed attempt to turn Maori into Brown Britons was also an attempt to solve their persisting disadvantages in health, education, economics and housing. Hunn himself did not see it as incompatible with some retention of Maori culture, narrowly defined. But the new policy was still fundamentally assimilationist, it envisaged state leadership rather than Maori leadership, and it ignored the lessons of history. Maori could organise themselves for reform, as they had done with Ngata's land-development schemes and the war effort. They would accept Pakeha help and some compromise with the state in the process. But they would not accept reform imposed upon them from without, especially if it envisaged the ultimate disappearance of Maori tribes and the Maori people as social, if not cultural, entities. A naive piece of land legislation, passed in 1967 and known as 'the last land grab', was the final straw. The political fuse for an explosion of Maori radicalism had been laid.

The first Maori protest publications appeared in 1968, and were followed in 1970 by the formation of the first activist group, Nga Tamatoa, which consisted primarily of young and educated Maori.[40] Some were influenced by international, and particularly American, developments in black activism. The Maori protest movement of the 1970s and 1980s also had characteristics in common with the other New Zealand activisms of the period, discussed in the next chapter, and was uneasily allied to some of them. But Maori activism tended to be less exclusively young, university educated and middle class than its Pakeha relatives. It usually had the support of some, though never of all, Maori elders and traditional leaders. On the other hand, it was seldom united within itself. Indeed, it was more prone to disunity than earlier Maori mass movements. All these characteristics were demonstrated by the first great national protest: the Land March (Hikoi) of 1975.

The march, from Cape Reinga in the Far North to Parliament in

Wellington, was intended to peacefully protest at, and raise awareness of, the loss of Maori land over many years. The technique of a hikoi was an old one – it was used by the resistance leader Titokowaru in 1867. Estimates of the number involved in 1975 vary from 30,000 to 40,000.[41] Led by eighty-year-old Whina Cooper, the march succeeded in its objectives. A splinter group conducted a sit-in in Parliament Grounds, much to Cooper's anger. Her biographer described this controversy as 'a tragedy for the cause of Maori protest'.[42] But it was a harbinger of things to come, and it did not prevent results. Northland politician Matiu Rata had become Minister for Maori Affairs in the third Labour government of 1972–75. He had his own schemes for Maori redress and at first opposed the march. But he eventually gave it his blessing and subsquently set up the Waitangi Tribunal to hear Maori claims to recompense for breaches of the treaty. For neither the first nor the last time, protest and politics worked hand in hand. The Treaty of Waitangi moved back towards centre stage in New Zealand history. But it was not there yet. The tribunal had no teeth, and the National government of 1975–84, under Robert Muldoon, had no intention of letting it grow any. One early member was told that the tribunal would only take up one or two days of his time per year.[43] Muldoon's role in a general backlash against Maori and other activisms is discussed in the next chapter.

The next major Maori protest occurred at Bastion Point, Orakei, in 1977–78. Orakei was the main marae of Ngati Whatua, of Auckland, who had sponsored the creation of the Pakeha town in the 1840s. In 1951, the marae was acquired compulsorily by the government under the Public Works Act. In 1977, the government moved to subdivide and sell some of the land. Ngati Whatua protesters occupied Bastion Point for several months but were evicted in May 1978 in a massive police operation in which 222 people were arrested.[44] Maori activism simmered, and exploded again in convergence with wider protest against a tour by the racially selected South African rugby team in 1981. The '81 Springbok tour, discussed in the next chapter, generated the worst civil violence in New Zealand since the Depression riots in 1932. Neither Maori nor the Treaty of Waitangi was the main issue, but Maori were quick to tell Pakeha protesters against the tour that they should have been.

Initially, Maori activists were undecided about the Treaty of Waitangi. Was it a fraud or was it a sacred covenant that had been repeatedly breached? Some tried illogically to have it both ways; most tended towards the latter view. Waitangi itself, in the Bay of Islands, was often a centre of protest, between 1971 and 1998, on 6 February each year when the signing of the treaty was commemorated. Governors-general were spat at and jostled, and on one occasion the visiting Queen Elizabeth herself received treatment that was arguably even worse: a whakapohane, or traditional insult involving the baring of buttocks in the direction of the offender. The buttocks belonged to the idiosyncratic Maori activist Dun Mihaka, who thereby made New Zealand's only original contribution to royal protocol, the 'one-bum salute'. There were many other protests at Waitangi and elsewhere, with particularly intense spasms 1975–84, and in the early 1990s, including the occupation of Wanganui's Moutoa Gardens for 79 days in 1995 by a large and determined group of Maori protesters.[45] Some activist publications pulled no punches: 'White people of *any* generation have no business being in this country.'[46] Others, like those of academic columnist Ranginui Walker, were impressively reasoned but sometimes no less hard-hitting.[47]

While feelings during some of these protests obviously ran very high indeed, people were seldom hurt. Dust flew on the national marae at Waitangi; blood did not. In the 1990s, in a technique pioneered by Hone Heke's amputation of the British flagstaff at Kororareka in 1844–45, Maori radicals attacked Pakeha icons: statues of John Ballance and George Grey, the America's Cup, and the lone pine on Auckland's One Tree Hill. Enraged Pakeha failed to register that such tactics would have delighted the authorities in Northern Ireland. Directed against objects rather than people, they were, in a sense indicators of moderation rather than extremism. There was considerable angry Pakeha reaction to Maori activism, but it tended to be inchoate and unfocused. There was also Pakeha sympathy, and it extended beyond radical activists. The established Christian churches, for example, aligned themselves with Maori protestors at the Waitangi demonstrations of 1983.[48] Outside Pakeha politics, a Maori Congress with representatives from 37 tribes was formed in 1990.[49] Inside the political system, Rata left Labour and formed his own party, Mana Motuhake, in 1980. It advocated Maori autonomy.[50] Those Maori who voted, however, stuck with Labour until the 1990s, when there was a revival of the politics of engagement and of the spreading of Maori representation across all major political parties. Helped by proportional representation reforms, Maori parliamentary representation in 1996 tripled to fifteen out of 120 MPs, or 12.5 per cent – only slightly below their share of the population.[51]

There was a downturn in Maori protest in the late 1980s, and another in the late 1990s. These appear to have been related to the teeth grown at last by the Waitangi Tribunal. In 1985, the restructuring Labour government made the tribunal's remit to hear Maori claims retrospective to 1840, and subsequently conceded the tribunal further powers. In 1986, to the alarm of some politicians on both sides of the House, the courts ruled that the sell-off of state assets had to take account of the Treaty of Waitangi and, therefore, of Maori interests. At last, some real redress followed, with Ngati Whatua receiving land and compensation in 1987 for the loss of Orakei. But it soon seemed that the Waitangi Tribunal would be swamped by the sheer number of claims. By 1989, there was a backlog of 180 claims; by 1999, the figure had grown to over 700.[52] Treaty law, research and settlement negotiation became quite an industry. It seemed to some as if money was flowing to Pakeha lawyers and historians – and to a Maori élite – rather than to the ordinary Maori who really needed it. But the 'Treaty industry' did encourage the government to begin direct negotiation with tribal groups. Negotiations commenced under Labour and were taken up by the succeeding National government with some enthusiasm. Progress was tortuous and contested, but there were some substantive results. Agreements over fisheries, in 1989–92, over Tainui claims in 1995 and over Ngai Tahu claims in 1998 made over capital and assets worth over $400 million to some Maori groups. This seemed far too low to some, and other groups remained out in the cold completely. But this at last was real money. It was now clear to all that the Treaty of Waitangi was worth somewhat more than the paper it was written on.

Hard-earned victories in politics and treaty settlements were accompanied by limited good news on the cultural front. Urbanisation dealt the Maori language a heavy blow, so heavy that in the 1970s it threatened to be terminal. As late as 1950, 50 per cent of Maori children spoke fluent Maori, because it was used daily in their homes if not their schools. By the mid-1970s, the total of fluent speakers, including adults, was less than 18 per cent.[53] In the 1980s, however, a series of developments gave some hope for revival. From 1981, kohanga reo, 'language nests', were established – pre-school institutions using the Maori language. Quality varied, but by the year 2000, 40,000 children had passed through kohanga, of which there were 690.[54] A Maori Language Commission was established in 1987. The number of fluent Maori-speakers continues to drop as the elders for whom it was a first language die off. But over half of Maori aged over sixteen in 1995 could speak some at least of their own language.[55] In the 1980s and 1990s, kohanga were joined by Maori-oriented classes and institutions at primary, secondary and tertiary levels. With some help from these, Maori educational performance improved. Between 1979 and 1993, the proportion of Maori leaving secondary school with no qualifications at all halved, from 65 to 33.5 per cent. The proportion of Maori students at university more than doubled between 1986 and 1993, from 3.6 to 8.4 per cent, and rose further to close on 10 per cent by the end of the 1990s.[56] These numbers were still not good. Qualification-free non-Maori were only 12.5 per cent of school-leavers in 1989, and because of their younger age structure Maori should be more like 20 per cent of tertiary students. But it remains true that the situation in the 1990s was improving significantly compared with the 1980s, let alone the 1960s. There were also exciting developments in both traditional and innovative Maori artistic culture, noted in Chapter Eighteen.

Opting Out?

The relatively good news for Maori on the political and cultural fronts in the last quarter of the twentieth century was coupled with very bad economic news, beginning about 1975 and picking up pace after 1984. This inverted the pattern of the previous 25 years, 1950–75, when political downturn had accompanied economic upturn. The Maori social response to the new economic pattern featured poverty, unemployment, massive crime rates and renewed alienation from the mainstream of New Zealand politics and economics. The Maori political response was cross-class but tended towards the small but growing Maori middle class. The social response was working class: a deeply problematic Maori 'populist activism', involving such things as high crime and a less benign segregation, an 'opting out'.

One feature of modern Maori society, which should not be papered over, is high crime. Maori crime rates were low in the nineteenth century – a fraction of Pakeha rates until the 1880s. They then began climbing while Pakeha rates dropped, and took the lead around World War One. In the period 1918–27, the Maori rate of arrests for assault was more than twice that for Pakeha.[57] Maori crime continued to rise, slowly but steadily. The Maori imprisonment rate in 1950 was 4.7 times the non-Maori rate. It climbed somewhat faster to 6.9 in 1965. It then rocketed to 9.5 times the rate in 1970 – as steep a rise in five years as in the previous fifteen. The imprisonment rate then fell back to 8.8 times the non-Maori level in 1975, then climbed again, quite sharply, to 12.1 in 1985, when Maori comprised half the prison population.[58] Maori crime rates then appear to have stabilised at a little below this peak, but they remain grossly disproportionate – Maori were over 44 per cent of the prison population in 1997.[59] The rise of Maori crime, in short, pre-dates urbanisation and therefore cannot have been caused by it. But after urbanisation got fully under way around 1950, the climb steepened, with two particularly sharp bursts in the late 1960s and in 1975–85.

How do we explain high Maori crime? Urbanisation boosted it from 1950 but did not cause it. Similarly, sheer economic disadvantage, a disproportion of Maori in the crime-prone lowest class, boosted high crime – in 1975–85 in particular – but is clearly not the only problem. Maori crime rocketed in the 1960s, when Maori were getting richer, as well as in the 1980s, when they were getting poorer. Discriminatory policing and judicial practice may be factors. In 1958, Maori were 7 per cent of the total population, 15.9 per cent of those arrested, 17.8 per cent of those convicted and 22.3 per cent of those imprisoned.[60] At each stage, it appears, the worst was more likely to happen to them than to non-Maori. But judicial and police discrimination seems likely to have been worse in the 1940s and 1950s than in the 1980s and

1990s, yet Maori imprisonment rates kept climbing. There were virtually no Maori police in the 1950s; there were many in the 1990s. We need to dig a little deeper. The later twentieth-century Maori crime boom is not the first New Zealand has experienced. Another occurred between the 1850s and the 1880s. It, too, starred young men, but in this case the crime-prone were Pakeha, not Maori. The root of this Pakeha crime problem was the weakening of an old set of social bonds that had discouraged crime, and the formation of new ones that accepted, even encouraged, certain types of crime. The old set weakened through migration and mobility, an 'atomising' or desocialising process; the new set was what I have described as 'crew culture'.[61] Can Pakeha crime in the nineteenth century help explain Maori crime in the twentieth?

The modern Maori equivalent of desocialisation was 'detribalisation', the weakening of kin links. People avoid crime, not primarily because it is illegal, but because of the disapproval of those who matter to them – in the traditional, rural Maori case, the kin group. When Maori – especially young male Maori – left their kin, or when the kin-based community dissolved because of economic pressure, constraints on their behaviour loosened. Both kin-group dissolution and the departure of young people occurred to some extent in the first half of the twentieth century – hence the slow rise in Maori crime to 1950. When urban migration did take off, detribalisation did so too, as did crime rates. A Maori social worker picked this up as early as 1959: 'to an extent, the younger Maori are detribalised'.[62] Urbanisation did not automatically result in detribalisation. From 1965, some tribes established urban marae in the cities as homes away from home. Even before this, the mass advent of motor transport facilitated the retention of links to the home marae through visits each way. A survey in the late 1980s indicated that 54 per cent of Maori in secondary urban centres and 41 per cent of those in the main urban centres had recently attended hui (gatherings) back home.[63] Some urban Maori were not lost to their tribes. Besuited Maori executives still sit trembling in their offices, dreading the next visit from a kaumatua (elder) who points his stick and says, 'We need you, boy.' But many *were* lost.

My guess is that detribalisation intersected with a regrouping of young Maori into a 'street culture' that licensed certain types of crime, like Pakeha crew culture before it. It is not purely Maori. Pacific Islanders and working-class Pakeha also feature large, but Maori do appear to feature largest of all. The most obvious expression of this street culture was 'patched' gangs, carrying uniform patches on their jackets, which became prominent from about 1970. The 'Stormtroopers' and 'Highway 61', founded in the 1970s, seem to have had large Maori memberships. The two largest and best-known gangs are almost entirely Maori: the 'Mongrel Mob', formed in the 1960s, and the more tightly organised 'Black Power' gang, formed in 1970. By their very nature, these gangs are not keen on inquiries from outsiders, and published research on them is limited.[64] But both quickly became substantial, with thousands of patched members and associates, a heavy involvement with organised crime and a strong (and well-organised) presence in prisons, which they are sometimes said to virtually run. In the 1980s, 'Black Power dominated Mount Eden and the Mongrel Mob controlled Paremoremo'. One survey in 1993 suggested that half of all male gang members, and a quarter of their female associates, had been to prison. Police in 1992 estimated that there were 6,000 gang members, two-thirds of them in ethnic gangs that were mainly Maori.[65] More recent estimates suggest that 'the gang network in New Zealand', associates as well as full members, 'comprised between 25,000 and 30,000 people'.[66]

These 'patched' gangs are only the best-organised and most prominent forms of a wider street culture. Informal neighbourhood gangs date from the 1950s, and a 'street kid' subculture emerged in the late 1970s. A 1997 Auckland study showed that this subculture survives, its participants now known as 'homies', and that it intersects with various kinds of informal local gangs, some of which are ethnic.[67] Pacific Islander gangs, descendants of the 'King Cobras' of the 1970s, are prominent, and so are Maori. The street culture may extend beyond even the least formal and most local of gangs into working-class Maori urban youth culture in general. Within the group, gang or not, mutual association to some extent replaces kin links, or at least the influence of older kin, and changes attitudes to crime. Some crimes remain unacceptable – stealing from fellow members and child-molesting, for example. But stealing from others, involvement with illegal drugs and violence within and without the culture are acceptable, in some cases even applauded by the peer group. This culture is not solely urban but does stem from the migrations and economic pressures that weakened the influence of elder-led kin groups. It borrows from overseas models but does so eclectically. Black Power took its name but not necessarily much else from black American activism. The Mongrel Mob has dabbled with Nazi slogans and salutes, an ironic epilogue to Maori Aryanism. Other groups have embraced forms of Rastafarianism.[68] Among the less endearing characteristics of this culture is a reinvention of Maori masculinity. Ostensibly modelled on the traditional Maori warrior, this can involve violence towards women and children, as exemplified in Alan Duff's eye-opening novel *Once Were Warriors* (1990). In fact, striking a child – though not necessarily a woman – was just about the last thing a traditional warrior would ever think of doing.[69] One suspects a cross-fertilisation of popular culture here. The New Warrior may conceal an Iwi Bloke. Whether the gangs and groups that comprise this 'street culture' can be seen as 'neo-tribes' is controversial. But they are a reality in late modern

New Zealand, and their subculture helps explain high Maori crime rates. They are not without rules, but their rules are not those of the mainstream of either Pakeha or traditional kin-based Maori society.

This crime-prone, resocialised street culture is allied to an even wider phenomenon, known as the 'black economy', or the 'informal economy'. Unsurprisingly, it is even harder to find out about than gangs. It operates outside the mainstream economy, and its demographic core is the long-term unemployed and underemployed. Again, though Pakeha and Pacific Islanders are by no means insignificant, Maori are massively over-represented. 'Black' economic activities can include perfectly innocent practices, such as gardening, other forms of home production, fishing and gathering, the receipt of legitimate welfare benefits, the bartering of goods and services, and the occasional sale of such things as fish or firewood. It also includes legal crimes that some populisms say are not social crimes: tax evasion, through 'cash jobs', for example; low-level benefit fraud; and other types of petty crime, notably cannabis production and sale. Curiously enough, this important modern New Zealand industry cannot be found in the indexes of the standard economic histories. A 1990 survey indicated that 43 per cent of people in the northern North Island had used cannabis, but half of these did so infrequently. In the black economy and in street culture, its use is common, as is its production, gifting and sale. Police seizures alone were valued at $700 million in 1995–96. Until the recent rise of hydroponic production, which can take place as easily in the city as the country, about a quarter of the New Zealand crop appears to have been produced in Northland. 'Cannabis use in Northland is extremely high compared to the rest of the country.'[70] The total value of the Northland crop has been estimated at anywhere between $140 million and $900 million a year.[71] The higher figures outrank Northland's other leading industries, dairying, tourism and beef farming.[72] The Far North is said to be the prime growing area. Intriguingly enough, this area had a higher rate of Maori unemployment yet a lower rate of Maori urban migration than the rest of Northland.[73]

The informal economy in general and the cannabis industry in particular need to be seen in perspective. Cannabis consumption is a 'crime' that at least half of New Zealanders between fifteen and 50 years of age have committed at least once. It is by no means clear that the drug is harmless, but a very good case can be made for suggesting that it is less harmful than the legal drug alcohol. Its production and distribution is clearly part-commercial, but there is also a major gift-giving or barter component – an interesting intersection between Western 'hippy' drug culture and traditional Maori practice. The decision to enter the informal economy also has to be seen in context. Until the mid-1970s, young Maori, Pacific Islanders and working-class Pakeha were given a clear message by the mainstream economy, whatever teachers or parents said to the contrary. The message was that they should leave school as soon as possible and get a high-paying unskilled job. After the mid-1970s, the message suddenly changed. It now read: if you do not have qualifications, you may well remain unemployed for the rest of your life, and it is your own fault. People were told to try harder to get jobs when there were no jobs, and they also had to cope with the powerful ideology of the work ethic, which implied that people without jobs were worthless. In this context, you had two options: give up and curl up into a little ball, or forget the work ethic and formal employment and go out and do a little fishing and grow a little dope. Self-righteous middle-class critics of the informal economy should consider what they themselves would have done in these circumstances.

The informal economy is not necessarily a moral problem, but it is a social one. Maori are grossly over-represented in it, yet it operates outside the mainstream of kin-based Maori society, as well as outside the mainstream of the pan-New Zealand socio-economy. The informal economy draws from the public purse, through welfare benefits, but does not contribute to it. It seems to correlate strongly with political alienation. One-third of Maori electors do not register for either the Maori seats or general seats. It has been estimated that, in the 1996 election, only half of eligible Maori actually voted.[74] This informal (non) political economy may tend to be self-perpetuating, devaluing education and employment in the eyes of a younger generation because their parents have had to do without both. It narrows the options of the individuals in it, and divides the country in a fundamental but largely unrecognised way. It deprives a substantial section of the community of political and economic citizenship. This is not the kind of autonomy that Maori activism seeks.

Maori in 2000 are vastly better off than they were in 1900. But they – and therefore the rest of New Zealand – confront persisting old problems of relative deprivation and the new problem of the post-1975 informal political economy. It is very tempting to see the Treaty of Waitangi settlements as the seeds of a solution to these problems. Some tribal leaders would vehemently disagree. They see the settlements as a matter of justice, not equity. Compensation should go to the injured parties, the tribes, and it should be entirely separate from any attempt to socially engineer a correction of Maori socio-economic disadvantage. Each tribal group understandably wants recognition and acknowledgement of its particular wrongs, not just compensation – hence the proliferation of claims to the Waitangi Tribunal, and their painfully slow processing. Taken to extremes, however, this view could theoretically result in a multi-million-dollar settlement going to the very few surviving members of an original tribe. There is a need to take account both of the fluid dynamics of tribe formation, which continue in the present as they did in the past, and the existence of non-tribal Maori organisations. If the settlement process happens to converge with a broader Maori-led strategy aimed at resolving Maori socio-economic problems, then why not? Such a strategy is clearly needed – for the sake of all New Zealanders – but it faces at least two obstacles. First, how do you get Maori to unite to produce and implement it? Second, how do you sell it to Pakeha, who need to actively support it yet keep their hands off the steering wheel?

In recent decades, there appears to have been a worrying diminution in the Maori capacity for united and effective action, at both regional and national levels. The 'social efficiency' that Maori society demonstrated in Ngata's land-development schemes in the 1930s and Paikea's Maori War Effort Organisation in the 1940s was extremely high. Compare this with the endemic bickering of some treaty claimant groups. One root of this problem is probably urbanisation, which may have weakened tribal structures even more than conquest, colonisation and poverty had done before it. There are also hints of a related breakdown in the Maori system of leadership. Traditionally, chiefs who inherited mana, or prestige, were respected and valued, but not necessarily followed. Effective leadership went to those who could get tasks done. There is a sense in which 'ineffective leaders' was a contradiction in terms, because they would have no followers. They ceased to be leaders when they set off to fish, fight or build a pa or canoe, looked behind them, and found that they were on their own. Leadership was based on what amounted to a continuous election. With institutionalisation and urbanisation, this system broke down and has not yet been effectively replaced. There is also a continuing tension between tribal and non-tribal organisations. The latter are sometimes assumed to be new and somehow illegitimate. In fact, a Maori proto-nationalism, expressed in supra-tribal prophetic movements, dates back to the 1850s. The Ratana Church, still a key Maori institution, is also supra-tribal, as are a number of new urban Maori organisations – and the national gangs, Black Power and the Mongrel Mob. Very clearly, non-tribal organisa-tions are not going to disappear. Just as Pakeha may have to learn to live with autonomous Maori, so Maori tribes may have to learn to live with non-tribal organisations.

The second obstacle to full Maori recovery is Pakeha. A substantial number of Pakeha are sympathetic towards Maori issues, and possibly even to some Maori autonomy. They are a minority, but quite a large one, extending well beyond radicals and left-liberals. A residue of the relatively benign Pakeha stereotype of Maori as 'honorary white' may be at work here, but increased intermarriage is probably also a factor. Urbanisation led to a great surge in inter-racial – and inter-tribal – marriage. By 1960, 42 per cent of all Maori marriages in Auckland were to Pakeha, and the proportion probably increased thereafter.[75] For every one of a half-million or more Maori, there is at least one Pakeha who is somehow connected to Maori – who has a Maori spouse, or in-laws or relatives. The hoary old notion that intermarriage will eliminate Maori–Pakeha difference in the marriage bed needs to be put to bed itself. But marriage *alliance*, the ancient Maori mechanism for easing permanent relations between groups, is still going strong. This positive, however, can shift almost imperceptibly into a negative. There is, perhaps, still a tendency for Pakeha to lean too much on Maori for cultural distinctiveness and for national symbolism. In my view, this sometimes goes beyond healthy cross-cultural borrowing, and it has fraught implications. If Pakeha believe that Maori is the only real New Zealand culture, they are less likely to be comfortable with Maori going their own way. A key obstacle to Pakeha support for a Maori resolution to Maori problems is the Pakeha identity crisis of the late twentieth century, discussed in the remaining two chapters.

For many Pakeha, possibly a narrow majority, these are not major issues. They believe that Maori socio-economic disadvantage is their own fault. Along with a few eminent Maori, such as 1970s politician Ben Couch and 1990s novelist Alan Duff, they feel that Maori should stop whingeing and pull themselves up by their own bootstraps. They agree with J. K. Hunn that separate Maori institutions are undesirable, and are hostile to any degree of Maori self-government – 'only Parliament makes the law'. New Zealand, in fact, has long had public authorities outside Parliament, of almost every shape and size – regional authorities, city councils, county councils, water boards, harbour boards and the rest. Would Maori authorities, responsible for particular issues in particular regions, really be the end of the world? New Zealand history suggests that Maori problems will never be solved except by Maori themselves, but they have to be given the necessary tools, which may include some cession of authority as well as resources. It is quite true that Maori have to pull themselves up by their own bootstraps. But this may require that they be given back some bootstraps first.

CHAPTER SEVENTEEN

Escape from Nappy Valley

In the bustling little cities of progressive colonial New Zealand, before the 1880s, most people walked to work. Cities were concentrated; what would now be called 'downtown' or the 'city centre' was just about it. From the 1880s, horse-drawn trams began a trend of urban spread, which picked up pace in the heyday of the electric tram, 1900s–30s. Some urban tram systems were very large, capable of moving thousands of people quite quickly and very efficiently, but only for a short distance. Trams were short-range transport. They extended cities, made possible a widening fringe of residential neighbourhoods around the city centre, and allowed more people to have the yards and gardens around their houses that they so desired. Industry also tended to be concentrated in the city centres, in factories that were several storeys high but did not take up too much precious space. People took the tram into these and other workplaces. Most work and much recreation took place downtown.

From the 1920s, new developments began to change the New Zealand cityscape. Assembly-line techniques required factories on one level, which took more space than was available in city centres. Industrial suburbs, such as Wellington's Lower Hutt and Auckland's Mount Wellington–Penrose, came into being. People could now both live and work in such places. Added to this, new forms of commuter transport emerged: electric trolley buses, from 1924; electric commuter railways from 1938; and motor buses, which were first introduced in 1904 but only flourished in the cities from the 1930s.[1] Above all, the motorcar, already pervasive in the country, became widespread in the cities from the late 1930s, and pervasive in the 1950s. By 1955, the car was the dominant form of commuter transport in Auckland.[2] These new forms of transport replaced the tram in most cities during the 1950s, though trams hung on in Wellington until 1964. In some cities, the car also displaced the commuter railway, which was in decline by the late 1950s.[3] New residential suburbs developed, town-sized clusters of quarter-acre sections with shops, as we have seen, but little industry of their own. They could be raw new subdivisions, short on public transport and public amenities, treeless and sterile. Or they could be converted urban-fringe villages. The swelling city engulfed a pre-existing kernel, which was eventually swamped like Maori villages before it, but still lent a little age and character to the new suburb. Johnsonville, near Wellington, for example, was a village of about 2,000 people until the late 1930s. An electric-train service and the sealing of the road to Wellington in 1938–39 established commutable links, followed by a motorway in 1951. Johnsonville quadrupled in size between 1956 and 1976, with most of its adult male inhabitants working outside the suburb.[4]

After 1945, these new suburbs, industrial and residential or simply residential, sprouted like mushrooms on the margins of Auckland, Wellington and Christchurch, and in those of the provincial towns, such as Hamilton, Tauranga and Palmerston North, that were experiencing high growth. Sometimes known as 'Nappy Valley', because of the preponderance of young familes, they were the crucible of modern New Zealand social history, producing several new types of New Zealander. They were also the chief location of one of that history's determining features: the baby boom.

Baby Boom, Baby Bust

Between 1945 and 1970, both Maori and Pakeha populations underwent their biggest demographic transitions of the twentieth century. Maori experienced a 'death bust', as we have seen. Pakeha experienced a 'baby boom'. Like the economic boom of the same period, it was long. It began about 1944 and peaked in 1961, when it is sometimes said to have ended. But a flow-on effect meant birth rates did not return to pre-war levels (and below) until the early 1970s. Unlike the economic boom, it was not that slow. Crude birth rates increased 50 per cent from 18 per 1,000 in 1936 to 27 in 1961. Total fertility rates (the size of the average family if the birth rates of that year had continued indefinitely) almost doubled, from just over two notional children to just over four.[5] The 'baby-boomer' cohort includes those born between 1945 and 1970. At almost 1.5 million, they are roughly twice as numerous as the pre-boom generation of 1920–45, and more numerous than the post-boom generation of 1970–95.[6] The baby-boomers are the people who run New Zealand today – and write its history – and they are the people who will overflow its hospitals and retirement homes in the future.

Why did the Pakeha baby boom happen? One obvious causal candidate is the after-effect of war itself – implied in the label 'post-war baby boom'. Delayed marriage and delayed family formation took place, as they had after World War One, boosting birth rates. But key features of the long baby boom were marriage and family formation at younger ages than before – the opposite of delay. The average age of women at marriage fell from 25 to 21 years, 1945–71. Older age groups initially bred more too, but only for the first couple of years after 1945. As after World War One, the 'delayed marriage' boost was modest and brief, lasting about two years – more baby blip than baby boom.[7] Another, attractively unromantic, possibility is that 'single women made haste to secure spouses from a war-depleted stock of eligible males'.[8] But the boom continued after the wartime husband barrel had been scraped, and going downmarket in the husband hunt does not explain the increased universality of marriage – between 1945 and 1971, the proportion of women ever married at age 39 increased from 85 to 95 per cent.[9] Postwar baby blips, from whatever cause, do not explain the long baby boom of the 1950s and 1960s. Another promising candidate is pro-natal ideology, advocating parenthood as one's first duty. Yet such an ideology had existed since the turn of the century, while birth rates had remained stubbornly low – the Great Mothers' Mutiny. The growing economy was no doubt a factor, but economic growth had not regularly increased birth rates in the past. The obvious does not take us very far in explaining the great baby boom.

More subtle postwar reflexes than delayed marriage were behind the baby boom. One was a vague but widespread urge to restore, to revert to 'pre-war normality'. The 'reversion' was to an *idealised* past, rather than the thing itself. Another unspoken aspiration, perhaps, was to deliver in the present the past as it should have been. Studies of fertility patterns suggest that parents look to their own childhoods when deciding whether to have children themselves. If the present seems likely to be better than the past, they are more likely to say yes. Parents, I suspect, wanted to give children what they feel they should have had themselves, to take a second bite of the apple, if only by proxy. Depression and war, 1929–45, was not a hard act for the present to beat. Above all, there was a widely recognised but understudied phenomenon: the rise of romantic marriage. This idealised the marriage process: 'falling in love', white wedding and honeymoon. It also involved a notion of long-term 'domestic bliss', 'housewife' breeding and housekeeping contentedly in her own modern home, equipped with the latest in electric servants. It romanticised not only marriage and women's domestic lives, but also childhood, parenthood and married men's lives, and it might be more accurate to describe it as a 'cult' of 'romantic domesticity'. Parenthood shifted from the strict and austere Dr Truby King model to the more humane, caring and educated Dr Spock model. Screaming brat was transubstantiated into cute toddler. Kiwi Bloke, except for half an hour in the pub each evening, was transformed into Family Man, earning the large wage that permitted his wife to stay at home.

It is strange that the early twentieth-century cult of domesticity, of scientific and patriotic motherhood, which was ineffective in encouraging births, has received more historical attention than the mid-twentieth-century cult of romantic domesticity, which was very effective. The beginnings of the latter in New Zealand can be dated back to the 1920s,[10] but the 1930s is a more likely time of origin, and the real flowering occurred from 1944, in association with the baby boom. As yet, we can only guess at the sources of this transformation in attitudes to marriage and family life. Low birth rates in the first decades of the century are thought to have corroded traditional pragmatic notions of marriage, whereby its main purpose was economic alliance and reproduction, although love might develop between spouses after marriage. Yet romantic marriage came half a century after the decline in birth rates, which dates from the 1880s. War itself, perhaps, 'generated a heightened consciousness of romantic love and conventional family roles'.[11] 'Domestic bliss' must have seemed attractive in comparison to the Western Desert, or to women's war work amidst austerity. New developments in the mass media are also likely to have been important, though whether they were primarily cause or consequence is not always clear.

During the 1930s and 1940s, films increasingly emphasised romance, radio became widespread and increasingly catered for domesticity, with special programmes aimed at housewife-listeners. A new genre of popular women's magazines, notably the *New Zealand Woman's Weekly*, founded in 1932, featured both romance and domesticity. Media images did not persuade the parents of the time to have more children, but they may have influenced the attitudes of the children they did have. Such messages increased in the 1950s and helped keep the boom going. The popular media reflect mass attitudes – otherwise they would not be popular – but they do not necessarily cause them. 'The *New Zealand Woman's Weekly* ran articles encouraging women to work for war and rehabilitation during the 1940s; to stay at home in the 1950s; to work part time in the 1960s and, by the 1970s and 1980s, to work full time in the name of equality.'[12] This could mean that women did what the *Woman's Weekly* and similar magazines told them to do. It could also mean that, in the interests of sales, such magazines told women what they wanted to hear. Men were not forced into marriage. They, too, married younger and more often, and were presumably as starry-eyed as women about marriage, but without benefit of the *Woman's Weekly*, Aunt Daisy and the radio serial *Portia Faces Life*.

Cinema may have had a more even impact on both genders than radio and magazines. Cinema became increasingly romantic, evocative and popular in the 1930s, with the advent of talking pictures. Silent movies could reach great heights of artistry and impact. When ocean waves were screened in the 1900s, 'the audience in the front rows leapt from their seats and dashed down the aisles towards the back to avoid being swamped'.[13] But once novelty wore off, identifying with silent stereotypes, romantic storylines and 'moods' may have been less easy than with talkies. Silent movies had to use accompanying piano music to evoke atmosphere. Scores developed a musical language of 52 'moods' to support action on the screen: Beethoven was the thing for escapes from cannibal islands; and Chopin for monotony. A drunken pianist once played 'For He's a Jolly Good Fellow' to accompany screen scenes of the resurrection of Christ.[14] Talkies boosted film-going in the 1930s and 1940s, and so perhaps did a need for escape from the dire external circumstances of war and depression. Cinema admission rates were higher between 1938 and 1949 (peaking at a staggering 23 per head in 1943–44) than they were in the 1950s, when the level was seventeen or eighteen per head. Television then reduced them to five per head by 1968–69.[15] The movies more people were seeing in the 1930s and 1940s were increasingly idealising romantic love and marriage. Another factor, I suspect, was the emergence of a new kind of youth culture, discussed later in this chapter, which at first cherished romantic marriage.

Our understanding of the rise of romantic domesticity is speculative, but it does seem to have been a key driver of the baby boom. Another, more tangible, driver was that the state at last put a substantial set of teeth behind its long-standing pro-natalist rhetoric. The teeth included the introduction of a universal family benefit in 1946, paid directly to mothers. Inflation was allowed to erode benefits from 1958, but they were initially substantial. Combined with tax exemptions for dependents, their value in 1947 has been calculated at 10 per cent of average net earnings – per child.[16] Three children would therefore boost the average net income by a third. There was also the new spasm of state assistance for home-ownership. The first Labour government preferred building state houses – 37,000 between 1935 and 1949 – and renting them out. Over 4,000 houses were built in 1949, and there were still 52,000 people on the waiting list.[17] The National government of 1949 sold off 20,000 of these houses and switched focus to helping people into their own homes – on a massive scale. This proved too popular a policy for the second Labour government, of 1957–60, to reverse. Instead, it further developed it by allowing for capitalisation of the family benefit to provide a deposit, and by making state loans even cheaper. The construction of state houses was diminished by this new emphasis on indirect help, but it did not end. Between the late 1930s and the early 1970s, the state built about 100,000 new houses and flats – about a quarter of the new housing stock of the period.[18] At peak, in 1961, 52 per cent of all dwellings were state-funded in some way.[19]

Another massive state attempt at social engineering was the post-World

War Two rehabilitation programme. This was larger and more successful than after World War One. No fewer than 49,000 ex-servicemen were helped into their own homes by 1955, and another 18,000 received state rental houses. Some 14,000 were helped into farms, and thousands more were financed through training of various kinds – 7,400 as carpenters alone.[20] This huge programme obviously privileged men over women – and servicemen over other men – and it has been suggested that it helped wind back wartime gains by working women.[21] But women did have indirect access to the state's rehabilitation largesse – through marriage. From all causes, home-owners grew from 56 to 70 per cent of all householders between 1945 and 1971.[22] For both men and women, marriage now often also meant a home of your own. Unsurprisingly, state pro-natalism with bribes worked a lot better than without. In 1929–45, it was unusually hard to provide a secure and affluent home for children. In 1945–70, it was unusually easy.

The wedding of romantic domesticity and massive state aid goes quite a long way towards explaining the baby boom. Another boom booster may have been an element of female populism, a mothers' mutiny in reverse, whereby young women sought greater freedom and adulthood in marriage and motherhood. This contradicts preconceptions, but the possibility of husbandly control may have compared favourably to the certainty of parental control in the minds of young women. The average age gap between husband and wife was narrowing, to between two and three years. Whereas young couples in the past had sometimes remained under a parental roof, or postponed marriage until they could get out from under it, they could now acquire their own homes. An alternative route to independence, flatting with other single people, had not yet become widely accepted. The romanticised images of wife and mother being inculcated by domestic media also functioned as symbols of adulthood, even independence. 'A home of her own' was not only an escape from rental housing but from parental housing. There might be a sense in which the mass entry into Nappy Valley was a search for independence rather than a turning away from it. Pakeha women entered Nappy Valley, wisely or not, more through choice than compulsion.

Baby boom was followed by baby bust. The boom peaked in 1961 and ended when birth rates reverted to pre-boom levels in the early 1970s. The drop was particularly sharp in the early 1960s and the early 1970s. It was these two five-year mini-busts that did the damage, accounting for three-quarters of the total fall in rates between 1961 and 1998. Decline was more gradual at other times, but generally steady. By 1998, the birth rate was 14.5 per 1,000 people, just over half the 1961 level.[23] Obvious reasons take us no further in understanding the bust than they did the boom. The contraceptive pill did first appear around 1960 – the sources differ between 1958 and 1962 – but did not become widely available until five years later.[24] New Zealand women then became very enthusiastic users, and the Pill made women-led fertility control much easier, but it did not cause the baby bust. Formal feminism encouraged women's control of fertility. But the great 'second wave' of formal feminism, discussed in the next section, did not get off the ground until 1970 – a decade after the bust began. Long-term economic downturn, another causal candidate, did not begin until 1973.

One factor behind the baby bust may have been the puncturing of the cult of romantic marriage, motherhood and domesticity. Marriages certainly became easier to escape from. The number of divorces rose from around 2,000 a year in 1960 to over 7,000 by 1980.[25] The rise of romantic domesticity in the 1950s had corresponded with the mass advent of 'electric servants', which prior to this had been the privilege of the upper middle class. Between 1939 and 1955, prices of these machines halved as a proportion of wages. The 1956 census showed that over half of all homes had electric stoves, refrigerators and washing machines. By 1966, 'New Zealand households had become the most electrified in the world'.[26] Electric servants must have made motherhood and domesticity seem more attractive at first, but there were clear downsides to Nappy Valley.

The flight of the servant meant that only 3 per cent of households had any kind of paid help with housework,[27] and men were of little use here. In 1976, only 42 per cent of women received any help from men with housework.[28] New, gentler and more educative, techniques of child-rearing could be demanding and time-intensive: Spock babies took more time than Truby King babies. Suburban houses were more spacious and better equipped, but also more isolated, than their urban predecessors. Potential sites for social interaction existed – school and church committees, other voluntary organisations, playcentres and kindergartens, part-time jobs, even Plunket itself, whose approach was softening at this time. But these sites were limited and access to them often depended on cars or public transport. Unless a family had two cars, which was still quite rare, a housewife's use of one depended on a working husband's ability and willingness to use public transport. As in the nineteenth century, access to a horse or car made a big difference to New Zealand women. Nappy Valley could be a lonely, unsatisfying and constrictive place. As late as 1981, a quarter of women had no personal access to money.[29] Two-thirds went out at night once a week or less, of whom one-third had not been out at night at all for the past month.[30] Some analysts these days tend to discount 'suburban neurosis', and neurosis may be too strong and deceptive a word. But for many women there must have been times when their bright new suburban home seemed more prison than paradise.

A second possible contributor to the baby bust may have been a shift in women's attitudes to their own future. During the 1950s, the ongoing increase in life expectancy must have become apparent. This could, and initially did, lead women to bear children early in the confidence that there would be plenty of time for a post-maternal life after they left the nest. The baby boom was partly a matter of *earlier* babies, rather than *more* babies, and once planned families were formed, the birth rate dropped. Later, a slow but steady upward shift in the medical view of the upper age limit of safe childbirth could lead to a decision for later marriage and child-bearing. The average age at marriage began moving back up from about 1970, from 21.7 years in 1971 to 27.1 in 1996.[31] Even before this, growing tertiary educational opportunities for women must have encouraged delayed child-bearing in the middle class at least. From 1963, the number of women going to university increased even faster than that of men.[32] Underneath this, perhaps, was a reversion to the old populist view that women's lives would consist of roughly equal spells of work and motherhood.

The third contributor to the baby bust was an interplay between the decline of the family wage, the rise of equal pay and the erosion of state pro-natalism, notably the family benefit.[33] Between 1936 and 1949, the women's minimum wage increased from 47 to 66 per cent of that of males.[34] Some historians feel that these nominal rates understate the actual gap, but the most recent research suggests they may overstate it. If that is so, there was a substantial improvement in women's remuneration compared with men's *before* the first of two big steps in legislation: equal pay for government employees in 1960. The root of this, it seems, was the decline of the concept of the family wage – the idea that men should receive enough to maintain a wife and three children in 'moderate comfort'. The key blow to this was the advent of the universal family allowance of 1946, which undermined the case against equal pay – namely the need for men to have a higher, 'family', wage. 'The universal family allowance of 1946, then, must be regarded as the major turning point for equal pay.'[35] In 1972 – again, before the second big step in equal-pay legislation that year – women were getting 73 per cent of male wages. After the legislation of 1972, the situation did not improve much at all. The Equal Pay Act of 1972 was not fully implemented until 1978, when women averaged 78 per cent of men's pay. In the late 1990s, the level was still only 81 per cent.[36]

At first, the family benefit helped compensate for the decline of the family wage. But it soon became clear that the family benefit was eroding too. Its value, combined with tax exemptions for dependents, declined from 10 per cent of the average wage in 1946 to 3.5 per cent in the early 1970s,[37] and state assistance for housing also declined rapidly after 1975. There is cruel irony here. The discriminatory problem had never been the 'family wage' in itself, but the fact that it was always men who got it. The universal family benefit reduced the need for the family wage, and contributed more than legislation to bringing about more equal pay. But the family benefit then shrank to insignificance – and eventually disappeared altogether in the late 1980s. Gradually, families lost both the family wage and the family benefit. The process began around 1960. It increasingly pressured women into the work-force, and so helped cause a baby bust that continues to the present.

The decline of romantic domesticity and of state pro-natalism leaves the present with a problem that, disconcertingly enough, would have been familiar to eugenicists earlier in the century. The decline in birth rates went furthest and fastest among Pakeha, especially middle-class city-dwelling Pakeha, who were also quite prone to emigration. With birth rates now well below replacement, the Pakeha middle class is now literally a dying breed. In effect, state action – and to some extent, public attitudes – have swung from explicit pro-natalism to implicit anti-natalism over the last 30 years. By the 1990s, apart from the very poor, who received targeted 'family support' and other assistance, there was neither the family wage nor the family benefit, nor state housing assistance, nor significant tax exemptions for dependents. The assumption is that a person on $60,000 a year with four dependents is as 'rich', and therefore as subject to tax, as someone on the same income with no dependents. This situation is sometimes justified by the curious observation that having children is a 'lifestyle choice', of no public benefit, like owning goldfish. But goldfish will not pay the taxes or staff the retirement homes of the future.

New Waves: Work and Feminism

As we saw in Chapter Five, formal feminism, the 'first wave' of the women's movement, had been a powerful force in New Zealand history between 1885 and 1905. Women's gains were subsequently reined in to some extent, but not completely. A 'New Woman' archetype survived, clearly outranked by the 'Wife and Mother', but still in there fighting, and surfacing occasionally. It was somehow predictable that the pioneer woman aviator of the 1930s, Jean Batten, should be a New Zealander. Yet the period 1910s–50s has been seen as something of a dark age for New Zealand feminism, and attempts to contest this image have not as yet been very convincing. The case for dating the advent of the 'second wave' of the women's movement, an important development in recent history, to the 1960s is a little stronger. But the first radical feminist groups emerged in Auckland and Wellington in 1970.[38]

Symbolically enough, they first hit the headlines with their liberation of men-only pubs, which was completed by about 1981 – twenty years after the demise of the colour bar.[39] The first women's liberation conference was held in 1972, the important magazine *Broadsheet* was established, and lesbian groups and magazines emerged the following year. About a hundred new women's organisations were formed in the 1970s, compared with twenty or so in the 1960s.[40] Second-wave feminism flowered in the 1970s and 1980s. It is interesting to note that both it and the first wave accompanied the two major systemic shake-ups of modern New Zealand history: the advents of recolonisation and decolonisation.

As with most such movements, second-wave feminism comprised different strands, notably liberal, lesbian, socialist and Maori. The liberal strand had the deepest historical roots, the broadest base and the fewest problems of hybridity – of combining feminism with some other cause. The lesbian strand tended towards radicalism. Lesbian feminism was also part of a general 'coming-out' of homosexuality, treated below. Socialist feminism, which was very prominent in the 1970s but less so in the 1980s, also had a dual character, and sometimes suffered from it: was the key enemy masculism or capitalism? It also suffered from internecine strife within the New Zealand left, which reached surprising levels of intensity in the late 1960s and 1970s. Another hybrid was Maori feminism, which had problems not only with its Pakeha feminist sisters but also with its Maori masculist brothers. The four strands often diverged and sometimes clashed, but they also converged, and between them had contributed to a substantial culture shift by the 1990s. Feminism's success here was obscured, but perhaps also enhanced, by a tendency to stereotype it on its extreme, to read 'feminist' as 'extremely radical activist feminist'. Extreme political correctness, of the type that recently saw an American federal employee disciplined for using the word 'niggardly', was used by the hostile to characterise the whole movement. One notorious New Zealand example was a demand for free 24-hour childcare – actually already available in the form of adoption. Such stereotyping is often used as an anti-feminist weapon, but is arguably double-edged. Recent studies suggest that many New Zealand women of the 1990s deny being 'feminist' in the stereotyped sense, but support most of the actual feminist agenda.[41] This agenda also has considerable male support, at least in theory.[42] The middle ground has shifted towards feminism, and the women's movement – helped, ironically, by its stereotyping enemies – can claim substantial credit for this.

Second-wave feminism operated on four main fronts: seeking more equal treatment in and through politics; battling for greater control by women of their own health and reproduction; tackling the problem of camouflaged but apparently endemic male violence towards women; and trying to end gender discrimination, notably in the workplace. Until 1933 and the election of Elizabeth McCombs as MP for Lyttelton, women's representation in the New Zealand Parliament was non-existent. Between 1933 and 1975, despite the efforts of Labour Cabinet minister Mabel Howard in the 1950s, it remained token. In the election of 1975, only 6 per cent of Labour candidates and 5 per cent of National candidates were female. From 1978, however, women's parliamentary representation rocketed – to 15 per cent in 1990 and to 30 per cent in 1996. Even the 1990 figure was high compared with Britain, Australia and the United States.[43] The 1999 figure of 31 per cent, coupled with the fact that the top four political and judicial positions were all held or about to be held by women, is internationally exceptional. Women in politics are sometimes discounted as 'honorary men', and it is true that women such as Britain's Margaret Thatcher are quite capable of leading governments that no-one would describe as feminist. But the numbers in New Zealand are now too high for this disclaimer. Complete parity in Parliament will probably require a change in traditional approaches to male work and parenthood. But, short of that, the surge of women into New Zealand politics 1978–99 has surely to be counted as a substantial success for the women's movement.

Formal feminism's second battle was over control of women's health and reproduction. This had many facets, including some feminisation of the medical profession, a renewal of the old contest between male-controlled hospital birth and female-controlled home birth, and the revelation of 'unfortunate experiments' at National Women's Hospital in Auckland in 1987.[44] The single issue that most united both the women's movement and opposition to it, however, was abortion. New Zealand had a long tradition of readily available abortion dating back to the first baby bust of the 1880s. It had quite a high degree of populist acceptance, but was illegal and therefore often carried out in dangerous circumstances. There was some provision for legal abortion if the health of the mother was clearly threatened, but it was minimal. The numbers involved were tiny until the late 1960s – 63 in 1965 – but from that time, attitudes of middle-class medics began to shift to match those of the working class. By 1969, there were 225 legal abortions. This was a very modest liberalisation – illegal abortions that year amounted to 4,000–5,000, and legal abortions in 1998 amounted to 15,000 (up from 10,000 in 1988). The overall proportion of abortions, legal and illegal, was probably dropping in the 1960s, as alternative means of fertility control such as the Pill proliferated.[45]

Yet the tiny increase of the late 1960s aroused traditionalist fears, and an anti-abortion movement emerged in 1970, in the shape of the Society for the Protection of the Unborn Child. The establishment of the first abortion clinic in 1974 was fuel to the flames, and SPUC squared off against the new feminism and its allies. There was an arson attack against an abortion clinic in 1976, legislation permitting abortions was tightened in 1977, and radical medic and polemicist Erich Geiringer responded with a book entitled *SPUC 'em All* in 1978.[46] A feminist network sprang up that facilitated travel to Australia for safe and legal abortions. Finally, from 1979, legal abortions became quite readily available. SPUC, however, did not give up, and claimed up to 70,000 members in 1991.[47]

The abortion issue introduces crucial interactions between formal feminism and two other major historical phenomena. One was populism. Scholarship on the abortion debate has yet to realise that abortion was quite readily available in New Zealand before the 1970s. It was a legal crime but, in populist circles, not a social crime. Juries sometimes declined to convict abortionists, and at least one acquittal was accompanied by cheers from the public gallery.[48] What happened in the 1970s was that formal practice was brought into alignment with informal practice. Formal feminism was most effective when it intersected with populist feminism. The second interaction was between feminism and its enemy, traditional moral conservatism, which was flowering at the same time – partly in reaction to feminism and other activisms, partly in reaction to the vaguely sensed traumas of decolonisation. With abortion, the reassertion of moral conservatism actually came first. The 'lash' (the modest increase in legal abortion in the late 1960s) preceded second-wave formal feminism, which was actually 'backlashing' against the SPUC backlash. One could say the same about the domestic purposes benefit of 1973, whose introduction had little to do with feminist agitation, and which had a precursor in 1968 in any case. In the mid-1970s, there was panic about the morality of single mothers on the DPB, and ludicrous state attempts to police it, through such techniques as counting shoes under beds, and toothbrushes. Here again, it was the moral right rather than the liberal left that actually took the initiative. Society was untightening from below, as it were. Conservatives resisted this, and were resisted in their turn by the activists.

The new feminism's third crusade was against domestic violence. The moral, conformist, family-oriented tight society had long had this skeleton in its closet. The closet was kept tightly closed until the 1970s, and the level is difficult to estimate. Male violence towards women featured prominently in divorce cases in late nineteenth-century Auckland.[49] A century later, even discounting sensationalist claims, the rate was still quite high. What seems the most reliable of several 1980s surveys suggests that about 16 per cent of women were hit by their male partners, half of them regularly.[50] To the 1970s, wife-beating was to a considerable extent accepted by both formal and populist male cultures – a salutary reminder that the latter is a very unreliable ally of left-liberalisms. In 1949, a judge chastised a defendant for beating his wife with an iron bar. He should, said the judge, have explained to his wife what she had done wrong and then beaten her with a reasonable-sized stick. 'While it might be proper for a man to beat his wife at times, he must beat her properly. I think it is proper that at times a man does so, and the Bible subscribes to and supports that statement, but the beating must be done as a service of love and not in temper.'[51] 'Giving the wife a bit of a clip round the ear-hole' was also considered acceptable in male popular culture. Its 1960s icon, Barry Crump, and his father Wally, were both master practitioners of this unedifying Kiwi folk art.[52]

Formal feminism attacked this problem by bringing it out into the open and so changing police and public attitudes, and by establishing 'women's refuges', at which beaten women and their children could obtain help and shelter. The first refuge was established in 1973 or 1974 (the sources differ). By 1985, there were 34, estimated to be helping about 22,000 women and children a year in various ways. By 1987, there were 48 refuges.[53] Publicising the issue also appears to have had some effect. A Hamilton study in 1981 indicated that only 4 per cent of men and 1 per cent of women found spouse-beating acceptable. By the late 1990s, police, prompted by the Domestic Violence Act of 1996, were at last beginning to take a more proactive attitude to domestic violence, hitherto seen by many as none of their business. Whether these efforts have actually reduced the problem is not clear. The broad pattern in violent crime is of massive increase between 1960 and the mid-1990s, followed by a minor downturn. Convictions for male assaults on women and children rose from 1,477 in 1989 to 4,395 in 1995, with a modest fall to 3,345 in 1998. Convictions for breaching non-molestation orders jumped from 268 in 1989 to 1,885 in 1998, a sevenfold increase. More active policing may explain the rise in convictions. But neither feminism nor policing have yet got to the roots of domestic violence in New Zealand.

Second-wave feminism's fourth and final battle was against gender discrimination of various kinds. Landmark legislative successes included the Matrimonial Property Act of 1976, which made divorce less of an asset-stripping experience for women, an act equalising welfare benefits in 1979, and equal-opportunities legislation in 1987–88. Equal-pay legislation, as we have seen, was implemented between 1972 and 1978. It is noticeable that some of these measures had 1960s precedents that pre-dated the women's movement. Equal pay in the public service was introduced in 1960, and there was some improvement in matrimonial property law in 1963. To some extent, second-wave formal feminism was reinforcing a pre-existing trend, and this was most apparent in the broad sphere of women and work.

The story here begins during World War Two, when women entered many occupations previously closed to them. Waged women increased in numbers from 180,000 in 1939 to a peak of 236,000 in 1943.[54] But this was still only a standardised participation rate of about 30 per cent, compared to 38 per cent in Britain and 51 per cent in Germany.[55] Moreover, women left their new jobs as the war ground to an end. Their participation rate quickly returned to pre-war levels and remained there until 1961, when a steep rise began. Most recent studies therefore emphasise the 'limitations of wartime change' for working women. 'The orthodox view now is that the war brought about no permanent change in women's paid labour.'[56] On this view, women did not get into the wartime workforce very much, and to the extent that they did, they soon left for Nappy Valley. 'Unleashing' during the war was very modest and was soon reined in.

However, the war did, it seems to me, help bring about three important and permanent changes in women's work. One was women's mass exodus from domestic service. This had always been work of last resort for New Zealanders, male and female, despite the fact that demand was high.[57] This servants' mutiny was an enduring feature of the populist compact. But, during the Depression, many women had been forced to the last resort. Almost 30,000 were working as domestic servants in 1936. This figure fell dramatically to 9,000 by 1945, and kept falling.[58] This happened despite some state and public pressure, which sought to have domestic service defined as essential war work and toyed with state intervention, as with the 1942 State Corps of Domestic Assistants.[59] 'Attempts to attract women into domestic work failed . . . young women with opportunities elsewhere showed a marked reluctance to settle for the domestic sphere.'[60] Domestic service persisted vestigially as part-time 'home help' or 'cleaning ladies', but the servant as such virtually disappeared. She did so before 'electric servants' such as electric stoves, fridges and vacuum cleaners became widespread, and it seems reasonable to conclude that she did so because women seized the change opportunity of World War Two.

The second wartime change was the entry of women into some new occupations, or their entrenchment of their position in older occupations. Women mechanics, tram and truck drivers were eased out after the war in favour of returned soldiers – women taxi drivers were at least 'farewelled at a celebratory dance'. Servicewomen, too, lost their jobs. Their rehabilitation consisted in courses in needlework, nutrition, 'Planning Your Trousseau' and 'Adjusting to Married Life'.[61] But women in banks and government services – the police, the Post Office, Railways and the civil service itself – kept their jobs or handed them on to other women. Securing a permanent place in the expanding public service was particularly important, and here women were helped by high labour demand. The civil service, traditionally considered highly desirable as a safe billet, became less popular with qualified males immediately after World War Two. There were fewer of them, owing to wartime casualties, and private sector opportunities seemed more attractive. The civil service had been treating all its women workers as temporary since 1921, and requiring them to resign at marriage since 1913. In this new context, it repealed the former provision in 1946, and the latter in 1948. The lesson that it could rely on women is likely to have been learned during the war, when the number the civil service employed more than tripled.[62]

In 1945, a quarter of the female 'clerks and administrators' employed by the civil service were married, and this symbolises the third wartime change.[63] During the war, a process began that made waged work by married women acceptable to women themselves and, more slowly, to the public in general. The shift was only partial. Full-time work was restricted mostly to women without school-age children. Women with school-age children could, it was thought, only work part-time, and women with pre-schoolers were under heavy pressure not to work at all. But the workforce-participation rate of married women more than doubled 1936–45, from 3.7 to 7.7 per cent, and this probably conceals a sharper and higher rise between 1939 and 1944. The trajectory thus modestly begun proved permanent. The participation rate doubled again, to 16 per cent by 1961, and increased further to 26 per cent ten years later. Put another way, married women comprised a quarter of the female workforce in 1951, and half in 1971.[64] These figures must represent a higher turnover of married women moving in and out of waged work. The low rate of women's overall participation in the workforce, single or married, between 1945 and 1961 was due to a substantial decline in single women working, as they opted for early marriage. It conceals a substantial movement of married women into – or back into – the workforce. By 1971, a period of waged work as well as motherhood – not instead of motherhood – was a significant part of most women's lives. Nappy Valley allowed for day-release into the dubious pleasures of waged work, and this in turn may help explain why women were willing to enter the Valley.

Between World War Two and the present, women's engagement with waged work seems to have gone through three stages of change. In the first stage, to 1961, the increase in married-women workers was compensated by the decrease in single-women workers, who took up motherhood or further education instead. During this stage, the overall female workforce-participation rate remained roughly static at around 26–27 per cent. In the second stage, 1961–76, a substantial rise began, to a participation rate of 36.6 per cent. This new surge into the workforce is unlikely to have been driven by sheer poverty. Poverty did exist, but it affected a small minority. Only 5–7 per cent of women in various surveys around 1970 defined themselves as being financially in need.[65] The times were prosperous and the demand for labour was high. While some women's historians suggest that domestic technology did not lower women's housework loads, this seems inherently unlikely, and a Canadian study suggests that mechanisation did improve domestic productivity.[66] But it also increased domestic costs, and may have encouraged women to enter the workforce to help pay for the new whiteware and other luxuries that had become necessities in terms of consumer expectations. Electric servants, then, lowered the amount of housework but not the total amount of women's work. The demand for labour, equal-pay legislation and the demise of the family wage also drove up women's wages as a proportion of male wages in this period – from 66.7 per cent in 1961 to 78 per cent in 1978 – a vastly higher increase that that of the next twenty years. Opportunities also broadened somewhat, and small minorities of women began to make their way into traditionally male professions. The minorities were small indeed – 2 per cent of lawyers in 1975, for example.[67] In this stage, women with pre-school children were still seldom found in the workforce. In 1972, there were only 1,714 childcare places in the whole country, and only 7 per cent of women with pre-schoolers worked full-time.[68]

Between 1978 and 2000, our third stage, women's engagement with work continued to increase, but with a more marked divergence between the experiences of middle-class and working-class women. Middle-class women shared fully in a renewed expansion of tertiary education, and seem poised to use this to invade male professions on a massive scale. Almost half of new lawyers in 1992 were female, compared with 2 per cent in 1975.[69] Among tertiary students graduating in 1998, females outnumbered males by 34,000 to 23,000, and their traditional orientation towards arts subjects had declined markedly. They outnumbered men in law, commerce and business, and medicine, and were nearly equal in sciences (2,055 men; 1,943 women). A few male strongholds remained – in engineering, for example – but even here women were 20 per cent of all graduates in 1998.[70] Glass ceilings and glass gateways persist, but these figures suggest that, if the economy recovers, twenty-first-century New Zealand will be rather a good place to be a middle-class career woman.

The last quarter of the twentieth century was much less promising for working-class women. Along with Maori and Pacific Islanders, they were first to the wall when economic downturn struck. Their participation increased, but was now driven by poverty, and the increase in the quantity of work was not matched by an increase in the quality. Women's wages as a proportion of men's increased only 3 per cent, 1978–98, compared with over 20 per cent 1961–78. Women were much more likely to be found in extremely low-paid work, and much of the increased work available was only part-time.

Full-time women workers increased only from 34 to 39 per cent of adult females, 1971–96, while part-time and full-time combined rocketed from 38 to 58 per cent. Added to this, unemployment hit women harder than men. Analysts blame the 1984 restructuring for this, but it was the earlier economic downturn resulting from decolonisation that was to blame. Between 1976 and 1986, the female unemployment rate was almost twice the male. Both rates increased thereafter but tended to converge, peaking in 1991 with male unemployment at 11 per cent and female unemployment at 14.9 per cent. Taking into account unemployment, women's participation in the full-time workforce actually fell from its 1986 peak, and had still not recovered ten years later.

All this means that the mass entry into waged work, and the substantial other achievements of the 'feminist revolution', have turned into something of a Judas kiss for many New Zealand women. A survey in 1993 indicated that 94 per cent of New Zealand women felt they had more freedom than their mothers, and they were right.[71] But they also had less money in real terms, and their engagement with waged work had not been matched by a male engagement with unwaged work. A survey of time use in 1999 indicated that, while women did about three-quarters of the waged work of men, they still did twice as much housework and three times as much childcare.[72]

Letting Out Lolita?

In 1953, only two years after the Waterfront Crisis of 1951, another revolt against the established order took place. It was centred at the Elbe Milk Bar in the Hutt Valley, and it consisted of an alleged mass outbreak of sex among schoolchildren. Fifty-nine adolescents were charged with 107 sex offences, and the government ordered a commission of inquiry into 'moral deliquency' led by Dr Oswald Mazengarb.[73] The Mazengarb Report appeared in 1954. It found that 'improper sexual behaviour among children' was 'extensive', especially in the big North Island cities, and that this was 'undermining the fabric of society'. Especially alarming was a 'new pattern' of 'female precociousness', whereby girls initiated sexual activity and seemed to be 'unconcerned or unashamed, and even proud, of what they had done'. A smaller sex epidemic was said to have occurred in 1952. The problem of adolescent moral rebellion also appeared in other places and in other forms in the early 1950s. There was the Parker–Hulme incident in 1954, where two Christchurch schoolgirls, thought to be lovers, killed one of their mothers when she tried to part them. There was a fatal stabbing involving juveniles in a milk bar in Auckland in 1955. There was also an alarming invasion of loud and unruly American music, known as 'rock and roll' from 1955, and an infestation by subversive American comics, estimated to number seven million a year.[74] Finally, there was the emergence of the 'Bodgie'. Male 'bodgies', or 'teddy boys', and female 'widgies' dressed a little strangely, frequented milk bars, rode motor scooters or motorcycles, and called the rest of the world 'squares'. They were also thought to be more prone to sex, violence, drink and crime than normal youths.

The tight society reacted fiercely. The government distributed a copy of the Mazengarb Report to every household in the country – the Government Printer's biggest job ever. Censorship legislation was tightened, radio enforced stricter standards, and cinema ushers were urged to police the back rows as in the 1920s. A handbook for concerned schools and parents, *The Bodgie: A Study in Abnormal Psychology*, was published.[75] Less laughably, capital punishment appears to have increased as an indirect response. Half of the eight executions of the 1950s occurred in 1955.[76] Moral panics about 'hooligan' and 'larrikin' boys and sexually permissive girls have been traced back to the 1890s, and could probably be traced back to the 1840s. Historians likewise dismissed the Mazengarb Report as mere moral panic: a 'great sexual hoax'. Moral panic implies two things: moralistic public alarm, with repressive intent; and the wild exaggeration of the object of panic, the making of mountain from molehill. The moral panic about adolescent behaviour in the early 1950s certainly had the first characteristic, but it is not clear that it had the second – it may have been more mountain than molehill. If you had the morals of Mazengarb, you may have been quite right to panic.

One overlooked statistic suggests a real postwar boom in teenage sex. The proportion of brides aged twenty or under doubled between 1939 and 1958, from 17 to 35 per cent.[77] Most marriages of sixteen- to nineteen-year-olds – 65 per cent in 1962 and 80 per cent in 1971 – resulted from pre-nuptial conception.[78] There was also a sharp rise in illegitimate births, reflected in a massive adoption boom dating from 1944. Between that year and 1980, 87,000 adoptions occurred, compared with 16,000 between 1881 and 1944.[79] Adoptions usually resulted from very young mothers being pressured into giving up babies born out of wedlock. In 1962, only 18.5 per cent of unmarried mothers kept their children.[80] Abortions also continued to be quite numerous. This was traditionally the resort of married women, but did involve some pregnant teenagers.[81] Young lovers sometimes used contraception. Among the 59 adolescents involved in the Mazengarb incident – quite a large number – 'not one of the girls involved became pregnant', because condoms were used.

If we combine this evidence (teenage brides, teenage unmarried mothers adopting out, teenage abortions, and teenage sex not resulting in conception) we appear to be looking at something quite substantial – a sexual semi-revolution ten or twenty years before it was supposed to have happened. Some rare solid evidence about the sexual practices of New Zealanders, a 1991 survey of over 2,000 adults, qualifies the picture somewhat.[82] The oldest surveyed, born between 1937 and 1946, and turning fifteen in the 1950s, first had intercourse at the median age of twenty years – male and female alike. In the next cohort, born between 1947 and 1956 and turning fifteen in the 1960s, there is a sharp drop in the age of first intercourse to eighteen years. At first sight, this contradicts the evidence in the previous paragraph, and counts against the notion of an upsurge in teenage sex in the 1950s. Yet, while the drop in age at first intercourse continues in the 1970s and 1980s, it is much steeper in the 1960s. For example, age at first sex for males drops 2.4 years between the 1950s and the 1960s, but only 0.3 and 0.5 years in the next two decades. Changes of this type tend to occur in big cities first, and then in the rest of the country. The evidence of a 1950s upsurge in teen sex in Auckland and Wellington, outlined in the previous paragraph, is quite strong. We may therefore have a modest two-step youth-sex revolution: big cities in the 1950s, and the rest of the country in the 1960s.

Early sex was only one expression of an emerging teenage subculture. Others occurred in music, slang, dress, group formation, entertainment and general style: The Bodgie had a long sequence of successors. The word 'teenager' was coined in the United States in 1945 for commercial marketing purposes, and was in wide use by the early 1950s.[83] There had been some distinct adolescent subculture before this, but the 'teen age', a transitional phase between childhood and adulthood seems to have become much more marked after World War Two. To some extent, this was a New Zealand manifestation of a world trend, or at least an Anglo-American trend. Bodgies and their successors were not indigenous. Their transition to New Zealand was made easier by the postwar opening-up of new gateways to the world, or at least to the Anglo-American world, described in Chapter Fifteen. One could add developments in the recording of popular music to these: the 1950s advent of the 'single' and the long-playing album.

The derivative nature of the emergence of the New Zealand teenager can be exaggerated. There was an element of convergent evolution as well as global connection. The beginning of the upsurge in teenage sex and teenage marriage actually pre-dates the advent of the Bodgie and rock and roll, and there is reason to believe that the advent of the 'teenager' does so too, although the word was not used. A prerequisite for the development of a new subculture, so obvious that it is easily overlooked, is the emergence of a new place for it to happen – a cultural 'site'. The key site for teenage culture seems likely to have been the secondary school. Secondary schooling in New Zealand developed in three phases. It was the activity of a small élite to about 1900, and of a large minority, still middle class, to the early 1930s. Then, in or around 1932, secondary schooling became a majority experience – an important and understudied watershed in social history.[84] For the first time, most adolescents spent a substantial and significant chunk of their lives surrounded by other adolescents. Before this watershed, on leaving primary school, most adolescents returned to the family or went out to work – both sites dominated by adults. After it, they had the cultural site to become teenagers – once the word was invented. The New Zealand 'teen age' was similar to, but not fundamentally derived from, American and British archetypes.

It remains true that the forms and fads of the new teenage culture were derived from overseas. The bodgies and widgies of the early 1950s were succeeded by motorcycle, street and ethnic gangs, rockers, hippies, and punks. All these were imported, yet local factors helped determine their reception. Hippies, for example, came later to New Zealand than elsewhere, from 1967, but lasted longer as alternative lifestyle communities in the Coromandel and the West Coast of the South Island. The most basic local factor was the existence of an audience. When blues and jazz, the predecessors of rock and roll, had come to New Zealand in the 1920s and 1930s, there was much less of a teenage subculture to listen to them. Rock and roll music came to New Zealand in 1955 from America – arriving here a little earlier than in Australia and Britain. Johnny Devlin, who became New Zealand's first rock star in 1957–59, was essentially an Elvis Presley impersonator. The shrieks of fans and the tumultuous welcomes that greeted his concerts were also imports, but as highly improper American imports they challenged both the tight society and the recolonial system. To some extent, American culture acted as a 'denomination of dissent', like the nineteenth-century Maori engagement with Judaism and the twentieth-century Catholic Irish engagement with rugby league.

A denomination of dissent would not have been needed unless dissent was desired, and the denomination did not have to be American. British anti-establishment models, such as punk rock, were used almost as often. Indeed, the New Zealand flirtation with punk youth culture, in the late 1970s, was said to be second in intensity only to Britain itself. One could suggest a residual recolonialism here – the pink-haired punk rocker as Robert Muldoon's folk equivalent, the last of the Better Britons. But I doubt that the comparison holds up. The attractiveness of overseas models, it seems to me, was not just that they were British or American, but that they were imported ways of expressing a local sense of youth difference, and perhaps of rebellion against the tight society. Devlin lost his shirt at some concerts to adoring fans. When he visited Invercargill in 1959, he also lost his pants. In 1965, another New

Zealand rock band, Ray Columbus and the Invaders, played at Invercargill, supporting a British band called the Rolling Stones. 'An over-patriotic audience gave the Invaders a rousing reception while pelting the Stones with eggs and tomatoes.'[85] Why Invercargill should have an even more extreme response to Devlin and the Rolling Stones than other New Zealand towns is a mystery. But it was certainly not because it had better connections with America.

Predictably enough, the new youth culture was gender-contested. Residual masculism remained quite powerful, and does so to this day. At school, boys continue to command more playground space and teacher attention than do girls. Some video games, films and toys are still rigidly gendered, and, until the 1990s, New Zealand popular music tended to be male-led. A new masculism arguably joined the old, most noticeably in the gangs, Maori and Pakeha, that flourished in various forms from about 1970. Like nineteenth-century crews before them, these male-dominated entities defined themselves largely in terms of not being effeminate. One could almost suggest that gangs were collectives designed to shore up a threatened sense of masculinity. Women associates were rarely allowed full membership, and at worst were treated with contempt and violence as sexual and domestic conveniences. Added to this, the economic downturn from the 1970s hit vulnerable groups hardest, with young women workers among them. The benefit cuts of 1991 were particularly hard on solo parents, who were mostly working-class women.

On the other hand, formal feminism shifted the middle ground especially among the young. As we have seen, the number of women who accepted the basic principles of feminism, such as gender equality though not necessarily sameness, was much greater – and more cross-class – than the number who would call themselves feminist. This qualified good news for women appears to have been joined by a populist feminist challenge to masculism, which takes the curious form of copying it. There are hints of a 1990s tendency in female popular culture, especially youth culture, to appropriate or co-opt male behaviours. The rate of increase in female alcohol and drug consumption is higher than among men, though it starts from a much lower base, and there is anecdotal evidence of yet another new subclass: the female 'hoon'. In the early 1990s, in the small Southland town of Mataura, a group of young women were observed driving aggressively through the streets, leering and yelling sexual innuendoes at passing males.[86] In a famous student pub in Dunedin, rowdy, hard-drinking rugby supporters are now female as well as male.[87] Male strip shows have grown in popularity, and are considered some-how more acceptable than female ones. At first sight, this may seem simply to add a female problem to a male one. Doubling the number of young hoons at a stroke is not necessarily a great feat of social engineering. But the result may be that, as such behaviour becomes less archetypally male, it becomes less useful in defining masculinity, and therefore less common. Populist feminism, as we have learned, does not necessarily behave in ways which formal feminism – or anyone else for that matter – would approve. But, even so, it can be effective in bringing about change.

Secondary schools were not the only emerging site for the development of youth cultures. Tertiary education followed a similar pattern, several decades behind. To 1945, universities were essentially in the same phase that secondary schooling had been before 1900: they were restricted to a small élite. From 1945, they entered the large-minority phase. The number of tertiary students (including those at teacher training colleges), doubled from under 10,000 in 1944 to almost 20,000 in 1960, and then climbed by 150 per cent to well over 50,000, now including polytechnic students, in 1975.[88] The total number of New Zealand university graduates in 1959 has been estimated at a mere 10,000. By 1981, there were 170,000. The Teenager had been joined by the Graduate as 'a new social class'.[89] Along with working women and teenagers, these were among the most significant of the escapees from that crucible of recent New Zealand social history: Nappy Valley.

Graduates were the core of a new young 'post-materialist' middle class, noted in Chapter Fourteen in the context of its taking over the Labour Party in the 1970s. Initially left-liberal on more or less everything, this new subculture split sharply on economics in the 1980s, as we have seen. New Right 'neo-liberals' contested leadership with left-liberals. But, outside economic policy, a left-liberal strand persisted even in the New Right. An early expression of New Right sentiment, the short-lived but popular New Zealand Party, which was prominent in the 1984 ousting of Muldoon, illustrates this. It was founded and dominated by wealthy entrepreneur Robert Jones, whom no-one could call 'post-materialist' or 'left-liberal'. Yet its policy on education and international relations, as against economics, was not just left-liberal, but left-radical. Left-liberals and neo-liberals have more in common than they would like to think, and both were products of the rise of the Graduate. In the 1970s and early 1980s, when the left-liberal strand was dominant, the Graduate contributed substantially to the flowering of various political activisms.

One of the most intriguing things about graduate subculture is the possibility that we ain't seen nothing yet. The 50,000 or so tertiary students of 1975 have exploded into something more like 250,000 as the twenty-first century opens. Tertiary education is now entering the majority-experience phase, as secondary schooling did in the 1930s. It may be that this new Graduate, Mark Two, will be a less volatile and innovative historical force than the Graduate, Mark One. University students in the 1990s certainly appeared less prone to activism than those of the 1960s and 1970s. Vocational and financial pressures are much greater; Mark Two has had to be much cheaper than Mark One. Opportunities for a 'liberal education' have declined. Nevertheless, a much larger site for the development of student-based youth culture has opened up in recent decades with the quantitative, if not qualitative, expansion of tertiary education. What its consequences may be is as yet more a matter for prophets than for historians.

The postwar Graduate Mark One has been seen as the key to modern New Zealand nationalism, to developing 'a population capable of generating its own norms'.[90] There is surely some truth in this. Apart from artistic culture and post-materialist politics, the new graduates energised, even if they did not begin, a fresh scholarly engagement with New Zealand studies – in history and sociology, for example. But modern New Zealand nationalism is a strange, ambiguous hybrid. The influence of an élite, even a large élite, can be overestimated, and so can the local character of their subculture. The Graduate formed new understandings of New Zealand but did not disseminate them very well, and spent much of his time talking to herself rather than to the rest of the population. Like New Right neo-liberalism, left-liberalisms were generally imported ideologies – feminism, socialism and even to some extent ethnic activism. On the other hand, as we have seen earlier in different contexts, the derivativeness of Pakeha culture can be overestimated and misunderstood. Ideas derived from Australia or America – or France or China – could be used as denominations of dissent to contest the dominant recolonial ideology. Some were, in any case, derived from 'Britonnic' or global cultures in which New Zealand was a shareholder as well as a borrower. Some of New Zealand graduate culture's answers to overseas questions were a little different from answers elsewhere.

In the 1950s and 1960s, as we saw in Chapter Ten, the tight society managed to fend off pressures for change, coming at it from within and without. In the later 1960s and 1970s, the pressures came from both sources with still more force, and the tight society began to crumble, by no means completely, but quite fast. A little controversy about 'mixed flatting', notorious at the time, illustrates the shift.[91] Male and female university students living together unsupervised was not on as far as the tight society was concerned. At Otago University in 1967, with rolls growing and traditional accommodation under pressure, a few resorted to 'mixed flats'. The university authorities clamped down on the practice. About 150 students staged a 'sleep-in' at a university building to protest at this, but support was limited. A 1964 survey had indicated that only 12 per cent of male students and 4 per cent of female students favoured mixed flatting. In the mid-1960s, then, the tight society was safely internalised, even in the minds of university students, the group theoretically most prone to radicalism. In 1971, the issue erupted again. This time close on half the students joined the protest. The general public's attitude had also softened somewhat, and the university buckled. 'By 1975, mixed sex student flats were generally seen as acceptable if not desirable.' Within ten years, the unacceptable had become commonplace. The NZBC tried to ban a song by environmentalist singer John Hanlon in 1974, because it contained the words 'randy schoolboy', but was laughed down by the public.[92]

By the early 1970s, ethnic difference was becoming visible on city streets, and so was youth difference, to a much greater and more subversive extent than in the 1950s and 1960s. Marijuana was 'widely used' by the early 1970s, and 'dope smokers all but advertised the fact'.[93] If this did lead you to court, you might have met James K. Baxter, long-haired, barefoot, bearded and raggedly dressed on the courtroom steps, and he would not have looked that unusual. The new youth demanded and received a modicum of political power – important evidence of an upward shift in status. The voting age was reduced from twenty-one to twenty in 1969, and then to eighteen in 1974. The cultural repertoire of the Teenager and the Graduate may have been imported, but they themselves, and their new status as a significant socio-cultural entity, were not. Between them, globalism and Nappy Valley were proving a match for the tight society. But would they prove a match for recolonisation?

Out on the Street

Of all the escapees from Nappy Valley, working women, teenagers, graduates, activists and liberals, the one that most riled moral conservatives was probably the Gay. If you wish to give a person frozen in 1960 a heart attack, then taking them to Auckland's annual Hero Parade may well be the best way to do it. It is not easy to discover where this particular difference 'came out' from. We know that a New Zealand history of homosexuality exists, but not much more. Male homosexuality was tolerated in traditional Polynesian societies, including the Maori. When Europeans arrived in New Zealand in 1769, in their male-only floating villages, Maori may have assumed that they were all gay – there are recorded cases of boys being offered as sexual hospitality.[94] In the 1820s, the missionary William Yate was alleged to have had sexual relations with between 50 and 100 young Maori males – not an insignificant percentage of the young male populations with which he would have interacted.[95] A certain Maori tolerance for homosexuality persists to the present. In the early 1980s, a study of 'drag queens' -- public transvestites – in Wellington found that they were mostly Maori, and that they were much more readily accepted by their families than were their European sisters. 'Interestingly, only the European drag queens reported a continuing parental rejection.'[96]

Yate's Maori partners apparently faced no sanctions, but Yate himself was hounded from the Church Missionary Society in terrible disgrace, and his name was an enduring embarrassment to his colleagues. Taking its lead from the missionaries, Pakeha society built up a substantial homophobia, and sometimes it found targets. There were seventeen convictions for 'unnatural offences' in 1872–80.[97] In 1893, as part of moral evangelism, New Zealand tightened its laws against homosexuality. It followed Britain in this, but for good measure added flogging and hard labour to the British penalty of life imprisonment. Parliament thought better of these refinements in the 1900s, but 'the penalty of life imprisonment for "sodomy" was retained until 1961'.[98] Occasional public revelations of homosexuality, such as one involving the mayor of Wanganui in 1920, led to outraged outcry against the 'pursuers of perverted and putrid pleasures'. In 1964, in a notorious incident, six youths beat a homosexual to death in Christchurch – and were acquitted.

Understandably enough, the embryonic literature on homosexuality maintains that 'the history of being gay in New Zealand is synonymous with persecution . . . until the 1960s every aspect of society damned gays'.[99] Even after the 1960s, New Zealand failed to follow Britain's 1967 decriminalisation of male homosexuality until 1986. Conservatives fought the measure to the death, alleging 800,000 signatures in their support, and are still fighting bitter rearguard actions over such issues as gay marriage. When the terrible AIDS epidemic hit New Zealand from 1984, at first primarily affecting homosexual men, some conservatives seemed almost to welcome it as God's punishment for perversion. One study seems to date the emergence of gay subculture to the 1980s and 1990s, which, internationally, would be very late indeed. Yet this picture of unremitting homophobia and the very recent development of gay subculture is not entirely convincing. It is true that sources are very hard to come by, on lesbianism in particular. One can resort to Amy Bock, who married Agnes Ottaway in 1907 while impersonating a wealthy gentleman. But the marriage only lasted four days before Bock's arrest for fraud, and the sources are coy on the issue of consummation.[100] There were a few other known cases of female cross-dressers, and one can put together a very short list of women with suspected lesbian dimensions to their lives, such as poet Ursula Bethell, the bohemian Auckland dancer Freda Stark, and the tragic young killers Juliet Hulme and Pauline Parker. Lesbianism was not illegal –

on the grounds that it was unimaginable – so there are not even court records to go on. It is, as yet, very hard to write much meaningful about the history of New Zealand lesbianism before the 1970s. But even a general historian can do just a little better on male homosexuality.

Apart from Maori, two British traditions imported into New Zealand in the nineteenth century tolerated male homosexuality. Sailors, reared on 'rum, sodomy and the lash', were one. They were very influential in the progressive colonising era, providing the majority of European visitors to New Zealand to about 1860. The English public school tradition was the second. Notions that these schools were 'hotbeds of buggery' are sometimes dismissed as urban myth, but homosexuality does seem to have been quite prevalent, if sometimes ritualised. One Eton housemaster 'having unexpectedly gate-crashed a soiree in the house library, was surprised to find himself surrounded by dancing naked prefects sipping gin and tonic'.[101] Did sailors and young gentlemen suddenly change their habits on reaching our fair shores? The seventeen criminal convictions of 1872–80 were probably not from such groups. Homosexuals were usually apprehended when they sexually approached 'straight' strangers. Homosexual groups, or subcultures, with agreed signs and meeting places, are therefore not likely to produce convictions. Such signs and places did exist in the New Zealand of the earlier twentieth century. Places included wharves, bars and cafés in Auckland, Wellington and Lyttelton. 'The Ward Baths in Rotorua were famous all over the gay world as a gay resort in the first decades of this century.'[102] Signs included having keys dangling from the back pocket. There is a hint of a cluster of homosexual police officers in 1950s Wellington,[103] and a magazine reported in 1955 that 'there are gangs of homosexuals who live together for the sake of perversion. You see these warped-brained men – and women too – wandering the streets or sitting idly in night cafes. Auckland has too many of them.'[104] But how many is 'too many'? Such media references were rare – even the word 'homosexual' featured seldom in the newspapers until the 1960s – but it is clear that gay culture in New Zealand existed well before the 1960s.

The picture of uniform and intense homophobia may also need qualification. There are occasional hints of a certain tolerance before the 1980s, though it was sometimes sniggering and contemptuous. Frank Sargeson's friends knew about his homosexuality, and sometimes joked about it at parties in the 1930s and 1940s. 'Backs to the wall, boys, here comes Frank.'[105] This was not pleasant, but it was not gay-bashing either. There was some respect for the prominent drag queen Carmen in early 1970s Wellington. A survey in Wellington and Hamilton in 1978 found that three-quarters of those interviewed had a fairly tolerant attitude to homosexuality and favoured its decriminalisation. The results indicated that 'the climate toward homosexuality is more favourable than many homosexuals, legislators, and others concerned with homosexual rights may believe'.[106] Homophobia did have a long and sorry history in New Zealand, but it varied over time, was never completely comprehensive and had ceased to be a majority position, at least in the cities, by the 1970s. This makes the intense campaign against homosexual law reform in the mid-1980s doubly interesting – it may have been *against* the grain of public opinion. Gay activists claimed that only 350,000 of the 800,000 signatures in the giant petition of 1986 were genuine. The anti-reform backlash also made a gay mountain out of what may be a gay molehill, helped by some gay activists who claimed a large constituency. The 1991 survey of sexual behaviour found that only 2.3 per cent of men and 1.8 per cent of women had ever had homosexual experiences. This is between a third and half of the levels found in Britain and the United States.[107] The campaign against homosexual law reform appears to have been a 'moral panic'. Unlike the Mazengarb Report alarum, this 'problem' was more molehill than mountain. Moral panics are most common and intense in times of cultural stress. In the 'molehill' type, a minor problem, or no problem at all, becomes a scapegoat for fear of change, all the more threatening because it is not understood.

Traditionalists had plenty to panic about in the New Zealand in and around the 1970s, and you did not have to be a traditionalist to be uneasy. This was the era of protest and the public attacks on accepted norms. Mass demonstrations shook the streets, mass petitions flowed and feelings ran high. Traditionalists sometimes struck back, sometimes struck first, and sometimes struck out at other things entirely: scapegoats. We have seen that a sense of sea change was widespread from the mid-1970s, but that people found it difficult to put a shape on it. The new volatility was manifested in many ways, one of them religious.

In 1967, a leading Presbyterian theologian, Lloyd Geering, was tried for heresy by the General Assembly of his church for saying that 'man has no immortal soul'. He was acquitted but then eased out of his post as Principal of the Presbyterian Theological College in 1971.[108] Geering's conservative opponents were alarmed by change, which for them took the shape of a further dramatic decline in church attendance, and felt it had to be resisted through the reassertion of traditional values. He himself and his liberal supporters were alarmed by precisely the same thing, but responded by trying to reform the church and make it relevant in the new world. The efforts of both parties were gallant but doomed. Between 1966 and 1996, Anglican adherence – let alone attendance – collapsed from 33.7 to 18.4 per cent;

Presbyterian from 21.8 to 13.4 per cent, and Methodism from 7 to 3.5 per cent. Even Roman Catholics diminished from 15.9 to 13.8 per cent.[109] All these figures would have been worse were it not for an inflow of Pacific Island immigrants, who were more religious than average. On the other hand, some fundamentalist denominations experienced a boom, a classic symptom of change trauma. Adherence to the Pentecostal churches rose fivefold between 1966 and 1981, with the biggest rise in the last five years of that period.[110]

Both conservative and liberal religion were in crisis from the 1970s, and so, perhaps, was New Zealand collective identity. From 1975, there was an upsurge in the populist use of various ethnic groups as scapegoats, similar to the spasm of Sinophobia in the 1890s and 1900s. Pacific Islanders from the late 1970s and East Asian migrants from the late 1980s were both victims of this, as we shall see in the next chapter. As we saw in the last, Maori activism and separatism could also generate populist Pakeha antagonism. One could see this as fear of the actual rise in immigrant and activist numbers, but this does not work for many rural communities and small southern towns. In these, there were no Pacific Islanders, Asians or Maori activists in 1975, and there were few in 2000 either. As with homosexuality, the antagonism persisted despite the virtual absence of its targets. Scapegoating 'Others', of course, indicates an insecure collective self. It provides someone to blame for change and shores up a threatened collective identity. New Zealanders were no longer Better Britons, so what were they? This remained unclear, but at least they knew they were not Pacific Islanders, Asians, Pakeha gays or Maori separatists. Robert Muldoon recognised this affronted populism and its nationalist subtext, and placed himself at the head of 'Rob's Mob', partly for political advantage but partly also from genuine sympathy. He, too, sensed mega-shift. He, too, could not bring himself to recognise it as decolonisation, but he could resist some of its manifestations. He led a crackdown on Pacific Island 'overstaying' in 1976–77 and on Maori activism – the Bastion Point protesters – in 1977–78. He also led resistance to some of the other protest movements.

The peak of the new public contestation came in the decade after 1976, but a precursor was protest against the Vietnam War, 1967–71. Most of the 339 street demonstrations 1967–70 were about this issue.[111] They and some subsequent protest involved the only two groups traditionally willing to hit the streets with their grievances: committed trade unionists and the radical left. Trade unions resisted an erosion of their power, gradual from 1975 and sharp from 1984. The old hard left fragmented from the mid-1960s, and the Communist Party's influence dwindled.[112] Some of the new groups, such as the Socialist Unity Party (formed 1966), were hardworking and well organised. They became quite influential in some unions and some protest movements. But what gave the protest era its force were an intersecting set of new groups, escapees from Nappy Valley: the liberal section of the growing middle class; university students and graduates; and a somewhat wider group of women, young people and men prepared to question long-accepted norms. Some of these groups had long existed but were insignificant in numbers, or kept their heads down, before the 1960s. It was these groups, the rank and file of the protest movements, not their activist leaders, old or new, who turned the protest era into a kind of liberal middle-class rebellion.

There were no fewer than seven major issues of contestation and protest in the 1967–85 period. Apart from the homosexual law reform issue and the Vietnam War, they included the abortion issue, discussed in the previous section, and the anti-nuclear movement, discussed in Chapter Fifteen. They also included Maori protests (Chapter Sixteen) and environmental protests (Chapter Eighteen). The last of the big seven liberal *v.* conservative contests, and arguably the most intense, was over the South African rugby union tour of 1981.

Maori exclusion from New Zealand rugby teams visiting South Africa dates back to 1919. When South Africa's Springboks did play a Maori team, during their tour of New Zealand in 1921, there was ill feeling. It stemmed from the racialist telegram quoted in Chapter Six, from South African allegations of rough Maori play, and from Maori allegations of South African insults. The Maori game was deleted from the next Springbok tour, of 1937, and in 1956 the strong Maori team was so harangued about the need for exemplary conduct that they allowed the Springboks to walk over them.[113] Even Pakeha New Zealanders had never liked Maori exclusion from tours to South Africa – not because of antagonism to the racialist South African system of apartheid or sympathy for black South Africans, but because of Maori status as Brown Britons. When Maori were again excluded from an All Black tour to South Africa, in 1960, this feeling produced substantial protests. Over 150,000 New Zealanders, mostly Pakeha, signed a petition advocating 'No Maoris, No Tour'. The tour went ahead anyway, but the South Africans were forced to allow Maori on the next tour, in 1970. South African rugby boss Danie Craven accepted that it was 'ridiculous' to compare Maori to black South Africans,[114] and the touring Maori were accorded the status of 'honorary Whites' – a position they had to some extent held in New Zealand for a long time. Edward Tregear's Aryan Maori thesis had finally been imposed on the South Africans. After 1970, Maori were demoted from text to subtext of the vexed issue of New Zealand sporting relations with South Africa.

During the 1970s, prompted especially by a police massacre of Blacks at Soweto in 1976, international feeling against the apartheid system hardened. Most international sporting bodies expelled the South Africans because their teams were racially selected, most countries banned their visits, and the New

Zealand Rugby Union came under pressure to do so too. Keen on their rugby, and satisfied by the inclusion of Maori, most New Zealanders were against such a course. In 1971–72, opinion polls showed huge majorities in favour of the scheduled Springbok tour of New Zealand in 1973.[115] Despite this, the Kirk government banned that tour, and this may well have been a factor in its downfall in 1975. However – despite Soweto – the 1976 All Black tour of South Africa went ahead with the blessing of the new Muldoon government. The All Blacks lost the test series, and the tour 'was a diplomatic disaster unprecedented in the country's history'.[116] In 1977, facing mounting threats of sports boycotts, Muldoon bowed to international pressure and signed the Gleneagles Agreement to discourage sports contact with South Africa. All other signatories believed this meant banning tours, but the 1981 Springbok tour of New Zealand went ahead anyway. Muldoon's 'discouragement' appears to have been merely nominal – despite claims to the contrary in a recent biography. Muldoon himself admitted that he was 'pleased that the tour went ahead'.[117]

Meanwhile, anti-tour feeling in New Zealand had been growing. Halt All Racist Tours (HART) and other radical activist organisations were gaining support, and there was also a vague but substantial anti-tour sentiment in society at large. Pro-tour majorities diminished in the late 1970s and, in a dramatic shift from 1971, polls in 1981 showed a balance of opinion against the tour. To the surprise of the government and police, who had budgeted less than $3 million to handle anti-tour protests, the tour was met not only with large-scale protest but also with non-violent yet active resistance. Feelings on both sides were intensified by two incidents. The second game of the tour, at Hamilton, was called off because of protests and threatened protests. Rugby supporters were enraged, and the police felt themselves to be humiliated. Determined to show that they could maintain 'the rule of law', they attacked demonstrators outside Parliament in Wellington. The one-sided 'Battle of Molesworth Street' enraged the protest movement in its turn, and the subsequent demonstrations, acts of sabotage and violence – from both sides, but especially the police – gained international media attention. In all, nearly 2,000 protestors were arrested.[118]

The tour set the new liberal middle class against a newly uneasy populism, which had both conservative middle-class and (normally apolitical) working-class elements. But there was a degree of nationalism on the populist side, and a degree of both populism and nationalism on the liberal side. That a country could be 'thrown into a state of near civil war'[119] over a few rugby games can bewilder people outside Wales, South Africa and New Zealand. In fact, rugby, as we have seen, had long been a major focus of New Zealand collective identity. Despite the partial revenge of 1956, the loss of 1976 meant that South Africa in 1981 remained the only country that had scored more victories than defeats against the All Blacks. Expunging this blot on the national escutcheon was a factor in pro-tour sentiment. It would not have been so intense against an equally racially selected team of Rhodesian easy-beats.

The anti-tour movement included a number of socialist activists, and they tended to be prominent in the leadership. Like Holland in 1951, Muldoon and his lieutenants alleged that communists and extremists were seeking to overthrow the state. Surveys show, however, that the majority of protesters were not activists or radicals, but liberal middle-class Labour supporters. Only 6 per cent of a large Wellington sample were frequent demonstrators.[120] Only a minority were university students or young people under 25. The numbers arrested alone greatly exceeded the number of communist activists in the whole country. Over a third (700) of those arrested were women – something that ranks with the Hero Parade as being unimaginable in 1960. New Zealand women – and the New Zealand middle class – had taken to the streets for the first time in history. Some were influenced by a desire to defend New Zealand's cherished, if dubious, international reputation for anti-racialism and racial harmony. Both pro- and anti-tour sentiment was largely a nationalist response to the trauma of major change. The two sides contested the definition of a New Zealandness that seemed under threat, yet did not quite realise that they were doing so.

What do we make of this diverse, inchoate but also strangely intense 'rebellion' and 'counter-rebellion' of the 1970s and 1980s, taken as a whole? One characteristic common to both is exaggerating the importance of leaders and formal organisations. This tendency is familiar to historians as the 'great man', or 'great woman' theory of history, in which big names subsume the small. In fact, it tends to be the following, not the leadership, that is the decisive variable. While the rebellion was obviously influenced by individual leaders and formal organisations – and by international trends – it had clear local demographic origins: in the new, educated and numerous middle class; and in exploding Maori numbers and urbanisation. Similarly, Rob's Mob made Muldoon at least as much as he made them. As we have seen, it was not always clear which was rebellion and which counter-rebellion, 'lash' or 'backlash'.

The 1970s–80s spasm of contestation and confrontation was, obviously enough, partly a product of international trends. Other countries had anti-war, anti-nuclear and (in Australia and Britain) even anti-tour protests. Other countries struggled over the issues of environmentalism and sexual liberation. Other countries had a burgeoning liberal middle class and a 'revenge of the cradle' by ethnic minorities, indigenous or not. But New Zealand's anti-tour, anti-nuclear, indigenous rights and possibly even environmental movements were exceptionally early and strong. Its resistance to liberalising abortion and homosexuality laws was exceptionally late and strong. Something was at work here other than the obvious issues themselves, and I suggest that it was a confused and confusing nationalism, or at least a response to a vaguely sensed decolonisation. Ironically enough, this was true of both liberal rebellion and conservative counter-rebellion.

In the 1960s, environmental, anti-tour and anti-nuclear movements were very small. Each broadened its support in the decolonising 1970s and 1980s as it became entwined with issues of nationalism. White New Zealand's good relations with its indigenous people, real and alleged, were considered a central plank of national identity, and this helped stimulate the anti-tour movement. Contesting rugby's position as the national game, and implicitly the Kiwi Bloke as the national archetype, was a motive for women protesters. Conversely, the centrality of rugby in national identity, and the need for national sporting revenge on South Africa, boosted the pro-tour forces. Anti-nuclear sentiment, as we have seen, progressed from a tiny minority to a majority between 1959 and 1989, as its association with national independence increased – the process was heavily loaded towards the post-1973 decolonising period. On the other side, scapegoating and moral panic are classic symptoms of a collective identity under stress. The moral panics over abortion in the 1970s and homosexuality in the 1980s, whatever the rights and wrongs of the issue, made mountains out of molehills. Mazengarb's frolicking teenagers in the 1950s had at least been quite numerous.

Victory in the feud between the right and left of the middle class went to the side that appealed most successfully to the populist centre, usually by beating the newly resonant drum of nationalism more loudly. The marker of victory for the protesters was when the actions they advocated were accepted by both major political parties. This happened after 1978 on abortion, in 1986 on homosexuality, and in 1989 on the nuclear issue. Sections of the populist working class, and even the conservative middle class, gradually came over to the liberal side. They did so more because of nationalism than liberalism.

Decolonisation then, had a social face as well as economic and geopolitical ones. The social face was more complex, contorted and contested, and has been even less recognised. New Zealand's 'war of independence' was also a civil war, fought over different responses to the same issue. Some compromise and reconciliation has been achieved, but some embers still smoulder. Pakeha New Zealanders have still to replace the secure sense of identity, as Better Britons, that they lost to decolonisation.

CHAPTER EIGHTEEN

One, Two, Many?

Mount Victoria rears above the city of Wellington like the Iron Duke's nose. A haunt of courting couples by night, by day it is a fine place for looking out, down, back and in. It is one of the best urban views on earth, if you can stand up in the wind. Wellington itself is compressed between hill and harbour, nature standing in for medieval walls to make an old-world sense of city, unlike the car-spread urban sprawls of Los Angeles or Auckland. It is smaller than it looks; fewer than 150,000 people live in the city itself and its immediate suburbs. But its bars, art places, office blocks and bureaucracy draw custom from the dormitory cities and suburbs strung up the Hutt Valley and the Kapiti Coast, and from the rest of the country. Tourists know Auckland and Christchurch better, but New Zealand is ruled from Wellington. Once this was also true of Western Samoa and at least the dining tables of middle-class London. The city still contains nominal monuments to recolonisation, such as Victoria University of Wellington and – until 1994 – the Queen Elizabeth the Second Arts Council of New Zealand, the dependently named official patron of cultural independence.

Your view is dotted with physical history, and you can read the city like an unedited book. In legend, the outlet from the harbour was made by duelling sea-monsters. The great explorer Kupe visited, though Cook missed out, and the place was named for Maori and British heroes Tara (as in Whanganui-a-Tara) and Arthur Wellesley (as in the 'Iron Duke' of Wellington). The old National Museum sat on the site of the near-civil war of 1913, but of course its collections did not hint at this. The big bell tower outside, the Carillon, is one of many symbolic tombs to the dead of World War One. The new museum, Te Papa, may look like an architect's wet dream, but it is a major tourist attraction and contains some real treasures, such as a postmodern Maori meeting house. The old rugby ground, Athletic Park, the world's ugliest cathedral, was dreaded by visiting teams, who were generally no match for wind, rain and New Zealanders. It is gone now, replaced by a modern Welling Tin. The Basin Reserve, once water, but made into near-solid land by the grace of an 1855 earthquake, is a delightful sports ground, but it has no parking. The Bank of New Zealand building, a black glass giant known colloquially as Darth Vader's Pencil Case, is monument both to old unionism and public/private enterprise. It took eleven years to build, owing to industrial troubles that helped sour the public towards unions, and is headquarters to a commercial bank twice saved by public money. You can also see the 'Government Village', a piquant name: stone Parliament; recently restored, old, massive, wooden Government Buildings (dating from 1876, with 143 rooms and 64 toilets, and now a Law School)[1]; and new plastic Beehive. The last looks to be a decolonial building but resulted from the suggestion of a visiting British architect in 1964.[2] The waterfront is at last linked up to the city centre after wharves and warehouses, made redundant by containers in the early 1970s, had lain useless for twenty years. Oriental Bay is also a complex metaphor: the compass says our Orient is the Occident; history orients us otherwise. A beautiful promenade, suggesting cosmo-politanism, its beach was made from meat-ship ballast.

Among Wellington's most distant domains are the Chatham Islands, 700 kilometres to the south-east. Peaty, windswept, rainy islands of about 100,000 hectares, they have their own strange beauty. The Chathams are the only part of New Zealand with different local time, they are different in other ways, too, and their inhabitants occasionally threaten to secede. But so does Auckland, and the Chathams are unmistakeably Kiwi, symbolising an older New Zealand. In 1956, the Queen's husband, Prince Philip, Duke of Edinburgh, visited the islands. Mainland New Zealand gossiped, half in embarrassment, half in delight, that he had been given tomato sauce in a beer bottle. You wave to all the locals you meet, and you can meet virtually all of them. There are only 750 of them in the whole group, making a living mostly from sheep and fish, especially crayfish. There is a pub, a bank, a general store, a radio station and four churches. You do not have to bother to lock your door, and you can legally hunt weka, a robust and cheeky bird, a kind of populist version of the iconic kiwi.[3]

The Chathams have skeletons in the closet. The islands were once inhabited by 2,000 Moriori, a Polynesian people derived from the mainland Maori. A peaceful folk, their tree carvings still evoke a sense of gentle spirituality even if not in the least spiritual. In 1835, they were unfortunate enough to encounter martial Maori, fresh from the intertribal Musket Wars, and were killed or enslaved. The 'last of the Moriori', Tommy Solomon, died in 1933, and the 'race' was long believed to have died with him. In fact, there are now again 2,000 people, mostly living on the mainland, of some Moriori descent. The Chathams are a *tri*-cultural society. Without intending to, the real Chathams Moriori helped keep alive the myth of the mainland Moriori, allegedly exterminated by the Maori before European contact. The real Moriori also irritate their Maori neighbours on the islands by making their own claims to the Waitangi Tribunal, and contesting local Maori claims of tangata whenua (people of the land) status. Angry Maori have been heard to say that they wished their ancestors had finished the job in 1835. On the Chathams, therefore, you can actually meet a creature even rarer than their famous black robin: the brown redneck.

Between Wellington and the Chathams lies a whole dimension of New Zealand that a general history can scarcely touch: the particularities of place and space, of each New Zealander's relationship with the land. These paragraphs on Wellington and the Chathams, few as they are, will have to represent hundreds of distinct local histories. But we can briefly explore some patterns in regionalism and in the interaction of New Zealanders and their landscape.

Towns and Arounds

One broad pattern in the regional history of New Zealand over the last century or so is the long swing in the demographic balance of power from South Island to North Island. Until the 1890s, the South was more populous, but the recolonial economic system changed all that. The dairying and meat-farming opportunities unleashed by refrigeration were mainly in the North Island, though, as we have seen, South Islanders came north to take some of them. By 1936, the North Island had twice the population of the South; by 1996 three times the population. An intriguing reverse shift is the small but increasing proportion of Maori living in the South Island. Because the South has grown much more slowly, old Pakeha cultural patterns show greater persistence. Aside from the Maori way of speaking English, the residual Scots burr of Otago and Southland is the only easily noticeable regional variation in New Zealand English. A 1940s study showed that Pakeha folklore, in the form of children's games, also persisted more strongly in the south.[4] Another difference, perhaps, is a stronger sense of regional identity in the south, as expressed in the writing of regional history, for example. Otago and Canterbury each have two substantial histories published since 1948; Auckland and Wellington have nothing comparable.[5]

Another broad pattern is the demographic decline of the countryside. New Zealand's level of urbanisation was already quite high for its day in 1881, at 40 per cent for Pakeha, and recolonisation boosted the trend. The non-Maori population was more than half urban by 1911. This of course makes the persistence of dominant rural stereotypes all the more striking. Farmer Backbone and the (rural) Kiwi Bloke have not been anything like the average New Zealand man for almost a century, if they ever were. One factor here, noted earlier, may be that recolonial Better Britain had to supply rural virtue, not just for itself but for Old Britain as well. A full admission that New Zealand, too, was mainly urban would have spoiled the ideological plot. New Zealanders, including Maori, were 68 per cent urban by 1926 and 80 per cent urban by 1971. The rate of urbanisation then slowed, and in 1996 stood at 85 per cent. Recolonisation and a global trend towards secondary and tertiary industry and away from primary industry were factors in the rise of the New Zealand town. Others included the improving efficiency of farm labour, through the grasslands revolution, and the advent of trams and then motor vehicles, which allowed cities to sprawl.

Since 1840, the three great epochs of New Zealand history – progressive colonisation, to the 1880s; recolonisation, to the 1970s; and decolonisation, from the 1970s – have had different effects on regions and localities. In the nineteenth century, 'progress' and its allied extractive industries treated regions quite even-handedly, despite the fact that some had gold and some did not. The urban races were quite evenly contested among the Big Four. Dunedin, Christchurch, and Auckland ran virtually neck and neck between the 1870s and the 1890s – only Wellington lagged well behind. Regions that later became marginal, such as Westland and Northland, had spasms of prosperity, mass extraction and bustling ports. Recolonisation created a firmer and longer-term divide between two sets of regions: the 'marginal' and the 'mainstream'. Marginal regions included Westland, Northland and the East Cape, and isolated smaller areas such as the Coromandel, Stewart Island, Mahia, the Marlborough Sounds, the Hauraki Gulf islands and the Chathams. They remained fairly static in population and economic growth, but also retained a distinctive character. One could add the 'high country' of various regions, especially in inland Canterbury and Otago. These areas were not necessarily poor, but their primary economic activity – the very extensive farming of sheep for wool – was among the few things that did not change between the colonial and recolonial eras. The rest of the country consisted of mainstream regions, the prime beneficiaries of the recolonial system. Some regions did better from recolonisation than others. Dunedin, the leading city under progressive colonisation, took Wellington's place as the laggard of the Big Four. North Otago and Southland developed their own protein ports at Oamaru and Bluff partly because of deficiencies in Dunedin's harbour. But, generally speaking, recolonisation reduced regional difference in the mainstream areas. There were similar sorts of farms, freezing works, dairy factories, provincial towns and protein ports from north to south. Regional identity was expressed more in sport than in lifestyles, politics or economics. There was less distinctiveness but more growth and prosperity than in the marginal regions.

Decolonisation, with its economic diversification, brought new life to some fortunate regions despite low overall growth. The new international tourism circuit brought wealth to, and buttressed difference in, its northern and southern capitals of Rotorua and Queenstown. Each represented a kind of idealised New Zealand, living tourist brochures. In Rotorua, Maori remained unusually central in both culture and economics. Even in the early 1980s, Queenstown scarcely seemed like part of New Zealand at all – its restrictions on shopping, drinking and dining were relaxed earlier than elsewhere. Other regions took to the bottle. The wine industry seems to be a particular stimulant to 'regional character'. First West Auckland, then Marlborough, then Hawke's Bay, then the Wairarapa, and now various other regions and subregions as well, are harvesting character as well as grapes. But elsewhere the news that decolonisation brought was not so good.

Recolonial New Zealand did contain extremes of wealth and poverty, but they were small and, in the tight society, they kept their heads down. Consumption was anything but conspicuous, even among the rich. One family was wealthy enough in the 1950s to own several brand-new cars, but they ensured that all were exactly the same make and colour so that nobody would know.[6] In the mainstream regions at least, poverty was quite rare. With decolonisation, wealth and, especially, poverty increased, and both also 'came out' into public prominence. Recent research suggests that the number of very rich families has not greatly increased over the past 30 years, and that 'new money' has long been more common than 'old money', or inherited wealth.[7] But old money has always been better at camouflaging itself than new. The crash of 1987 hurt the very rich, but the fairly rich continued to do quite well, and New Zealand's cherished relative equality of income distribution began to crumple. During the 1980s, reported the Department of Statistics, 'the purchasing power of the top income quintile increased by 10 per cent compared with a decline of between 4–6 per cent in the bottom three quintile groups'.[8] In 1993, 'the top 20 per cent of households currently receive 45 per cent of all gross income, up from 35 per cent in the late 1970s'. 'The real spending power of those in employment between 1987 and 1992 rose by 7 per cent for the wealthiest 20 per cent and fell by 2.9 per cent for the poorest quintile.'[9] Whether that poorest quintile is now in actual poverty is hotly debated. The debate seems to suffer from the myth of 1984: the assumption that all major economic change must date from the restructuring beginning in that year. One must also note that it does not take account of the informal economy – supermarket takings in Kaitaia might be a more accurate measure of wealth in the Far North than nominal income statistics. Yet the case for the mass advent of what in New Zealand terms can be reasonably defined as poverty is strong. The downturn came in the mid-

1970s, though worsened from 1984 and the welfare-benefit cuts of 1991.

A survey in 1984, before restructuring, suggested that 'a quarter of a million were living in relative poverty' with insufficient disposable income to visit a doctor when needed, or spend more than two days away from home a year. Systematic statistical research contests the definition of poverty, usually putting it at around 50–65 per cent of average incomes. Even the most conservative analyses, commissioned by Treasury in the early 1990s, suggest that between 4.4 per cent and 7.8 per cent of the population lived in poverty. The most recent and comprehensive analysis available, on the other hand, using a higher definition, indicates that 20.5 per cent of the population lived in poverty in 1994. Deciding between these estimates is not easy for a non-specialist, but as I write, anecdotal evidence comes to the rescue. Each year, the Auckland City Council kindly provides a special service. It collects the large items of junk, such as broken furniture and old timber, that are not normally taken by the rubbish trucks. As the piles build up on middle-class streets, old vans and cars from working-class streets begin to cruise by – not too early or little will have been put out, and not too late because the best will be gone. Most of the junk never makes it into the city council trucks. One could explain this in terms of a waste-not, want-not mentality, or the Kiwi eye for a bargain. But would this have happened on this scale in 1960? One must conclude with regret that poverty has made it into the reforged paradise. It may be relative more than absolute, and it may be more common in big cities, where access to the informal economy is restricted. But the big cities are getting bigger, especially the biggest of all: Auckland.

Perhaps the most striking pattern in modern New Zealand regional history is the rise of Auckland, which took place in two stages. In 1881, Auckland ranked third in size of the Big Four, with Dunedin and Christchurch ahead of it and only Wellington behind. Auckland took the lead in 1886, and kept it and increased it thereafter. But as late as the 1950s, Auckland was only first among peers. Christchurch did quite well from recolonisation, and Wellington did very well. Between 1881 and 1945, Auckland and Wellington grew at much the same rate, each increasing over eightfold. In 1951, Auckland was less than twice as big as Christchurch and little more than 50 per cent bigger than Wellington. By 1996, at almost a million people, it was three times the size of either. It had shifted from first among peers to New Zealand's only really big city. Like it or not, the Big Four is becoming the Big One. Quite a number of New Zealanders do not like it.

One factor behind Auckland's rise was the late but massive growth of its agricultural hinterland. The problems solved by the second and third stages of the grasslands revolution, notably mineral deficiency and land that was good but inaccessible to land-borne phosphate fertiliser, were particularly acute in Auckland. It therefore benefited most from their solution – the addition of cobalt from the 1930s and aerial topdressing from the 1940s. Between 1921 and 1961, the Auckland provincial region's grasslands doubled in acreage, while those of the rest of the country stayed roughly static.[10] Auckland shared the early development of assembly-line manufacturing with Christchurch and Wellington's Hutt Valley. But from the 1940s, Auckland increasingly took the lead from its manufacturing rivals. The key to this was the advent of import controls in 1938. It made sense to import components to the place where most would be both assembled and sold. Auckland's port was already the busiest in the country in the 1920s, and it became increasingly dominant in imports, though not exports. This was part of a tendency for Auckland to act as New Zealand's main gateway to the world. Wellington remained the hub of domestic air traffic, as it had been of domestic shipping. Protein and other bulky exports such as wool and timber used the nearest large port. But the world increasingly flowed into New Zealand through Auckland. The opening of the Panama Canal in 1914, which made Auckland closer to Britain, was the first step in this. The two world wars favoured the efficiency of a single gateway to New Zealand, and Auckland benefited from this too. The opening of the international airport at Mangere in 1966 was another step. This airport handled the great bulk of New Zealand's international air traffic from the outset and, despite the building of international airports at Christchurch and Wellington, it still does.

Decolonisation appears to be increasing the dominance of Auckland, almost as though it is struggling to grow into a substitute for recolonisation's London. Manufacturing, business, external and internal migration, and overseas tourism have concentrated more on Auckland than ever over the past 25 years. Auckland's share of shoe factories, for example, increased from 39 to 59 per cent between 1978 and 1988.[11] Auckland's share of the international tourist trade increased markedly in the period 1982–92, when the 'main tendency' in the regional distribution of overseas visits was 'towards a greater concentration on Auckland and less frequent visits to most other destinations'.[12] There are signs of strain, however. The 1990s witnessed major water and power crises, increasing pollution of the harbours and the steady rise of traffic congestion, which seems similar to that of a city two or three times the size. Public transport still relies on motor buses for the most part, development of the waterfront came strangely late, and there are major problems with the cultural infrastructure as well. Auckland has three times the population of Wellington, yet Wellington has three times the professional theatre of Auckland.

One root of Auckland's problems is its artificial division into four separate cities, though this itself is an improvement on the situation in 1970, when the urban area was governed by 32 territorial authorities and 23 boards.[13] An Auckland Regional Council was established in 1963 but still has less power than the four city councils. Different areas of Auckland do have different needs, but this can surely be catered for without dismembering what is an obvious organic whole. Local government reform has always been a vexed issue in New Zealand. 'Those local bodies earmarked for extinction almost universally bellowed that they were too good to die.'[14] Yet the case for a united Auckland is so obvious and urgent that it is hard to avoid the suspicion that central government in Wellington prefers to divide and rule. Auckland's rise has created some resentment in the rest of the country. But the hard fact is that Auckland's problems are increasingly New Zealand's problems, and vice versa.

Despite these problems, overseas tourists are not the only people to prefer Auckland. Virtually all categories of overseas migrants do so too, as do internal migrants, Maori and Pakeha. Immigrant preference is discussed in the next section; Maori preference in part stems simply from Auckland's proximity to the densest concentrations of Maori population in Northland, Waikato and the Bay of Plenty. Pakeha preference is more complicated. Until the 1980s, one could say that internal migrants were simply going where the jobs were: Auckland. But internal migration to Auckland continued in the 1980s, and even in the 1990s, though at a diminishing rate.[15] This happened despite the facts that unemployment was normally lower in Wellington, and that Auckland, with its high housing costs, was just about the worst place in the country in which to be poor. There may be another factor behind the drift north: a better fit between Auckland and an idealised and persistent Pakeha urban-ruralism, including the desire to combine city dwelling with 'outdoor living' and outdoor recreation.

The boat, the bach, the beach and the barbecue extend the list of sites of Pakeha folk culture, begun in Chapter Twelve. They represent a modern populist engagement with the New Zealand landscape. Boats and baches (holiday homes) can be expensive items, and they tend towards the middle class. But they are quite widespread in that class, and, in the 1950s and 1960s at least, were more accessible to workers than in most countries. Baches were often self-built, or adapted from old army huts, and sometimes located on public land. There were at least 33,000 baches in New Zealand in the 1970s, up from 7,000 in the 1920s.[16] Many were used by more than one nuclear family. In the middle-class Wellington suburb of Khandallah in the 1970s, 12 per cent of households owned a holiday home and 8 per cent owned a boat. In the neighbouring working-class suburb of Johnsonville, 4 per cent owned a holiday home and 5 per cent owned a boat.[17] Boat-ownership in both classes is much more common in Auckland. In the 1960s, Auckland accounted 'for over 80 per cent of New Zealand's total yachting population'.[18] Beaches and barbecues were obviously still more widely accessible. Auckland's climate, though by no means the best in New Zealand in terms of sunshine hours, does have warmer weather than the rest of the Big Four. Combined with better access to boats and beaches if not baches, this made the desired Kiwi mix of urban-outdoor living more viable in Auckland.

The four Bs were one populist New Zealand engagement with the landscape. The holiday was another. There appears to have been little research into the history of domestic tourism, but we can assume that the prerequisites of the classic Kiwi holiday away from home included the paid holiday period of one or two weeks and of the motorcar. The mass advent of both dates to the 1920s for the middle class and to the late 1930s and 1940s for the working class. The peculiar institution of the motor camp arrived in the 1920s, organised by local authorities. By 1927, there were 60 registered motor camps, providing camp sites, caravan sites and simple cabins as well as cooking and toilet facilities.[19] Holidaying in these was cheap, and camping, hunting and fishing trips were also much more accessible to the working class than in other countries. Like attitudes to work, this modern Pakeha recreation pattern shows clear descent from colonial populism, according to which workers should be able to hunt and fish like lords. The American and Australian patterns are likely to be similar but not the same. Visitors, even from these countries, were surprised by recolonial New Zealand's total closedown over the Christmas holidays, as well as during the weekend. Free weekends and holidays were seen as a God-given right. Whether this particular Pakeha tradition, and the mass engagement with the natural heritage that it permitted, can survive decolonisation's reshuffling of work, holidays and shopping hours remains to be seen.

Populist engagement with the landscape through recreation sometimes converged, and sometimes clashed, with a more middle-class and moral evangelist version: 'rational recreation' and environmentalism. 'Rational recreation' was adult play, licensed by being seen as a form of moral self-improvement, and often involving engagement with the 'natural heritage'. One shape of 'rational recreation' in New Zealand was the mountain-oriented sports of tramping, climbing and skiing. All three date from the nineteenth century but experienced their first major surge in popularity in and around the 1920s. The first tramping club was formed in 1919; ski clubs proliferated from 1930; and in 1931 twenty clubs practising all three sports and located mostly in the cities formed the Federated Mountain Clubs. These mountain sports involved younger middle-class adults of both sexes. Rational recreation was the text; subtexts included an almost spiritual relationship with nature and, perhaps, a sneaking desire to escape from the tight society for a few days. Climbing was 'that ennobling sport', not mere 'peak bagging' but 'joyous pilgrimages'.[20] Despite the frequent presence of married women as chaperones on tramping trips, there were rumours of 'ungentlemanly behaviour' and 'amorous couples'. One club was described as an 'eminently successful matrimonial agency'.[21]

In the 1920s, mountain sport was restricted to the middle class, but in the 1930s it made a foray into full moral evangelism by trying to improve the workers. This stemmed partly from the efforts of Bill Parry, a minister in the first Labour government, who evangelised rational recreation with 'almost religious zeal'. Labour's legislation on working hours and holidays supplied the necessary leisure for the working class, and in 1937 more legislation established a Physical Welfare and Recreation Council. The state became involved in supplying cheap holidays through the Group Travel Association, especially for mothers – rest and recreation for workers on the 'kitchen front'. A 'Socialist Sporting Paradise' joined the never-ending list of Kiwi utopias. The other source of rational recreation's foray into populism was New Zealand Railways, which, in the 1920s and 1930s, responded to the threat of the motorcar by getting serious about domestic tourism and day trips. In the early 1930s, it organised 'Mystery Tramps', involving up to 1,200 city-dwellers. They also involved littering, noise and fun. This was too much for moralist authority, and mystery tramps tailed off from 1932.

The rise of mountain sports in the 1920s appears to have been associated with the modest flowering of a conservationist or environmentalist move-ment. Forest conservation measures actually began in 1877, but were at first largely driven by economics. Forests needed to be conserved to supply lumber for the future, to assist water catchment and to prevent the erosion of farmland. Legislation in 1908, which restricted milling, was too little, too late for the great northern kauri forests. A campaign against soil erosion, to which about half of New Zealand was subject, was mounted from the late 1930s, but there was nothing environmentalist about it. It was seen as 'a war against nature', intended to prevent nature striking back against farmland.[22] Scenic areas seemingly of no direct economic use were protected from 1894, when the Tongariro National Park was established. A substantial system of national parks and reserves grew up, and was consolidated and developed from the 1950s, totalling about 4 million hectares or one-sixth of the country by 1972. One park, dating from 1905, encompasses the whole of Fiordland.

New Zealand's first major environmentalist publication was Herbert Guthrie-Smith's book *Tutira* (1921). A sheep farmer, Guthrie-Smith was scathing about the devastation his own kind had wrought on the New Zealand landscape. Less well remembered is his emphasis on the resilience of some native flora, such as the fern. Like its natives, New Zealand nature was not easily conquered.[23] Guthrie-Smith represents an environmentalist strand in Pakeha thought that emerged in the 1920s. What became the Forest and Bird Protection Society was set up in 1923. Mountaineers and trampers, who needed wilderness, were natural allies of environmentalism. The Christchurch activist Harry Ell supported both environmental issues and decorous tramping. He developed a system of trails and rest houses in the area around Christchurch, including the 'Sign of the Takahe'.[24] A tinge of moral evangelism persisted in environmentalism. The National Parks Authority in the 1950s insisted that users of the parks behave in a 'cleanly and decent manner'. They were not to use 'foul, abusive, indecent or obscene language or be intoxicated, noisy or riotous, or in any way misbehave'. Bathing suits, of course, were to be worn for swimming in streams along the trail.[25] As late as 1972, environmentalists objected to campers drinking and dancing rather than 'national parking' (their phrase) in a restrained and moral way.[26] Populists engaged in hunting, fishing, camping and amoral tramping, are unlikely to have been impressed by attitudes of this kind. Barry Crump, for example, was surely a 'national parker's' nightmare. Yet they are likely to have outnumbered environmentalist users of the wilderness. One can chart wilderness use to some extent through the grim statistic of fatal accidents in mountain recreation. These ran at two or three a year between 1890 and 1920, then climbed in the 1920s and 1930s to between five and ten a year, dipped in the war years of the 1940s, then climbed again in the 1950s to ten or twelve a year.[27] We can tell that it was populist hunters doing the dying, as well as rational recreationists, because the leading cause of death was gunshot wounds.

From the outset, environmentalism had a tinge of nationalism as well as moralism. If you were looking for something uniquely New Zealand, glancing at the bush or the mountains was the easiest way to find it. The influence of the landscape on literature and painting between the 1930s and the 1950s is well known. But until the 1970s this remained very much a proto-nationalism. Even with its tramping allies, environmentalism itself was also weak. Its triumphs did not extend beyond wilderness, small islands and mountaintops. Until the 1970s, almost all conservationists 'timid before the authority of agricultural and timber interests, focused their efforts on the islands and high-elevation wildernesses'.[28] The numbers involved remained very small and very middle class. A 1967 survey of climbers at Mount Cook found that 90 per cent were male and 60 per cent were university students or graduates, who made up about 5 per cent of the general population at the time.[29] From the late 1960s, however, environmentalism flowered and became a force in politics. A 'back-country boom' took place, which doubled the use of national parks between 1966 and 1972, and quadrupled visits to some scenic areas between 1970 and 1985.[30] In politics, the environmentalist Values Party was formed in 1972 – internationally early. Although the first-past-the-post electoral system prevented 'green' representation in Parliament until 1996, environmental issues became increasingly hard for the two main parties to ignore.

The event that both reflected and triggered this shift was the 'Save Manapouri' campaign of the 1960s and early 1970s. In 1960, the state had struck a deal with an Australian company to produce aluminium using cheap power generated from Lake Manapouri in Fiordland National Park. This was originally planned to raise the level of the lake by up to 30 metres, with obvious impact on the lake itself and the surrounding countryside. There were petitions against this in 1960 and 1965, but the protests really took off in 1969 and peaked in 1971, with Save Manapouri committees 'all over the country', and a petition of 264,000 signatures.[31] The National government backed down in late 1971, and the incoming third Labour government confirmed the decision the following year. Like other activists, environmentalist activists deserve credit for their efforts, but this should not be allowed to obscure the other forces at work. The escape of the Graduate from Nappy Valley itself created the activists. The issue was another in which activism was reinforced by populism: you did not have to be a raving greenie to dislike the idea of our lakes and national parks being destroyed for the benefit of an Australian commercial concern. The Save Manapouri campaign and the associated rise of environmentalism were further reflections of an inchoate new nationalism, a response to vaguely sensed decolonisation. It was not simply that John Hanlon penned the protest song 'Damn the Dam', but that people bought it. When populism and nationalism converged with environmentalism and left-liberalism, they made a force that was very hard to stop. New Zealand discovered this not only over Manapouri but also over nuclear issues in the late 1980s. We may learn the lesson again in the current debate on genetic engineering.

New Migrations

The war against Japan of 1941–45 gave Australia an even greater scare than it gave New Zealand. Two Australian towns, Darwin and Broome, were bombed into ruins, and the bloody campaign in New Guinea could quite easily have taken place in Queensland. After the war, Australian politicians were able to persuade a dubious public that Australia must 'populate or perish', and large-scale immigration began. The immigrant hunt aimed first at Northern Europeans, especially Britons, but the supply of these soon ran low – partly because of New Zealand competition. In the 1950s and 1960s, the hunt shifted to Southern Europeans – Greeks, Italians and Yugoslavs – who immigrated in very substantial numbers. In the 1970s and 1980s, the hunt shifted again, to East Asians. The 'Aryan Australian' immigration policy, therefore, ended in the 1950s, and the 'White Australian' policy ended in the 1970s. Australian ethnic liberalism can easily be exaggerated. The author of Australia's 'open door' policy, Labour politician Arthur Calwell, was also author of the immortal line 'Two Wongs do not make a White'.[32] Yet New Zealand managed to edge out even Australia in the persistence of a racialist immigration policy.

The 'Aryan New Zealand' immigration policy identified in Chapter Seven persisted in practice at least until 1974, and arguably until 1986. There were exceptions. Family reunification migration became somewhat easier, even for Chinese New Zealanders, from about 1950. This enabled existing ethnic minorities to reinforce themselves to a limited extent. The Chinese-born population increased from 5,000 to 12,000 between 1945 and 1971, and the Indian-born from 1,500 to 7,000 – still tiny minorities.[33] After 1945, New Zealand participated in various international resettlements of refugees. But it did so very cautiously. It took fewer than 5,000 European refugees from World War Two, and only 6,000 refugees from the Indo-Chinese wars of the 1970s – in proportion to population, one-third as many as Australia.[34] A mean-minded attitude to refugees persisted until the late 1990s, and family reunification immigration was not big either. Consequently, by far the largest category of immigrants to New Zealand remained the British, who in 1996 still constituted almost 40 per cent of overseas-born New Zealanders (including a relatively few Irish). Counting other Europeans and Australians, the 'European' or 'white' proportion of the overseas-born totalled over 60 per cent. These 'new Europeans' were the largest of three major components of a new migration that brought close on a million fresh people into New Zealand between 1945 and 1999. The sheer scale of these new migrations is obscured by an insistence on 'net immigration' as the key statistic. Especially after 1970, almost as many people emigrated as immigrated, a substantial exodus, mainly to Australia, where about 400,000 New Zealanders now live. Net immigration was therefore modest. From 1986, the immigrants included an increasing proportion of East Asians, the second major category of new New Zealanders, who now total about 5 per cent of the population. The third major category was known as the 'Pacific Islanders', now also about 5–6 per cent of the population.

Although substantial New Zealand involvement in the islands of the South Pacific dates from 1890, the Island peoples did not move into New Zealand in any numbers until after World War Two. Even in 1956, the total Pacific Islands-born population was only 8,000 – little more than the Chinese-born population at the time.[35] The big inflow began in the 1960s, and by 1976 there were over 60,000 Pacific Islanders in New Zealand. By 1996, the figure had reached over 200,000 – many by now New Zealand-born. Some groups of these people were New Zealand citizens, with free right of entry – Cook Islanders, Niueans and Tokelauans. In 1966, these groups comprised 47 per cent of the Pacific Islands population; by 1991 the figure was 29 per cent.[36] The depth and permanence of these peoples' relationship with New Zealand is indicated by the fact that the great majority of them live in New Zealand rather than the home islands.[37] The single biggest group of Island immigrants were Samoans, now comprising about half the Pacific Island population, whose main inflows came a little later. After Western Samoa gained independence from New Zealand in 1962, Samoans entered on a negotiated quota system. Their right of entry was fiercely contested in the courts in 1979–82.[38] A third group were the Tongans, who had no colonial connection with New Zealand at all – the Kingdom of Tonga had been a protectorate of Old Britain. Yet they, too, entered in substantial numbers, though later than the other two main groups. By 1996, there were over 30,000 Tongans in New Zealand. Most Samoans and Tongans still live in their home countries, but not by much.

Like other immigrants, Pacific Islanders tend to concentrate in urban Auckland, where about two-thirds of them live. In 1996, they made up 6 per cent of the population of New Zealand, but 13 per cent of the population of Auckland. Immigrants initially preferred Auckland because it was where the jobs were. When this ceased to be true, they still preferred it because it was where their co-patriots were. Living in the same city enhanced the chances of ethnic persistence. As we have seen, it facilitated occupational and residential clustering. Pacific Islanders comprise up to half the population of some South Auckland suburbs. Concentrating in the big city also enhances other mechanisms of ethnic persistence. Island foods are more readily available than elsewhere; ethnic magazines have a bigger market – there were said to be five Samoan newspapers in Auckland in the early 1990s.[39] The key ethnic organisation is the church. Pacific Islanders remain much more religious than other New Zealanders. In a sense, the fact that Pakeha are rejecting churchgoing makes it a 'denomination of dissent', a site for the survival of difference. Pacific Christianity seems rather like Maori Christianity in that it merges imported and indigenous elements, and church and community. In Samoa, each village is said to have its own church, typically several times as large as it needs to be, just as was the case in Maori villages in the nineteenth century.[40] The church symbolises community pride, unity and capacity for collective action. The transfer of this communal/religious ethos from the islands to Auckland is by no means complete, but it does appear to be quite impressive. Other traditions that had to some extent made the jump are the willingness to contribute work and money to communal causes, and the authority of family, elders and – in the Samoan case at least – of hereditary chiefs, or matai. There are hints of a rift between Island-born and New Zealand-born over such traditions.[41] Like other young immigrants before them, young Pacific Island New Zealanders can find traditional authority oppressive. As with Maori, there may be an element of intergenerational rebellion in Pacific 'street culture'.

The attitude of both Pacific Islanders and New Zealanders in general to a 'Pacific identity' is problematic. Pacific Islanders are understandably irritated by the tendency of other New Zealanders to conflate their identities. Samoans, it is claimed, are as different 'from the Cook Islanders as the British are from the French'.[42] This may overstate the case, but substantial differences exist among, and even within, the island peoples. Cook Islanders from the smaller islands of Mangaia and Aituaki were less likely to cluster in Auckland than those from Raratonga. Aituakians clustered in the early 1960s in the booming timber town of Tokoroa.[43] Bloody clashes between Samoan and Tongan gangs occasionally made headlines. Yet a compound 'New Zealand Pacific' culture is in some respects an exciting possibility – in artistic culture, for example. As for New Zealanders in general, they sometimes talk the talk about being a Pacific nation, but it is not clear that they walk the walk. The Pacific was essentially an empty space to be crossed for recolonial New Zealand, and decolonisation does not seem to have improved the situation much. Diplomatic representation expanded from 1972, and Pacific Studies centres were belatedly established at New Zealand universities in the 1980s. But, to the early 1990s at least, New Zealand's share of Pacific Islands' economic activity was actually diminishing – in shipping, banking and tourism, for example.[44]

Until the mid-1970s, the inflow of Pacific Island peoples was actively encouraged by the New Zealand state and by New Zealand business. The overoptimistic assumption that Pacific Islanders would somehow 'fit in' to Maori society because all were Polynesian was a factor, as was the colonial connection with all but Tonga. As the entry of Tongans suggests, however, the key factor was the need for labour during the years of the Golden Weather, 1945–73. Assistance schemes focused on young men and women, and it was initially assumed that their stay would be temporary – a 'guest worker' system similar to that of the Turks in West Germany. Problems similar to those of urban Maori migrants developed quite quickly. Houses were overcrowded and inadequate. Some 45 per cent of the Cook Islands households in Auckland in 1966 had no inside toilet, and 30 per cent had no hot water, although only 23 per cent had no television.[45] Desocialisation through the migration of single youths, and resocialisation into 'street culture', meant that crime rates were quite high. But they were not as high as for Maori. The migration of whole families picked up in the 1960s, and there was also some transfer of Island institutions, such as churches. Pacific Island average incomes were quite close to the general average and seem initially to have withstood economic downturn rather better than Maori.[46] There was some discrimination but, to the early 1970s, Pacific Islanders were highly regarded by Pakeha as workers, though not necessarily as neighbours. One analysis in 1970 was quite positive about the re-establishment of Polynesian settlement. 'Islanders have experienced little hostility to non-white labour and have integrated reasonably smoothly in the New Zealand economic framework.'[47]

From the mid-1970s, that fulcrum of change in modern New Zealand history, attitudes to Pacific Island immigration worsened dramatically. This was most clearly expressed in the 'overstayer affair' of 1976–77, when there was a sudden crackdown on Pacific Islanders who had overstayed their entry permits or ignored conditions about not working. There was a clear element of racialism here. The Auckland police chief advised that people who did not look like New Zealanders should carry passports. Notorious 'dawn raids' were carried out on Pacific Island homes. Pacific Islanders actually comprised a minority of overstayers, but a majority of arrests for overstaying. New immigration was also restricted. About 24,000 Pacific Islanders immigrated in 1971–76, but only 7,000 in 1976–81.[48] There was also an element of moral panic. The upsurge of hostility to Pacific Island immigration is usually attributed to economic downturn beginning in the mid-1970s. But in 1976–77 this had yet to fully bite. Unemployment was still below 1 per cent, and other New Zealanders could not logically blame Pacific Island immigration for the loss of jobs they had not yet lost. It seems likely to me that the intensified antagonism to Pacific Islanders was part of the scapegoat hunt caused by the Pakeha identity crisis that accompanied decolonisation – all the more because decolonisation was not acknowledged. Pacific Islanders were not to be the only scapegoats.

'Asian', even the more accurate 'East Asian', conflates still more disparate cultures than does 'Pacific Islander'. East Asian groups in 1996 comprised about 5 per cent of New Zealand's population, or 173,000 people.[49] By far the largest groups are ethnic Chinese, from China itself, Hong Kong, Taiwan and elsewhere; and ethnic Indians, from India, Bangladesh and Fiji. Smaller but still significant groups include Koreans, Filipinos, Japanese, Vietnamese and Indonesians. There is another divide within the category 'Asian' that equals ethnicity in importance: between 'old Asians' and 'new Asians'. The former group is very long established in New Zealand. As we have seen, the first Indian settled among Maori in Northland before 1810, and a substantial Chinese presence dates from the 1860s. These groups have roots in New Zealand that are older than those of many Pakeha – indeed, a case can be made for including them in the concept 'Pakeha'. Because much Asian immigration before 1986 was a matter of family reunification, 'old Asian' families included virtually all the Asians in New Zealand in 1966, except for some Colombo Plan university students. Even as late as 1986, they were the majority of Asians in the country. In both years, all Asians in New Zealand amounted to only around 1 per cent of the population.[50] From 1986, however, a much larger new wave arrived that within ten years quintupled the Asian population. Still only fifteen years old, this development is one area where the historical jury is genuinely still out. Some of these people were im- poverished peasant refugees. Many were middle class, well educated and reasonably affluent.

For the same reasons as other migrant groups, new Asian New Zealanders concentrate in Auckland, where they comprise about 10 per cent of the population. They, too, cluster occupationally – when they can get jobs – and residentially. For example, the Auckland suburb of Otahuhu is the capital of Vietnamese New Zealand, with Vietnamese restaurants, warehouses, barber, nightclub and billiards room.[51] East Auckland is the favoured location for Hong Kong Chinese, who tend to be wealthier.[52] Korean migrants, who suddenly began entering in substantial numbers in 1991, are also middle class and prefer the North Shore of Auckland.[53] Problems of unemployment and discrimination, noted below, may be pressuring the poorer new Asian groups into developing an 'informal economy' of their own. There is anecdotal evidence of participation in illegal fishing, illegal immigration and even organised crime. While 10 per cent of Vietnamese in Auckland in 1991 designated themselves as unemployed, 21 per cent drew the unemployment benefit.[54] One must also note the intriguing phenomenon of 'educational immigration'. More by luck than good management, English-language education has become an internationally desirable commodity, and New Zealand has just about the cheapest available. It is especially cheap if a student immigrates and so avoids paying full fees. Over 77 per cent of Indonesian immigrants in New Zealand, who come from the more affluent Christian minority of their home population rather than the Muslim majority, are attending educational institutions, and most have nuclear family still living in Indonesia.[55] Some 30 per cent of the students at the University of Auckland are Asian, but very few of these pay full international fees. To this extent, New Zealand immigration policy's attempt to outwit the East Asian middle classes by persuading them to bring us their money appears to have backfired.

Such issues should be discussed, but they are fraught with the risk of stereotyping and exaggeration. 'Educational immigration' is not necessarily a bad thing, because even if participants return, they do so with an understanding of New Zealand that should be good for our relations with their home countries in the future. The new Asians were actively sought by the New Zealand government, through various schemes to encourage an inflow of skills and capital. For example, the Business Immigration Policy of 1986 brought in over 10,000 middle-class Asians by 1990.[56] This hearty formal welcome, however, was not matched by the informal welcome. At the practical level, the new Asians expected there to be suitable jobs available – why else should New Zealand seek skilled immigrants? Instead, they found that unemployment was high and that there were difficulties in accessing those that were available. Language barriers were a problem for some groups, though not for Hong Kong and Singapore Chinese, or middle-class Indians. Another problem was the reluctance of some employers and some professional associations to accept Asian qualifications. The medical profession claims that it is protecting New Zealand standards, but the inferiority of the medical schools in Hong Kong and Singapore to those in New Zealand is not obvious. Still more serious is the apparent failure to use the new Asians to help expand exports to their countries of origin. Such people are obviously the best source of language and other skills for this purpose, and can rapidly develop a good knowledge of New Zealand as well. Some are employed in the tourist industry, handling the needs of tourists of their particular ethnic groups. But how many new Asian New Zealanders are employed by public and private organisations engaged in expanding trade with East Asia?

A significant amount of populist anti-Asian sentiment was evident in New Zealand in the late 1980s and 1990s. It lacks even the dubious logic of antagonism to Pacific Island immigration or Maori urbanisation. Asian neighbours do not increase crime rates or lower house prices. If it were based on some subliminal fear of swamping by a different culture, anti-Asian sentiment should be restricted to Auckland, but it is not. I am not convinced that this is a matter of simple racism, however. As noted in Chapter Seven, antagonism towards Asian immigration, which principally took the form of Sinophobia, was quite intense in New Zealand in the 1890s and 1900s, but diminished thereafter. In the 1950s, 1960s, and 1970s, old Asians appear to have experienced minimal discrimination. Some groups, such as the old Chinese of Dunedin, Wellington and Auckland, achieved a high degree of community acceptance, though they did not necessarily fully assimilate. Yet, from the 1980s, such Chinese New Zealanders found themselves subject to the slogan 'Asians go home'. They had not changed, but mainstream New Zealand had.

The third and largest major category of postwar immigrants were the 'new Europeans'. These included a substantial inflow of Dutch immigrants, 1945–75. The first small echelon were white colonists from the Dutch East Indies, which became independent as Indonesia after World War Two. Some Dutchmen had difficulty in getting their Indonesian wives and children past the New Zealand immigration gate. All cases, announced the gatekeepers in 1952, 'would be considered on their merits and the degree of colour involved'.[57] The main Dutch inflow, however, came from the metropolitan Netherlands and was assisted and organised by its government and New Zealand's, with the main spasm in the 1950s and the last in 1972–76.[58] The total inflow was almost 40,000 people, and estimates of the number of New Zealanders of Dutch descent in the early 1990s ranged from 80,000 to 100,000, making the Dutch roughly equal to Dalmatians as the largest 'continental European' New Zealand ethnic group.[59] Dutch immigrants were thought to be highly assimilable, and they did indeed tend to be economically successful. But they were also desired because they were Aryan – good Germanic genes but without the politics. Just as Maori tribal history can reach back over a gap of several centuries to link up with an early explorer, so Dutch in New Zealand sometimes described themselves as inheritors of Abel Tasman's 'legacy'.

Australian immigration was quite significant until the mid-1970s – the flow reversed thereafter – and there was some white South African immigration in the 1990s. But by far the largest category of postwar immigrants were Britons. Between 1948 and 1976, about 100,000 British immigrants were assisted in by the New Zealand government. The 1950s and 1960s inflows were known as 'Ten-pound Poms' after the small sum they themselves had to contribute to their expenses. There was a surprisingly large late burst of assisted British immigration 1972–75, when 22,000 were brought in.[60] Other Britons came to New Zealand under their own steam. Between 1951 and 1961, 40,000 Britons were assisted out, while another 150,000 came independently or through family migration.[61] In 1965–70, while assisted British immigration was below 15,000, total British immigration was 80,000.[62] In 1976, the number of British- and Irish-born was about 300,000, or about 10 per cent of the population. This was up from 180,000 – also about 10 per cent of the population – in 1945, when war and depression had reduced all immigration to its nadir. Here was the ethnic dimension of recolonisation's last stand. In all years the numbers of Welsh and Irish were small – 8,000 and 17,000 respectively in 1976.[63] Anglo-Scots New Zealanders were reinforced; Irish New Zealanders were not. Unlike the Ten-pound Poms, independent British migrants continued to come after the great mid-1970s watershed, though in a diminishing stream. In 1996, British- and Irish-born

New Zealanders totalled 230,000, or almost 7 per cent of the population, and this may understate the size of the British ethnic minority. In the 1996 New Zealand census, 407,000 people, or 11 per cent of the population, defined themselves as British and Irish.[64] This appears to mean that some native-born New Zealanders still define themselves as British.

Like other immigrants, the new New Zealand British concentrated in Auckland and, to a lesser extent, Wellington, and clustered residentially and occupationally. In 1971, their capital was the North Shore in Auckland, where 18.3 per cent of the population were British-born. They were over-represented in manufacturing – especially in tobacco for some reason – and, interestingly enough, in the state services. As always, they were attracted by the myths as well as the actualities of New Zealand life. In 1992, New Zealand was still being advertised in Britain as a paradise for Britons, a place where 'health and education are free and a 16 oz. steak and a litre of wine cost £2.70'.[65] One little peculiarity among British immigrants was a propensity for alphabetic friendship, friends whose names all began with the same letter. The ships on which they came had their multiple-berth cabins allocated alphabetically, and people became life-long friends with their cabin-mates. They encountered a 'curiously ambivalent attitude towards pommies' – a love-hate relationship.[66] They came partly because they thought that New Zealanders would be like them. New Zealand sought them under the same delusion. Yet in the later 1970s, 'Pommie stirrers' in the union movement in particular came quite close to joining Pacific Islanders as public scapegoats.

It is hard for a general historian to say much more about recent British immigration to New Zealand, because it appears to be virtually unstudied. If quizzed on the identity of their largest immigrant group in the year 2000, how many New Zealanders would answer correctly? The answer is the British, who outnumber the next largest groups, the Samoans and ethnic Chinese, by at least two to one. New Zealand's biggest immigrant group is camouflaged by the illusion of familiarity. Recolonisation casts its long shadow into the present.

Te Pakeha?

In 1984, a major exhibition of New Zealand art and craft toured the museums of some major American cities, including New York and Chicago, then returned for a triumphal home tour. The queues were long. The exhibition, known as *Te Maori*, showcased traditional Maori material culture, including carving and weaving. It was sometimes associated with traditional perform-ances of kapa haka, group action songs and dances. If you met someone who still thought that Maori culture was simple, primitive or undistinctive, you could simply say, 'Go to see *Te Maori*.' Having seen it, your cynic might concede that traditional Maori artistic culture is rich and distinctive, but ask if it is not also frozen in 1769. Where is the innovation that marks a living culture? There was and is some risk of freezing. Cultures under siege retreat to their citadels. But the traditional arts persist strongly; they are not museum pieces but are alive in the present. Carving is strong, if not necessarily fully traditional, and so is kapa haka – witness the performance of massed young people at the Aotearoa Festival of Traditional Maori Performing Arts, biennial since 1972. In 1994, 72 groups competed in this festival, watched by 15,000 people.[67] Furthermore, as the siege gradually lifts, a modern Maori artistic culture is joining the traditional.

There is considerable intersection between the lists of leading New Zealand novelists and leading Maori novelists. Witi Ihimaera, Patricia Grace, Alan Duff and Keri Hulme would appear on both lists. Cliff Whiting's pastel marae at the national museum is nothing if not innovative. In popular culture, comedian Billy T. James made Maori jokes as no Pakeha could, followed by other Maori comics, and the television series *Mai Time* is a lively Maori/populist hybrid. Maori are over-represented among professional dancers and actors. They are heavily over-represented among professional singers, of whom they comprise 32 per cent compared with 15 per cent of the general population.[68] This derives less from some intrinsic talent than from a culture that lends itself to fresh approaches and artistic confidence. An enhanced *Te Maori* in the present might involve all these elements, as well as traditional arts and crafts. If so, it would be both impressive and dynamic. Maori have social, economic and political problems, as we have seen. But their culture is looking fairly healthy. Cultural vigour and collective identity tend to feed off each other, so the latter, for all its tribal and pan-tribal fissures, is quite strong too. But what about Pakeha? Could we mount an enhanced *Te Pakeha*, showcasing a vibrant non-Maori artistic culture? What would be in it, and would it be different from cousin cultures across the seas?

Our chances are certainly better than they would have been during the depths of the recolonial era. In recent times there has been a substantial upsurge in New Zealand cultural production, highbrow and low. A case could be made for dating its origin to the 1940s and 1950s. The centenary celebrations of 1940 had a strong cultural and historical component, but were unfortunately upstaged by a mediocre Austrian painter named Adolf Hitler. Continuous state support for arts and literature began in 1946, when the first Labour government and its enlightened bureaucrat, Joseph Heenan, instituted a Literary Fund and a Symphony Orchestra.[69] There were also developments in popular culture from 1948, when the first New Zealand record was produced, 'Blue Smoke', by Ruru Karaitiana. Other recordings followed, drawing on a long-standing tradition of dance bands and country music, and newer strands imported from America – first the Hawaiian sound, then rock and roll. *Landfall* and its brave domestic expatriates pushed hard in literature, as we have seen, but did not greatly impinge on public consciousness. Bruce Mason began a long career writing and performing solo plays, the New Zealand Ballet was established, and a professional theatre group, New Zealand Players arose. But it also fell. These were significant developments, but it would be pushing it to portray the 1940s and 1950s as a time of major take-off in artistic culture.

A better case can be made for the 1960s. A long-standing craft tradition began to consolidate, professionalise and gain public acceptance in this decade, whereas in the 1950s there had been 'some consumer resistance to the local product'.[70] Art education improved; painting began to find its feet, for the first time since a flowering in the 1930s. The first 'post-provincial', or post-expatriate, novelists, such as Maurices Shadbolt and Gee, emerged, as did a crop of new publishers. Janet Frame and James K. Baxter became public figures. All combined were well outsold by Barry Crump, who was in turn well outsold by the Mills & Boon chapter in the long history of New Zealand pan-British fiction. Indigenous radio drama became significant, and the first professional theatres emerged. An Arts Advisory Council was formed in 1960, followed by a National Library in 1965 and a Dance School in 1967. There were other firsts, and it may be fair to see the 1960s as the pioneering decade. But the big shifts in culture as in economics came in the 1970s.

Television, which had hitherto concentrated on setting itself up, at last began to produce substantial local content from the early 1970s. Indeed, the ratio of local drama to hours broadcast was probably higher than in the present. Quality was mixed, costs were high, and a 'rort' mentality prevailed in some quarters. Broadcasting executives found it necessary to attend 40 overseas conferences a year, and to use 2 per cent of all domestic air flights in 1977.[71] But New Zealanders were at last seeing themselves on the small screen. They were also seeing themselves on the large screen. Only five feature films were made between 1940 and 1972 – and one of them was a remake; 120 features have been made since 1975.[72] A state-funded Film Commission, established in 1978, along with various tax breaks, boosted this celluloid explosion, but nine features had already been made earlier in the 1970s. Experimental film-making began in the late 1960s, and avant-garde New Zealand expatriate artists such as Len Lye and Billy Apple made reputations overseas.[73]

Development in theatre, art galleries and museums, and the New Zealand publication of novels was also considerable. The output of novels between 1965 and 1991 was twice as great as in all the years before. Eight New Zealand novels were published in 1979; 40 in 1995.[74] New art galleries and museums opening in the 1960s and 1970s numbered 88, compared with thirteen in the 1940s and 1950s.[75] Playmarket, an organisation for developing and marketing play scripts, was set up in 1973. Lively professional theatre scenes emerged in Wellington and Auckland, with a few state-supported professional theatres elsewhere as well, and middlebrow playwright Roger Hall broke box-office records. Popular music arguably developed most of all, and increased its standing in the public mind. In 1980, Robert Muldoon could pronounce that one leading group, Misex, was not culture at all. But by 1984 another leading group, Split Enz, had achieved national icon status, which one member, Neil Finn, still enjoys. The breakup of Split Enz in that year occasioned the *New Zealand Herald*'s first-ever editorial about a local rock group.[76] By 1999, the 'cultural sector' as a whole was quite big: it contributed about 3 per cent, or $3 billion, to GDP and employed over 50,000 people, a huge increase on the 1950s.

How distinctive is this newly active Pakeha culture? Not very, suggests a 1988 study. 'There are not enough of us and we have too few original stories to tell. Whether we like it or not (and we should like it) we are an integral part of universal culture.'[77] 'We have assumed that we can make uniquely New Zealand films but these have been false hopes . . . our inspiration remains Hollywood.' Popular music, central in youth culture, was especially derivative. 'All New Zealand music (from classical to country and western) is derivative.'[78] 'New Zealand musicians still feel awkward extolling the joys of Friday night in Huntly.'[79] This study rejects 'the flawed premise that there is such a thing as a pure and unique New Zealand popular music'. This seems to me to misunderstand and oversimply a complex cultural phenomenon. Much of Pakeha culture *was* derivative, but derived from a pan-British compound culture to which New Zealand had contributed its mite. Some, such as Crump's capping yarns, descends from compound folk cultures that belong as much to New Zealand as to the other co-owners, such as Australia. And some does seem to be developing distinctive Kiwi sounds and distinctive Kiwi styles. The delusion that New Zealand has 'too few original stories to tell' is a quintessentially recolonial one, though now made in relation to American rather than British culture.

The cultural upsurge is good news, and it has elements of distinctiveness and benign hybridity. But there are problems. The Pakeha 'cultural revolution' is incomplete and constrained, underfunded and hampered by the small size of its market. Professional artists are selected as much for their willingness to live in poverty as for their talent. 'Highbrow' and 'lowbrow' remain unreconciled, reluctant to see each other as necessary partners. Quality control is mixed, and so is the level of self-confidence. The view that there is no such thing as Pakeha culture can still be heard; the use of Maori as a cultural crutch still persists; and many Pakeha dislike even their own name.

'Pakeha' is a Maori word dating from 1814. It is sometimes said to have originated as a derogatory term, but this is unlikely. The most probable original meaning was 'imaginary pale-skinned beings'.[80] Even if it was originally derogatory, words are allowed to change their meanings. The terms 'Welsh' and 'Black', for example, have outgrown derogatory origins. In the mid-nineteenth century, Maori applied 'Pakeha' to all Europeans, whether living in New Zealand or Vienna. But in common usage it now means New Zealanders of European descent. For some, recent European immigrants are not Pakeha until they have committed themselves to New Zealand. A shrinking, but still substantial, proportion of Pakeha reject the term, preferring 'New Zealand European' or simply 'New Zealander'.[81] Theoretically, Maori, Pacific Island and Asian New Zealanders could also describe themselves simply as 'New Zealanders', but they do not. Of about 200 people in one 1992 survey who insisted on using only 'New Zealander' to describe themselves, 97 per cent were Pakeha.[82] Rejecting 'Pakeha' implicitly rejects other ethnic groups as well, as in the phrase 'We're all New Zealanders'. We *are* all New Zealanders, but we are other things as well. You are allowed more than one collective identity, although ideally the set should be mutually compatible, telescoping into each other. The same person can be an Irish New Zealander, a Pakeha and a New Zealander. Multiple identities can enrich and strengthen New Zealandness, and not necessarily weaken it, just as separate but intertwining strands strengthen a rope. The persisting assertion of homogeneity, the unease about ethnic pluralism, and the delusion that pluralism must mean disunity, are residues of recolonial ideology.

The late twentieth-century upsurge in arts was arguably matched by an upsurge of interest in the past. History, too, has its 'brows'. Its highbrow equivalents were the scholarly monographs produced by academics and public historians. Here, too, there was a modest take-off from the 1950s, and a larger one from the 1970s. History's 'lowbrow' consists of both 'popular' historical writing and 'heritagism' – a popular interest in the past reflected in such things as membership of local historical societies and public visits to historic sites and museums. 'Lowbrow' history may well be more culturally important than 'highbrow', and to understand either we need briefly to reach further back into the history of history. In the nineteenth century, under progressive colonisation, New Zealand historical writing was quite lively, as noted in Chapter Eleven. A. S. Thomson and W. P. Reeves penned classics the next half-century was unable to match. Most nineteenth-century history books were more notable for industry than quality. But these early New Zealand historians did not deprecate the brevity of their subject; they celebrated it. It corroborated the presumed trajectory of the future: onwards and upwards. Recolonisation produced four different responses in history and heritagism. One was simple neglect, which persisted to the mid-1970s. As Keith Sinclair put it in 1979:

> It has often been said that New Zealand is a country without a history – and is all the happier for that. Certainly, it is true that its inhabitants *know* no history, or only a few scraps . . . New Zealanders in general do not want anything from the past. Self-conscious, educated New Zealanders want any past, so long as it is not their own.[83]

The second recolonial response, which one might call historiographical 'subimperialism', was to see New Zealand history as a subordinate branch of British imperial history. New Zealand history was modestly useful for teaching civic duty and patriotic loyalty – to Britain as well as New Zealand. The 1920s and 1930s school text *Our Nation's Story*, in which 'Our Nation' was Britain and 'Our Country' was New Zealand, is the classic text of this strand of historical thought. But it also had eminent academic champions, such as James Hight and William Morrell. They were the equivalents of the 'happy exiles' of recolonial literature discussed in Chapter Eleven.

Another pair of recolonial approaches to history were more positive. One, which we could call 'founder studies', laundered and reinvented, but also preserved, the Pakeha past for the purposes of the present. Its doyens included Thomas Hocken and Robert McNab. It was especially active in the 1890s and 1900s, when many communities celebrated silver jubilees and it was feared that old settlers would soon pass away without recording their memories. This approach emphasised *founders*, the virtuous and moral pioneers who had laid such a sound basis for the present. Its practitioners tended to write out the ruthless, disreputable but dynamic elements of nineteenth-century history. Early sojourners and settlers were divided into two categories: respectable, who made it into history, and 'degenerate', who did not – 'nothing need be recorded of them'.[84] This retrospective taming of nineteenth-century New Zealand history lasted a long time. It had a 'popular' heritage dimension too – 'Early Settlers' Associations' and 'Old Colonists' Museums'. But, except possibly in Otago, whose receding future stimulated interest in its leading past, the breadth of impact of the 'Old Settler' movement does not seem to have been huge after the 1900s.[85]

The final recolonial approach to history, one that romanticised race relations, was connected to the 'Smithing' and 'whitening' of Maori culture, discussed in Chapter Six. It sought to inject both interest and harmony into

New Zealand history by focusing on benign Maori–Pakeha relations, the origins of the 'race relations paradise'. Its leading practitioners, 1900s–30s, included James Cowan and T. Lindsay Buick, and its key iconic events were the New Zealand Wars of 1845–72 and the Treaty of Waitangi of 1840. Each was portrayed as a romantic and exciting drama with a happy ending. There was, however, a semi-nationalist subtext to the work of Cowan, Buick, Hocken and McNab. They claimed that New Zealand did have a history that was interesting and important. They pushed their barrows uphill into mounting public disinterest, and so did their equivalent in heritagism, Vernon Reed.

Reed was a Northland lawyer and politician who devoted much of his life to preserving and enhancing James Busby's old house at Waitangi, on whose lawn the iconic treaty of 1840 had been signed.[86] From 1911, mostly as a Reform MP whose party was in government, Reed repeatedly lobbied Cabinet to preserve what he saw as New Zealand history's most sacred place, the Treaty House and its grounds. For twenty years he was completely unsuccessful, but in the summer of 1931–32 he was able to infect the visiting Governor-General, Charles Bledisloe, with his own enthusiasm. Bledisloe promptly bought the Treaty House and gifted it to the nation, and the grand opening was held in 1934 – with Apirana Ngata's help. But it was Vernon Reed who ran the show for the next twenty years, without payment or expenses, and who tried gallantly to get New Zealanders to visit their most sacred site. Reed had problems with World War Two, when the army took over Waitangi, and with the fact that the few thousand visitors he did get 'largely ignored' the donations box. But in 1948, after 37 years of trying, he finally persuaded the government to provide some money – an annual grant of £1,000.

Reed now set about developing Waitangi as what was in effect the nation's first 'heritage park', to cultural heritage as a national park is to natural heritage. He proposed that the army buildings be used to house schoolchildren who would come to Waitangi for an intensive course in their nation's heritage at 'this sacred spot'. 'Early history should be the pride of the nation . . . instilled into the minds of the people.' In 1948, a large dormitory and other accommodation was constructed as 'a school lodge'. In 1950, as new Reed schemes to build tearooms, a museum and a hotel of local stone were maturing, Waitangi was taken over by the Department of Lands and Survey. Reed's development plans were put on hold. Lands and Survey decided to develop parts of the Waitangi Reserve for farming. Stock grazed the Treaty House grounds, and the school lodge, designed to educate young New Zealanders about their history, was 'converted into a manure shed'.

I am aware of the dangers of presentism, of portraying the recolonial era as a dark age for New Zealand historical literature and heritage, to which the present is the solution. But the triumph of farming over history at Waitangi in the 1950s seems hard to argue with. There has been considerable improvement in the recent past. As it did with artistic culture, decolonisation brought an upsurge of interest in history and heritage. Even as Reed and Waitangi suffered humiliation in the 1950s and 1960s, the Historic Places Trust was set up and the National Archives were established. Good history books began to trickle out, from outside as well as inside academia. As in artistic culture, a stronger upsurge occurred from the 1970s and 1980s, and continues to the present. But, as with artistic culture again, flies remain in the ointment.

I have discussed the problems and achievements of current historical scholarship elsewhere.[87] The achievement is very considerable – indeed, it provides the sources that have made this book possible. But there is, I think, a persistent reluctance to accept the realities of recolonisation and a tendency to focus instead on the more independent national history we would like to have happened. Outside scholarship, the message from past and present to each other is considerably worse. Though the Treaty House grounds are no longer a sheep farm, an investigation in 2000 found 'a deep lack of knowledge of the country's icon heritage attractions' among the public at large.[88] Secondary school pupils still engage with New Zealand history to a stunningly limited degree. In 1999, of 65,000 pupils who sat School Certificate, fewer than 9,000, or 14 per cent, did history of any sort. Of 46,000 doing Sixth Form Certificate, only 10 per cent did history. Of 27,000 sitting the University Bursary exam, 5,000 did history. This amounted to a slightly healthier 18 per cent but, of these, over 60 per cent did Early Modern British history, 'Tudors and Stuarts', with less than 40 per cent doing New Zealand history – in fact some schools do not offer it in the seventh form.[89] In short, the vast majority of New Zealand senior secondary school students still have little knowledge of their own country's past. One reason for this cultural self-lobotomy is depressingly simple. Education has been underfunded since 1975. The money, and the teacher time and energy, for new textbooks and retraining is not easy to find. But the problem also stems from the recolonial system, and from a failure to fully recognise it or its legacies.

Artistic culture, highbrow and low, and heritage, highbrow and low, are only two of the strands from which twenty-first-century New Zealand is being woven. Others include this book's cast of characters, some of which have been mistaken for skeletons and locked in closets. From the closet labelled 'Tight Society' come its stalwarts: Farmer Backbone, Race Mother, Moral Evangelist and Better Briton. From the closet marked 'Old Subversions' come the Kiwi Bloke, the Wild Child, the Resilient Maori and the old 'New Woman', or Populist Feminist. From the closet marked 'New Subversions' comes the Teenager, the Graduate, the Left-Liberal and the Right-Liberal, and the Even Newer Woman. The characters dance in patterns: the drift north, the rise of Auckland, baby boom and baby bust, fast monopod economy, slow quadruped economy, the various 'comings-out'. Another pattern is the persistence, and then revival, of difference in the homogenous society, not only by Maori but also by various other Others, old and new. Class shapes and reshapes, sometimes ducking its head below the surface of history, but never quite going away. New gateways to the world open, some slowly, some fast, allowing serpents to slither into the reforged paradise, and a Kiwi exodus to slither out. But one pattern looms high above the rest: recolonisation, whose rise, reign and fall is the master variable of modern New Zealand history.

My own mixed feelings about recolonisation may already be evident to the reader, and I wish to confess openly to them. I have to acknowledge it was a remarkable historical phenomenon: an amazing transcending of distance, a spatial miracle that made light of 12,000 miles and plugged London almost as firmly as Auckland into the New Zealand socio-economy. For almost a century, 1880s–1970s, it made New Zealand a virtual Scotland. As a comparative historian, I am intrigued by the possibility that the New Zealand pattern of progressive colonisation and recolonisation may help unravel problems in the histories of Canada and Australia, which also appear to have undergone both processes. This might also extend to the United States, where the Midwestern and far-western states arguably played New Zealand to New York's London, and at much the same time. As a New Zealand historian, I have to recognise that recolonisation had many benefits as well as costs. As a New Zealand historian uneasily engaged with the present, I have to accept that the system also has left legacies benign as well as malign, the useful as well as the redundant.

Yet as a New Zealander I cannot help being enraged by some aspects of my country's voluntary neo-colonialism. The terrible toll of World War One need not have been so high, the tight society need not have been so tight. I take no pleasure in renewing the life in print of such recolonial gems as William Lane's wish that New Zealand remain 'chief among the children', or Anthony Eden's 'dear old men' who would do anything for him and for Mother Britain. Up to a point, I share the motives of New Zealand's 'post-colonial' historians who, since Keith Sinclair in the 1950s, have handled recolonisation largely by evading it. We historians differ on our dating of New Zealand's twenty-first birthday, the advent of national maturity and independence. Did it happen in 1856, 1869, 1907, 1915, 1935 or 1947? – to which list I would add 1973. But we agree that no-one likes snapshots of them clinging to mother being displayed at the twenty-first birthday party, especially if the snapshots were taken at age nineteen. Not only historians but also society at large appear to feel that the embarrassingly tight old links with Britain, for a century the 'North Island' of the New Zealand–British system, are better ignored and forgotten. So why has this book made such a meal of recolonisation and its alter ego, Better Britonism, returning to them again and again?

One reason is that recolonisation is in fact a key determinant of New Zealand's modern history, without which much of that history cannot be understood. The modest good news about Maori–Pakeha relations, for example, is inexplicable without knowledge of the recolonial need for racial harmony and homogeneity – and for that suitably whitened touch of distinctiveness to give Better Britain a 'golden tinge'. New Zealand's war efforts, economy and culture can only be fully understood in their recolonial context. Sinophobia in the 1900s, liberalism and populism in the 1980s, and feminism and the state in both periods also need their context: systemic mega-shift, the rise and fall of recolonisation. The 1880s and the 1970s, which mark the shift from progressive colonisation to recolonisation, then from recolonisation to decolonisation, are great fulcrums on which many changes balance. To adapt a phrase, trying to explain modern New Zealand history without reference to recolonisation is like trying to explain a rugby game without reference to the ball.

My second reason for rejecting the evasion of recolonisation is that it has benign legacies as well as malign ones, and that the former may be particularly useful in the immediate future. The imminent possibility of fresh waves of globalisation is a commonplace of contemporary comment. Has New Zealand emerged at long last from the shadow of recolonisation only to have its nascent cultural maturity and national independence washed away by globalising tides? The threat of globalisation may be exaggerated – the world system still needs differences and identities. But the incoming waves are substantial even so. If New Zealand wishes to surf them rather than be swamped by them, it so happens that it has a surfboard ready to hand – the benign legacies of recolonisation. The English language, by a fortunate accident the Esperanto of the twenty-first century, is only the most obvious. There is also the deep-seated infrastructure of economic and cultural hybridity, the capacity to operate like locals in two places at once. This comes with long experience of expatriate games, and a capacity for New Zealanders living overseas to remain connected in various enriching ways. The Kiwi exodus of the last quarter-century is a 'brain drain' at one level, a potential 'worldwide web' at another. There are few countries – Ireland is one possible exception – that have New Zealand's long and intense experience of transnationalism. We may as well use it.

My final reason for rejecting the evasion of recolonisation is that this evasion has unnecessarily marred our recent past and, to some extent, our present. In economics it led, as we have seen, to the misdiagnosis of the problems of the last quarter-century. Good or bad, restructuring in itself was never going to compensate for the disconnecting of the town-supply district from its town. In culture, recolonisation has left us with an acute case of the tall-poppy syndrome and a flawed capacity for self-assessment. It is almost as though we still expect that the really tall poppies should be in London, and that London will handle our cultural quality control. These problems are less likely to be resolved if we fail to recognise their recolonial roots. The failure to recognise the legacies of recolonisation, good and bad, and to recognise the traumatic but exciting process of decolonisation for what it is, may prevent us from realising the full potential of that process. The failure to recognise recolonisation's rise and fall has also left many New Zealanders insecure. They are uncertain about their capacity to manage change, to reject the bad and accept the good, or even to tell the difference between them. They are uneasy about burgeoning pluralism, partly because no-one has explained to them that it was the old homogeneity and conformism that was artificial, and not the new 'coming-out' of difference. They are uncomfortable about their identity, unsure about whether they are Pakeha, New Zealanders or Europeans, about how the three fit into each other, and about what they actually mean. These are malign legacies not so much of recolonisation itself, but of the failure to understand it. For the sake of our future as well as our past, New Zealanders must face up to the realities of our modern history. Recolonisation is a ghost that can be laid only by confronting it.

REFERENCES

Full referencing is impossible in a work of this kind, because most paragraphs are distilled from many sources. The policy followed here has been to reference quotations, most statistics and many particular points, with more general sources acknowledged where this seems particularly warranted. Books cited are published in New Zealand unless otherwise specified.

Abbreviations

AEHR Australian Economic History Review
AJHR Appendices to the Journals of the House of Representatives
ENZ An Encyclopedia of New Zealand, ed. A. H. McLintock, 1966
DNZB Dictionary of New Zealand Biography, vol. 1, eds W. H. Oliver & Claudia Orange, 1990; vols 2, 3, 4, ed. Claudia Orange, 1993, 1996, 1998
HS New Zealand: A Handbook of Historical Statistics, ed. G. T. Bloomfield, Boston, 1984
NZJH New Zealand Journal of History
OYB Official Yearbook of New Zealand
TPNZI Transactions and Proceedings of the New Zealand Institute

Prologue

1. *ENZ*, vol. 1, 476. Also see R. G. Keam, *Tarawera: The Volcanic Explosion of 10 June 1886*, 1988; Rotorua Museum and Art Gallery, *Tarawera Eruption Centennial Exhibition Guidebook*, 1986.
2. *NZ Herald*, 12 June 1886.
3. James Belich, *Making Peoples: A History of the New Zealanders from Polynesian Settlement to the End of the Nineteenth Century*, 1996.
4. Recent discoveries of bones of the Polynesian rat said to date back further than 1,000 years have not convinced most experts that they indicate continuous early settlement. See Richard

N. Holdaway, 'A Spatio-temporal Model for the Invasion of the New Zealand Archipelago by the Pacific Rat *Rattus exulans*', *Journal of the Royal Society of New Zealand*, 29 (1999), 91–105, and various papers presented at the New Zealand Archaeological Association Conference, 1999.
5. J. A. Froude, *Oceana, or England and Her Colonies*, London, 1886, 282, 212, 228.
6. *HS*, 275, 283.
7. Ibid., 58.
8. Froude, *Oceana*, 203.
9. See *Making Peoples*, 318. Note the difference between ethnic groups as a percentage of Pakeha, and as a percentage of the total population, including Maori and Chinese.
10. *Making Peoples*, 409.

Part 1: Introduction

1. Malcolm Saunders, *Britain, the Australian Colonies and the Sudan Campaigns of 1884–5*, Armidale, 1985, esp. chapter 3.
2. Personal communications, London, 1981–82.
3. Malcolm McKinnon, *Independence and Foreign Policy: New Zealand and the World Since 1935*, 1993, 206–7.
4. Timothy McIvor, *The Rainmaker: A Biography of John Ballance*, 1989, 108.
5. Rookes to George Grey, 28 April 1886, Grey Collection, R19, Auckland Public Library.
6. See, e.g., W. B. Sutch, *Poverty and Progress in New Zealand: A Reassessment*, 1969; David Bedggood, *Rich and Poor in New Zealand: A Critique of Class, Politics, and Ideology*, 1980. Also see Charles Reid, 'The Politics of Development: Neo-Marxist Approaches to New Zealand History', MA thesis, University of Canterbury, 1990.

7. W. P. Morrell, *New Zealand*, London, 1935.
8. Keith Sinclair, *A History of New Zealand* (London, 1959, and many subsequent editions), *A Destiny Apart: New Zealand's Search for National Identity*, 1986.

Chapter 1: God's Lone Country

1. R. C. J. Stone, *The Father and His Gift: John Logan Campbell's Later Years*, 1987, 112.
2. Gary Hawke, *The Making of New Zealand: An Economic History*, 1985, 5, 55, 82; Rollo Arnold, *The Farthest Promised Land: English Villagers, New Zealand Immigrants of the 1870s*, 1981, 339–41; Miles Fairburn, *The Ideal Society and Its Enemies: The Foundations of Modern New Zealand Society, 1850–1900*, 1989, chapter 4.
3. R. J. Campbell, '"The Black Eighties": Unemployment in New Zealand in the 1880s', *AEHR*, 16 (1976), 69.
4. Fairburn, *Ideal Society*, 96–97.
5. Campbell, 'Black Eighties', 69.
6. Erik Olssen, 'Towards a New Society', in W. H. Oliver & B. Williams (eds), *The Oxford History of New Zealand*, 1981.
7. Fairburn, *Ideal Society*, 84 (Fairburn quotes the claims to discount them).
8. Paul Husbands, 'The People of Freeman's Bay 1880–1914', MA thesis, University of Auckland, 1992, 80–81.
9. See, e.g., Stevan Eldred-Grigg, *A Southern Gentry: New Zealanders Who Inherited the Earth*, 1980, *Otago*, 1984, 91; Adela Stewart, *My Simple Life in New Zealand*, London, 1908.
10. *HS*, 267–68; *OYB*, 1990, 608; Hawke, *Making of NZ*, 73.
11. Ibid., 71.
12. Wolfgang Rosenberg, 'Capital Imports and Growth: The Case of New Zealand-Foreign Investment in New Zealand, 1840–1858', *Economic Journal*, 71 (1961), 94.
13. Ibid., p. 95. Also see C. G. F. Simkin, *The Instability of a Dependent Economy: Economic Fluctuations in New Zealand, 1840–1914*, Oxford, 1951, 83–84.
14. H. J. Hanham, 'New Zealand Promoters and British Investors, 1860–1895', in Robert Chapman & Keith Sinclair (eds), *Studies of a Small Democracy*, 1963, 64–65.
15. These figures are calculated from John M. Gandar, 'New Zealand Net Migration in the Latter Part of the Nineteenth Century', *AEHR*, 19 (1979), 162, 167. Other estimates are higher.
16. David Thorns & Charles Sedgewick, *Understanding Aotearoa/New Zealand: Historical Statistics*, 1997, 38.
17. Arnold, *Farthest Promised Land*, 339–42.
18. All these figures are approximate and are calculated from *HS*, 54, 169–70.
19. Duncan Waterson, 'Transport in New Zealand, 1900–1930', in R. F. Watters, (ed.), *Land and Society in New Zealand*, 1965, 121–22.
20. *DNZB*, vol. 1.
21. Stone, *The Father*, 210 and passim.
22. *DNZB*, vol. 1.
23. R. C. J. Stone, *Makers of Fortune: A Colonial Business Community and its Fall*, 1973, 130; Keith Sinclair & W. F. Mandle, *Open Account: A History of the Bank of New South Wales in New Zealand*, 1961, 87.
24. R. C. J. Stone, *Russell McVeagh: The First 125 Years of the Practice of Russell McVeagh*, 1991, 62–67.
25. *OYB*, 1990, 573.
26. Calculated from *HS*, 405.
27. Stone, *Makers of Fortune*, 71.
28. Stone, *The Father*, 212–13.
29. Hawke, *Making of NZ*, 83.
30. Peter Shaw, *New Zealand Architecture: From Polynesian Beginnings to 1990*, 1991, 59.
31. Michael Bassett, *Sir Joseph Ward: A Political Biography*, 1993, chapters 2–3.
32. Timothy McIvor, *The Rainmaker: A Biography of John Ballance*, 1989, 236.
33. Trevor Wilson, *The Rise of the Liberal Party in New Zealand, 1877–1890*, 1951, 25.
34. Seddon, quoted in Dick Scott, *Years of the Pooh-Bah: A Cook Islands History*, 1991, 105. Also see R. M. Burdon, *King Dick: A Biography of Richard John Seddon*, 1955.
35. Keith Hancock, cited in Bassett, *Ward*, 194.
36. McIvor, *The Rainmaker*; Bassett, *Ward*.
37. Keith Sinclair, *William Pember Reeves: New Zealand Fabian*, Oxford, 1965; Tom Brooking, *Lands for the People? The Highland Clearances and the Colonisation of New Zealand: A Biography of John McKenzie*, 1996. Carroll as yet lacks a modern biography.

38. *HS*, 80.
39. McIvor, *The Rainmaker*, e.g. 209; David Hamer, *The New Zealand Liberals: The Years of Power, 1891–1912*, 1988, 28. For examples of contemporary feeling against banks and land monopoly, see George W. Cole, *The Financial Condition of New Zealand*, 1887, and Robert Lashley, *The Cause of, and the Cure for, the Exodus*, 1891.
40. Hamer, *NZ Liberals*, 82.
41. James Holt, *Compulsory Arbitration in New Zealand: The First Forty Years*, 1986, 21.
42. On the Maritime Strike, see Conrad Bollinger, *Against the Wind: The Story of the New Zealand Seamen's Union*, 1968; Neill Atkinson, 'Auckland Seamen and Their Union, 1880–1922', MA thesis, Univesity of Auckland, 1990; H. Roth, *Trade Unions in New Zealand*, 1973, 9–16; Erik Olssen, *A History of Otago*, 1984, 109–12.
43. See, e.g., Sinclair, *Reeves*, chapter 7; Roth, *Trade Unions*; Erik Olssen, 'The "Working Class" in New Zealand', *NZJH*, 8 (1974); 'Social Class in Nineteenth-Century New Zealand', in D. Pitt (ed.), *Social Class in New Zealand*, 1977; C. Campbell, 'The "Working Class" and the Liberal Party in 1890', *NZJH*, 9 (1975), 41–51.
44. Ibid., 47–49; Roth, *Trade Unions*, 18.
45. See Erik Olssen, *Building the New World: Work, Society and Politics in Caversham, 1880s–1920s*, 1995.
46. Cited in Olssen, *History of Otago*, 111.
47. Wilson, *Rise of the Liberal Party*, 31.
48. Hamer, *NZ Liberals*, 29.
49. Cited in Wilson, *Rise of the Liberal Party*, 36.
50. D. Beaglehole, 'The Structure and Course of Politics in Nineteenth-Century Wellington', Victoria University M.A. thesis, 1987, 150–74.
51. Hamer, *NZ Liberals*, 49–50.
52. Bassett, *Ward*, 171.
53. Leslie Lipson, *The Politics of Equality: New Zealand's Adventures in Democracy*, 1948, 292–93.
54. Quoted in Burdon, *King Dick*, 52.
55. McIvor, *The Rainmaker*, 26; Hamer, *NZ Liberals*, 88.
56. Hamer, *NZ Liberals*, 144, 173.
57. Bassett, *Ward*, 29, 144–45, 130.
58. Hamer, *NZ Liberals*, 82–84, 225–26.
59. W. J. Gardner, 'The Rise of W. F. Massey, 1891–1912', *Political Science*, 13/1 (1961), 17.
60. Hamer, *NZ Liberals*, 202. Also see Jack H. Nagel, 'Populism, Heresthetics, and Political Stability: Richard Seddon and the Art of Majority Rule', *British Journal of Political Science*, 23 (1993); *DNZB*, vol. 2; Burdon, *King Dick*.
61. W. P. Reeves, *The Long White Cloud: Ao Te Roa*, 1973 (orig. 1898), 301.
62. Michael Bassett, *The State in New Zealand, 1840–1984*, 1998, 120, based on estimates by Keith Rankin.
63. *OYB*, 1893, 426.
64. *HS*, 24; J. D. Gould, 'The Twilight of the Estates, 1891 to 1910', *AEHR*, 10 (1970), 11.
65. Cited in Ian McLaren, 'The Politics of Secondary Education in Victorian New Zealand', in R. Openshaw & D. McKenzie (eds), *Reinterpreting the Educational Past: Essays in the History of New Zealand Education*, 1987, 71.
66. Kerry Howe, *Singer in a Songless Land: A Life of Edward Tregear*, 1991, 87–88.
67. See W. P. Reeves, *State Experiments in Australia and New Zealand*, 1902; Holt, *Compulsory Arbitration*.
68. Quoted in Howe, *Singer in a Songless Land*, 126.
69. *HS*, 147.
70. Bassett, *The State in New Zealand*, 1, 81. Also see Lipson, *Politics of Equality*; Alan Henderson, *The Quest for Efficiency: The Origins of the State Services Commission*, 1990.
71. Patricia Grimshaw, *Women's Suffrage in New Zealand*, 1987 edn, chapter 2.
72. Bettina Bradbury, 'From Civil Death to Separate Property: Changes in the Legal Rights of Married Women in Nineteenth-Century New Zealand', *NZJH*, 29 (1994).
73. See E. J. Tapp, 'Australian and New Zealand Federation', *Historical Studies*, 5/19 (1952); F. L. W. Wood, 'Why Did New Zealand Not Join the Australian Commonwealth in 1900–1901?', *NZJH*, 2/2 (1968); Adrian Chan, 'New Zealand, the Australian Commonwealth and "Plain Nonsense"', *NZJH*, 3/2 (1969); Miles Fairburn, 'New Zealand and Australasian Federation, 1883–1901: Another View', *NZJH*, 4/2 (1970); Keith Sinclair, 'Why New Zealanders Are Not Australians: New Zealand and the

Australian Federal Movement, 1881–1901', in Sinclair (ed.), *Tasman Relations: New Zealand and Australia 1788–1988*, 1988; Sinclair, *Destiny Apart*, esp. chapter 8.

74. Rollo Arnold, 'Family or Strangers? Trans-Tasman Migrations, 1870–1900', in *Australia and New Zealand: Aspects of a Relationship*, Proceedings of the Stout Research Centre 8th Annual Conference, 1991.

75. Rollo Arnold, 'The Dynamics and Quality of Trans-Tasman Migration, 1885–1910', *AEHR*, 26 (1986), 3.

76. John Martin, *The Forgotten Worker: The Rural Wage Earner in Nineteenth-Century New Zealand*, 1990, 47.

77. John Molony, *The Penguin History of Australia*, Melbourne, 1988, 185.

78. Erik Olssen, 'Lands of Sheep and Gold', in Sinclair (ed.), *Tasman Relations*, 48.

79. Hamer, *NZ Liberals*, 261.

80. Sinclair, *Destiny Apart*, 111–13.

81. Ibid., 116.

82. Brian Easton, 'The Economic Relationship Between Australia and New Zealand', in *Australia and New Zealand: Aspects of a Relationship*, Proceedings of the Stout Research Centre 8th Annual Conference, 1991; *HS*, 292–93, 310–11.

83. Sinclair, *Destiny Apart*, 119.

84. Ibid., 120.

85. Molony, *History of Australia*, 189.

86. Graeme Davison et al. (eds), *The Oxford Companion to Australian History*, Melbourne, 1998, 243–44.

87. Charles Dilke, *Greater Britain: A Record of Travel in English-Speaking Countries During 1866 and 1867*, London, 1968, vol. 1, 398.

88. Easton, 'Economic Relationship'; *HS*, 293–94.

89. Sinclair, *Destiny Apart*, 120–21.

90. Allen Curnow (ed.), *The Penguin Book of New Zealand Verse*, 1960, 27n.

Chapter 2: The Recolonial System

1. B. L. Evans, *A History of Agricultural Production and Marketing in New Zealand*, Palmerston North, 1969, 104.

2. *HS*, 280–86; *NZ Digest of Statistics*, 1983, 111.

3. *The Sterling Area: An American Analysis*, London, 1951, 117.

4. Richard Perren, *The Meat Trade in Britain 1840–1914*, London, 1978, 3.

5. R. C. O. Mathews et al., *British Economic Growth, 1856–1973*, Stanford, 1982, esp. 554; Paul Johnson (ed.), *Twentieth Century Britain: Economic, Social and Cultural Change*, London, 1994, 3.

6. H. C. G. Mathew, 'The Liberal Age', in Kenneth O. Morgan, (ed.), *The Oxford History of Britain*, Oxford, 1988, 531–33; S. Pollard, *The Development of the British Economy, 1914–1980*, 3rd edn, London, 1988, 86.

7. R. S. Sayers, *A History of Economic Change in England, 1880–1939*, London, 1967, 109; Perren, *Meat Trade*, 3.

8. All quotes in this paragraph are from C. Anne Wilson, *Food and Drink in Britain*, Chicago, 1991. Also see I. C. Barker et al. (eds), *Our Changing Fare: 200 Years of British Food Habits*; Thomas Brydone, in *OYB*, 1893, 195.

9. Marylin J. Campbell, 'Runholding in Otago and Southland, 1848 to 1876', MA thesis, University of Otago, 1981, 355–61.

10. *NZ's Heritage*, 50, 1376.

11. Quoted in ibid., 1379.

12. Marvin Sundstrom, 'Dairy Industry Developments in Canada and New Zealand Circa 1900', *NZ Geographical Society Conference Proceedings*, 12, 207–11.

13. R. C. J. Stone, 'The New Zealand Frozen Meat and Storage Company: A Pioneer of Refrigeration', *NZJH*, 5 (1971), 175.

14. *OYB*, 1893, 202, 193; Also see Evans, *Agricultural Production*, 86, 115, 152–53.

15. *HS*, 280–86.

16. J. D. Gould, 'The Occupation of Farm Land in New Zealand, 1874–1911', *Business Archives and History*, 5 (1965), 139.

17. Perren, *Meat Trade*, 186–87.

18. Donald Denoon, *Settler Capitalism: The Dynamics of Dependent Development in the Southern Hemisphere*, Oxford, 1983, 101, 104.

19. Sinclair & Mandle, *Open Account*, chapter 8.

20. J. D. Gould, *The Grassroots of New Zealand Farming*, 1974. Also see Evans, *Agricultural Production*; F. R. Callaghan & D. O. W. Hall, 'Refrigeration', *NZ Centennial Surveys*, 12, 1940.

21. Mervyn Palmer, 'William Soltau Davidson: A Pioneer of New Zealand Estate Management', *NZJH*, 7 (1975),

148–64; *DNZB*, vol. 2; *NZ's Heritage*, 51, 1409–10; 50, 1373–79; Geoffrey G. Thornton, *New Zealand's Industrial Heritage*, 1982, 109.

22. Stone, 'New Zealand Frozen Meat and Storage Company', *NZJH*, 5 (1971), 171–84; *DNZB*, vol. 2: Brydone, Davidson, Grigg; *NZ's Heritage*, 40, 1108–9; 51, 1409–10; 50, 1373–79; Thornton, *Industrial Heritage*, 109–11.

23. Hawke, *Making of NZ; DNZB*, vol. 2: Chew Chong; A. P. C. Bromley, *Hawera District Centenary*, 1981, 184; Sundstrom, 'Dairy Industry Developments'; Mary Boyd, *City of the Plains: A History of Hastings*, 1984, 98; Sinclair & Mandle, *Open Account*, chapter 8. Complaints about 'fishy' butter did not die away completely until 1911. H. G. Philpot, *A History of the New Zealand Dairy Industry, 1840–1935*, 1937, 135.

24. Richard Wolfe, *Well Made New Zealand: A Century of Trademarks*, 1987, 105.

25. Evans, *Agricultural Production*, 82; Stephen Barnett & Richard Wolfe, *New Zealand! New Zealand! In Praise of Kiwiana*, 1989, 153.

26. Hawke, *Making of NZ*, 76.

27. Keith Robbins, *Nineteenth-Century Britain: Integration and Diversity*, Oxford, 1988, 125.

28. Hanham, 'NZ Promoters', 76–77; Hawke, *Making of NZ*, 64–65.

29. See J. Critchell & J. Raymond, *A History of the Frozen Meat Trade*, London, 1912; H. Belshaw et al., *Agricultural Organisation in New Zealand*, Melbourne, 1936; Philip Hereford, *The New Zealand Frozen Meat Trade*, 1932; Evans, *Agricultural Production*; Cyril Loach, *A History of the New Zealand Refrigerating Company*, 1970; Dick Scott, *Stock in Trade: Hellaby's First Hundred Years, 1873–1973*, 1973; Richard Perren, 'The Retail and Wholesale Meat Trade 1880–1939' and Forest Capie, 'The Demand for Meat in England and Wales Between the Two World Wars', in Derek J. Oddy and Derek S. Miller (eds), *Diet and Health in Modern Britain*, London, 1985; Perren, *Meat Trade*.

30. Loach, *NZ Refrigerating Co.*, 95.

31. Perren, *Meat Trade*, 178–79; Hereford, *NZ Frozen Meat Trade*, 60.

32. Scott, *Stock in Trade*, 121.

33. Loach, *NZ Refrigerating Co.*, 93.

34. Boyd, *Hastings*, 94–96; *DNZB*, vol. 2; Hereford, *NZ Frozen Meat Trade*, 71–72; Perren, *Meat Trade*, 178.

35. R. P. Davenport-Hines & Judy Slinn, *Glaxo: A History to 1962*, Cambridge, 1992.

36. Evans, *Agricultural Production*, 175. Also see Philpott, *NZ Dairy Industry*, 293–94.

37. McLean, *The Southern Octopus: The Rise of a Shipping Empire*, 1990, 178. Also see *OYB*, 1893, 334–36; *ENZ*, vol. 3, 'Shipping'; Evans, *Agricultural Production*, 106–7; David Johnson, *New Zealand's Maritime Heritage*, 1987.

38. McLean, *Southern Octopus*, 177 and passim; Daniel R. Headrick, *The Tentacles of Progress: Technology Transfer in the Age of Imperialism, 1850–1940*, New York, 1988, 18–45; *OYB*, 1893, 335–37.

39. Perren, *Meat Trade*, 190; Evans, *Agricultural Production*, 107; Johnson, *Maritime Heritage*, 129.

40. F. B. Stephens & C. R. Barnicoat, 'Marketing of Meat', in H. Belshaw et al., *Agricultural Organisation in New Zealand*, Melbourne, 1936, 638–41.

41. F. B. Stephens, 'Processing and Marketing of Dairy Produce', in ibid. Also see Steven J. Keillor, 'Agricultural Change and Crosscultural Exchange: Danes, Americans, and Dairying, 1880–1930', *Agricultural History*, 67 (1993); Sundstrom, 'Dairy Industry Developments'.

42. Perren, 'Retail and Wholesale Meat Trade', *Meat Trade*, 195, 204 and passim.

43. Capie, 'Demand for Meat'.

44. Quoted in Stone, 'NZ Frozen Meat and Storage Co.', 172.

45. Bassett, *Ward*.

46. *NZ's Heritage*, 51, 1410.

47. Sinclair & Mandle, *Open Account*, chapter 8; Joan Burnett, 'The Impact of Dairying on the Landscape of Lowland Taranaki', in R. F Watters (ed.), *Land and Society in New Zealand: Essays in Historical Geography*, 1965; *NZ's Heritage*, 57, 1575–81; Gould, 'Occupation of Farmland', 140–41.

48. Eric Olssen, 'Lands of Sheep and Gold', in Sinclair (ed.), *Tasman Relations*, 47, citing research by Peter Brosnan; Sinclair & Mandle, *Open Account*, 145, 166.

49. Quoted in Thornton, *Industrial Heritage*, 2.

50. *OYB*, 1893, 131–32.

51. W. B. Sutch, *Colony or Nation?*, Sydney, 1966, 29. Also see his *The Quest for Security in New Zealand*, and *Poverty and Progress in New Zealand: A Re-assessment*, 1969 (orig. 1941), 99–100.

52. Eric Olssen. 'Towards a New Society', in Geoffrey Rice (ed.), *The Oxford History of New Zealand*, 2nd ed., 260. The other figures are calculated from *HS*.

53. Richard Hill, *The Iron Hand in the Velvet Glove: The Modernisation of Policing in New Zealand 1886–1917*, 1995, chapter 20.

54. *HS*, 220.

55. Reid Perkins, 'Photography in New Zealand 1892–1904', Research essay, Victoria University of Wellington, 1993; William Main & John B. Turner, *Photography in New Zealand: From the 1840s to the Present*, 1993, 37.

56. Headrick, *Tentacles of Progress*.

57. See James Watson, '"Plus ca Change . . .": Changing Technology and New Zealand's Dependence', *Historical News*, 51, 1985.

58. See, e.g., *OYB*, 1893, 100; Robert Stout, *New Zealand*, Cambridge, 1911, 20.

59. Hill, *Iron Hand*, chapter 22.

60. Stone, *Father and His Gift*.

61. From Blanche Baughan, 'A Bush Section', in Harvey McQueen (ed.), *The New Place: The Poetry of Settlement in New Zealand 1852–1914*, 1993, 201.

62. See, e.g., Joseph Ward, 1901, quoted in Hamer, *NZ Liberals*, 139; Charles A. Wilson, *Around New Zealand*, 1925, Preface; *OYB*, 1960, 40.

63. Hamer, *NZ Liberals*, 60.

64. Michael Burgess, 'Imperial Federation: Continuity and Change in British Imperial Ideas, 1869–91', *NZJH*, 17 (1983), 60–80, 63.

65. Publications associated with the Australasian displays at London exhibitions in 1862 and 1886. Quoted in Jonathan Easthope, 'Imaging Ourselves: The Projection of Pakeha Culture Overseas, 1870–1925', MA thesis, Victoria University of Wellington, 1995, 103ff.

66. Sinclair, *Destiny Apart*, 137, 79, quoting Lane, 1901 and 1911.

67. Ibid., 12.

68. Wilson, *Around New Zealand*, 14. Also see Belich, *Making Peoples*, 300; Sinclair, *Destiny Apart*, 81–83.

69. Fiona Hamilton, 'Founding Histories: Some Pakeha Constructions of a New Zealand Past in the Late Nineteenth and Early Twentieth Centuries', MA thesis, University of Auckland, 1999.

70. Quoted in ibid., 127.

71. Jock Phillips, *A Man's Country? The Image of the Pakeha Male: A History*, 1987, 141–42.

72. Sinclair, *Destiny Apart*, 140.

73. Phillips, *A Man's Country?*, 146.

74. D. O. W. Hall, *The New Zealanders in South Africa 1899–1902*, 1949.

75. Gary Clayton, 'Defence Not Defiance: The Shaping of New Zealand's Volunteer Force', DPhil thesis, University of Waikato, 1990.

76. Brian Sutton-Smith, *A History of Children's Play in New Zealand, 1840–1950*, 1981, 177–81; J. H. Murdoch, *The High Schools of New Zealand: A Critical Survey*, 1943, 198–200; Roy Shuker, *The One Best System? A Revisionist History of State Schooling in New Zealand*, 1987, 102.

77. Reeves, *Long White Cloud*, 297.

78. Michael Hoare, '"Our Comrades Beyond the Seas": Colonial Youth Movements 1820–1920', *Turnbull Library Record*, 12 (1979), 86.

79. Quoted in Sutton-Smith, *Children's Play*, 68.

80. Sinclair, *Destiny Apart*, 173.

81. Paul Baker, *King and Country Call: New Zealanders, Conscription and the Great War*, 1988, 12. Also see Hill, *Iron Hand*, chapter 23.

82. In Ian McGibbon, *The Pathway to Gallipoli: Defending New Zealand 1840–1915*, 1991, 222.

83. *ENZ*, vol. 3, 559.

84. Sinclair, *Destiny Apart*, 137–38.

85. Wolfe, *Well Made New Zealand*.

86. H. W. Orsman (ed.), *The Oxford Dictionary of New Zealand English*, 1997, 92.

87. Terry Sturm, 'Popular Fiction', in Sturm (ed.), *The Oxford History of New Zealand Literature*, 1998, 495.

88. A. H. Reed, *The Story of New Zealand*, 1974 (orig. 1945), 137.

89. John Macmillan Brown, 'Epilogue', in James Hight (ed.), *The Cambridge History of the British Empire*, vol. 7, part 2, Cambridge, 1933.

90. See *DNZB*, vol. 1. Also see John Taylor, *Consuming Identity: Modernity and Tourism in New Zealand*, 1998; Douglas

Pearce, *Tourist Organizations*, Harlow, Essex, 1992, chapter 8.

91. Easthope, 'Imaging Ourselves', 35.
92. Taylor, *Consuming Identity*, 10.
93. Easthope, 'Imaging Ourselves', 32.
94. Ibid., 27
95. James Cowan, 1906–07, quoted in Hamilton, 'Founding Histories', 131.
96. Bassett, *Ward*, 150; *NZ's Heritage*, 1316.
97. See Easthope, 'Imaging Ourselves' and 'Exhibiting Ourselves' exhibition at Te Papa Tongarewa/Museum of New Zealand.
98. Stephen Constantine (ed.), *Emigrants and Empire: British Settlement in the Dominions Between the Wars*, Manchester, 1990, 2.
99. Perren, 'Retail and Wholesale Meat Trade', 61.
100. *OYB*, 1893, 202.
101. Wolfe, *Well Made New Zealand*, chapter 6.
102. Sean Glynn & Lana Booth, *Modern Britain: An Economic and Social History*, London, 1996, 29.
103. Stephens, 'Processing and Marketing', 684.
104. Perren, *Meat Trade*, 193–94.

Chapter 3: Trouble in Paradise

1. Hill, *Iron Hand*, chapter 20.
2. *DNZB*, vol. 2.
3. Jeremy Mouat, 'The Ultimate Crisis of the Waihi Gold Mining Company', *NZJH*, 26 (1992), 184–203.
4. Eric Olssen, *The Red Feds: Revolutionary Industrial Unionism and the New Zealand Federation of Labour 1908–1913*, 1988. The following account of the industrial conflicts of 1912–13 draws in particular on this work and on Hill's *Iron Hand*. A lively but less reliable account of the Waihi Strike is Stanley Roche, *The Red and the Gold: An Informal Account of the Waihi Strike, 1912*, 1982.
5. Mouat 'Ultimate crisis'; Olssen, *Red Feds*, 142–43.
6. Hill, *Iron Hand*, chapter 19.
7. Quoted in Olssen, *Red Feds*, 137.
8. Ibid.
9. *DNZB*, vol. 3.
10. Olssen, *Red Feds*, 154–55; Hill, *Iron Hand*, chapter 19.
11. Quoted in ibid., chapter 20.
12. Ibid., chapter 19; Olssen, *Red Feds*,

chapter 12; *DNZB*, vol. 3: F. G. Evans.
13. Harry Holland, *The Tragic Story of the Waihi Strike*, 1913, 106, 193.
14. McLean, *Southern Octopus*, 120–4.
15. Quoted in Olssen, *Red Feds*, 181.
16. Quoted in Hill, *Iron Hand*, chapter 20.
17. Jim McAloon, 'Working Class Politics in Christchurch 1905–1914', MA thesis, University of Canterbury, 1986, 240 (photograph).
18. Quoted in Christopher Pugsley, *Gallipoli: The New Zealand Story*, 1984, 44.
19. Olssen, *Red Feds*, 193.
20. Howe, *Tregear*, 193.
21. Graeme Dunstall, *A Policeman's Paradise?: Policing a Stable Society 1918–1945*, 1999, 50.
22. Hill, *Iron Hand*, chapter 20; Olssen, *Red Feds*, chapter 14.
23. Pat Lawlor, *Confessions of a Journalist*, 1935, 20.
24. Hill, *Iron Hand*, chapter 20.
25. Olssen, *Red Feds*, 184.
26. Atkinson, 'Auckland Seamen'; Olssen, 'The Seamen's Union and Industrial Militancy', *NZJH*, 19 (1985), 14–37; Bollinger, *Against the Wind*.
27. Walter Carruthers, letter 1917, in Jock Phillips et al. (eds), *The Great Adventure: New Zealand Soldiers Describe the First World War*, 1988, 275. Also see Baker, *King and Country Call*, 107–9 (This section draws heavily on Baker's book.)
28. Howe, *Tregear*, 196.
29. W. S. Austin, 'The Senussi Campaign', in H. T. B. Drew, *The War Effort of New Zealand*, 1923.
30. See, e.g., John Terraine, *The Smoke and the Fire: Myths and Anti-myths of War, 1861–1945*, London, 1980.
31. This view features in the diaries and letters of a great many soldiers. See, e.g., Nicholas Boyack, *Behind the Lines: The Lives of New Zealand Soldiers in the First World War*, 1989; Phillips et al., *Great Adventure*; Sinclair, *Destiny Apart*, chapter 11. For officers' views, see C. Pugsley, *On the Fringe of Hell: New Zealanders and Military Discipline in World War One*, 1991, 191, 253; A. E. Byrne, *Official History of the Otago Regiment, NZEF, in the Great War*, 1921, 226–27.
32. Wira Gardiner, *Te Mura o Te Ahi: The Story of the Maori Battalion*, 1992, 19; Pugsley, *Gallipoli* and *Fringe of Hell*.

33. See, e.g., Alan Moorehead, *Gallipoli*, London, 1956, 242.

34. Pugsley, *Fringe of Hell*, 190–91, 253.

35. See, e.g., Byrne, *Otago Regiment*, 96–108.

36. Ibid., 93.

37. See J. Belich, 'War', in Colin Davis & Peter Lineham, (eds), *The Future of the Past: Themes in New Zealand History*, 1991.

38. N. M. Ingram, *Anzac Diary: A Nonentity in Khaki*, 1987, 65.

39. J. L. Sleeman, 'The Supply of Reinforcements During the War', in Drew, *NZ War Effort*, 11; *HS*, 51. The figure sometimes given, 200,000, is incorrect.

40. Fiona J. Hall, '"The Greater Game": Sport and Society in Christchurch during the First World War, 1914–18', MA thesis, University of Canterbury, 1989, 18.

41. Baker, *King and Country Call*, 51 and passim.

42. Ibid; Sinclair, *Destiny Apart*, chapter 15.

43. Baker, *King and Country Call*, 30.

44. Pugsley, *Gallipoli*, 34; Baker, *King and Country Call*, 21. Also see Hall, 'Greater Game'.

45. Baker, *King and Country Call*, 242.

46. Ibid., 58–63.

47. Pugsley, *Fringe of Hell*, 153.

48. Baker, *King and Country Call*, 202–09 and passim; Hill, *Iron Hand*, chapter 23; Pugsley, *Fringe of Hell*, 153.

49. Quoted in Baker, *King and Country Call*, 66.

50. Ibid., 115, 113.

51. Ibid. On marriage rates, also see *HS*, 70.

52. Pugsley, *Fringe of Hell*, 217.

53. Jane Tolerton, *Ettie: A Life of Ettie Rout*, 1992, 151; Boyack, *Behind the Lines*, 131–46; Pugsley, *Fringe of Hell*, 156–65.

54. Tolerton, *Rout*, 150–55.

55. Pugsley, *Fringe of Hell*, 161.

56. William Taylor, *The Twilight Hour*, 1978, 24.

57. Pugsley, *Fringe of Hell*, 161.

58. Belich, 'War'.

59. Ingram, *Anzac Diary*, passim; Cecil Malthus, *Anzac: A Retrospect*, 1965, 69; Taylor, *Twilight Hour*, 70; Baker, *King and Country*, 36.

60. Pugsley, *Fringe of Hell*, 348 (graph).

61. Bernard Freyberg, quoted in Paul Freyberg, *Bernard Freyberg, VC: Soldier of Two Nations*, 1991, 136.

62. Archibald Baxter, *We Will Not Cease*, 1980 edn.

63. Taylor, *Twilight Hour*, 67, 93–94; Pugsley, *Fringe of Hell*, 271–72.

64. Robin Hyde, '"Starkie": Outlaw of the NZEF', 1935, reprinted in Gillian Boddy & Jacqueline Mathews (eds), *Disputed Ground: Robin Hyde, Journalist*, 1991, 294–98.

65. Boyack, *Behind the Lines*, 152–58.

66. Pugsley, *Fringe of Hell*, 383–92; Boyack, *Behind the Lines*, 159–63; Cedric Mentiplay, *A Fighting Quality: New Zealanders at War*, 1979, 31.

67. Quoted in J. Cowan, *The Maoris in the Great War*, 1926, 157; Pugsley, *Fringe of Hell*, 289–90.

68. Alec Hutton, in Phillips et al., *The Great Adventure*, 252.

69. Malthus, *Anzac*, 99.

70. Cited in Pugsley, *Gallipoli*, 68, 75.

71. Boyack, *Behind the Lines*, 17 and passim. Also see Phillips, *A Man's Country?*, 190–91.

72. Boyack, *Behind the Lines*, 163–67; Pugsley, *Fringe of Hell*, 286–88.

73. Ian McGibbon, *The Pathway to Gallipoli: Defending New Zealand, 1840–1915*, 1991, 250.

74. Ibid., 255.

75. Boyack, *Behind the Lines*, chapter 6; Pugsley, *Fringe of Hell*, 296–98 and passim.

76. Pugsley, *Fringe of Hell*, 227.

77. Sleeman, 'The Supply of Reinforcements'; Pugsley, *Fringe of Hell*, 235; Baker, *King and Country Call*, e.g., 135, 229.

78. Pugsley, *Fringe of Hell*, 236.

79. McGibbon, *Pathway to Gallipoli*, 250–53.

80. Michael J. Field, *Mau: Samoa's Struggle for Freedom*, 1991, 14. Also see S. J. Smith, 'The Seizure and Occupation of Samoa', in Drew, *The War Effort*.

81. McGibbon, *Pathway to Gallipoli*, 251.

82. Evans, *Agricultural Production*, 107.

83. McGibbon, *Pathway to Gallipoli*, chapter 15.

84. Quoted in ibid., 226.

85. Captain Hall-Thompson, 'The Work of the Philomel', in Drew, *NZ War Effort*.

86. *OYB*, 1990, 666; McGibbon, *Pathway to Gallipoli*, 257.

87. Baker, *King and Country Call*, 43.

88. Bassett, *Ward*, 232.

89. Baker, *King and Country Call*, 138.

90. Ibid., 229.

91. Sleeman, 'The Supply of Reinforcements'.

92. Baker, *King and Country Call*, 135.
93. Peter Lineham, 'The Nature and Meaning of Protestantism in New Zealand Culture', *Turnbull Library Record*, 26/1 (1993), 69; Ashley Gould, 'Soldier Settlement in New Zealand After World War I: A Reappraisal', in J. Smart & T. Woods (eds), *An Anzac Muster*, Melbourne, 1992, 128.
94. Geoffrey Rice, *Black November: The 1918 Influenza Epidemic in New Zealand*, 1988, 2 and passim.
95. See Peter O'Connor, 'Sectarian Conflict in New Zealand, 1911–1920', *Political Science*, 19/1 (1967); Rory Sweetman, *Bishop in the Dock: The Sedition Trial of James Liston*, 1997, 'New Zealand Catholicism and the Irish Issue 1914–1922', in W. J. Sheils & Diana Wood (eds), *The Churches, Ireland and the Irish*, Oxford, 1989; *DNZB*, vol. 3: Elliott, Henry Cleary, James Kelly. For an example of sectarian rhetoric, see J. Dickson, *Shall Ritualism and Romanism Capture New Zealand? Their Ramifications in Protestant Churches*, 1912.
96. Quoted in O'Connor, 'Sectarian Conflict', 10.
97. See Sweetman, 'New Zealand Catholicism and the Irish Issue'.
98. See Patrick O'Farrell, *Vanished Kingdoms: Irish in Australia and New Zealand*, Sydney, 1990.
99. Quoted in O'Connor, 'Sectarian Conflict', 8–9.
100. W. J. Gardner, 'W. F. Massey in Power', *Political Science*, 13/2 (1961), 26.
101. Sweetman, *Bishop in the Dock*, 112.
102. Maureen Sharpe, 'Anzac Day in New Zealand 1916–39', *NZJH*, 15/2 (1981), 97. Also see Orsman (ed.), *Dictionary of New Zealand English*, 11–13.
103. R. M. Burdon, *The New Dominion: A Social and Political History of New Zealand, 1918–1939*, 1965, 18.
104. *ENZ*, vol. 3, 67.
105. Chris Maclean & Jock Phillips, *The Sorrow and the Pride: New Zealand War Memorials*, 1990.
106. See, e.g., Allan Davidson & Peter Lineham, *Transplanted Christianity: Documents Illustrating Aspects of New Zealand Church History*, 1989, 249, 295, 298.
107. Sharpe, 'Anzac Day', 102.
108. Alistair Thomson, 'The Anzac Legend: Exploring Myth and Memory in Australia', in Raphael Samuel & Paul Thompson (eds), *The Myths We Live By*, London, 1990, 73. Also see K. S. Inglis, 'Anzac and the Australian Military Tradition' in *Revue Internationale d'Histoire Militaire*, 72 (1990), 1–18.
109. Maclean & Phillips, *Sorrow and Pride*, 104.
110. *DNZB*, vol. 2: Massey; Sweetman, *Bishop in the Dock*, 119.
111. R. Openshaw, 'Imperialism, Patriotism, and Kiwi Primary Schooling Between the Wars', in J. A. Mangan (ed.), *Benefits Bestowed? Education and British Imperialism*, Manchester, 1988, 114.
112. *Our Nation's Story: A Course of British History*, [c. 1925].

Part 2: Introduction

1. Quoted in Stevan Eldred-Grigg, *New Zealand Working People, 1890–1990*, 1990, 71.
2. See Leon Poliakov, *The Aryan Myth: A History of Racist and Nationalist Ideas in Europe*, London, 1971.
3. *OYB*, 1990, 666.
4. *HS*, 336; *OYB*, 1893, 426.
5. Bassett, *The State in New Zealand*, 147 and passim.

Chapter 4: Social Harmony: The Touch of Class

1. Stevan Eldred-Grigg, 'Whatever happened to the gentry? The large landowners of Ashburton county, 1890–6', *NZJH*, 11 (1977) and *Southern Gentry*.
2. *HS*, 24; J. D. Gould, 'The Twilight of the Estates, 1891 to 1910', *AEHR*, 10 (1970), 11.
3. Ibid., 11.
4. Ibid., 12.
5. J. Belich, 'The Effects and Significance of the Lands for Settlement Acts on the Large Landowners: Some Suggestions Towards an Interpretation', research essay, Victoria University of Wellington, 1977.
6. Quoted in E. Yvonne Spiers, 'Preston Runholding in the Maniototo and the Mackenzie, 1858–1917', MA thesis, University of Otago, 1987, 101. Also see

Herbert Guthrie-Smith, *Tutira: The Story of a New Zealand Sheep Station*, Edinburgh and London, 1921, 386–87.

7. *OYB*, 1893, 333.
8. McLean, *The Southern Octopus*, 155, 169.
9. Bassett, *Ward*.
10. Belich, 'Lands for Settlement Acts', 25–26.
11. On the rise of white-collar work see, Paul Meuli, 'Occupational Change and Bourgeois Proliferation: a Study of New Middle-Class Experience in New Zealand, 1896–1926', MA thesis, University of Otago, 1977.
12. See *Making Peoples*, 406.
13. J. H. Murdoch, *The High Schools of New Zealand: A Critical Survey*, 1943, 4.
14. Roy Shuker, *The One Best System? a Revisionist History of State Schooling in New Zealand*, 1987, 53; Murdoch, *High Schools*, 24.
15. Shuker, *One Best System?*, 54.
16. On schooling, see, apart from the works cited above, Roger Openshaw and David McKenzie (eds), *Reinterpreting the Educational Past: Essays in the History of New Zealand Education*, 1987; David McKenzie et al., *Scholars or Dollars? Selected Historical Case Studies of Opportunity Costs in New Zealand Education*, 1996; H. Roth, *George Hogben*, 1952; *HS*, 112–13; *DNZB* articles on school principals.
17. Sandra Coney, *Standing in the Sunshine: A History of New Zealand Women Since They Won the Vote*, 1993, 225.
18. *HS*, 132–37. Also see Melanie Nolan, '"Politics Swept under a Domestic Carpet"? Fracturing Domesticity and the Male Breadwinner Wage: Women's Economic Citizenship, 1920s–1940s', *NZJH*, 27 (1993), 206 n. 40.
19. Peter Hodge, 'The Army of Opportunity? Social and Military Backgrounds of the NZEF Officers in the Great War, 1914–1918', Research essay, Victoria University of Wellington, 1994, 26; Olssen, *History of Otago*, 154.
20. Roberta Nicholls, 'Elite Society', in David Hamer and Roberta Nicholls (eds), *The Making of Wellington, 1800–1914*, 1990, 225.
21. *AJHR*, 1911, B-17A.
22. M. D. N. Campbell, 'The Evolution of Hawkes Bay Landed Society 1850–1914', PhD thesis, Victoria University of Wellington, 1972; Spier, 'Preston Runholding'; *AJHR*, 1905, B-24C.
23. Elvin Hatch, *Respectable Lives: Social Standing in Rural New Zealand*, Berkeley, 1992.
24. Stephen Constantine, 'Immigration and the Making of New Zealand, 1918–1939' in Constantine (ed.), *Emigrants and Empire*, Manchester, 1990.
25. Fiona J. Hall, '"The Greater Game"', esp. 255–58.
26. Quoted in Margaret Tennant, *Paupers and Providers: Charitable Aid in New Zealand*, 1989, 148.
27. Hatch, *Respectable Lives*, 164.
28. *HS*, 168.
29. Allan Bell and J. Holmes, *New Zealand Ways of Speaking English*, 1990, 27.
30. *DNZB*, vol. 1.
31. Roth, *Trade Unions*, 3.
32. My analysis of the importance of craft draws heavily on Erik Olssen's *Building the New World: Work, Politics and Society in Caversham, 1880s–1920s*, 1995.
33. James Watson, 'An Independent Working Class?' in John E. Martin and Kerry Taylor (eds), *Culture and the Labour Movement*, 1991.
34. Bollinger, *Against the Wind*, chapter 4; Atkinson 'Auckland Seamen', 33–38.
35. Olssen, 'Social Class in Nineteenth-Century New Zealand', in Pitt (ed.), *Social Class in New Zealand*, 1977, 37; C. Campbell, 'The "Working Class" and the Liberal Party in 1890', *NZJH*, 9 (1975), 45; Roth, *Trade Unions*, 10.
36. Holt, *Compulsory Arbitration*, 21.
37. Quoted in Olssen, *Caversham*, 177.
38. McLean, *The Southern Octopus*, esp. chapters 7–9.
39. Ibid. and Bollinger, *Against the Wind*, chapter 4.
40. Quoted in Roth, *Trade Unions*, 15.
41. Hamer, *NZ Liberals*.
42. Bert Roth, 'Labour Day in New Zealand' in John Martin and Kerry Taylor (eds), *Culture and the Labour Movement: Essays in New Zealand Labour History*, 1991.
43. Olssen, *Red Feds*, 41–44.
44. Ibid., 200, 39.
45. *HS*, 57.
46. Olssen, *Caversham*, 114.
47. Conrad Bollinger, *Grog's Own Country: History of Liquor Licensing in New Zealand*, 1959, 45.
48. Boyd, *Hastings*, 248.
49. Calculated from *HS*, 167–68.

50. Campbell, 'The "Working Class" and the Liberal Party', 43.
51. For figures from 1891, see *HS*, 144 and *OYB*, 1990, 363. The rise 1886–1891 is assumed from the increase in farm holdings.
52. Calculated from Thorns and Sedgwick, *Historical Statistics*, 62. Also see Meuli, 'Occupational Change and Bourgeois Proliferation'.
53. Quoted in Ian McLaren, 'The Politics of Secondary Education in Victorian New Zealand', in Openshaw and McKenzie, *Reinterpreting the Educational Past*, 68. Also see *DNZB*, vol. 1.
54. David McKenzie, 'The Growth of School Credentialling in New Zealand 1878–1900', in ibid. Also see Howard Lee, 'The Junior Civil Service Examination Reconsidered . . . ', in Openshaw and McKenzie, *Reinterpreting the Educational Past*; *HS*, 112–13; Campbell, 'The "Working Class" and the Liberal Party'; J. L. Ewing, *Development of the New Zealand Primary School Curriculum, 1877–1970*, 1970.
55. Olssen, *History of Otago*, 105; also see 110 and *Caversham*. For parallel developments in Australia see Raymond Markey, 'Race and Organized Labor in Australia, 1850–1901', *The Historian*, 58 (1996).
56. In addition to the works cited below, see Coney, *Standing in the Sunshine*, and Melanie Nolan, *Breadwinning: New Zealand Women and the State*, 2000.
57. Calculated from *HS*, 132–37 and Thorns and Sedgwick, *Historical Statistics*, 79.
58. Olssen, *Caversham*, 76.
59. L. C. Duncan, 'A "New Song of the Shirt"?: A History of Women in the Clothing Industry in Auckland', 1890–1939', MA thesis, University of Auckland, 1989, 31.
60. Shannon Brown, 'Female Office Workers in Auckland 1891–1936', MA thesis, University of Auckland, 1993, 24.
61. *HS*, 131–33.
62. Olssen, *Caversham*, 76.
63. Olssen, *Red Feds*, 97; Holt, *Compulsory Arbitration*, 127.
64. Olssen, *Caversham*, 52–53.
65. Judi Boyd and Erik Olssen, 'The Skilled Workers; Journeymen and Masters in Caversham, 1880–1914', *NZJH*, 22 (1988), 118–34; Olssen, *History of Otago*, 103–113.
66. Eldred-Grigg, *New Zealand Working People*, 32, 55–56.
67. See Atkinson, 'Auckland Seamen', esp. 11–24, 34–45; Olssen, *Red Feds*, passim.
68. *HS*, 147; Olssen, *Red Feds*, 217.
69. Quoted in ibid., 121.
70. *HS*, 147.
71. Miles Fairburn in 'Why did the New Zealand Labour Party Fail to Win Office Until 1935?', *Politicial Science*, 37 (1985).
72. See Bruce Brown, *The Rise of New Zealand Labour: A History of the Labour Party of New Zealand*, 1962; Barry Gustafson, *Labour's Path to Political Independence: The Origin and Establishment of the New Zealand Labour Party, 1900–1919*, 1980; Erik Olssen, 'The Origins of the Labour Party: A Reconsideration', *NZJH*, 21 (1987).
73. Jack Vowles, 'From Syndicalism to Guild Socialism: Some Neglected Aspects of the Ideology of the Labour Movement' in John Martin and Kerry Taylor (eds), *Culture and the Labour Movement: Essays in New Zealand Labour History*, 1991.
74. R. C. J. Stone, 'The Unions and the Arbitration System, 1900–1937' in Chapman and Sinclair (eds), *Studies of a Small Democracy*, 212.
75. Stephen Robertson, 'The Link that Binds the Movement: The Story of the New Zealand Worker and the New Zealand Labour Movement, 1916–1935', research essay, Victoria University of Wellington, 1995.
76. Arnold Pickmere, *In Thy Toil Rejoice: The Story of J. J. Patterson, Taranaki Pioneer*, 1990. The next four paragraphs draw heavily on this book.
77. Malcom McKinnon (ed.), *New Zealand Historical Atlas*, 1997, 61.
78. Hamer, *NZ Liberals*, chapters 4–5.
79. Hatch, *Respectable Lives*, esp. 34 and 58.
80. *ENZ*, vol. 1, 17.
81. Hatch, *Respectable Lives*, 11.
82. Norah Keating and Heather Little, *Generations in Farm Families: Transfer of the Family Farm in New Zealand*, 1991, 45.
83. Tom Brooking, '"Larkrise to Littledene": The Making of Rural New Zealand Society, 1880s–1939', unpublished paper kindly provided by the author, 42.
84. Ibid., 39.
85. *HS*, 167.

86. Keating and Little, *Generations in Farm Families*, 1.
87. Ashley Gould, 'Soldier Settlement in New Zealand after World War I: A Reappraisal' in J. Smart and T. Woods (eds), *An Anzac Muster*, Melbourne, 1992.
88. Martin, *Forgotten Workers*.
89. Boyd, *Hastings*, 135–36.
90. Reeves, *State Experiments*, vol. 1, 361.
91. E. J. Riches, quoted in B. D. Graham, 'The Country Party Idea in New Zealand Politics 1901–1935' in Willis and Airey (eds), *Studies of a Small Democracy*, 197–98.
92. John Banks, interview with the author, 1990.
93. See *Making Peoples*, chapter 14.
94. On Massey see W. J. Gardner, 'The Rise of W. F. Massey, 1891–1912', and 'W. F. Massey in Power, 1912–1925', both *Political Science*, 13 (1961), and *DNZB*, vol. 2.
95. Massey's twofold strategy was identified by Miles Fairburn in 'Why did the New Zeland Labour Party Fail?' and 'The Farmers Take Over' in Keith Sinclair (ed.), *The Oxford Illustrated History New Zealand*, 1990. The housing flank of the strategy was earlier identified by Anthony Ward, 'Aspects of New Zealand Housing 1920–1930', MA thesis, Victoria University of Wellington, 1977.
96. Thorns and Sedgwick, *Historical Statistics*, 111.
97. *HS*, 113.
98. Shuker, *One Best System?*, 54, 61.
99. Murdoch, *High Schools of NZ*, 59–60.
100. M. F. Lloyd Prichard, *An Economic History of New Zealand to 1939*, 1970, 317. Fairburn, 'Why did the NZ Labour Party Fail?', 121; Ward, 'Aspects of New Zealand Housing'.
101. Fairburn, 'The Farmers Take Over'.
102. Thorns and Sedgwick, *Historical Statistics*, 148.
103. Ibid., 79.

Chapter 5: Moral Harmony: A New Crusade

1. Shelley Griffiths, 'Feminism and the Ideology of Motherhood in New Zealand, 1896–1930', MA thesis, University of Otago, 1984, 48–49.
2. Hill, *Iron Hand*, chapter 9.
3. N. J. Elliot, 'Anzac, Hollywood and Home: Cinemas and Film-Going in Auckland, 1909–1939', MA thesis, University of Auckland, 1989, 126–30, 90; Richard S. Joblin, 'The Breath of Scandal: *New Zealand Truth* and Interwar Society, 1918–39', MA thesis, University of Canterbury, 1990, 136–37.
4. Hill, *Iron Hand*, chapters 1, 5, 13.
5. Quoted in Coney, *Standing in the Sunshine*, 147.
6. Sutton-Smith, *History of Children's Play*, 153–54; John Marshall, *Memoirs*, vol. 1, 1983, 219.
7. Quoted in Griffiths, 'Ideology of Motherhood', 45–6.
8. Peter Luke, 'Suicide in Auckland, 1848–1939', MA thesis, University of Auckland, 1982, 169–71.
9. Stevan Eldred-Grigg, *Pleasures of the Flesh: Sex and Drugs in Colonial New Zealand, 1840–1915*, 1984, 165.
10. Jean Marie O'Donnell, 'Female Complaints: Women's Health in Dunedin, 1885–1910', MA thesis, University of Otago, 1991, 120.
11. Barbara Brookes, 'Women and Madness: A Case Study of the Seacliff Asylum,' in Brookes et al. (eds), *Women in History*, vol. 2, 1992, 141.
12. Quoted in Michael Belgrave, '"Medical Men" and "Lady Doctors": The Making of a New Zealand Profession, 1867–1941', PhD thesis, Victoria University of Wellington, 1985, 304.
13. See ibid., 301–05.
14. Ibid., 304–05.
15. Hill, *Iron Hand*, chapter 7.
16. Quoted in Griffiths, 'Ideology of Motherhood', 147, 132–35.
17. Eldred-Grigg, *Pleasures of the Flesh*, 188–89.
18. Hill, *Iron Hand*, chapters 1–8, 13.
19. Barbara Brookes, 'A Weakness for Strong Subjects: The Women's Movement and Sexuality', *NZJH*, 27 (1993), 146.
20. Hill, *Iron Hand*, chapter 1.
21. Belgrave, '"Medical Men"', 187–88.
22. Quoted in Eldred-Grigg, *Pleasures of the Flesh*, 125.
23. 'Report of the Committee of Inquiry into Mental Defectives and Sexual Offenders', *AJHR*, 1925, H31-A, 28.
24. A. J. Harrop, in Reeves, *Long White Cloud*, 367.
25. Coney, *Standing in the Sunshine*, 70; Phillipa Mein Smith, *Maternity in*

Dispute: New Zealand 1920–1939, 1986; Philip Fleming, 'Eugenics in NZ', MA thesis, Massey University, 1981; W. A. Chapple, *The Fertility of the Unfit*, 1902.

26. Truby King, *The Evils of Cram*, Dunedin, 1906, 156–58.

27. Sinclair, *Destiny Apart*, 223.

28. Linda Bryder, *Not Just Weighing Babies: Plunket in Auckland 1908–1998*, 1998.

29. Erik Olssen, 'Truby King and the Plunket Society', and 'Analysis of a Prescriptive Ideology', *NZJH*, 15 (1981), 3–23.

30. Quoted in Griffiths, 'Ideology of Motherhood', 27.

31. Mein Smith, *Maternity in Dispute*, 2.

32. Hugh Jackson, *Churches and People in Australia and New Zealand*, 1987, 117. For other adherence and attendance statistics see A. K. Davidson and Peter J. Lineham, *Transplanted Christianity: Documents Illustrating Aspects of New Zealand Church History*, 1995; *HS*, 115.

33. H. C. D. Somerset, *Littledene: A New Zealand Rural Community*, 1938, 49–50.

34. Peter Lineham, 'How Institutionalised was Protestant Piety in 19th Century New Zealand?', *Journal of Religious History*, 13, (1985).

35. Davidson and Lineham, *Transplanted Christianity*, 197.

36. Brian Gilling, 'Retelling the Old, Old Story: A Study of Six Mass Evangelistic Missions in 20th Century New Zealand', PhD thesis, University of Waikato, 1990; Peter Lineham, 'Religious Fundamentalism in Auckland in the 1920s', seminar paper, 26 March 1998, University of Auckland History Department.

37. Jackson, *Churches and People*, 112.

38. *NZ's Heritage*, 100 and 93.

39. Gordon Slatter, *On the Ball: The Centennial Book of New Zealand Rugby*, 1970, 328.

40. Gil Dymock (ed.), *Good Morning New Zealand: News Stories of the Day from the 1930s*, 1990, 11, 44.

41. Andre Siegfried, *Democracy in New Zealand*, intro. by David Hamer, 1982, 322.

42. Davidson and Lineham, *Transplanted Christianity*, 215–16.

43. Ibid., 181.

44. Ibid., 242–43.

45. Jackson, *Churches and People*, 66–74. Also see Pauline O'Regan, *Aunts and Windmills*, 1991, 158–59.

46. Quoted in Christopher Van Der Krogt, 'Exercising the Utmost Vigilance: The Catholic Campaign Against Contraception in New Zealand During the 1930s', *Journal of Religious History*, Oct. 1998.

47. Sandra Coney, *Standing in the Sunshine*; *DNZB*, vol. 2; Judith Devaliant, *Kate Sheppard: A Biography*, 1992.

48. Anne Else (ed.), *Women Together: A History of Women's Organisations in New Zealand*, 1993, 571–72.

49. See, for example, Raewyn Dalziel, 'Presenting the Enfranchisement of New Zealand Women Abroad', in Caroline Daley and Melanie Nolan (eds), *Suffrage and Beyond: International Feminist Perspectives*, 1994.

50. Patricia Grimshaw, *Women's Suffrage in New Zealand*, 1987.

51. *DNZB*, vol. 2.

52. *OYB*, 1893, 149–50; *HS*, 50.

53. D. McKenzie et al., *Scholars or Dollars?*, 68.

54. Grimshaw, *Women's Suffrage*, 3; *OYB*, 1893, 149–50; Coney, *Standing in the Sunshine*, 193; W. J. Gardner, *Colonial Cap and Gown: Studies in the Mid-Victorian Universities of Australasia*, 1979.

55. Sutton-Smith, *History of Children's Play*, 164–66.

56. Ibid.

57. Luke, 'Suicide in Auckland', 69–80.

58. Dymock, *Good Morning NZ*, 21.

59. *HS*, 414–15.

60. Jennifer Carlyon, 'Friendly Societies 1842–1938: The Benefits of Membership', *NZJH*, 32 (1998), 130–31.

61. David Thompson, 'Taking the Long View on Pensions', *NZJH*, 32 (1998), 119–20.

62. Dulcie Gillespie-Needham, 'The Colonial and His Books: A Study of Reading in 19th Century New Zealand', PhD thesis, Victoria University of Wellington, 1971, 257–58.

63. Bollinger, *Grog's Own Country*; *ENZ*, vol. 2: Prohibition; J. Cocker and J. Malton Murray (eds), *Temperance and Prohibition in New Zealand*, London, 1930.

64. Davidson and Lineham (eds), *Transplanted Christianity*, 181.

65. A. R. Grigg, 'Prohibition: The Church and Labour', *NZJH*, 15 (1981), 140.

66. Auckland WCTU, 1888, quoted in Davis and Lineham, *Transplanted Christianity*, 218.
67. Richard Newman, 'New Zealand's Vote for Prohibition in 1911', *NZJH*, 9 (1975), 52–71; A. R. Grigg, 'Prohibition and Women: The Preservation of an Ideal and a Myth', *NZJH*, 17 (1983), 144–65.
68. Bollinger, *Grog's Own Country*, 48–49.
69. Olssen, *History of Otago*, 142, 144.
70. Bollinger, *Grog's Own Country*, 37.
71. Phillips, *Divorce in New Zealand*, chapter 4.
72. A. R. Grigg, 'Prohibition and Women'.
73. Miles Fairburn, *The Ideal Society and Its Enemies*, 207–08.
74. Belgrave, '"Medical Men"', 146–47.
75. Linda Bryder, '"A Health Resort for Consumptives": Tuberculosis and Immigration to New Zealand, 1880–1914', *Medical History*, 40 (1996), 453–71.
76. Thorns and Sedgwick, *Historical Statistics*, 40.
77. Ibid., 113.
78. Derek A. Dow, *Safeguarding the Public Health: A History of the New Zealand Department of Health*, 1995, 24 and passim.
79. Geoffrey Rice, 'Public Health in Christchurch 1875–1910: Mortality and Sanitation', in Linda Bryder (ed.), *A Healthy Country: Essays on the Social History of Medicine in New Zealand*, 1991. Also see Dow, *Safeguarding the Public Health*, and 'Life in the Cities', *NZ's Heritage*, 67.
80. *HS*, 97.
81. Mein Smith, *Maternity in Dispute*, 1.
82. Coney, *Standing in the Sunshine*, 60–61; Mein Smith, *Maternity in Dispute*, 53.
83. Quoted in O'Donnell, 'Female Complaints', 129.
84. Linda Bryder, 'If Preventable, Why Not Prevented? The New Zealand Response to Tuberculosis, 1901–40', in Bryder, *A Healthy Country*. Also see Dow, *Safeguarding the Public Health*, passim, and F. S. Mclean, *Challenge for Health: A History of Public Health in New Zealand*, 1964, chapter 16.
85. Margaret Tennant, 'Missionaries of Health: The School Medical Service During the Inter-War Period', in Bryder, *A Healthy Country*. Also see Bronwyn Dalley, *Family Matters: Child Welfare in Twentieth-Century New Zealand*, 1998.
86. Olssen, *Caversham*, 45, 253.
87. See Weintraud Ernst, 'The Social History of Psychiatry in 19th-Century New Zealand' in Bryder, *A Healthy Country*; Bronwyn Labrum, 'Looking Beyond the Asylum: Gender and the Process of Committal in Auckland, 1870–1910', *NZJH*, 26 (1992), 125–44; *OYB*, 1990, 247; *HS*, 98.
88. Margaret McClure, *A Civilised Community: A History of Social Security in New Zealand, 1898–1998*, 1998, 34.
89. *DNZB*, vol. 3.
90. Tennant, *Paupers and Providers*, 158.
91. Luke, 'Suicide in Auckland', 166, 43–56.
92. Tennant, *Paupers and Providers*, 149.
93. Tolerton, *Rout*.
94. Somerset, *Littledene*, 44–46.
95. Joblin, 'The Breath of Scandal', 20, 112. Unless otherwise specified, all quotations in the following four paragraphs are from *Truth*, quoted in Joblin.
96. Ibid., 255.
97. Grant, *On A Roll*, 83, 126.
98. Gillespie-Needham, 'The Colonial and His Books', 414 and passim.
99. Griffiths, 'Ideology of Motherhood', 33.
100. Helen Smyth, *Rocking the Cradle: Contraception, Sex, and Politics in New Zealand*, 2000, 11.
101. Megan Hutching, '"Mothers of the World": Women, Peace and Arbitration in Early Twentieth-Century New Zealand', *NZJH*, 27 (1993), 173–85.
102. Calculated from Griffiths, 'Ideology of Motherhood', 311.
103. Ian Pool and F. Tiong, 'Sub-National Differentials in the Pakeha Fertility Decline: 1876–1901', *New Zealand Population Review*, 17 (1991), 46–64. Also see *OYB*, 1990, 139; *HS*, 64–67.
104. *OYB*, 1893, 73.
105. James Gibson, cited in Pool and Tiong 'Pakeha Fertility Decline', 46. Also see B. J. Kirkwood, 'Population and Social Policy' in R. J. Warwick Neville and C. J. O'Neill (eds), *The Population of New Zealand*, 1979.
106. Wally Seccombe, 'Starting to Stop: Fertility Decline in Britain', *Past and Present*, 126 (1990), 151–88.
107. Pool and Tiong, 'Pakeha Fertility Decline'; Griffiths, 'Ideology of Motherhood', 213.
108. *OYB*, 1990, 174, 138.

109. Griffiths, 'Ideology of Motherhood', 311.
110. Department of Statistics, *Trends and Patterns in New Zealand Fertility, 1912–83*, 1986, 15.
111. Seccombe, 'Starting to Stop'.
112. Griffiths, 'Ideology of Motherhood', 219–24.
113. F. M. L. Thompson, *The Rise of Respectable Society: A Social History of Victorian Britain*, London, 1988, 61.
114. Jackson, *Churches and People*, 145.
115. Renee Levesque, 'Prescribers and Rebels: Attitudes to European Women's Sexuality in New Zealand, 1860–1916', in Barbara Brookes et al., *Women in History: Essays on European Women in New Zealand*, 1986, 7. Also see Coney, *Standing in the Sunshine*, 73–75; Griffiths 'Ideology of Motherhood', 224–30.
116. Levesque, 'Prescribers and Rebels', 4.
117. Lynley Hood, *Minnie Dean: Her Life and Crimes*, 1994.
118. Joblin, 'The Breath of Scandal', 231–32.
119. Quoted in Orsman, *Dictionary of New Zealand English*: 'Baby Farming'.
120. *HS*, 65–67.
121. Jeanine Graham, 'Child Employment in New Zealand', *NZJH*, 21 (1987), 62–78.
122. Pool and Tiong, 'Pakeha Fertility Decline'.
123. Boyd, *Hastings*, 139.
124. Dalziel, 'Presenting the Enfranchisement of New Zealand Women Abroad', 51; *OYB*, 1990, 67.
125. Brown, 'Female Office Workers', 73.
126. J. H. Murdoch, *The High Schools of New Zealand: A Critical Survey*, 1943, 130–31, 78–79.
127. Brown, 'Female Office Workers'.
128. Olssen and Levesque, 'Towards a History of the European Family in New Zealand', in Penny Koopman-Boyden (ed.), *Families in New Zealand Society*, 1978, 11; Levesque, 'Prescribers and Rebels', 6–7.
129. Charlotte Macdonald (ed.), *The Vote, the Pill and the Demon Drink: A History of Feminist Writing in New Zealand, 1869–1993*, 1993, 7. Also see Roberta Nicholls, 'The Collapse of the Early National Council of Women of New Zealand, 1896–1906', *NZJH*, 27 (1993), 157–72.
130. Gardner, *Colonial Cap and Gown*, 106.
131. See Jock Phillips, *A Man's Country?*

Chapter 6: Racial Harmony (1): Merging Maori?

1. Evelyn Stokes, *A History of Tauranga*, 1980, 313.
2. See, for example, Hazel Petrie, 'The "Lazy Maori": Pakeha Representations of a Maori Work Ethic, 1890–1940', MA thesis, University of Auckland, 1998; 'Maori' in Orsman, *Dictionary of New Zealand English*.
3. For an account of the Bennett incident, see Lloyd Jones, 'Images of the Maori in the Pakeha Press: Pakeha Representations of Maori in the Popular Print Media, 1935–1965', MA thesis, University of Auckland, 1998, chapter 2.
4. *DNZB*, vol. 3, 51.
5. Andrew Armitage, *Comparing the Policy of Aboriginal Assimilation: Australia, Canada, and New Zealand*, Vancouver, 1995, 171, 195.
6. Quoted in John Forster, 'The Social Position of the Maori', in Erik Schwimmer (ed.), *The Maori People in the Nineteen-Sixties*, 1968, 104.
7. McClure, *A Civilised Community*, 18–19, 25–28; Tennant, *Paupers and Providers*, 99–100.
8. M. P. K. Sorrenson, *Integration or Identity: Cultural Interaction in New Zealand Since 1911*, 1971, 19.
9. Report of the Native Department, *AJHR*, 1920, G-9.
10. J. Cowan, *The Maoris in the Great War*, 1926; M. P. K. Sorrenson, 'Modern Maori: The Young Maori Party to Mana Motuhake', in Keith Sinclair, *The Oxford Illustrated History of New Zealand*, 1990, 331.
11. Geoffrey Rice, *Black November: The 1918 Influenza Epidemic in New Zealand*, 1988, 103.
12. Ibid., 122.
13. Ibid., 110–11.
14. Quoted in Michael King, *Whina*, 1983, 82.
15. Peter Buck, quoted in Michael King, *Te Puea*, 1977, 99.
16. See *Making Peoples*, chapter 11.
17. Judith Binney et al., *Mihaia: The Prophet Rua Kenana and his Community of Maungapohatu*, 1979; Peter Webster, *Rua and the Maori Millennium*, 1979.
18. On the King Movement, see relevant *DNZB* essays; Lindsay Cox, *Kotahitanga: The Search For Maori Political Unity*,

1993; Pei Te Hurunui Jones, 'Maori Kings' in Schwimmer, *The Maori People in the 1960s.*

19. King, *Te Puea*, 61.

20. *DNZB*, vol. 3: Mahuta.

21. King, *Te Puea*, 45–53.

22. King, *Te Puea*, 77–96.

23. Michael King, *Maori: A Photographic and Social History*, 1983, 164.

24. *HS*, 117; *DNZB*, vol. 3; J. M. Henderson, *Ratana: The Origin and Story of the Movement*, 1963, 71.

25. Ibid., 62.

26. Ralph Love, 'The Politics of Frustration: the Growth of Maori Politics in the Ratana-Labour Era', PhD thesis, Victoria University of Wellington, 1977.

27. *DNZB*, vol. 4: Parire Paikea.

28. Cox, *Kotahitanga*, 118.

29. *HS*, 117.

30. King, *Whina*, 90–91.

31. *DNZB*, vol. 4: Hirini Christy.

32. Ian Barber, 'Between Biculturalism and Assimilation: The Changing Place of Maori Culture in the Twentieth-Century New Zealand Mormon Church', *NZJH*, 29 (1995), 153, 155.

33. Henderson, *Ratana*; Cox, *Kotahitanga*, 118.

34. King, *Te Puea*, 120.

35. Henderson, *Ratana*, 44.

36. Kay Boese, *Tides of History: Bay of Islands County*, 1977, 124.

37. Ibid., 126. Also see Cox, *Kotahitanga*, 43, 61–78, and Keith Sinclair, *Kinds of Peace: Maori People after the Wars 1870–85*, 1991.

38. M. P. K. Sorrenson, (ed.), *Na To Hoa Aroha: From Your Dear Friend: The Correspondence between Sir Apirana Ngata and Sir Peter Buck, 1925–50*, 1986–7, vol. 1, 13 (hereafter *Buck–Ngata Letters*).

39. Calculated from Tom Brooking, '"Busting up" the Greatest Estate of All: Liberal Maori Land Policy, 1891–1911', *NZJH*, 26 (1992), no. 1, 78–98.

40. For biographical details on Carroll, Pomare, and Ngata see relevant essays in *DNZB* and *ENZ*; *Buck–Ngata Letters*; J. F. Cody, *Man of Two Worlds: Sir Maui Pomare*, 1953; Eric Ramsden, *Sir Apirana Ngata and Maori Culture*, 1948.

41. *Buck–Ngata Letters*, vol. 1, 144.

42. G. V. Butterworth, *End of An Era: The Department of Maori Affairs 1840–1989*, 1989, 16.

43. *Buck–Ngata Letters*, vol. 2, 17.

44. G. V. Butterworth, 'A Rural Maori Renaissance? Maori Society and Politics 1920 to 1951', *JPS*, 81 (1972), 160–194.

45. King, *Whina*, 122.

46. *Buck–Ngata Letters*, vol. 3, 90 and passim. Also see Ramsden, *Ngata and Maori Culture*, 42.

47. *DNZB*, vol. 4.

48. *Buck–Ngata Letters*, vol. 3, 260 and passim.

49. Ibid., vol. 1, 160.

50. *HS*, 112–113.

51. Quoted in J. M. Barrington and T. M. Beaglehole, *Maori Schools in a Changing Society*, 1974, 137.

52. Ibid., 255, 258.

53. On the native schools see *DNZB* biographies of Pope and W. W. Bird; Barrington and Beaglehole, *Maori Schools*; and Judith Simon (ed.), *Nga Kura Maori: The Native Schools System, 1867–1969*, 1998; 'Maori language and the Pakeha Education system – a historical outline', unpublished typescript, 1982.

54. Letter to *Bay of Plenty Times*, 1882, quoted in Stafford, *Te Arawa*, 512.

55. Quoted in Hazel Petrie, 'The "Lazy Maori"', 115.

56. Froude, *Oceana*, 232–238.

57. Rangitiaria Dennan, *Guide Rangi of Rotorua*, 1968, 15–20. Also see Stafford, *Te Arawa*, 505–12.

58. Adela Stewart, *My Simple Life in New Zealand*, 70.

59. *DNZB*, vol. 3; Dennan, *Guide Rangi*, 20–21.

60. See Philippa Galbraith, 'Colonials in Wonderland: The Colonial Construction of Rotorua as a Fantasy Space', MA thesis, University of Auckland, 1992, and John Taylor, *Consuming Identity: Modernity and Tourism in New Zealand*, 1998.

61. *Buck–Ngata Letters*, vol. 1, 184n.

62. Ibid., vol. 1, 17, 34 (editor's intro.).

63. Ibid., vol. 1, 182–183.

64. W. K. Jackson and G. A. Wood, 'The New Zealand Parliament and Maori Representation', *Historical Studies*, 11 (1964), 383–96.

65. This quotation and all those in the next paragraph are from Tregear, *The Aryan Maori*, 1885.

66. A. S. Atkinson, 'The Aryo-Semitic Maori', *TPNZI*, 19 (1886), 552–76.

67. See M. P. K. Sorrenson, *Manifest Duty: The Polynesian Society over One Hundred Years*, 1992.
68. Howe, *Tregear*, 64.
69. Sinclair, *A Destiny Apart*, 197–99.
70. Max Herz, *New Zealand: The Country and the People*, London, (trans. from German), 1912.
71. *Auckland Star*, 30 June 1927, quoted in Petrie 'The "Lazy Maori"'.
72. Pearl and Ernest Beaglehole, 'The Maori' in *Making New Zealand: Pictorial Surveys of a Century*, 1940.
73. Jones, 'Images of the Maori', 103.
74. G. L. Pearce, *The Story of the Maori People*, 1968, 11.
75. J. Condliffe and W. Airey, *Short History of New Zealand*, 1960, 9.
76. Reed, *Story of New Zealand*, 1974, 25–26.
77. Joblin, 'The Breath of Scandal', 135, 143–49.
78. E. C. Buley, *A Child's History of Anzac*, London, 1916, 164.
79. Stewart Firth and Robert Darlington, 'Racial Stereotypes in the Australian Curriculum', in J. A. Mangan (ed.), *The Imperial Curriculum: Racial Images and Education in the British Colonial Experience*, London and New York, 1993, 83.
80. Quoted in Warwick Roger, *Old Heroes: The 1956 Springbok Tour and the Lives Beyond*, 1991, 36.
81. Quoted in Harry Bioletti, *The Yanks are Coming: The American Invasion of New Zealand, 1942–1944*, 1989, 157–58.
82. Quoted in Angela Ballara, *Proud to be White? A Survey of Pakeha Prejudice in New Zealand*, 1986, 55.
83. Coney, *Standing in the Sunshine*, 281. Also see ibid., 248; Sinclair, *A Destiny Apart*, 190–94; *The Kia Ora Coo-ee*, March–December 1918 (1981 reprint); Charles A. Wilson, *Around New Zealand*, Auckland, 1925; J. M. Thomson, *The Oxford History of New Zealand Music*, 1991, e.g. 212; Leonard Bell, *Colonial Constructs: European Images of Maori, 1840–1914*, 1992.
84. Sinclair, *Destiny Apart*, 190 passim.
85. Reeves, *The Long White Cloud*, original 1898 edn, 55–57, 1924 edn, 62.
86. W. P. Smith, *The Lore of the Whare-Wananga*, 1913–15; *DNZB*, vol. 2: Te Matorohanga.
87. *Buck–Ngata Letters*, vol. 2, 78.

88. *Buck–Ngata Letters*, vol. 3, 262.
89. Peter Buck, *Vikings of the Sunrise*, Philadelphia, 1938; also *Buck–Ngata Letters*, vol. 1, 104; vol. 3, 262.
90. See James Cowan, *The Maoris in the Great War*, 1926; Wira Gardiner, *Te Mura o Te Ahi: The Story of the Maori Battalion*, 1992; J. B. Condliffe, *Te Rangi Hiroa*, 1971; Baker, *King and Country Call*, 213–21; P. S. O'Connor, 'The Recruitment of Maori Soldiers, 1914–1918', *Political Science*, 19 (1967).
91. Pomare, in Preface to Cowan, *Maoris in the Great War*, ix–x.
92. Scott, *Years of the Pooh-Bah*, 131–42.
93. *DNZB*, vol. 3: Katerine Parata.
94. 'The Maori in Rugby Football', *Official Match Programme, Australia Versus New Zealand Maoris*, Wellington, 1919. I am grateful to Paul Hamer for supplying a copy of this.
95. John Nauright, 'Sport, Manhood, and Empire: British Responses to the New Zealand Rugby Tour of 1905', *International Journal of the History of Sport*, 8 (1991), 242.
96. Slatter, *On the Ball*, 162.
97. L. M. Rogers (ed.), *The Early Journals of Henry Williams, 1826–40*, 1961, 268.
98. 'Athletics', *ENZ*, vol. 1.
99. *Dominion*, 13 June 1922.
100. *Truth*, 12 June 1930.
101. *Buck–Ngata Letters*, vol. 1, 250–51; vol. 2, 44.
102. Ibid., vol. 1, 178–80.
103. *DNZB*, vol. 2, 207.
104. *Buck–Ngata Letters*, vol. 3, 120–36.
105. James Belich, 'Myth, Race and Identity in New Zealand', *NZJH*, 31 (1997).
106. *Buck–Ngata Letters*, vol. 1, 178–80.
107. Ibid., vol. 1, 64–65.

Chapter 7: Racial Harmony (2): Unmaking the Difference

1. Donald Harman Akenson, *Half the World From Home: Perspectives on the Irish in New Zealand 1860–1950*, 1990.
2. R. Wenthold, quoted in Richard Thompson, *Race Relations in New Zealand*, 1963, 16.
3. Stuart William Greif, *The Overseas Chinese in New Zealand*, Singapore, 1974, interviews, 122–55.
4. Ernest Beaglehole, 'The Maori Now', in Erik Schwimmer, *The Maori People*

in the 1960s, 352.

5. See Malcolm D. Prentis, *The Scottish in Australia*, Melbourne 1987, 115, 153; G. L. Pearce, *The Scots of New Zealand*, 1976, 160–61.

6. *ENZ*, vol. 2, 727.

7. Atholl Anderson, *Race Against Time: The Early Maori-Pakeha Families and the Development of the Mixed Race Population in Southern New Zealand*, 1991.

8. Pearce, *Scots of New Zealand*, 151–52; Maureen Molloy, 'Friends, Neighbours and Relations: The Practice of Kinship in Waipu, New Zealand, 1857–1911', *Journal of Family History*, 14 (1989).

9. Susan Butterworth, *Chips off the Auld Rock: Shetlanders in New Zealand*, 1997.

10. Calculated from Pearce, *Scots of New Zealand*, 141–42, and *HS*, 54.

11. Pearce, *Scots of New Zealand*, 142.

12. Ibid., 149. Also see Tom Brooking, '"Tam McCanny and Kitty Clydeside": The Scots in New Zealand', in R. A. Cage (ed.), *The Scots Abroad: Labour, Capital, Enterprise*, London, 1985; Prentis, *The Scottish in Australia*.

13. Hatch, *Respectable Lives*, 135.

14. *HS*, 79.

15. Olssen, *Caversham*, 23; Keith Ovenden, *A Fighting Withdrawal: The Life of Dan Davin*, 1996, chapter 3; Anna Rogers, *A Lucky Landing: The Story of the Irish in New Zealand*, 1996, 103.

16. Hill, *Iron Hand*, chapters 2 and 9. On Irish publicans see Rogers, *Lucky Landing*, chapter 9.

17. Akenson, *Half the World From Home*, 171–72.

18. See ibid.; Jackson, *Churches and People*; O'Farrell, *Vanished Kingdoms*.

19. See, e.g., Akenson, *Half the World from Home*, 42.

20. *OYB*, 1893, 145.

21. Hill, *Iron Hand*, 138; Sean Brosnahan, 'The "Battle of the Borough" and the "Saige o Timaru": Sectarian Riot in Colonial Canterbury', *NZJH*, 28 (1994).

22. Lyndon Fraser, '"Ties that bind": Irish Catholic Testamentary Evidence from Christchuch, 1876–1915', *NZJH*, 29 (1995), 72.

23. Akenson, *Half the World From Home*, chapter 4.

24. Peter O'Connor, 'Sectarian Conflict in New Zealand, 1911–1920', *Political Science*, 19 (1967), 5.

25. Thorns and Sedgwick, *Historical Statistics*, 38; *HS*, 73–77.

26. Stephen Constantine, 'Immigration and the Making of New Zealand, 1918–39', in Constantine, *Emigrants and Empire*, 139–40.

27. Robert A. Huttenback, *Racism and Empire: White Settlers and Colored Immigrants in British Self-Governing Colonies, 1830–1910*, Ithaca, 294.

28. James N. Bade, (ed.), *The German Connection: New Zealand and German-Speaking Europe in the Nineteenth Century*, 1993, 39.

29. Marian Minson, 'Trends in German Immigration to New Zealand' in ibid.

30. *OYB*, 1960, 68.

31. Hill, *Iron Hand*, chapter 23.

32. Cabinet Paper 4, September 1950, CP (50) 905, National Archives, Wellington.

33. *Hovding: Magazine of the New Zealand-Norway Society*, 13 (1983); *ENZ*, vol. 2, 627.

34. W. D. Borrie, *Immigration to New Zealand 1854–1938*, Canberra, 1991 (orig. 1939), 129.

35. Andrew D. Trlin, *Now Respected, Once Despised: Yugoslavs in New Zealand*, 1979, 27; personal communications with Steve Jelicich.

36. R. A. Lochore, *From Europe to New Zealand: An Account of our Continental Settlers*, 1951.

37. Quoted in Trlin, *Now Respected*, 76.

38. Judith Bassett, 'Colonial Justice: The Treatment of Dalmatians in New Zealand During the First World War', *NZJH*, 33 (1999).

39. Cabinet Paper, op. cit.

40. A. D. Trlin, 'The Yugoslavs' in K. W. Thomson and A. D. Trlin (eds), *Immigrants in New Zealand*, 1970, 77–78.

41. Greif, *The Overseas Chinese in New Zealand*, 113.

42. M. Taker, 'The Asians' in Thomson and Trlin, *Immigrants in NZ*, 39.

43. Ibid., 39.

44. Michael Trotter and Beverley McCulloch, *Unearthing New Zealand*, 1989, 120–22.

45. Manying Ip, *Dragons on the Long White Cloud: The Making of Chinese New Zealanders*, 1996, 42. Also see Manying

Ip, *Home Away From Home: Life Stories of Chinese Women in New Zealand*, 1990, 181, n. 17.

46. Peter O' Connor, 'Keeping New Zealand White', *NZJH*, 2 (1968), 45.
47. Cabinet Paper, op. cit. 'Chinese Immigration', 6.
48. Quoted in Fred Turnovsky, *Turnovsky: Fifty Years in New Zealand*, 1990, 96.
49. Burdon, *King Dick*, 227.
50. Quoted in David Pearson, *A Dream Deferred: The Origins of Ethnic Conflict in New Zealand*, 1990, 93.
51. Wolfe, *Trademarks*, 61; Sutton-Smith, *Children's Play*, 85–86.
52. Marshall, *Memoirs*, vol. 1, 190.
53. Hill, *Iron Hand*, chapter 13.
54. Cabinet Paper 9, February 1951, CP (51) 137, National Archives, Wellington. On Sinophobia in general see O' Connor, 'Keeping New Zealand White'; Pearson, *Dream Deferred*; Huttenback, *Racism and Empire*; and Sean Brawley, 'No "White Policy" in New Zealand: Fact and Fiction in New Zealand's Asian Immigration Record, 1946–1978', *NZJH*, 27, (1993).
55. R. A. Lochore, *From Europe to New Zealand*; Thomson and Trlin, *Immigrants in New Zealand*, e.g. 74.
56. Tregear, *Aryan Maori*, 90.
57. Quoted in Jacqueline Leckie, 'In Defence of Race and Empire: The White New Zealand League at Pukekohe', *NZJH*, 19 (1985), 108. On Aryanism in India see Joan Leopold, 'British Applications of the Aryan Theory of Race to India, 1850–70', *English Historical Review*, 89 (1974), and 'The Aryan Theory of Race in India, 1870–1920', *Indian Economic and Social History Review*, 7 (1970).
58. Turnovsky, *Fifty Years in New Zealand*, 90–95.
59. Tregear, *Aryan Maori*, 90.
60. Wolfe, *Trademarks*, 8, 18–23.
61. See *DNZB* and W. H. McLeod, *Punjabis in New Zealand: A History of Punjabi Migration 1890–1940*, 1986, 140–41.
62. See Odeda Rosenthal, *Not Strictly Kosher: Pioneer Jews in New Zealand*, Wainscott, N.Y., 1991, 171–72.
63. Quoted in Jacqueline Leckie, '"They Sleep Standing Up", Gujaratis in New Zealand to 1945', PhD thesis, University of Otago, 1981, 602.
64. Quoted in Ip, *Dragons*, 109.
65. See Paul Spoonley, *The Politics of*

Nostalgia: Racism and the Extreme Right in New Zealand, 1982.
66. James Ng, *Windows on a Chinese Past*, vol. 2, 1995, 9.
67. *DZNB*, vol. 2.
68. *ENZ*, vol. 2, 630.
69. Cabinet Paper, op. cit.
70. Leckie, '"They Sleep Standing Up"', 41–57.
71. Trlin, *Now Respected*, 28–31.
72. I. H. Burnley, 'The Greeks', in Thomson and Trlin, *Immigrants in NZ*, 101; *ENZ*, vol. 2, 628.
73. Butterworth, *Chips off the Auld Rock*, 4.
74. Burnley, 'The Greeks', 107.
75. Trlin, *Now Respected*, 144.
76. McLeod, *Punjabis in NZ*, 74.
77. Molloy, 'Friends, Neighbours, and Relations'.
78. Burnley, 'The Greeks'.
79. Trlin, *Now Respected*, passim, and 'The Yugoslavs'.
80. McLeod, *Punjabis in NZ*.
81. Leckie, '"They Sleep Standing Up"', 302 and passim.
82. H. B. Levine, 'Making Sense of Jewish Ethnicity: Identification Patterns of New Zealanders of Mixed Parentage', *Ethnic and Racial Studies*, 6 (1993), 327.
83. McLeod, *Punjabis in NZ*, 86.
84. Greif, *Overseas Chinese*, 136–42. Also see Trlin, *Now Respected*, chapter 8; Levine, 'Making Sense of Jewish Ethnicity', 329.
85. Leckie, '"They Sleep Standing Up"', and McLeod, *Punjabis in NZ*.
86. Ibid., 118.
87. Hans-Peter Stoffel, 'The Dalmatians and their Language in New Zealand', in *Atlas of Languages of Intercultural Communication: Trends in Linguistics Documentation*, 13, 1996, and 'Dialect and Standard Language in a Migrant Situation: The Case of New Zealand Croatian', *New Zealand Slavonic Journal* (1994). Copies kindly provided by the author.
88. *HS*, 79.
89. Belich, *Making Peoples*, 448. Also see Angus Ross, *New Zealand's Aspirations in the Pacific in the Nineteenth Century*, Oxford, 1964.
90. Ron Crocombe, *Pacific Neighbours: New Zealand's Relations with Other Pacific Islands*, 1992, 115.
91. Dick Scott, *Years of the Pooh-Bah*, 77, 90–91, 206; relevant *DNZB* essays; P. H.

Carson, 'The Cook Islanders', in Thomson and Trlin, *Immigrants in NZ*.

92. See Judith Huntsman and Antony Hooper, *Tokelau: An Historical Ethnography*, 1996; Terry Chapman, *Niue: A History of the Island*, 1982.

93. M. J. Field, *Mau: Samoa's Struggle for Freedom*, 1991.

94. Mary Boyd, 'Racial Attitudes of New Zealand Officials in Western Samoa', *NZJH*, 21 (1987), 139–55; I. C. Campbell, 'New Zealand and the Mau in Samoa: Reassessing the Causes of a Colonial Protest Movement', *NZJH*, 33 (1999), 92–110.

95. See Malama Meleisea, *The Making of Modern Samoa; Traditional Authority and Colonial Administration in the History of Western Samoa*, Suva, 1987; M. J. Field, *Mau*; Hermann Hiery, 'West Samoans between Germany and New Zealand 1914–1921', in *War and Society*, 10 (1992).

96. Meleisea, *Making of Modern Samoa*, 172.

97. Field, *Mau*, 218.

98. Ibid., 92–110, 126, 200–01.

99. Field, *Mau*, 69.

100. See Hiery, 'West Samoans', 64–66.

101. See Field, *Mau*, chapter 14; Dunstall, A *Policeman's Paradise?*, 150–51.

102. *Buck–Ngata Letters*, vol. 1, 72–74.

103. On New Zealand and the Pacific Islands, apart from the sources cited above, see relevant *DNZB* and *ENZ* essays; *The Pacific Islands Yearbook*, 1994; Angus Ross (ed.), *New Zealand's Record in the Pacific Islands in the Twentieth Century*, 1969; Office For Tokelau Affairs, *Matagi Tokelau: History and Traditions of Tokelau*, 1991; Hill, *Iron Hand*, 390–94; J. W. Davidson, *Samoa mo Samoa: The Emergence of the Independent State of Western Samoa*, Melbourne, 1967; Hermann Hiery and John MacKenzie (eds), *European Impact and Pacific Influence: British and German Colonial Policy in the Pacific Islands and the Indigenous Response*, London, 1997.

Part 3: Introduction

1. Statistics from htp://www. ramhb.co.nz/artdeco/earthquake.htm; *ENZ*, vol. 1, 475; Boyd, *Hastings*, chapter 12.

2. John Mulgan, *Report on Experience*, 1967, 10.

Chapter 8: Depression and Labour

1. Robert Holland, 'The British Empire in the Great War', in Judith M. Brown and Wm. Roger Louis (eds), *The Oxford History of the British Empire*, vol. 4: *The Twentieth Century*, Oxford, 1999, 117.

2. P. J. Cain & A. G. Hopkins, *British Imperialism: Crisis and Deconstruction, 1914–1993*, London, 1993, 73.

3. D. K. Fieldhouse, 'The Metropolitan Economics of Empire', in Brown & Louis, *Oxford History of the British Empire*, vol. 4, 100–02.

4. Quoted in Angus Ross, 'New Zealand and the Commonwealth to 1939', in *The Commonwealth: Its Past, Present and Future*, New Zealand Institute of International Affairs, 1973, 7.

5. W. David McIntyre, 'Imperialism and Nationalism', in Rice (ed.), *Oxford History of New Zealand*, 345.

6. Ross, 'New Zealand and the Commonwealth', 11.

7. Fieldhouse, 'The Metropolitan Economics of Empire', 102; D. Baines, 'Recovery from the Depression in Great Britain, 1932–9', in Anne Digby et al., *New Directions in Economic and Social History*, vol. 2, London, 1992, 194, 198–99.

8. Richard Perren, 'The Retail and Wholesale Meat Trade', 50.

9. Sean Glynn and Lana Booth, *Modern Britain: An Economic and Social History*, London, 1996, 80.

10. See figures in H. Belshaw (ed.), *Agricultural Organisation in New Zealand*, Melbourne, 1936, chapters 29–30.

11. Ibid., 641.

12. *HS*, 293–94, 312–13.

13. *HS*, 156.

14. John E. Martin (ed.), *People, Politics and Power Stations: Electric Power Generation in New Zealand 1880–1990*, 1991, 124.

15. James Watson, *Links: A History of Transport and New Zealand Society*, 1996, 172; *HS*, 248–49.

16. Bill Laxon, 'The Golden Age of Shipping in the Trade Between Britain and New Zealand 1911–1940' in David Johnson and Peter Dennerly (eds), *Half A World Away*, 1998.

17. *Statistical Report on the Trade and Shipping of the Dominion of New Zealand, 1929–36*, Part 2, x, xii.

18. *HS*, 189.
19. R. M. Burdon, *The New Dominion: A Social and Political History of New Zealand Between the Wars*, 1965, 54.
20. Ross Galbreath, *DSIR: Making Science Work for New Zealand*, 1998, chapters 1 and 3.
21. *HS*, 166–68, 185.
22. Kenneth B. Cumberland and James W. Fox, *New Zealand: A Regional View*, 1964, 42.
23. *Making New Zealand*, 1940, vol. 1, no. 11, 2.
24. Galbreath, *DSIR*, 13.
25. Ibid., chapters 1 and 10; *ENZ*, vol. 3, 185. Also see J. D. Atkinson, *DSIR's First Fifty Years*, 1976.
26. See M. E. Hoare, 'The Relationship Between Government and Science in Australia and New Zealand', *Journal of the Royal Society of New Zealand*, 6 (1976), 392.
27. Galbreath, *DSIR*, 65. Also see chapters 1 and 3.
28. Nerida Jane Elliott, 'Anzac, Hollywood and Home: Cinemas and Film-Going in Auckland, 1909–1939', MA thesis, University of Auckland, 1989.
29. *HS*, 125; Elliott, 'Anzac, Hollywood and Home', 9.
30. *HS*, 261.
31. Burdon, *New Dominion*, 308–09.
32. Patrick Day, 'American Popular Culture and New Zealand Broadcasting: The Reception of Early Radio Serials', *Journal of Popular Culture*, 30 (1996), 204.
33. Peter J. Coleman, 'New Zealand Liberalism and the Origins of the American Welfare State', *Journal of American History*, 69 (1982).
34. The statistics and quotations in this paragraph are from Elliott unless otherwise cited.
35. Elliott, 'Anzac, Hollywood and Home', 88–89.
36. Day, 'American Popular Culture', 206.
37. Ibid. Also see Peter Downes and Peter Harcourt, *Voices in the Air: Radio Broadcasting in New Zealand*, 1976.
38. Zane Grey, *Tales of the Angler's Eldorado: New Zealand*, London, 1926, 25–26.
39. T. T. N. Coleridge, *Our Motoring Heritage*, 1973, 35.
40. *OYB*, 2000, 288.
41. See Downes and Harcourt, *Voices in the Air*; Ian Carter, *Gadfly: The Life and Times of James Shelley*, 1993; C. G. Scrimgeour and John A. Lee, *The Scrim–Lee Papers: C. G. Scrimgeour and John A. Lee Remember the Crisis Years, 1930–40*, 1976.
42. Scrimgeour in ibid., 63–64.
43. Quoted in Malcolm Kay, *The Inside Story of Farmers'*, 1950, 217.
44. David Grant, *Bulls, Bears, and Elephants: A History of the New Zealand Stock Exchange*, 1997, 138.
45. C. Westrate, quoted in John Macrae and Keith Sinclair, 'Unemployment in New Zealand During the Depression', *AEHR*, 15 (1975), 36; Keith Rankin, *Unemployment in New Zealand at the Peak of the Great Depression*, 1995, 28.
46. John E. Martin, 'The Removal of Compulsory Arbitration and the Depression of the 1930s', *NZJH*, 28 (1994), 124–44.
47. *Monthly Abstracts of Statistics*, 1929 and 1933; Thorns and Sedgwick, *Historical Statistics*, 138; *HS*.
48. Gordon Ell, *New Zealand Traditions and Folklore*, 1994, 92.
49. R. C. J. Stone, '"Sinister" Auckland Business Cliques, 1840–1940', *NZJH*, 21 (1987), 45.
50. W. P. Morrell, *New Zealand*, London, 1935, 190.
51. Bruce Brown, 'From Bulk Purchase to Butter Disputes: New Zealand's Trading Relations with Britain', in Robert Patman (ed.), *New Zealand and Britain: A Special Relationship in Transition*, 1997, 42.
52. Denis Trussell, *Fairburn*, 1984, 130–32.
53. Dymock, *Good Morning New Zealand*, 148.
54. Tony Simpson, *The Sugar Bag Years*, 1990, 15.
55. Barbara Brookes, 'Housewives' Depression: The Debate over Abortion and Birth-Control in the 1930s', *NZJH*, 15 (1981), 123.
56. See Sutch's biographical essay on Coates in *NZ's Heritage*, 79; J. C. Beaglehole, *New Zealand: A Short History*, London, 1936, 94, 152.
57. Hawke, *Making of New Zealand*, 131.
58. *NZ's Heritage*, 71 (Coinage); Dymock, *Good Morning New Zealand*, 94.
59. Roth, *Trade Unions*, 51.
60. Erik Olssen, 'Depression and War', in Keith Sinclair, (ed.), *The Oxford Illustrated History of New Zealand*, 1990, 215.

61. Michael Bassett, *Coates of Kaipara*, 1995, 243. The rest of this paragraph also draws on Bassett, though the conclusion differs.

62. James Watson, 'No Mean City? Christchurch's Labour City Council During the Depression, 1927–35', *NZJH*, 23 (1989), 127.

63. R. C. J. Stone, *The First 125 Years of the Practice of Russell McVeagh*, 1991, 132.

64. Graham Dunstall, *A Policeman's Paradise?*, 86–97; Watson, 'No Mean City?'.

65. Trussell, *Fairburn*, 117.

66. Bassett, *Coates*, 229.

67. Barrie MacDonald and David Thompson, 'Mortagage Relief, Farm Finance and Rural Depression in New Zealand in the 1930s', *NZJH*, 21(1987), 228–50.

68. Barry Gustafson, *His Way: a Biography of Robert Muldoon*, 2000, 27.

69. A. D. Ward, 'Aspects of New Zealand Housing During 1920–1930', MA thesis, Victoria University of Wellington, 1977, 136–38.

70. Fairburn, 'Why did the New Zealand Labour Party Fail to Win Office until 1935?', 121.

71. Bruce Brown, *The Rise of New Zealand Labour*, 1962, 185, n. 4.

72. McLure, *A Civilised Community*, 111–21.

73. Quoted in Hamish Keith, *A Lovely Day Tomorrow: New Zealand in the 1940s*, 1991, 8.

74. Francis G. Castles, *The Working Class and Welfare: Reflections on the Political Development of the Welfare State in Australia and New Zealand, 1890–1980*, 1985, 32. Also see David Thompson, *Selfish Generations? The Ageing of New Zealand's Welfare State*, 1991, which emphasises NZ welfare's universalism more than Castles.

75. Castles, *The Working Class and Welfare*, 24.

76. On import controls see Hawke, *Making of NZ*, chapter 9, and C. Westrate, *Portrait of a Modern Mixed Economy*, 1959, chapter 9.

77. Keith Sinclair, *Walter Nash*, 1976, 170; W. Rosenberg, 'Capital Imports and Growth: The Case of New Zealand: Foreign Investment in New Zealand, 1840–1958', *Economic Journal*, 71 (1961), 98–99.

78. Bassett, *Coates*, 219.

79. *HS*, 312–13.

80. Sinclair, *Nash*, 184, 186.

81. Ibid., 166. Also see Richard Davis, 'New Zealand Labour Government and the ALP, 1939–40: an Image of Independence', *Electronic Journal of Australian and New Zealand History*, 1996.

82. Malcolm McKinnon, *Independence and Foreign Policy: New Zealand and the World Since 1935*, 1993, chapter 2.

83. Quoted in Barry Gustafson, *From the Cradle to the Grave: A Biography of Michael Joseph Savage*, 1986, 182, 208.

84. Susan Skudder, '"Bringing it home": New Zealand Responses to the Spanish Civil War, 1936–9, PhD thesis, University of Waikato, 1986, 31–47. Also see Sinclair, *Nash*, 387, n. 50; F. L. W. Wood, *The New Zealand People at War*, 47; W. B. Sutch, *The Quest for Security in New Zealand 1840–1966*, 1966, 205n.

85. Nancy Taylor, *The Home Front*, 1986, vol. 1, 17; Gustafson, *Savage*, 249.

86. Sinclair, *Nash*, 199.

87. On Lee see Erik Olssen, *John A. Lee*, 1977; John A. Lee, *Simple on a Soap-Box*, 1963; Scrimgeour and Lee, *Scrim–Lee Papers*; Gustafson, *Savage*; Brown, *Rise of NZ Labour*, chapter 10; Davis, 'New Zealand Labour Government'.

88. Gustafson, *Savage*, 254.

89. Written prior to the publication of Michael Bassett and Michael King, *Tomorrow Comes the Song: a Life of Peter Fraser*, 2000. See Margaret Clark (ed.), *Peter Fraser: Master Politician*, 1998. James Thorn, *Peter Fraser: New Zealand's Wartime Prime Minister*, London, 1952 is mere hagiography.

90. Gustafson, *Savage*, 270.

91. Ibid, 200–01.

Chapter 9: New Zealand in World War Two

1. John McLeod, *Myth & Reality: The New Zealand Soldier in World War II*, 1986; J. Belich, 'War'; Glyn Harper, *Kippenberger: An Inspired New Zealand Commander*, 1997.

2. Keith Jeffery, 'The Second World War' in Brown and Louis (eds), *The Oxford History of the British Empire*, vol. 4.

3. Ian McGibbon, 'New Zealand's Strategical Approach', in John Crawford

(ed.), *Kia Kaha: New Zealand in the Second World War*, 2000, 12.

4. H. L. Thompson, *New Zealanders with the Royal Air Force*, 1953–9, vol. 2, 10.

5. W. Wynne Mason, *Prisoners of War*, 1954, 1. For a fascinating account by a New Zealand pilot interned in neutral Ireland see Bruce Girdlestone, 'Prisoner of the Green', in Anna Rogers (ed.), *The War Years: New Zealanders Remember 1939–45*, 1989.

6. *ENZ*, vol. 3, 574–76; Thompson, *New Zealanders with the Royal Airforce*; *Evening Post*, 12, 18 April 1941.

7. Geoffrey Bentley, *RNZAF: A Short History*, Reed, 1969, 40.

8. Calculated from John Robertson, *Australia at War, 1939–45*, Melbourne 1981, 54.

9. Peter Dennerly, 'The Royal New Zealand Navy', in Crawford, *Kia Kaha*, 109.

10. Calculated from Thompson, *New Zealanders with the Royal Airforce*, vol. 2, 455.

11. Ibid., 7–9.

12. See Ibid.; Bentley, *RNZAF*; *ENZ*, vol. 1, 585–86.

13. Bentley, *RNZAF*, 144–45.

14. *ENZ*, vol. 3, 575–76 and vol. 1, 585–86.

15. Geoffrey Cox, *A Tale of Two Battles: A Personal Memoir of Crete and the Western Desert*, London, 1987, 173.

16. Harper, *Kippenberger*, 147.

17. McLeod, *Myth & Reality*, 62–63.

18. Vladimir Peniakoff, *Popski's Private Army*, London, 1953, 56, 21, 201.

19. Mulgan, *Report on Experience*, 14.

20. *Documents Relating to New Zealand's Participation in the Second World War*, 1949, vol. 2, 20.

21. *Evening Post*, 19–23 April 1941. Also see Taylor, *Home Front*, vol. 1, 290–91.

22. Cedric Mentiplay, *A Fighting Quality: New Zealanders at War*, 1979, 51.

23. McLeod, *Myth & Reality*, 50, 127, 49. Also see Freyberg, *Bernard Freyberg*.

24. Brooke, quoted in Arthur Bryant, *The Turn of the Tide*, London, 1957, 431.

25. See, e.g., F. W. Von Mellenthin, *Panzer Battles 1939–45*, London, 1956, 63, 122–33.

26. Baron Von der Heydte, *Daedalus Returned: Crete 1941*, London, 1958, 181.

27. Geoffrey Cox, *A Tale of Two Battles*; Freyberg, *Bernard Freyberg*; Also see Belich, 'War'.

28. McLeod, *Myth & Reality*, 16.

29. Ibid., 177.

30. Quoted in Harper, *Kippenberger*, 163.

31. McLeod, *Myth & Reality*, 158.

32. Harper, *Kippenberger*, 181–82.

33. Wira Gardiner, *Te Mura o Te Ahi: The Story of the Maori Battalion*, 1992, chapters 8–10, 14.

34. W. G. Stevens, *Problems of 2 NZEF*, 1958, 126, 149.

35. Mulgan, *Report on Experience*; Keith Ovenden, *A Fighting Withdrawal*; Harper, *Kippenberger*, 270.

36. Stevens, *Problems*, 158.

37. J. T. Burrows, *Pathway Among Men*, 1974, 180.

38. S. D. Waters, *The Royal New Zealand Navy*, 1956, 411–13.

39. John Robertson, *Australia at War*, Melbourne, 1981, 24.

40. Albert Ellis, *Mid-Pacific Outposts*, 1946.

41. J. V. T. Baker, *War Economy*, 1965, 372–73.

42. Sydney D. Waters, *Ordeal By Sea: The New Zealand Shipping Company in the Second World War*, London, 1949, 174.

43. Taylor, *Home Front*, vol. 1, 329.

44. U-862 journal quoted in *Sunday Star*, 23 August 1992.

45. Report of British High Commissioner, 19 February 1942, British Cabinet Papers CAB 66/24, 188, Public Record Office, London; Oliver A. Gillespie, *The Pacific*, 1952, 61.

46. Christoper Thorne, *The Issue of War: States, Societies and the Far Eastern Conflict of 1941–5*, London, 1985, 272. Also see King, *Te Puea*, 207.

47. I. Kawase, Reminiscences, 1965, MS Papers 683, Alexander Turnbull Library.

48. Gillespie, *The Pacific*, 74.

49. McLeod, *Myth & Reality*, 162, 111; Stevens, *Problems*, 29, 43.

50. Freyberg, *Bernard Freyberg*, 256.

51. Quoted in ibid., 236.

52. All quotes from *Documents*, vol. 2, 308–27.

53. F. W. Perry, *The Commonwealth Armies: Manpower and Organisation in Two World Wars*, Manchester, 1988, 185.

54. See S. H. Capon, 'The "Hamilton Furlough Mutiny": An Analysis of the Implementation and Consequences of the 1943 Furlough Scheme', MA thesis, University of Waikato, 1986, from which these quotations are drawn.

55. A. S. Helm, *Kiwis on Tour in Egypt and Italy*, 1949, 10. Also see McLeod, *Myth & Reality*, chapter 10.

56. See Gillespie, *The Pacific*; *Documents*, vol. 3; John Crawford, 'A Campaign on Two Fronts', in Crawford, *Kia Kaha*.

57. McGibbon, 'New Zealand's Strategical Approach', 15–16.

58. Alister McIntosh, Secretary of External Affairs, quoted in Ian McGibbon (ed.), *Undiplomatic Dialogue: Letters Between Carl Berendsen and Alister McIntosh*, 1993, 23–24.

59. Fraser to Churchill, 19 Nov. 1942, *Documents*, vol. 2, 142–44.

60. *Documents*, vol. 3, 233.

61. McGibbon, 'New Zealand's Strategical Approach', 17–18.

62. Berendsen, in McGibbon, *Undiplomatic Dialogue*, 36–38.

63. Report of British High Commissioner, 26 January 1942, British Cabinet Papers, 66/21, 38, Public Record Office, London.

64. David Day, *The Great Betrayal: Britain, Australia, and the Onset of the Pacific War 1939–42*, Sydney, 1988, 72.

65. Robertson, *Australia at War*, 213.

66. Bentley, *RNZAF*, 40–41.

67. *Documents*, vol. 3, 206–66.

68. Gillespie, *The Pacific*, 195–96.

69. Fraser to Churchill, 17 March 1942, *Documents*, vol. 2, 41–42.

70. Quoted in Capon, 'The "Hamilton Furlough Mutiny"', 136.

71. George Brasell, *Boats & Blokes*, 1991, 81–85.

72. Dunstall, *A Policeman's Paradise?*, 329–30.

73. Report of British High Commissioner, 26 January 1942, British Cabinet Papers, 66/21, 38, Public Record Office, London.

74. Malcolm Kay, *The Inside Story of Farmers'*, 257.

75. Taylor, *Home Front*, vol. 1, 289–90.

76. Ibid, vol. 1, 540–46. Also see Eve Ebbett, *When the Boys were Away: New Zealand Women in World War II*, 1984, chapter 14.

77. Wynne Mason, *Prisoners of War*, 358–59; Vincent O'Sullivan, *Shuriken*, 1985; Mike Nicolaidi, *Featherston Chronicles: A Legacy of War*, 1999.

78. Quoted in Harry Bioletti, *The Yanks are Coming: The American Invasion of New Zealand 1942–44*, 1984, 72.

79. Denys Bevan, *United States Forces in New Zealand, 1942–1945*, 1992, 370–71.

80. All quoted in Bioletti, *The Yanks are Coming*.

81. *Evening Post*, 31 December 1983.

82. Taylor, *Home Front*, vol. 1, chapter 14; David B. Atwool, 'Enemies and Allies: Changing Stereotypes Portrayed in New Zealand During the Second World War', MA thesis, University of Waikato, 1986, chapter 4.

83. Dunstall, *A Policeman's Paradise?*, 332.

84. Bioletti, *The Yanks are Coming*, 151; King, *Te Puea*, 212.

85. Ebbett, *When the Boys were Away*, 159.

86. Jock Barnes, quoted in Bioletti, *The Yanks are Coming*, 89–90.

87. Quoted in Coney, *Standing in the Sunshine*, 316.

88. Taylor, *Home Front*, vol. 1, 644; Hamish Keith, *A Lovely Day Tomorrow*, 16–18.

89. Calculated from Ebbett, *When the Boys were Away*, 165 and Taylor, *Home Front*, vol. 2, chapter 20.

90. Coney, *Standing in the Sunshine*, 317.

91. Thorne, *The Issue of War*, 253.

92. Quoted in Taylor, *Home Front*, vol. 2, 1287.

93. John E. Martin, 'Total War?', in Crawford, *Kia Kaha*, 234.

94. Taylor, *Home Front*, vol. 1, 427.

95. Baker, *War Economy*, chapter 8.

96. Ibid., 79.

97. Boyd, *Hastings*, 241; *NZ's Heritage*, 2542.

98. Taylor, *Home Front*, vol. 2, 734–41, 757, 767, 777; Baker, *War Economy*, chapters 4, 6, 7.

99. Ibid., 123; Hawke, *Making of New Zealand*, 251, says factory output doubled.

100. Baker, *War Economy*, 175.

101. Ibid., 370.

102. *HS*, 312.

103. Baker, *War Economy*, 265.

104. Ibid., chapter 10.

105. Ibid., chapter 12.

106. Michael Bassett, *The State in New Zealand 1840–1984: Socialism Without Doctrines?*, 1998, 14.

107. Commissioner Cumming, quoted in Dunstall, *A Policeman's Paradise?*, 313.

108. Ibid., 305; Taylor, *Home Front*, vol. 2, chapter 19.

109. Taylor, *Home Front*, vol. 1, 243, 220–21, 233–34.

110. Dunstall, *A Policeman's Paradise?*, 307–08.

111. Taylor, *Home Front*, vol. 2, chapter 18.
112. David Grant, *Out in the Cold : Pacifists and Conscientious Objectors in New Zealand during World War II*, 1986; Ian Hamilton, *Till Human Voices Wake Us*, 1984; Taylor, *Home Front*, vol. 1, chapters 5–7.
113. Ibid, 246; Grant, *Out in the Cold*, 133–34 and 238.
114. Ibid., 12; Barry Gustafson, 'The Labour Party', in Hyam Gold (ed.), *New Zealand Politics in Perspective*, 1992, 265. Also see Sinclair, *Nash*, 208–09.
115. Taylor, *Home Front*, vol. 1, 50.
116. Ibid., 454–64.
117. Maxine Iversen, 'Inextricable Links: Pakeha Perceptions of Identity and their Relationships with Britain at the Time of the Statute of Westminster', MA thesis, University of Auckland, 1996, 60–63.
118. Kay, *The Inside Story of Farmers*', 277–78.

Chapter 10: Golden Weather?

1. Jock Phillips, 'New Zealand Celebrates Victory', in Crawford, *Kia Kaha*.
2. McKinnon, *Independence and Foreign Policy*, 76–77.
3. Sidney Holland, quoted in Michael Bassett, *Confrontation '51: The 1951 Waterside Dispute*, 1972, 170.
4. See *DNZB*, vol. 4; 'F. P. Walsh: Industrial Strongman', *NZ's Heritage*, 93; *ENZ*; Barry Gustafson, *The First Fifty Years: A History of the National Party*, 1986, 60; Roth, *Trade Unions in New Zealand Past and Present*, 1973; Bassett, *Confrontation '51*; Sinclair, *Nash*, chapter 22.
5. Marshall, *Memoirs*, vol. 1, 167; Sinclair, *Nash*, 265.
6. Bassett, *Confrontation '51*, 40.
7. Ibid., chapter 3.
8. See, e.g., Roth, *Trade Unions*, 78; 'Sidney George Holland', *NZ's Heritage*, 91; Bassett, *Confrontation '51*, 11, 113. Bassett does note that the number of strikers in 1913 was proportionately larger.
9. Ibid., 91.
10. *Dominion Sunday Times*, 26 July 1991; Jock Barnes, *Never a White Flag: Jock Barnes, Waterfront Leader*, 1998.
11. Bassett, *Confrontation '51*, 186.
12. Roth, *Trade Unions*, 78.
13. Quoted in Bassett, *Confrontation '51*, 83.
14. Roth, *Trade Unions*, 151.
15. Bassett, *Confrontation '51*, 168–69.
16. Marshall, *Memoirs*, vol. 1, 172; Bassett, *Confrontation '51*, 170.
17. *ENZ*, vol. 2, 794; Kerry Taylor, '"Our Motto, No Compromise": The Ideological Origins and Foundation of the Communist Party of New Zealand', *NZJH*, 28 (1984).
18. Roth, *Trade Unions*, 158–60.
19. Sinclair, *Nash*, 285.
20. Bassett, *Confrontation '51*, 87.
21. Sinclair, *Nash*, 285–86.
22. Marshall, *Memoirs*, vol. 1, 167; Barnes interview in Bioletti, *The Yanks are Coming*, 88–90.
23. Bassett, *Confrontation '51*, 91–92, 207; Marshall, *Memoirs*, vol. 2, 176–77.
24. Bassett, *Confrontation '51*, 94, 76, 183.
25. Roth, *Trade Unions*, 72.
26. Marshall, *Memoirs*, vol. 2, 155.
27. See Margaret Clark, (ed.), *Sir Keith Holyoake: Towards a Political Biography*, 1997.
28. Marshall, *Memoirs*, vol. 2, 152.
29. Hawke, *Making of NZ*, 178–79. Also Westrate, *Portrait of a Modern Mixed Economy*, 285.
30. Hawke, *Making of NZ*, 179.
31. Westrate, *Modern Mixed Economy*, 298.
32. *New Zealand Farmer*, August, 1982, 203–04; *HS*, 185.
33. Galbreath, *DSIR*, chapters 1, 3, 4.
34. *HS*, 282.
35. Ibid., 218; Hawke, *Making of NZ*, 237.
36. Evans, *Agricultural Policy*, 144–45.
37. Hawke, *Making of NZ*, 231.
38. Ibid., 244.
39. Pollard, *British Economy*, 289; Paul Smith, *Twist and Shout: New Zealand in the 1960s*, 1991, 46.
40. Coleridge, *Our Motoring Heritage*, 6. Other, less specialised, sources say 1926.
41. Hawke, *Making of NZ*, 260, 314.
42. Ibid., 273.
43. Ibid., 268–69.
44. *OYB*, 1960, 623; *OYB*, 1972, 478.
45. Thorns and Sedgwick, *Historical Statistics*, 79.
46. McKinnon, *Independence and Foreign Policy*, 99.
47. *ENZ*, vol. 3, 429.
48. Baker, *War Economy*, 185–87.
49. L. Lipson, *The Politics of Equality: New Zealand's Adventures in Democracy*, Chicago, 1948, 367–68.
50. Precise figures vary, but see Bassett, *State*

in *New Zealand*, 14 and passim; Gustafson, *Muldoon*, 238, 245.

51. Alan Henderson, *The Quest for Efficiency: The Origins of the State Services Commission*, 1990, 397–98.

52. Quoted in Eldred-Grigg, *NZ Working People*, 219.

53. Roth, *Trade Unions*, 141.

54. Marshall, *Memoirs*, vol. 2, 154.

55. Thorns and Sedgwick, *Historical Statistics*, 108.

56. *HS*, 246.

57. Martin, *People, Politics and Power Stations*.

58. Brasell, *Boats & Blokes*, 159–68; Martin, *People, Politics and Power Stations*, chapter 9.

59. 'The New Towns' in *NZ's Heritage*, 91.

60. *OYB*, 1990, 565.

61. *NZ's Heritage*, 92.

62. David Grant, *On A Roll: A History of Gambling and Lotteries in New Zealand*, 1994, 126.

63. Quoted in ibid., 227.

64. See Bollinger, *Grog's Own Country*.

65. Brian Easton, *In Stormy Seas: The Post-War New Zealand Economy*, 1997, 183.

66. Stuart Perry, *The Indecent Publications Tribunal: A Social Experiment*, 1965.

67. Redmer Yska, *All Shook Up: The Flash Bodgie and the Rise of the New Zealand Teenager in the Fifties*, 1993, 104.

68. McGibbon, *Undiplomatic Dialogue*, 108–09, 125, 145, 181, 230.

69. Hawke, *Making of NZ*, 220.

70. Quoted in Michael Macky, 'New Zealand and the Decline of British Power, 1939–56', MA thesis, University of Auckland, 1999, 97. Also see Iversen, 'Inextricable Links', 22.

71. W. David McIntyre and W. J. Gardiner, *Speeches and Documents in New Zealand History*, Oxford, 1971, 295.

72. Berendsen, in McGibbon, *Undiplomatic Dialogue*, 94–95.

73. Berendsen, in ibid., 247.

74. Macky, 'New Zealand and the Decline of British Power', 32.

75. Ibid., 9.

76. McKinnon, *Independence and Foreign Policy*, 115.

77. Ian McGibbon, 'New Zealand's Intervention in the Korean War, June–July 1950', *The International History Review*, 11 (1989), 278–79. Also see McGibbon, *Politics and Diplomacy*, 1992.

78. Macky, 'New Zealand and the Decline of British Power', 42.

79. Ibid., 45.

80. McIntosh, in McGibbon, *Undiplomatic Dialogue*, 252–53.

81. Iversen, 'Inextricable Links', 52, n. 20.

82. Macky, 'New Zealand and the Decline of British Power', 72.

83. McKinnon, *Independence and Foreign Policy*, 81.

84. Quoted in ibid., 145–46. Also see McGibbon, *Undiplomatic Dialogue*, 146n.

85. Department of State, despatch from Wellington, 9 December 1957.

86. W. H. Oliver, *The Story of New Zealand*, London, 1960, 244.

87. Quoted in McKinnon, *Independence and Foreign Policy*, 179–80.

88. *NZ's Heritage*, 95.

89. J. C. Beaglehole, 'The Development of New Zealand Nationality', *Journal of World History*, 2 (1954), 106–23.

90. Quoted in McKinnon, *Independence and Foreign Policy*, 180.

91. Oliver, *Story of NZ*, 234.

92. Ian Richards, *To Bed At Noon: The Life and Art of Maurice Duggan*, 1997, 82.

Part 4: Introduction

1. Mike Harding, *When the Pakeha Sings of Home: A Source Guide to the Folk and Popular Songs of New Zealand*, 1992, 38.

Chapter 11: The Expatriate Game

This chapter has some referencing peculiarities. I have used, but not cited, my own 30 years of random reading in New Zealand literature. For the whole chapter, I draw heavily on two important recent compendia: Terry Sturm (ed.), *The Oxford History of New Zealand Literature*, 1991 and 1998 editions (page references are to the first edition unless otherwise specified) and Roger Robinson and Nelson Wattie (eds), *The Oxford Companion to New Zealand Literature*, Melbourne, 1998.

1. Peter Luke, 'Suicide in Auckland', 87.

2. M. A. E. Hammer, '"Something Else to Live For": Sport and the Physical Emancipation of Women and Girls in Auckland 1880–1920', MA thesis, University of Auckland, 1990, 1–2.

3. Keith Sinclair, 'New Zealand Literary History', *NZJH*, 12 (1978), 69.

4. J. C. Reid, in *NZ's Heritage*, 57, 1595–96. Also see Eric McCormick, *Letters and Art in New Zealand*, 1940.

5. Lawrence Jones, 'The Novel', and Mac Jackson, 'Poetry: Beginnings to 1945', in Sturm, *Oxford History of NZ Literature*, 117, 122, 360.

6. Robinson and Wattie, *Oxford Companion to NZ Literature*, 283.

7. Quoted in Dennis McEldowney, 'Publishing, Patronage, and Literary Magazines', in Sturm, *Oxford History of NZ Literature*, 547.

8. Mac Jackson, 'Poetry: Beginnings to 1945', 357.

9. Sinclair, *Destiny Apart*, 54; T. M. Hocken, *A Bibliography of the Literature Relating to New Zealand*, 1909.

10. Jock Phillips, 'Musings in Maoriland – or was there a Bulletin School in New Zealand?', *Historical Studies*, 20 (1983), 522.

11. Robinson and Wattie, *Oxford Companion to NZ Literature*, 249.

12. Karen Sherry, 'Popular Entertainment in Auckland 1870–71', *Australasian Drama Studies*, 18 (1991), 22.

13. Howard McNaughton, 'Drama' in Sturm, *Oxford History of NZ Literature* (2nd edn) 328–29.

14. Peter Downes, *Shadows on the Stage: Theatre in New Zealand: The First 70 Years*, 1975, 61. Adrienne Simpson and Peter Downes, *Southern Voices: International Opera Singers of New Zealand*, 1992, 3. Also see Adrienne Simpson, 'Opera in the Antipodes: A Forgotten Aspect of the Nineteenth-Century Trans-Tasman Entertainment Industry', *NZJH*, 27 (1993), 61–74.

15. Simpson, 'Opera in the Antipodes', 73.

16. Thompson, *History of NZ Music*, 52.

17. Ibid., passim.

18. Lydia Wevers, 'The Short Story' in Sturm, *Oxford History of NZ Literature*. See also V. S. O'Sullivan, (ed.), *Katherine Mansfield: New Zealand Stories*, 1997, *DNZB*, vol. 2.

19. *DNZB*, vol. 2; Robinson and Wattie, *Oxford Companion to NZ Literature*, 66–67; *ENZ*, vol. 2, 622.

20. Dymock, *Good Morning NZ*, 160.

21. Adela Stewart, *My Simple Life in New Zealand*, 25.

22. See Mark Stocker, review of Buchanan et al., *Frances Hodgkins: Paintings and Drawings*, in *Bulletin of New Zealand Art History*, 16 (1995), 59; E. H. McCormick, *Portrait of Francis Hodgkins*, 1981.

23. Quoted in Ovenden, *A Fighting Withdrawal*, 275.

24. Trussell, *Fairburn*, 93–94.

25. Quoted in Pat Lawlor, *Confessions of A Journalist*, 239–40.

26. Quoted in ibid., 170.

27. John Mulgan, *Report on Experience*, 17.

28. Allen Curnow, 'New Zealand Literature: The Case for a Working Definition', in Wystan Curnow (ed.), *Essays on New Zealand Literature*, 1973.

29. See, for example, R. S. Broughton, 'Three New Zealand Poets in the 1920s' in Curnow, *Essays on NZ Literature*.

30. Quoted in Lawrence Jones, 'The Novel', in Sturm, *Oxford History of NZ Literature*, 124, 134–35.

31. Quoted in Vaughan Yarwood, '"Shibboleth of Empire": Attitudes to Empire in New Zealand Writing, 1890–1930', MA thesis, University of Auckland, 1982, 132.

32. Thompson, *History of NZ Music*, 94.

33. Michael King, *Frank Sargeson: A Life*, 1995, 255.

34. Charles Brasch, *Indirections: A Memoir, 1909–1947*, 1980, 407.

35. Janet Frame, *An Angel at My Table*, 1984, 70.

36. See Rachel Barrowman, *A Popular Vision: The Arts and the Left in New Zealand, 1930–50*, 1991.

37. Trussell, *Fairburn*, 113.

38. Michael King, *Wrestling with the Angel: A Life of Janet Frame*, 2000, 112.

39. Robinson and Wattie, *Oxford Companion to NZ Literature*. Also see Lynley Hood, *Sylvia! A Biography of Sylvia Ashton-Warner*, 1988.

40. King, *Sargeson*, 213.

41. Sinclair, 'NZ Literary History', 74. Also see Trussell, *Fairburn*; Gordon Ogilvy, *Denis Glover: His Life*, 1999.

42. King, *Sargeson*, 287.

43. Quoted in Trussell, *Fairburn*, 221, 234.

44. Except where otherwise cited, this paragraph and the next draw on Robinson and Wattie, *Oxford Companion to NZ Literature*.

45. See Belich, *Making Peoples*, 436.

46. Marshall, *Memoirs*, vol. 1, 46–47.

47. Terry Sturm, 'Popular Fiction' and Betty Gilderdale, 'Children's Literature', in

Sturm, *Oxford History of NZ Literature*.
48. Simpson and Downes, *Southern Voices*.
49. *NZ's Heritage*, 80; *NZ Herald*, 20 June 1997.
50. Dennis McEldowney, 'Publishing, Patronage, Literary Magazines', in Sturm, *Oxford History of NZ Literature* (2nd edn), 652.
51. In the form of Air Marshal Hayr.
52. Alan Mulgan, *From Track to Highway: A Short History of New Zealand*, 1944, 116–17.
53. *ENZ*, vol. 1, 575–604.
54. *Oxford Today*, 2 (1990), 47.
55. Heather Roberts, *Where Did She Come From? New Zealand Women Novelists, 1862–1987*, 1989.
56. See James Belich, 'Race in New Zealand: Some Social History of Ideas', Macmillan Brown Lecture Series, 1994.
57. Ian Cox and Mike Whitall, *Rutherford: The Early Years*, 1991. Also see J. Campbell, *Rutherford: Scientist Supreme*, 1999.
58. S. H. Jenkinson, *New Zealanders and Science*, 1940, chapter 10.
59. Robin J. H. Clark and Michael J. Kelly, 'New Zealand, New Zealanders, and the Royal Society', *Notes Received, Royal Society*, 48 (1994), 263–81.
60. Galbreath, *DSIR*, 109, 139.
61. Ross Galbreath, 'The Rutherford Connection: New Zealand Scientists and the Manhattan and Montreal Projects', *War in History*, 2 (1995), 306–19.
62. Jenkinson, *New Zealanders and Science*, 2.
63. *Sunday Times*, 18 June 1995.

Chapter 12: Life During History

1. Gillian Green, *New Zealand: A Guide for New Settlers*, 1988.
2. Austin Mitchell, *The Half-Gallon, Quarter-Acre, Pavlova Paradise*, 1972.
3. *HS*, 104–08.
4. Jeremy Salmond, *Old New Zealand Houses, 1800–1940*, 112.
5. *HS*, 260–61, 248.
6. Paul Pascoe, 'Houses', *Making New Zealand*, 1940, 14.
7. Ibid.
8. Quoted in Christine Dann, 'Sweet William and Sticky Nelly: Sex Difference in New Zealand Gardening and Garden Writing', *Women's Studies International*

Forum, 15 (1992), 239. Also see Mathew Bradbury (ed.), *A History of the Garden in New Zealand*, 1995.
9. Salmond, *Old NZ Houses*, 131.
10. Quoted in Dann, 'Sweet William and Sticky Nelly', 246.
11. Ibid., 246.
12. H. C. D. Somerset, *Littledene: Patterns of Change*, 1974, 105.
13. H. C. D. Somerset, *Littledene: A New Zealand Rural Community*, 1938, 24, also 20.
14. *New Zealand Historic Places*, July 1998, 69; Salmond, *Old NZ Houses*, 211; Peter Shaw, *New Zealand Architecture*, 132–33.
15. Phyllis Herder, 'Ladies a Plate: Women and Food' in Julie Park (ed.), *Ladies a Plate: Change and Continuity in the Lives of New Zealand Women*, 1991, 160.
16. Salmond, *Old NZ Houses*, 204.
17. *OYB*, 1990, 458.
18. Geoffrey Cox, *Eyewitness: A Memoir of Europe in the 1930s*, 1999, 26.
19. See, e.g., Somerset, *Littledene: Patterns of Change*, 107.
20. Allan Davidson and Peter Lineham (eds), *Transplanted Christianity: Documents Illustrating Aspects of New Zealand Church History*, 1987, and Censuses of New Zealand.
21. Somerset, *Littledene: Patterns of Change*, 181.
22. Hans Mol, *The Fixed and the Fickle: Religion and Identity in New Zealand*, 1982, 83.
23. Danielle Sprecher, 'The Right Appearance: Representations of Fashion, Gender, and Modernity in Inter-War New Zealand, 1918–39', MA thesis, University of Auckland, 1997.
24. Malcolm Kay, *Inside Story of Farmers'*.
25. *OYB*, 1990, 586–87.
26. R. S. Odell, 'Manufacturing', *Making New Zealand*, no. 15, 17.
27. Fiona McKergow, 'Opening the Wardrobe of History: Dress, Artefacts, and Material Life of the 1940s and 1950s', in Bronwyn Dalley and Bronwyn Labrum (eds), *Fragments: New Zealand Social and Cultural History*, 2000.
28. David Ausubel, *The Fern and the Tiki: An American View of New Zealand National Character, Social Attitudes, and Race Relations*, North Quincy, Massachussets, 1977.
29. Tim Hazledine, *Taking New Zealand*

Seriously: The Economics of Decency,
1998, 123–24.

30. Dymock, *Good Morning NZ*, 162.

31. Quoted in Trussell, *Fairburn*, 265.

32. Phillips, *A Man's Country*, 225, 265, 249–51.

33. *NZ's Heritage*, 83.

34. Colin Hogg, *A Life in Loose Strides: The Story of Barry Crump*, 2000, 36–37.

35. See Belich, *Making Peoples*, 431.

36. Colin Hogg, *Crump*. Also see Barry Crump, *A Good Keen Man*, 1960, and *Hang On A Minute Mate*, 1961.

37. Hogg, *Crump*, 35.

38. Quoted in ibid., 45.

38. Ian Cross, *The Unlikely Bureaucrat: My Years in Broadcasting*, 1988, 19–20.

40. *OYB*, 1990, 241.

41. Sinclair, *A Destiny Apart*, 75, 230.

42. Recent exceptions to the neglect of the history of childhood include Helen May, *The Discovery of Early Childhood*, 1997; Claire Toynbee, *Family, Kin and Community in New Zealand, 1900–1930*, 1995.

43. Dugald J. Macdonald, 'Children and Young Persons in New Zealand Society', in Peggy Koopman-Boyden (ed.), *Families in New Zealand Society*, 1978. Also see Mary Trewby, *The Best Years of your Life: A History of New Zealand Childhood*, 1995, e.g. 50.

44. Quoted in Linda A. Pollock, *Forgotten Children: Parent-Child Relations from 1500 to 1900*, 1983, chapter 1. Note that Pollock is summarising an historical orthodoxy with which she disagrees.

45. Quoted in Sutton-Smith, *History of Children's Play*, 20.

46. Dominick Cavallo, *Muscles and Morals: Organized Playgrounds and Urban Reform, 1880–1920*, Philadelphia, 1981, esp. 55–83; Christina Hardyment, *Dream Babies: Child Care from Locke to Spock*, Oxford, 1984, 104.

47. Ibid., 8–9.

48. Mary Ann Barker, *Station Life in New Zealand*, 56–58. For other examples see S. J. Goldsbury, 'Behind the Picket Fence: The Lives of Missionary Wives in Pre-Colonial New Zealand', MA thesis, University of Auckland, 1986.

49. James Walvin, *A Child's World: A Social History of English Childhood, 1800–1914*, London, 1982, chapter 2.

50. Barker, *Station Life in NZ*, 58.

51. Jackson, *Churches and People*, 159.

52. Eldred-Grigg, *Pleasures of the Flesh*, 241.

53. For examples, see Jackson, *Churches and People*, 160–61.

54. Sally Anne Maclean, 'Nga Tamariki O Te Rohe Waikato: Maori Children's Lives in the Waikato Region 1850–1900: a Case Study', MA thesis, University of Waikato, 1990.

55. See, for example, Ovenden, *A Fighting Withdrawal*, chapters 1–2.

56. Charlotte MacDonald, *A Woman of Good Character: Single Women as Immigrant Settlers in Nineteenth-Century New Zealand*, 1990, 159; Pool and Tiong, 'Sub-national Differentials in the Pakeha Fertility Decline', 46–64.

57. Sutton-Smith, *History of Children's Play*, 121.

58. *New Zealand Handbook* 1875, quoted. *OYB*, 1990, 269.

59. D. McKenzie, H. Lee, and G. Lee, *Scholars or Dollars?*, chapters 2 and 3.

60. Sutton-Smith, *History of Children's Play*, 61 and passim.

61. Orsman, *Dictionary of NZ English*.

62. Quoted in Sutton-Smith, *History of Children's Play*, 32.

63. Ibid., 175.

64. *In Those Days: a Study of Older Women in Wellington*, 1982, 14–15; Sarah Ell (ed.), *The Lives of Pioneer Women in New Zealand*, 1993, 73; Sutton-Smith, *History of Children's Play*, 137.

65. Ibid., 128.

66. Ibid., 85–92.

67. Zorica Anzulovich, personal communication.

68. Sutton-Smith, *History of Children's Play*, 79–80. All quotes in the next four paragraphs are from Sutton-Smith, ibid., unless otherwise cited. Also see his *The Folkgames of Children*, Austin, 1972.

69. See Belich, *Making Peoples*, 428.

70. S. J. Goldsbury, 'Behind the Picket Fence', 38, 52. Also see 107.

71. Pauline O' Regan, *Aunts and Windmills*, 1991, 16–18.

72. Sutton-Smith, *History of Children's Play*, 71–72.

73. Ibid., xv.

74. Ibid., 47, 188.

75. *ENZ*, vol. 3, 697–702. Also see S. G. Culliford, *New Zealand Scouting: The First Fifty Years, 1908–1958*, 1958; Michael E. Hoare, *Faces of Boyhood: An*

*Informal Pictorial Record of the Boys'
Brigade in New Zealand, 1886–1982*,
1982; Mary Iles, *65 Years of Guiding,
1908–73: The Official History of the Girl
Guides Association, New Zealand*, 1976;
Sandra Coney, *Every Girl: A Social
History of Women and the YWCA in
Auckland, 1885–1985*, 1986.

76. Michael Rosenthal, *The Character
Factory: Baden-Powell and the Origins of
the Boy Scout Movement*, New York, 1984.

77. Ibid.

78. Canterbury Girl Guides, *The Great
Game: Girl Peace Scouts and Girl Guides
of the Canterbury Province from 1908*,
1990, 18.

79. Peggy Armstrong and Denise Jackson,
Toys of Early New Zealand, 1990.

80. Mary Trewby, *The Best Years of your Life*,
100–05.

Chapter 13: Games People Play

1. By economist Brian Gaynor, *NZ Herald*,
30 September 2000. The rest of this litany
of sporting triumphs is drawn from a
wide variety of sources especially *ENZ*;
Making New Zealand; *NZ's Heritage*, and
DNZB.

2. Sinclair, *Destiny Apart*, 230.

3. John Nauright and Jayne Broomhall, 'A
Woman's Game: The Development of
Netball and a Female Sporting Culture in
New Zealand, 1906–1970', *International
Journal of the History of Sport*, 11 (1994),
388.

4. Hocken, *Bibliography of Literature
Relating to NZ*, 460.

5. George Ranstead, *A Right Royal Hunt
With the Waikato Hounds*, 1991, 16, 45.

6. 'Boxing', in *ENZ*, vol. 1; *DNZB*, vol. 2.

7. J. G. McLean, 'Summer Sports', *Making
New Zealand*, 26.

8. M. A. E. Hammer, '"Something Else to
Live For"', 20–23; Coney, *Standing in the
Sunshine*, 160.

9. Joblin, 'Breath of Scandal', 191.

10. Kent Pearson, 'Meanings and Motivation
in Sport', in John Hinchcliff (ed.), *The
Nature and Meaning of Sport in New
Zealand*, 1978.

11. L. M. Rogers (ed.), *The Early Journals of
Henry Williams, 1826–40*, 1961, 268;
Armstrong and Jackson, *Toys of Early
New Zealand*, 72.

12. J. A. Mangan, *Athleticism in the Victorian

and Edwardian Public School*, Cambridge,
1981.

13. See relevant articles in *ENZ*.
(Significantly these are still the most
comprehensive summary of NZ sporting
history.)

14. 'Cricket' in Tony Mason (ed.), *Sport in
Britain: A Social History*, Cambridge,
1989; Eric Dunning and Kenneth Sheard,
*Barbarians, Gentlemen, and Players: A
Sociological Study of the Development of
Rugby Football*, Oxford, 1979, 177–81.

15. *DNZB*, vol. 2. Also see R. T. Brittenden,
Great Days of New Zealand Cricket, 1958.

16. See Greg Ryan, 'New Zealand', in Brian
Stoddart and Keith Sandiford (eds), *The
Imperial Game: Cricket, Culture, and
Society*, Manchester, 1998.

17. J. M. Golby and A. W. Purdue, *The
Civilisation of the Crowd: Popular Culture
in England, 1780–1900*, London, 1984,
166.

18. D. O. Neely, *100 Summers: The History of
Wellington Cricket*, 1975, 19; *DNZB* and
ENZ articles on school principals.

19. Hill, *Iron Hand*, chapters 3 and 13.

20. Boyd, *Hastings*, 152.

21. D. J. Mulvaney, *Cricket Walkabout: The
Australian Aboriginal Cricketers on Tour,
1867–8*, London, 1967.

22. Hammer, '"Something Else to Live For"',
29.

23. J. G. Mclean, 'Summer Sports', 26.

24. Coney, *Standing in the Sunshine*, 252–53.

25. Catherine Smith, '"Control of the Female
Body": Physical Training at Three New
Zealand Girls' High Schools,
1880s–1920s', *Sporting Traditions*,
13 (1997), 67.

26. John Nauright, 'Netball and the Creation
of a Female Sporting Culture in New
Zealand', *Journal of Physical Education*,
29 (1996).

27. Charlotte Macdonald, 'Netball New
Zealand', in A. Else (ed.), *Women
Together: A History of Women's
Organisations in New Zealand*, 1993, 431.

28. Coney, *Standing in the Sunshine*, 243.

29. Ibid., and Macdonald, 'Netball New
Zealand', 433.

30. *NZ's Heritage*, 92; *ENZ*; Coney, *Standing
in the Sunshine*, 250–51; *Evening Post*,
31 October 1995.

31. Reeves, *State Experiments*, vol. 1, 137;
Hammer, '"Something Else to Live For"',
24–28.

32. From 'The Girls of Ninety-One', *New Zealand Graphic and Ladies Journal*, 2 January 1892, 9, quoted in ibid.
33. Ibid., 3.
34. *OYB*, 1990, 347.
35. Calculated from ibid.
36. Coney, *Standing in the Sunshine*, 242.
37. Hammer, '"Something Else to Live For"', 97; Coney, *Standing in the Sunshine*, 242.
38. Hammer, '"Something Else to Live For"', 147. Also see Fiona J. Hall '"The Greater Game".
39. Coney, *Standing in the Sunshine*, 255.
40. Warwick Roger, *Old Heroes: The 1956 Springbok Tour and the Lives Beyond*, 1991, 10 and passim.
41. Gordon Slatter, *On the Ball: The Centennial Book of NZ Rugby*, 1970, 345.
42. T. P. McLean quoted in Roger, *Old Heroes*, 4. Also see McLean's article in *NZ's Heritage*, 96.
43. Roger, *Old Heroes*, 49, 161–62.
44. Dunning and Sheard, *Barbarians, Gentlemen, and Players*, chapter 1.
45. Ibid.; Gareth Williams, 'Rugby Union' in Mason, *Sport in Britain*; Goldby and Purdue, *Civilisation of the Crowd*.
46. Williams, 'Rugby Union'.
47. Phillips, *A Man's Country?*, 88.
48. S. A. G. M. Crawford, 'A Social History of Sport in 19th-Century Otago', in J. Hinchcliff, *The Nature and Meaning of Sport in NZ*, 38 (citing research of G. D. Connon and S. J. Haycock).
49. Williams, 'Rugby Union'.
50. *NZ's Heritage*, 43.
51. Slatter, *On the Ball*, 143.
52. Ibid., 66; *ENZ*.
53. *OYB*, 1990, 347.
54. Crawford, 'Social History of Sport in 19th-Century Otago', 37.
55. *100 Years of Taranaki Rugby 1885–1985*, 1985, 2.
56. Sutton-Smith, *The Folkgames of Children*, 152–55. Also see Armstrong and Jackson *Toys of Early NZ*, 71.
57. H. J. Maverley, 'Early Days Rugby in New Plymouth', in *100 Years of Taranaki Rugby 1885–1985*, 26–27.
58. Quoted in Phillips, *A Man's Country?*, 95.
59. Lynn McConnell, *Something to Crow About: The Centennial History of the Southland Rugby Football Union*, 1986, 271–72.
60. Hammer, '"Something Else to Live For"', 2–3.

61. Slatter, *On the Ball*, 51.
62. Ibid., 95.
63. Williams, 'Rugby Union'.
64. Hall, '"The Greater Game"', 116.
65. Slatter, *On the Ball*, 356.
66. *Dominion*, 2 August 1992.
67. Joblin, 'Breath of Scandal', chapter 5.
68. Slatter, *On the Ball*, 282.
69. Hall, '"The Greater Game"', 119–31, 230.
70. Slatter, *On the Ball*, 119.
71. Ibid., chapter 4.
72. Geoff Fougere, 'Sport, Culture and Identity: the Case of Rugby Football', in David Novitz and Bill Willmott (eds), *Culture and Identity in New Zealand*, 1989.
73. R. H. Chester and N. A. C. McMillan, *Centenary: 100 Years of All Black Rugby*, 1984, 73.
74. Phillips, *A Man's Country?*, 110.
75. Quoted in John Nauright, 'Sport, Manhood, and Empire: British Responses to the New Zealand Rugby Tour of 1905', *International Journal of the History of Sport*, 8 (1991), 246.
76. Slatter, *On the Ball*, 357.
77. Sinclair, *Destiny Apart*, 147.
78. *Punch*, quoted in Slatter, *On the Ball*, 276–77.

Part 5: Introduction

1. *OYB*, 1990, 114.
2. *Erebus: The Aftermath*, screened TVNZ 1987; Gordon Vette, *Impact Erebus*, 1983; Peter Mahon, *Verdict on Erebus*, 1984; Stuart MacFarlane, *The Erebus Papers*, 1991. Also see *NZ Herald*, 26 and 28 August 1999.
3. Quoted in Downes and Harcourt, *Voices in the Air*, 153.

Chapter 14: 1984 and All That

1. Michael Bassett, *The Third Labour Government: A Personal History*, 1976, 208.
2. Ibid., 142.
3. Barry Gustafson, *Muldoon*, 169.
4. Muldoon, interviewed by the author, 1990.
5. Gustafson, *Muldoon*.
6. Thorns and Sedgwick, *Historical Statistics*, 111.
7. Bassett, *Third Labour Government*, 191.
8. Gustafson, *Muldoon*, 240.

9. Sinclair, *History of NZ*, 316.
10. Thorns and Sedgwick, *Historical Statistics*, 119.
11. Gustafson, *Muldoon*, 251.
12. McKinnon, *Independence and Foreign Policy*, 172–75.
13. W. P. Reeves, 'The "New" Foreign Policy: A Dissenting View', in Stephen Levine (ed.), *New Zealand Politics: A Reader*, Melbourne, 1975, 437.
14. Gustafson, *Muldoon*, 225, 215.
15. R. D. Muldoon, *The Rise and Fall of a Young Turk*, 1974, 5.
16. Gustafson, *Muldoon*, 324.
17. Ibid., 117 and passim. Bassett, *Third Labour Government*, 33, 63, 244.
18. Gustafson, *Muldoon*, 273.
19. Ibid., 238, 245.
20. See ibid., 287 and Hazledine, *Taking New Zealand Seriously*, 43.
21. See, e.g., *Industrial Development Conference 1960: Background Papers*, 1960.
22. See David Orwin, 'Conservatism in New Zealand', PhD thesis, University of Auckland, 1999.
23. Gustafson, *First Fifty Years*, 1986, 241.
24. Gustafson, 'The Labour Party', 269.
25. Bassett, *Third Labour Government*, 254–63. The suggestion that the CIA were involved in Kirk's death was allegedly made by Bob Harvey in 2000. Harvey was president of the Labour Party, but the party quickly disavowed the suggestion.
26. G. A. Wood, 'The New Zealand News Media', in Levine, *NZ Politics*, 265–66.
27. Marshall, *Memoirs*, vol. 2, 35, 175.
28. Grant, *On a Roll*, 226.
29. Gustafson, 'The Labour Party', 264.
30. Gustafson, *First Fifty Years*, 26.
31. Ibid., chapter 5, and *Muldoon*, 49. Also see G. A. Wood, 'The National Party', in Gold, *NZ Politics in Perspective*.
32. Gustafson, 'The Labour Party'; Jack H. Nagel, 'Social Choice in a Pluralitarian Democracy: The Politics of Market Liberalization in New Zealand', *British Journal of Political Science*, 28 (1998).
33. Gustafson, *Muldoon*, chapter 22; David Lange, interview with the author, 1990.
34. Jane Kelsey, *The New Zealand Experiment: A World Model for Structural Adjustment?*, 1997, 245; James, *Turning Point*, 175.
35. Ibid., 241–42; Nagel, 'Social Choice'.
36. Marcia Russell, *Revolution: From Fortresss to Free Market*, 1996, 152; Grant, *History of the NZ Stock Exchange*, 308; James, *Turning Point*, 178.
37. Grant, *History of the NZ Stock Exchange*, 285, 345, 356.
38. Financial analyst Brian Gaynor, quoted in Russell, *Revolution*, 150; *OYB*, 2000, 503.
39. Grant, *History of the NZ Stock Exchange*, 284, 307.
40. Ibid., 304.
41. Stone, *Making of Russell McVeagh*, 227.
42. Gaynor, quoted in Russell, *Revolution*, 150.
43. James, *New Territory*, 182.
44. See in particular Paul Dalziel, 'The Reserve Bank Act', in Brian Roper and Chris Rudd (eds), *Oxford Readings in New Zealand Politics*, 1993.
45. Kelsey, *The NZ Experiment*, 119.
46. Nagel, 'Social Choice'.
47. See ibid.; Kelsey, *The NZ Experiment*; *OECD Economic Surveys: New Zealand*, Paris, 1999, 128–33; Henderson, *Quest for Efficiency*, chapter 12; Stephen Franks, 'Rigorous Privatisation: The New Zealand Experience', *The Columbia Journal of World Business*, 23 (1993), 1; 'Where and How the Assets Went', *Dominion Sunday Times*, 24 June 1990.
48. *OECD Economic Surveys*, 129–33.
49. Kelsey, *The NZ Experiment*, 184.
50. John Gould, *The Rake's Progress? The New Zealand Economy Since 1945*, 1982, 227.
51. Harvey Franklin, *Cul De Sac: The Question of New Zealand's Future*, 1985, 102; Roger Douglas, *There's Got to be a Better Way! A Practical ABC to Solving New Zealand's Major Problems*, 1980.
52. Roger Douglas, *Unfinished Business*, 1993, 221, 225.
53. Merman M. Schwartz, 'Reinvention and Retrenchment: Lessons from the Application of the New Zealand Model to Alberta, Canada', *Journal of Policy Analysis and Management*, 18 (1997), 405–6.
54. Nagel, 'Social Choice'.
55. James, *New Territory*, 152.
56. Marshall, *Memoirs*, vol. 1, 219.
57. Bassett, *The State in NZ*.
58. Lipson, *Politics of Equality*, 283.
59. Quoted in Bassett, *The State in NZ*, 133–34.

60. Stone, '"Sinister" Auckland Business Cliques'.
61. Quoted in Bassett, *The State in NZ*, 186.
62. G. H. G. McDougall, 'Marketing: The Issues for New Zealand', in George H. Hines (ed.), *Business in New Zealand Society*, 1973, 116.
63. S. R. H. Jones and D. R. Paul, 'Concentration and Regulation in the New Zealand Brewing Industry, 1850–1970', *AEHR*, 31 (1992), 88.
64. David Irving and Kerr Inkson, *It Must Be Wattie's! From Kiwi Icon to Global Player*, 1998, 34, 44.
65. Steve Britton et al., *Changing Places in New Zealand: A Geography of Restructuring*, 1992, 63–69.
66. Ibid., 30.
67. Geoffrey Blainey, *A Land Half Won*, Melbourne, 1980, 253.
68. Britton et al., *Changing Places*, 45.
69. Kelsey, *The NZ Experiment*, 144.
70. Very personal communication.
71. Ibid.
72. Bassett, *The State in NZ*, 191, 336.
73. David Thompson, *Selfish Generations?*, 1991.
74. *OYB*, 1990, 141.
75. Bassett, *The State in NZ*, 19.
76. Thorns and Sedgwick, *Historical Statistics*, 105.
77. *OYB*, 2000, 397.
78. Srikanta Chatterjee, 'The Balance of Payments and Exchange Rates', in Stuart Birks and Srikanta Chatterjee, *The New Zealand Economy*, 1992, 255.
79. Calculated from Thorns and Sedgwick, *Historical Statistics*, chapter 4.
80. Bassett, *The State in NZ*, 288.
81. These statistics are drawn from Thorns and Sedgwick, *Historical Statistics*, 111, 144, and *OYB*, 2000, chapter 9.
82. Stuart Birks, 'Economic Growth in New Zealand', in Birks and Chatterjee, *New Zealand Economy*, 40.
83. Thorns and Sedgwick, *Historical Statistics*, 81.
84. Hazledine, *Taking NZ Seriously*, 34.
85. David McLoughlin, 'Why Won't the Economy Fly?', *North and South*, July 1993.

Chapter 15: Rainbow's End

1. *ENZ*, vol. 1, 252; *OYB*, 1990, 340.
2. *OYB*, 1990, 170.
3. *OYB*, 2000, 261. Also see Claudia Bell, *Inventing New Zealand: Everyday Myths of Pakeha Identity*, 1996, chapter 6.
4. *OYB*, 2000, 119, 261.
5. Ian H. Driscoll, *Flight Path South Pacific*, 1972, 61.
6. Ibid., 104.
7. *HS*, 256.
8. Ibid.; *OYB*, 2000, 476. Also see Watson, *Links*, 228–39.
9. *OYB*, 2000, 259.
10. Ibid.
11. Quoted in W. R. Williams (ed.), *Looking Back to Tomorrow*, 1985, 83, facing 129, 40.
12. *OYB*, 2000, 262, 277.
13. Jock Phillips, 'New Zealand and the ANZUS Alliance: Changing National Self-Perceptions, 1945–88', in Richard W. Baker (ed.), *Australia, New Zealand and the US: Internal Change and Alliance Relations in the ANZUS States*, New York, 1991, 185–87.
14. Geoff Leyland, *A Foreign Egg in Our Nest? American Popular Culture in New Zealand*, 1988, 61–63.
15. Jonathan Easthope, 'Home away from Home: The Recent History of Overseas Travel by New Zealanders to Britain, c. 1960–1975', Honours research essay, Victoria University of Wellington, 1993.
16. *OYB*, 2000, 260.
17. *NZ's Heritage*, 104.
18. McKinnon, *Historical Atlas*, 100.
19. W. Jackson, *Withdrawal from Empire*, London, 1986.
20. 'Expatriates', *ENZ*, vol. 1.
21. Watson, *Links*, 184.
22. S. Pollard, *The Development of the British Economy, 1914–1980*, London, 1988, 287.
23. Molly Melhuish, 'Energy and Social Policy' and Geoff Bertram, 'Rents in the New Zealand Energy Sector', in *Report of the Royal Commission on Social Policy*, 1988, vol. 4, 271, 318.
24. Pollard, *Development of the British Economy*, 283.
25. See D. K. Fieldhouse, 'The Metropolitan Economics of Empire', in Brown and Louis, *Oxford History of the British Empire*, vol. 4, and P. J. Cain and A. G. Hopkins, *British Imperialism: Crisis and Deconstruction 1914–1990*, London, 1993, 284–85.
26. Pollard, *Development of the British Economy*, 326–27. Also see *OYB*, 1976, 543.

27. Paul Brassley, 'Output and Technical Change in Twentieth-Century British Agriculture', *The Agricultural History Review*, 48 (2000), 60–84.

28. Pollard, *Development of the British Economy*, 275–77.

29. Merwyn Norrish, in Malcolm Templeton (ed.), *An Eye, an Ear, a Voice: Fifty Years in New Zealand's External Relations 1943–1993*, 1993, 135–36.

30. Juliet Lodge, *The European Community and New Zealand*, London, 1982.

31. Ibid., 8, 43.

32. Bruce Brown, 'From Bulk Purchases to Butter Disputes', in Robert G. Patman (ed.), *New Zealand and Britain: A Special Relationship in Transition*, 1997, and 'New Zealand in the World Economy', in Brown (ed.), *New Zealand in World Affairs III, 1972–1990*, 1999.

33. Lodge, *European Community and NZ*, e.g. xii.

34. Marshall, *Memoirs*, vol. 2, 100–03.

35. Lodge, *European Community and NZ*, 207.

36. Brown, 'NZ in the World Economy', 28.

37. Ibid., 27.

38. Brown, 'From Bulk Purchase to Butter Disputes', 49.

39. Brown, 'NZ in the World Economy', 28–29.

40. Quoted in John Dyson, *Sink the Rainbow! An Enquiry into the 'Greenpeace Affair'*, 1986, 89.

41. Personal communication from Owen Wilkes.

42. James M. McCormick, 'Healing the American Rift with New Zealand', *Pacific Affairs*, 68 (1995).

43. Michael C. Pugh, *The ANZUS Crisis: Nuclear Visiting and Deterrence*, Cambridge, 1989.

44. McKinnon, *Independence and Foreign Policy*, 281; Nicola Dawn Costello, 'New Zealand's Nuclear-Free National Identity: The Evolution of an Image', MLitt, University of Auckland, 1995, chapter 3.

45. William T. Tow, 'The Anzus Dispute: Testing US Extended Deterrence in Alliance Politics', *Political Science Quarterly*, 104 (1989), 128.

46. Thorns and Sedgwick, *Historical Statistics*, 109.

47. McKinnon, *Independence and Foreign Policy*, 198–99, 203 and 'Realignment: New Zealand and its ANZUS Allies', in Brown, *NZ in World Affairs III*, 159.

48. Gustafson, *His Way*, 230.

49. Brian Sinclair, paraphrased by Malcolm McKinnon (who disagrees) in 'Realignment: NZ and its ANZUS Allies', 144.

50. Costello, 'New Zealand's Nuclear-Free National Identity', 32 and passim.

51. William Watts, 'Australia, New Zealand and the US: Mutual Perceptions' in Baker, *Australia, New Zealand and the US*; Roderic Alley, 'The Public Dimension', in Brown, *NZ in World Affairs III*, 303.

52. Douglas Porch, *The French Secret Services: From the Dreyfus Affair to the Gulf War*, New York, 1995, 460–61.

53. Dyson, *Sink the Rainbow*, 9.

54. Michael King, *Death of the Rainbow Warrior*, 1986, 193.

55. Ramesh Thakur, 'A Dispute of Many Colours . . .', *World Today*, 42, December 1986.

56. Dyson, *Sink the Rainbow*, 184–85, 164.

57. Watts, 'Australia, New Zealand and the US'.

58. McKinnon, *Independence and Foreign Policy*, 298.

59. Michael Szabo, *Making Waves: The Greenpeace New Zealand Story*, 1991, 128–30.

60. Most of these details are from Graeme Davison et al. (eds), *The Oxford Companion to Australian History*, Melbourne, 1998.

61. Brian Easton, 'The Economic Relationship between Australia and New Zealand', *Australia–New Zealand: Aspects of a Relationship*, 1991.

62. Stephen Hoadley, 'Trans-Tasman Relations: CER and CDR' in Brown, *NZ in World Affairs III*.

63. Ian McGibbon, 'From Anzac Pact to Anzac Frigates: The Australia/New Zealand Relationship since the Second World War', in *Australia–New Zealand: Aspects of a Relationship*.

64. *OYB*, 2000, 104.

65. Howe, *Singer in A Songless Land*, 181.

66. Peter McPhee, 'An Australian View of New Zealand' in Sinclair, *Tasman Relations*, 291.

67. Peter Pierce, in Robinson and Wattie, *The Oxford Companion to NZ Literature*, 33–34. Also see Terry Sturm, 'The Neglected Middle Distance: Towards a

History of Trans-Tasman Literary Relations', in Sinclair, *Tasman Relations*.

68. James Cowan, 'Domett and his work *Ranolf and Amohia*', *New Zealand Illustrated Magazine*, 5 (1901), 214–23.

69. Hazledine, *Taking New Zealand Seriously*.

70. Peter Norman, *The Meat in the Sandwich*, 1998, 76.

71. D. M. Horsley, 'New Zealand and Japan: Trade Relations 1928–58', MA thesis, University of Canterbury, 1990, 124.

72. Norman, *Meat in the Sandwich*.

73. A. M. Gorrie, 'New Zealand's Trade Future in Japan: A Preliminary Statement', *Proceedings of the 4th New Zealand Geography Conference*, 1965, 237–44.

74. Dick Scott, *Stock in Trade*, 162.

75. *OYB*, 1977, 548.

76. Statistics calculated from *HS*, 268–82 and *OYBs*.

77. Evans, *Agricultural Production and Marketing*, 89.

78. *New Zealand Pocket Digest of Statistics*, 1983, 15.

79. *OYB*, 2000, 516.

80. Marshall, *Memoirs*, vol. 1, 52.

81. *OYB*, 1990, 443–44; *OYB*, 2000, 408, 518.

82. *OYB*, 1990, 612; *OYB*, 2000, 543.

83. Gould, *The Rakes Progress?*, 75.

84. *OYBs*, op. cit.

85. See, e.g., Hugh Templeton, *All Honourable Men: Inside the Muldoon Cabinet, 1975–1984*, 1995, 68; Edwin B. Slack 'Socio-Economic Aspects of Fishing', in G. H. Hines (ed.), *Business and New Zealand Society*, 1973, 278.

86. *OYB*, 1990, 481.

87. *HS*, 99.

88. Slack, 'Socio-Economic Aspects of Fishing'.

89. *OYB*, 1972, 432–33.

90. Irving and Inkson, *It Must Be Watties!*; Boyd, *Hastings*.

91. I. J. Warrington and G. C. Weston (eds), *Kiwifruit Science and Management*, 1990.

92. Quoted in Barbara Fill, 'Report on James Busby', 1987, 45.

93. Dick Scottt, *Winemakers of New Zealand*, 1964; Eric Ramsden, *James Busby: The Prophet of Australian Viticulture*, Sydney, 1940.

94. Andy West, 'Brief History of the Red Meat Industry', Ernst and Young paper, n.d., kindly supplied by the author, 23.

95. *HS*, 320; *OYB*, 2000, 305–10; Taylor, *Consuming Identity*, 4; *Evening Post*, 23 June 1999.

96. Paul Cloke and H. C. Perkins, 'Pushing the Limits: Place Promotion and Adventure Tourism in the South Island of New Zealand', in H. C. Perkins and Grant Cushman, *Time Out? Leisure, Pleasure, and Recreation in New Zealand and Australia*, 1998.

97. Eric Pawson and Simon Swaffield, 'Landscapes of Leisure and Tourism', in ibid., 266.

98. *Sunday Times*, 10 January 1993.

99. David Simmons and Neil Leiper, 'Tourism Systems in New Zealand and Australia', in Perkins and Cushman, *Time Out?*, 92.

100. Douglas Pearce, *Tourist Organisations*, Harlow, Essex, 1992, 166.

101. Templeton, *All Honourable Men*, 68.

102. *Report of the Accommodation/Liquor Inquiry*, 1979, 25.

103. Taylor, *Consuming Identity*, 9. Also see Tourism New Zealand's 1999 '100% Pure New Zealand' publicity campaign.

104. Pearce, *Tourist Organisations*, 158–59.

105. Birks & Chatterjee, *The NZ Economy*, 233. Figures on p. 226 differ somewhat, presumably because different definitions are used.

106. *OYB*, 2000, 517.

107. Dennis Rose, 'Manufacturing', *Pacific Viewpoint*, 32 (1991), 176.

108. Marshall, *Memoirs*, vol. 2, 205.

109. Hoadley, 'Trans-Tasman Relations', 183–84; Templeton, *All Honourable Men*, 136–38.

110. Britton et al., *Changing Places in New Zealand*, 109.

111. *OECD Economic Surveys*, 12.

112. *OYB*, 2000, 277.

113. *Sunday Star-Times*, 22 October 2000.

114. Michael D. Myers, 'Can Kiwis Fly? Computing in New Zealand', *Communications of the ACM*, 39 (1996).

115. M. S. Kaiser, 'A New Industry for New Zealand' in W. R. Williams (ed.), *Looking Back to Tomorrow*, 161–62.

116. Jim Bolger, *A View from the Top*, 1998, 259.

117. Hazledine, *Taking NZ Seriously*, 123–24.

118. R. P. Davenport-Hines & Judy Slinn, *Glaxo: A History to 1962*, Cambridge, 1992, chapter 5.

119. Jack Ilott, *Creating Customers: The Story of Ilott Advertising New Zealand: 1892–1982*, 1982, 47, 65.

120. Evans, *Agricultural Production and Marketing*, 122.

Part 6: Introduction

1. *OYB*, 2000, 288.
2. Thorns and Sedgwick, *Historical Statistics*, 135.
3. Mitchell, *Half-Gallon*, 21.
4. *OYB*, 2000, 318.
5. Thorns and Sedgwick, *Historical Statistics*, 131; *OYB*, 2000, 242.

Chapter 16: Resurgent Maori

1. Michael King, *Whina*, 1983, 166.
2. Gil Dymock, *Good Morning NZ*, 62.
3. Ian Pool, *Te Iwi Maori: A New Zealand Maori Population, Past, Present, and Projected*, 1991, 112.
4. Michael King, *Maori: A Photographic and Social History*, 1983, 201.
5. Turbott, quoted in F. S. McLean, *Challenge for Health: A History of Public Health in New Zealand*, 1964, 206.
6. King, *Whina*, 125n.
7. See Colin Feslier, 'Maori Attitudes to the Disposal of Human Waste and the Continuation of These Beliefs as a Major Public Policy Issue of the Present Day', Research essay, Victoria University of Wellington, 1998.
8. Mclure, *A Civilised Community*, 85, also see 111–15 and Gael Ferguson, *Building the New Zealand Dream*, 1994, 169, 216.
9. Pool, *Te Iwi Maori*, 116.
10. Bryder, 'If Preventable, Why Not Prevented?', 125.
11. Dow, *Safeguarding the Public Health*, 166.
12. McLean, *Challenge for Health*, 215.
13. Ian Prior, 'Health', in Schwimmer, *The Maori People in the 1960s*, 279.
14. McLean, *Challenge for Health*, 218.
15. Pool, *Te Iwi Maori*, 120.
16. King, *Whina*, 66–67.
17. Quoted in Alexandra McKegg, 'The Maori Health Nursing Scheme: An Experiment in Autonomous Health Care', *NZJH*, 26 (2), 1992, 154.
18. King, *Whina*, 168. Also see *DNZB*, vol. 4.
19. Mason Durie, *Whaiora: Maori Health Development*, 1994, 49.
20. Dow, *Safeguarding the Public Health*, 111.
21. Quoted in Simon, *Nga Kura Maori*, 125.
22. Helena Barwick, *The Impact of Economic and Social Factors on Health*, 1992, 54.

23. Pool, *Te Iwi Maori*, 124, citing Brosnan.
24. Ibid., 207. Also see 153–59.
25. G. V. Butterworth, *The Maori People in the New Zealand Economy*, 1974, 29.
26. Joan Metge, *A New Maori Migration*, London, 1964, 128.
27. King, *Maori*, 257.
28. Donna Awatere, 'Cultural Imperialism and the Maori', unpublished paper, 1982.
29. I. H. Kawharu, in Schwimmer, *The Maori People in the 1960s*, 176.
30. M. P. K. Sorrenson, 'Modern Maori: The Young Maori Party to Mana Motuhake', in Sinclair, *Oxford Illustrated History*, 345.
31. Metge, *A New Maori Migration*, 117.
32. Lisa Davies, *Women's Labour Force Participation in New Zealand: The Past 100 Years*, 1993, 86.
33. Sorrenson, 'Modern Maori', 345.
34. Paul Spoonley, 'Racism and Ethnicity', in Paul Spoonley et al., *New Zealand Society: a Sociological Introduction*, 1990, 94.
35. Greg Blanden, et al., *Land-Based Production in Northland*, 1995, 57.
36. See Claudia Orange, 'The Price of Citizenship? The Maori War Effort', in Crawford, *Kia Kaha*, and 'A Kind of Equality: Labour and the Maori People 1935–1949', MA thesis, University of Auckland, 1977; Love, 'Politics of Frustration'.
37. Hirini Kaa, 'Te Wiwi Nati: The Cultural Economy of Ngati Porou', MA thesis, University of Auckland, 2000.
38. Orange, 'Price of Citizenship', 243. Also see Butterworth, *End of an Era*, 19–20.
39. Ibid., 21–23; M. P. K. Sorrenson, *Integration or Identity: Cultural Interaction in New Zealand Since 1911*, 1971, 39; J. K. Hunn, *Report on the Department of Maori Affairs*, 1961.
40. R. J. Walker, 'The Genesis of Maori Activism', *Journal of the Polynesian Society*, 93 (1984), 267–81.
41. Ibid., 277, and *OYB*, 2000, 139.
42. King, *Whina*, 228.
43. Paul Temm, *The Waitangi Tribunal: The Conscience of the Nation*, 1990, 3.
44. See *Orakei (Bastion Point): Case Study of a Claim to the Waitangi Tribunal*, 1990.
45. Paul Moon, *The Occupation of Moutoa Gardens*, 1996.
46. Donna Awatere, *Maori Sovereignty*, 1984, 66.

47. Ranginui Walker, *Nga Tau Tohetohe: Years of Anger*, 1987; Also see Walker's *Ka Whawhai Tonou Matou: Struggle Without End*, 1990.

48. National Council of Churches, *What Happened at Waitangi*, 1983.

49. Lindsay Cox, *Kotahitanga: The Search For Maori Political Unity*, 1993, 140–93.

50. Author interview with Matiu Rata, 1990.

51. *OYB*, 2000, 139.

52. Jane Kelsey, *A Question of Honour? Labour and the Treaty, 1984–1989*, 1990; *OYB*, 2000, 140. On the Treaty claims process also see I. H. Kawharu (ed.), *Waitangi: Maori and Pakeha Perspectives on the Treaty of Waitangi*, 1989; Andrew Sharp, *Justice and the Maori: The Philosophy and Practice of Maori Claims in New Zealand since the 1970s*, 1996.

53. Bruce Biggs, 'The Maori Language Past and Present', in Schwimmer, *The Maori People in the 1960s*, 75; *Dominion*, 13 December 1994; Richard A. Benton, 'Bilingual Education and the Survival of the Maori Language', *Journal of the Polynesian Society*, 93 (1984).

54. *OYB*, 2000, 146.

55. *Evening Post*, 13 December 1995.

56. Thorns and Sedgwick, *Historical Statistics*, 146–47; *OYB*, 2000, 138.

57. Calculated from statistics kindly provided by Miles Fairburn.

58. Thorns and Sedgwick, *Historical Statistics*, 133.

59. *OYB*, 2000, 253. Also see Te Puni Kokiri, 'A Statistical Profile of Maori Participation and Achievement in Education', [1996?]

60. Sorrenson, 'Modern Maori', 340.

61. See Belich, *Making Peoples*, chapter 16, and Fairburn, *Ideal Society*, 1989.

62. Roi Te Punga, in *Te Ao Hou*, 1959, quoted in Lloyd Jones, 'Images of Maori in the Pakeha Press', 82.

63. *Report of the Royal Commission on Social Policy*, 1988, vol. 1, 433.

64. See Bill Payne, *Staunch: Inside the Gangs*, 1991; Pahmi Winter, '"Pulling the Teams Out of the Dark Room": The Politicisation of the Mongrel Mob', in Kayleen and Cameron Hazlehurst, *Gangs and Youth Subcultures: International Explorations*, New Brunswick and London, 1998.

65. Ibid., 245.

66. *New Zealand Herald*, 1 March 2001.

67. *Local Authorities and Gang Problems*, 1997.

68. David Pearson, 'From Communality to Ethnicity: Some Theoretical Considerations on the Maori Ethnic Revival', *Ethnic and Racial Studies*, 11 (1988), 168–91.

69. See Belich, *Making Peoples*, 100.

70. Lauren Waller, et al., *Cannabis Highs and Lows: Sustaining and Dislocating Rural Communities in Northland*, 1998, 33.

71. Ibid., 35.

72. *Tai Tokerau: Regional Profile Supplement: Training Opportunities*, Education and Training Support Agency, 1997, 16.

73. Greg Blanden et al., *Land-Based Production in Northland*, 53–57.

74. *OYB*, 2000, 139; Pita Rikys, unpublished paper on urban Maori, copy kindly supplied by the author.

75. John Harre, 'Maori Pakeha Intermarriage', in Schwimmer, *The Maori People in the 1960s*, 118–19. Also see Harre, *Maori and Pakeha: A Study of Mixed Marriages in New Zealand*, 1966.

Chapter 17: Escape from Nappy Valley

1. Watson, *Links*, 172–74.

2. McKinnon, *Historical Atlas*, 75.

3. Gordon Troup, *Steel Roads of New Zealand*, 1973, 283.

4. David Pearson, *Johnsonville: Community and Change in a New Zealand Township*, Sydney, 1980.

5. *OYB*, 1998, 92; Also see Ian Pool and Richard Bedford, *Macro Social Change in New Zealand: Historical and International Contexts*, 1996, 19–20, and 'The People of NZ', in *Report of the Royal Commission on Social Policy*, 1988, vol. 1.

6. Calculated from *OYB*, 1990 and 2000, 141 and 100.

7. Gordon A. Carmichael, 'Post-War Trends in Female Labour Force Participation in New Zealand', *Pacific Viewpoint*, 16 (1975); Thorns and Sedgwick, *Historical Statistics*, 40–41; Smyth, *Rocking the Cradle*, chapter 6.

8. Carmichael, 'Post-War Trends in Female Labour Force', 82.

9. Ibid., 91.

10. Olssen and Levesque, 'Towards a History of the Family', in Koopman-Boyden, *Families in New Zealand Society*, 13.

11. Helen May, *Minding Children, Managing Men: Conflict and Compromise in the*

Lives of Postwar Pakeha Women, 1992, 43.

12. Ibid., 11.

13. Elliott, 'Anzac, Hollywood and Home', 93.

14. Thompson, *History of NZ Music*, 159–62; Elliott, 'Anzac, Hollywood and Home', 137.

15. *HS*, 125.

16. Quoted in Melanie Nolan, *Breadwinning: New Zealand Women and the State*, 2000, 272.

17. Keith, *A Lovely Day Tomorrow*, 24.

18. Calculated from *HS*, 224–25, 108.

19. Ferguson, *Building the New Zealand Dream*, chapter 4.

20. Taylor, *The Home Front*, vol. 2, 1270–83.

21. May, *Minding Children, Managing Men*, 50.

22. Thorns and Sedgwick, *Historical Statistics*, 148.

23. *OYB*, 2000, 98.

24. E. Geiringer, 'Attitudes to Birth Control in New Zealand', in *Populations, Resources and Environment in NZ: Papers of a National Symposium*, 1972; Macdonald, *The Vote, the Pill and the Demon Drink*, 143; Smyth, *Rocking the Cradle*, 44.

25. Roderick Phillips, *Divorce in New Zealand: A Social History*, 1981, 58; *Report of the Royal Commission on Social Policy*, vol. 1, 131.

26. Coney, *Standing in the Sunshine*, 214; Martin, *Power, People and Politics*, 131. Also see Jean Marie O'Donnell, '"Electric Servants" and the Science of Housework: Changing Patterns of Domestic Work, 1935–56', in Barbara Brookes et al., *Women in History 2*, 1992; May, *Minding Children, Managing Men*, 114.

27. Society for Research on Women in New Zealand, *Urban Women*, 1982, 72.

28. May, *Minding Children, Managing Men*, 265–77.

29. Ibid., 244.

30. *Urban Women*, 202.

31. 'Many Changes in Women's Status', Statistics New Zealand press release, 8 March 1999.

32. Judith Aitken, *A Woman's Place? A Study of the Changing Role of Women in New Zealand*, 1980, 82.

33. This paragraph and the next draw heavily on Nolan, *Breadwinning*. Also see Prue Hyman, 'Equal Pay for Women in New Zealand: History and Evaluation',

Victoria Economic Commentaries, 10 (1993).

34. Nolan, *Breadwinning*, 188.

35. Ibid., 236.

36. *OYB*, 2000, 317.

37. Nolan, *Breadwinning*, 272.

38. See Christine Dann, *Up From Under: Women and Liberation in New Zealand 1970–85*, 1985; Macdonald, *The Vote, the Pill, and the Demon Drink*, chapter 7.

39. Coney, *Standing in the Sunshine*, 129.

40. Else, *Women Together*, 575–76.

41. Jenifer Curtin and Heather Devere, 'A Plurality of Feminisms', in Helena Catt and Elizabeth McLeay, *Women and Politics in New Zealand*, 1992; Prue Hyman, 'New Zealand Since 1984: Economic Restructuring: Feminist Responses, Activity and Theory', *Hecate*, 20 (1994); *Evening Post*, 7 January 1993.

42. *Report of the Royal Commission on Social Policy*, vol. 1, 533–46.

43. Elizabeth McLeay, 'Women's Parliamentary Representation: A Comparative Perspective', in Catt and McLeay, *Women and Politics*; Coney, *Standing in the Sunshine*, chapter 2; *OYB*, 2000, 37–38.

44. See Sandra Coney, *The Unfortunate Experiment*, 1988.

45. *OYB*, 1990 and 2000, 243, 191; Erich Geiringer, *SPUC 'em All: Abortion Politics*, 1978.

46. Ibid., 21.

47. Jacqueline Owens, 'Abortion Politics', in Catt and McLeay, *Women and Politics*, 108.

48. Coney, *Standing in the Sunshine*, 73.

49. Phillips, *Divorce in New Zealand*, chapter 4.

50. Cited in Jane Ritchie and James Ritchie, *Violence in New Zealand*, 1990, 32.

51. Quoted in Smyth, *Rocking the Cradle*, 75.

52. Hogg, *Crump*.

53. J. and J. Ritchie, *Violence*, 36; Dann, *Up From Under*, chapter 9. Also see Justice Department, *Report on Domestic Violence*, 1993; and *OYB*, 2000, 244, 246.

54. Deborah Montgomerie, 'Re-assessing Rosie: World War II, New Zealand Women and the Iconography of Femininity', *Gender and History*, 8 (1996), 111. For a similar estimate see D. M. Brosnahan, 'A Woman's Place: Changing Attitudes to the Role of Women in Society During World War

Two in New Zealand', MA thesis, University of Canterbury, 1987, 29. Also see Montgomerie, 'The Limitations of Wartime Change: Women War Workers in New Zealand', *NZJH*, 23 (1989), 68–86.

55. R. J. Overy, *War and Economy in the Third Reich*, Oxford, 1994. The best NZ figure for comparison seems to be in Carmichael, 'Post-War trends in Female Labour Force', 80. *OYB*, 1998, 306, appears to calculate participation on a different basis.

56. Nolan, *Breadwinning*, 198.

57. See Belich, *Making Peoples*, 331, 387–88.

58. Melanie Nolan, '"Politics Swept Under a Domestic Carpet"?', 206, n. 40.

59. Nolan, *Breadwinning*, 132, and see 190.

60. Brosnahan, 'A Woman's Place', 104.

61. Ibid., 113–20.

62. Ibid., passim; Henderson, *Quest For Efficiency*; Nolan, *Breadwinning*, 220–21.

63. Ibid., 220.

64. Carmichael, 'Post-War trends in Female Labour Force'.

65. *Urban Women*, 146.

66. Tanis Day, 'Capital-Labor Substitution in the Home', *Technology and Culture*, 33 (1992), n. 2.

67. Coney, *Standing in the Sunshine*, 237.

68. *Urban Women*, 91, 182.

69. Coney, *Standing in the Sunshine*, 237.

70. *OYB*, 2000, 228. Also see *NZ Herald*, 10 August 2000.

71. *Evening Post*, 7 January 1993.

72. *OYB*, 2000, 118.

73. Janet Soler, 'That "Incredible Document" Commonly Known as the Mazengarb Report', *Sites*, 19 (1989); Coney, *Standing in the Sunshine*, 174–75; Yska, *All Shook Up*, 63–70.

74. Trewby, *Best Years*, 145.

75. A. E. Manning, *The Bodgie: A Study in Abnormal Psychology*, 1958.

76. *ENZ*, vol. 1, 308; Yska, *All Shook Up*, 170. Also see Marshall, *Memoirs*, vol. 1, 221–24.

77. *OYB*, 1960, 90.

78. Carmichael, 'Post-War Trends in Female Labour Force', 92, n. 20.

79. *OYB*, 2000, 98; Anne Else, '"The Need is Ever Present": The Motherhood of Man Movement and Stranger Adoption in New Zealand', *NZJH*, 23 (1989).

80. Nolan, *Breadwinning*, 270.

81. Smyth, *Rocking the Cradle*, 152.

82. Peter Davis and Roy Lay-Yee, 'Early Sex and its Behavioral Consequences In New Zealand', *Journal of Sex Research*, 36 (1999), 135–44.

83. Yska, *All Shook Up*, 57.

84. Shuker, *One Best System?*, 54.

85. John Dix, *Stranded in Paradise: New Zealand Rock 'N' Roll, 1955–1988*, 1988, 28 and 47.

86. Kirsten Lovelock, 'Men and Machines: Manufacturing Work Sites in Mataura, Southland', in Robin Law et al. (eds), *Masculinities in Aotearoa/New Zealand*, 1999, 121–22.

87. Anna Kraak, 'It takes Two to Tango: The Place of Women in the Construction of Hegemonic Masculinity in a Student Pub', in ibid.

88. Thorns and Sedgwick, *Historical Statistics*, 144.

89. Phillips, 'New Zealand and the ANZUS Alliance', 189–90.

90. Ibid.

91. David Wilson, 'Mixed Flatting and the Student Revolt Against Paternalism', MA thesis, University of Otago, 1994.

92. Dix, *Stranded in Paradise*, 143–44.

93. Ibid., 106, 159.

94. See, for example, Anne Salmond, *Two Worlds: First Meetings Between Maori and Europeans, 1642–1772*, 1991, 251.

95. Judith Binney, 'Whatever Happened to Poor Mr Yate? An Exercise in Voyeurism', *NZJH*, 9 (1975).

96. Rana Waitai, 'Modes of Dress: Drag Queens in Wellington', in Michael Hill et al., *Shades of Deviance: A New Zealand Collection*, 1983.

97. Eldred-Grigg, *Pleasures of the Flesh*, 50.

98. Phil Parkinson, 'Sexual Law Reform: The New Zealand Experience from Wolfenden to the Crimes Bill 1989', *Sites*, 19 (1989), 7–13.

99. Nigel Gearing, *Emerging Tribe: Gay Culture in New Zealand*, 1997, 12, 15.

100. *DNZB*, vol. 2. Also see Julie Glamuzina, *Out Front: Lesbian Political Activity in Aotearoa 1962–1985*, 1993; Coney, *Standing in the Sunshine*, 170–71.

101. Peter Parker, 'Lads' loves and t–boys', review of Alisdare Hickson, *The Poisoned Bowl: Sex, Repression and the Public School System*, Constable, 1995, *Times Literary Supplement*, 12 May 1995.

102. Phil Parkinson, 'Lesbian and Gay Archives in New Zealand: A Minority Gathers its Own History', *Archifacts*, 4 (1984), 8.

103. Julie Glamuzina and Alison J. Laurie, *Parker and Hulme: A Lesbian View*, 1991, 152.

104. Quoted in Coney, *Standing in the Sunshine*, 171.

105. Quoted in King, *Sargeson*, 252.

106. Richard Bowman, 'Beyond the Pink Triangle: The New Zealand Public's Atttitude Towards Homosexuality', in Hill et al., *Shades of Deviance*, 109.

107. Davis and Lay-Yee, 'Early Sex and its Behavioral Consequences in New Zealand'.

108. See James Veitch, 'Christianity: Protestants Since the 1960s' in Peter Donovan, *Religions of the New Zealanders*, 1990.

109. New Zealand Censuses. Also see Alan E. Webster and Paul E. Perry, *The Religious Factor in New Zealand Society*, 1989.

110. New Zealand Censuses. Also see D. Thompson in Davidson and Lineham, *Transplanted Christianity*, 315–16.

111. 'The Politics of Discontent', *NZ's Heritage*, 100.

112. Eldred-Grigg, *NZ Working People*, 209.

113. Warwick Roger, *Forgotten Heroes*.

114. Greg Ryan, 'Anthropological Football: Maori and the 1937 Springbok Rugby Tour of New Zealand', *NZJH*, 34 (2000). Also see Malcom Templeton, *Human Rights and Sporting Contact: New Zealand Attitudes to Race Relations in South Africa, 1921–94*, 1998.

115. Mckinnon, *Independence and Foreign Policy*, 240.

116. Ibid., 243.

117. Templeton, *Human Rights and Sporting Contact*, 202; Gustafson, *Muldoon*, 311. 'The Tour: Ten Years On', TV One documentary, 1991.

118. Geoff Chapple, *1981: The Tour*, 1984, 314. Also see *56 Days: A History of the Anti-Tour Movement in Wellington*, 1982; Louise Greig, 'The Police and the Tour', and Rachel Barrowman, 'A Report on the Molesworth Street Incident' both in *The Police and the 1981 Tour*, 1985; Ross Meurant, *The Red Squad Story*, 1982.

119. *Evening Post*, 10 July 1991.

120. Peter King and Jock Phillips, 'A Social Analysis of the Springbok Tour Protestors', in *Counting the Cost: The 1981 Springbok Tour in Wellington*, 1982, 10.

Chapter 18: One, Two, Many?

1. *Historic Places*, 57, (March 1996).

2. Shaw, *NZ Architecture*, 175.

3. On the Chathams see *Sunday Star-Times*, 8 January 1995; *OYB*, 2000, 141; Michael King, *Moriori: A People Rediscovered*, 1989. I visited the islands in 1997.

4. See Sutton-Smith, *A History of Children's Play*.

5. A. H. McLintock, *The History of Otago: The Origins and Growth of a Wakefield Class Settlement*, 1949; Erik Olssen, *A History of Otago*, 1984; J. Hight et al., *A History of Canterbury*, 3 vols, 1957–71; Stevan Eldred-Grigg, *A New History of Canterbury*, 1982.

6. Keith Sinclair, *Half Way Round the Harbour: An Autobiography*, 1993, 123.

7. Tim Hazledine and John Siegfried, 'How Did the Wealthiest New Zealanders Get So Rich?', *New Zealand Economic Papers*, 31 (1997).

8. Cited in Charles Waldegrave et al., 'An Overview of Poverty Research in New Zealand', *New Zealand Sociology*, 12 (1997), 226.

9. Kelsey, *The New Zealand Experiment*, 258.

10. Calculated from *HS*, 169.

11. Britton et al., *Changing Places*, 135.

12. Martin Oppermann, 'Regional Aspects of Tourism in New Zealand', *Regional Studies*, 28 (1994).

13. Graham W. Bush, *Local Government and Politics in New Zealand*, 1980, 50. Also see Bush, *Decently and in Order: The Centennial History of the Auckland City Council*, 1971.

14. Bush, *Local Government*, 50.

15. *OYB*, 2000 94; Richard Bedford et al., 'Migration in New Zealand 1986–1996: A Regional Perspective', *New Zealand Journal of Geography*, 16 (1997).

16. *HS*, 10.

17. Pearson, *Johnsonville*, 43.

18. *ENZ*, vol. 3, 694–97.

19. Burdon, *New Dominion*, 109–10.

20. J. D. Pascoe, 'The Mountains', *Making New Zealand*, no. 10.

21. Quoted by Kirstie Ross, 'Signs of Landing: Pakeha Outdoor Recreation

and the Cultural Colonisation of New Zealand', MA thesis, University of Auckland, 1999, 33. The next paragraph is also drawn from this thesis.

22. Michael Roche, '"The Land we Must Hold": Soil Erosion and Soil Conservation in Late 19th and 20th Century New Zealand', *Journal of Historical Geography*, 23 (1997), 447–58. Also see Michael Roche, *Land and Water: Water and Soil Conservation and Central Government in New Zealand, 1941–88*, 1994.

23. Guthrie-Smith, *Tutira*. Also see *DNZB*, vol. 3, and G. Wynn, 'Remapping Tutira: Contours in the Environmental History of New Zealand', *Journal of Historical Geography*, 23 (1997), 418–46.

24. *DNZB*, vol. 3.

25. Ross, 'Signs of Landing', 107.

26. William R. Catton, Jr, 'The Use of Open Space in New Zealand', *Populations, Resources and Environment in NZ*: Papers of a National Symposium, 1972.

27. Margaret Johnston and Eric Pawson, 'Challenge and Danger in the Development of Mountain Recreation in New Zealand, 1890–1940', *Journal of Historical Geography*, 20 (1994), 179.

28. Geoff Park, *Nga Ururoa: The Groves of Life: Ecology and History in a New Zealand Landscape*, 1995, 317.

29. Catton, 'The Use of Open Space in NZ'.

30. P. J. Devlin et al. (eds), *Outdoor Recreation in New Zealand*, 1995, vol. I, 33–34; David Thom, *Heritage: The Parks of the People*, 1989, 190.

31. Ibid., 188–89. Also see Neville Peat, *Manapouri Saved! New Zealand's First Great Conservation Success Story*, 1994.

32. Davison et al., *Companion to Australian History*: Calwell biography.

33. Thorns and Sedgwick, *Historical Statistics*, 55.

34. *ENZ*, vol. 2, 130–34; Patrick Ongley and David Pearson, 'Post-1945 International Migration: New Zealand, Australia and Canada Compared', *International Migration Review*, 29 (1995).

35. Thorns and Sedgwick, *Historical Statistics*, 55–56.

36. Ibid., 56.

37. Kerry Howe, 'New Zealand's Twentieth-Century Pacifics: Memories and Reflections', *NZJH*, 34 (2000).

38. William Tagupa, 'Law, Status, and Citizenship: Conflict and Continuity in New Zealand and Western Samoa, 1922–82', *Journal of Pacific History*, 29 (1994), 19–35.

39. Ron Crocombe, *Pacific Neighbours: New Zealand's Relations with Other Pacific Islands*, 1992, 136.

40. Malama Meleisea and Penelope Schoeffel, 'Samoan Families in New Zealand: The Cultural Context of Change', in Vivienne Adair and Robyn Dixon (eds), *The Family in Aotearoa/New Zealand*, 1998, 159.

41. Cluny Macpherson, 'Would the Real Samoans Please Stand Up? Issues in Diasporic Samoan Identity', in Deborah Ball and Ian Pool (eds), *The Building Blocks of National Identity: Population in New Zealand History*, 1998.

42. Meleisea and Schoeffel, 'Samoan Families in New Zealand', 173.

43. P. H. Curson, 'The Cook Islanders', in Thomson and Trlin, *Immigrants in New Zealand*, 181–82.

44. See Crocombe, 56–68.

45. Curson, 'The Cook Islanders', 188–90.

46. Cluny MacPherson, 'Pacific Islanders', *Pacific Viewpoint*, 32 (1991), 139–46.

47. Curson, 'The Cook Islanders', 186.

48. *Report of the Royal Commission on Social Policy*, 1988, vol. 1, 82.

49. *OYB*, 2000, 108.

50. Thorns and Sedgwick, *Historical Statistics*, 55.

51. Trung Tran, 'From the Mekong Delta to the Auckland Isthmus', in Hon-key Yoon (ed.), *Vietnamese, Indonesian, and Hong Kong Migrants in Auckland*, 1997.

52. Rachael Boswell, 'Kowloon to Vim Valley', in ibid.

53. Hon-key Yoon, 'Searching for Korean Identity in New Zealand', in Ball and Pool (eds), *Building Blocks of National Identity*.

54. Tran, 'From the Mekong Delta', 39–40.

55. Mayumi Torgersen, 'Orang Indonesia di Auckland', in Yoon, *Vietnamese, Indonesian, and Hong Kong Migrants*.

56. Ongley and Pearson, 'Post-1945 Immigration'.

57. Hank Shouten, *Tasman's Legacy: The New Zealand-Dutch Connection*, 1992, 68–69.

58. *HS*, 77.

59. Schouten, *Tasman's Legacy*, 257.

60. *HS*, 76–77.

61. McKinnon, *Historical Atlas*, 76.

62. Ibid., and *OYB*, 1972, 69.
63. *HS*, 79.
64. *OYB*, 2000, 108, 111.
65. Quoted *Evening Post*, 6 July 1992.
66. Ashley Cunningham, *Sheila: Happy Wanderer*, 1991, 55, 60.
67. *New Zealand Cultural Statistics*, 1995, 73.
68. *The Heart of the Nation: A Cultural Strategy for Aotearoa New Zealand*, Report of strategic working group, 2000, 11.
69. *DNZB*, vol. 4.
70. Crafts Council of New Zealand, *Mau Mahara: Our Stories in Craft*, 1990, 124.
71. Ian Cross, *The Unlikely Bureaucrat*, 36. At the opposite end of the broadcasting hierarchy, my experience as a labourer on *The Governor*, a controversial 1977 series about the career of George Grey, tends to confirm Cross's view.
72. *OYB*, 1990, 328; *OYB*, 2000, 288.
73. Roger Horrocks, 'Alternatives: Experimental Film-Making in New Zealand', in Jonathan Dennis and Jan Bieringa (eds), *Film in Aotearoa New Zealand*, 1992, 60.
74. Fergus Barrowman (ed.), *The Picador Book of Contemporary New Zealand Fiction*, London, 1996, vii.
75. Calculated roughly from Keith W. Thomson, *Art Galleries and Museums of New Zealand*, 1981.
76. Tony Mitchell and Roy Shuker, 'Music Scenes and National Identity: Popular Music and the Press in Aotearoa/New Zealand', *New Zealand Sociology*, 12 (1991), 106.
77. Leyland, *A Foreign Egg in Our Nest?*, 35.
78. Ibid., 75.
79. Ibid., 76.
80. Orsman, *Dictionary of New Zealand English*, 567–69.
81. See Pearson, *A Dream Deferred*, chapter 12.
82. David Huges et al., *A Question of Ethnicity: The Meanings of 'New Zealander'*, 1996, 19.
83. Keith Sinclair, 'History in New Zealand', in John A. Moses (ed.), *Historical Disciplines and Culture in Australasia: An Assessment*, St. Lucia, Qld, 1979.
84. Quoted in Fiona Hamilton, 'Founding Histories: Some Pakeha Constructions of a New Zealand Past in the Late Nineteenth and Early Twentieth Centuries', MA thesis, University of Auckland, 1999, 123.
85. Chris Hilliard, 'Island Stories: The Writing of New Zealand History 1920–1940,' MA thesis, University of Auckland, 1997, 28.
86. Vernon Reed, *The Gift of Waitangi: A History of the Bledisloe Gift*, 1957, from which all quotes in the next two paragraphs are taken.
87. James Belich, 'Colonization and History in New Zealand', in Robin W. Winks (ed.), *The Oxford History of the British Empire*, vol. 5: *Historiography*, 1999.
88. 'Heart of the Nation', 43.
89. 'Pau Misa, Lloyd Ashton, and Siobhan Wilson, 'Why Hide our History?', *Mana Magazine*, 36, October–November 2000, 22–32.

INDEX

abortion, 183, 498–9
Adams, Arthur, 330, 332
adoption, 505
Advances to Settlers measures, 128
aerial topdressing, 309, 526
Agriculture, Department of, 60, 249
air travel, 427
Aitken, W. E., 294–5
Akenson, Donald, 218, 222
Alanbrooke, Lord. *See* Brooke, General Alan
All Black tours: (1905), 386–7, 387–8; (1960) 516; (1970) 516; (1976) 517
Allen, C. R., 333
Allen, James, 110, 111, 112
Allen, Colonel Stephen, 239
Allenby, General, 108
Alliance of Labour, 145, 146
aluminium smelter, 401, 531
American popular culture, 251–4, 428–9
American troops in New Zealand, 287, 289–92
America's Cup, 392, 407, 479
Anglican Church, 198, 202
Angus, Rita, 334
anti-communist hysteria, 303
anti-nuclear movement/policies, 435–40
Anzac Day, 116–18, 316
ANZUS treaty, 318, 319, 321, 399, 435–40
Apple, Billy, 541
Arawa, 202, 212
Arbitration Court, 398
Arthur, Sir Basil, 395

The Aryan Maori (Tregear), 207, 231, 516
Aryanism, 206–10, 211, 230–2
Ashton-Warner, Sylvia, 336–7
Asians in New Zealand, 535–7
assembly plants, 312
asset sales, 410
assimilation, 218, 219, 233, 477
asylums, 159, 176
Atkinson, Arthur, 208
Atkinson, Harry, 38, 41, 49
Auckland, 523, 525–7, 533
Auckland Ladies Benevolent Society, 132
Auckland Lunatic Asylum, 176
'Aunt Daisy', 253
Australia, 46–52, 254, 318, 440–3, 453–5, 531–2
Australian immigrants in New Zealand, 538
automobiles. *See* motorcars
Ayson, Hugh, 237

'baby boom', 489–93
'baby bust', 493–6
baby farming, 184
Baden-Powell, Robert, 366
Baker, Louisa, 339
Balfour Declaration (1926), 246
Ball, Murray, 342, 350
Ballance, John, 28, 38, 41, 42, 46, 128, 479
Balneavis, Te Raumoa, 201
Bank of New Zealand, 63, 407
banks and banking, 32, 63, 257, 260–1, 407, 409, 416, 417
Barker, Lady, 358

Barnes, Harold 'Jock', 299, 300, 301, 302, 305, 306
Barrowclough, General H. E., 285
Basham, Maud, 253
Bastion Point, Orakei, 478, 479
Batchelor, Dr Ferdinand, 159
Batten, Jean, 496
Baughan, Blanche, 76, 330, 334
Baxter, Archibald, 106
Baxter, James K., 332, 338, 511, 541
Beaglehole, J. C., 257
Bean, C. E. W., 107
beef exports, 309, 445, 447
Bellamy, Henry, 137
Bennett, Dr Harry, 190–1
Berendsen, Carl, 318, 319
Bethell, Ursula, 512
birth rate, 161, 181–6, 489–96
'black' economy, 484–5
Black Power, 482–4
Blair, William, 71
Blake, Peter, 392
Bledisloe, Charles, 214, 545
blood sports, 371
'Blue Smoke' (Ruru Karaitiana), 540
Blue Star Line, 65
Bluff, 523
Board of Maori Ethnological Research, 203
Bock, Amy, 512
bodgies, 505, 506
Boer War, 79–80
Bolger, Jim, 408, 458, 466
Borthwick's, 63
boxing, 371–2
Boy Scouts, 365–6
Boys' Brigade, 365, 366
Bracken, Thomas, 328, 331, 332
Bragato, Romeo, 451
Brasch, Charles, 335, 337
Brierley (the company), 407–8
Britain. See decolonisation; 'recolonisation'
British immigration to New Zealand, 83, 532, 538–9
broadcasting. See radio; television

Brooke, General Alan, 276
Brydone, Thomas, 56
Buchanan, 436–7, 438
Buck, Peter, 200, 201, 211, 213, 238, 470
Buckle Street riot (1913), 94
Buick, T. Lindsay, 545
Bulletin, 329–30
Burchfield, Robert, 342
Burrow, Brigadier J. W., 279–80
Busby, James, 170, 451
Business Roundtable, 411, 412

Calwell, Arthur, 532
Cameron, Robina, 470
Campaign for Nuclear Disarmament, 435
Campbell, John Logan, 32, 36, 76, 129, 288
Canada, 254
Canberra Pact (1944), 318, 321
cannabis growing and consumption, 484–5, 511
Canterbury and Otago Association Limited, 60
Canterbury Frozen Meat and Dairy Produce Export Company, 61
capital punishment, 505
Carman, Dulce, 339
Carmen (drag queen), 513
Carroll, James, 39, 194, 199, 200–1, 205, 206, 210, 213
cars. See motorcars
cartelism, 425–7
Casali, Kim, 342
casein, 309, 445, 446, 447
Caversham, 134–5, 144
Cavour, Count, 111
Cawthron Institute, 249
Caxton Press, 334
censorship, 294, 317–18, 505
CER, 441, 455
Chamier, George, 327
Chatham Islands, 449–50, 521–2
Chelsea Sugar Refinery, 255
Chew Chong, 61, 70, 231
'Chicago School', 411

Child Welfare Act 1925, 176
childhood, 356–67
Chinese in New Zealand, 227–9, 231, 232–3, 234, 362, 532, 536, 537
Christchurch, 174, 523, 525
Christchurch Beautifying Society, 349
Christ's College (Christchurch), 130
church-going, 350–1, 514–15
Churchill, Winston, 110, 286–7
cinema, 251, 252, 491–2
City of Glasgow Bank, 32
Civic (Auckland picture theatre), 251
Clarke, John, 350
classes. See farm sector; gentry; working class
Cleal, Charles, 326
Cleary, Bishop Henry, 116, 165
Clifford, Charles, 132
Closer Economic Relations, 441, 455
Coalition government (1931–35), 254, 256
Coates, Gordon, 196, 201, 249, 254, 256–7, 258–9, 264
cobalt deficiency, 249, 309, 526
cold war, 298, 304
Colonial Observatory, 249
Columbus, Ray, 508
Commerce Act 1986, 416
Common Agricultural Policy, 431, 432, 434
communications technology, 427–8
Communist Party, 257
compulsory military service, 298
compulsory unionism, 262, 306
conservationist movement, 529–31
contraception, 162, 165, 178, 183, 494
Cook Islanders in New Zealand, 534
Cook Islands, 212, 237
Cooper, Whina, 196, 468, 478
corporatisation, 409
Couch, Ben, 487
Courage, James, 332
Cowan, James, 443, 545
Cowley, Joy, 340
Cox, James, 177
Craven, Danie, 379, 516

'crew culture', 18–19, 176–8, 482
cricket, 372–4, 375
Crimes Act 1908, 305
croquet, 373, 375
Crown Lynn Potteries, 293
Crump, Barry, 338, 350, 354–6, 500, 530, 541
Crump, Wally, 500
Cullen, John, 90, 92, 94, 226
Curnow, Allen, 332, 334
Curtin, John, 284
cycling, 375

Dairy Board, 311
dairy-produce exports. See casein; milk powder; 'protein industry'
Daldy, Amey, 166
Dalmatians in New Zealand, 225–7, 233, 234, 235, 236, 293, 362
Dannevirke, 225
Darrell, George, 328
Darwin, Charles, 162, 344, 372
Davidson, William Soltau, 56, 57, 64
Davin, Dan, 223, 279, 332, 337, 342
Davis, Sir Ernest, 415
Davis Pool (of British shipping companies), 65
De Montalk, Geoffrey, 333
Dean, Williamina ('Minnie'), 184
death, premature, 173–6
decolonisation, 425–60, 474, 519, 524
deer, 309, 448
defence spending, 437
'demon drink', 170–3
Depression. See Great Depression (1929–35)
Devanney, Jean, 330, 332
Devlin, Johnny, 507
Divorce Act 1898, 45, 166
Dix, P. R., 328
Dodd, Lynley, 340
Doidge, Frederick, 320
'domestic bliss', 490–3
domestic education, 187
domestic purposes benefit, 397–8
domestic service, 131, 133, 186, 501

domestic violence, 499–500
Domestic Violence Act 1996, 500
Domett, Alfred, 327
Dominion Breweries, 415
'dominionism', 116–18
Don, Alexander, 232
Donnelly, Ian, 333–4
Douglas, Major Clifford, 261
Douglas, Roger, 405–6, 407, 408, 412
Downes, Alex, 373
DPB, 397–8
Duff, Alan, 483, 487, 540
Duggan, Eileen, 335
Duggan, Maurice, 321
Dunedin, 53, 56, 57, 60, 61
Dunedin, 523, 525
Dutch immigrants in New Zealand, 538

economic boom (1945–72), 307–13
economic growth, 308, 423–4, 456–60
economic policy, 400–2, 406–9, 410
Economic Stabilisation Commission,
   294, 295
Eden, Anthony, 266, 283–4, 547
Eden, Dorothy, 340
Edendale Dairy Factory, 60, 61
education, 130–1, 154, 222, 397, 421–2,
   506–7
Education Act 1877, 130
eight-hour day, 133, 134, 136
electricity, 248, 315, 494, 501
Elizabeth II, Queen, 320–1, 478–9
Ell, Harry, 530
Elliott, Howard, 114, 115, 116
Ellis, William Webb, 380, 384
Ellison, Edward, 237
Ellison, Tom, 212
emigration (from Britain to New
   Zealand), 83, 532, 538–9
Empire Air Training Scheme, 273
Empire Marketing Board, 250
Employers Federation, 92
Employment Contracts Act 1991, 411
environmentalism, 529–31
equal-opportunities legislation, 500
Equal Pay Act 1972, 495

Erebus disaster (1979), 391
'eugenics', 162
European Economic Community
   (EEC), 397, 429–35
Evans, Frederick George, 91
exchange rate, 405, 408–9
exhibitions, 83
export diversification, 309–10,
   443–60
extractive industries, 69–70, 73, 74. *See
   also* 'progress industry'; 'progressive
   colonisation'

Fairburn, A. R. D. (Rex), 256, 258, 336,
   337
Falklands War (1982), 27–8, 399–400
family benefit, 492, 495–6
family wage, 495–6
Farjeon, Benjamin, 327, 339
farm sector, 146–56, 262, 308–11, 400,
   402–3
Federated Mountain Clubs, 528
Federation of Labour (FOL), 299, 303
Federation of Labour ('Red Feds'),
   88–90, 93, 95, 137
feminism: 'first-wave', 166–8; 'second
   wave', 496–504
Fiji, 282, 283, 455
film-making, 340, 341, 541
financial institutions, 62–3
Finn, Neil, 542
Firth, J. C., 36
Firth, J. P., 374
fishing industry, 449–50
FitzRoy, Charles, 48
FitzRoy, Robert, 48
Fitzsimmons, Robert, 371–2
Fletcher, James, 295
Forbes, George, 254, 256
foreign-exchange crisis (1984), 405
Forest and Bird Protection Society,
   530
forestry, 315, 448–9
Frame, Janet, 332, 336, 541
France, 436, 438–9
Fraser, Isabel, 450

Fraser, Peter: arrested for sedition, 94; and Aryan Maori thesis, 208; character, 268, 295; Deputy Prime Minister, 264, 267, 268; at founding of United Nations Organisation, 318; Minister of Health, 469; Prime Minister, 279–80, 283, 284, 286–7, 294, 298, 300, 304, 305, 318, 437; relations with Te Puea, 196; relations with Walsh, 295, 299
free trade, 410
Freyberg, General Bernard, 274, 276, 277–8, 283, 284
Friedman, Milton, 411
Friendly Societies, 169, 178
Frikart, Eliza, 159
From Europe to New Zealand (Lochore), 230
Froude, James Anthony, 16–17, 18
Fuchs, Vivian, 392

Gallup poll (1948), 83, 84
Galton, Francis, 162
Galway, Viscount, 265
gambling, 316–17
gangs, 482–4
Garrard, Phyllis, 340
Garrick, James, 177
Gee, Maurice, 541
Geering, Lloyd, 514
Geiringer, Erich, 499
gender discrimination, 143–4, 500
gentry, decline of, 127–33
George, Henry, 137
Germans in New Zealand, 224–5
Ghormley, Admiral, 283
Gillespie, O. A., 333
Gillies, Sir Harold, 342
Gipps, Governor, 48
Girl Guides, 366
Girls' Life Brigade, 366
Glaxo, 64, 446, 459
Gleneagles Agreement (1977), 517
globalisation, 425–9
Glover, Denis, 337
goat farming, 447–8

'God Defend New Zealand', 331
Godley, Lady, 110
Godley, General Sir Alexander, 92–3, 97, 107, 211
golf, 373, 375
Gould, Bryan, 345
Government Life Insurance Office, 416
Governor-General, position of, 246
Grace, Patricia, 540
graduate subculture, 509–11
Graham, Doug, 466
'grasslands revolution', 248–9, 308–9
Great Depression (1929–35), 254–9, 263–4
Great Fleet, 208, 211, 214
Great Strike (1913), 92–5, 144
'Great Tightening', 121–5
Greek Orthodox Church, 235
Greeks in New Zealand, 225, 233, 234, 235
Greenpeace New Zealand, 436, 440
Grey, George, 49, 236, 479
Grey River Argus, 403
Grey, Zane, 253
Grigg, John, 61, 132
Grossman, Edith Searle, 330
Group Travel Association, 529
growth. *See* economic growth
Gudgeon, Walter, 237
Gunn, Dr Elizabeth, 175
Guthrie-Smith, Herbert, 529–30

Haig, Field Marshal Sir Douglas, 97
Halberg, Murray, 368
Hall, Sir John, 166
Hall, Roger, 341, 542
Halt All Racist Tours (HART), 517
Hamilton, Adam, 295
Hanlon, John, 511, 531
Harris, Dick, 333
Hassett, J. P., 94
Hastings, 374
Hawkins, Allan, 406
Hayward, Henry, 252
Hazledine, Tim, 458
Health Department, 174

health services, 174, 421–2
Heard, Colonel, 94
Heath, Sir Frank, 250
Heberly, Jacob, 213
Hector, James, 249
Heenan, Joseph, 540
Heke, Hone, 199, 479
Hellaby's, 445–6
Hempton, J. H., 368
Herangi, Te Puea. *See* Te Puea Herangi
Herries, William, 190
Hewitt, F. S., 368
Hight, James, 544
Hillary, Edmund, 368, 392
Historic Places Trust, 546
history and the historical, 543–6
Hobson, Lieutenant-Governor William, 48
Hocken, Thomas, 544, 545
hockey, 373, 375
Hodge, Merton, 341
Hodgkins, Frances, 332, 332–3
Hogben, George, 130
Holden, Anne, 340
holidays, 527–8
Holland, Harry, 88, 91, 146, 259
Holland, Sidney, 295, 298, 300, 301, 303, 305, 307, 319, 320, 437
Holyoake, Keith, 307, 314–15, 392, 437
home ownership, 154–5
homosexual law reform, 410, 512
homosexuality, 511–14
Hororata, 281
horticulture, 450–1
hospitals, 174, 421–2
housework, 494
housing, 154–5, 347–50, 397, 492–3
Howard, Mabel, 498
Howes, Edith, 340
Hulme, Juliet, 504, 512
Hulme, Keri, 540
Hume, Fergus, 327–8, 332, 339
Hunn, J. K., 477, 487
Hunn Report (1961), 477
Hyde, Robin, 332, 336
hydro-electric power, 315

Ihimaera, Witi, 540
immigration policy, 216, 223–32, 235, 532–9
Imperial Agricultural Bureaux, 250
imperial preference, 66–7
imports and import controls, 264, 311–12
Indians in New Zealand, 227, 231, 233, 234, 235, 236, 532, 536, 537
Indonesians in New Zealand, 536
Industrial Conciliation and Arbitration Act 1894, 44
industrial conflict: (1912–13), 87–95; (1951), 299–307; (1970s), 398–9
influenza epidemic (1918), 112–13, 193, 196, 239
'informal' economy, 484–5
information technology, 428
Ingram, Private N. M., 98, 105
insanity, 176
'interest-group capture', 418–21
international affairs, 399–400
international labour movement, 136–7
investment, 456
Irish in New Zealand, 41, 221–3, 233
Italians in New Zealand, 225, 233

Jackson, Peter, 340, 341
James, Billy T., 540
Japan, 445
Jehovah's Witnesses, 294
Jews in New Zealand, 231, 235
Joll, T. L., 61
Jones, Frederick, 285
Jones, Robert, 509
Jordan, Bill, 265, 266
Joseph, George, 339
Joyce, William ('Lord Haw-Haw'), 288

Kaihau, Henare, 195
Kalman, Yvonne, 340
Karaitiana, Ruru, 540
Kawase, Isamu, 282
Kawerau, 315
Kawiti, Maihi Paraone, 199
Kawiti, Te Ruki, 199

Kermadec Islands, 236
King, Dr Frederic Truby, 159, 162–3, 186, 357, 365, 366, 490
King Movement, 194–6
Kingsford-Smith, Charles, 164
Kippenberger, General Howard, 277, 279
Kirk, Norman, 320, 395, 398, 399, 437
Kissinger, Henry, 435
Kitchener, Lord, 80, 250
'Kiwi Bloke'/'Kiwi Joker', 354–6
kiwifruit, 450–1
'knowledge-based industries', 457–8
kohanga reo, 480
Komet, 280, 281
Korean War (1950–53), 298, 318, 319
Koreans in New Zealand, 536
Koroki, King, 195, 196
Kotahitanga, 195, 199

Labour governments: (1935–49), 259–69, 298, 492; (1957–60), 436, 492; (1972–75), 394–5, 396–402, 436, 455, 517, 531; (1984–90), 405–10
Labour Party, 136, 146, 197, 259, 404
lamb exports. *See* 'protein industry'
Lancaster, G. B., 339
Land March (1975), 477–8
Landfall, 335, 541
Lands and Survey, Department of, 545
'Lands for Settlement' Acts, 44, 128, 129, 132
Lane, William, 77–8, 81, 334, 547
Lange, David, 405, 407, 408, 436
Latter-day Saints. *See* Mormon Church
Lawlor, Pat, 320, 333
League of Nations, 246
Leavitt, Mary, 170
Lebanese and Syrian Christians, 227
Lee, John A., 264, 267–8
Legislative Council, 42–3
Leitch, George, 328
Liberal government (1891–1912), 38–46, 128
licensing laws, 171, 316, 317, 410, 414

Lincoln Agricultural College, 249
Lion Breweries, 415
Liston, James, 114
literature, 327–8, 329–41, 540, 541–2
Liverpool, Lord, 92
local government, 410
Lochore, Dr R. A., 225, 226, 230
Lodge, Juliet, 433, 434
Long Depression/Stagnation (c.1879–95), 32–8
Lord of the Rings (film), 340
The Lore of the Whare-wananga (Smith), 210–11
Lovelock, Jack, 368
Low, David, 342
'lucky generation', 419–20
Lutheran Church, 224
Lye, Len, 541
Lyster's Opera Company, 328
Lyttleton, Edith, 339

McCahon, Colin, 334, 337
McCarthy, Senator, 304
McCombs, Elizabeth, 498
McCormick, Eric, 337
McDonald, Ginette, 350
McGregor, Dr Duncan, 175
McIndoe, Sir Archibald, 342
McIntosh, Alister, 318
Macintosh, Sir Robert, 342
McIntyre, Donald, 342
McKenzie, John, 39, 41, 129
Mackenzie, Thomas, 90
McLagan, Angus, 299
McLay, Jim, 396
McNab, Robert, 544, 545
Mahon, Peter, 391
Mahuta, King, 195
Mahy, Margaret, 339–40
Major, Malvina, 342
Malayan Emergency, 319
male culture, 352–6
Malone, Colonel W. G., 97
Malthus, Cecil, 105, 107
Mana Motuhake, 479
Manapouri, Lake, 531

Mander, Jane, 335, 336
Maning, Frederick, 330
Mansfield, Katherine, 330, 332, 334
manufacturing, 71–4, 293, 312, 453–5
Maori: activism, 475–80; cash incomes, 469–70; crime rates, 481–4; culture, 539–40; disengagement, 194–9; educational performance, 480; engagement, 200–5, 211–15; health, 468–9, 470; housing, 468, 473; land alienation, 200–20; land development schemes, 202–3, 473, 486; language, 203, 203–4, 480; non-tribal organisations, 486; occupational clustering, 473–4; population growth, 466–71; resurgence, 466–87; rugby, 212–13; sanitation, 468; subsistence economics, 469–70; supposed Aryan origin, 206–10, 211; survival and recovery, 191–4; symbolism, 209–10, 213–14; unemployment, 474; urban migration, 471–4; 'White Maori' stereotype, 206–15; in World War One, 211–12; in World War Two, 278–9, 297, 475–6
Maori Affairs, Department of, 476
Maori Battalion, 278–9, 476
Maori Language Commission, 480
Maori–Pakeha relations, 189–91, 486–7
Maori Purposes Fund, 203
Maori War Effort Organisation (MWEO), 297, 475–6, 477, 486
Maori Women's Welfare League, 470
Maoriland Worker, 101, 137
marching girls, 375–6
marijuana. *See* cannabis growing and consumption
Maritime Strike (1890), 40, 41, 90, 135–6, 137
Marris, C. A., 333
Marsh, Ngaio, 339–40, 340
Marshall, John, 307, 340, 403, 414, 433, 434, 455
Marx, Karl, 137
Mason, Bruce, 541

Mason, R. A. K. (Ron), 334, 336
Massey Agricultural College, 249
Massey, William: acts against strikers (1913), 92, 94; 'British Israelite', 118; education and housing policies, 154–6; 'Farmer Bill', 152, 154; opposed to Chinese immigration, 228; Prime Minister in Reform government, 90; Protestant, but not sectarian anti-Catholic, 115–16; supports government science, 249; and World War One, 106, 109, 111–12, 113
'Massey's Cossacks', 92, 148
masturbation, 158–9, 175, 176
Matrimonial Property Acts: 1884, 45; 1976, 500
Mau movement, 239, 240
Maui gas field, 401
Mazengarb Report, 504
Meat Research Institute, 250
mechanics' institutes, 178–9
medical profession, 160–1
Mège-Mouriès, Hippolyte, 432
Mellors, Joseph, 344
Messenger, Elizabeth, 340
Methodist Church, 198, 380
'middle-class capture', 418
Mihaka, Dun, 479
militarism, 79–81
milk in schools, 470
milk powder, 309, 445, 446, 447
Millar, J. A., 41
Mills & Boon, 340
Mills, Dr Daisy Platt, 158
Mission Vineyards, 451
Mitterand, François, 439
mixed flatting, 510–11
Mongrel Mob, 482–4
moral evangelism, 159–70, 528–9, 530
Mormon Church, 198
Morrell, W. P., 29, 544
Morrin, Thomas, 36
Morris, William, 137, 304
Moss, Frederick, 237
'Mothers' Mutiny', 181–6

motorcars, 248, 253, 254
mountain sports, 528–9
Mounted Rifles Brigade, 109
Moutoa Gardens, Wanganui, 479
Moyle, Colin, 396
Muldoon, Robert: Bastion Point
    protesters, 515; CER, 400, 455;
    Common Agricultural Policy of
    EEC, 434; defence spending, 437;
    deregulation/liberalisation moves,
    400, 413; Falklands War (1982), 28,
    399–400; foreign-exchange crisis
    (1984), 405; Gleneagles Agreement,
    517; leader of recolonisation's 'last
    stand', 394, 395, 413; military
    alliances, 437–8; Misex, 542; Pacific
    Island 'overstayers', 515; political
    character and approach, 395–6,
    412–13, 437–8; 'Rob's Mob', 438,
    515, 518; snap election (1984), 405,
    509; Springbok tour (1981),
    517–18; superannuation scheme,
    398; supplementary minimum
    prices, 447; 'Think Big' projects,
    401–2, 413; unemployment, 398;
    unions, 398–9; Waitangi Tribunal,
    478
Mulgan, Alan, 333, 334
Mulgan, John, 275, 279, 334, 336, 342
Muller, Mary Ann, 166
music, 328–9

NAFTA, 441, 455
Napier earthquake (1931), 243
Nash, Walter, 264–5, 267, 305, 318, 320,
    436, 477
Nathan, Joseph, 64
National Archives, 546
National Bank of New Zealand, 63, 407
National Council of Women, 166, 187–8
National Defence League, 80
National governments: (1949–57),
    298–9, 307, 476, 492; (1960–72),
    307, 436, 531; (1975–84), 395,
    396–402, 436, 476, 478, 517;
    (1990–93), 408, 410–11

National Library, 307, 541
national parks, 529, 530
National Party, 305, 402–4
National Women's Hospital, 498
Native Affairs, Department of, 476
Native schools, 203–4, 471
Nauru, 281
Nazism, 230–1, 238
Nelson Brothers, 64, 65, 136
Nelson, Frederick, 64
Nelson, Olaf, 239
Nelson, William, 64, 152
netball, 375
New Right revolution (1984–93),
    394–424, 474. *See also*
    'Rogernomics'
New Zealand (battle-cruiser), 80, 81, 110
New Zealand Alliance, 171
New Zealand and Australia Free Trade
    Agreement, 441, 455
New Zealand and Australian Land
    Company, 60, 61
New Zealand Athletics Association, 370
New Zealand Ballet, 541
New Zealand Breweries, 415
New Zealand Business Roundtable,
    411, 412
New Zealand citizenship, 318–19
New Zealand Communist Party
    (CPNZ), 303
New Zealand Conference Lines, 65
New Zealand Dairy Board, 64
New Zealand Division, 274–80, 283–7
New Zealand Expeditionary Force, 2nd,
    274
New Zealand Film Commission, 541
New Zealand Frozen Meat and Storage
    Company, 61
New Zealand Legion, 257
New Zealand Literary Fund, 540
New Zealand Meat Board, 459
New Zealand Party, 509
New Zealand Players, 541
New Zealand Rail, 417–18
New Zealand Refrigeration Company,
    61, 63

New Zealand Rugby Football Union (NZRFU), 383
New Zealand Shipping Company, 65
New Zealand Symphony Orchestra, 540
New Zealand Wars, 545
New Zealand Woman's Weekly, 491
newspapers, 403
Nga Puhi, 212
Nga Tamatoa, 477
Ngai Tahu, 202, 480
Ngapua, Hone Heke, 199
Ngata, Apirana: brilliantly subversive co-operation with Pakeha, 206, 214–15, 466; calls for a Maori bishop, 198, 202; on Chinese, 228, 231; on Henare Kaihau, 195; land development scheme, 202–3, 470, 473; leader in Young Maori Party, 194, 199, 200–6; Maori recruitment in World War One, 211; the 'Mussolini of Maori football', 213; political career, 201–3, 475; relations with Te Arawa and Rotorua, 205; sceptical of, yet willing to exploit, 'Great Fleet' myth, 211, 214; and TB vaccine, 469; and Waitangi, 214
Ngati Kahungunu, 212
Ngati Porou, 192, 193, 202, 212, 476
Ngati Tuwharetoa, 202
Ngati Whatua, 473, 478, 479
Niemeyer, Otto, 250
Niue, 212, 237
Norsewood, 225
North, J. J., 165–6
Northland, 484
nuclear-free movement/policies, 435–40

Oamaru, 523
Ocean Island, 281
O'Connor, Peter, 223
oil industry, 417
oil shocks (1970s), 396–7, 401, 429–30
old age pensions, 45, 169, 177. See also superannuation

One Tree Hill, Auckland, 479
opera, 328–9
Orakei, 478, 479
Orion, 280, 281
ostrich farming, 447–8
Otara, 473
Ottawa Agreement (1932), 247, 252, 253, 264, 349, 431
Ottaway, Agnes, 512
Our Nation's Story, 118, 544
overseas debt, 421
'overstayer affair' (1976–77), 515, 535
Owen, Richard, 304
Owen, Robert, 137
Oxford (North Canterbury), 164, 179

Pacific Islanders in New Zealand, 464, 482–3, 484, 532–5
Pacific Islands, 236–40
Pai Marire, 197
Paikea, Paraire, 475, 476
painting, 334
Pakeha: culture, 540–3; ethnicity, 217–23
'Pakeha treaty'. See 'populist compact'
Parker, Pauline, 504, 512
Parnell, Samuel Palmer, 133, 136
Parry, Bill, 319, 529
Patterson, George, 146–7
Patterson, James, 147–8, 151
Paul, J. T., 294
Peacocke, Isabel, 339, 340
Pearse, Richard, 74
Peel, Colin, 340
Peniakoff, Colonel Vladimir ('Popski'), 275
Pensions Act 1898, 45, 169, 177
Pereira, Fernando, 439
Philomel, 110
Phoenix, 334
Physical Welfare and Recreation Council, 529
Playmarket, 542
Plunket Society, 163, 365
Police Offences Amendment Act 1951, 305

Polynesian Society, 208
Pomare, Maui, 200, 201, 206, 211, 212, 213, 470
Pope, James, 203, 470
'Popski', 275
popular culture, 346–67
'populist compact', 22–3, 397
Porritt, Arthur, 368–9
possums, 309
Post Office, 409
Post Office Savings Bank, 416
Poutapu, Piri, 203
poverty, 524–5
premarital sex, 187, 504–6
premature death, 173–6
Prince of Wales Cup, 213
privatisation, 410
Privy Council, 392
producer boards, 311
'progress industry', 17–19, 523. See also extractive industries
'progressive colonisation', 16–17, 32–8, 523
prohibition, 164, 170–3
promotion campaigns (of tourism, emigration, export trade), 81–5
proportional representation, 408, 479
'protein industry', 54–75
Protestantism, 114–16
Pryor, William, 92
Public Health, Department of, 470
public health system, 174–5
Public Service Association, 315
public works (1950s and 1960s), 315–16
Punch, 387–8
Pyke, Vincent, 327

Queenstown, 524
Quentin, Dorothy, 339

rabbits, 308–9
'race suicide', fear of, 161–3
racism, 143, 535
radio, 251, 252, 253, 254
Rainbow Warrior, 438, 439

Ranfurly Shield, 386
Rangitane, 280
Rata, Matiu, 478, 479
Ratana Church, 196–9, 486
Ratana-Labour alliance, 197, 475, 476–7
Ratana, Tahupotiki Wiremu (the Mangai), 197, 198–9, 471
Reagan, President Ronald, 406
'recolonisation', 29–30, 53–86, 138, 394–404, 523, 547–9
recreations, 527–31
Reed, Vernon, 545–6
Rees, Rosemary, 339
Reeves, William Pember, 39, 43, 44, 80, 83, 128, 152–3, 210, 228, 330, 376, 543
Reform government (1912–28), 130
Reform Party, 87, 152
regions, history of, 522–7
religion, 163–6, 514–15
research and development, 421, 423
Reserve Bank, 257, 409
returned servicemen, 152, 493
Returned Servicemen's Association, 296, 316
Richardson, General G. S., 109, 238–9
Richardson, Ruth, 408, 410
Rickard, Eva, 196
Rickard, Harry, 328
Rikiriki, Mere, 197
Ringatu religion, 194
riots: (1913), 94; (1932), 257–8
Roberts, 'Big Jim', 145, 146
'Rogernomics', 406–8. See also New Right revolution (1984–93)
Rolleston, William, 43
Roman Catholic Church, 198, 222–3
'romantic domesticity', 490–3
Rommel, General, 274, 275
Roosevelt, President F. D., 287
Ross Dependency, 391
Rotorua, 202–5, 524
Rotorua, Lake, 202
Rout, Ettie, 178
rowing, 375

Roxburgh, 315
Royal Air Force, New Zealanders
    serving in, 272–4
Rua Kenana, 194
Ruatara, 210
rugby, 374, 375, 378–88
Russell, Major-General A. H., 97–8,
    107
Russell, Thomas, 36, 61, 62, 63
Rutherford, Ernest, 344, 345, 383

Sabbatarianism, 164. *See also*
    weekends
Samoa, 108, 109–10, 238–40
Samoans in New Zealand, 533, 534
sanitation, 173–4, 468
Sargeson, Frank, 335, 337, 513
Satchell, William, 330, 334
Savage, Michael Joseph, 259–60, 265,
    267, 268, 269
'Save Manapouri' campaign, 531
Scandinavians in New Zealand, 224,
    225
Scanlan, Nellie, 339
'Scarecrow Ministry' (1887–90), 38
Schmidt, Hermann, 74
Scholefield, Dr Guy, 226
School Dental Service, 175–6
School Journal, 118
School Medical Service, 175–6
School of Maori Arts and Crafts,
    Rotorua, 203
schooling. *See* education
science establishment, 249–51
Scientific and Industrial Research,
    Department of (DSIR), 250–1
scientists, 344
Scots in New Zealand, 41, 219–21, 233,
    234
Scott, Mary, 339
Scrimgeour, Colin, 253
Seacliff Asylum, 159
Seamen's Union, 299
secondary industries, 71–4
sectarianism, 114–16, 222–3
Security Intelligence Service, 295

Seddon, Richard: and 'God's Own
    Country', 43; imperialism, 80, 236;
    legislates for pensions, 177; Liberal
    leader, 43; mausoleum, 249;
    'Minister for Football', 387; New
    Zealand militarism, 80; populist
    politician, 38, 41–2, 43; secondary
    schools, 130; sets up Liberal and
    Labour Federation, 136; sets up
    maternity hospitals, 174; walking
    public opinion poll, 130, 228;
    women's suffrage, 45
'selfish generation', 419–20
Semple, Bob, 88, 89, 146, 305
sex discrimination, 143–4, 500
Shadbolt, Maurice, 541
Shand, Gwitha, 375
share-market crash (1987), 406–8
Shaw, G. B., 368
sheep-meat exports. *See* 'protein
    industry'
Shelley, Professor James, 253
Sheppard, Kate, 166, 170, 175
Shetlanders in New Zealand, 220
shipping companies, 65–6, 74
shopping, 316, 351–2
Sievwright, Margaret, 166
Sinclair, Keith, 29, 80, 81, 256, 265, 267,
    337, 338, 398, 544
Sisam, Kenneth, 342
six o'clock closing, 316, 317, 414,
    441
skiing, 528–9
Skinner, Tom, 314, 399
Slatter, Gordon, 384
Smith, Stephenson Percy, 208
Snell, Peter, 368
'social capital', 458–60
social change (1960–2000), 463–5
Social Credit, 257, 260–1
Social Credit News, 294
'Social Purity' movement, 160
Social Security Act 1938, 261–2
Socialist Unity Party (SUP), 303
Society for the Protection of the
    Unborn Child, 498–9

Soler, Joseph, 451
Solf, Wilhelm, 238, 240
Solomon, Tommy, 521
South African immigrants in
    New Zealand, 538
South-East Asian Treaty Organisation
    (SEATO), 319
Southland, 223
Spee, Admiral, 108, 109–10
Split Enz, 542
Spock, Dr, 357, 490
Spofforth, 'Demon', 329, 369
sport, 368–88; New Zealand's
    excellence in, 368–70; in relation to
    society, 370–8; women in, 375–8
Springbok tours: (1921), 209, 516;
    (1937), 516; (1956), 378–9; (1981),
    478, 516–19
Stark, Freda, 512
Stark, James Douglas, 106
state, role of, 313–16, 409–10, 416–17,
    417–23
state-owned enterprises, 409–10
Statute of Westminster (1931), 246,
    318–19, 441
steel mill, 401
sterling system, 431
Stewart, Adela, 205, 332
Stewart, Downie, 256, 257
Stewart, General K. L., 277–8
Stoney, Henry Butler, 327
Stout, Anna, 131, 166
Stout, Robert, 38, 49, 228
Sudan war (1884–85), 27–8
Suez Crisis (1956), 429, 319–20
'sugarbag years', 255
suicides, 158, 168–9, 177
Sullivan, 'Big Bill', 306
Summers, Essie, 340
superannuation, 398, 421. *See also* old
    age pensions
Surafend, 108
Sutch, W. B., 72, 257, 266, 401
Sutton-Smith, Brian, 361, 365, 382
swimming, 372, 375
Syme, Sir Ronald, 342

Taiapa, Hone, 203
Taiapa, Pine, 203
Taingakawa, Tupu, 195, 199
Tainui (iwi), 476
Tainui, Emma, 193
Talboys, Brian, 396
Tamasese Lealofi, Tupu, 239
Tamehana, Wiremu, 195
Taranaki, 70–1, 249
Tarawera eruption (1886), 15, 205
Tasman Empire Airways Limited
    (TEAL), 427
Tasman world: New Zealand's
    departure from, 46–52, 137; revival
    of, 440–3
Taupo, Lake, 202
Tawhiao, King, 195
tax reform, 409
Taylor, Waring, 36
Te Arawa, 192, 193, 204–5
Te Atairangikaahu (Maori queen),
    196
Te Kanawa, Kiri, 342
Te Kauwhata winery, 451
Te Kooti, 200
Te Matorohanga, 210–11
Te Puea Herangi, 195–6, 199, 206, 470,
    471
Te Rata, King, 195
Te Ua Haumene, 197, 199
teenage culture, 504–9
Telecom, 409, 416
television, 426–7, 541
temperance movement, 170–3
tennis, 373, 375
Terry, Lionel, 228–9
Thatcher, Charles, 328, 330
Thatcher, Margaret, 406, 434, 498
theatre, 328–9, 341
'Think Big' projects, 401–2, 453–4,
    456–7
Thompson, David, 419
Thompson, G. M., 250
Thomson, Arthur Saunders, 330, 543
Thomson, John, 335
The Times, 434

Tirakatene, Eruera, 197, 475, 476
Titokowaru, 147, 478
Tokelau, 237
Tomorrow, 334
Tongans in New Zealand, 533, 534
Tooley Street, 64–5
topdressing, 309, 526
Topp Twins, 350
tourism, 81–3, 452–3
Towers and Company, 63
Tracey, Mona, 340
Trade Union Congress, 300
trades unions. *See* unions
tramping, 528–9, 530
'transaction costs', 458–60
Treasury, 411, 412
Treaty of Versailles, 246
Treaty of Waitangi, 199, 478, 479–80,
    485, 545
Tregear, Edward, 44, 92, 93, 95, 144,
    207, 210, 228, 230, 442, 516
Truth, 102, 115, 179–80, 209, 372, 384,
    388
tuberculosis, 175, 468–9
Tuohy, Patrick. *See* Walsh, Fintan
    Patrick
Turangi, 315
Turbott, Dr Harry, 467, 468, 469
Turner, C. W., 65
Tutira (Guthrie-Smith), 529–30
typhoid, 469
Tyser Line, 65

U–862, 280, 281, 288
unemployment, 398, 421, 474
Union Shipping Company, 65, 129, 135
unions, 88–90, 92, 93, 95, 133, 134, 137,
    145, 262, 299, 300, 303, 306, 398–9,
    411
United Federation of Labour, 92
United government (1928–31), 254
United Nations Organisation, 318
United-Reform Coalition. *See* Coalition
    government (1931–35)
unmarried mothers, 183–4
Urewera, 193, 194

USA: military alliance with, 318, 319,
    321, 399, 435–40; trade with, 445–6
'user pays', 409, 411

Values Party, 531
venereal disease, 103–4
Vestey Brothers, 63, 65
Vietnam War, 321, 515–16
Vietnamese in New Zealand, 536
Vikings of the Sunrise (Buck), 211
Vogel, Julius, 38, 46, 231, 236

W. and R. Fletcher. *See* Vestey Brothers
Wade, Constable, 91
Waihi Strike (1912), 87–91
Waikato (region), 249
Waikato (tribes), 196, 212
Waipu (Northland), 220, 234
Waitangi, 478, 545–6, 546
Waitangi Tribunal, 410, 478, 479–80,
    485–6
Waitere, Tene, 205
Wakefield, Edward Jerningham, 330
Walker, John, 368
Walker, Ranginui, 479
Walrond, Violet, 375
Walsh, Fintan Patrick, 267, 295, 299,
    301, 303, 304, 306, 314
Wanganella, 315
Wanganui Collegiate, 130
Ward, Sir Joseph: and Australian
    federation, 49; composition of
    Cabinet (1908), 41; donates battle-
    cruiser to British navy, 80; good
    relations with business, 129;
    opposed to Chinese immigration,
    228; overseas borrowing, 46;
    political phoenix, 38–9; succeeds
    Seddon, 43; supports government
    science, 249; and World War One,
    106, 109, 111
waterfront dispute (1951), 299–307
Watt, Hugh, 395
Wattie's, 415–16, 450
wealth, 524–5
Webb, Beatrice, 326

Webb, Paddy, 88, 137, 146
Webb, Sidney, 326
Weddell (William) and Company, 63
weekends, 316. *See also* Sabbatarianism
Welburn P. G. Butterman (bovine
    mega-sire), 308, 311
Wellington, 520–1, 522, 523, 525
West, Joyce, 340
Westland, 222
Whitaker, Frederick, 36
white-collar work, 155–6
White Feather Leagues, 99–100
'White Maori' stereotype, 206–15
White, Margaret Matilda, 210
White Ribbon, 180
Wilding, Anthony, 369
Williams, William, 372
Williams, Yvette, 368
Williamson, J. C., 328
Winder, Mavis, 339
wine industry, 451
Wolf, 110
women in the workforce, 143–4, 297–8,
    501–4
Women's Christian Temperance Union,
    170
Women's Health League, 470
women's refuges, 500
women's suffrage, 45, 166
Wool Board, 311
wool exports, 446–7
Woollaston, Toss, 334
working class, making of, 133–46
working men's clubs, 178–9
workplaces, 352–4

Works, Ministry of, 315–16
World War One, 95–112, 192–3, 196,
    211–12
World War Two, 270–96; American
    troops in New Zealand, 287, 289–
    92; censorship, 294; conscientious
    objectors, 295; Crete, 274, 276,
    277–8, 283; 'Crusader' offensive,
    274; Economic Stabilisation
    measures, 294, 295; Egypt, 274; El
    Alamein, 275; 'enemy aliens', 295;
    Featherston incident (1943), 289;
    'furlough affair', 285, 288; Greece,
    274, 276, 283, 284; home front,
    287–96; manpowering regulations,
    294, 476; Maori Battalion, 278–9,
    476; Mediterranean theatre, 274–80,
    283–7; Monte Cassino, 275; New
    Zealand Division, 274–80, 283–7;
    New Zealanders in RAF, 272–4;
    Security Intelligence Service, 295;
    Singapore, 281, 284; threat of
    Japanese invasion, 280–7, 296; war
    at sea, 280–1; war effort, 292–6
Wright, David McKee, 330, 332
Wright, Noni, 341

Xena Warrior Princess, 340

Yate, William, 511–12
Yates, Elizabeth, 45
Young Maori Party, 194, 199, 200–6
Young Men's Christian Association, 365
youth culture, 504–9
Yugoslavs. *See* Dalmatians

PARADISE

REFORGED